CHILD DEVELOPMENT

CHILD DEVELOPMENT

SHYAM SUNDER SHRIMALI

RAWAT PUBLICATIONS

Jaipur • New Delhi • Bangalore • Mumbai • Hyderabad • Guwahati

ISBN 81-316-0181-1 (HB)
ISBN 81-316-0182-X (PB)

Published by
Prem Rawat for Rawat Publications
Satyam Apts., Sector 3, Jawahar Nagar, Jaipur 302 004 (India)
Phone: 0141 265 1748 / 7006 Fax: 0141 265 1748
E-mail: info@rawatbooks.com
Website: www.rawatbooks.com

New Delhi Office
4858/24, Ansari Road, Daryaganj, New Delhi 110 002
Phone: 011 2326 3290

Also at Bangalore, Mumbai, Hyderabad and Guwahati

Printed at Nice Printing Press, New Delhi

To my respected father, a great scholar of Sanskrit, who has ever been a source of inspiration to me in writing whatever I have been able to.

CONTENTS

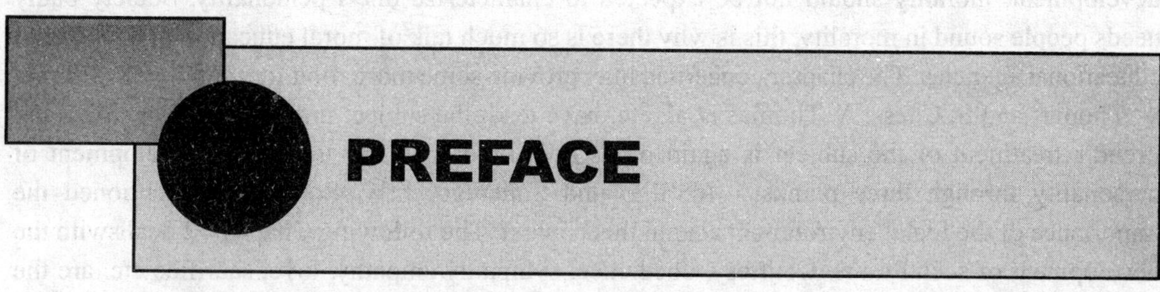

PREFACE

No subject could appeal more than "Child Development" to a person who retired as a teacher after serving for more than 42 years, and, one who had been associated with the teaching of Psychology to postgraduate students of Education; and to a person who still considers himself as a teacher though past 75 he is. A person who is not developed – physically, mentally, emotionally and so on, would feel his life to be a hard problem to bear, and, for society he would be an undesirable burden, or, one turned to be like a rogue animal.

As the process of development sets in since prenatal stage, the book deals with the factors which affect the development of the child at the embryonic stage; the classic book *Child Development & Personality,* authored by Paul Henry Mussen, John Janeway Conger and Jerome Kogan provided very important information regarding the subject. The name of L.W. Sontag should also be mentioned in this respect.

The period of life up to five, is crucial so far the process of development is concerned, this is why the book has attempted to trace development of the child, mainly, up to five years of age; and separate chapters have been devoted for the child's development in various fields such as physical, intellectual, emotional, moral etc. Lop-sided physical or intellectual development can only result in a personality neither desirable for the person himself nor for the society. While chapters third to sixth are on the child's physical development, the seventh is devoted to intellectual development. J.P. Guilford's book – *The Nature of Human Intelligence;* C.L. Hull's – *Mind, Mechanism and Adaptive Behaviour* and A.M. Leahy's book *Nature-Nurture & Intelligence,* and some others were found to be containing useful matter regarding child's intellectual development. Chapter 8 deals with the development of language; this author has incorporated a lot many observational results of his own while penning this and some other chapters. But the name of Jean Piaget deserves to be mentioned with a feeling of great thankfulness, as I have depended too much on him for writing on the development of intelligence and reasoning.

Though in this book there are separate chapters on emotional and moral development, the overt and covert relationship of the two has been highlighted therein. Without desirable emotional development, morality should not be expected to characterize one's personality. Society badly needs people sound in morality, this is why there is so much talk of moral education at the level of educational agencies. The chapter concerned may provide some more food for thinking. D. Elkind, A. Thomas and S. Chess, A. Thomas et al. etc. have dealt the subject in their own way. Sigmund Freud's treatment of the subject is again of its own kind – he has traced the development of personality through three planks – Id, Ego and Superego. L.W. Sontag has mentioned the importance of the foetal environment also in this context. The following Chapter 12 deals with the development of social traits. Courtesy, obedience, sympathy/empathy, love, sacrifice etc. are the social qualities which parents and teachers should be expected to help develop. Harriet L. Rheingold, R.C. Challman, P.J. Greenberg and a few others were consulted in this respect. A person physically strong, and mentally sharp if is not positively developed emotionally, and in social traits, may prove a big menace to the society.

Chapter 15 suggests what really the term all-round development indicates; a term which many educational institutions claim to be their objective; actually, in many cases, the function of education has been dwarfed to forcing the child to cram some undigested pieces of information, which tantamounts to blocking a child's development. Chapter 16 deals with some general abnormalities in a child, which parents and teachers have to face; remedies have also been suggested. Adolescence is a critical period that in due course, each one passes through; a non-psychological and injudicious handling of an adolescent may negatively affect his/her development, it is the subject-matter of Chapter 17. Sigmund Freud and Jean Piaget's theories of child development are discussed at length in Chapters 18 and 19. Chapters 20 and 21 present a good model of child education. The book ends with the chapter entitled "Ideas that I am seized with", it carries the author's freely expressed ideas developed because of a long theoretical and practical association to pedagogy or to education in general.

Shyam Sunder Shrimali

CHAPTER

1 SCIENTIFIC METHODS AND CHILD PSYCHOLOGY

Chapter Outline

- Case Study
- Limitations and Resources of a Case Study
- Contribution of Case Study
- Longitudinal Study
- Cross-section Study
- Observation
- Review Questions

For centuries, Psychology remained confused with Philosophy; it could not evolve its independent identity as long as it continued to be considered as the "Science of Soul". Later, it began to be considered as the "Science of Mind". But the problem remained the same; 'Mind' is as abstract as 'Soul'; none having any form or colour; so, the study of mind was as difficult as that of soul. The Psychology was then defined as "Science of Consciousness". The difficulty with this definition was that Psychology happens to be concerned with not only the 'conscious mind' but with 'Sub-conscious' and 'unconscious' as well, thus the definition was found to be incomplete. It was relinquished in favour of modern definitions; first those given by the behaviourists, such as C Woodworth, E Watson, Charles E Skinner, and others; who all defined Psychology as a "Science of Behaviour"—behaviour physical and mental, as stimulated by the environment of the organism. The study of behaviour enabled the psychologists to be more and more objective in their conclusions. Psychology assumed the nature of a positive science depending more and more on experiments and other scientific methods for its findings. Observation of behaviour of an organism under a particular setting of circumstances, became an important method of investigation in Psychology. But the Gestalt School of Psychology added the missing aspect in the study of behaviour—the affective side was non-existent for the behaviourists. The gestaltists, Max Wertheimer, Kurt Koffka and Wolfgang Kohler solved the problem as to why different people behave differently in response to the same stimulation, under similar circumstances—they taught that each mind has its own evolution, thus remaining one single whole in spite of its adapting to every new experience, thus showing dynamism. As an impact of Gestaltism, the psychologists started observing the individual as a whole, and not in isolation in one particular response only.

The psychologists, while studying the behaviour of an individual, established the importance of the sub-conscious and unconscious mind. Thus, the points of reference were increased, and were made more penetrating in case of studies of children also. The psychologists equipped with this background, adopted varied scientific methods to study the bahaviour of children. The main among them being—Case Studies, Longitudinal and Cross-section Studies, the Observation Technique and Experimentation. It would be in the fitness of things, to define and explain each one of these, giving some examples, how different psychologists used different methods to reach to their conclusions in their studies of children.

CASE STUDY

A case provides an example of an individual who alone, or a group of like individuals, studied in their present conditions and situations.

A case provides an example of an individual who alone, or a group of like individuals, studied in their present conditions and situations. The point of study happens to be how the child behaves under certain circumstances, that it is living in at present. The psychologists have also to find out the reasons which make it behave in the way that it does. The experimenter may change the factors eliciting certain behaviours from the child to see how different stimulations cause a change in the mode and way of bahaviour that is evidenced in the child. With the result that all findings or conclusions happen to be in reference to a single individual child or a group of similar children; and, they all show how the different factors related to nurture, would be affecting a child whose growth and development have been of a certain category.

Carter G Wood and Douglas E Scates define the 'case study' in their book *Methods of Research* as follows:

"The essential procedure of the case study method is to take account of all pertinent aspects of one thing, or situation, employing as the unit for study an individual, an institution, a community or any group, considered as a unit."

They further say, "The complex situation and combination of factors involved in the given behaviour are examined to determine the existing status and to identify the causal factors operating."

In the same book, characteristics and skills of a satisfactory Case Study have been enumerated. Summarising the same, they may be put as under:

1. **Continuity** The steps in a case study must be in such a continuous succession of time that the entire study may provide a complete picture of growth or development; each succeeding step must serve as a complementary process for the previous one.
2. **Completeness of data** The data should be based on the observation of all aspects of the child's development, whatsoever the field may be—sensory-motor (or physical), cognitive or emotional activities.
3. **Validity of data** Information regarding the date of birth, and the prenatal milieu that the mother was living in, must be verified through records where they are maintained in an authentic way.
4. **Confidential recording** "The difficulties of individual teachers of pupils, in relation to discipline, failure, achievement, or mentality", are to be regarded as problems to be treated in a confidential manner.
5. **Scientific synthesis** One important part of the report is the interpretation of the evidence. It should be done in a convincing way; mere enumerating the data will not make it so. The causal factors for a proper diagnosis, will have to be identified. Likely developments will have to be considered, or treatment to check undesirable development will have to be decided—these two form the part of diagnosis. All these are the parts of a scientific synthesis.

The essential procedure of the case study method is to take account of all pertinent aspects of one thing, or situation, employing as the unit for study an individual, an institution, a community or any group, considered as a unit.

LIMITATIONS AND RESOURCES OF A CASE STUDY

In conducting a case study on a child, the researcher has especially to work under certain limitations, mainly related to resources. If his subject is a neonate, or a very young baby, it can in no way extend its direct co-operation in the work of garnering data. The researcher can adopt neither the device of interview nor the technique of some test to get information regarding the child—his subject may even have no language to express himself; and if the subject has grown old enough to have developed his language, a child should not be expected to co-operate consciously as much as a mature subject can do. One very important method that will do, is the observation method. It is through observing the behaviour of the child that the researcher can realise a problem worth working upon. Sometimes, the researcher may find it difficult **to define a problem in clear-cut terms.**

Likewise, the researcher may have **difficulty in the formulation of a shrewd hypothesis.** If the first step, that is, the identification of a problem, is weak, it will, naturally, have its effect on the formulation of the hypothesis. And, hypothesis is, what gives direction to the efforts of the researcher. But formulation of a shrewd hypothesis in case of researches in social science, in general, is difficult, and it is all the more so in a case where the subject is a child with no verbal expression of his own.

For the accuracy of the findings, the **accuracy of instruments** employed for measurement, is a must. Accurate instruments for measurement in social researches, in general, and in case of child psychology, in particular, are not easy to find. Very few instruments are available to a child psychologist, his subject being not matured enough for him to expect any conscious co-operation from him; the researcher cannot handle him at his will, or at a time that suits him. The questionnaire, the test schedules and so on, can be of no use to a researcher until the child has grown up enough to comply with, and respond positively to the directions of the researcher.

For the accuracy of the findings, the **accuracy of instruments** employed for measurement, is a must. Accurate instruments for measurement in social researches, in general, and in case of child psychology, in particular, are not easy to find.

As the researcher in field of child psychology, has to work under these limitations, he will have to make very **skilful use of the few tools** that are available to him. Observation is the main tool in case of children younger than two years of age. So observation must be objective and keen, lest anything important should miss the notice of the researcher, and, fail him in reaching to a correct conclusion or finding. The observation also needs to be patient and long.

The researcher should make use of only **the standardised units of measurements.** This is essential not only in case of child psychology but in case of all kinds of researches. Likewise, **the terminology should also be uniform**—if it is not so, there is every chance for confusion.

As mentioned previously, a case study may be related to a single child, but for reaching to some verified conclusion, it is essential that **the sampling should be adequate;** adequate in the sense, that the conclusions should be based on the study of a good number of cases, all alike in age and, in other variables.

The findings may not be correct if a correct classification is not made; to be able to do this, the researcher needs to use only **sound techniques for classification.**

The analysis of data is directly related to the hypothesis that the researcher works with. **The data will have to be analysed so as to enable the researcher to verify the correctness of the hypothesis from different angles.** The analysis should have the characteristics of clarity and compatibility.

The final step is the reporting. There should be **a well organised system for reporting.** By the time the researcher reaches to this stage, he will be in possession of very valuable findings, but the same will be of no use if they are not shaped in a well arranged system of communication. This tests the skills of the organisation in the art of communication. The report should have proper sections and sub-sections as required for the analysis of data. The reporting should make a clear mention of all the steps that the researcher has worked through. It should bring home clearly to the reader, as to what was the object of the researcher; what steps he had worked upon to achieve the same; what tools and instruments were employed for the work; what data he could collect and to what effect, that is, a lucid reporting should mention his findings in the last section.

To quote and refer to the book *Methods of Research* (Carter V Good and Douglas E Scates) here again, will be useful:

"Case study is essentially an intrusive investigation of the particular unit represented, where case work refers especially to the remedial, corrective or developmental procedures that appropriately follow diagnosis of the causes of maladjustment or of approved behaviour; case work and case study, therefore, are complementary processes even though they may not be performed by the same person or agency."

"Case study is essentially an intrusive investigation of the particular unit represented, where case work refers especially to the remedial, corrective or developmental procedures that appropriately follow diagnosis of the causes of maladjustment or of approved behaviour; case work and case study, therefore, are complementary processes even though they may not be performed by the same person or agency."

The cycle of steps as given in the said book are as follows:

1. recognition and determination of the status of phenomenon to be investigated;
2. collection of data relating to the factor of circumstances associated with the given phenomenon;
3. diagnosis or identification of causal factors as a basis for remedial or developmental treatment;
4. application of remedial or adjustment measures;
5. subsequent follow-up to determine the effectiveness of the treatment applied.

A case study when conducted to know the nature of growth of a child, may adopt a variety of techniques according to the age of the child. To study the prenatal behaviour of the child, experimental and laboratory techniques are used—generally with animal foetuses as subjects; limited experiments on, and extensive observations of premature human infants are also done. The researcher's main sources of data happen to be: (*i*) experiments on infants; (*ii*) direct measurements; (*iii*) observations; and (*iv*) ingenious techniques, such as—one way vision screens, video recording, the Gessel observation dome, and the stabilimeter. When children have grown older, are school-going, the use may be made of a number of tests available: test-schedules or tools are available (or may be developed or standardised) for the measurement of sensorimotor development, span of attention, language-development, intelligence, memory, interest, attitude, aptitude, capacity of reasoning etc. In case of older children, paper and pencil tests are effective techniques; but in case of children who do not know reading and writing, such techniques are not feasible. Sociometric techniques are also very useful for the study of older children or adolescents. Social relationships can be diagrammed while the older children are busy in playing some dramatic roles.

On the basis of what N Thanulingan describes about case study method in his book *"Research Methodology in Social Sciences"*, we can arrive at the following points:

1. The method aims at deep and detailed study of the unit.
2. It covers a wide cycle of time, and, it makes the study comprehensive.
3. The sample may either be a single individual or more to a big number. In case, the sample is consisted of more than one individual, they all must be of the same age.
4. The researcher, mainly, has to depend on his power of observation, and sense of logic.
5. The method demands a deeper probe, and a keen insight on the part of the researcher.
6. For the collection of data, regarding different aspects of growth and development, the researcher should use different techniques and tools; such as, personal documents, life-histories, observation, and others. In case of older children or adolescents, interviews, questionnaires, schedules, and a variety of tests may be adopted for gathering data.
7. Then the data are integrated, and are analysed. The data should be classified as dominant, less dominant and neutral.
8. When the data have been classified and analysed, then the same must be explained and interpreted. The interpretation must be logical, and in a convenient form. The report should mention results or the conclusions arrived at, in definite terms. The researcher should also tell what methods or techniques were employed by him. A complete report must contain all these points.

CONTRIBUTION OF CASE STUDY

1. To professionals, working in the fields of medicine, education, juvenile delinquency, and a number of other social sciences, very significant findings have been made available through case studies. Findings are available, tabulated under different categories, in terms of source of reference—age, sex, race, problem, intelligence, social grade, economic status and so on; some categories may be based on the inter-relationship of different factors.

2. For the evaluation of progress, case study is an important method. The efficacy of the measures adopted for a desirable change, can only be known through a case study. For example, there is a boy under ten, who is referred to a habit-clinic, where he undergoes certain measures arranged by the clinic. Now, to evaluate what change has come about, and what is the amount of change, the researcher will have to study the child at different stages of age; report of changes may also be sought from parents, teachers, and from other concerned sources.
3. Group patterns as existing in different families, classes, schools and communities, can be studied in a proper way through the method of case study. So immense has been the contribution of this method in this respect.
4. The professional courses need vast material for the purpose of instruction, which has only been available as a result of case studies. In fact, a significant portion of most of the books on psychology—social, criminal or educational, medicine or management, is made up from conclusions of case studies.
5. For the illustration and verification of statistical results, findings of case studies are very helpful. As for example, detailed case histories, have revealed many important facts related to twin resemblance, to identical twins reared together, fraternal twins reared together, non-twin siblings reared together and apart, unrelated children reared together, and, as a sample of the general population together, they supplement the statistical results.
6. There are bureaus or agencies which may be hired for findings that are significant for professionals and government departments. These findings, generally happen to be the results of case studies. Results of case studies are published in book-form, as they are very helpful in formulating generalisations. Very useful body of knowledge is available in the form of reports of case studies.

In the field of child psychology, in particular, and in education and social areas in general, statistical and experimental studies do not have so important a role, as they do in physical sciences, where the problem may be related to managerial or other practical aspects. In case of social sciences, purpose happens to be, not only to reveal some facts as is the case in physical sciences, but to make the concerned social institution work in a more effective manner, so that the desired goal may be achieved.

Researchers, in the field of child psychology, have to pool from the results of the efforts done in different fields related to the child or adolescent.

The field may be a child guidance clinic, an institution related to the work of a psychiatrist, a sociologist or a social worker. Such a researcher may make use of home, school, a recreational programme or of a child placement agency for resources.

Some examples of the case study are:

1. Through a case study observing the behaviour of infants, six months old, Gibson, E and Walk, RR, could reveal important facts regarding their reactions to the perception of depth—"an infant avoids a stimulus which suggests a sudden increase in depth". (*The Visual Cliff*, 1960).
2. Harlow, HF through his case studies could establish the fact that increase in stimulation is reinforced, and leads to learning.
3. It was through case studies of individual pre-school children that Sears, Macoby and Levin could make clear how children move from the stage of fear of the environment to the development of conscience. (*Patterns of Child Learning*).
4. Ebbs, JH et al., investigated the effect of malnutrition on pregnant mothers and their born babies with a sample of 210 subjects—90 in the experimental groups and 120 in the controlled group—through a case study; the book is, *The Influence of Improved Prenatal Nutrition Upon the Infant.*
5. Piaget's suggestion that training for comprehension of certain subject matter (physics, for example) should be delayed until the child's thinking is more formal and less concrete—was based on his case studies.
6. It was through case studies that Helen Koch ("Attitudes of young children toward their peers as related to certain characteristics of their siblings.") could report that the school boys with older sisters tended to develop more feminine attributes than boys with older brothers; on the other hand, girls with older brothers had masculine attributes.
7. Levy's demonstration that "over protective" mothers, who are highly permissive with their infants (breast-feeding for a long time, cuddle them, etc.) may actually retard their acquisition of mature responses—is an example of case study. (Levy, DM: *Maternal Overprotection*).
8. Piaget observed children of different age groups, at different times; he observed their intellectual behaviour; and, concluded that the era of conceptional intelligence, may be broken up into four developmental stages. (*The Growth of Logical Thinking*).

LONGITUDINAL STUDY

In the preceding paragraphs, it was mentioned that in a case study, one individual, or a group of identical or similar individuals, is the sample. In the case study, such a sample is studied in the prevailing physical and social conditions, that is, under the conditions as are there, at present; but in a Longitudinal Study, the same sample continues to be studied for a longer period with changing conditions. For example, if a one-year-old child is studied, or a group of children of the same age, that is, of one-year, is studied to know what special characteristics are found in a child of one year, conceived and reared in a particular setting of conditions- it is CASE STUDY; but if the same sample continues to be studied till the subject or subjects of the sample, attain the age of three, to observe what physical or mental or affectional changes take place with the advancement of age, with the natural process of maturity and development, it becomes a Longitudinal Study.

In a Longitudinal Study, the same sample continues to be studied for a longer period with changing conditions

The following are the special points related to a Longitudinal Study:

1. It goes beyond the present milieu of the sample to trace the special characteristics that develop along the advancement of age.
2. A longitudinal study is the study of development—physical, cognitive or/and emotional.
3. In a longitudinal study, only one variable that is, the age, or time limit alters; all others remain the same.
4. A longitudinal study, is a case study covering a wider spectrum that emerges as the sample develops with age.
5. A longitudinal study takes more time in its being complete than is the case in regard to the case study; the former being related to a longer span of time than the latter does.
6. Both, in a case study and in a longitudinal study, the physical and social conditions, remain the same throughout the period of study; in the latter case, the sample changes in chronological age while in the former, the objective is to study the sample as it behaves during the current period of time.
7. A longitudinal study provides us data for comparison between physical, cognitive or/and emotional development of a sample, as is the case at present, with what takes place with the advancement of age, at different periods of life.
8. A longitudinal study is to reveal the facts regarding the impact of age on the samples; a case study is to know the impact of physical or social environments on the samples, as they are at present.

Carter V Good and Douglas E Scates in their "*Methods of Research*" thus describe the longitudinal approach:

The longitudinal approach to investigation of the weight of school children is to follow a particular group of pupils or the same individual year after year through repeated measurements. The resulting series of measurements, therefore, represents growth sequences for the same group of children or same individual.

"The longitudinal approach to investigation of the weight of school children is to follow a particular group of pupils or the same individual year after year through repeated measurements. The resulting series of measurements, therefore, represents growth sequences for the same group of children or same individual. Expressed otherwise, such a longitudinal study is a series of rather closely spaced cross-sections for the particular group or individual.............growth investigations of the same subjects should be conducted with the measurements made *seriatim*."

The book makes mention of some special characteristics of the longitudinal technique which make it different from other techniques:

1. The sample may be an individual or a group of small number of individuals.
2. If the sample is consisted of more than one individual, they all must be alike in all respects.
3. The longitudinal study spreads over a certain period of time, the period may be one year or more. The average development of the group that occurs during the different stages of the period, is measured; the development may be in the form of gain in height and weight; acquiring certain motor skills or language or the faculty of reasoning or emotional stability, and so on.
4. The study enables the researcher to compare the average stages of development between successive age groups. The development of a single individual may be assessed whether it is normal or not comparable with the average growth and development of the age group, year after year.
5. A longitudinal study is directly related to a situation, and does not depend on laboratory experiments.
6. The repeated measurements of the same individual or of the same group of individuals year after year, will indicate the trends of development in one or more fields. If the trends do not suggest the development to be normal, a thorough diagnosis may be required.
7. Average states of growth and development of the same group, year after year, provide norms to compare with the growth and development of a single subject or each individual subject of the group.
8. As a longitudinal study may be related to any length of time, its results are likely to be affected by certain "unpredictable and uncontrollable" events; maybe, some "death, illness, moving of families, and changes in the co-operation of children and parents

with the investigator" and so on. This fact has to be reckoned with, while measuring growth and development, or forming conclusions.

Longitudinal study also reveals the fact that "children grow at different rates and reach similar development levels at different ages. Individual curves for vocabulary growth, for example, as reported in baby biographies differ markedly from the usual growth curves based on cross-section studies." (*Methods of Research*). It also deals with the inter-relationship of different variables that affect the growth or development of the child. The co-operation of specialists, working in various fields, has been an important contributory factor in the achievements made through longitudinal studies—the Stanford Genetic Studies of Genius and the Berkley Growth Study of mental, motor and physical development from birth to maturity, could be possible only because of such a co-operation.

There are certain difficulties which the researcher, conducting a longitudinal study, has to endure with:

- During a long-term investigation, many of the original subjects, have to be eliminated because of one or the other reason. Of course, the investigator will have to see to it that elimination occurs only when it is unavoidable; and he will also have to see that the elimination does not affect the validity of results.
- Generally, it is not possible that the same personnel continue with the work as the study may continue for a pretty long period, hence the problem of the maintenance of satisfactory working relationship with subjects.
- Non-comparability or uncertain psychological equivalence of tests that are used at different age levels in a study through childhood to adolescence, is also a difficulty.
- The motivation of children may change during the repeated testing that goes on over a period of months or years; with the result that sometimes their performance may become perfunctory.
- In a longitudinal study, administration of tests—mental or physical, is repeated at different levels of age; scoring of test results, also goes on along with it, so there is a great chance of errors in the repeated measurements.
- Though standardised tests are adopted, nevertheless, results may vary because of varied experience of groups.
- When the study continues for a long period of years, sometimes, less efficient and less experienced hands also have to be associated with the work, which definitely impedes the recording and manipulation of data.

- The investigator or investigators need to take account of the principle of regression, to avoid the mistakes of interpretation to the minimum possible level.

Some examples of the longitudinal study are:

1. The important conclusions to which Fantz, RL reached (*The Origin of Form Perception and Pattern Vision in Young Infants*) regarding the changes that occur in the perception of forms and patterns of vision during infancy, were the results of a longitudinal study. He found that "during 1 to 15 weeks of age most infants prefer to gaze at complex patterns rather than simple stimuli".
2. Escalona, S and Heider, GM in *Prediction and Outcome* remarked as conclusion:

   "Children who had been awkward in their motor movements, and, had not displayed vigorous motor activity during infancy, were retarded as pre-schoolers, in level of motor development, motor co-ordination................some aspects of infant activity...........are precursors of future behaviour."

   This was the result of their longitudinal study.
3. Roger Brown and Ursula Bellugi provided excellent insights into the development of grammar through longitudinal observations.
4. Through a longitudinal study, Irwin (Irwin, OC) found that children who were exposed to books between the ages 13 to 30 months, had larger vocabularies from 17 months on, than did children of the same age, who had not been so exposed.
5. Growth trends and adjustments can only be known through a longitudinal study; Thomson, GC got his book *Child Psychology: Growth Trends and Adjustments*, published in 1952.
6. In Australia, Wheeler did his study in 1961, and confirmed that as a child grows older, he chooses parents less often, and tends more to choose imaginary compositions of desirable qualities or blends of admired traits abstracted from more than one real person ....the self-concept becomes more objective and stable.
7. Yarrow, LJ did his research in the dimensions of maternal care. It was a longitudinal study on 96 infants to know how maternal care (stimulation) boosts development in infancy.

"Children who had been awkward in their motor movements, and, had not displayed vigorous motor activity during infancy, were retarded as pre-schoolers, in level of motor development, motor co-ordination ....some aspects of infant activity...........are precursors of future behaviour."

CROSS-SECTION STUDY

"The cross-section technique requires at least a single measurement for each individual within the particular groups represented; as, when height is measured for each pupil in the first six grades of a public school system.

The central tendency for each of the six grades can be calculated; the results representing 'norms' of growth in height, or, growth trends from grade to grade or year to year, although these central tendencies are not appropriate 'norms' of growth for heights of an individual case,................." (*Essentials of Educational Research—Methodology and Design* by Carter V Good).

The cross-section technique requires at least a single measurement for each individual within the particular groups represented; as, when height is measured for each pupil in the first six grades of a public school system. The central tendency for each of the six grades can be calculated; the results representing 'norms' of growth in height, or, growth trends from grade to grade or year to year.

The above quotation describes the following characteristics of the cross-section study:

Sample Groups belonging to different categories, with one important factor differing in each case, together make the sample with a wide spectrum; or the minimum, at least groups of two categories, must be there to make the study cross-sectional.

As for example, if height of the subjects is to be measured with the objective of finding out what are the different factors—genetic or environmental, which have their impact upon height, then the different categories of the groups may be identical twins reared apart; children of the same family reared apart, and so on. Such a study only can reveal the facts how far genes have their impact on heights; how biological causes, such as the secretion of the related hormone and others affect it; and how socioeconomical status of a family, upon which depends the nourishment and care of the children, affects the growth. Likewise, cognitive or intellectual development, or emotional stability of children belonging to cross-sectional categories, may also be studied to know how nature and nurture act upon development in these fields.

Methods In a cross-section study, too, the method is the same as is employed for a case study; in the former the case studies are spread over a big number of individuals or groups belonging to different sections or categories, while, a case study relates itself to a single unit—even if the sample consists of more than one individuals, they all must be alike in all respects.

Objective A case study is done to know the impact of a single variable—may it be related to nature or nurture, on the growth and development of a single individual or that of a single unit of identical individuals; whereas a cross-section study aims at knowing the central tendency of growth or development through the measurement of a single item of growth or development in individuals grouped in different categories or sections.

A case study is to enable the researcher to know what are the factors that affect the growth or development of an individual, or, of individuals of one single category: the cross-section study is useful for fixing "norms" of growth or development, which may not exactly describe the mode of growth or development of an individual subject, as a case study does.

A cross-section study is the study of subject/subjects with one variable being different in each section of them, the variable whose impact on the subject/subjects, is to be studied. When the researcher aims at finding out what physical, mental or/and emotional changes come about because of the change in the chronological age of a subject, he may take the sample of subjects varying in age but similar in all other variables related to their environment.

Some examples of the cross-section study are:

1. Macfarline, Allen and Honzik conducted their studies on different groups of children—varying in age, dependability and the behaviour of the mother and other elders towards them; and through such cross-section studies could conclude that jealousy is "a normal response to actual, supposed or threatened loss of affection."
2. Breckenridge and Vincent's cross-section study led them to conclude that physical defect of vision causes undesirable emotional development.
3. Waston, G reported the results of his cross-section study covering different age groups, and, belonging to families of varying sub-cultures in "*Some personality differences in children related to strict or permissive parental discipline*"— the lower class children preferred the immediate material rewards of money and other tangible possession; upper middle-class children preferred for the long range goals of fame and power over others. These preferences persist in adolescence, and, may be later even.
4. Jersild's conclusion—"at all levels .... children differ decidedly in their susceptibility to fear." is based on his cross-section studies.
5. McCarthy, Dorthea through cross-section studies, related to different groups and classes of society, came to the conclusion that development of language depends on the amount and nature of stimulation that the environment provides. (*Research in Language Development—Retrospect and Prospect*).
6. The studies conducted by Kriuchkova and Ostrouskaia and Kaplan to verify the facts regarding individual differences in learning abilities at early ages, were cross-sectional as they were conducted on different groups varying in sex, nutrition, somatic conditions, seasonal influences, and so on.

   And, as the studies continued on the same groups as they grew in age, should be considered longitudinal as well.
7. Gesell's classical studies of fear were all cross-sectional as they were conducted on children of different age groups, to know how the nature and object of fear differ with age.
8. Fielder's study of young public school children with hearing defects, was also a cross-sectional study; the children belonging to families of different socioeconomic classes being the subjects.

OBSERVATION

Observation is fundamental in research. The basic elements of scientific facts are revealed through observation. It is the most important technique that can be used in a research method. Observation is useful at every stage of a research method. In the activity of observation, the researcher can make use of each of his sense organs related to sight, hearing, smell, touch and taste. The facts that are revealed through the experiences of these sense organs, help in locating the problem. "Alert" and "Skilful" observation yields clues which help in constructing theoretical solution for the problem. The researcher can find an evidence to substantiate his hypothesis only through careful and accurate observations:

Observation is fundamental in research. The basic elements of scientific facts are revealed through observation. It is the most important technique that can be used in a research method. Observation is useful at every stage of a research method.

"From the inception of an inquiry to the final confirmation or rejection of his proposed problem solution, a research worker relies on observation to keep him on the trail to truth." (*Understanding Educational Research. An Introduction,* Deobald B Van Dalen).

From the inception of an inquiry to the final confirmation or rejection of his proposed problem solution, a research worker relies on observation to keep him on the trail to truth.

Nature of observation Depends upon the problem that is to be investigated into. If a problem is simple, so will be the nature of observation; a complex scientific problem will require a well-planned complicated device of observation—the significant and relevant aspect of the phenomenon, and a certain situation, and some definite time, etc., have to be selected. An observation may be direct, but in a complicated situation, it has to be indirect. The use of precision procedure will be required for a close scrutiny.

The type of instruments to be used, will also depend upon the nature of the problem. And, finally, the report will have to be presented in a form which may sustain public verification.

Factors involved in an observation If psychologically considered, the procedure of observation involves four factors: 1. Attention, 2. Sensation, 3. Perception, and 4. Conception (*Understanding Educational Research*).

1. **Attention** Attention is the process of selection. When the researcher observes the phenomenon, a number of aspects of it, and many other objects may gather together against his sense organ; a throng of stimulants may be there, he will have to select only the most relevant object or aspect for channelising to the cortex, and this is attention, a mental function of bringing an object to the centre of consciousness. For the successful handling of the technique of observation, attention is an important factor to make use of. It is a necessary condition; it indicates a "state of alertness" or a "mental set.............. which assumes so as to sense or perceive (only) selected events, conditions, or things".

Table 1.1 Research methods—A comparative view

	Case Study	*Longitudinal Study*	*Cross-section Study*
Sample	Single individual or a group of similar individuals.	Single individual or a group of similar individuals.	Different groups each varying at least in one important variable from the other or others.
Objective	• To reveal the factors (related to nature and nurture) which make the subject of the sample behave as he or she does.	• To reveal the trend of growth and development. • To assess the efficacy of the remedial measures taken.	• To study how different groups, each varying in one important variable from the other, behave under the same conditions.
Time reference	• The study relates to the current time. • Conclusions are made in reference to the past.	• The researcher starts with the present and traces through to the future. • Conclusions are made in reference to the past.	• A cross-section study is also a study of the present or prevailing conditions as in a case study with the only difference that it is a case study with a wide spectrum of the sample. • Conclusions are made in reference to the past.
Techniques and Tools #	• Observation • Interview • Questionnaire • Test-schedules etc.	• Observation • Interview • Questionnaire • Test-schedules etc.	• Observation • Interview • Questionnaire • Test-schedules etc.

\# The nature of technique depends upon the age and physical and mental maturity or development of the subject/subjects.

There is likelihood that some errors may occur in the process of attention:

- The researcher may be so obsessed with his hypothesis that he may develop a mind set which looks out for the bases which can only support his hypothesis. The researcher would be looking for the facts which can only support his proposed solution to the problem. The researcher should, rather, investigate all the significant aspects of the situation so as to be able to detect the unsuspected facts.
- The researcher should guard against such personal factors which may interfere with his work. He will have to control such

characteristics of the subject that may obstruct the work of effective observation.

- If the subject for investigation is too big, too small, too fleeting or too chaotic to be perceived with the senses, there would be more chances for the occurrence of errors in the work; so a proper subject should be selected, or special instruments be employed looking to the nature of the subject.

2. **Sensation** An object in the external environment of man, stimulates some of his sense organs. That in turn, stimulates the concerned sensory nerves; the sensory nerve impulses reach the brain, and man experiences the event. The event may be of some shape, having different qualities; a sound, varied in tone or pitch; a pressure; pain, warmth or cold, etc. He senses something as sweet, sour, salty or bitter; or distinguishes sweet smell from foul smell because of the experience of the event through sense organs. But our sense organs have their limitations:

   - They cannot be reliable tools for exact measurements of speed, size, intensity or distance; they are poor tools for making comparisons.
   - A sense organ may be defective, thereby, rendering its experience incorrect; and, the observation will be distorted. Congenital colour blindness or tone deafness would affect the observation if colours are to be distinguished or tones to be differentiated.
   - In a state of fatigue, emotional arousal, or under the impact of some drug, sense organs may suffer temporary impairment.
   - Sense organs may also grow less reliable because of age or illness.

   To compensate the limitations of sense organs, special instruments have to be made use of; microscope, amplifying tube, polygraph, and a lot of other latest gadgets and devices have been made available by the science of our day "to extend the range and clarity" of the researcher's observations.

   The researcher should make sure that his senses are working efficiently, "he is getting clear, undistorted, normal signals from his phenomena." He will have to guard against the extraneous stimuli which may make it difficult for him to experience the significant stimuli.

3. **Perception** To experience an event—a shape, a sound, an odour, something as warm or cold; or sweet or sour is not enough—such an experience will be meaningless until and unless it is interpreted in light of the past experiences; only then one can identify the shape

to be that of a cow; the sound that of a telephone; the odour that of a flower; the warmth that of sun or cold that of snow; or taste that of sugar, or, of an unripe mango, Deobold B Van Dalen remarks, "Observation is more than experiencing sensations. Observation is sensation plus perception." He further writes, "Perception is the art of linking what is sensed with some past experience, to give the sensation meaning."

There are some factors or situations which may distort perception, make it less clear, or render it wrong, and so on.

- The memory of the observer may fail him, and, he may associate his present experience with an experience of the past that is not at all related with the present one. The interpretation will be wrong if an association of the present sensation is made with a past perception under some misunderstanding.
- If the observer makes inferences on the basis of insufficient sensory cues, he is very much likely to commit mistakes.
- One more likely pitfall is the too strong a personal interest which would make the observer to be on a look out only for things he likes to see.
- Because of his "private passions" or "pre-conceptions", the observer may ignore some stimuli or interpret them in a partial way.
- A lot of other things are there which distort the perceptions of an observer; his "emotions, motivations, prejudices, mental sets, sense of value, physical conditions, and errors of inference"—are some such things that need to be guarded against by an observer.

4. **Conceptions** "Conception is the intellectual process of removing blocks to perception...". Sometimes, it so happens that a person fails to recognise a thing that his sense or senses experience; he cannot tell what is what—his past experiences also fail to guide him in making any definite meaning of his experience. In such a situation, he resorts to intellectual exercises giving a free hand to his imagination to exhaust all possibilities; of course, his visualisation would be affected by self-concept, social milieu, and other related factors and, the result will be the construction of imaginary concepts.

For a researcher who adopts observation as a technique, it is essential to make use of all these four psychic phenomena in a proper way, lest his revelations should be distorted. The researcher should be cautious that his observations are not distorted because of subjectivity. Deobold B Van Dalen has suggested six things in this respect:

(*i*) The researcher should have **a wide knowledge** of the background of the field that his problem is related to. It is only then he can decide what facts he should look for, and how he can find those facts.

(*ii*) The researcher needs to remain **mentally 'alert' and 'questioning'** all through till the process of observation continues. He also needs ample practice in examining all the aspects of the phenomena in their proper perspective.

(*iii*) **Varied observational instruments and procedures** are available, it is for the investigator to select only those which best suit his objective. He should be proficient too, in the use of the same.

(*iv*) The observer may make **use of the computerised counters or calculators, ACR and VCR, oscillographs and others.** For preserving records, any amount of data may be fed in the memory of the computer with ease, and, in the shortest possible time. Fax and internet services are also very helpful to the observer in communicating his material to his colleagues, and, in getting similar communications from other sources.

(*v*) The observer should, first, make a complete list of items that he is to observe; the order for the observation of these items, should also be fixed. When all details regarding the modalities of the procedure, and, the approach for the procedure, have been chalked out; all tools and instruments have been readied for use, the researcher should start working in right earnest. **No delay in compilation work** can ever be allowed.

(*vi*) The work of reporting is very important, otherwise, the findings of the observer will fail to be communicated in the way he intends the same to be. The scientific observations made by him, **should be reported in precise form, and, using exact words and exact terminology only.**

The observer, generally, observes the overt behaviour of his subject in appropriate situations, and, when the subject is in normal conditions; but sometimes, he may need to find out how his subject behaves physically, mentally or psychically when under some stress, or in tension. To observe his subject with some special set of factors operating upon him, he needs to use anecdotal forms, and other tools for adopting projective methods to reveal facts regarding the convert behaviour and the mind set of his subject. Interviews and questionnaires may also serve as tools in such a study.

REVIEW QUESTIONS

***Q*.1.** What are the characteristics of "case study"?

***Q*.2.** What are the limitations of "case study"?

***Q*.3.** What are the special features of "longitudinal study as a research methodology? "

***Q*.4.** Supposing yourself as a research scholar, describe which methodology, would you prefer for a study related to Child Development; also give reasons for your preference.

***Q*.5.** Make a chart showing characteristics of the research methods—case study, longitudinal study and cross-section study.

CHAPTER 2

GROWTH AND DEVELOPMENT—DEFINED AND EXPLAINED

Chapter Outline

- The Principle of Common Direction of Growth/Development
- The Principle of Continuity
- The Principle of Sequential Development
- The Principle of Maturation or Readiness
- The Principle of Developmental Pace
- The Principle of Individual Differences
- Differing Rates of Growth
- Review Questions

Since conception, the process of growth and development continues; it goes on sometimes slowly and sometimes rapidly. The single cell grows into a full-sized foetus before it is delivered. The process of growth becomes all the more rapid when the child has been born. What are the principles of growth and development, their patterns—we shall deal in this chapter. First, we shall see what these two terms **Growth** and **Development** connote.

The increasing of an organ or limb of the body, in size and weight, is its growth. Division of each cell, and, their growing into thousands in number, or their changing into tissues, blood or bone, is part of the process of development. The process of growth and development goes on simultaneously; for development, growth is also required up to a certain age. Growth is essential to enable the organism to bear the strain which the process of development causes. After a certain age, the process of growth ceases, but development may continue beyond it. An organism is said to have attained maturity in a certain field where the zenith of growth has been reached.

It is in the nature of the organism to grow and develop. Growth and development are the important characteristics of a living organism. As the baby grows in age, it is expected to perform more and more functions; the functions continue to become more and more difficult and complicated. To be able to do all this, development—physical, mental and emotional, is essential; the growth of the body, of its different organs or parts, is also essential for the development.

Development can be defined as the emerging and expanding of capacities of the individual to provide progressively greater facility in functioning. The child increases in motor skills from his uncertain first steps to a high proficiency in skilled games at adolescence; from physiological instability to stability; from his first babbling in infancy to manipulation of language in abstract thinking; from confusion of self to inanimate objects to a clear realisation of himself as a person; from the immature child to the man and woman who is able to reproduce.

Brekenridge et al.[1] have defined "Development" in the following words: "Development can be defined as the emerging and expanding of capacities of the individual to provide progressively greater facility in functioning. The child increases in motor skills from his uncertain first steps to a high proficiency in skilled games at adolescence; from physiological instability to stability; from his first babbling in infancy to manipulation of language in abstract thinking; from confusion of self to inanimate objects to a clear realisation of himself as a person; from the immature child to the man and woman who is able to reproduce."

The history of **physical growth** of human organism begins when it is in the form of a very minute dot which we call **Protoplasm,** only 13 millimetre in size. When the embryo is a month old, its length becomes 6 millimetre. In the second month, it starts having human shape; it grows six times in length and five hundred times in weight. By about 20th week, the mother starts feeling the movement of the foetus; now it weighs nearly one pound. The gaining in of the embryo/foetus in weight, and, its increase in length, is its "growth"; and its ability to make movements, is its "development", motor development which syncronises with the physical growth of the foetus. During the first three years of the infant's life, the growth happens to be very rapid; and so does his development in—physical or mental fields. In the first year, the weight becomes three times than what it was at the time of birth. When the child of 6 or 7 months, shows the development of eye-hand co-ordination in grasping things, the mother feels happy to see; by one year, he can feed himself with spoon and cup; by 18 months, he can exercise control over anal and uretheral sphincters; in due course, the child starts not only running and hopping but doing somersaults and other complicated physical movements which are the sure indicators of rapid physical or motor development—development of balance and co-ordination. Along with this development, mental development also takes place. After birth, the child can only gradually develop the function of sensing things or events, as his skeletal-muscular-neurological growth and development take place, so also develops the area of his gaining experiences through his sense organs because with age, increases his

1. *Child Development: Physical and Psychological Growth Through Adolescence.*

mobility and capability to handle things with increasing skill and in varied ways. Development of language is the most important stage in the process of development. The child's perception increases, and his mental abilities and expression also increase accordingly. Jean Piaget has traced the cognitive development through four stages which will be dealt with later in the book.

Maturity Maturity is the stage in the process of growth or development, when one is fit or ready to perform some particular function, or to learn some particular thing. Psychologists, through their observations and experiments, have concluded that an attempt made to make the young child learn a thing, for which a stage of maturity or readiness has not been reached by him, will only result in frustration on the part of the trainer. A baby cannot have control over his anal and urethal sphincters before he is 18 months old; cannot put one block over the other before he is 2 years old, cannot tell colour effects before the age of 3 to 4; and according to Piaget, "conceptual schemas become organised into interrelated systems" only during the period between two to seven years, which Piaget has called **Operational period** and the problem solving stage begins by about the age of eleven years only. These are the stages when the related skeletal-muscular-neurological systems achieve the required maturity for different physical and cognitive activities referred to above. If efforts are made to make the child do the activities for which "readiness" (maturity) is not there, the efforts are sure to fail, frustrating the one who expects such a performance, and the child too suffers harassment, with deleterious effects to follow.

In books on child development, we find a chart showing agewise growth and development of the child, but the figures show only the average positions which, of course, are predictable. Individual differences are there, because of which the elders often complain about their youngsters not showing enough maturity in accordance with their age. It is to be understood that individuals do not keep the same pace of physical growth and development. The recurring remarks of others regarding their inability, incompetence to do what others of their age can do, develop a self-concept which makes them suffer from inferiority complex and frustration.

In spite of individual differences in growth and development, there is a common, or generally common, pattern of growth and development; there are seven principles working therein:

1. The Principle of Common Direction of Growth/Development;
2. The Principle of Continuity;
3. The Principle of Sequential Development;
4. The Principle of Maturation or Readiness;

5. The Principle of Developmental Pace;
6. The Principle of Individual Differences; and
7. Differing Rates of Growth.

THE PRINCIPLE OF COMMON DIRECTION OF GROWTH/DEVELOPMENT

Though pace of development or growth varies from individual to individual, and in different periods of life, the degree of development or growth may also vary yet the direction of development or growth remains the same in all cases. It is the head of the embryo which develops its shape first; and it does not change so much in size as is the case in regard to other parts of the body after the birth of the baby. The internal organs, such as heart and lungs, develop to their full functional capacity at a very early stage; the outer parts develop later on. So, the direction of development may be said to be from head to legs, and, from interior towards the exterior.

THE PRINCIPLE OF CONTINUITY

According to growth and development, the life of an individual is, generally, divided into four parts: (1) Infancy, from birth to 5 years; (2) Later Childhood, from 5 years to 12 years; (3) Adolescence, from 12 years to 18 years of age; and (4) Adulthood, from 18 years and onwards. Though it has been surveyed how growth and development occur during these different periods of life, nevertheless, it is not the case that growth and development of one particular period of life cease to continue as soon as the period of one stage ends; the process of growth or development is a continuous feature of human life, or, of any organism, and, continues from the very beginning, and crosses over from the boundary of one period to the other. Of course, there is an average age by which, generally, an organ or limb or system of human body reaches its maturity and can perform its function very well, that may be expected from one of that age. And, even if one has not become matured enough to perform a certain action by the age which according to the norms of growth and development, one of that age should be able to do, it should not be concluded that the process of growth and development has now ceased for ever; the process should be expected to continue beyond that limit of age—it is the Principle of Continuity.

THE PRINCIPLE OF SEQUENTIAL DEVELOPMENT

In spite of there being a similar pattern of growth and development in all cases, the pace and degree vary according to individual differences; nevertheless, the sequence of growth and development is the same in all cases. By the sequence being the same, we mean, in all individual cases some parts or organs grow in size, weight, first, and others, after that. A child cannot stand until it has developed the capacity to sit; so the sequence of development is that the child learns sitting first before it can stand; it learns standing first before it can walk. The sequence of the appearing of the deciduous teeth is the same in all cases, and so is the sequence of their falling—some fall first, some after them, and the others still later. During the first three years, the child rapidly grows in size and weight; but there is a sequence in this development too, as to which part grows first and which later. Likewise, a common sequence is found in regard to bodily changes before it is the period of actual pubescence. And, if there is a case where the sequence is not the same, it should be taken as an exception. [Figs. 2.1 (*a*), (*b*), (*c*)].

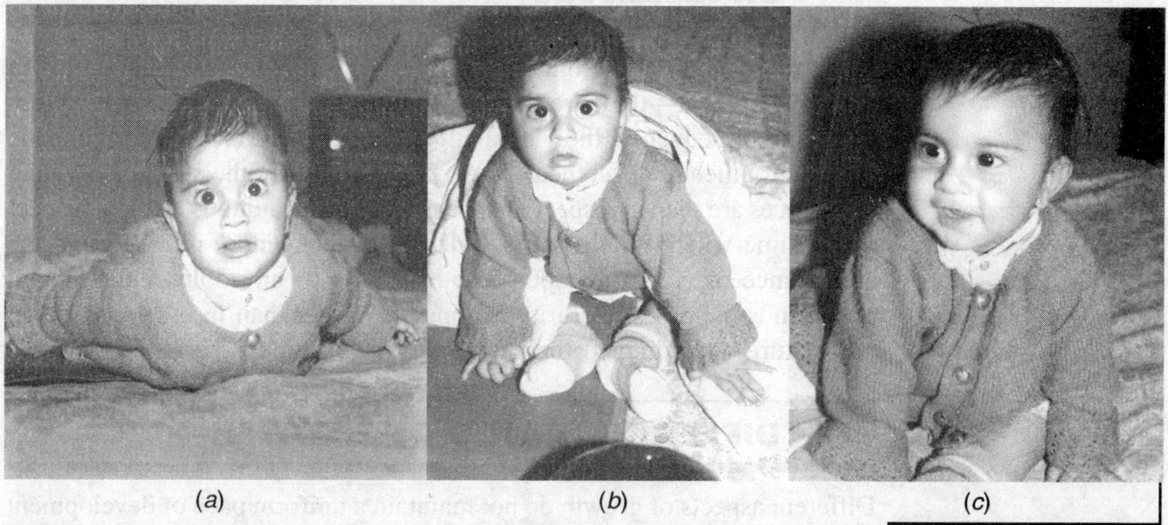

(*a*) (*b*) (*c*)

Figure 2.1 (*a*), (*b*), (*c*) The principle of sequential development has been shown here.

THE PRINCIPLE OF MATURATION OR READINESS

A human being has to perform a number of functions in his life. Some of them happen to be very difficult or complicated requiring full skeletal-muscular-neurological development. Nature first matures the child's muscles and nerves, to enable him to perform a function for which such sort of maturity is essential. This maturity is time-bound; for different kinds of functions different sorts of skeletal-muscular-neurological development is required. No amount of efforts to train a child to do something for which he has not achieved maturity or readiness, can enable him to do the same.

THE PRINCIPLE OF DEVELOPMENTAL PACE

Maturity indicators do not appear at regular intervals. Infancy is a period of accelerated growth when maturity indicators appear in various aspects of growth. During the pre-school and early school years, the pace of growth slackens; it is a period of decelerated growth. But even during the period of decelerated growth, significant bodily, mental and affectional changes take place. There is a spurt of growth in height with the beginning of adolescence. Certain phases have accelerated growth before "they taper off to the adult level."

THE PRINCIPLE OF INDIVIDUAL DIFFERENCES

We have been talking of individual differences in all references to growth and development—they are there in spite of the facts of common pattern and common sequence. Individual differences are natural because of genetic and environmental differences that one has from the others. The individual differences are seen in respect of appearing of the deciduous teeth, in respect of the time when a child starts walking independently, in respect of the appearance of signs of puberty both in case of an adolescent boy and a girl. In some cases, maturity is apparent earlier than in others, some do not mature according to their age, they lag behind others.

DIFFERING RATES OF GROWTH

Different aspects of growth do not maintain a uniform pace of development all the time. By the age of 12 months, the child uses 3 to 5 words, but during the next 3 to 4 months, he may not acquire any new words; it may be because of his energy being utilised in acquiring the skill of locomotion. It is also likely that he may forget what words he had already acquired. This continues even during the period of adolescence. The scholastic progress may be adversely affected during this period because of the excessive energy being utilised in the process of rapid growth and development; social and emotional factors also affect the school work.

Parts of body grow with varying rates during the different periods of life. Nervous systems grow rapidly during the early years. Along with this growth, there occurs rapid development in the skill of control over bodily manipulations; and, expansion of intellectual capacities. During early adolescence, there takes place rapid growth of genital system—"social sexual interests and emotional capacities increase concurrently or *soon afterward*."

In Table 2.1, the concept of growth and development has been defined.

Table 2.1 Distinguishing Growth and Development

Growth	*Development*
1. Growth is *concrete* change in size and weight.	1. Development includes growth but *abstract changes* are also referred to by this term.
2. Growth is a kind of development.	2. Development is wider, and includes growth also.
3. Physical growth, in some cases, may be a pre-condition for motor, mental or cognitive development.	3. Development may take place without any concrete/physical growth.
4. Growth is only physical.	4. Development may be physical, mental or emotional.
5. Growth becomes apparent through increase in size and weight of some organ/limb.	5. Development is perceived through behaviour, too.

GENERAL FACTORS AFFECTING RATE AND PATTERN OF GROWTH AND DEVELOPMENT

In the foregoing paragraphs, some general patterns of growth and development have been given, but in some cases, we find deviations from them. There are certain factors responsible for these deviations. In some cases, genetic accidents happen to be the causes; and because of this, change occurs in the rate as well as pattern of growth and development. If there is interference, especially, during the prenatal period when the foetus develops its organs and systems of the body, it would mark its permanent impact on the growth and development of the child after birth. The child would become mentally retarded if there has been brain damage during the prenatal period, or during the early days of infancy. If after birth, the baby does not get an environment which can fully satisfy his physical and psychological needs, it also thwarts the growth and development of the child; his fundamental needs must get full gratification. Ingalls (1960) has underlined the importance of nutrition, activity, rest, psychological challenges, opportunity to learn, security in affection, an adequate and understanding discipline, and so on, in the realisation of the potentialities ingrained by nature. If all these factors are congenial, the development will be fast and to the possible extent. There can be no healthy growth if the child is not getting adequate feeding. Psychological deprivations would also cause the production of damaged personality. Radiation and pollution are other factors which affect the growth and development in a seriously adverse manner. Cretinism may also be caused because of lack of iodine-salt, with iodine is the remedy.

A child deprived of the warmth of affection, and who is feeling insecure, may develop fear and anxiety as a part of his nature, and the result will be a neurotic personality. Such a personality may also be suffering from grudges or explosive tempers. On the other hand, if a child gets adequate diet, an environment of affection and security, good teaching and other favourable factors in his circumstances, he will develop to his full potential.

Fortunately, human personality has great resilience—because of which it can make up temporary retardations "provided, the disturbing factors are removed in time; or the accident damage is not too devastating." An environment of too much protection is also not desirable as it would give the child no opportunity to develop immunity to life's ordinary germs. And, an excessively coddled child is also likely to grow spoilt. For the development of desirable resistance and moral strength, circumstantial adversities are also helpful, if these are not too severe.

REVIEW QUESTIONS

***Q.*1.** How can you distinguish growth from development?

***Q.*2.** The pace of development differs from person to person, but there are certain principles which are operative in case of each individual whatsoever. What are they?

***Q.*3.** Describe in brief the following:
(*i*) the principle of common direction
(*ii*) the principle of sequential development

***Q.*4.** Which part of the body of an embryo does develop first? Choose the correct option:
(*a*) feet (*b*) hands (*c*) head (*d*) heart

***Q.*5.** The human organism begins its life as a
(*a*) zygote (*b*) protoplasm
(*c*) chromosome (*d*) cytoplasm

ANSWERS TO OBJECTIVE TYPE QUESTIONS

***Q.*4.** (*c*) ***Q.*5.** (*b*)

CHAPTER

3 PRENATAL DEVELOPMENT

Chapter Outline

Man is one of the most complicated creations of nature. Centuries of observations and researches have revealed, the many important factors working into the creation and development of Man. The variables affecting his development, have been put into two categories—Nature and Nurture. There are five major agents inclusive in these two categories:

Two are related to Nature—1. Genetically determined biological variables, and, 2. Non-genetic biological variables.

Three are related to Nurture—3. The child's past learning; 4. The immediate physical environment; and, 5. The general social and cultural milieu in which the embryo/foetus develops.

GENETICALLY DETERMINED BIOLOGICAL VARIABLES

The individual begins its life when the sperm cell from the father penetrates the wall of an ovum, the egg, from the mother. An intricate maturational process, called mitosis, sets in as a result of the fertilisation of an ovum by a sperm. The original fertilised ovum divides and subdivides itself until thousands of cells have been produced. These cells begin to assume different functions, forming themselves as parts of different systems of the body of the organism; the systems, of course, become perceivably operative in due course of time. A few of these systems are the nervous, the skeletal, the muscular and the circulatory. In the beginning, the embryo appears like an expanding ball; gradually it takes its shape—the head, eyes, trunk, arms and legs begin to appear. Approximately, in nine months' time, the embryo becomes ready for birth. (Fig. 3.1).

(*a*) HOW FAR AN ORGANISM IS THE PRODUCT OF HEREDITY?

The life of an organism begins with conception. The moment the tiny sperm penetrates the wall of the ovum, it releases 23 minute particles of chromosomes. At about the same time, the inner core of the ovum, the nucleus, breaks up releasing 23 chromosomes. These are further subdivided, and, are called "genes"—these are the carriers of heredity. It is in these 46 chromosomes that the child's physical heritage from his parents, is contained.

Geneticists differ in their views as to what is transmitted. Lamarck wrote his book on this subject, titled as *Philosophie Zoologique*, and it was published in 1773. During the eighteenth century, the speculation was that the mother's singing ability, and the father's mathematical ability were also transmitted. Weismann (1889) hit hard at such speculations, and asserted that only the germ cells (chromosomes and genes) are unchangeable, the rest of the body may be changed; the germ cells are passed on from the parents at the time of conception. Researches done on this subject later on, also verified the conclusion of Weismann. So, we can say that biological destinies are unchangeable. [Only under special circumstances, genes may change, or, be destroyed—this can happen as a result of atomic blasts, or, because of direct radiation from X-ray].

(*b*) HOW HEREDITARY TRANSMISSION OCCURS?

The fertilised egg cell goes on splitting and multiplying into lengthwise halves, and the same polarising towards the centre—the process is called "Polarisation". The halved chromosomes keep shifting to the opposite sides of the cell. Then, the cell divides itself down the centre. Each new cell, thus created, contains the same 46 chromosomes as the original cell does. This process of the creation of new cells, is repeated again and again as the organism develops. Even when the myriad cells of the human body have assumed their special functions as tissue, bone, blood and muscle, each cell contains the same original 46 chromosomes of the fertilised ovum.

Fig. 3.1 Different stages of development of the embryo / foetus.

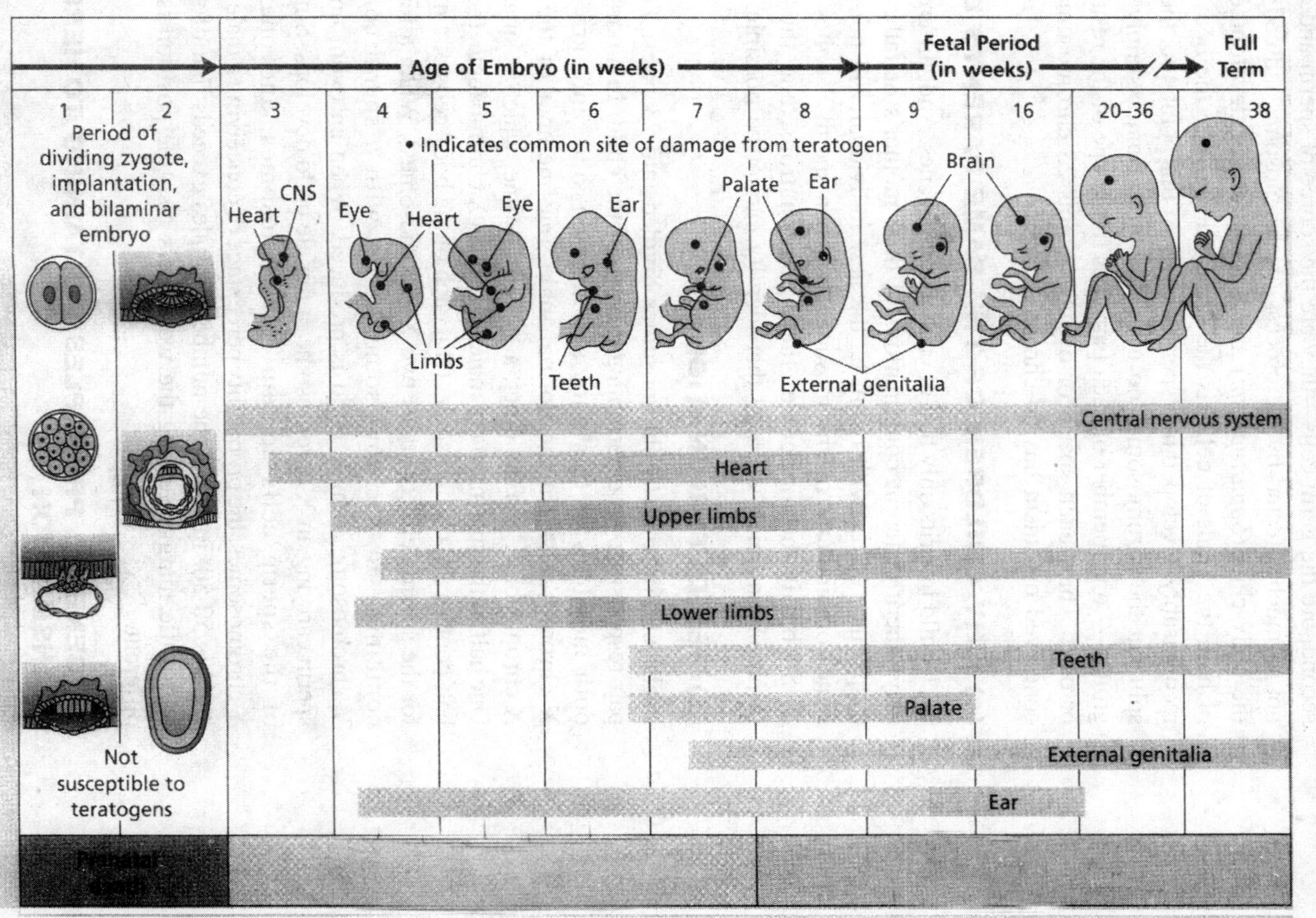

These cells are of two kinds—first, the body cells, they are called *Somatoplasm,* and they make up nerves, muscles, bones and organs. The second, are the germ cells—they are the source of sperm and ova and are not so much affected by the process of chromosome and cell division as the body cells (*Somatoplasm*) are. The pattern of development, in case of both the kinds of cells, is the same till the time the body cells have recognisably developed into sperm or ova. At this point, too, the germ cells split but the chromosomes do not—46 chromosomes simply divide into groups—"one member of each pair goes to the one of the resulting sperm or ova." Thus, each sperm or ovum contains 23 chromosomes; and the conceived organism has 46 chromosomes.

(*c*) WHY CHILDREN OF THE SAME PARENTS DIFFER?

Each child inherits only half of each parent's genes. And, different children may inherit different combinations of their mother's or father's genes—if sperm A unites with ovum C, the new individual will not possess the same combinations of chromosomes as when sperm B unites with ovum C. So big is the number of these combinations, and the process of combination being so rapid that identity cannot be possible.

(*d*) SEX DETERMINATION

Each cell contains 46 chromosomes divided into 23 pairs. There is one pair responsible for determining the sex of the child. In a normal female, both members of this pair, are large in size, and, are called the X chromosomes. In the normal male, one member of the pair is an X chromosome, and the other, a Y chromosome, which is smaller in size. One half of the sperms of the male contain an X chromosome; the remaining half contain a Y chromosome. [But each of the body cells of a male, except for the sperm cells, contains two X chromosomes]. When a female ovum containing an X chromosome, unites with a sperm containing a Y chromosome, a male child is produced. When an ovum unites with a sperm carrying an X chromosome, a female child develops. Since one half of the sperm cells contain X chromosomes, and one half, the Y chromosomes, the probability percentage of conceiving a male or a female child is 50-50. In India, the number of males exceeds that of the females by a little margin; among the westerners also the position is not much different.

(*e*) GENERAL PRINCIPLES PERTAINING TO HEREDITARY TRANSMISSION

We can derive some general principles on the basis of the experiment conducted by Mendel, an Austrian monk, in 1857. He worked on two strains of peas—the red flowering and the white flowering. He found that when plants of a pure red strain were mated with those of a pure white strain, in the second generation, all the offspring would be red. But if they were mated with each other, the third generation would average as three red flowering and one of white flowering strain. The general principles derived are as follows: [these have been summarised by Schienfeld]

1. The inherited characteristics are produced by genes [Mendel calls the same as "factors"]. They pass unchanged from one generation to another.
2. In each individual, these genes are found in pairs. When in a pair, the two genes are different, one of them happens to be "dominant" and the other "recessive".
3. When seeds are formed in any individual, the members of each pair of genes, segregate out independently of the other pairs. But one of every two mated genes will be from each parent to each offspring.

But the geneticists of our days do not much rely upon the findings of Mendel; his results were ignored even during his own days. It was realised that the mechanisms of heredity transmission were much more complicated than what had appeared first:

1. Characteristics depend on complex combinations of gene pairs rather than a single pair.
2. The behaviour of genes cannot be described only as dominant and recessive; they behave in many other ways also; and their effects vary according to the prevailing conditions. Some effects, such as, eye colour, hereditary baldness in men, certain kinds of night-blindness, and some forms of diabetes are quite simple; but others are not so; as for example, mental deficiency depends upon a number of pairs of genes that happen to be present in a particular combination.

The behaviour of genes cannot be described only as dominant and recessive; they behave in many other ways also; and their effects vary according to the prevailing conditions.

NON-GENETIC BIOLOGICAL VARIABLES

What kind of personality, a human organism, would develop into, also depends upon certain other factors related to the anatomy and physiology of a particular human being. In the body, there are a variety of systems; such as nervous system, muscular system, digestive system, blood-circulatory system, respiratory system, and other systems. Then, there are a number of biochemicals affecting the functioning of these systems—the chemicals generally secrete from different kinds of glands. Though, broadly speaking, these systems, chemicals and other substances of the body, are the same in human beings, yet differences are there, important enough to notice, which have their impact in the development of the human organism. They all, together, make the non-genetic variables working into the process of development of the child since its prenatal period.

But this categorisation of variables, is for the convenience of study, as the fact is that one category of variables is not free from the impact of the other category of variables—the kind of genes have their effect on the nature and functioning of the non-genetic biological variables which include in them the different physiological systems and biochemical substances.

"Zygote" is the first fertilised ovum, and is consisted of one cell only. It is surrounded by a thin membrane; its nucleus remains floating in a fluid substance called "Cytoplasm". The nucleus contains the chromosomes and genes inherited from the parental sperm and ovum. After a few hours, the "Zygote" divides itself into two new cells; each of these two new cells divides itself into two cells again—the process is repeated—2 cells, 4 cells, 8 cells, 16 cells, 32 cells and so on..... .

The occasion when a sperm from a male pierces the wall of an ovum or egg from a female, the factors working in the process, are purely physiological. "Zygote" is the first fertilised ovum, and is consisted of one cell only. It is surrounded by a thin membrane; its nucleus remains floating in a fluid substance called **"Cytoplasm"**. The nucleus contains the chromosomes and genes inherited from the parental sperm and ovum. After a few hours, the **"Zygote"** divides itself into two new cells; each of these two new cells divides itself into two cells again—the process is repeated—2 cells, 4 cells, 8 cells, 16 cells, 32 cells and so on..... .

Tendrils begin to grow around the outside of the **trophoblast (the outer layer of the small cavity formed within uterus)**. The extensions of the tendrils reach into the blood spaces formed within the maternal tissue. With this, sets in the period of prenatal development, or the period of the embryo. The process of development of the embryo is dependent on its relationship with the mother. During this process, the biological factors play very important roles—the nature of the functioning of the different bodily systems and the variety of biochemical substances of the mother, have their indirect impact on the on-growing embryo.

1. **Amniotic fluid** keeps the embryo floating in it, and, thereby protects the embryo from any possible physical shock that the mother may have.
2. **Umbilical cord** joins a section of the uterine wall where the uterus and the chorion join. Umbilical cord is called **the life line of the embryo**; it extends from it.
3. Two arteries carry blood from the embryo to the placenta; and one vein carries blood from the placenta to the infant.

Two arteries carry blood from the embryo to the placenta; and one vein carries blood from the placenta to the infant.

Though no direct neural connection exists between the embryo and the mother yet various nutrient substances, mainly sugars, fats, and some protein elements permeate from the mother's blood into the embryo through the **placenta**. Waste products, such as carbon-dioxide and metabolites, can also pass through the placenta. Some vitamins, and a few disease germs may also have their entry into the embryo through the placenta—and may affect its development. The disease germs most likely to affect thus, are those of diptheria, typhoid, influenza and syphilis. This is why, these diseases may sometimes be considered as hereditary.

Do the feelings, ideas, moods or intentions of the mother affect the embryo? There is no channel for the transmission of the same from the mother to the embryo; not a single fibre crosses the placental barrier. "The infant is, in fact, completely shut off from its mother, save for the exchange of simple chemical nutrients and wastes through a screen so fine that it will pass nothing but the smaller molecules of matter".[1]

Nevertheless, a mother's emotional state may affect her child indirectly. The physiological functionings of the child may be affected by the same. When the mother is emotionally aroused, a number of physiological reactions occur—adrenal gland becomes more active, more adrenaline hormone is released. Some other chemical agents are also released into the mother's blood stream. Some of these substances may pass through the placenta, and, affect the physiological processes going on in the unborn child. The embryonic period extends from conception to 8 weeks. During this period, though neuromotor activities do not happen to be well-defined, nevertheless, the period is critical so far the development of the integrity of the nervous system is concerned. And, as such, the mechanical (e.g., falling of the mother downstairs) or chemical (e.g., overdosing of some drug) causes may interfere with the development of the unborn child. Such an interference may cause permanent nervous system damage. If the mother contracts a disease like German Measles, the child may grow mentally deficient.

RH FACTORS

If the mother and the foetus are genetically incompatible in their blood types, they may be biochemically incompatible, too. The baby may be "RH-positive", and, the mother "RH-negative". In such a case, the child's red blood corpuscles may contain a substance which makes the blood agglutinate in response to a specially prepared serum while its mother's blood may lack this substance. The "RH-positive" of the child may produce certain substance called antigens which enter into the mother's circulation through the placental barrier. Antibodies are then produced in her blood. The same then pass back into the circulatory system of the foetus. This causes damage destroying his red cells and preventing the normal distribution of oxygen. Tragic consequences in the form of miscarriage, still birth or death shortly after birth may be the results. And, if the child survives, he may be partially paralysed or mentally deficient as a result of *erythroblastosis,* or brain damage caused because of inadequate oxygen supply during the crucial development period.

"RH-positive", and, the mother "RH-negative". In such a case, the child's red blood corpuscles may contain a substance which makes the blood agglutinate in response to a specially prepared serum while its mother's blood may lack this substance.

1. Mussen, Paul Henry, Conger John Janeway, Jerom Kagan. *Child Development and Personality,* 1964.

Fortunately, RH-is not incompatible in mother and child almost in all cases. Incidence of erythroblastosis is only 1 in 200 cases. First born children are not, usually affected, since the development of antibodies in the mother takes some time. But the subsequent children are more likely to suffer if the mother's RH-blood types are not the same as that of the child.

But now antidote is available to prevent the disastrous effects of RH-incompatibility—mother is injected after delivery when the incompatibility has been detected.

A woman planning marriage should consult her physician to find out the RH-group of herself as well as of her prospective husband. If the RH-types are known at this stage, measures are available to minimise the evil effects of the RH-incompatibility to the possible extent.

Incompatibility between the mother and the foetus for A, B or O blood substances, may cause similar consequences, as mentioned in case of RH-incompatibility. But the percentage of incidence is much smaller.

THE CHILD'S PAST LEARNING

Now, we start considering how Nurture affects the growth and development of the child who is still unborn. Really speaking, the growth and development of the child—during prenatal and postnatal periods, is the result of the interaction between Nature and Nurture. The latter may further boost the natural course of growth and development, the process of natural growth and development may become more rapid, more effective and stronger if congenial conditions are provided for the Nature to function. Conditions, physical and social, together make the Nurture. In the absence of proper Nurturing, the normal functioning of Nature will be thwarted, and growth and development will be adversely affected.

The prenatal period has been broadly divided into two parts; the first, extending up to 8 weeks, is that of embryonic stage; and during the second stage, we call the child as foetus. It is during this second period, when the unborn child begins to respond to the tactile stimulation, starts distinguishing different tastes, and to react to sounds and odours. These are the kinds of learnings with which the child is born; and, the same have been called here as Past Learning. In the *Mahabharat,* there is a reference that Abhimanyu, the son of Arjun, learnt to enter into the Chakravyuh—an impenetrable arrangement for positioning the soldiers—while he was still in the womb of his mother. This may not be a total truth, a mere mythical anecdote, though, it may be; nevertheless, it alludes to a fact that learning may also take place when the child is still a foetus. A few days ago, the author happened to read in a newspaper that an electronic device, smaller in size than a pager, has been developed, through which sounds may be communicated to the unborn child. The gadget is attached to the stomach. It is also being claimed, that this device has been experimented on a big sample. Still, we are right in doubting it till the same is recognised by the world of science.

The mind of the child is not a blank slate even when it is born. There happen to be an umpteen number of impressions related to different sense organs. Though the foetus does not get much chances to react to the external phenomena, to the experiences that different sense organs get, impressions are made on the mind of the unborn child. These impressions enable even the new born child, to react promptly to the various visual, auditory or other experiences received through the sense organs. To some of these reactions, we call reflex actions, but others are learned. Of course, the amount of such learning, called here "Past Learning", is, generally, small or limited, and, the nature of it is simple, even then their impact on future development of the child is significant.

Had the genetic factor (the Nature) only been significant, there would not have been so much difference in the IQ of fraternal and identical twins—Newman[2] et al. found the average difference to be 9.9 points in case of fraternal twins, and 5.9 in case of identical twins. Jones[3] also gives weight to environmental similarity.

All these psychologists studied the impact of the external environment on the intellectual development of the young children, but we are concerned here with the prenatal period of the child, when the external environment (Nurture) can exert its influence on the foetus, only indirectly, through what impressions the mother gets, and how she reacts to the same. The suitability of the environment of the mother would have a positive impact upon the growth and development of the unborn child, though the impact on the unborn child cannot so easily be experimentally verified.

The Nature causes a rapid growth in the foetus; the length increases from 3 inches by the end of the 3rd month, to 10 inches in a period of 16 to 20 weeks (6 months); the weight grows to 8 or 9 ounces; the trunk flexes and the head extends; motor functions become more differentiated. Thus, the foetus becomes more fit for learning through his sense organs, which increasingly become operative during this period. If Nurture is congenial, it would be a facilitating factor in the process of learning. However, Nurture has not much scope to enhance the process of learning till the child is born.

THE IMMEDIATE PHYSICAL ENVIRONMENT

The physical environment that the pregnant mother lives in, is an important

2. Newman, Freeman and Holzinger. *Twins: A Study of Heredity and Environment.*
3. Jones, HF. *Environmental Influence on Mental Development.*

factor affecting the growth and development of the embryo/foetus. Here again, the physical environment would have its first effect upon the mother of the unborn child, and through the former, the latter would be affected. The physical environment consists of air, food, drug, mother's diseases and the general impact of the surroundings on the mind and body of the pregnant woman and her unborn child in the womb.

(*a*) **Air** Pure and sufficient air should be available to the expectant mother for the proper functioning of the respiratory system, and, the purification of the blood. Otherwise, the mother may develop different ailments which would impair the growth and development of the embryo/foetus. Inadequate supply of pure air and improper ventilation may, also, lead to asphyxia. During labour, the position of the baby should be monitored carefully. Sometimes, due to its wrong position, the baby could have breathing problems.

(*b*) **Malnutrition of the mother** We are well aware of the fact that the unborn child has its feeding through its mother, so malnutrition of the mother will affect the growth and development of the unborn child. The mother should have balanced diet, with all the needful nutrients available in it. The expectant mother needs to keep herself healthy, using nourishing food in adequate quantity, so that she may deliver a healthy baby. The embryo/foetus is fed through the umbilical cord which contains two arteries for the blood of the mother to flow into the embryo/foetus to nourish it; the mother's blood must contain the essential nutrients for the proper growth and development of the unborn child. The semipermeable membrane of the placenta, also has its important role in the supply of oxygen and nutrients to the foetus. The placenta allows an exchange of oxygen and nutrients to be passed from the mother to the foetus, linked by the umbilical cord.

A study was conducted on 210 pregnant women of a clinic, who were having inadequate diet during the first 4 or 5 months of pregnancy. The diet of 90 of them was supplemented and made adequate from a nutritional point of view; that of the remaining 120, was kept nutritionally deficient throughout their pregnancies. The comparison of the effect of maternal diets upon the course of pregnancy and the condition of the infants during the first few months of their life, in case of both the groups, revealed important facts:

1. The mothers of the "good-diet" group, were good in health during the entire period of their pregnancies.
2. Complications, such as anaemia, toxaemia, threatened and actual miscarriages, premature births and still births, were much more frequent in the "poor-diet" group.

3. The women of the "good-diet" group, on an average, had to remain in the labour room for five hours less.
4. The infants of the first group (good-diet group), were in a better health condition during the first two weeks after their births.
5. The infants of the first group also had smaller incidences of major illnesses, such as, pneumonia, ricket, tetany, anaemia, and minor diseases, like cold, bronchitis during the entire first six months.

The findings of the investigators who worked on maternal malnutrition, were published under the title *The influence of improved prenatal nutrition upon the infant.* Those associated with the work were Ebbs, JH; Brown, A; Tisdall FF; Moyle, WH and Bell, M. Another important work, related to this field, was entitled as *The influence of prenatal diet on the Mother and Child*—the investigators were Ebbs, JH; Tisdall, FF and Scott, WA. *The clinical significance of nutritional deficiencies in pregnancy* by Tompkins, W'I', is also an important work on the subject.

Insufficient protein in the mother's diet, may cause premature birth and neural defects in the infant. The findings are important:

".....Foetus obtains its nutritional requirements prior to the maternal organisms, and, draws upon maternal storages. When these storages are depleted to a point of deficiency in the mother, the baby will fail to obtain the necessary elements."

".....foetus obtains its nutritional requirements prior to the maternal organisms, and, draws upon maternal storages. When these storages are depleted to a point of deficiency in the mother, the baby will fail to obtain the necessary elements."

(*c*) **Drug** Narcotics, and dosages of some drugs, may prove very harmful to the expectant mother, and, may thwart or distort the development of the foetus. They permeate the mother's blood stream, whence they are transmitted to the foetus, affecting its development. Temporary dysfunctions may be the result. We see some neonates to be often drowsy, or showing signs of oversedation—this may happen as an effect of barbiturate drugs or when other such preparation is given during labour. Respiratory difficulties may be caused because of the use of these drugs. A study of the cases of twenty mothers who had been given second sodium, was conducted, and it was found that because of its use, the cardiac activity of the neonates, was in a depressed condition for two days after birth, they seemed sluggish and drowsy.

The blood of the foetus may become overloaded with such drugs if the same are given in heavy dosages to the mother; and may result in asphyxiation leading to permanent brain damage or mental impairment.

If the mother smokes, it may bring about such chemical reactions that accelerate the heart rate, though any permanent heart or circulatory impairment may not be caused. Large therapeutic doses of radium or Roentgen (X-ray) may prove injurious; it may precipitate abortion.

(*d*) **Mother's diseases** Though there is an effective barrier to protect the embryo/foetus from the possible contagion or effect of any maternal disease, yet in rare cases, babies are born with smallpox, measles, mumps or chickenpox transmitted from their mother. The incidence of the transmission of syphilitic spirocetes is as high as 24 per cent. If the prospective mother contracts Rubella (German Measles) within the first 3 or 4 months of pregnancy, it may damage the foetus considerably—deaf-mutism, cardiac-lesions, cataracts or some form of mental deficiency may be caused because of it. Even if the attack is not very serious, foetal malformations may be caused. Mother's continuous illness for more than a week, may cause a similar harm.

(*e*) **Effects of pregnancy or delivery disturbances** Researches conducted on the basis of hospital files, have revealed/verified the important fact that mental retardation in children, in a high percentage of cases, were found to be related to pregnancy or delivery disturbances. Incidences of mental retardation are much higher in case of premature births than in mature deliveries. In some cases of mental retardation, physiological disturbances during pregnancy seem to be the cause. The most common among the physiological disturbances, are bleeding, toxaemia, disturbances in blood circulation and kidney function during the late stages of pregnancy. Length of labour and the type of operative procedures were not found to be important factors affecting the infants that were born. Majority of epileptic children had mothers who had experienced pregnancy disturbances. Speech disorders or muscular tics, were not found to be the results of disturbed pregnancy or abnormal delivery.

People belonging to lower classes of society suffer more incidences of pregnancy difficulties and premature births than those who are socially and financially well off.

The mother's age at the time of conception and delivery is also an important factor to consider. A study of the records, reveals the fact that child and maternal mortality is low if the age of the mother ranges between 23 and 29. A higher proportion of retarded children are born to mothers who are either under 20 or above 35.[4] Difficulties are caused because of the reproductive organs being not fully or adequately developed in case of younger women, and, because of

4. Pasamanic, B, Lilienfeld, AM: *Association of Maternal and Foetal Factors with Development of Mental Deficiency.*

progressive decline in reproductive functioning in case of elderly women who deliver first infant when they are 35 or over. The production of defective ova (eggs) is more likely in case of older women. Such elderly mothers may develop complications during their deliveries, and, are likely to have a more difficult and longer labour thereby, also, affecting the infant being born. Deliveries in case of such younger and elderly women, are more likely to require operative and caesarean sections.

Mongolism is a condition of severe mental retardation.

Mongolism is a condition of severe mental retardation. It is associated with certain physical features, such as oblique or slit eyes, and disorderly growth of the skull bones. Incidences of Mongolism are higher in case of children born to older women than to the younger ones. The main cause of Mongolism has been found to be chromosomal abnormality. On the basis of microscopic study of thc cclls takcn from the bone marrow of the Mongoloid children, it has been established that each cell of a Mongoloid has 47 chromosomes rather than 46, as is the case in each normal child.

Each cell of a Mongoloid hac 47 chromosomes rather than 46, as is the case in each normal child.

(*f*) **The birth process** Birth is an event of tremendous importance. The infant is displaced from a calm, quiet and secure environment of the uterus; into a "blooming, brizzing confusion of the outside world." The event has both psychological and physical significance. The psychologists consider it to be a major event affecting the infant's sense of security—the occasion proves to be one which provides prototype for all future anxieties. Specific birth injuries may cause permanent impacts on the physique and psyche of the child. Abnormally long and difficult labour, instrumental delivery, obstetrical mishandling may cause immense harm to the neonate, both physically and psychologically. The central nervous system may be damaged as a result of anoxia or haemorrhage of the blood vessels of the brain. As a consequence, there may occur motor and mental defects.

Lack of oxygen (anoxia) during the delivery process, birth injury, some pathological abnormalities in the brain may result in "cerebral palsy". "Cerebral palsy" appears in the form of motor defect; sometimes, it is not evident soon after birth. In this disease, some important areas of the brain are damaged. Adequate supply of oxygen is necessary before, during, and after the birth of the child—as lack of it may cause anoxia or asphyxiation, which may result in the degenerative changes in the brain cells leading to mental retardation. The sensitivity of the traumatised infant is blunted, and he becomes less sensitive to pain, the process of maturation in motor integration is delayed or thwarted; and his response to visual stimulation becomes inadequate.

(*g*) **Premature birth** Premature birth is a traumatic event for the infant. If premature birth is unduly prolonged or precipitous, the infant is subjected to unusual stress. Incidence of mental, motor or emotional disturbances are much higher among the premature children. Such a child happens to be extremely fragile and unprepared for extrauterine life.

A comparative study was conducted upon 500 prematurely born children vis-a-vis a control group of 490 full-term children. The lighter the weight, the more is the likelihood of some mental or neural defect. At 40 weeks of age, over 16 per cent of the prematures and 8 per cent of the normals, showed neurological defects of the serious type; and, the motor activities of the children were mainly affected by them. To know the long-term consequences, a study was done on children aged between 4 to 10. The prematures were not found retarded in size, but there were greater incidences of eye-defects. The mean IQ of the prematures was 94, while that of the normals, was 107. In most of the cases, no deficit was witnessed in body growth of the prematures, but in later years, they were found to be more apt to manifest behaviour abnormalities. The abnormalities were of the nature of highly developed auditory or visual sensitivity, speech difficulties, baby talk or mispronunciation; or awkward movement, or poor motor co-ordination; activity extremes—overactive or sluggish; difficulties in sphincter control; too much dependence upon mother; either extremely flighty or badly sticking to work and acutely shy.

All these difficulties may also develop in consequence to some postnatal experiences, and, such experiences proved to be rather, more important factors. If the family environment is not stimulating enough, or if they are overprotected by the parents, many other psychological problems may result. Intelligence and personality tests were administered to 22 children of the age between 8 and 19; no permanent effect of premature birth was found. Of course, because of emotional problems, they failed to make the optimal use of their intellectual abilities.

THE GENERAL SOCIAL AND CULTURAL MILIEU IN WHICH THE EMBRYO/FOETUS DEVELOPS

The foetus, of course, is not immediately affected by the milieu outside. It is first the mother who is affected. The blood of the mother is affected because of increase in the secretion of certain harmones, thereby, increasing the pulse rate or disturbing the functions of digestive or respiratory systems. The diet of the mother, and the overall social or cultural environment of the family, have their effects on the growth and development of the foetus.

The socioeconomic environment of the family is a relevant factor in the process of growth and development of the foetus. A mother living in a small and congested house, surrounded by a dingy or dirty physical environment, giving out foul smell and polluted air, can hardly maintain good health. She may have to work long and continuous—doing domestic chores and (may be) working as a wage servant, she can hardly spare any time to relax. Nor she can afford a balanced diet, nourishing enough to supply calories in the required amount. The nutrient-deficit diet, polluted and foul air, a noisy and disturbing house, leave the prospective mother a tired, gloomy, morbid or diseased woman. Such a state of affair is sure to affect the growth and development of the organism lying in her uterus, since the feeding of the organism is done through the umbilical cord, connecting the foetus to the blood arteries of the mother via the placenta.

A house where there is no peace, its occupants, though members of the same family, lack in a sense of belongingness; where squabbling is a routine, and, the husband is insensitive to the feelings and needs of his wife, a prospective mother, the husband may be a drunkard, treats his wife cruelly, and, would cause a severe strain to the pregnant woman, she would be obsessed with a feeling of fear and anxiety. Emotions such as anger, fear and anxiety cause more secretion of hormones, such as, adrenalin, more liberation of chemicals such as acetylcholine and epinephrene into the mother's blood stream. Cell metabolism is also affected. All this, changes the composition of the blood of the mother, and, of the foetus through the placenta. These substances change the circulatory system of the foetus. These changes may result in irritation to the foetus. LW Sontag found that if the mother continues suffering a state of high emotional stress for several weeks, the bodily movement of the foetus increases several times. Its activity continues at an increased level throughout the entire period. Heightened irritability would continue for hours together. Infants who are born to unhappy and upset mothers, have high activity levels. Sontag[5] writes: "Such ... an infant is from the beginning a hyperactive, irritable, squirming, crying child, who cries for his feeding after every two or three hours, instead of sleeping through his four-hour feeding period. Because, his irritability affects control of his gastrointestinal tract, he empties his bowels at unusually frequent intervals; spits up half his feedings, and, generally makes a nuisance of himself. He is, to all intents and purposes, a neurotic infant when he is born."

"Such ... an infant is from the beginning a hyperactive, irritable, squirming, crying child, who cries for his feeding after every two or three hours, instead of sleeping through his four-hour feeding period. Because, his irritability affects control of his gastrointestinal tract, he empties his bowels at unusually frequent intervals; spits up half his feedings, and, generally makes a nuisance of himself. He is, to all intents and purposes, a neurotic infant when he is born."

Such an infant may have severe feeding problem; being unable to retain food, would grow "emaciated" and "dehydrated."

5. Sontag, LW. *The Significance of Foetal Environmental Differences.*

When the expectant mother is extremely tired, there is uncommon abdominal pressure; or when the atmosphere remains disturbed by repeated and violent sounds, the movements of the foetus are considerably increased.

Maternal emotional tensions may produce colic in the neonate; and the neonate cries continually because of pain. Abnormal delivery may also be a cause for high amount of anxiety. Maternal anxiety and emotional unrest during pregnancy, may thwart the usual course of foetal development and growth; and the neonate may become handicapped.

Maternal attitudes There can be no congenial atmosphere for the foetus to grow in a normal course, and to have desirable impressions to serve as "past learnings" after birth, if the sub-culture of the family is not of a good sort. It is common experience in India that the poor and the slum-dwellers have more offspring though the attitude of the mother, generally, does not happen to be welcoming for the foetus because of the torturing penury of the family, and, also because of the attitudes of other members of the family towards the act of conceiving. A woman who resents of being pregnant, is more likely to be upset when she becomes so. Marital conflict, generally, leads to the development of the attitude of resentment. If the woman is not well-adjusted with her in-laws, or, her husband, even then she would not like the idea of conceiving.

If the girl is not mature enough so far her age is concerned, even then she may resent. If the woman is satisfied with the marital relationship with her husband, she would have positive attitudes towards pregnancy, which is so helpful in the proper growth and development of the embryo/foetus. The woman must feel financially secured, emotionally satisfied with her husband, and culturally compatible with him. Families with no education even up to the minimum needful level, which are culturally backward, and, are ignorant of proper sex education, are financially and emotionally impoverished, and where the elder children are forced to take care of their younger siblings, generally, have women with a negative attitude towards pregnancy. A strong negative attitude towards pregnancy, generally, develops psychosomatic reactions, characterised by nausea, vomiting, backaches, etc. The infants of such women also exhibit behavioural abnormalities like irregular eating, too frequent bowel movements, gas pains, inability to sleep at night, and too much crying.

The author read an article published in the Ist January 1996 issue of the *Times of India*, wherein was given that a quarter of the estimated five lakh who die each year from pregnancy-related causes, nearly 99 per cent of these occur in the developing nations—this verifies the fact that socioeconomic status is an important factor for the successful or wholesome delivery.

NATURE–NURTURE

The previous sections dealt with the factors of Nature and Nurture that affect the growth and development of the embryo/foetus. In the first category, we considered two factors—(*i*) Genetic and (*ii*) Non-genetic biological factors; and, under Nurture, three factors were discussed (*i*) Past learning, (*ii*) Immediate physical environment, and (*iii*) Social and cultural milieu. This section is to clarify the relationship between Nature and Nurture. Nurture supports and accelerates the work of Nature. If there is a proper harmony between the two, the process of growth and development, will continue unhindered and the pace would be as fast as it, normally, can be. Of course, if the factors of Nature, are not wholesome, Nurture can do something to correct the same, or to lessen the effect of the same to some extent—but Nurture cannot turn a pig into a lion; the effects of Nature cannot be nullified altogether. Though the behaviourists claim to the contrary:

"Give me a dozen healthy infants, well-formed, and my own specified world to bring them up; and I'll graduate to take any one at random and train him to become any type of specialist I might select—doctor, lawyer, merchant, chief, and yes, even beggarman and thief, regardless of his talents, peculiarities, tendencies, abilities, vocations, and race of ancestors. There is no such thing as inheritance of capacity, talent, temperament, mental constitution and characteristics".

But it is an extreme view to reject altogether, the inescapable impact of Nature in the development of personality. Mental deficiency in the form of cerebral selerosis is caused by the co-existence of two specific recessive genes, and no amount of medical care or training by the mother or teacher of the child suffering from it, can make any improvement. Heredity or Nature also plays an important role in the physical or body-build of an individual; but the impact of environment or Nurture in this respect, is not altogether absent—Nurture may help or hinder the work of Nature. Nature does its work through genes. The work of genes, is never direct; we cannot study it directly but only derivatively. Secondly, genes and other non-genetic biological factors, which together make Nature in regard to the growth and development of the individual, can never work without having the effect of environment or Nurture on them. So the approach to study the impact of Nature and Nurture on the development of personality, should not be as, which particular characteristic of personality is due to Nature, and which due to Nurture; the approach should rather be—"How" Nature has affected the growth and development of a particular characteristic or trait of personality, and, "How" Nurture has played its role in the same process. Of course, in respect of some developments, the role of Nature may be very-very important, and that of Nurture may not be very substantial; in case of others, the fact may be just reverse. Nevertheless, we should not forget that Nature and Nurture are not to be studied as antithesis to each other, but, rather, the one as complementary to the other; generally, one affects the work of the other. There are only a few cases where Nurture appears to be helpless in changing or even affecting the course of Nature—the comparative study of the amount of effect of each of them in the process of growth and development, may make us remark this.

The impact of environment on the growth, is quite important. Environment or Nurture affects height and weight. Obesity is mainly the result of rich diet and less physical work, again the environmental factors, or Nurture. Over-protection by parents may lead to the development of such dietary styles which result in obesity.

Physical and psychological processes are affected by reasons which are environmental. A person, whose efforts to satisfy his drive representative deeds or others, are obstructed time and again, gets angry. One who does not feel assured of his security, becomes obsessed with fear. Anger and fear adversely affect the functions of different body systems, and glands, secreting important chemical substances. With the result that blood pressure rises, the throat dries, and the pulse rate increases. But also anger and fear do not affect all alike—those who are highly reactive, they are more affected, and express more severe and persistent reactions. And, how much reactive one's nervous system is, depends upon the factors related to Nature that is genetic and non-genetic biological factors. The proportion of effect of the factors—those related to Nature, and, those to Nurture, became evident through the investigations conducted on two different categories of subjects. The first being, that of identical twins, and the second, that of the non-identical twins. The average difference in blood pressure in case of identical twins, was 5.1; while in case of non-identical twins, it was 8.4. Likewise, a difference was found in each of the other cases—pulse rate, breathing, salivation and perspiration. Investigations revealed the comparative impact of Nature, and Nurture in all these cases.

A number of identical twins were found to be more consistently and closely related than the non-identical siblings. And, siblings were found to be having many more things in common than did the unrelated children, "... there is a genetic factor in autonomous nervous system functioning".[6] Under psychological stress, some individuals become hypertensive while others do not—maybe, because of different genetic factors.

Longevity Longevity is also a field where genetic factor plays an important role. Studies conducted to see the effect of genes on longevity, revealed the fact that in case of identical twins there was an average difference of 36.9 months when they survive beyond 60 years of age, while in case of non-identical twins the difference was 78.3 months.

6. Jost, H and Sontag, LW. *The Genetic Factors in Autonomic Nervous System. Psychosomatic Medicine.*

Motor ability Researchers studied a sample of identical twins vis-a-vis that of a non-identical one. The study revealed that the impact of genetic factor was important in this field also. The timings for the beginning of sitting and of walking, were much more similar in case of identical twins than in case of non-identical twins. Likewise, there was significant similarity in the patterns of eye-movements while reading, in case of identical twins, which was not found to be the case with fraternal twins.

Physical defects and diseases Causes for hearing and visual defects have, in most cases, been found to be hereditary. There are diseases which transmit from parents to their children, for example, diabetes and haemophilia. There is controversy regarding the causes of numerous other diseases. The fact is, there are a number of diseases which are the results of the combined effect of heredity and environment.

Mental defects and retardation All of us come across many cases of congenital mental defects—the impact of environment can bring about little or no improvement in such cases. Gross mental disorders or deterioration in intelligence, are caused by hereditary factors. Infantile amaurotic familial idiocy is caused by a peculiar hereditary defect in the nerve cells of the brain and spinal cord. The cells swell and become full of fat; this may result in paralysis, blindness or mental deficiency. The infant may not survive long. "This disorder appears to be caused by the inheritance of a specific recessive gene from both the mother and father, and occurs most often when the parents themselves are close relatives." (Stern, C: *Principle of Human Genetics, 1960*).

Phenylketonuria is another hereditary syndrome. This disease is caused by deficiency of enzyme, with the result that metabolic functioning is adversely affected. A toxic chemical accumulates in the body, which causes damage to the nervous system, and leads to mental deterioration. If the ailment is diagnosed early, the harmful effects may be minimised through special diet. Though the disease is genetically determined, the process is not completely irreversible.

Mental disorder Certain kinds of mental disorders are caused by genetic factors. General paresis is an example. It is partial paralysis. "Huntington's Chorea" is another mental disease. It is a progressive hereditary disease and affects the adults. The patient makes involuntary jerky movements, and progressive dementia develops. Syphilis of the central nervous system is caused by infection or similar agents affecting the body from outside; but in many cases, it passes from parents to their offspring.

There are a number of mental disorders which fall into two categories—(*i*) Psychosis (a general term for any serious disorder where the patient shows lack of insight), and (*ii*) Psychoneurosis (when a patient has a faulty response to the stresses of life). There is less agreement among the psychologists as to which factors (related to Nature or Nurture) are more significant in causing these mental disorders. Some experts viewed them as entirely dependent on environmental factors—mainly those related to early life experiences; while some attribute the same to the hereditary defects.

One of the commonest forms of functional psychosis is Schizophrenia: The Schizophrenic manifests defects in logical thinking, and in emotional responsiveness. An ordinary person would term such a person as "crazy". Some experts attribute early child-parent relationship to be the main factor in the development of this disorder. The majority of psychologists consider Schizophrenia to be the "reaction of a biological organism to its environment; although they may differ widely concerning the relative importance attributable to heredity and environmental influences in its determination". Kallmann, FJ (*The Genetic Theory of Schizophrenia*) studied 794 cases of Schizophrenia, and concluded: "the more closely one is genetically related to a Schizophrenic, the greater are one's chances of developing the disorder .... the genetic factor is probably recessive." Even then, the importance of environmental factors, is suggested by the data given by Kallmann. 91 per cent monozygotic (identical) twins of Schizophrenic patients developed mental disorder, when reared in a like general environment, but only 78 per cent did so when reared in a different environment. However, a sudden development of a schizophrenic breakdown, with no trace of it in the patient's earlier life, should be taken as influenced by genetic factors.

Intelligence of a child is considered to be dependent both on genetic (NATURE) and environmental (NURTURE) factors.

Intelligence Intelligence of a child is considered to be dependent both on genetic (NATURE) and environmental (NURTURE) factors. To be definite regarding the percentage of effect of each kind, is well-nigh impossible. Burks[7] and Leahy[8], through their studies, revealed that relationships between children and their parents, were higher than those between children and their foster parents.

To assess the impact of genetic factors on IQ, Newman, Freeman and Holzinger conducted studies (*Twins: A study of heredity and environment*) and came to the conclusion that there was a difference of 9.9 points in IQ in case of fraternal twins, and, of 5.9 points in case of identical twins. Newman, Freeman and Holzinger found a correlation of 0.76 between the IQs of identical twins reared in different environments, and 0.63 between those of non-identical twins reared together.

Shields, J and Slater, E published their findings in their book titled as *Heredity and Psychological Abnormality*. They studied 40 pairs of identical twins reared apart and found that in a non-verbal intelligence test, in case of each pair, there was a correlation of 0.77.

7. Burks, BS. *The Relative Influence of Nature and Nurture upon Mental Development; A comparative study of foster parent–foster child resemblance and true parent–true child resemblance.*
8. Leahy, AM. *Nature, Nurture and Intelligence.*

In another study of the children of foster homes, the average correlation between children's IQ and that of their natural parents, was found to be ranging between 0.50 and 0.60. And, that of the foster children and their foster parents, it was lower than 0.50. Thus in intelligence, the children resemble their natural parents more than their foster parents. The studies conducted by Burks and Leahy, led to similar conclusions. Honzik and Marjorie, P[9] found that upto four years of age, there was little or no relationship between the child's IQ and the education of its true or foster parent. From age 6 onward, the correspondence between the IQ of the child and the education of the true mother or father, was about 0.35, while in case of foster parent's education, it was almost zero.

Personality Pearson, K compared the inheritance of mental and moral character in man, with the inheritance of physical character, and he found that an average correlation was, 0.52 between siblings in traits, such as, vivacity and temper. "We are forced to the conclusion that the physical and psychical characteristics in man, are inherited within broad lines in the same manner and with the same intensity."

Jones[10], disagreeing to this conclusion, remarks: ".... a given degree of resemblance may (theoretically) be obtained not only through the influence of a common heredity, but also through the effects of living in a common environment."

".... a given degree of resemblance may (theoretically) be obtained not only through the influence of a common heredity, but also through the effects of living in a common environment."

In a number of studies, the correlations of identical twins were found to be higher than those of fraternal twins; these correlations were higher regarding physical traits than in the comparison of intelligence. A large battery of tests was given to cover 600 children ranging from 10 to 15 years of age, and consisted of (*i*) identical twins reared together; (*ii*) fraternal twins reared together; (*iii*) non-twin siblings reared together, and apart; (*iv*) unrelated children reared together, and apart, and (*v*) a sample of a general population; and the researchers[11] found:

- intelligence had genetic influence;
- timidity and confirmity were the traits which bore the influence of heredity (in contrast to rebellious tendencies);
- most of the traits that were studied, did not reveal a genetic influence.

Gottesman, II in his doctoral thesis[12] found some evidence of a genetic factor in introversion.

9. Honzik and Marjorie, P. *Developmental Studies of Parent–Child Resemblance in Intelligence.*
10. Jones, HE. *Environment Influence on Mental Development.*
11. Cetell, RA, Stice GF, Kristy, NF. *A First Approximation to Nature–Nurture Ratio for Eleven Primary Personality Factors in Objective Tests.*
12. *The Psychogenetics of Personality.*

REVIEW QUESTIONS

Q.1. Complete the following sentences:

(*i*) As soon as the tiny ..... penetrates the wall of the ovum, it releases 23 minute particles of ..... .

(*ii*) The chromosomes are further divided, and are called ..... , they are the carriers of ..... .

(*iii*) The 'polarization' is the process when the fertilised egg cell goes on ..... and ..... into lengthwise halves.

(*iv*) The main non-genetic factors affecting the development of the human organism are:

different systems, such as nervous system, ... system, ... system; and a number of biochemicals secreting from different kinds of ..... .

(*v*) After a few hours, the ..... divides itself into two new cells; each new cell again divides itself into ..... cells till the number goes to ...... chromosomes.

Q.2. Describe the functions of the following:

(*i*) Amniotic fluid (*ii*) Umbilical cord

(*iii*) Placenta (*iv*) Cytoplasm

Q.3. What is heredity? How does it affect the pre-natal development of an organism?

Q.4. When is a male child produced, and when a female one? Describe in detail.

Q.5. What is meant by RH factors? How is erythroblastosis caused?

Q.6. How is an embryo/foetus affected by the diet and the physical and mental conditions of the prospective mother?

ANSWERS TO OBJECTIVE TYPE QUESTIONS

Q.1. (*i*) sperm, chromosomes,

(*ii*) genes, heredity,

(*iii*) splitting, multiplying,

(*iv*) muscular, digestive, glands,

(*v*) zygote, two, 46.

CHAPTER 4

PHYSICAL GROWTH AND DEVELOPMENT DURING FIRST YEAR

Chapter Outline

- Congenital Differences Among Neonates
- Basic Needs
- Sensory Development
- Response Capabilities
- Motor Development in the First Year
- Locomotion
- Manipulation
- Speech Development
- Observations
- Environment and Language
- Review Questions

The baby's leaving the womb of its mother, and its delivery into the wide open world, is a tremendous change into the environment of it. The neonate has to make some immediate adaptations; previously, food was readily got entered into its body, now it has to have oral feeding—a new learning which has to be made immediately after birth. The neonate has to digest its food, eliminate and excrete—all this involves many systems of the body, and the same rapidly develop for a proper functioning of them. The physical growth of the child also happens to be very rapid during this period; for the development of physical functioning, the growth of the body is essential. The child who at the time of birth was only 20 inches in length, and 6 to 8 pounds in weight, rapidly gains in both; in six months time, its weight becomes double, and in a year, three times. Throughout the first year, the body growth remains very rapid. Physical development in all respects, also happens to be rapid. Many new motor functions are initiated, and they develop, sometimes marvellously during this period (Fig. 4.1).

The child who at the time of birth was only 20 inches in length, and 6 to 8 pounds in weight, rapidly gains in both; in six months time, its weight becomes double, and in a year, three times.

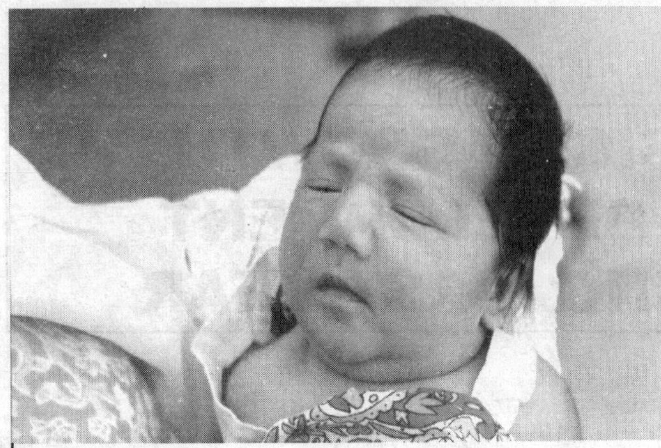

Figure 4.1
Your world is too noisy, dazzling and full of commotion; I can't see it straightway.

A number of biological needs arise after birth. So, the body grows and develops accordingly. "After birth, the number of environmental stimuli impinging on the infant and affecting his status, is multiplied several times. Passing from a parasitic to a position of some independence, some of his needs to be met partially by himself.......".[1] Before we go into the details of physical growth and development, it seems to be proper, to look into the fact of general congenital differences among children, at birth.

CONGENITAL DIFFERENCES AMONG NEONATES

The congenital differences start appearing since birth. Differences that are related to sensory thresholds, become apparent through the motor activities of the child. Marked differences may be witnessed in the physiological reactions. Many of the motor activities during this period, happen to be spontaneous but congenital or hereditary differences are found, too. Some show "frequent and vigorous thrashing of arms and legs while others lie still and quiet." Some infants show restlessness while asleep, but some show minimal activity. Sex differences can be noticed even since that early period—the activities of male infants, generally, happen to be higher and more vigorous than that of the female infants. These early activities of the infants, have great relevance with their development—"an extremely active and motorically energetic infant, might be more apt to become physically aggressive in the pre-school years (speculation is that, such a state shows the child's inability to control and modify the effect of strong needs and states of internal tension)."[1]

The development of the organism depends, to a large extent, upon the way it reacts to its environment. The infant who is congenitally very active, interacts more promptly and vigorously to the stimuli that are received at the sensory thresholds. The way a child reacts to environmental stimuli, is also affected by the way the child is handled. The child's behaviour develops as it responds to its environment. If a child is phlegmatic and quiet, it would have responsiveness with an environment, not so wide as does an active and irritable child. An active child would attract others more,

1. Mussen, Paul Henry; Conger, John Janeway; Jorome Kagan. *Child Development and Personality*.

to share reactions to the same environment. An active child may be recognised even in its crib as it can be seen there turning and kicking restlessly. An active child would be cooing, crying and smiling more than does a placid, unreactive child.

Infant's behaviour develops as it reacts to its environment. The infant's needs and the parent's attitudes and handling of it, are important factors to influence the process of development of the infant. Other elders who respond to it, also influence the development. Restrictive parents may become easily irritated towards a child who is active, taking such a behaviour as frightening or bad. A noisy, active infant is more likely to excite its mother for a hard attitude. "An energetic, athletic father may be cross and irritable with a placid infant but accepting with a more active, responsive one." Thus, the level of activity of the child, affects the reactions of the parents, and the same in turn affects the development of the child: "Children who had been awkward in their motor movements, and, had not displayed vigorous motor activity during infancy, were retarded as pre-schoolers, in level of motor development, motor co-ordination............some aspects of infant activity....are precursors of future behaviour."[2]

"Children who had been awkward in their motor movements, and, had not displayed vigorous motor activity during infancy, were retarded as pre-schoolers, in level of motor development, motor co-ordination ....some aspects of infant activity....are precursors of future behaviour."

SENSATION

Sensation is the experience that the infant has at or through its sensory threshold; it may be visual, auditory, olfactory, gustatory or tactile. The sensory thresholds happen to be quite capable of responding to the appropriate environmental stimuli, even when the child is born. Congenital differences are evident in the amount of responsivity; some children are quick in responding to a stimulation, while others may require higher intensity of stimulation to make them responsive.

An experiment was conducted on babies ranging up to 5 days of age, to see how they would respond to a tone of constant intensity. The rates of their heart beating were also marked. And, it was found that some adopted to the changed situation earlier than others who continued flexing legs and arms for long. It was also evidenced that the new born female babies were less sensitive to pain, than were the new born male babies.

PHYSICAL REACTIONS AND DEVELOPMENT

Much depends upon the way the child reacts to physical stress. For the neonate, hunger is the general source of tension or stress. The four main bodily systems are involved in the reaction—the gastrointestinal tract, the skin, the respiratory apparatus and the cardiovascular system (that is, heart and blood vessels). Under stress, the heart rate increases, the temperature of the skin rises, some even vomit, and "break out with a rash", the face

2. Escalona, S, Heider, GM. *Prediction and Outcome*, New York Basic Books, 1951.

or skin may flush markedly as a result of increase in blood pressure and the widening (dilation) of the small blood vessels. If such a behaviour occurs with great frequency during the first year of the child, his development is sure to be affected by it. Psychosomatic symptoms may appear; in some cases, ulcers, asthma or allergies may be the result.

BODILY GROWTH

Norms are there to know the height and weight of a child at a particular age; but these are averages; wide variations are there in individual cases. The rate of growth varies greatly. Here, only a general picture of development is meant to be given. Sex differences are also there—the full time male infants weigh a little more than the full time female infants; there is difference in height also. A full time male baby is about 20 inches tall, and, weighs 7.5 pounds at birth. Nutrition of the expectant mother, is an important factor to affect the tallness and the weight of the foetus or the neonate. The first year of the child witnesses rapid increase in height and weight. By the end of the first year, the average height of the child becomes 28 inches (one-third growth) and the weight, 20 pounds (three times growth) [Table 4.1].

Nutrition of the expectant mother, is an important factor to affect the tallness and the weight of the foetus or the neonate.

Table 4.1 Growth and Caloric Requirements

Age	*Approximate Daily Weight Gain (g)*	*Approximate Monthly Weight Gain (g)*	*Growth in Length Circumference (cm/mo)*	*Growth in Head Circumference (cm/mo)*	*Recommended Daily Allowance (kcal/kg/day)*
0-3 mo	30	2 lb	3.5	2.00	115
3-6 mo	20	1¼ lb	2.0	1.00	110
6-9 mo	15	1 lb	1.5	0.50	100
9-12 mo	12	13 oz	1.2	0.50	100
1-3 yr	8	8 oz	1.0	0.25	100
4.6 yr	6	6 oz	3 cm/yr	1 cm/yr	90-100

Source Adapted from National Research Council, Food and Nutrition Board. Recommended Daily Allowances. Washington, DC, National Academy of Sciences 1989; Frank D, Silva M, Needlman R: Failure to thrive: Myth and method. *Contemp Pediatr* 10:1/4, 1993.

BODY PROPORTIONS

Vast changes occur in the body proportions during the first year and the growth happens to be very rapid. At birth, the legs of the infants are about one-fifth the size of the leg of an adult. Since 8 weeks of age, the growth rate of legs is accelerated. The head and face grow more slowly, than do the other parts of the body. The size and shape of the skull, too undergoes change. The total length of the head and face of a 3 month old foetus is about one-third of the total length of the body; length of the same at birth, is less than one-fourth; and in adulthood, it is about one-tenth.

SKELETAL DEVELOPMENT

Soft cartilage tissues turn into bones as a result of ossification. Ossification is the result of the hardening of cartilages, mainly due to the deposition of minerals. The process of ossification begins during the prenatal period, and continues, in case of some bones, till late in adolescence. Some bones may break easily while others do not, even though they are very soft. Individual differences may also be seen in case of ossification or development of bones. The timing and the rate of ossifications vary from child to child—some bones develop early while others late, and, take more time in ossification. Of the total 28 bones of hand and wrist, three develop earlier than the rest, though in comparison to the bones of the other parts of the body, the bones of the hands and wrist ossify earlier. When a child is born, its skull has six fontanelles (membraneous space in infant's skull); they ossify gradually. The process is not completed till the child is 2 years old. Growth and development of bones is a bit faster in case of female children than male children. Racial differences are also perceivable in case of skeleton growth. Some children are broad-framed, and have faster growth rate than others. The rate and nature of ossification also depends on the factor of heredity, though the same are also affected by malnutrition, illness, allergies, and other problems.

> The total length of the head and face of a 3-month-old foetus is about one-third of the total length of the body; length of the same at birth, is less than one-fourth, and in adulthood, it is about one-tenth.

> Soft cartilage tissues turn into bones as a result of ossification.

TEETH

Variation is also found in case of eruption of teeth. Some have a particular type of teeth erupted earlier while others have the same teeth erupt later. Some deciduous teeth appear earlier, and, others later. Generally, by about the age of 1 year, and through the age of nine months, these teeth can be seen. The first tooth, the lower front one, generally appears by the time the child is 7 months old. There is no co-relation between the eruption of teeth and the height, weight or muscle-mass of the child. Again, the girl goes ahead of the boy child, in case of the eruption of teeth also. Genetic factor also has its impact on the timing and nature of the eruption of teeth.

MUSCLES

A continuous growth occurs in case of muscles since the time the child is born. In the beginning, the muscle fibres happen to be small in size—in length, breadth and thickness. With age they gain in all these respects. The process of growth may continue till adulthood, when the gain made in weight of the muscles, may be forty times of what it was at birth. During the first year, the striped or skeleton muscles are not fully under the control of the child.

All the different muscles do not develop at the same rate. The muscles that are near the hands and the neck, have a tendency of developing earlier. A male child has a greater proportion of muscles than a female child does; this difference holds on later also.

BASIC NEEDS

A child has some such physiological needs, the satisfaction of which are essential for the survival. These are his basic needs. The degree and nature of the child's development depends upon the way these needs are taken care of in a "self-regulatory" manner; but 'hunger' and 'thirst' are not such needs, and so are important in the process of early learnings of the child. First, let us take the needs which are taken care of automatically through reflex actions.

NEED FOR OXYGEN

Oxygen is inhaled through a reflex mechanism, the neonate achieves the adult level respiratory stabilisation within the first few days of birth.

The drive rarely needs to be high for having an adequate supply of oxygen. The neonate may have irregular and shallow breathing, but if its breathing is noisy, it may be an indication of the child's having contracted croup, asthma, or other infection.

TEMPERATURE REGULATION

Before delivery of the child into the external environment, the amniotic fluid keeps the body temperature of the organism fairly stable. After delivery, an automatic mechanism continues to operate to maintain the body temperature stable, but because of so much variations in the temperature of our atmosphere, the elders have to be careful as to when to shut a window, and when it should be opened, when the child needs extra protection against cold by way of putting a blanket about its body, and so on. Sometimes, even the use of some drug may become essential to maintain the body temperature of the child to a certain level.

NEED FOR SLEEP

Neonates on an average spend 80 per cent of their time in sleep. By the time the baby is one year old, the time is reduced to 50 per cent. The rhythms and depths of sleep also go on changing. For the first 3-4 weeks, the average infant has 7–8 short naps in 24 hours; the number is reduced to between 2 and 4 longer periods of sleep by 6 weeks of age. By 28 weeks, most children, generally, have a long stint of sleep during night only. A one-year-old child would not require more than two or three short naps during the day, but his night-time sleep happens to be a long and unbroken one.

> "For the first 3–4 weeks, the average infant has 7–8 short naps in 24 hours; the number is reduced to between 2 and 4 longer periods of sleep by 6 weeks of age. By 28 weeks, most children, generally, have a long stint of sleep during night only. A one-year-old child would not require more than two or three short naps during the day, but his night-time sleep happens to be a long and unbroken one.

Though individual differences in regard to the periods and rhythms of sleep may be found but, generally, as the child grows in age, the number of naps (or rhythms per day) goes on reducing, and the period of long sleep goes on increasing.

The parents will have to see to it that the sleep of the child is not disturbed because of noise, inclement weather conditions, or other physical disturbances—a sound and full sleep is very much needed for the health of the child. It is through sleep that the body regulates itself. It is through sleep that the body accumulates energy for the performance of different physical and mental functions, though a part of energy released because of metabolism, is consumed, even when the organism is asleep, in the all-time going on functionings of some of the systems of body. It is through sleep, that an equilibrium is maintained in the chemical constitution and physiological processes of the body.

NEED FOR ELIMINATION

In the beginning, the passing of urine or faeces, is purely a reflex action. The neonate has frequent and irregular eliminations. By the time the child is about 4 weeks old, the frequency is, generally, reduced to 3 to 4 times a day. The bowel movements, ordinarily, occur at the wakening time of the child.

During the beginning weeks, enough control of sphincters do not happen to be there, but by and by this control increases, and, by the time, the child is 8 weeks old, the frequency of bowel movements is reduced to two times only—one, when the child awakes, and second, when the mother is to start feeding it, or, during the feeding. When the child is about 16 weeks old, there, generally, happens to be a definite interval between the feeding and the evacuation times.

Toilet training is important, which each parent seriously imparts through inhibition and suppression. Lot of patience and skill are required on the part of the guardians while helping the child to learn toilet discipline as to when one may defecate or urinate. Patience is necessary because no amount of training can enable the child to exercise control over his anal and urethral sphincters, until these have got the needful level of neuromuscular maturity. For a successful learning of toilet discipline, reflex actions will have to be substituted by voluntary control—a skilful parent can adopt an effective device to help the child learn it. Breckenridge[3] et al. write that by the end of first year, the bowel training is complete.

Until the child is toilet-trained, the sporadic bowel movements of the child may prove very tiring for the mother. And, her annoyance may make

3. Marain E Breckenridge, E Lee Vincent. *Physical Physiological Growth Through Adolescence.*

her irritable in her responses towards such a behaviour of her child; this further accentuates the problem, as the child may himself grow aggressive, and cause more trouble for the mother, by way of bowel movements, when it is the most unsuitable time for the same. So, it needs to be reiterated that if the parent loses patience in regard to imparting toilet-training, the child may grow peevish forever.

HUNGER AND THIRST

Satisfaction of hunger and thirst is among the most important drives of a neonate. If these are not satisfied timely, the child becomes very irritable. Undue delay in feeding the child, upsets the mood of the child, and he reacts with violent crying, blushing of face or entire body and the child may not even accept feeding in such a situation. If the mother, for whatever reasons, is unable to respond positively to the child who needs to be fed, the child would grow pessimistic, and would be having no feeling of belongingness, which is so essential for a proper emotional development.

> By 4 weeks of age, the average intake is 18 to 25 ounces. The intake increases to 35 ounces when the infant is 6 to 8 weeks of age. Solid food should be started when the child is about 20 weeks old. Cereals and vegetables may form a regular part of his diet.

The earliest learnings of the child, are closely related with the way his/her needs of hunger and thirst are satisfied. If they are satisfied timely and properly, it will be an important factor in the desirable physical development of the child. It affects his emotional development, too. The child should not often be required to undergo a long period of stress under hunger and thirst. If it so happens for a long period, it may make the child irritable and aggressive.

The pattern of feeding varies from society to society; it may vary from family to family depending upon the socioeconomic status of the family. Even then, norms are available to guide us as to how much to feed and how often to feed. An American new born infant, on an average, has seven or eight feedings a day. By 4 weeks of age, the average intake is 18 to 25 ounces. The intake increases to 35 ounces when the infant is 6 to 8 weeks of age. As the child advances in age, the amount of intake, naturally increases, but the frequency decreases. Solid food should be started when the child is about 20 weeks old (the time and manner of weaning the infant to solid food vary from culture to culture)—cereals and vegetables may form a regular part of his diet. To a child who is one-year-old, three meals a day, are required. Food given to the infant should be nutritious, healthy and at the same time, appealing so that the child will eat it eagerly and willingly.

> To a child who is one-year-old, three meals a day, are required.

Cleanliness of the environment, mood and health of the mother, are also factors to be taken into consideration, as they too affect the physical and emotional development of the child, especially, when he depends upon breast-feeding. During the period when the mother breast-feeds her child, she, herself, requires proper nourishment.

SENSORY DEVELOPMENT

Jean Piaget has described the first stage of child's development as sensory motor stage. The motor development of the child is very much related to his sensory development. It is through the senses that the child receives stimuli from the environment. The promptness and intensity of responses, depend upon the acuity of senses. If the sense organ concerned, grasps an experience promptly and intensively, so will be the responses of the organism. A child can learn nothing unless he receives experiences through his senses—the senses of vision, audition, smell, taste and touch. These sense organs have been called the sense-thresholds, because it is there that the process of sensing or receiving an experience begins, otherwise a long neuromuscular system is involved; and it makes the affected or concerned body part or part of the organ active, and thus goes on the development of motor control and motor skills.

VISION

In the human embryo, the development of the essential neural mechanism, begins during the third week of prenatal life. When the infant is born, the neuromuscular apparatus involved in the vision does not happen to be perfect. Important studies have been conducted on the responses to visual stimuli; and, the facts revealed may be summarised as under:

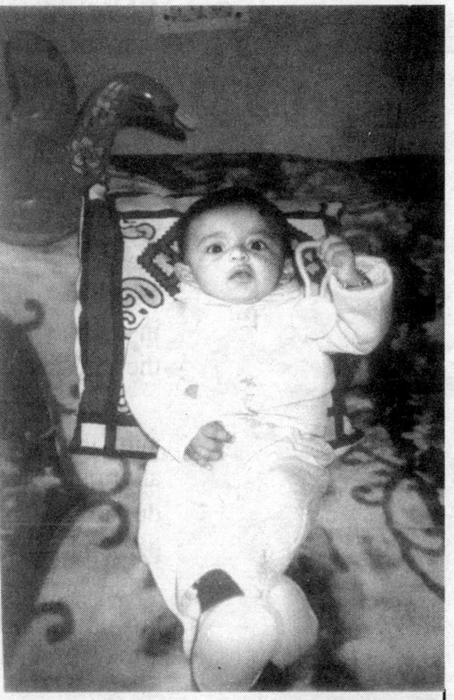

Figure 4.2 A 2.5-month-old child has very little perception.

(*i*) *The pupiliary reflex* The child contracts its pupil in response to light; it is a reflex action that needs no learning but occurs automatically. At birth, this response happens to be sluggish but perfection in this response is achieved in the first few weeks of birth.

(*ii*) *Visual pursuit* In the beginning, a child cannot concentrate its vision on an object; but soon he develops response to this effect. Though a change of vision, from one object to another in a quick movement, does not happen to be a possibility till the child is about 16 weeks old, yet visual pursuit movement may be marked in a child who is about 15 days old, especially in case, where the stimuli are some nearing coloured spots or some such a thing.

(*iii*) *Co-ordination of the two eyes* We may have seen that the neonate, for many days after its birth, cannot look at an object with both eyes concentrating immediately upon it as soon as it is brought to its vision—proper co-ordination of the two eyes develops in 7 or

8 weeks' time when the convergence or binocular fixation becomes "smooth and continuous"; though convergence "in a series of jerking movements" starts occurring even after a few hours of birth.

(*iv*) *The ciliary muscles* The ciliary muscles of the neonate do not happen to be mature enough so as to catch images properly. But gradually, as the child grows, these muscles also develop, the functioning of the eye, goes on improving rapidly. Fantz[4] found in his experiments that up to about 15 weeks after birth, the preference of the child continued to be for complex patterns, such as a checkerboard or a bull's eye; simple structures, such as a circle, a square or a triangle, rarely diverted his gaze to look at them. Nearly up to 8 weeks of time, between a striped pattern and bull's eye, the preference of the infant was for the former, but after 8 weeks the preference was shifted to the bull's eye.

In an experiment, three faces were shown to 49 infants, of ages from 4 days to 6 months, to mark their reactions to these three different stimuli. It was found that the infants looked longest at the real face, somewhat less at the scrambled one, and the third face which was no better than a black patch, was typically ignored. From this, it can be concluded that the unlearned preference of the child is always for the complex or varied patterns, rather than for "simple and relatively homogeneous stimuli".

An infant's visual apparatus matures very rapidly. To assess the visual acuity of a child, an object of his preference will have to be used. Through experiments, it was found that as a baby grew in age, the visual acuity developed to such a level that a six month old child, from a distance of 10 inches, could concentrate his vision on a stripe that was only 1/64 inch in width—the experimenter had been decreasing the width of stripes as the child was growing in age.

An infant avoids a stimulus of sudden increase in depth. A terrestrial animal would avoid the side which has a sharp "drop-off" or cliff;[5] likewise an infant, 6 months old, also avoids a surface which has a sudden dropping down depth. There are some animals who have a capability of depth perception from the very first day; the chicken and the goat are such animals.

So, in the end, it can be summed up that some aspects of visual preception are unlearned, while others develop early during the first year.

HEARING

At the time of birth, the hearing mechanism, happens to be sufficiently well developed to be functional. Even then, nature protects the neonate

4. Fantz, RL. *The Origin of Form Perception and Patterns Vision on Young Infants.*
5. Gibson, E, Walk, RR. *The Visual Cliff.*

in case there is a sudden onslaught of a very loud sound—the mid-ear mucus, or obstruction of the external auditory canal, works as protector. Poor hearing during the early natal days, may be there because of these reasons.

Sounds, lasting longer, have greater effect than those which are of very short durations such as for a second or so. A sound which lasted for 15 seconds, elicited more bodily movements, caused faster respiration, and closing of eyelids. If the sound continued for a duration much longer than this, first there was response which later on subsided because of such a long duration of the sound.

Loud sounds proved stronger stimulants and elicited more bodily movements, closing of eyelids, and changing of respiratory rates. Bridger[6] in an experiment on 50 neonates, ranging in age between 1 to 5 days, found that they responded differently to different frequencies. "A tone of a given pitch was sounded repeatedly until babies ceased responding to it", and then, the pitch of the tone was changed, though the loudness was the same, and there was a response; bodily movements were increased, and there was also increase in the rate of heart palpitation.

OLFACTION

The investigators found that the little babies responded differently to pleasant and unpleasant smells. The neonate would suck its thumb when there was a pleasant odour, such as that of *anise oil*. It turned away its head, and made grimaces, when the smell was unpleasant. If there was a greater saturation of odours, the baby would make more movements.

GUSTATION

The experiments found that the neonates did not give any indication of having felt any difference in taste among solutions of different kinds, that is, that of sugar, salt, citrate, and so on, when applied to their tongues—so poor happens to be the taste sensitivity in the beginning. However, a two weeks old child made clear, positive (sucking) response to sugar, and negative (grimacing) to quinine and citric acid. The experiments were conducted by Pratt KC et al.[7] Another investigator found "a moderately full baby is a better discriminator than the very hungry infant."[8]

THERMAL SENSITIVITY

The neonate becomes more active when it is colder, but the activity level is reduced when the object touching its leg is made hotter by 5 to 6 degrees

6. Bridger, WH. *Sensory Habitation and Discrimination in the Human Neonate.*
7. Pratt, KC, Nelson, AL, Sun, KH. *The Behaviour of the New Born Infant.*
8. Jensen, K 1932.

from a neutral point of 33°C. Cold stimuli (11°C or 12°C below the neutral point), when applied to the legs, increased head movements, accelerated breathing; and irregular pulse followed when stimulation was applied to the forehead.

It was also found that milk warmer than 50°C, colder than 23°C made the infant squirm and suck irregularly. Of course, in this respect also individual differences are found.

PAIN

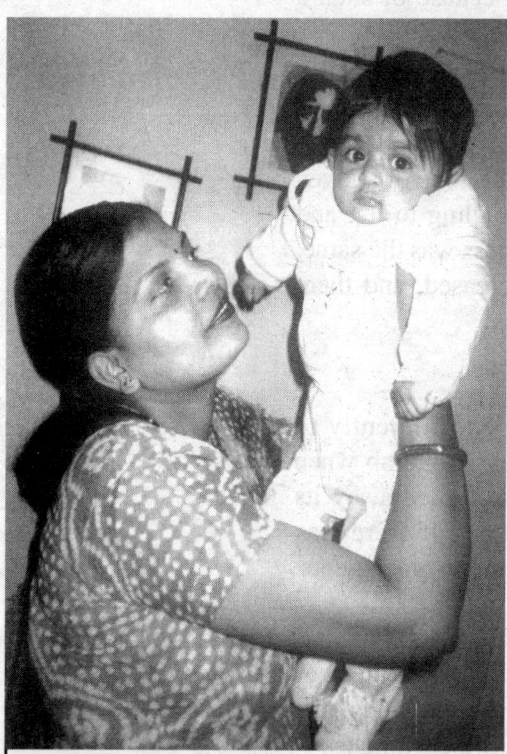

Figure 4.3
The picture illustrates nystagmus while being held upright.

There is no localised area in the brain which can receive and integrate pain producing stimulation. Learning plays a significant role in this respect. Pain sensitivity happens to be present in some degree even at the time of birth, but it grows sharper during the first few days. Number of pain stimuli decreases during the period from birth to 8 days but the sensitivity grows sharper. Constitutional differences, of course, are found there. A female child is more sensitive to the stimulation of pain; the more sensitive to the stimulation of pain one is, the more susceptible to the feeling of fear and anxiety he would be.

STATIC, KINESTHETIC SENSITIVITY

If a neonate is held upside down, or jarred, or its spatial position is changed, it will make generalised postural adjustment. Body rotation or prone placement on a table, may stimulate nystagmus[9] (oscillation of eyes). If the infant is held upright with its feet resting upon a flat surface, it would alternate stepping. Thus, from the very beginning, the child has the tendency of maintaining upright posture; this tendency proves helpful in enabling the child to walk in due course of time (Fig. 4.3).

RESPONSE CAPABILITIES

We observe that even the newly born infant can make many complex sensory-motor responses to the various stimuli, and with the increase in size of the body and development of the central nervous system, and other biological changes, the capability of the child to respond more promptly,

9. P Henry et al. *Child Development and Personality.*

more strongly and skilfully, increases. The infant makes sucking movements when their lips or cheeks are stimulated. The neonate contracts its pupils in response to bright lights or flashes though it had no such experience prenatally. The reflex actions are unlearned; but, actions like sucking a bottle, are learned. All the reflex actions have survival values—pupillary movements, swallowing, opening and closing of eyes, crying, rejecting food, coughing, vomiting, turning away the face in moments of irritation, and assuming resting and sleeping positions when the position is irritating—are such responses. These unlearned movements help the child in making adjustments to his new environment; in keeping himself healthy, and protecting from deleterious effects.

Some reflex actions are localised, in which only a part of some organ of the body is involved. The child flexes its hand when it is pricked or slapped. If there is a pressure on finger or palm, the child closes the hand tightly—this is grasp reflex. At birth, the grasp reflex is very strong but weakens after a few weeks. The big toe extends and the other fingers of the foot fan out if the foot is stroked; technically this is called Babinski reflex. When the child changes the position of its body, he needs to balance his head accordingly—this is head balancing reflex. The penis of the male child becomes erect, testes are raised if there is stimulation in the interior of the thigh. These are a few examples of the localised reflex actions/ responses, which have immense biological significance for the survival of the organism.

MOTOR DEVELOPMENT IN THE FIRST YEAR

As the child continues to grow in age, a lot of new motor abilities are added. The child rapidly gains in size and weight; the muscles grow not only in size but in strength also, and so do the bones. The central nervous system grows marvellously, and, its abilities to perform actions goes on increasing till it can perform very complex actions demanding great skills and mental functioning, or fine physical-mental co-ordination. Some motor skills seem to develop automatically as a result of maturity, but in their development, too, the role of practice happens to be quite significant. [see Tables 4.2 and 4.3].

Gesell, Amatruda and McGrow did classic work in this field; those who are interested in all the minute details regarding the development of the vast number of motor abilities, may consult the same; here, a few of them are being dealt with in brief.

Table 4.2 Key Developmental Milestones: Gross Motor

Age	*Milestone*
3 months	Neck holding
5 months	Sitting with support
8 months	Sitting without support
9 months	Standing with support
10 months	Walking with support
11 months	Crawling (Creeping)
12 months	Standing without support (1 year)
13 months	Walking with support
18 months	Running
24 months	Climbing staircase
36 months	Riding tricyle

Table 4.3 Key Developmental Milestones: Fine Motor

Age	*Milestone*
4 months	Grasps a rattle or rings when placed in hand
5 months	Reaches out to an object and holds it with both hands (intentional reaching with *bidextrous* grasp)
7 months	Holding objects with crude grasp from palm (*palmar* grasp)
9 months	Holding small object, like a pellet, between index finger and thumb (*pincer* grasp)

LOCOMOTION

CRAWLING AND CREEPING

Ames[10], through his long and patient observations, discovered 14 stages through which the child grows, before he is able to crawl and creep properly. The series begins with the thrusting out of one knee forward beside the body by about the age of 28 weeks. The median age for crawling is

10. Ames, LB. *The Sequential Patterning of Prone Progression in the Human Infant*.

34 weeks (Fig. 4.4); it is, generally, the time when a child starts moving about with its abdomen in contact with the floor. The locomotive skill in crawling is perfected by the time of 49 weeks.

Figure 4.4
A 8-month-old child likes to crawl.

SITTING

Ability to assume the sitting posture is not the result of some reflex action. The ability to sit, develops very early. A child of say, 3 or 4 months, can be seated with support, for a short stint. By the age of 7 or 8 months, the child can sit without support. Once the child has achieved this ability, the skill to do it develops rapidly. A 8-month-old child can keep sitting independently for a long time.

STANDING AND WALKING

The most remarkable work in this regard is that of McGrow[11], Thomson's[12] article is also an important contribution. The child matures gradually till he is able to walk. To be able to stand with support is the first stage in the direction (Fig. 4.5); and it is achieved by about the age of 38 weeks. The elders can help the child to step on forward, of course, in a very rude and awkward manner supporting it with a finger or so. When the child is 62 weeks old, it can stand alone independently. It may be taken as the last stage in the development of motor skill; and another two weeks or so (by 64 weeks of age) the child is able to walk with no support of any kind required. These are the median ages, individual variations, of course, are there. Some walk as early as 9 months, and some as late as 18 months. "There is always merging of patterns, and parts of patterns both in the degree of perfection of the action and in the frequency of occurrence." In their observations, the investigators also found that in many cases, there would be regression to less mature responses. In the development of the capabilities

Figure 4.5
A 10-month-old child can stand with support.

11. McGrow, MB. *Growth, A Study of Johnny and Jimmy*.
12. Thomson, H. *Physical Growth.*

" .... Experience affects not only the ages at which motor items appear but also their very form."

to sit, stand and walk, it is maturation of neuromuscular systems that has major impact. Environmental conditions should, of course, not be impeding the course of nature. Practice can also help in the natural course of locomotive development. It is a fact that if there is nothing to thwart the course of neuromuscular development, the child would achieve the capability to sit, to stand and to walk, even if no special training for the same is imparted to it, to have the skill for these motor activities. Dennis[13] for the sake of experiment, prevented two female twin children to sit till they were nine months old; they were kept lying on their backs, and could get no chance to sit ever. Then, the restrictions were removed, and it was found that the twins very rapidly made up for the retarded period. The most retardation was witnessed in case of sitting. At 37 weeks, they were given opportunities to sit; at first they failed to sit, but after some days they could do this. Dennis[14] concluded:

"..................... Experience affects not only the ages at which motor items appear but also their very form."

MANIPULATION

Manipulative ability develops through a series of stages as does the locomotive skills. The infant first only looks at an object. If the object moves about, the infant follows it with his eyes but still cannot reach to it. Then, the infant stretches his arms in the general direction of the object, makes slow, awkward and angular reaching movements involving mainly shoulder and elbow action. It is by 20 weeks of age that the child may reach to the object. The children who are older, have more direct approach towards the object. Now, in the manipulation, that is, in taking hold of the object, the wrist and the hand participate. With the development of neuromuscular-skeletal systems and with practice in successive steps, the number of superfluous steps decreases, and the infant has a direct access to the object of its attraction. It is by 9 months of age that the infant can, thus, reach directly to the object and can have an effective grasp. Halversion, HM through a systematic study of prehension in infants, made some important conclusions, he used cinema records for the purpose.

Illingworth traced the development of the manipulative skill of the hand as follows:

- 40 weeks: Finger-Thumb apposition; can pick-up pellet between finger and thumb.
- 44 weeks: Places one block after another into a box.

13. Dennis, W. *Causes of Retardation Among Institutional Children.*
14. Dennis, W. *Infant Development under Conditions of Restricted Practice and of Minimum Social Stimulation,* 1941.

- 48 weeks: Gives blocks to the mother.
- 52 weeks: Mouthing nearly stopped. Begins throwing objects on the floor.
- 1 year: Mature grasp of cube; feeding oneself with spoon and a cup.

My own granddaughter Shivangi left mouthing when she was about 10 months old, and also, started pointing with her fingers, catching them by moving the thumb opposite to fingers.

DEVELOPMENT TRENDS

It is in the nature of the organism to develop. Development is essential for its survival, for enabling it to perform functions which are beneficial for a wholesome life. In spite of there being individual differences in the degree and timings of developments, the trends of development are common.

(*i*) *Cephalocaudal* Development starts, first from head, and then develop the organs, which are below the head, towards feet; the trend is from head to foot. It is called *Cephalocaudal.* The foetus first starts moving its head; after birth also, it is head which the neonate first starts manipulating. Then develops visual fixation. Eye-hand co-ordination follows it. And, it is only lastly that the child can manipulate its feet in standing and walking. Thus, the whole trend of development of locomotion and manipulation moves from head to foot.

(*ii*) *Proximodistal* The development of motor responses also has the trend of "from the entire to periphery"; this trend is called *Proximodistal*. It is the heart and lungs which become functional first in case of an embryo; the organ which are outside or lying on the periphery of the body, develop their operational capacity later on. When the child develops the capacity to take hold of an object, the shoulders and the elbows first develop the manipulative skill, and the wrists and the hands do this later on. The upper arm and the upper leg, come under control first, and the lower arm and the lower leg later on.

> "The gross awkward movements of early grasping are replaced by more precise, refined movements of the thumb and forefinger. Locomotion is initially accompanied by excess bodily movements, but these decrease gradually until the appropriate muscles and limbs are involved."

(*iii*) *From mass to specific* In the beginning, when the infant is attracted towards an object, and is inclined to take hold of it, his entire body becomes locomotive. Gradually, the child develops the capacity to take hold of the object, reducing the involvement of the number of limbs and their parts; and lastly, only that part of his arm is involved which is directly related to the function. Thus, the reduction of involvement of parts of the body, has the trend of—from larger to smaller muscles.

"The gross awkward movements of early grasping are replaced by more precise, refined movements of the thumb and forefinger.

Locomotion is initially accompanied by excess bodily movements, but these decrease gradually until the appropriate muscles and limbs are involved."[15]

SPEECH DEVELOPMENT

Phonemes are the fundamental elements of a language. They include the basic vowels and consonants; the sounds (p) and (b) are the examples of phonemes. In the beginning, the child automatically produces many phonemes in his babblings. Refining in their articulation occurs as learning takes place. "The infant's earliest sounds are primarily reflex ones, associated with automatic responses, such as, breathing, swallowing and hiccoughing"—still the child cannot express any particular need. A one-month-old infant automatically makes primitive sounds which are the consequences of the reflex functioning of his respiratory and visual systems. The average baby under 2 months of age has 7 phonemes in its sound repertoire; at 6 months, 12; at a year, 18. (An adult American has 35 phonemes in his speech). This shows that the expansion of the infant's speech catalogue happens to be very rapid. The infant produces most of the vowel elements during the second quarter of the first year. He produces half of the consonants also during this period. Throughout the first year, the number of vowels produced, exceeds the number of consonants that the child uses, during this period the ratio being 5:1 at the beginning. This discrepancy goes on reducing until after first year.

"A child cannot learn verbal responses until he is old enough and mature enough to learn them. Maturation sets the pace. With a normal environment, the child's speech awaits a step-by-step unfolding of the growing process......"

About 90 per cent of the earliest consonant sounds are glottals. By the end of the first year, these sounds constitute only about 30 per cent of the total consonants that the child produces.

The development of sound patterns, has relationship with maturity, with changes in neuromuscular systems, and, with other anatomical changes, which together constitute the physical development of the child. There are sounds, in the production of which, oral cavity has to assume a particular shape; if the child is in a sitting posture, the production of the same is facilitated. The pattern of speech development is the same in all races and nationalities.

"A child cannot learn verbal responses until he is old enough and mature enough to learn them. Maturation sets the pace. With a normal environment, the child's speech awaits a step-by-step unfolding of the growing process. Consequently, we find a succession of developmental stages that are quite

15. Paul Henry Mussen et al. *"Child Development and Personality"*.

similar in all children. By manipulating the environment of the child, we can modify or delay his language development........................." (Miller, GA: *Language and Communication*).

Speech is a complex function as it involves lungs, wind pipe, larynx, roof of the mouth, tongue, jaws and lips. These are the physical parts involved in the process; besides these, it is very much related to sensation and preception, later, to conception. Here, we are to see how much of speech development occurs during the first year.

Initially, the child has no language; he receives a lot of speech sounds at the auditory threshold. The same being without any past references, convey no meaning whatsoever. In due course of time, some of the speech sounds become sensible because of contextual/past references. The child catches language word-by-word through the context that the word is used in. Repeated use of the same word, in the same context, enables the child to know what it conveys. In this way, the speech sounds which were only experiences at the auditory threshold in the beginning, start having some meaning for the child. The second stage in the development begins when the child attempts using the perceived vocabulary in his own way through babbling. The elders improve his expression even when they imitate and repeat his expression. The process goes on through listening and imitating the elders.

OBSERVATIONS

I had been observing the development of the vocalisation of my 10 months old granddaughter, Shivangi. First, she produced monosyllabic sounds with reduplication "Ma-Ma" (मां—Mother); and, then bi-syllabic ones. So far as I could mark, the first sounds produced were glottal—"Ga"; "Ka"; followed by bi-libial—"Pa-Pa"; "Ba-Ba" ("पा-पा"; "बा-बा") and dental sounds, such as "Da-Da" ("दा-दा"—grandfather). Shivangi started with bi-syllabic nouns—"Pa-Pa"; "Da-Da" etc. I heard her utter the verb "*De-De*" ("दे-दे"—give-give) for the first time when she was to be 11 months old after 14 days. About that same time, she also uttered the word—"*Aa-ja*" (come on); a verb, a word of two syllables. It was the same age when she started walking—going forward two or three steps. By the time she was only a little less than one year, she gave the impression of uttering the word "Neha"—the name of her aunt who she was very much fond of. Earlier, she had started calling her uncle, "*Cha-Cha*".

In response to my question "Will you eat *Pauha* (an eatable made of rice)"?, she, for the first time nodded along with uttering the sound "Hmu" ("हूं")—she was about 14 months old then.

She was rapidly improving the inventory of her vocabulary. What I could mark was that, first adjective she added to her vocabulary, was "*Gande*" ("गन्दे"—bad). I felt that impact of elder siblings in the development of language, was very important. Shivangi's elder sister, Ishita would often use the word "*Gande*" when she was displeased with someone. I heard Shivangi utter this for the first time when she was about 14 months old.

A lot of research is still required to say with certainty as to what is the exact order of development in language. So, as far as the use of nouns, verbs, adjectives, and others is concerned, the impression that I have got is, that the child first starts uttering nouns or interjections, then verbs and after that adjectives and others.

ENVIRONMENT AND LANGUAGE

Observations led the researches to conclude that the more motivating an environment is, more vocally expressive the child will grow. In a family, where the parents and elder siblings spend adequate time fondling the infant, talking and smiling to him, and encouraging him with a smile or a kiss or a pat when the child attempts at his own vocalisation—both the frequency of vocalisation and the number and variety of sounds, happen to be greater than in case of a child where the parents are too busy to spare adequate time to their child and, the environment is not motivating enough. A family of a working class illiterate parents, generally, can provide less motivating environment for the child to develop his language than does a family of middle or upper class parents who are well educated too.

"It has also been found that rewarding the 7 months old child's utterances by smiling and touching his abdomen after each sound leads to an increase in the amount of infant vocalisation." (Reingold, Harriet, Gewirtz, J and Ross H. *Social Conditioning of Vocalisations in the Infant*).

Individual differences are found here, too, some children start vocalisation earlier than others; in some cases development of language happens to be more rapid than in others.

As has been mentioned above, the environment of the child and the behaviour of the parents and elder siblings of the family, are two important factors bearing upon the development of language of the children. It is through the earliest vocalisations or the absence of the same that the fact whether a child is dumb or deaf, is revealed. Shirley recorded that the first distinct phoneme was uttered at the median age of 8 weeks. He also found that the median age, by which a child appeared to be attempting something like talking, was 25 weeks; singing tones appeared at the mean age of 32 weeks, and expressive sounds at 38 weeks.

First distinct phoneme was uttered at the median age of 8 weeks. Shirley also found that the median age, by which a child appeared to be attempting something like talking, was 25 weeks; singing tones appeared at the mean age of 32 weeks, and expressive sounds at 38 weeks.

If a child is not congenitally retarded, he improves his expression through experience or imitation. Imitation generally begins by the time the child is about 9 months old. Earlier he has, in general, only such reflex expressions which are results of the automatic functions of the respiratory system and the vocal apparatus. At the beginning stage, the child imitates only those sounds, for refinement and proper articulation, which have been constituting his babblings so far. As a result of maturation, new combinations of sounds develop.

From our general impression, we can say that a child, generally, utters his first meaningful word during the last quarter of his first year. During this period, the child, generally, utters monosyllabic words which he would, usually reduplicate—"bye-bye"; "ma-ma"; "da-da"; and so on.

The first words that the child speaks, would be nouns or interjections, but they would do the function of a whole sentence. When the child says "mamma", he means, "where is the mother?" This single word can convey other meanings also, depending upon the situation that the word is used in, or upon the accompanying behaviour of the child.

Some investigations have reported that if a child, first, engages himself in mastering the skill of walking, it would slow down the pace of his linguistic development............ speech development is held in abeyance at the time when motor progress is most rapid.

Till the end of the first year, the child's volume of comprehension happens to be bigger by far, than the volume of his expression. The number of words that the child has potentiality to say, far exceeds the number of words that he actually utters. The frequency and the quality of a young child's language products, much depend upon the desire of the child to speak, and, the reward that he receives for his language products.

REVIEW QUESTIONS

***Q*.1.** At the time of birth, a full time normal male baby, generally has a height of:

(*a*) 15 inches (*b*) 30 inches
(*c*) 20 inches (*d*) none of these

***Q*.2.** At the end of first year, in general, the weight would be: [Note: 1 pound = 0.4536 kg]

(*a*) 4 pounds (*b*) 7.5 pounds
(*c*) 20 pounds (*d*) 15 pounds

***Q.*3.** At the end of the first year, in general, the height of a normal male baby would be

(*a*) 28 inches (*b*) 20 inches

(*c*) 40 inches (*d*) 35 inches

***Q.*4.** At the time of birth, the average weight of a full time baby happens to be

(*a*) 7.5 pounds (*b*) 13 pounds

(*c*) 14 pounds (*d*) none of these

***Q.*5.** Complete the sentences:

(*i*) In the first year, a baby gains .... times in weight, and .... in height.

(*ii*) At birth, the legs of an infant are about .... the size of the leg of an adult; the growth is accelerated since ..... weeks of age.

(*iii*) The total length of the head and face of a 3 month old foetus is about ...... of the total length of the body; length of the same at birth, is less than ....

(*iv*) Soft cartilage tissues turn into bones as a result of .....

(*v*) At the time of birth, a child has six .... in its skull.

***Q.*6.** What are the basic needs of a neonate? How are they related to the growth and development of the child?

***Q.*7.** Describe in brief the sensory development of a baby during the first year of a child.

***Q.*8.** What are the milestones in the gross motor development of a baby during the first year?

ANSWERS TO OBJECTIVE TYPE QUESTIONS

***Q.*1.** (*c*)

***Q.*2.** (*b*)

***Q.*3.** (*a*)

***Q.*4.** (*a*)

***Q.*5.** (*i*) three times,

(*ii*) one third,

(*iii*) one fifth, 8,

(*iv*) ossification,

(*v*) fontanelles

CHAPTER 5 PHYSICAL GROWTH AND DEVELOPMENT DURING SECOND YEAR

Chapter Outline

- Muscular and Nervous Systems
- Motor Development
- Development of Senses and Perceptions
- Development of Language
- Review Questions

The second year of the child is also a period of rapid physical growth and development though the growth is not so rapid as it is during the first year. During this period, the child gains 4 inches in height, and 4 to 5 pounds in weight; while his gains during the first year of his life are 6 to 9 inches in height, and, 14 to 15 pounds in weight. A child of 2 years, on an average, has the height of 32 to 33 inches, and weighs approximately 28 pounds. In general, a positive relation between height and weight continues up to 12 years of age [NCHS standards are given in Table 5.1].

Bones also increase in size and number. They become modified in texture. More bones have become calcified now, than was the case during the first year. Somewhere between the age of 12 and 18 months, the bones become hardened and fused. The soft membrane spots in the skull, which we call fontanelles, generally, close. The second year is also the period when the deciduous teeth erupt.

Body proportion During this period, the upper part of the body, happens to be heavier than the lower. The head happens to be the heaviest than any other single part of the body. It appears to be too large for the body. Skull (cranicum) is much larger and so out of proportion to the face. Arms are too long; legs, hands and feet are too short.

Various parts of the body, develop at different rates. They develop in such a way that, in due course, proportion between different parts of the

Table 5.1 Weight (kg) by age of boys aged 2–5 years (NCHS standards)

Age		Percentiles													Standard Deviations							Age	
Yrs	Mths	3rd	5th	10th	20th	30th	40th	50th	60th	70th	80th	90th	95th	97th	–3 S.D.	–2 S.D.	–1 S.D.	Median	+1 S.D.	+2 S.D.	+3 S.D.	Yrs	Mths
2	0	10.2	10.5	10.9	11.4	11.8	12.1	12.3	12.8	13.2	13.8	14.5	15.1	15.5	9.0	10.1	11.2	12.3	14.0	15.7	17.4	2	0
2	1	10.3	10.6	11.0	11.6	11.9	12.2	12.5	13.0	13.4	14.0	14.7	15.3	15.7	9.0	10.2	11.4	12.5	14.2	15.9	17.6	2	1
2	2	10.4	10.7	11.2	11.7	12.1	12.4	12.7	13.2	13.6	14.2	14.9	15.5	15.9	9.1	10.3	11.5	12.7	14.4	16.1	17.8	2	2
2	3	10.6	10.9	11.3	11.9	12.3	12.6	12.9	13.4	13.8	14.4	15.1	15.7	16.1	9.1	10.4	11.7	12.9	14.6	16.3	18.0	2	3
2	4	10.7	11.0	11.5	12.0	12.4	12.8	13.1	13.6	14.0	14.6	15.3	16.0	16.4	9.2	10.5	11.8	13.1	14.8	16.6	18.3	2	4
2	5	10.8	11.1	11.6	12.2	12.6	13.0	13.3	13.8	14.2	14.8	15.5	16.2	16.6	9.3	10.6	12.0	13.3	15.1	16.8	18.5	2	5
2	6	10.9	11.2	11.7	12.3	12.8	13.2	13.5	14.0	14.4	15.0	15.7	16.4	16.8	9.4	10.7	12.1	13.5	15.3	17.0	18.7	2	6
2	7	11.0	11.4	11.9	12.5	13.0	13.3	13.7	14.1	14.6	15.2	15.9	16.6	17.0	9.4	10.9	12.3	13.7	15.5	17.2	19.0	2	7
2	8	11.1	11.5	12.0	12.7	13.1	13.5	13.9	14.3	14.8	15.4	16.1	16.8	17.2	9.5	11.0	12.4	13.9	15.7	17.4	19.2	2	8
2	9	11.3	11.6	12.2	12.8	13.3	13.7	14.1	14.5	15.0	15.6	16.4	17.0	17.4	9.6	11.1	12.6	14.1	15.9	17.6	19.4	2	9
2	10	11.4	11.7	12.3	13.0	13.5	13.9	14.3	14.7	15.2	15.8	16.6	17.2	17.6	9.7	11.2	12.7	14.3	16.0	17.8	19.6	2	10
2	11	11.5	11.9	12.4	13.1	13.6	14.0	14.4	14.9	15.4	16.0	16.8	17.4	17.8	9.7	11.3	12.9	14.4	16.2	18.0	19.8	2	11
3	0	11.6	12.0	12.6	13.3	13.8	14.2	14.6	15.1	15.6	16.2	17.0	17.6	18.0	9.8	11.4	13.0	14.6	16.4	18.3	20.1	3	0
3	1	11.7	12.1	12.7	13.4	13.9	14.4	14.8	15.3	15.8	16.3	17.2	17.8	18.2	9.9	11.5	13.2	14.8	16.6	18.5	20.3	3	1
3	2	11.9	12.3	12.9	13.6	14.1	14.6	15.0	15.4	15.9	16.5	17.3	18.0	18.5	10.0	11.7	13.3	15.0	16.8	18.7	20.5	3	2
3	3	12.0	12.4	13.0	13.7	14.3	14.7	15.2	15.6	16.1	16.7	17.5	18.2	18.7	10.1	11.8	13.5	15.2	17.0	18.9	20.7	3	3
3	4	12.1	12.5	13.1	13.9	14.4	14.9	15.3	15.8	16.3	16.9	17.7	18.4	18.9	10.2	11.9	13.6	15.3	17.2	19.1	21.0	3	4
3	5	12.2	12.6	13.3	14.0	14.6	15.1	15.5	16.0	16.5	17.1	17.9	18.6	19.1	10.3	12.0	13.8	15.5	17.4	19.3	21.2	3	5
3	6	12.4	12.8	13.4	14.2	14.8	15.2	15.7	16.2	16.7	17.3	18.1	18.8	19.3	10.4	12.1	13.9	15.7	17.6	19.5	21.4	3	6
3	7	12.5	12.9	13.6	14.3	14.9	15.4	15.8	16.3	16.9	17.5	18.3	19.0	19.5	10.5	12.3	14.1	15.8	17.8	19.7	21.7	3	7
3	8	12.6	13.0	13.7	14.5	15.1	15.6	16.0	16.5	17.0	17.7	18.5	19.2	19.7	10.6	12.4	14.2	16.0	18.0	19.9	21.9	3	8
3	9	12.7	13.2	13.8	14.6	15.2	15.7	16.2	16.7	17.2	17.9	18.7	19.4	19.9	10.7	12.5	14.4	16.2	18.2	20.1	22.1	3	9
3	10	12.9	13.3	14.0	14.8	15.4	15.9	16.4	16.9	17.4	18.0	18.9	19.7	20.1	10.8	12.6	14.5	16.4	18.4	20.4	22.4	3	10
3	11	13.0	13.4	14.1	14.9	15.5	16.1	16.5	17.0	17.6	18.2	19.1	19.9	20.3	10.9	12.8	14.6	16.5	18.6	20.6	22.6	3	11
4	0	13.1	13.6	14.3	15.1	15.7	16.2	16.7	17.2	17.8	18.4	19.3	20.1	20.5	11.0	12.9	14.8	16.7	18.7	20.8	22.8	4	0
4	1	13.2	13.7	14.4	15.2	15.9	16.4	16.9	17.4	17.9	18.6	19.5	20.3	20.8	11.1	13.0	14.9	16.9	18.9	21.0	23.1	4	1
4	2	13.4	13.8	14.5	15.4	16.0	16.5	17.0	17.6	18.1	18.8	19.7	20.5	21.0	11.2	13.1	15.1	17.0	19.1	21.2	23.3	4	2
4	3	13.5	14.0	14.7	15.5	16.2	16.7	17.2	17.7	18.3	19.0	19.9	20.7	21.2	11.3	13.3	15.2	17.2	19.3	21.4	23.6	4	3

Contd....

Age		Percentiles													Standard Deviations							Age	
Yrs	Mths	3rd	5th	10th	20th	30th	40th	50th	60th	70th	80th	90th	95th	97th	−3SD	−2SD	−1SD	Median	+1SD	+2SD	+3SD	Yrs	Mths
4	4	13.6	14.1	14.8	15.7	16.3	16.9	17.4	17.9	18.5	19.2	20.1	20.9	21.4	11.4	13.4	15.4	17.4	19.5	21.7	23.8	4	4
4	5	13.8	14.2	15.0	15.8	16.5	17.0	17.5	18.1	18.7	19.4	20.3	21.1	21.6	11.5	13.5	15.5	17.5	19.7	21.9	24.1	4	5
4	6	13.9	14.4	15.1	16.0	16.6	17.2	17.7	18.2	18.8	19.5	20.5	21.3	21.8	11.6	13.7	15.7	17.7	19.9	22.1	24.3	4	6
4	7	14.0	14.5	15.2	16.1	16.8	17.3	17.9	18.4	19.0	19.7	20.7	21.5	22.1	11.8	13.8	15.8	17.9	20.1	22.3	24.6	4	7
4	8	14.2	14.6	15.4	16.3	16.9	17.5	18.0	18.6	19.2	19.9	20.9	21.8	22.3	11.9	13.9	16.0	18.0	20.3	22.6	24.8	4	8
4	9	14.3	14.8	15.5	16.4	17.1	17.7	18.2	18.8	19.4	20.1	21.1	22.0	22.5	12.0	14.0	16.1	18.2	20.5	22.8	25.1	4	9
4	10	14.4	14.9	15.7	16.6	17.3	17.8	18.3	18.9	19.6	20.3	21.3	22.2	22.7	12.1	14.2	16.3	18.3	20.7	23.0	25.4	4	10
4	11	14.6	15.0	15.8	16.7	17.4	18.0	18.5	19.1	19.8	20.5	21.6	22.4	23.0	12.2	14.3	16.4	18.5	20.9	23.3	25.6	4	11
5	0	14.7	15.2	16.0	16.9	17.6	18.1	18.7	19.3	19.9	20.7	21.8	22.6	23.2	12.3	14.4	16.6	18.7	21.1	23.5	25.9	5	0
5	1	15.8	15.3	16.1	17.0	17.7	18.3	18.8	19.5	20.1	20.9	22.0	22.9	23.4	12.4	14.6	16.7	18.8	21.3	23.7	26.2	5	1
5	2	15.0	15.5	16.2	17.2	17.9	18.5	19.0	19.6	20.3	21.1	22.2	23.1	23.7	12.6	14.7	16.9	19.0	21.5	24.0	26.5	5	2
5	3	15.1	15.6	16.4	17.3	18.0	18.6	19.2	19.8	20.5	21.3	22.4	23.3	23.9	12.7	14.8	17.0	19.2	21.7	24.2	26.7	5	3
5	4	15.2	15.7	16.5	17.5	18.2	18.6	19.3	20.0	20.7	21.5	22.6	23.6	24.2	12.8	15.0	17.1	19.3	21.9	24.5	27.0	5	4
5	5	15.4	15.9	16.7	17.6	18.3	18.9	19.5	20.2	20.9	21.7	22.8	23.8	24.4	12.9	15.1	17.3	19.5	22.1	24.7	27.3	5	5

body, may grow the adult level. Now, the head grows much more slowly in comparison to other parts of the body. Facial skeleton grows relatively larger. The rate of growth of arms and legs, happens to be more rapid than in case of other parts of the body. This is especially the characteristic of growth between birth and two years of age. The arms become larger than the legs.

MUSCULAR AND NERVOUS SYSTEMS

During the second year, muscular and nervous systems gain in strength marvellously. The potentiality of their movements and function develop with great rapidity. The child can make new movements; his movements become finer and more precise. With the development of the nervous system, potentiality for such movements, also increases. Brain is the crucial part of the central nervous system. At the time of birth, it weighs 350 grams. By the end of second year, its weight is 1,000 grams, which is three-fourth of its weight in an adult.

The nervous system, as a whole, grows complex and highly differentiated. The nerve fibres develop from a state of immaturity to the one when they are having better protective fatty shield—the process is called *Myelinisation.*

MOTOR DEVELOPMENT

Walking The child continuously gains in physical strength as he grows in body size, and this development is essential for his being able to perform the motor activities that are initiated or refined during this period. 'Walking' is an important locomotor activity which the child learns during the second year. The child has to pass through a number of phases before he achieves the skill of walking independently; sitting, crawling, creeping, standing and walking with support are the stages which precede 'walking'. A child cannot walk without support until he has achieved the needful neuromuscular maturation for the same; even for the accomplishment of the preceding phases, maturation of a different kind is required. "Changed body proportions, advanced neural development, and increased muscle strength" along with proper practice, are crucial for progress in all these locomotor activities. Dennis[1] says that absence of complete practice may retard locomotor development.

The average age, when a child can stand and walk with support is 12 months. A child of 14 months can stand alone. By 15 months, he starts

1. Dennis, W. *Causes of Retardation among the Institutional Children.*

walking, though still awkwardly and cautiously but without support. In this respect, individual differences are so much that, some start walking as early as 10 months, and, some not until 2 years of age. There are many factors which may delay the development of locomoteor ability. Severe illness is one of them. By 20 months of age, a child can walk up and down the stairs with assistance, and without assistance by the time the child is 2 years old. Bayley[2] et al studied 61 children through repeated measurements, to know the amount of development during the first three years of the child.

Any attempt made to advance the development of these skills, before the needful neuromuscular maturity for the same has been achieved, is bound to fail. Practice, no doubt is important. It can enhance the pace of development but only if neuromuscular maturity, in case of each locomotor skill, takes its own time to be achieved. With age and practice, co-ordination between walking and climbing improves; waste movements are eliminated, steps become longer and more rapid, they become stronger also. A variety of motor skills develop during this period—reaching to things, grasping them, self-feeding and handling objects of different shapes and sizes. A child of 2 years, may also be interested in block building, and may do pretty well. Through experiments and observations, it was established that even children, 15 months of average age, could build a stable tower of 2 cubes; insert a pellet into a bottle, and place a round block into a farmboard, while by the age of 12 months, none of these skills were found to be there. By the time a child is 18 months old, he can throw a ball and construct a tower using three blocks. A two-year-old child can kick a ball; turn the pages of a book, insert 3 blocks in a farmboard, and, build a column six to seven cubes high. Children ranging between the age of 1 to 3, have been described as notorious handlers of objects; it is the way to satisfy their curiosity, and thus to go on learning rapidly [see Table 5.2].

Illingworth, while tracing the development of motor skills since the very beginning, confirms that a child of 18 months, automatically reaches out with much accuracy, to the near objects; can put one block on top of the other. A child of 2 years may also start scribbling with a pencil, crayon or paints; may enjoy smacking and rolling bits of clay or dough. However, a behavioural problem arises during this period, the child picks up dirty, tiny objects by this time, the eyes and hands have learnt to work together with co-ordination.

THUMB SUCKING

Thumb sucking is another behavioural problem, which may not be apparently so serious at the beginning, but later on parents, generally try

2. Bayley, Nancy, Devis, FC. *Growth in Bodily Size and Proportions during the First Year. Three Years: Developmental Study of Sixty-one Children by Repeated Measurements.*

Table 5.2 Developmental Milestones in the First 2 Years of Life

Milestone	*Average Age of Attainment (mo)*	*Developmental Implications*
Gross Motor		
Head steady in sitting	2.0	Allows more visual interaction
Pull to sit, no head lag	3.0	Muscle tone
Hands together in midline	3.0	Self-discovery
Asymmetric tonic neck reflex gone	4.0	Child can inspect hands in midline
Sits without support	6.0	Increasing exploration
Rolls back to stomach	6.5	Truncal flexion, risk of falls
Walks alone	12.0	Exploration, control of proximity to parents
Runs	16.0	Supervision more difficult
Fine Motor		
Grasps rattle	3.5	Object use
Reaches for objects	4.0	Visuomotor coordination
Palmar grasp gone	4.0	Voluntary release
Transfers object hand-to-hand	5.5	Comparison of objects
Thumb-finger grasp	8.0	Able to explore small objects
Turns pages of book	12.0	Increasing autonomy during book time
Scribbles	13.0	Visuomotor coordination
Builds tower of two cubes	15.0	Uses objects in combination
Builds tower of six cubes	22.0	Requires visual, gross, and fine motor coordination
Communication and Language		
Smiles in response to face, voice	1.5	Child more active social participant
Monosyllabic babble	6.0	Experimentation with sound, tactile sense
Inhibits to "no"	7.0	Response to tone (nonverbal)
Follows one-step command with gesture	7.0	Non-verbal communication
Follows one-step command without gesture (e.g. "Give it to me")	10.0	Verbal receptive language

Contd....

Milestone	Average Age of Attainment (mo)	Developmental Implications
Speaks first real word	12.0	Beginning cf labelling
Speaks 4–6 words	15.0	Acquisition of object and personal names
Speaks 10–15 words	18.0	Acquisition of object and personal names
Speaks two-word sentences (e.g. "Mummy shoe")	19.0	Beginning grammaticisation, corresponds with 50+ words vocabulary
Cognitive		
Stares momentarily at spot where object disappeared (e.g. yarn ball dropped)	2.0	Lack of object permanence (out of sight, out of mind)
Stares at own hand	4.0	Self-discovery, cause and effect
Bangs two cubes	8.0	Active comparison of objects
Uncovers toy (after seeing it hidden)	8.0	Object permanence
Egocentric pretend play (e.g. pretends to drink from cup)	12.0	Beginning symbolic thought
Uses stick to reach toy	17.0	Able to link actions to solve problems
Pretend play with doll (gives doll bottle)	17.0	Symbolic thought

hard to wean the child from it. Affectional insecurity may be a cause for it. By the time a child turns 4, and if he has learnt more satisfactory use of the hands, he would give up thumb sucking. "The habit will phase out as time passes on, and the child learns 'grown-up' ways to find his security and his place in the world." Contact with his parents may also prove helpful.

Thumb sucking may cause protrusion of the front teeth[3]. The observed instances make us believe that, malocclusion spontaneously corrects itself when thumb sucking is stopped early. Parental interference may prolong the period of thumb sucking, and increase the intensity of the force of sucking.

PREFERENCE IN THE USE OF HANDS

....."there is more of ambidextrality (use of both hands) and left-handedness among boys than among girls since girls are more tractable, and less resistant to adults and cultural pressures"—the social pressure to eat and write with right hand, happens to be more in case of girls. Accordingly, to one opinion, the side to which infant, generally, moves while assuming neck tonic reflex position, may be the side of his handedness.

During the second year, a child starts feeding himself; and his skill in doing this increases with age. More accuracy is witnessed with no falling of any food particle of food, or dirtying of the mouth area. It is only when a child is thus seen feeding himself that the parents can learn if the child is using left hand in the activity rather than the right one. Some parents, try to force the child to use the right hand. There is a difference of opinion, regarding the forcible use of right hand. Glaser (1953) and some others are against such an interference. They consider the cause to be neurological. According to them, there is a certain hemisphere in the brain which controls this and if the working of it is interfered with, this may adversely affect the development of speech and other fine motor activities of the child, which so rapidly develop, especially, during the ensuing period up to 5 years of age. Some are of the view that to conclude anything with definiteness in this regard, is not possible. Social and cultural factors may also affect people's opinion regarding it. Hildreth, GH[4] opines:

....."there is more of ambidextrality (use of both hands) and left-handedness among boys than among girls since girls are more tractable, and less resistant to adults and cultural pressures"—the social pressure to eat and write with right hand, happens to be more in case of girls. Accordingly, to one opinion, the side to which infant, generally, moves while assuming neck tonic reflex position, may be the side of his handedness.

A fairly vast majority of a population uses right hand because of the genetic neurological factors, and the social and cultural pressures. Though Trankell, in a study, found that the left-handed children worked in the same manner as the right-handed children; nevertheless, it has been suggested that children should be encouraged to use the right hand but they must

3. Silliman, JH. *Thumb Sucking and the Oral Structures.*
4. Hildreth, GH. *Development and Training of Hand Dominance: Developmental Problems Associated with Handedness. Training of Handedness.*

not be forced to do it. Thomson[5] warns: "A decision to change a left-handed child to a right-handed should be considered a major readjustment for the child, and a programme not to be instituted without serious caution and psychological planning." Jersild, AT[6] also cautions against the unfavourable after-effects which such a shift involves.

DEVELOPMENT OF SENSES AND PERCEPTIONS

When a child is born, it has its sense organs: eyes, ears, nose, tongue and skin, with full potentiality to develop constantly, rather rapidly, so as to enable it to grow into the most sensitive and sensible being on earth. It reaches to that stage, only after passing through a series of developmental processes and stages. Murphy[7] writes: "The transformation of an apparently dimly seeing, chaotically moving, avidly sucking, yet sleepy neonate into a smoothly co-ordinated alert and constructive adult involves many processes, not all of which we understand."

In this chapter, our objective is only to see how a child develops its senses during the second year of its life. In the last chapter, we read that the neonate's sense organs initially lead to no perceptions, that is no meaningful interpretations of the impressions got at the sense thresholds. It is only gradually that the accumulating sense-impressions in the central nervous system, start giving meanings. The sensations become perceptions when they convey meanings. Along with the development of nervous system, the sense organs, too, become more operative and their functions grow more meaningful. The development of the physical organs, and, of those which are related to motor activities, helps the child further in coming with contact to a wider world, thereby enriching the accumulation of sense impressions into the central nervous system. The intelligence of the child depends upon this accumulation, upon the quantum and nature of sense impressions, more and more of which develop into perceptions as the child grows into age.

As already mentioned in the previous chapter, during the first few postnatal weeks, the child learns the use of sense organs which are for seeing, hearing, tasting, smelling and for tactile impressions. By the time the child attains the age of 1 year, his sense organs are not only fully operative but are also serving as thresholds to the conduits for the transmission of the sense impressions into the central nervous system or the brain. As the child advances in age, the number of stimuli from the external world—both physical and social—increases. The sense organs continuously grow more and more skilful in their responses to these stimuli. The baby, thus,

5. Thomson GC. *Child Psychology: Growth Trends and Adjustments*, 1952.
6. Jersild, AT. *Child Psychology.*
7. Murphy, LB, et al. *The Widening World of Childhood: Paths Toward Mastery*, 1962.

reacting to the stimuli, develops intellectually; the intellectual development is planned to be dealt in a separate chapter to follow.

An organism is moved to behave in a certain way because of stimuli received from the external environment, as well as because of internal needs of the body such as caused by hunger, fatigue, thirst and a lot of others. The acquity of sense organs increases because of their responding to the external stimuli as well as to the impressions made by the internal needs of the body. Organs of functions, such as, hands, feet, and so on, become operative as a result of stimuli, which the sense organs receive. The functions of organs help in their rapid development. The feelings of hunger, of fatigue, of need for movement, for well-being and security or of discomfort or insecurity—all are internal impressions which, too evoke bodily reactions.

Though reactions go on being modified continuously, yet the inter-sensory development does not happen to be perceptible before the age of three. It is only later, that an equivalence relationship is established among visual, haptic and kinesthetic sense modalities. The perception of size is not still fully developed; a one-year-old child would pack up his tiny doll's nursing bottle, preparing his muscles in the same way as he would do in case of his own full-sized bottle. Still, he is so young that he may hold out his hand to catch his ball—the perception of distance has still not been developed. This also shows that his perception of shape has still not achieved maturity. The child cannot make correct perception of size, shape, height and the like. He may be seen trying to put an object into something hollow, though the hollow space is too small for the object to be put into it. Likewise, he may do the mistake of trying to put a round object into a hollow which is square in shape. Still, he does not have the conception that a bigger object will occupy more space; nor, he can recognise the shape of an object, in reference to the shape of the hollow where it is to be put into.

A child who is almost two years old, would like, and, be greatly benefited playing with toys such as blocks of different shapes and sizes; hollow cubes which fit into each other. Such toys, accidentally, and later purposefully, give chances to the children, to compare sizes of different toys, and also their shapes. They help in the development of perception as to which object is bigger and which is smaller; which toys are of the same shape and which differ in shapes and how.

The overall impact of the development of sense organs and of perception may be seen in the motor activities of the child, which continues to grow finer, accurate; the self-confidence of the infant, also continues to grow. Though, as already mentioned above, it would be too early to expect a child of 2 years to have achieved too much of maturity as regards sense organs and perceptions.

DEVELOPMENT OF LANGUAGE

The development of language and the development of intellect are co-related, but this relation is evident at a later stage. Up to two years of age, no significant co-relation between the two could be found by the researchers, this is why, the development of language is being dealt with, in this very chapter.

The development of language starts with the production of PHONEMES by the child. The phonemes are the basic single sounds which individually convey no meaning or sense. The production of MORPHEMES by the child, marks the second stage of language development. Morphemes are such meaningful words, which can convey some sense or meaning. Each morpheme has some phonemes which together make some sense; and if any of its phoneme is dropped, it would cease to give any meaning. A child begins with the production of phonemes, and learns to unite them in different patterns, in imitation to his elders, in such a way that they become meaningful—organisation of phonemes which we call morphemes. During the second year, the repertoire of phonemes increases rapidly. The researchers have reached to a general conclusion about the age-wise average number of phonemes, that the repertoire of a child contains: 18 phonemes can be pronounced by a one year old child; 25 phonemes, when the child is 23 months old. Throughout the first year, the vowel sounds dominate, during the second year, the situation is reversed—the average number of vowels pronounced by a child of 23 months, is 11, while he can pronounce 14 consonants. Among the number of consonants, the nasals (m, n, n̲)—have a greater proportion; the proportion of fricatives (f, v, s, z, ...) decreases. Sounds produced, restricting the air with the two lips (bilabials); and those produced by touching the front tongue to the teeth ridge (alveolars), become more frequent; while those produced from throat or by touching the back of the tongue to the velum (velars), decrease in number. These changes are attributable to physical maturity. As during the last quarter of the first year, the child starts using solid food which makes the jaws do a lot of experience in chewing, and the same helps in the development and stimulation of jaw muscles and dentition. The physical changes, thus involved, result in enabling the child to utter such sounds more and in a better way, in which the role of the jaw muscles, is greater. During the second year, when the child has got the four upper and the four lower teeth erupted, he is in a better position to utter dental and post-dental consonants. McCarthy[8] writes: "It is only after respiration has been satisfactorily established, after the child has assumed the erect posture, has ceased to

8. McCarthy, D. *Language Development in Children.*

Table 5.3 Key Developmental Milestones: Language

Age	*Milestone*
1 month	Turns head to sound
3 months	Cooing
6 months	Monosyllables ('*ma*', *ba*')
9 months	Bisyllables ('*mama*', '*baba*')
12 months	Two words with meaning
18 months	Ten words with meaning
24 months	Simple sentence
36 months	Telling a story

be nursed, has begun to use solid food, after the frontal incisors have erupted, that the onset of true speech is observed." (See Table 5.3).

Language is affected by the social environment of the child. For example, when the child hears his name pronounced repeatedly to call him, he starts comprehending what that particular word stands for—though he himself may not utter that word till the time he is also physically matured enough to do the same. Likewise, he grasps the meanings of the words 'milk', 'water' and others—which are so repeatedly spoken, though he can speak out these words only much later. The number of words, he can comprehend happens to be greater by far than the number of words he can utter; this is why a child who is only a little older than a year can follow the directions and commands given by the elders, though his own verbal expression is very limited as yet. In many cases, his single word—monosyllabic or disyllabic at the most, stands for the whole sentence; when he utters the word "Ma-Ma", he may mean, "Ma-Ma, lift me up in the lap"; or "Ma-Ma give me the toy"; or, "Ma-Ma, feed me": so on and so forth.

When my granddaughter was about 2 years old, she could speak a few full sentences with a correct syntax—"पापा डांटते है।" (*Papa dant-te hain*—Papa is rebuking); "मुझे दई (for "dalia"—porridge) खाना है।" (*muje dai khanna hai*—I am to eat the porridge.) etc. In the beginning, the child uses words which represent a single object or event. When he uses the word "apple" it indicates his learning that it is something edible, having a definite shape, a red or green (with parts of it yellow) in colour. When he says—"पापा गया।" (*papa gaya*—Papa has gone), he is communicating a complete sense—representing some event. A little later, he can use words which represent some class of objects or events; examples may be "खाना, खाना है" (*khana khana, hai*—the food is to be eaten); here the first "खाना" (*khana*—food) is noun which represents a class of objects. Thus, the child's ability to communicate with others goes on increasing. His greatest prize is that others are understanding him, his needs or desires are readily fulfilled because of his speech—it proves to be the highest motivation to the child to further

Table 5.4 Development of Language

1. First distinct phoneme is uttered by the medium age of 8 weeks [Shirley]
2. Attempt at something like Talking — 25 weeks
3. Singing tones appear — 32 weeks
4. Expressive sounds appear — 38 weeks

(First meaningful bisyllabic words are uttered during the last quarter of the First year]

SEQUENCE

REFLEX SOUNDS [Phonemes]
(18 in number by 1 year)

↓

MONOSYLLABIC WORDS
(Morphemes made of Nouns, Interjections)

↓

MONOSYLLABIC WORDS (Verbs)

↓

MONOSYLLABIC WORDS (Qualifying-Adjectives)

↓

MONOSYLLABIC/BISYLLABIC WORDS
(Adverbs of different types)

Note: A child of about 23 months, produces Morphemes made of about 25 phonemes. First it uses Bilabial, then Alveolars — more frequently. After that, the child uses Dentals and Post-Dentals.

The second year is a period of fast Linguistic Development

↓

PREPOSITIONS
by two and half years of age

↓

SENTENCES OF TWO/THREE
or even Four Words... between 2½ and 3 years

↓

SOMETIMES SENTENCES OF 6 TO 8 WORDS
by 4 years of Age
(The use of Inflections and Relational words begins)

FACTORS AFFECTING LINGUISTIC DEVELOPMENT

(*i*) Parents (*ii*) Peers
(*iii*) School (*iv*) Wider Social Milieu

improve his speech, capability to communicate. "The second year is marked by swift and dramatic improvements in language ability".

The child has an average vocabulary of 272 words by the time he is two years old.

The child has an average vocabulary of 272 words by the time he is two years old.[9] Of course, individual differences are present. These may be congenital or environmental. Some may get very motivating environment, where they get to listen and imitate with due encouragement provided, while some other parents or elders, may not be able to spare much time, may not be having the mood for playing with and talking to their children with a cheering up spirit. Counting words used by children, 2 years of age, in their spontaneous talks, during periodic routine examinations, revealed the fact that individual differences may be as wide as some using 126 words while the fewest used by a child, were only 6 words.

The context in which a word is used helps the child to learn its sense. When the child is engaged in doing something and his mother says — "Stop"; and the way she utters this word, makes it comprehensible to the child. Though initially, it would not be grasped as a discrete word, yet later on, it joins the child's repertoire of passive vocabulary. It is natural that the passive vocabulary exceeds in number, by far, to the active vocabulary of the child. At two years, the child can comprehend a great number of words while, at the time, is unable to use the same. [See Table 5.4].

REVIEW QUESTIONS

***Q.*1.** "The second year of the child is also a period of rapid physical growth and development". Illustrate in detail to verify the above statement.

***Q.*2.** What may cause the problem of "Thumb-sucking"? What should the guardian do to wean the child from it?

***Q.*3.** Glaser is against forcing a left-handed child for making use of the right hand only.

Give your opinions regarding this problem suggesting measures for a remedy.

***Q.*4.** Tick the correct answer

(*i*) The acquity of sense organs increases

(*a*) because of nutritive food

(*b*) through physical exercise

---

9. Smith, ME. *An Investigation of the Development of the Sentence and the Extent of Vocabulary in Young Children.* (According to this book, the average vocabulary of a child at different stages of the age is as under—1 year: 3 words; 15 months: 19 words; 18 months: 22 words; 21 months: 118 words; 2 year: 272 words.

(*c*) through therapeutic measures

(*d*) because of sense organs responding to overt and covert stimuli.

(*ii*) What is the average number of vowels and consonants that a child of two years should be expected to produce?

(*a*) 11 and 14 (*b*) 18 and 25

(*c*) 10 and 15 (*d*) 20 and 25

(*iii*) Which part of the body does grow slower than the other parts?

(*a*) arms (*b*) legs

(*c*) head (*d*) chest

***Q*.5.** What type of environment may help in a proper development of the language of a child? Also give the sequence of his linguistic development.

ANSWERS TO OBJECTIVE TYPE QUESTIONS

***Q*.4.** (*i*) (*d*) (*ii*) (*a*)

(*iii*) (*c*).

CHAPTER 6

PHYSICAL GROWTH AND DEVELOPMENT DURING FIFTH YEAR

Chapter Outline

- Body Growth and Body Proportions
- Neuromuscular-Skeletal Changes
- Factors Contributing to Physical Health and Growth
- Development of Intersensory Perception
- Fine Motor Activities
- Development of Physical Functioning
- Stuttering
- Measures which May Help Cure the Defect or Prevention
- Review Questions

The period of growth from the second year to the fifth, is characterised by rapid development. Parents and elders at home, find it amazing to see how the baby has transformed into a very active, naughty toddler. The child now, is a bundle of energy, seemingly tireless and always up to something. It is quite marvellous to see the progress that the child makes in the field of mobility, handling objects, language, and other activities. The development, of course, is a process of nature but it may be accelerated or decelerated or thwarted due to unfavourable environmental conditions.

Sometimes, parents and the elders at home would be surprised to see how the baby who as a neonate, two years back, apparently had little or no involvements in external world, has grown into a naughty handler of things. The child keeps moving about all the time, holding one thing after another, throwing this and that, babling something or the other—the sense of which can be grasped by the listeners only at times; especially, the mother may feel the pauseless activities of the child as tiring. Nevertheless, the progress that the child makes in the field of mobility, and, in handling objects, and in producing sounds so varied in nature, makes all feel—"it's quite marvellous".

BODY GROWTH AND BODY PROPORTIONS

The average height of a 3 year old male child is 38 inches and weight, 33 pounds. The female child is also, almost of the same height (37.6") and weight (32.5 pounds). By the time, the child attains 5 years of age, he stands about 43.6 inches tall, and is heavier than the girl, but the latter is roughly comparable to the boy. Even at the stage, prediction is fairly possible regarding the mature height. At birth, the male baby has 28.6 per cent of mature height; and the female baby 39.9 per cent; at 5, the same become 61.8 and 66.2 per cent, respectively. "Boys, in one study, generally, gained slightly more than twice as much in height during 2½ to 3½ year period of rapid growth as they did in the preceding and following periods covering 2 to 4 years."[1] [Tables 6.1 (*a*), 6.1 (*b*), 6.1 (*c*) and 6.1 (*d*)].

> "Boys, in one study, generally, gained slightly more than twice as much in height during 2½ to 3½ year period of rapid growth as they did in the preceding and following periods covering 2 to 4 years."

Progress in height tends to be more regular than in weight. Weight is more variable because it includes soft tissues, water as well as bones, and is easily susceptible to external factors; as such the impact of home, school and community in bringing about evenness in the tenor of progress in weight, is always very important. The home, the school and the community as a whole will have to plan properly so that the needs of the children may be met in a desirable way. [Tables 6.2 (*a*) and 6.2 (*b*)].

By five, the upper parts of the body approximate the adult size. The growth of the upper parts slows down earlier, and the points of their maturity are reached much earlier. The lower parts keep a rapid pace of growth. During the pre-school period, the growth of the head, which together with the face, was already of the size of less than one-fourth of the entire body at the time of birth, marks a very slow pace. Growth of limbs, happens to be quite rapid. Compared to it, the growth of trunk may be termed as intermediate. By 6, the body proportion becomes almost the same as that of an adult. The facial features undergo little or no change after the age of 6. Sex differences are found not only in average height and weight but in the composition of tissues also; the girls have more fatty tissues, and the boys have the heavier muscles. [See Fig. 6.1 and Table 6.3].

1. Stolz, HR, Stolz, LM. *Somatic Development of Adolescent Boys.*

Table 6 ®®®.1 (*a*) Length or Height (cm) of Indian children from birth to 6 years

Boys								*Girls*						
Percentiles								*Percentiles*						
3rd	*10th*	*25th*	*50th*	*75th*	*90th*	*97th*	**Age (Months)**	*3rd*	*10th*	*25th*	*50th*	*75th*	*90th*	*97th*
47.55	48.20	49.25	50.38	51.18	52.23	53.28	**0**	47.46	48.39	49.26	50.27	51.25	52.06	53.10
56.34	57.36	58.20	59.36	60.57	61.99	63.75	**3**	55.75	57.12	58.06	59.10	60.32	61.47	62.90
62.49	63.70	64.64	65.86	67.24	68.74	70.76	**6**	61.55	63.62	64.31	65.45	66.77	68.13	69.70
56.80	68.08	69.30	70.60	71.99	73.42	75.40	**9**	65.59	67.48	68.78	70.04	71.48	72.27	74.43
70.06	71.37	72.92	74.32	75.67	76.98	78.82	**12**	68.64	70.70	72.23	73.49	74.98	76.54	78.04
75.55	77.00	79.02	80.67	82.01	83.25	84.94	**18**	73.82	76.18	78.08	79.77	81.20	82.90	84.42
80.14	81.83	84.09	86.00	87.46	88.86	90.33	**24**	78.22	80.86	83.03	84.97	86.58	88.42	90.16
84.01	85.99	88.33	90.51	92.18	93.90	95.90	**30**	81.99	84.88	87.24	89.93	91.26	93.23	95.30
87.30	89.60	91.93	94.35	96.32	98.46	100.77	**36**	86.00	88.39	90.88	93.26	95.37	97.45	99.82
90.17	92.77	95.09	97.73	100.01	102.60	105.24	**42**	88.32	91.54	94.12	96.68	99.04	101.20	103.98
92.79	95.64	98.00	100.80	103.41	106.41	109.33	**48**	91.19	94.47	97.13	99.82	102.41	104.61	107.63
95.32	98.32	100.85	103.74	106.67	110.97	113.06	**54**	94.08	97.34	100.08	102.87	105.51	107.51	110.87
97.90	100.94	103.85	106.74	109.93	113.36	116.43	**60**	97.15	100.30	103.13	105.99	108.78	110.91	113.87
100.71	103.62	107.18	109.95	113.33	116.67	119.46	**66**	100.56	103.49	106.45	109.34	112.04	114.05	116.38
103.89	106.47	111.04	113.59	117.04	119.06	122.16	**72**	104.46	107.06	110.22	113.09	115.53	117.35	118.73

Table 6.1 (*b*) Height (cm) Mean and Percentiles of Indian Boys and Girls (5–18 Years)

Boys								*Girls*						
			Percentiles								*Percentiles*			
Mean	*3rd*	*10th*	*25th*	*50th*	*75th*	*97th*	*Age (Year)*	*Mean*	*3rd*	*10th*	*25th*	*50th*	*75th*	*97th*
107.1	97.9	100.4	103.8	106.7	109.9	116.4	**5.0**	106.0	97.2	100.3	103.1	106.0	108.8	113.8
110.4	100.7	103.6	107.2	109.9	113.3	119.5	**5.5**	109.4	99.6	103.5	105.0	108.1	112.2	116.4
113.7	103.7	106.9	112.0	114.2	118.0	125.9	**6.0**	113.0	102.1	106.1	108.8	112.5	115.9	123.3
117.5	106.1	109.6	113.5	117.3	120.7	128.4	**6.5**	115.4	104.5	108.4	111.1	114.9	118.4	126.0
118.6	108.5	112.0	115.9	119.7	123.0	130.8	**7.0**	118.2	107.1	110.7	113.7	117.4	121.3	129.3
121.6	110.9	114.2	117.8	121.6	125.2	133.2	**7.5**	120.2	109.7	113.1	116.4	120.3	124.4	132.8
124.1	113.3	116.3	119.7	123.6	127.4	135.8	**8.0**	122.7	112.3	115.5	119.3	123.2	127.5	136.4
126.4	115.2	118.6	121.9	125.7	129.8	138.5	**8.5**	126.2	115.0	118.1	122.2	126.2	130.7	139.8
130.4	118.0	120.9	124.2	128.2	132.5	141.4	**9.0**	128.6	117.8	120.9	125.1	129.2	133.8	143.1
131.5	120.3	123.4	126.7	130.8	135.3	144.5	**9.5**	131.9	120.6	123.6	128.0	132.3	136.9	146.2
134.7	122.7	125.9	129.4	133.6	138.3	147.7	**10.0**	134.8	123.4	126.5	130.8	135.2	139.8	149.0
137.6	125.1	128.6	132.2	136.6	141.5	151.0	**10.5**	137.9	126.1	129.3	133.7	138.1	142.7	151.7
139.6	127.5	131.2	135.6	139.6	144.7	154.3	**11.0**	141.3	128.8	132.1	136.4	140.9	145.4	154.2
142.3	129.9	133.9	138.0	142.7	147.9	157.5	**11.5**	144.3	131.4	134.8	139.0	143.5	147.9	156.5
144.7	132.4	136.6	141.0	145.8	151.1	160.8	**12.0**	146.7	133.9	137.4	141.5	146.0	150.3	158.5
147.9	134.9	139.3	143.9	148.9	154.2	163.9	**12.5**	149.9	136.3	139.8	143.8	148.3	152.5	160.4
150.3	137.4	142.0	146.8	152.0	157.3	166.9	**13.0**	151.4	138.5	142.1	145.9	150.4	154.4	162.1
154.9	140.0	144.7	149.7	154.9	160.2	169.7	**13.5**	153.2	140.6	144.1	147.8	152.2	156.2	163.5
158.0	142.6	147.4	152.4	157.6	162.9	172.3	**14.0**	153.6	142.4	145.9	149.4	153.8	157.6	164.7
161.4	145.2	149.9	155.0	160.2	165.4	174.7	**14.5**	154.8	144.1	147.4	150.8	155.1	158.8	165.8
164.3	148.0	152.4	157.4	162.5	167.7	176.8	**15.0**	155.0	145.5	148.6	151.8	156.0	159.7	166.5
165.5	150.8	154.9	159.6	164.6	169.6	178.5	**15.5**	155.4	146.6	149.3	152.6	156.6	160.4	167.1
167.1	153.6	157.9	161.6	166.3	171.2	179.8	**16.0**	155.8	147.5	149.7	152.9	156.8	160.4	167.4
167.9	156.6	159.4	163.3	167.7	172.4	180.7	**16.5**	156.0	148.0	149.7	152.9	156.5	160.5	167.6
168.6	159.6	161.5	165.0	168.7	173.1	181.2	**17.0**	157.1	148.3	149.8	153.0	157.0	160.5	168.0
169.4	162.7	163.4	167.5	169.3	173.4	181.1	**17.5**							
169.8	161.0	164.0	168.8	169.8	173.4	181.6	**18.0**							

Source: Physical and sexual growth of affluent Indian children from 5 to 18 years of age. Agarwal DK, Agarwal KN, Upadhyay SK, et al. *Indian Pediatrics* 1992; 29: 1203–1284

Table 6.1 (*c*) Weight (kg) of Indian Children from Birth to 6 Years (Boys and Girls)

Boys								Girls						
Percentiles								Percentiles						
3rd	*10th*	*25th*	*50th*	*75th*	*90th*	*97th*	*Age (Months)*	*3rd*	*10th*	*25th*	*50th*	*75th*	*90th*	*97th*
2.54	2.69	3.01	3.14	3.49	3.72	4.04	**0**	2.53	2.66	2.95	3.15	3.41	3.76	3.93
4.78	4.95	5.29	5.65	6.04	6.41	6.71	**3**	4.50	4.79	5.04	5.44	5.91	6.25	6.63
6.24	6.50	6.86	7.35	7.77	8.24	8.64	**6**	5.86	6.25	6.54	7.03	7.59	7.94	8.44
7.17	7.56	7.95	8.49	8.94	9.49	10.06	**9**	6.79	7.24	7.62	8.13	8.70	9.10	9.64
7.80	8.32	8.75	9.32	9.80	10.42	11.17	**12**	7.47	7.96	8.45	8.96	9.55	9.96	10.5
8.86	9.58	10.08	10.71	11.26	12.02	13.06	**18**	8.57	9.10	9.81	10.36	10.91	11.49	12.17
9.77	10.59	11.18	11.89	12.53	13.43	14.66	**24**	9.44	10.08	10.91	11.55	12.18	12.87	13.73
10.56	11.43	12.11	12.90	13.65	14.69	16.02	**30**	10.14	10.87	11.80	12.57	13.33	14.15	15.23
11.25	12.14	12.91	13.78	14.66	15.83	17.20	**36**	10.75	11.56	12.42	13.48	14.40	15.32	16.66
11.89	12.78	13.64	14.60	15.60	16.88	18.28	**42**	11.31	12.22	13.23	14.31	15.40	16.44	18.03
12.51	13.41	14.36	15.39	16.51	17.89	19.30	**48**	11.90	12.89	13.90	15.12	16.37	17.50	19.35
13.12	14.09	15.11	16.19	17.43	18.88	20.34	**54**	12.58	13.64	14.63	15.94	17.31	18.53	20.64
13.77	14.88	15.96	17.07	18.40	19.90	21.46	**60**	13.40	14.53	15.47	16.82	18.26	19.55	21.89
14.48	15.82	16.95	18.05	19.46	20.97	22.71	**66**	14.43	15.62	16.50	17.80	19.25	20.59	23.10
15.28	16.98	18.10	19.19	20.65	22.14	24.16	**72**	15.73	16.96	17.78	18.94	20.28	21.67	24.30

Table 6.1 (*d*) Weight (kg) Mean and Percentiles of Indian Boys and Girls (5–18 Years)

Boys								*Girls*						
	Percentiles								*Percentiles*					
Mean	*3rd*	*10th*	*25th*	*50th*	*75th*	*97th*	***Age (Year)***	*Mean*	*3rd*	*10th*	*25th*	*50th*	*75th*	*97th*
17.4	13.8	14.9	16.0	17.1	18.4	21.5	**5.0**	17.0	13.6	14.6	15.6	16.8	18.2	21.1
18.4	14.5	15.8	17.0	18.1	19.5	22.7	**5.5**	17.9	14.0	15.2	16.0	17.4	18.8	22.2
19.2	15.2	16.2	18.0	19.0	20.7	25.4	**6.0**	18.7	14.1	15.7	16.4	17.8	19.2	23.7
20.6	15.7	17.4	18.6	20.0	21.9	27.7	**6.5**	19.6	14.4	16.1	16.9	18.3	19.9	25.4
21.0	16.2	18.2	19.4	21.0	22.9	29.7	**7.0**	20.5	14.8	16.4	17.3	19.0	20.9	27.5
22.4	16.8	18.7	20.0	22.0	23.9	31.6	**7.5**	21.7	15.3	16.9	18.0	19.9	22.2	29.8
23.5	17.5	19.1	20.7	22.6	25.0	33.5	**8.0**	23.0	15.9	17.2	18.7	20.8	23.6	32.3
24.5	18.2	19.7	21.3	23.5	26.3	35.5	**8.5**	24.9	16.4	17.8	19.6	22.0	25.3	34.9
26.5	19.2	20.3	22.0	24.4	27.7	37.7	**9.0**	25.8	17.1	18.7	20.7	23.5	27.2	37.7
26.8	19.9	21.2	22.9	25.6	29.4	40.1	**9.5**	27.5	18.3	19.7	22.1	25.1	29.3	40.5
28.7	20.9	22.3	24.1	27.0	31.3	42.7	**10.0**	29.6	19.5	21.0	23.6	26.9	31.4	43.4
30.8	21.9	23.5	25.5	28.7	33.4	45.4	**10.5**	31.9	20.9	22.4	25.3	28.9	33.7	46.4
31.9	22.9	24.9	27.1	30.6	35.6	48.2	**11.0**	34.3	22.3	24.0	27.1	30.9	36.0	49.3
33.8	24.1	26.3	28.9	32.7	37.9	51.1	**11.5**	36.8	23.7	25.6	28.9	32.9	38.4	52.2
35.4	25.3	27.9	30.7	34.8	40.3	54.1	**12.0**	38.7	25.1	27.3	30.8	35.0	40.7	55.1
37.9	26.7	29.6	32.7	37.1	42.7	57.1	**12.5**	41.9	26.5	29.0	32.6	37.1	42.9	57.9
39.4	28.1	31.3	34.7	39.4	45.1	60.0	**13.0**	42.6	27.9	30.7	34.5	39.1	45.1	60.7
43.2	29.6	33.1	36.8	41.8	47.6	63.0	**13.5**	45.2	29.3	32.4	36.2	41.0	47.1	63.2
44.7	31.2	34.9	38.8	44.1	50.0	65.9	**14.0**	45.7	30.7	34.0	37.8	42.7	48.9	65.7
48.1	32.9	36.7	40.9	46.3	52.4	68.7	**14.5**	46.6	32.1	35.5	39.3	44.3	50.5	67.9
51.0	34.6	38.6	42.8	48.5	54.6	71.4	**15.0**	48.0	33.4	36.9	40.6	45.7	51.8	70.0
52.4	36.5	40.3	44.7	50.5	56.8	73.9	**15.5**	48.9	34.6	38.2	41.7	46.8	52.9	71.8
54.0	38.5	42,.1	46.5	52.4	58.8	76.3	**16.0**	49.2	35.7	39.3	42.5	47.7	53.6	73.3
55.0	40.6	43.8	48.1	54.0	60.6	78.5	**16.5**	49.4	36.7	40.1	43.0	48.2	54.0	74.6
56.6	42.8	45.9	50.0	55.5	62.3	80.5	**17.0**	50.0	37.6	40.7	43.3	48.4	53.9	75.9
56.9	45.2	46.9	52.0	57.2	63.7	82.2	**17.5**							
59.7	47.6	48.3	54.0	58.6	64.9	83.6	**18.0**							

Table 6.2 (a) Weight by Length[1]

Recumbent Length	Boys' Weight Percentiles, kg and (lb)							Girls' Weight Percentiles, kg and (lb)						
	5th	10th	25th	50th	75th	90th	95th	5th	10th	25th	50th	75th	90th	95th
Boys and Girls Younger than 4 years[2]														
48-50 cm (19-19¾ in)			2.86 (6¼)	3.15 (7)	3.50 (7¼)					3.02 (6¾)	3.29 (7¼)	3.59 (8)		
50-52 cm (19¾-20½) in)			3.16 (7)	3.48 (7¼)	3.86 (8½)					3.25 (7¼)	3.55 (7¾)	3.89 (8½)		
52-54 cm (20½-21¼ in)			3.25 (7¾)	3.88 (8½)	4.28 (9½)					3.56 (7¾)	3.89 (8½)	4.26 (9½)		
54-56 cm (21¼-22 in)	3.49 (7¼)	3.65 (8)	3.95 (8¾)	4.34 (9½)	4.76 (10½)	5.13 (11¼)	5.33 (11¾)	3.54 (7¾)	3.64 (8)	3.93 (8¾)	4.29 (9½)	4.70 (10¼)	5.02 (11)	5.21 (11½)
56-58 cm (22-22¾ in)	3.90 (8½)	4.09 (9)	4.43 (9¾)	4.84 (10¾)	5.29 (11¾)	5.69 (12½)	5.88 (13)	3.93 (8¾)	4.05 (9)	4.37 (9¾)	4.76 (10½)	5.20 (11½)	5.55 (12¼)	5.77 (12¾)
58-60 cm (22¾-23½ in)	4.37 (9¾)	4.58 (10)	4.94 (11)	5.38 (11¾)	5.84 (12¾)	6.28 (13¾)	6.47 (14¼)	4.38 (9¾)	4.50 (10)	4.85 (10¾)	5.27 (11½)	5.73 (12¾)	6.12 (13½)	6.36 (14)
60-62 cm (23½-24½ in)	4.88 (10¾)	5.10 (11¼)	5.49 (12)	5.94 (13)	6.42 (14¼)	6.88 (15¼)	7.08 (15½)	4.85 (10¾)	4.99 (11)	5.37 (11¾)	5.82 (12¾)	6.30 (14)	6.70 (14¾)	6.95 (15¼)
62-64 cm (24+-25¼ in)	5.43 (12)	5.65 (12½)	6.05 (13¼)	6.52 (14¼)	7.02 (15½)	7.50 (16½)	7.72 (17)	5.35 (11¾)	5.50 (12)	5.91 (13)	6.39 (14)	6.89 (15¼)	7.30 (16)	7.55 (16¾)
64-66 cm (25¼-26 in)	5.99 (13¼)	6.20 (13¾)	6.62 (14½)	7.11 (15¾)	7.63 (16¾)	8.13 (18)	8.36 (18½)	5.87 (13)	6.03 (13¼)	6.47 (14¼)	6.97 (15¼)	7.48 (16½)	7.90 (17½)	8.15 (18)
66-68 cm (26-26¾ in)	6.55 (14½)	6.76 (15)	7.19 (15¾)	7.70 (17)	8.23 (18¼)	8.75 (19¼)	8.99 (19¾)	6.38 (14)	6.56 (14½)	7.02 (15½)	7.55 (16¾)	8.07 (17¾)	8.50 (18¾)	8.75 (19¼)
68-70 cm (26¾-27¼ in)	7.10 (15¾)	7.31 (16)	7.75 (17)	8.27 (18¼)	8.82 (19½)	9.35 (20½)	9.62 (21¼)	6.89 (15¼)	7.08 (15½)	7.56 (16¾)	8.11 (17¾)	8.64 (19)	9.08 (20)	9.33 (20½)
70-72 cm (27½-28¼ in)	7.63 (16¾)	7.84 (17¼)	8.28 (18¼)	8.82 (19½)	9.39 (20¾)	9.93 (22)	10.21 (22½)	7.37 (16¼)	7.58 (16¾)	8.08 (17¾)	8.64 (19)	9.18 (20¼)	9.63 (21¼)	9.88 (21¾)
72-74 cm (28¼-29¼ in)	8.13 (18)	8.33 (18¼)	8.78 (19¼)	9.33 (20½)	9.92 (21¾)	10.48 (23)	10.77 (23¾)	7.82 (17¼)	8.05 (17¾)	8.56 (18¾)	9.14 (20¼)	9.68 (21¼)	10.15 (22½)	10.41 (23)
74-76 cm (29¼-30 in)	8.58 (19)	8.78 (19¼)	9.24 (20¼)	9.81 (21¾)	10.43 (23)	10.99 (24¼)	11.29 (25)	8.24 (18¼)	8.49 (18¾)	9.00 (19¾)	9.59 (21¼)	10.14 (22¼)	10.63 (23½)	10.91 (24)

Recumbent Length	Boys' Weight Percentiles, kg and (lb) 5th	10th	25th	50th	75th	90th	95th	Girls' Weight Percentiles, kg and (lb) 5th	10th	25th	50th	75th	90th	95th
76-78 cm (30-30¾ in)	9.00 (19¾)	9.21 (20¼)	9.68 (21¼)	10.27 (22¾)	10.91 (24)	11.48 (25¼)	11.78 (26)	8.62 (19)	8.90 (19½)	9.42 (20¾)	10.02 (22)	10.57 (23¼)	11.08 (24½)	11.39 (25)
78-80 cm (30¾-31½ in)	9.40 (20¼)	9.62 (21¼)	10.09 (22¼)	10.70 (23½)	11.36 (25)	11.94 (26¼)	12.25 (27)	8.99 (19¾)	9.29 (20½)	9.81 (21¾)	10.41 (23)	10.97 (24¼)	11.51 (25¼)	11.85 (26)
80-82 cm (31½-32¼ in)	9.77 (21½)	10.01 (22)	10.49 (23¼)	11.12 (24½)	11.80 (26)	12.39 (27¼)	12.69 (28)	9.34 (20½)	9.67 (21¼)	10.19 (22½)	10.80 (23¾)	11.37 (25)	11.93 (26¼)	12.29 (27)
82-84 cm (32¼-33 in)	10.14 (22¼)	10.39 (23)	10.88 (24)	11.53 (25½)	12.23 (27)	12.83 (28¼)	13.13 (29)	9.68 (21¼)	10.04 (22¼)	10.57 (23¼)	11.18 (24¾)	11.75 (26)	12.35 (27¼)	12.72 (28)
84-86 cm (33-33¾ in)	10.49 (23¼)	10.76 (23¾)	11.27 (24¾)	11.93 (26¼)	12.65 (28)	13.26 (29¼)	13.56 (30)	10.03 (22)	10.41 (23)	10.94 (24)	11.56 (25½)	12.15 (26¼)	12.76 (28¼)	13.15 (29)
86-88 cm (33¾-34¾ in)	10.85 (24)	11.14 (24½)	11.67 (25¾)	12.34 (27¼)	13.07 (28¼)	13.69 (30¼)	14.00 (30¾)	10.39 (23)	10.78 (23¾)	11.33 (25)	11.95 (26¼)	12.55 (27¼)	13.19 (29)	13.57 (30)
88-90 cm (34¾-35½ in)	11.22 (24¼)	11.53 (25½)	12.08 (26¾)	12.76 (28¼)	13.50 (29¼)	14.13 (31¼)	14.44 (31¾)	10.76 (23¾)	11.17 (24½)	11.74 (26)	12.36 (27¼)	12.98 (28½)	13.63 (30)	14.01 (31)
90-92 cm (35½-36¼ in)	11.60 (25½)	11.94 (26¼)	12.52 (27½)	13.20 (29)	13.94 (30¼)	14.58 (32¼)	14.90 (32¾)	11.16 (24½)	11.58 (25½)	12.17 (26¼)	12.80 (28¼)	13.45 (29¾)	14.10 (31)	14.45 (31¾)
92-94 cm (36¼-37 in)	12.00 (26½)	12.37 (27¼)	12.97 (28½)	13.65 (30)	14.40 (31¾)	15.05 (33¼)	15.39 (34)	11.59 (25½)	12.02 (26½)	12.63 (27¾)	13.27 (29¼)	13.95 (30¾)	14.61 (32¼)	14.92 (33)
94-96 cm (37-37¾ in)	12.42 (27½)	12.81 (28¼)	13.45 (29¾)	14.14 (31¼)	14.88 (32¾)	15.54 (34¼)	15.90 (35)	12.05 (26½)	12.48 (27½)	13.12 (29)	13.77 (30¼)	14.48 (32)	15.14 (33½)	15.42 (34)
96-98 cm (37¾-38½ in)	12.88 (28½)	13.28 (29¼)	13.96 (30¾)	14.66 (32¼)	15.39 (34)	16.06 (35½)	16.43 (36¼)	12.55 (27¾)	12.98 (28½)	13.64 (30)	14.31 (31½)	15.04 (33¼)	15.71 (34¾)	15.99 (35¼)
98-100 cm (38½-39¼ in)	13.37 (29½)	13.78 (30½)	14.50 (32)	15.21 (33½)	15.94 (35¼)	16.62 (36¾)	17.00 (37½)	13.10 (29)	13.51 (29¾)	14.19 (31¼)	14.87 (32¾)	15.63 (34½)	16.32 (36)	16.64 (36¾)
100-102 cm (39¼-40¼ in)	13.90 (30¾)	14.30 (31½)	15.06 (33¼)	15.81 (34¾)	16.54 (36½)	17.22 (38)	17.60 (38¾)	13.68 (30¼)	14.08 (31)	14.77 (32½)	15.46 (34)	16.25 (35¼)	16.96 (37½)	17.39 (38¼)
102-104 cm (40¼-41 in)	14.48 (32)	14.85 (32¼)	15.65 (34½)	16.45 (36¼)	17.18 (37¼)	17.87 (39½)	18.24 (40¼)							

Table 6.2 (*b*) Weight by Length[1]

Recumbent Length	*Boys' Weight Percentiles, kg and (lb)* 5th	10th	25th	50th	75th	90th	95th	*Girls' Weight Percentiles, kg and (lb)* 5th	10th	25th	50th	75th	90th	95th
Boys and Girls: Prepuberscent														
90-92 cm	11.70	11.97	12.59	13.41	14.35	15.25	15.72	11.45	11.67	12.28	13.14	14.11	14.98	15.74
(35½-36¼ in)	(25¼)	(26½)	(27¾)	(29½)	(31¾)	(33½)	(34¾)	(25¼)	(25¾)	(27)	(29)	(31)	(33)	(34¾)
92-94 cm	12.07	12.36	13.03	13.89	14.84	15.87	16.41	11.86	12.10	12.74	13.63	14.63	15.57	16.42
(36¼-37 in)	(26½)	(27¼)	(28¾)	(30½)	(32¾)	(35)	(36¼)	(26¼)	(26¾)	(28)	(30)	(32¼)	(34¼)	(36¼)
94-96 cm	12.46	12.77	13.49	14.38	15.34	16.45	17.06	12.26	12.53	13.21	14.12	15.14	16.13	17.05
(37-37¾ in)	(27½)	(28¼)	(29¾)	(31¼)	(33¼)	(36¼)	(37½)	(27)	(27½)	(29)	(31¼)	(33½)	(35½)	(37½)
96-98 cm	12.87	13.21	13.98	14.89	15.87	17.01	17.69	12.66	12.97	13.70	14.62	15.66	16.69	17.65
(37¾-38½ in)	(28¼)	(29)	(30¾)	(32¾)	(35)	(37½)	(39)	(28)	(28½)	(30¼)	(32¼)	(34½)	(36¾)	(39)
98-100 cm	13.31	13.67	14.48	15.43	16.41	17.56	18.29	13.06	13.42	14.19	15.13	16.19	17.24	18.23
(38½-39¼ in)	(29¼)	(30¼)	(32)	(34)	(36¼)	(38¾)	(40¼)	(28¼)	(29½)	(31¼)	(33¼)	(35¼)	(38)	(40¼)
100-102 cm	13.77	14.15	15.00	15.98	16.98	18.11	18.89	13.48	13.88	14.69	15.65	16.73	17.80	18.80
(39¼-40¼ in)	(30¼)	(31¼)	(33)	(35¼)	(37½)	(40)	(41¾)	(29¼)	(30½)	(32½)	(34½)	(37)	(39¼)	(41½)
102-104 cm	14.25	14.65	15.54	16.65	17.57	18.67	19.50	13.91	14.36	15.21	16.20	17.28	18.38	19.38
(40¼-41 in)	(31½)	(32¼)	(34¼)	(36½)	(38¼)	(41¼)	(43)	(30¼)	(31¾)	(33½)	(35¼)	(38)	(40½)	(42¼)
104-106 cm	14.76	15.18	16.10	17.13	18.18	19.25	20.12	14.36	14.85	15.75	16.75	17.86	18.98	19.98
(41-41¾ in)	(32½)	(33½)	(35½)	(37¼)	(40)	(42½)	(44¼)	(31¼)	(32¼)	(34¾)	(37)	(39¼)	(41¼)	(44)
106-108 cm	15.30	15.73	16.68	17.74	18.82	19.86	20.76	14.84	15.37	16.30	17.33	18.46	19.62	20.61
(41¾-42½ in)	(33¼)	(34¾)	(36¼)	(39)	(41½)	(43¾)	(45¼)	(32¼)	(34)	(36)	(38¼)	(40¼)	(43¼)	(45½)
108-110 cm	15.85	16.31	17.28	18.37	19.49	20.51	21.45	15.35	15.91	16.87	17.94	19.09	20.30	21.29
(42½-43¼ in)	(35)	(36)	(38)	(40½)	(43)	(45¼)	(47¼)	(33¼)	(35)	(37¼)	(39½)	(42)	(44¾)	(47)
110-112 cm	16.43	16.91	17.90	19.02	20.18	21.22	22.18	15.90	16.48	17.47	18.56	19.76	21.03	22.03
(43¼-44 in)	(36¼)	(37¼)	(39½)	(42)	(44½)	(46¼)	(49)	(35)	(36¼)	(38½)	(41)	(43½)	(46¼)	(48½)
112-114 cm	17.04	17.53	18.54	19.70	29.91	21.98	22.98	16.48	17.09	18.08	19.22	20.47	21.81	22.84
(44-45 in)	(37½)	(38¼)	(40¼)	(43½)	(46)	(48½)	(50¼)	(36¼)	(37¼)	(39¼)	(42¼)	(45¼)	(48)	(50¼)
114-116 cm	17.66	18.18	19.20	20.39	21.66	22.82	23.85	17.11	17.72	18.72	19.91	21.23	22.67	23.73
(45-45¾ in)	(39)	(40)	(42¼)	(45)	(47¼)	(50¼)	(52½)	(37¼)	(39)	(41¼)	(44)	(46¼)	(50)	(52¼)
116-118 cm	18.32	18.85	19.89	21.11	22.45	23.73	24.80	17.77	18.40	19.40	20.64	22.04	23.60	24.71
(45¾-46½ in)	(40½)	(41½)	(43¼)	(46½)	(49½)	(52¼)	(54¼)	(39¼)	(40½)	(42¼)	(45½)	(48½)	(52)	(54½)

Recumbent Length	Boys' Weight Percentiles, kg and (lb) 5th	10th	25th	50th	75th	90th	95th	Girls' Weight Percentiles, kg and (lb) 5th	10th	25th	50th	75th	90th	95th
118-120 cm	18.99	19.55	20.60	21.85	23.28	24.73	25.83	18.48	19.11	20.11	21.42	22.92	24.62	25.81
(46½-47¼ in)	(41¾)	(43)	(45½)	(48¼)	(51¼)	(54½)	(57)	(40¼)	(42¼)	(44¼)	(47¼)	(50½)	(54¼)	(57)
120-122 cm	19.70	20.28	21.34	22.63	24.15	25.80	26.96	19.22	19.85	20.87	22.25	23.88	25.73	27.03
(47¼-48 in)	(43½)	(44¾)	(47)	(50)	(53¼)	(57)	(59½)	(42¼)	(43¾)	(46)	(49)	(52¼)	(56¼)	(59½)
122-124 cm	20.43	21.03	22.11	23.45	25.07	26.96	28.18	19.99	20.64	21.68	23.13	24.91	26.95	28.37
(48-48¾ in)	(45)	(46¼)	(48¼)	(51¼)	(55¼)	(59½)	(62¼)	(44)	(45½)	(47¼)	(51)	(55)	(59½)	(62½)
124-126 cm	21.20	21.82	22.92	24.32	26.05	28.18	29.50	20.80	21.47	22.54	24.09	26.05	28.27	29.87
(48¾-49½ in)	(46¼)	(48)	(50½)	(53½)	(57½)	(62¼)	(65)	(45¼)	(47¼)	(49¼)	(53)	(57½)	(62¼)	(65¼)
126-128 cm	21.99	22.64	23.77	25.24	27.10	29.48	30.92	21.65	22.34	23.47	25.11	27.28	29.71	31.51
(49½-50½ in)	(48½)	(50)	(52½)	(55¼)	(59¼)	(65)	(68¼)	(47¼)	(49¼)	(51¾)	(55¼)	(60¼)	(65½)	(69½)
128-130 cm	22.82	23.50	24.67	26.22	28.21	30.86	32.44	22.53	23.25	24.46	26.22	28.63	31.28	33.33
(50½-51¾ in)	(50¼)	(51¾)	(54½)	(57¼)	(62¼)	(68)	(71½)	(49¼)	(51¼)	(54)	(57¼)	(63)	(69)	(73½)
130-132 cm	23.69	24.59	25.62	27.26	29.41	32.31	34.07	23.44	24.22	25.52	27.40	30.09	32.99	35.33
(51¼-52 in)	(52¼)	(53¼)	(56½)	(60)	(64¼)	(71¼)	(75)	(51¼)	(53½)	(56¼)	(60½)	(66¼)	(72¾)	(78)
132-134 cm	24.59	25.32	26.62	28.38	30.68	33.82	35.81	24.38	25.22	26.66	28.68	31.68	34.84	37.53
(52-52¾ in)	(54¼)	(55¼)	(58¼)	(62½)	(67¼)	(74½)	(79)	(53¼)	(55½)	(58¼)	(63¼)	(69¼)	(76¼)	(82¼)
134-136 cm	25.53	26.30	27.68	29.58	32.05	35.40	37.67	25.35	26.28	27.88	30.06	33.41	36.84	39.93
(52¾-53½ in)	(56¼)	(58)	(61)	(65¼)	(70¼)	(78)	(83)	(56)	(58)	(61½)	(66¼)	(73¼)	(81¼)	(88)
136-138 cm	26.51	27.32	28.80	30.86	33.51	37.05	39.65	26.34	27.39	29.19	31.54	35.29	39.01	42.54
(53½-54¼ in)	(58½)	(60¼)	(63½)	(68)	(74)	(81¼)	(87½)	(58)	(60½)	(64¼)	(69½)	(77¼)	(86)	(93¼)
138-140 cm	27.53	28.38	29.99	32.23	35.08	38.77	41.74							
(54¼-55 in)	(60¼)	(62½)	(66)	(71)	(77¼)	(85½)	(92)							
140-142 cm	28.59	29.48	31.25	33.70	36.75	40.55	43.97							
(55-56 in)	(63)	(65)	(69)	(74¼)	(81)	(89½)	(97)							
142-144 cm	29.70	30.64	32.58	35.27	38.54	42.39	46.32							
(56-56¾ in)	(65½)	(67½)	(71¾)	(77¼)	(85)	(93½)	(102)							
144-146 cm	30.86	31.85	34.00	36.95	40.45	44.29	48.80							
(56¼-57½ in)	(68)	(70¼)	(75)	(81½)	(89¼)	(97¼)	(107½)							

Source: 1. Data are those of the National Centre for Health Statistics (NCHS) Health Resources Administration. Department of Health Education and Welfare.
2. Data are based on studies of the Fels Research Institute. Yellow Springs Off
3. Data are based on the Health Examination Surveys of the NCHS.

Table 6.3 Length, Weight and Head Circumference by Age for Boys and Girls Birth to 36 Mo

	Boys' Percentiles								Girls' Percentiles						
	5th	*10th*	*25th*	*50th*	*75th*	*90th*	*95th*	*Measurement*	*5th*	*10th*	*25th*	*50th*	*75th*	*90th*	*95th*
	46.4	47.5	49.0	50.5	51.8	53.5	54.4	Length mm	45.4	46.5	48.2	49.9	51.0	52.0	52.9
	(18¼)	(18¼)	(19¼)	(20)	(20½)	(21)	(21½)	(in)	(17¼)	(18¼)	(19)	(19¼)	(20)	(20½)	(20¼)
Birth	2.54	2.78	3.00	3.27	3.64	3.82	4.15	Weight kg	2.36	2.58	2.93	3.23	3.52	3.64	3.81
	(5½)	(6¼)	(6½)	(7¼)	(8)	(8½)	(9¼)	(lb)	(5¼)	(5¼)	(6½)	(7)	(7¼)	(8)	(8½)
	32.6	33.0	33.9	34.8	35.6	36.6	37.2	Head C. cm	32.1	32.9	33.5	34.3	34.8	35.5	35.9
	(12¼)	(13)	(13¼)	(13¼)	(14)	(14½)	(14¼)	(in)	(12¼)	(13)	(13¼)	(13½)	(13¼)	(14)	14¼)
	50.4	51.3	53.0	54.6	56.2	57.7	58.6	Length cm	49.2	50.2	51.9	53.5	54.9	56.1	56.9
	(19¾)	(20¼)	(20¾)	(21½)	(22¼)	(22¼)	(23)	(in)	(19¼)	(19¼)	(20½)	(21)	(21½)	(22)	(22½)
1 mo	3.16	3.43	3.82	4.29	4.75	5.14	5.38	Weight kg	2.97	3.22	3.59	3.98	4.36	4.65	4.92
	(7)	(7½)	(8½)	(9½)	(10½)	(11¼)	(11¾)	(lb)	(6½)	(7)	(8)	(8¾)	(9½)	(10¼)	(10¼)
	34.9	35.4	36.2	37.2	38.1	39.0	39.6	Head C. cm	34.2	34.8	35.6	36.1	37.1	37.8	38.3
	(13¾)	(14)	(14¼)	(14¾)	(15)	(15¼)	(15½)	(in)	(13½)	((13¼)	(14)	(14¼)	(14½)	(15)	(15)
	56.7	57.7	59.4	61.1	63.0	64.5	65.4	Length, cm	55.4	56.2	57.8	59.5	61.2	62.7	63.4
	(22¼)	(22¾)	(23½)	(24)	(24¾)	(25½)	(25¾)	(in)	(21¾)	(22¼)	(22¼)	(23½)	(24)	(24¾)	(25)
3 mo	4.43	4.78	5.32	5.98	6.56	7.14	7.37	Weight kg.	4.18	4.47	4.88	5.40	5.90	6.39	6.74
	(9¾)	(10½)	(11¾)	(13¼)	(14½)	(15¼)	(16¼)	(lb)	(9¼)	(9¼)	(10¼)	(12)	(13)	(14)	(14¼)
	38.4	38.9	39.7	40.6	41.7	42.5	43.1	Head C. cm	37.3	37.8	38.7	39.5	40.4	41.2	41.7
	(15)	(15¼)	(15¾)	(16)	(16½)	(16¾)	(17)	(in)	(14¾)	(15)	(15¼)	(15½)	(16)	(16¼)	(16½)
	63.4	64.4	66.1	67.8	69.7	71.3	72.3	Length, cm	61.8	62.6	64.2	65.9	67.8	69.4	70.2
	(25)	(25¼)	(26)	(26¼)	(27½)	(28)	(28½)	(in)	(24¼)	(24¼)	(25¼)	(26)	(26¼)	(27¼)	(27¼)
6 mo	6.20	6.61	7.20	7.85	8.49	9.10	9.46	Weight, kg	5.79	6.12	6.60	7.21	7.83	8.38	8.73
	(13¾)	(14½)	(15¾)	(17¼)	(18¼)	(20)	(20¼)	(lb)	(12¾)	(13½)	(14½)	(16)	(17¼)	(18½)	(19¼)
	41.5	42.0	42.8	43.8	44.7	45.6	46.2	Head C, cm	40.3	40.9	41.6	42.4	43.3	44.1	44.6
	(16¼)	(16½)	(16¾)	(17¼)	(17½)	(18)	(18¼)	(in)	(15¼)	(16)	(16½)	(16¼)	(17)	(17¼)	(17½)
	68.0	69.1	70.6	72.3	74.0	75.9	77.1	Length, cm	66.1	67.0	68.7	70.4	72.4	74.0	75.0
	(26¾)	(27¼)	(27¼)	(28½)	(29¼)	(30)	(30¼)	(in)	(26)	(26½)	(27)	(27¾)	(28½)	(29¼)	(29½)
9 mo	7.52	7.95	8.56	9.18	9.88	10.49	10.93	Weight, kg	7.00	7.34	7.89	8.56	9.24	9.83	10.17
	(16½)	(17½)	(18¾)	(20¼)	(21¼)	(23¼)	(24)	(lb)	(15½)	(16¼)	(17½)	(18¾)	(20¼)	(21¼)	(22½)
	43.5	44.0	44.8	45.8	46.6	47.5	48.1	Head C. cm	42.3	42.8	43.5	44.8	45.1	46.0	46.4
	(17¼)	(17¼)	(17¼)	(18)	(18¼)	(18¼)	(19)	(in)	(16¾)	(16¾)	(17¼)	(17½)	(17¼)	(18)	(18¼)

	Boys' Percentiles								Girls' Percentiles						
	5th	*10th*	*25th*	*50th*	*75th*	*90th*	*95th*	*Measurement*	*5th*	*10th*	*25th*	*50th*	*75th*	*90th*	*95th*
	71.7	72.8	74.3	76.1	77.7	79.8	81.2	Length, cm	69.8	70.8	72.4	74.8	76.3	78.0	79.1
	(28¼)	((28¼)	(29¼)	(30)	(30½)	(31½)	(32)	(in)	(27½)	(27¼)	(28½)	(29¼)	(30)	(30¼)	(31¼)
12 mo	8.43	8.84	9.49	10.15	10.91	11.54	11.99	Weight, kg	7.84	8.19	8.81	9.53	10.23	10.87	11.24
	(18½)	(19½)	(21)	(22½)	(24)	(25½)	(26½)	(lb)	(17¼)	(18)	(19½)	(21)	(22½)	(24)	(24¼)
	44.8	45.3	46.1	47.0	47.9	48.8	49.3	Head C, cm	43.5	44.1	44.8	45.6	46.4	47.2	47.6
	(17¾)	(17¾)	(18¼)	(18½)	(18¾)	(19¼)	(19½)	(in)	(17¼)	(17¼)	(17¼)	(180)	(18¼)	(18½)	(18¾)
	77.5	78.7	80.5	82.4	84.3	86.6	88.1	Length, cm	76.0	77.2	78.8	80.9	83.0	85.0	86.1
	(30½)	(31)	(31¼)	(32½)	(33¼)	(34)	(34¼)	(in)	(30)	(30½)	(31)	(31¼)	(32¼)	(33½)	(34)
18 mo	9.59	9.92	10.67	11.47	12.31	13.05	13.44	Weight, kg	8.92	9.30	10.04	10.82	11.55	12.30	12.76
	(21¼)	(21¼)	(23½)	(25¼)	(27¼)	(28¼)	(29½)	(lb)	(19¼)	(20½)	(22¼)	(23¼)	(25½)	(27)	(28¼)
	46.3	46.7	47.4	48.4	49.3	50.1	50.6	Head C, cm	45.0	45.6	46.3	47.1	47.9	48.6	49.1
	(18¼)	(18½)	(18¼)	(19)	(19½)	(19¼)	(20)	(in)	(17¼)	(18)	(18¼)	(18½)	(18¼)	(19¼)	(19¼)
	82.3	83.5	85.6	87.6	89.9	92.2	93.8	Length, cm	81.3	82.5	84.2	86.5	88.7	90.8	92.0
	(32½)	(32¼)	(33¼)	(34½)	(35½)	(36¼)	(37)	(in)	(32)	(32½)	(33¼)	(34)	(35)	(35¼)	(36¼)
24 mo	10.54	10.85	11.65	12.59	13.44	14.29	14.70	Weight, kg	9.87	10.26	11.10	11.90	12.74	13.57	14.08
	(23¼)	(24)	(25¾)	(27¼)	(29¼)	(31½)	(32½)	(lb)	(21¾)	(22½)	(24½)	(26¼)	(28)	(30)	(31)
	47.3	47.7	48.3	49.2	50.2	51.0	51.4	Head C, cm	46.1	46.5	47.3	48.1	48.8	49.6	50.1
	(18½)	(18¾)	(19)	(19¼)	(19¼)	(20)	(20¼)	(in)	(18¼)	(18¼)	(18½)	(19)	(19¼)	(19½)	(19¼)
	87.0	88.2	90.1	92.3	94.6	97.0	98.7	Length, cm	86.0	87.0	88.9	91.3	93.7	95.6	96.9
	(34¼)	(34¾)	(35½)	(36¼)	(37¼)	(38¼)	(38¼)	(in)	(33¼)	(34¼)	(35)	(36)	(37)	(37¼)	(38¼)
30 mo	11.44	11.80	12.63	13.67	14.51	15.47	15.97	Weight, kg	10.78	11.21	12.11	12.93	13.93	14.81	15.35
	(25¼)	(26)	(27¾)	(30¼)	(32)	(34)	(35¼)	(lb)	(23¼)	(24¾)	(26¼)	(28½)	30¼)	(32¼)	(33¼)
	48.0	48.4	49.1	49.9	51.0	51.7	52.2	Head C, cm	47.0	47.3	48.0	48.8	49.4	50.3	50.8
	(19)	(19)	(19¼)	(19¾)	(20)	(20¼)	(20½)	(in)	(18½)	(18½)	(19)	(19¼)	(19½)	(19¼)	(20)
	91.2	92.4	94.2	96.5	98.9	101.4	103.1	Length, cm	9.0	91.0	93.1	95.6	98.1	100.0	101.5
	(36)	(36½)	(37)	(38)	(39)	(40)	(40½)	(in)	(35½)	(35¼)	(36¼)	(37¼)	(38½)	(39¼)	(40)
36 mo	12.26	12.69	13.58	14.69	15.59	16.66	17.28	Weight, kg	11.60	12.07	12.99	13.93	15.03	15.97	16.54
	(27)	(28)	(30)	(32½)	(34½)	(36¾)	(38)	(lb)	(25½)	(26½)	(28¼)	(30¼)	(33¼)	(35¼)	(36½)
	48.6	49.0	49.7	50.5	51.5	52.3	52.8	head C, cm	47.6	47.9	48.5	49.3	50.0	50.8	51.4
	(19¼)	(19¼)	(19½)	(20)	(20¼)	(20½)	(20¼)	(in)	(18¼)	(18¼)	(19)	(19½)	(19¼)	(20)	(20¼)

These data are those of the National Centre for Health Statistics (NCHS). Health Resources Administration. Department of Health, Education, and Welfare. They were based on studies of the Fels Research Institute. Yellow Springs, Ohio Metric data have been smoothed by a least cubic spline technique. For details see Hamill PVV, Drizd TA, Johnson CL. et al: NCHS growth curves for children, birth-18 yr . *United States Vital Health Statistics* 1977 (Nev 165) I–IV pp 1–74, 1979)

NEUROMUSCULAR-SKELETAL CHANGES

Skeletal, nervous and muscular systems rapidly grow towards maturity. More and more cartilage in the child's skeletal system develops into bones. The size and number of bones also increase. They also become harder. The set of deciduous teeth becomes complete up to the age of three; now the child can eat adult food.

Significant muscular development occurs during this period. Upto the age of 4, the muscular growth of the child, happens, roughly proportionate to the overall body-growth of the child. After 4, there is a spurt in the growth of muscles. They grow at a much faster rate—a time comes when 75 per cent of the weight of the body happens to be that of the muscles. The large muscles develop more than do the smaller ones; it may be because of the fact that in the activities of the child, the larger muscles are more involved. The smaller muscles, need to be activated only in case of finer activities. Strength and muscular development, very much depend on the general health of the child, his constitution, habits of eating, sleeping and activity.

"They grow at a much faster rate — a time comes when 75 per cent of the weight of the body happens to be that of the muscles. The large muscles develop more than do the smaller ones; it may be because of the fact that in the activities of the child, the larger muscles are more involved. Strength and muscular development, very much depend on the general health of the child, his constitution, habits of eating, sleeping and activity.

The more developed a child is physically, the more he would be able to participate in strenuous activities, in games and physical activities lasting for longer stretches of time—such activities demand endurance, also, on the part of the child. With age, respiration becomes deeper and slower; heart also slows down, and becomes stable. Blood pressure increases steadily. The nervous system develops rapidly during the nursery school years. The brain has 75 per cent of its adult weight by the time the child is two years old, and 90 per cent when he is 6 years old. Myelination is completed, first in the lower parts, and then, in the higher brain centres. The process is completed before the child attains 6.

The brain has 75 per cent of its adult weight by the time the child is two years old, and 90 per cent when he is 6 years old.

With all these physiological changes and neuromuscular-skeletal maturities, the child's nature of reaction to infection, also changes; the condition of body temperature remains more stable than was the case in infancy; less possibility of serious heart symptoms than as it was during the first two years.

FACTORS CONTRIBUTING TO PHYSICAL HEALTH AND GROWTH

There are many factors which affect the physical growth and development of the child, but the same may be classified into four categories.

1. FAMILY-LINE, HEREDITY (RACE)

"The moment of conception, when the parents' cells fuse, and when a unique biological pattern is fixed, is the most important moment in the life of a child. At that time a pattern for future growth and development of the individual is set."

[Child Development—Physical and Psychological Growth Through Adolescence: Brekenridge, E Marian and Vincent, E Lee].

The potentialities of the child are something which the child is born with. To what extent the same will be realised, depends upon the kind of postnatal environment of the child. Direction of development is also dependent upon his environment. If the child does not get a congenial environment for the realisation of his inherited potentialities, which are an endowment of nature, a part or the whole of some potentialities may be depressed—"a potential genius may become a moron" because of brain injury. However, it depends upon the endowments of nature as to how he will make use of his environment [nurture]. Musical environment may be very stimulating for one whose pitch and tune discriminations are sensitive, and, who is also, emotionally, able to respond to music. On the other hand, a child who has not been so equipped by nature or heredity, will not be able to be benefited even by the congenial environment. Two children, brought up in a similar environment may not grow up to the same level in different fields of growth and development because of the hereditary differences. One, who by birth, is intellectually superior to the other endowed less in intellectual potentialities, will be able to exploit his environment in a better way. Some defects and deficiencies may be congenital, transmitted in the family-line from generation to generation and will prove such hurdles in the growth and development of the child, as can hardly be removed. Again, there may be a case where one may succeed in achieving a certain level of growth and development, in spite of the environment not being so suitable, only because of this better heredity.

> Some individuals are more susceptible to certain diseases because of "certain genetic combinations". Tuberculosis, diabetes or certain mental illnesses are common diseases.

Some individuals are more susceptible to certain diseases because of "certain genetic combinations". Tuberculosis, diabetes or certain mental illnesses are common diseases; but these diseases may be there also where no such family history is available.

For example, tuberculosis may be caused (*i*) because of exposure to tubercle bacillus; (*ii*) because of genetic make-up; or (*iii*) because of unhygienic living conditions and nutrition. Some people are born with such a poor resistance, that even the best possible environment may not prove to be very protective for them. Diabetes is a hereditary disease but it, too may develop, partly because of one's diet, and, partly because of one's physical conditions of living—though a family history may not exist. Some disease or injury to pancreas, may also cause diabetes. If a child has got constitutionally a weak nervous system, he may develop certain types of mental illness because of a certain environmental factor. Soldiers posted at very difficult places, difficult because of inclement weather conditions, may be due to great altitudes or desert or other geographical reasons; and also because of living lonely, far-far away from their near and dear ones, have been found, sometimes to have developed some or the other sort of mental illness. Even the best psychological constitution may break down, because of strong nervous strain.

If a child has a familial tendency towards disease, then the environmental factors need to be more carefully controlled. Sleeping, eating, activities, adjustments to one's circumstances and to people are all included in the environment. Children with constitutional weaknesses, require particular help in meeting their needs. Every child needs to be developed in such a way that he can assume his responsibilities to his satisfaction and to the satisfaction of others who are concerned. Children having hereditary or some sort of congenital problem, may be having inborn constitutional frailty and need particular help. Such children are more likely to suffer from undue fear and anxiety. All genetic differences are produced because of differences in physiological processes of cells. By means of these processes, tissues and organs emerge, and they arrange themselves into a harmonious whole which bears the unique characteristics of the individual. Certain abnormalities may be caused by abnormal chromosomal behaviour. For example, if instead of 46, there are 47 chromosomes, the child will be a mongoloid, and, characterised by some specific abnormalities in structure. His physical and mental developments are also retarded.

Height, pigmentation, longevity, degree of intelligence, and resistance to disease much depend upon the different genetic processes.

One single characteristic may be the result of many genes; as genes do not act in isolation by themselves, but they react with the cytoplasm of the cell. The genes also act upon one another. Nevertheless, it is one single gene which first becomes active in the process, that involves other genes, and the cytoplasm of the cell. Height, pigmentation, longevity, degree of intelligence, and resistance to disease much depend upon the different genetic processes. The regular metabolic process, may also be affected by inborn subnormal genetic interference. The excessive secretion of the phenylpyruvic acid in the urine, causes mental impairment; pigmentation of the hair is also a little disturbed by it—the condition thus developed, is called Phenylketonuria. Phenylketonuria is a hereditary defect caused by the genes inherited from both the parents. A special diet may go a long way to treat the condition.

Some genes are changed by mutation—though it occurs rarely. Sex chromosome, X and Y, produce characteristics that are sex-linked. Some characteristics are sex-limited, for example, Baldness is limited to males only. Baldness is an example which verifies sex control or modification. If rickets is caused in spite of rich intake of vitamin D, the genetic action may be responsible for the same. A genetic action may not have its full impact on the growth and development of the child, if the impact of environment is to the other effect. A good example of the impact of environment is the height, which differs from race to race, and country to country. Mark the difference in height between that of an American, and of a Japanese.

A genetic action may not have its full impact on the growth and development of the child, if the impact of environment is to the other effect. Mark the difference in height between that of an American, and of a Japanese.

2. SOCIOECONOMIC STATUS, HEALTH, FAMILY, SURROUNDINGS

Broadly speaking, Nurture includes all—diet, child-care in general, family surroundings, health conditions of the child and other members of the family. All these reflect the socioeconomic status of the family. So, socioeconomic status is an important factor which has a great role to play in the processes of growth and development. The impact of heredity (Nature) and that of family-environment (Nurture) or environment of thc surroundings of the child in general, happen to be so interlocked, that it is very difficult to assess to what degree each has separately affected the growth and development of the child. Of course, the impact of each should be studied separately, to realise the importance of each factor.

First, we shall see how illness may affect the growth and development of the child. During the period of illness, the growth of height is slowed, or may even be suspended. So, long periods of illness would have their permanent effect on the process of growth. Severe illness affects metabolic processes, and, it adversely affects the growth of heights. Prolonged illness also affects the muscles; they lose some of their tone and grow flabby. If the harm caused by illness is not timely corrected, fatigue would be very frequent and the postures of the body would be distorted. Even bones are affected by some long serious illnesses, and the results may be rickets or even infantile paralysis. Illness may produce anaemia. Frequent lowered fatigue after illness, may be due to lowered haemoglobin cover.

Genuine recovery from illness, therefore, means not only to be free from the symptoms of illness but also return to the state of positive health. Even after the disappearance of the symptoms of illness, the parents should be in no hurry in sending their child to school, if the illness has been of the serious nature. For some days, the body lacks its usual reserve of energy, and because of that, tiredness becomes very frequent.

A prolonged rheumatic fever may cause damage to heart; scarlet fever may affect the kidneys in a bad way, or, deafness may be the sequel of this fever; poliomyelitis may cause paralysis, and encephalitis may damage the brain. Physical therapy may help a little in modifying these handicaps, and, in enabling the child to adjust himself to the situation. So, all efforts should be made for the prevention of these diseases.

Socioeconomic status, in general, is such an important factor, upon which depends the diet, condition of the house and its sanitary arrangements, the locality of the house, and the general living standard of a family. Meredith (1951), after many studies, concluded that boys of the professional and major managerial classes were taller and heavier than those of the unskilled and semiskilled classes.

Socioeconomic status, in general, is such an important factor, upon which depends the diet, condition of the house and its sanitary arrangements, the locality of the house, and the general living standard of a family. All these are very much relevant when we consider the growth and development of the child. Material well-being offers physical development. Meredith (1951), after many studies, concluded that boys of the professional and major managerial classes were taller and heavier than those of the unskilled and semiskilled classes—"diet, housing conditions, health practices, occupational demands and selective mating are possible contributing factors."

However, it is not always easy to determine as to what extent environment has affected growth and development in a certain case. This is because, the rich and the poor, the educated and the uneducated are equally affected by a congenital or chronic disease. Some chronic diseases occur later in adulthood, with a much higher percentage of evidence among the poor. Fielder (1951), in an attempt to survey the possible causes of hearing defects among the young school-going children, found that the great majority of such children were from the families with low socioeconomic status, and, were under-privileged. Even parents of some of them were found to be suffering from long-term malnutrition and chronic diseases. Children, belonging to families with low socioeconomic status, generally, lack in vigour and ambition which are necessary to improve their condition. Some children will not be having even normal intellects because of unsuitable family conditions—hereditary, nutritional and social factors, all may be contributing to thwart the normal course of physical growth and development. Poverty may be compelling some children to do hazardous jobs. They suffer from malnutrition as the food they take does not happen to be containing the necessary ingredients in sufficient quantity. There are families which cannot afford food, milk, fruit in required quantity for their children and others. Lack of vitamins, minerals, fats, protein, carbohydrates and so on, causes diseases of different nature, which in consequence, adversely affect the growth and development of the child. In some cases, because of lack of education, the desirable conception regarding food, may not be there in the family.

Vitamin A is essential for normal growth, formation of skin, glands and bones, and for the proper functioning of eye sight.

For example, Vitamin A is essential for normal growth, formation of skin, glands and bones, and for the proper functioning of eye sight. Its deficiency causes imperfect calcium metabolism, formation of teeth, cartilage, imbalance of the intestinal flora and night blindness. The amount of essential intake for infants, is 1,500 IU, and for children ranging between 2 and 5 years, it is 2,000 to 5,000 IU; adults require 5,000 IU daily. Its sources are liver, butter, margarine, milk, eggs, yellow and orange fruits, green vegetables, cod liver oil and halibut liver oil.

Deficiency of Vitamin B results in loss of appetite, impaired digestion of starches, constipation and diarrhoea, and beri-beri. Severe deficiency of this vitamin results in various nervous disorders and loss of co-ordinating power of muscles. More specifically, lack of B_2 causes cheilosis, weakness and impaired growth; niacin deficiency results in pellagra, gastrointestinal disturbances, and mental disturbance. Cyanocobalamin deficiency results in anaemia.

Deficiency of Vitamin B results in loss of appetite, impaired digestion of starches, constipation and diarrhoea, and beri-beri.

Sources of vitamins B and a larger number of its related vitamins are as follows:

Thiamine (B_1): Wheat germ, bread, pork, potatoes, liver, milk; *Riboflavine* (B_2): liver, eggs, milk; *Nicotine acid* (*Niacin*): Yeast, liver, bread, wheat germ, milk, kidney; *Pyridoxine* (B_6): meat, fish, milk, yeast; Biotin: liver, yeast, milk, butter; *Pantothenic acid*: liver, yeast, eggs, and many other foods; *Cyanocobalamin* (B_{12}): liver, kidney, eggs, fish; *Folic Acid*—(also called Vitamin Bc): green vegetables, liver, mushrooms, yeast.

Daily intake of vitamin B and the related vitamins, as recommended for the different age groups, is as under:

	Infants (mg)	*Children (mg)*	*Adults (mg)*	*Lactation*	
				General (mg)	*Pregnancy (mg)*
Thiamine	0.4 to 0.5	0.7 to 1.8	1.0 to 1.6	1.3	1.7
Riboflavine	0.4 to 0.9	1.0 to 2.0	1.4 to 2.5	2.0	2.5
Niacins	6.0 to 7.0	8.0 to 21.0	17 to 21		15

Deficiency of Vitamin C results in lowered vitality; flaccid joints; dental caries; lowered resistance to infection; fibrous tissue abnormalities. Severe deficiency results in haemorrhage, anaemia, and scurvy.

Deficiency of Vitamin C results in lowered vitality; flaccid joints; dental caries; lowered resistance to infection; fibrous tissue abnormalities. Severe deficiency results in haemorrhage, anaemia, and scurvy.

Sources of Vitamins C (ascorbic acid): Citrus fruits; rose-hip syrup, black currants, fresh vegetables, tomatoes.

Vitamin C increases resistance to infection; it keeps the skin in a healthy condition; it improves the circulation, the condition of gums and of other body tissues, and promotes healing of wounds.

Recommended daily intake of Vitamin C:

Infants (mg)	*Children (mg)*	*Adults (mg)*	*Lactation*	
			General (mg)	*Pregnancy (mg)*
30	35 to 100	70	100	150

Vitamin D is essential for the proper utilisation of calcium and phosphorus, and thus directly influences the structure of bones and teeth.

Blood chemistry is also affected by it. Elderly people, living in temperate areas, and more especially, the dark skinned people, may fail to synthesise this vitamin in sufficient quantity.

Deficiency of vitamin D results in interference with calcium and phosphorus metabolism; weakness and irritability. Its severe deficiency in children may cause rickets, and osteomalacia in adults.

Deficiency of vitamin D results in interference with calcium and phosphorus metabolism; weakness and irritability. Its severe deficiency in children may cause rickets, and osteomalacia in adults.

Its sources are—butter, egg yolk, fish liver oils and oily fish, yeast. The vitamin can be synthesised by the skin under the stimulus of sunlight or ultraviolet light.

Recommended daily intake of Vitamin D:

Infants (IU)	*Children (IU)*	*Adult*	
		Pregnancy (IU)	*Lactation (IU)*
400	400	400	400

Note: Where there is sufficient sunlights available, its deficiency, generally, does not occur.

Vitamin E may have its effect on the ageing process.

Vitamin E About the physiological activity of this vitamin, an exact and detailed knowledge is still lacking. Animal experiments have suggested that it is related to reproductive cycle and fertility. It may have its effect on the ageing process. It is available in most foods, particularly in green vegetables.

Vitamin K It is responsible for the biosynthesis of prothrombin and for maintaining plasma prothrombin levels.

Vitamin K is found in green leafy vegetables and in liver.

Regarding the per day needful quantity of this vitamin, nothing is known with definiteness. Nevertheless, it has been suggested that the daily intake of children should be 1 microgram.

Protein is necessary for the growth of the body and for the repair of the body tissues. They are found as amino acids formed by the combination of carbon, nitrogen and oxygen in various quantities. Beans, meat, eggs, fish and milk are rich in proteins.

Carbohydrates are organic compounds, and derive from sugar and starch. They provide energy to the body.

Carbohydrates are organic compounds, and derive from sugar and starch. They are made of carbon, hydrogen and oxygen. Carbohydrates provide energy to the body.

Fat stores energy and protects body against cold. Lard or butter are rich in fat.

Fat is the white or oily substance in the body. It stores energy and protects body against cold. Especially, the type of food which supplies proteins and vitamins A and D, generally, happens to be fats. Lard or butter and other oily substances used for cooking, are rich in fat. Fat is a necessary part of diet because it contains vitamins and energy giving calories. Fat may be available either from animals, that is animal fats; or from vegetables, that is vegetable fats. Butter, meat, cream, and other milk products. fall in the first category, and are saturated fatty acids. Animal fats are more likely to raise the level of cholesterol in the blood to the risky point, while the vegetable fats in the diet keep down the level of cholesterol in the blood, and so, lessen the risk of atherosclerosis. To believe that a low fat diet can always reduce weight, is a misconception. Saturated fat may prove harmful in some cases, as it contains the largest possible amount of hydrogen.

> *Minerals* are inorganic substances, and are needed by the body for growth and for its proper functioning. The most important among them are calcium, iron, phosphorus, and iodine.

Minerals are inorganic substances, and are needed by the body for growth and for its proper functioning. The most important among them are calcium, iron, phosphorus, and iodine. Calcium is found in cheese, milk and green vegetables; it helps the growth of bones, and helps in blood clotting. Iron is found in bread and liver; it helps in producing red bloods cells. Phosphorus is found in bread and fish; it is also helpful in the growth of bones and the metabolism of fats. Iodine is found in ordinary salt and in fish. It is essential for the functioning of thyroid gland. Its deficiency may cause goitre.

> *Water* is very much essential for life. 50 per cent of our body is made up of water. A normal adult needs 2.5 litres (5 pints) of fluid each day.

Water is very much essential for life. 50 per cent of our body is made up of water. A normal adult needs 2.5 litres (5 pints) of fluid each day. Water taken into the body, is passed out as urine or sweat.

There are families to whom even pure drinking water is not available easily in a sufficient quantity. The water that they consume, may not be clean and hygienic as it may contain harmful organic and inorganic substances. Such a water would cause diseases of different sorts, and the same would adversely affect the growth and development of the child. The utensils used for storing and drinking water, should be clean and free of germs and other harmful substances.

For the proper growth and development, wholesome living conditions and habits are essential. The wholesome living includes not only dietary pattern or food style but clothing and housing too. Clothes should be clean through timely and proper washing, and, should not be too tight to obstruct the growth of body. The house should be airy, with proper ventilation for the fresh air to enter and the exhaled air to pass out. If possible, proper sunlight should also come into the house, according to the need of the season. Care needs to be taken to keep the house free of dinginess and dampness. Slum-dwellers or those compelled to living in narrow and dirty locations, cannot escape heaps of filth lying around and a foul smell emanating from the same. The people living there, generally, happen to be prone to different ailments and the children are the first to fall prey to infections.

3. EMOTIONS

Affection, especially of the mother for her child, is a great motivating factor in the process of development. It affects the biological chemistry of the

Emotions affect the biological chemistry of the child — the activity of glands or secretion of hormones is affected by the emotions of the child, or by the emotions and feelings of mother and other elders of the family to which the child reacts.

child - the activity of glands or secretion of hormones is affected by the emotions of the child, or by the emotions and feelings of mother and other elders of the family to which the child reacts. A background of love and security is a great help in the normal growth and development of the child. Its absence may affect the process of development adversely. If the needs of the child are satisfied in time and in a proper way; if the room of the child is well—stocked with play things—these too serve as factors for keeping the child in a good mood, that is in keeping him emotionally satisfied and happy. A stimulating family environment is very much needed for keeping the child emotionally healthy. The warmth of affection and a feeling of security, indirectly, help in the process of child's development.

4. OTHER EXTRINSIC REASONS

Various longitudinal studies on growth were conducted at the University of Michigan. It was found that "children of the same family tend to show a notable similarity in their patterns of growth." Bayer and Bayley (1961) studied shifts in growth pattern. Growth was induced by the use of 17 alpha-ethyl–19 non-testosterone or methandrostenoline. Growth was accelerated. In 7 of the 16 boys, there was gain in height because of treatment; two of the four girls, were likewise benefited. The treatment was continued over a period of six months. In case of three boys and two girls, there was no gain because of this treatment.

"There are some children, who, in spite of the best environments, are underweight, perhaps have poor muscular tone or are just not robust. When such a child is seen with his parents, he may be recognised as a cliff off the old block."[2]

"There are some children, who, in spite of the best environments, are underweight, perhaps have poor muscular tone or are just not robust. When such a child is seen with his parents, he may be recognised as a cliff off the old block."

School should also be included into the extrinsic reasons that affect the growth and development of the child. There was a time, when the general practice in India was to send children to school at around five years of age. Now, majority of the children are admitted into the nurseries by the age of three. So, the impact of school, in the process of child's development, has become very important. If there are a lot of nursery toys and other items of playing and physical activities, which can stimulate the children to indulge in different sorts of physical and mental activities, they would help in the development of the child.

Contrary to this, if schools still run as institutions, where only 3 Rs (reading, writing and arithmetic) are taught, and the children have to follow a strict routine, then the environment cannot be considered to be one conducive to the wholesome development of the child. If the physical environment is not hygienic, comfortable and pleasant, it may have negative

2. Brekenridge, E, Marian and Vincent, E Lee. *Child Development.*

impact on the normal process of development. "The school should do everything possible to provide a physical environment which is conducive to the physical well-being and working efficiency; an atmosphere which is conducive to mental health, and in which stimulation to learn is provided without nervous tension." The site for the school, the plan of the building, the equipment for the use of the students and the teachers, all are important. The school, should be functional, adaptable and aesthetic. Nemir, A suggests that a school should be planned in such way, whose space, light, heat, ventilation, toilet facilities, locker space and equipment for work are provided in a manner which allows for safety, health and comfort of pupils and teachers. Desks and chairs should be such where the child may sit comfortably in proper posture. "Bad postural habits cause physical and psychological difficulties."

Figure 6.1
Free activity leads to physical as well as cognitive development.

Health services should be child centered rather than defect-centered. They should be family-oriented too. "Home-school understanding and co-operation are generally accepted as basic to smooth continuity of growth, as the child moves from the home into the new and different environment of the school." The child moves back and forth between home and school experiences. Parents differ in their ambition, and expectations from the school but they should not forget that a school has to attend to the needs and comforts of many of its students. Partially, it cannot be always possible to attend to all the less important needs of all individual students. Therefore, school and home co-operation is a must to cater to the needs of the children. Under a democracy, a parent has a right to expect many things from the state, essential for the growth and development of the child. At the same time, if the attitude of the parent towards an institution of the state, as a school is not proper, it may sabotage anything the latter may be doing for the welfare of the child. "Home-school contact should be a conscious part of the programme of every school." Report-cards may serve as a means to keep the parents/guardians, informed of the developmental condition or needs of the child. The formal card system may be dispensed with if there is a regular system of having a personal conference with parents, to inform them of the developmental conditions and needs of their wards.

"Bad postural habits cause physical and psychological difficulties."

"Home-school contact should be a conscious part of the programme of every school."

DEVELOPMENT OF INTERSENSORY PERCEPTION

With the advancement of age, separate sensory modalities improve in their interactions to one another. The reaction of each sense organ to the stimulus that it receives from the external environment, improves in its kind because of the continuous improvement of its own functioning, as well as, because of the improvement of other sensory modalities with which this sense organ interacts. Berch and Lefford explored uniform relationships among visual; haptic and kinesthetic sense modalities for geometric form of recognition in normal children of school age.

[The authors have used the term "haptic for the input of information received through the active manual exploration" of an object].

Such an exploration involves tactile, kinesthetic and surface movement sensations. In handling an object, the fingers of the subject become very much active. "Haptic sense modalities are the results of the movements of wrists, elbows, shoulder joints or sometimes of all the muscles of the complete arm in handling an object. The intersensory judgment of identical forms, improves with age. Much advancement takes place in case of visual-haptic judgments, by the time the child is 8 years old. Depth perception improves fairly rapidly after 3.

Perception of size goes on improving rapidly since the time the child becomes first aware of the presence of general objects and their situations. A general reaction is replaced by the reaction of specific parts of the body. The child takes some time when he can separate the size of an object from its shape while having a visual preception of the same. During the period from 3 years to 5 years, there occurs rapid improvements in the perception of shape, size, height and the like. By two and a half years, a child can pick up the biggest without trial and error, then the next biggest, likewise, he can pick up the smallest object. When he has, thus, developed the perception of size, he can pile up blocks into a tower; can develop different figures by joining, or putting blocks or parts inside one another with least or no error. Now, the child has learnt how much space each object occupies. Even then, in some cases, confusion of size persists even up to the age of five.

"One can see them for a moment, forgetting to realise the size of tiny doll furniture and attempting to sit on it themselves, only to look surprised, and often a little sheepish, because they failed to react accurately to this quality to the object because the child sees himself less than he sees other objects; he usually misjudges his own size."

Perception of shape also takes its time to develop. Similarity and dissimilarity of shapes; nature and amount of likeness and unlikeness can be judged only through learning. A child of 18 months would indiscriminately throw a square into a round and vice-versa, but, by the time a child is about 3, he can wisely work upon a formboard which, of course, offers a good challenge to him. First, he can differentiate squares, circles and triangles, then diamonds, crosses and more complicated shapes. In Binet-Terman mental test, a child of 5 could copy a square with a pencil in three trials. A child of less than 4 years of mental age, could scribble, could draw a careless figure resembling an irregular circle. A diamond imposes difficulty even for a child of 6 to 7 years of mental age. Accuracy of inter-model discrimination, is assessed to find out the mental age of a child. This ability depends upon the ability to translate eye-hand co-ordinated, into kinesthetic performance. Such a test should be given only to a child who is not younger than 5 years of age though maturity in this respect is reached only later on.

FINE MOTOR ACTIVITIES

As the child grows in age, he achieves more ability and proficiency in performing physical activities, requiring quick sensory judgment and better co-ordination of senses between or among themselves, and of the sensory organs with the organs, of action. Sometimes, in performing a particular action only a specific part of an organ of action, needs to be activated. Thus, the child grows proficient in performing actions which are of finer sorts, and complicated in nature.

A child of two can eat solid food, but for sometime he remains a slow and deliberate chewer. His control over the urethral sphincters, is almost complete by the end of second year. Sex-typing becomes apparent during the period between second and the fifth year of the child through the games that he or she likes to play. A female child would like to play with dolls; would put on daintily the feminine-looking clothes. She would also like to play house-keeping activities. The children, during this period, learn the anatomical difference between the two sexes. The female children easily get more items of play as they happen to be related to the child-rearing or house-keeping which they see their mother or sister/sisters engaged in. The male children cannot get so many occasions of observing their male parent or male sibling/siblings engaged into their sex-specific activities-this is a factor which explains why sometimes, we find male children to be indulging more into acts of mischief.

The female children easily get more items of play as they happen to be related to the child-rearing or house-keeping which they see their mother or sister/sisters engaged in.

The world of games and work that the child enters now, demands more of neuromuscular skills, more control over one's body. He likes driving bicycle, roller skating, and other games. Initiation of training may be made in dance and swimming, too. The kindergarten school children with whom the author had been associated, could learn some *Yoga asan* in a proper way. Swinging chair, ladder and slide and see-saw were the very much liked instruments of play for the kindergarteners of our school. Most of the small children of the school could very well learn the physical exercises, which they were expected to perform on the occasion of a function of the school. Of course, due consideration to their age and tenderness had been given while selecting exercises for them. It was realised that children preferred fine motor activities to the just outdoor games. The children who learnt a particular physical activity, would assume a swaggering gait, and, speak in a pre-emptory manner.

Body co-ordinations and acquisition of good motor skills, are essential for everyone, for survival, and a dignified living in society. Acquiring of such skills only, can enable one to perform one's adult chores smoothly and in a dignified manner. Efficiency of movements is required for the performance of routines of daily life—driving a car or some vehicle, is one of such efficiencies. Man needs creative activities for enjoyment, and may be for a living as well—all of which demand the acquisition of fine motor skills, and, intersensory co-ordination. Good physical health is an essential condition, for the acquisition of these skills. Proper feeding, hygienic home and school environment plus free and congenial environment for games and other physical activities, are important factors for a good physical health.

DEVELOPMENT OF PHYSICAL FUNCTIONING

None the less, physical growth and development is a natural process, [which, of course, needs to be boosted through proper Nurture]. With the growth of body, new bodily functions are required to be done, for which physical development automatically takes place. The beating of heart becomes stronger, slower and more regular. The digestive process takes more time, and, is not easily disturbed. The urethral sphincters are now strong enough to retain urine longer. The body temperature remains, generally, stable. The composition of the blood remains more constant. Due to these changes—efficiencies and homeostatis, older children and adults can more easily adjust to changed environments and routines. Periods of their work and play become longer without including much fatigue. Some children have higher levels of globin than others, have larger tonsils, adenoids, and more lymph glands.

The protection of ears and eyes is important in all ages. The ear is well-developed at birth. The inner and middle ear have reached, practically, to the adult size when the child is born. In the young children, the eustachian tube which connects the ear with the throat, is short, wide and straight, and so allows, relatively, an easy passage for the bacteria to pass from the throat to the ear—this is why the incidence of ear infection is higher in young children. All necessary precautions should be taken to prevent ear infections which may lead to the impairment of hearing.

The eye continues to develop through all the years of growth. The sight of the child depends upon the growth of his eyeball. Eyeball is the receptor part of the eye; it is a round ball of tissue through which light passes. To be more precise, the rays of light, enter the eye through cornea, pass through the pupil, are refracted through the aqueous humor on to the lens, which then focuses the rays through the vitreous humor onto the retina at the back of the eyeball. Impulses from the retina pass along the optic nerve to the brain. Myopia or shortsightedness is the result of unusual growth of the eyeball. The development of binocular vision is essential for a correct judgment of distance; it is the ability to see with both eyes at the same time, it gives a stereoscopic effect. Depth perception cannot develop without binocular vision. The health of the eye is very much dependent on the general health. So, much care needs to be taken about the nutrition of the child, about the sanitary conditions or hygienic conditions that the child is reared under. The knowledge of the proper use of the eye is essential, both in normal conditions and when the child is ill. The prints for the child should be larger; and frequent relief from close work should be provided to the child.

"The degree of effectiveness depends upon the processes of growth and maturation, and the quality of the body tissues. Good bones, firm muscles and sound organs are invaluable as a basis for a happy, satisfying life."

The heart grows rapidly till the child is 4 years of age, then the rate of growth slows down, until the child is ten. Then again, there is an increase in the rate of growth until it reaches the peak stage. The weight of the heart is very much related to the capacity to bear the strain of competitive sports; and to the pattern of growth in strength.

Physical growth does not mean only growth in height and weight but it also includes all those changes within the tissues and organs of the body. These changes are necessary for a healthful living of the child, and for increase of the effectiveness of the use of the body—so these changes take place in a normal course.

"The degree of effectiveness depends upon the processes of growth and maturation, and the quality of the body tissues. Good bones, firm muscles and sound organs are invaluable as a basis for a happy, satisfying life."[3]

3. E Marian and Vincent, E Lee. *Child Development—Physical and Psychological Growths through Adolescence.*

A knowledge of the different physical or biological changes taking place during different periods of the child growth, can be a good guide in deciding the needs and routines of the child. The nature and amount of his physical activities and rest, as well as the type of nutrition that should be given to him. Such a knowledge is also helpful in deciding prerequisites of the child, for his healthful and happy living. All precautionary measures may be taken in light of such a knowledge, so that the growth and development of the child may be smooth and full.

STUTTERING

Stuttering is a speech defect which has been found, generally, developing during this period of development. When the child makes involuntary stops and repetitions in speaking, we call it his stuttering. The stutterer makes spasmodic repetitions of certain sounds; for example; "t-t-too" or "c-c-cold", and so on. In general, peak comes at two and a half to three years of age.

Reasons: Johnson W has enlisted the following reasons for the development of stuttering:

(*i*) too much pressure exerted on the child for his weaning from bottle to cup;

(*ii*) mental strain caused because of very strict toilet training;

(*iii*) the reaction of the listener, especially of the parent, to the child's non-fluency of speech;

(*iv*) the child's degree of non-fluency as objectively determined;

(*v*) the child's sensitivity to his own hesitation in speech;

(*vi*) the parental or listener's attitude towards it.
In some cases stuttering has been found to have increased when the child joins his first school...............;

(*vii*) because of the child's difficulty in adjusting to the new authority;

(*viii*) because of difficulty in adjusting to other children;

(*ix*) because of difficulty in adjusting to the routine of the school;

(*x*) in 5 to 10 per cent cases, stuttering begins when an attempt is made to convert a left-handed to the right-handedness.

"The nervous tension created may spill over into fingernail biting, a reversion to thumb-sucking, a relapse to toilet habits, or, frequently, into stuttering."

MEASURES WHICH MAY HELP CURE THAT DEFECT OR PREVENTION

(*i*) Reactions of the parents and of the others should be such as not to make the stutterer conscious of his speech defect.

The listeners should give the impression of finding nothing unusual in the speech of the stutterer or the stammerer.

(*ii*) Bluemel has suggested that therapy for stutterers and stammerers should attempt at the reorganising of the speech, rather than at removing "the multiple symptoms of these disturbances."

(*iii*) Weaning from bottle to cup, or toilet training should not be so strict as to cause too much strain to the child.

(*iv*) The treatment of the teachers, especially, toward the new entrants should be such that they may adjust to the teachers and other children and to the routines of the school without feeling much strain. The behaviour of the staff, coming in contact with the child, should be assuring in regard to security and affection.

(*v*) No attempt should ever be made to wean the child from left-handedness to right-handedness.

(*vi*) The stimulating and encouraging environment may go a long way in setting the thing right.

REVIEW QUESTIONS

***Q*.1.** "At that time a pattern for future growth and development of the individual is set."

What is that time, and how does it set a pattern for future growth and development? What are the postnatal factors that affect the growth and development of the child? Describe in brief.

***Q*.2.** Write the vitamins, deficiency of which causes the following ailments:

Night blindness ....
Loss of appetite ....
Flaccid joints ....
Dental caries ....
Beri-beri ....

***Q.*3.** Write three sources of each Vitamin and of the ingredients mentioned here:

Vitamin D (1) ..... (2) ..... (3) .....

Vitamin A (1) ..... (2) ..... (3) .....

Protein (1) ..... (2) ..... (3) .....

Carbohydrates (1) ..... (2) ..... (3) .....

***Q.*4.** Complete the following sentences:

(*i*) At birth the male baby has .... per cent of mature height, and the female baby .... per cent.

(*ii*) At 5, the height of the male baby becomes .... per cent and that of the female baby .... per cent of a mature person.

(*iii*) According to Johnson, too much pressure on a baby for weaning from bottle to cup feeding may also cause ....

(*iv*) A normal adult needs .... litres of fluid each day.

(*v*) Phosphorous is found in .... and ......

(*vi*) Daily intake of Vitamin B in case of children is .... to .... mg.

***Q.*5.** What is meant by Intersensory Perception? Describe its gradual development up to 5 years of age.

***Q.*6.** Write measures for curing stuttering–a speech defect.

ANSWERS TO OBJECTIVE TYPE QUESTIONS

***Q.*2.** A, B, C, C, B

***Q.*3.** (*i*) fish, (*ii*) butter, (*iii*) yeast

(*i*) milk, (*ii*) green vegetables, (*iii*) yellow and orange fruits

(*i*) beans, (*ii*) meat, (*iii*) milk

(*i*) sugar, (*ii*) starch, (*iii*) a compound of carbon, hydrogen and oxygen

***Q.*4.** (*i*) 28.6, 39.9, (*ii*) 61.8, 66.2, (*iii*) stuttering, (*iv*) 2.5 litres, (*v*) bread, fish (*vi*) 0.7 to 1.8

CHAPTER 7

COGNITIVE/INTELLECTUAL DEVELOPMENT DURING CHILDHOOD

Chapter Outline

- **What is Intelligence?**
- **Symbolic Schemas**
- **Intellectual Development and Play**
- **Review Questions**

When the child is born, it does not happen to be conscious regarding the whole gamut of animate and inanimate objects, that make up its surroundings. Though the child possesses all the five senses which are the means for cognition of these various objects, still the objects are meaningless for the neonate. A thing that is seen, a sound that strikes the neonate's ears, the smell that is inhaled along with air, anything which is cold or warm, or soft or hard to touch, though stimulates the child, yet no meaningful interpretation ensues. Sensation is there but it conveys no meaning. As the child grows in age, the brain starts interpreting in terms of size and shape, in terms of relationships and interrelationships. Up to two years of age, the child does not happen to be conscious of all these attributes of objects that strike his senses. The reactions, so long, happen to be the motor ones only. The objects of the external world do not seem to evoke any apparent mental reactions in the beginning; they stimulate only sensorimotor activities. Piaget has named this first stage of cognitive development, as Sensorimotor Development, a stage commencing since birth and continuing up to two years of age. During this stage, almost each stimulus happens to be from the external environment, and, few or none from the internal world of the brain of the child. The external stimulant affects the child through his senses, and it becomes apparent through the motor activities of the child. In the beginning, the actions of the child impress

A thing that is seen, a sound that strikes the neonate's ears, the smell that is inhaled along with air, anything which is cold or warm, or soft or hard to touch, though stimulates the child, yet no meaningful interpretation ensues. Sensation is there but it conveys no meaning. As the child grows in age, the brain starts interpreting in terms of size and shape, in terms of relationships and interrelationships.

Piaget has named this first stage of cognitive development, as Sensorimotor Development, a stage commencing since birth and continuing up to two years of age.

Piaget has subdivided the sensorimotor period of cognitive development into six stages.

as reflex actions. Gradually, we begin to feel, that learning is taking place in case of the child too, who is still not two years of age. Piaget has subdivided the sensorimotor period of cognitive development into six stages.

Stage–1 (0–1 M) is the stage of The Use of Reflexes.

Stage–1 (0–1 M) It is the stage of The Use of Reflexes, "Many behavioural responses of the newborn child are innate, but they are not all rigid and predictable like the knee jerk." Sucking is a good example. Sucking, generally, occurs when the mouth, lips or cheeks of the young infant, are touched. The child nuzzles the source of stimulation, and when it is within its mouth, there is the action of sucking being done repeatedly. But AL Baldwin is right when he writes, "Sucking movements may occur without any apparent stimulus to the mouth region. On the other hand, some infants may not suck even if the nipple is put directly into the mouth".[1] Moreover, the child may suck on any object—a finger, a toy, or even a spot on the skin. After some time, the child would reject all such objects except the nipple. Piaget considers this development to be the development of a behaviour rooted into the reflexes. He distinguishes schemas from reflexes as the former are not innate like the latter.

"Sucking, grasping, the visual accommodations and eye movements", are the early important reflex behaviours.

"Sucking, grasping, the visual accommodations and eye movements, and those having to do with hearing and phonation" are the early important reflex behaviours. The end results in all these cases, happen to be pre-determined. The only development that takes place during this first stage is that these reflexes stabilise, become general and more discriminating.

Stage–2 (1–4M) The First Acquired Adaptations.

Stage–2 (1–4M) The First Acquired Adaptations. It is during the second stage that such behaviours appear which are the results of first new adaptations. The first behaviour thus acquired, is thumb sucking. Though it is not the case that thumb sucking has not occurred previously. It may have occurred even prenatally, but it is only during this period that a set of behavioural adjustments develops which enables him effectively to bring his thumb to his mouth, and to keep the thumb there. Some states of affairs are brought about, prolonged and repeated through the child's behaviour as has never been done before—first new adaptations are identified; "circular responses and schemas are identified by the result they produce".

The word schema is very important for Piaget as it is a particular kind of SCHEMA which initiates, directs and controls a particular kind of behaviour caused by some stimulus.

The word schema is very important for Piaget as it is a particular kind of SCHEMA which initiates, directs and controls a particular kind of behaviour caused by some stimulus, or which is a reaction to some particular type of stimulus. I would like to explain the term SCHEMA as the total effect caused to the whole nervous system of the organism, when it reacts to some particular stimulus received from the external world, through one or more of the senses of the organism. As a result of the development of a Schema related to a particular behaviour, each such behaviour has its own set of stabilising adjustments. Whenever the stimulus which initially

1. Baldwin AL. *Theories of Child Development, p. 204.*

evoked the behaviour of reaction reappears, it is because of the development of the schema through repeated reactions to the stimulus that the organism is able to behave in an effective way. Each new situation presents a new stimulus which demands a new set of stabilising adjustments or a schema to enable the organism to react effectively.

Now, how does such a schema develop? Each sensation that an organism receives through one or more of his senses, is the assimilation, or taking in something from the environment. This affects the nervous system or the brain of the organism in such a way that it becomes changed.

This change in the set of stabilsing adjustments in respect to a particular stimulus, is the adaptation. Such an adaptation becomes evident only through the behaviour of the organism. The behaviour becomes changed because of adaptation which, itself, is the result of assimilation. This changed behaviour is the accommodation. With the help of these three terms—Assimilation, Accommodation and Adaptation, Piaget has described the continuum of cognitive development. And, cognitive development may be measured on the basis of the bulk of the repertoire of schemas and their nature.

Thumb sucking is a "primary circular response". Primary, because part of this behaviour is innate, but part of it is acquired, too; the systematic thumb sucking is the result of adaptations. 'Circular' because the same behaviour is repeated under the circumstances that had initially evoked it. But even the repetitions bring about something new in the experience which was earned because of the initial response, and a schema develops for each set of behaviour to initiate, direct, prolong and control it. Repetitions make response to the same stimulus, more effective, and the improved behaviours have been called "secondary circular responses" by Jean Piaget.

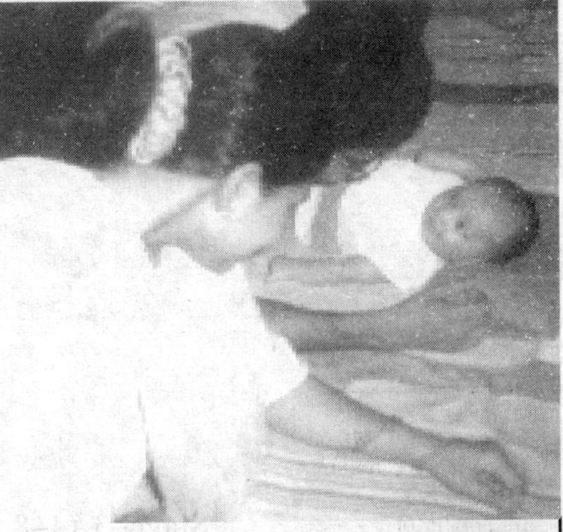

Figure 7.1
This figure shows two of the three sensorimotor behaviours : Looking at an object and prehension.

The main sensorimotor behaviours of the stage are: (*i*) Thumb sucking; (*ii*) looking at objects, and (*iii*) prehension (Fig. 7.1).

(*i*) Thumb is the part of the child's hand, so no extra schemas other than that which enables the child to suck the thumb, is required in the behaviour. Sucking of objects other than the thumb, can only be possible when the schemas which enable it to look at different objects of the environment, and to prehend or grasp them, have been developed.

(*ii*) Coming to the second sensorimotor behaviour, that is looking at an object which the child accidentally happens to see in his environment; it should be mentioned that looking is not the same

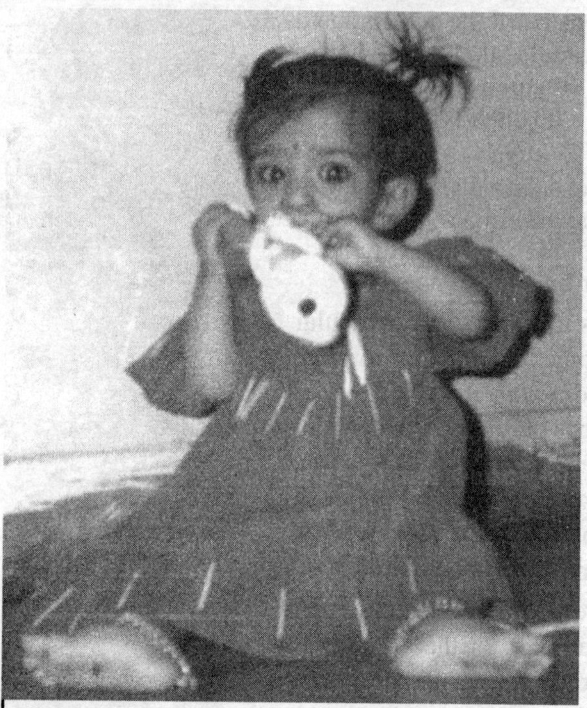

Figure 7.2
Two sensorimotor behaviours : Sucking and prehension are depicted here.

as seeing. Looking is not the mere fixation of the eyes, it is also following the contours of the object (this behaviour in the latter stages, enables the child to recognise the shapes of objects). During the second stage, the child looks only at sights or luminous spots—the perception of an object becomes possible only at the third stage when the child can realise the existence of objects as detached from itself.

(*iii*) The third type of behaviour as mentioned above, that is prehension or grasping of objects, is not possible until the child can look at objects. "Recognitory assimilation is especially important in the visual behaviour ......".[2] (Fig. 7.2). Though grasping is possible even for neonate; if an object is placed on the palm of a child, he would grasp it tightly. However, it would not keep its hold for long as it goes on closing and opening its hand after each short interval. The schema for holding on an object for longer time, develops only during the second stage. But the child still makes no attempt to reach to an object. The schema to enable the child to do this, develops only during the third stage. Such a behaviour shows a co-ordination in visual, (sometimes auditory also) tactual and motor actions. The stage second is a transit for stage third. This is the stage when we can only witness a co-ordinated development of schemas related to actions which are visual, auditory, tactual and motor.

Stage–3 (4–8 M) Secondary Circular Reactions—beginning of intentional adaptations.

Stage–3 (4–8 M) Secondary Circular Reactions—beginning of Intentional Adaptations. The most important development during this stage, is the desire to do something. It precedes an action which is intended to satisfy the desire. It is the stage when a child, also, looks for objects which have been lost from his sight. A desire to prehend such an object, evokes the child for reaction; and, it is only during this stage when the child's behaviour provides an apparent evidence of the existence of internal stimulus. With the assimilation of experience from the external world, some

2. Baldwin AL. *Theories of Child Development,* p. 206.

need may start to be felt so the child intends to do something, before it actually starts behaving in the way which can satisfy the need. This intermediary time between assimilation and accommodation, is the time of 'Intentional Adaptation' as Piaget puts it. Piaget observed "the prolongation of accommodation movements to recapture a lost object"—the desire arises before the child actually starts behaving in a way which enables it to recapture the lost object.

It is the stage of secondary circular responses; these responses are more novel than the ones made during the second stage, the stage of primary circular responses. As already mentioned, thumb sucking is an example of primary circular response, as it is a "piece segregated from an already existing stable behaviour pattern" whereas "moving the right arm up and down, is not part of any previous circular response". Piaget's Laurent gives regular shakes to rattle balls repeatedly, stretching his right arm, it is an example of secondary circular response. The shaking of the celluloid balls, is the external reward which motivates Laurent to resort to the circular behaviour of swinging his right arm regularly. Piaget insists that the balls are still not objects for the child but, merely sights. It is for the sight of swinging balls that the child moves its arm. Gradually, the means and the end are differentiated; the subjective action and the external results are distinguishable. It is during this stage that individual differences in the development of schemas begin. The repertoire of schemas expands tremendously, depending upon the experiences that the external circumstances provide. It is the stage when secondary circular responses establish themselves in a great number. Nevertheless, it cannot be said that the conception of casual relationship between an action and its consequence, is properly established during this third stage of the sensorimotor development.

Acquisition does begin of the conception of a stable world where objects do "maintain their identity and move around in a continuous space". The development of visual motor—prehensive behaviours, the learning of new schemas that reproduce or prolong an interesting event—are the important characteristics of the stage. A child handles an object for the development of an event that is interesting, though the handling happens to begin accidentally. The motor activity of the child is in relation to an object which is visual. By the time the child is about 7 months old, the child begins to stretch out its hand for its prehension. The child can recover an object which is only partially out of sight, and which is recoverable only through the prolongation of the same motor behaviour. For it, it is also essential that the object remains in the same trajectory.

Stage–4 (8–12M) Acquisition of Instrumental Behaviour and Active Search for the Vanished Object

Stage–4 (8–12M) Acquisition of Instrumental Behaviour and Active Search for the Vanished Object. It is the stage for the first appearance of instrumental schemas. The schemas are used as means to achieve some ends. Even the child can use old schemas to achieve its ends in the new situation. Piaget remarks that, Laurent pushed aside, for the first time, an obstacle in the way to reach to its target when she was at O; 7(13).[3] It is during this stage that the child starts making an active search for the object which is no longer visible. It means, he is developing the conception of the permanence of objects. Now, he realises that the object which has vanished from his sight, still exists. The child's "pushing aside the hand or pounding the cushion is a separate schema". It is "preliminary to reaching for the object".

Piaget uses the term "mobility of schemas" by which he means, schemas which are used as means to serve the consummatory schemas. The consummatory schemas may be different on different occasions, but the organism may use the same set of stabilised schemas, under different situations, as "manipulation aspect" of the behaviour though the "motivational aspect" may differ each time. Thus, one more important development of the period is the separation of the "manipulative aspect" from the "motivational aspect". The "manipulative aspect" represents the well-practised pattern of behaviour. In the beginning, it is essential that the manipulative aspect must be interesting or challenging, and such a one which can free the organism from the instigating situation. But later on, when it has become part of the repertoire of the child's voluntary behavioural actions, it can be used in all sorts of situations, both enjoyable and otherwise.

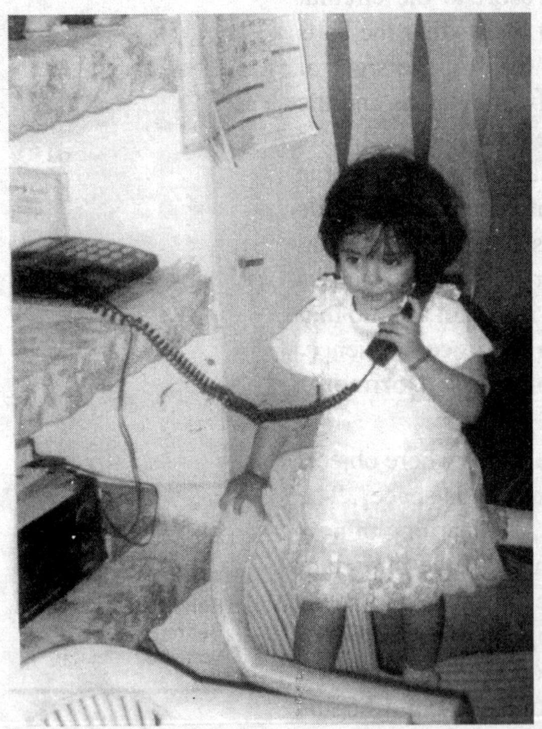

Figure 7.3
Children enjoy imitating their elders.

It is the stage when the child learns in an independent way from its model. It would close and open its fist in imitation of its father only when it has already developed a schema for doing the same by itself. The child imitates sounds also. Imitations of a child also reflect the new mobility of schemas. An imitative action is prepared voluntarily, and is never a result of direct instigation (Fig. 7.3).

Piaget remarks that an important addition to the development of concept of an object, is that the child reaches for the invisible object at the place where only it has just succeeded in finding out. Piaget's Laurent searches for the object not under the blue pillow where it has really been hidden but under the red one because the last time it was found hidden there. During this stage, the concept of the permanence of object is fully

3. Piaget, Jean. *Origins of Intelligence*, p. 217.

established, but still the child lacks the notion that "displacements in space form groups". This notion develops during the next stage.

Stage–5 (12–18 M)
Tertiary Circular
Reactions and the
Discovery of New
Means.

Stage–5 (12–18 M) Tertiary Circular Reactions and the Discovery of New Means. A child of about one year, not only goes on repeating an action on the same pattern but an element of newness is also introduced into it. Variations are not always accidental but are the results of the child's deliberations also. In his book *Origins of Intelligence*, Piaget has given an illustration of the tertiary circular response.

By the time Laurent is 0; 10(2) old, he throws a case of soap not because the "Objective phenomenon of the fall" interests him, but because the very act of letting go interests him; He limits himself to reproducing of the same result, and this constitutes the secondary reaction. It is only when Laurent has attained the age of 0; 10(10) that this reaction becomes tertiary. On that day, Laurent lets a small piece of bread fall continually as he continues breaking it off into fragments. Now, he pays no attention to "the act of letting go" but it is the body in motion that makes him watch it with interest. Next day also, Laurent resumes the experiment of the previous day by first grasping a celluloid swan, a box, etc., then stretching out his arm, and letting them fall. He distinctly varies the position, sometimes holding the object obliquely, sometimes in front or behind his eyes, and so on. He observes the spatial relations, then he modifies the situation.

Out of the well-established schemas, new variants develop. They are, rather, intentionally developed for adaptation to new situations. The child's ability of creating new variations, proves to be of great value in the solution of problems.

"The ability to profit from pure accidents, is first observed in stage 3 of the infant's development".

Even we, the elders, many a time, stumble upon a solution, rather than reaching to it in a well-thought-out plan. In case of children, they can never think ahead of a solution to the problem that they are facing. "The ability to profit from pure accidents, is first observed in stage 3 of the infant's development".[4] Stage 5 is the time when the responses of the child may be, and, generally are, tertiary circular; the child improves its behaviour through trial and error. Reference to an episode mentioned by Piaget, in his famous book *Origins of Intelligence*, would make the point clearer still. There is an object on a pillow. The object is beyond the reach of the child. While struggling for access, the corner of the pillow is hit, and it moves. Further hits make the pillow move again and again. At last, the pillow is in such a position that the child prehends it. The solution of the problem, is all accidental. Notwithstanding, the result helps in further advancing the learning of the child, that if base of an object is moved, the object will also move.

4. Baldwin AL. *Theories of Child Development,* p. 215.

Figure 7.4
The youngest one lacks the mental representation of the external world, yet to be developed in a child of her age.

This stage is important also because the child now can imitate actions of others; prior to it he could do so only in regard to an action, schema for which was already in its repertoire.

The tertiary circular response of the child may also help it in understanding the relationship of an object and the space that it is situated in. Previously, the child's interest was only in the letting go of objects, but now his interest is in the trajectory of the falling object. The falling of the object is an occasion for the child to learn more about the continuous nature of space; and about the relationship between the varying acts and the corresponding varying results.

The fifth stage is also important because the child can learn to fill in the gaps in the arrangement of his schemas, on the basis of feedback. To illustrate, the child is to hit with his hand the three balls hanging down at different heights from three different pieces of string. He attempts to do it by turn, at each ball. His actions teach him, to which height and with what force he needs to raise and move his arm.

There is also improvement in the concept of object. During stage 4, the child would look for the hidden object, only where it was found out last time, and, not at the place where the object was hidden last of all. Now, he would search the object at the place where it was last hidden. Still, the child cannot cope with invisible movements, that is, the child lacks inference that movement of the object may have continued invisibly. If some object is hidden in the closed fist of someone, and, the same is dropped under a pillow; the closed fist is taken out and neared to the child. The child will vigorously try to open it for the object, as the dropping out of the object under the pillow was an action done invisibly. Mental representation of the external world is still not involved. There is no imagery, no anticipation, and so on." It represents the peak of the purely sensorimotor adaptations in the infant's development. During the last, the stage 6, no new principles are involved, of course, the sensorimotor schemas get more refined, elaborate and complete.

Stage–6 (18–24 M) : Internal Representation of Actions in the External World.

Stage–6 (18–24 M) : Internal Representation of Actions in the External World. This stage "marks the beginning of cognitive representation". The child can mentally picture to itself how an event would develop. It can follow internally, along the trajectory a thing would move, and can anticipate the results. The external imitation can be deferred as it first has internal imitation. And, imitation may continue even when the model has disappeared. All this enables the child, sometimes to find solutions to problems without trial and error. The final location of an object can be anticipated by way of filling in invisible portions of an object's trajectory. "The ability to represent events internally, requires, of course, some intuitive understanding of the nature of objects, the relationships between different paths of space, and some understanding of casualty".

Now, we shall describe the two observations made by Piaget. One is related to the behaviour of Jacqueline when she was in stage 5; and the other, to that of Lucience who was in the stage 6. Both were facing the same problem—putting a watch chain into a matchbox through an opening slightly less than 1/2 inch by 1 inch.

Jacqueline puts one end (2 to 4 cm of it) of the chain in the matchbox through the narrow opening. Then, she takes hold of the next segment at a point 5 cm away from the end of the first segment already put inside. And, while she gets ready to do the same with the third segment, the chain slides out with a sound. The child made such an attempt fourteen times with no success. By the time it was the tenth attempt, she was tired, and may have given up further attempts. But the observer put the chain inside without letting the child see how it was done. Seeing the chain inside, Jacqueline continued her attempts. The sixteenth one was a success—this time Jacqueline had grasped the chain nearer the middle, and it took the form of two entwined cords. The seventeenth attempt was the exact repetition of the preceding movement—she pulled the chain together grasping it at the middle and put both ends together.

But the 18th attempt was again a failure as now she adopted the procedure as had been done initially. The observer marked the following characteristics in the behaviour of Jacqueline when she was passing through stage 5:

- Solutions were mostly reached at by accident—but then she took advantage of the same, and improved her behaviour as per the demand of the situation.

But Lucienne behaved in a different way when she was in stage 6. In face of the same problem, she first puts one end of the chain inside, and the rest is pulled inside by and by, and she succeeded. But she failed in her second and the third attempts.

In her fourth attempt, Lucienne spreads the chain flat on the floor, and, then rolls up the whole round into the shape of a ball. This is put in the match box, and the attempt was a success.

The fifth attempt had a short resumption, and was alike the first one, but soon the child corrected herself.

Lucienne's successful attempt was characterised by the following special features:

- the success was not accidental;

- imagination played an important part in the success as she must have constructed the solution in her imagination and carried it out. "This ability to form a mental representation of events is the hallmark of stage 6, and the end of infancy".

During this stage, the child can picture events mentally, and, this ability helps it in searching objects that have disappeared, and, in understanding spatial relations. The child must acquire the insight that "space is a continuous medium within which all displacements of objects occur. Objects may take various paths to an end point and return to the starting point either by retracing the path or by taking another one".

Mental representation is essential to trace the invisible path, which the object that has disappeared, must have followed. For the genuine intuitive understanding of objects in space, mental representation of events is a must. The child can solve problems involving displacement of objects, because of this ability. For the cognition of an object or of an event, the child must also picture itself as someone existing separate from the object or event in the external space. Only through such a perception of oneself, one can know how one would walk to reach to the kitchen crossing the courtyard. The child can develop a picture of itself, before its mental eye, showing its journey to the kitchen. The child develops the ability to do this only during stage 6.

WHAT IS INTELLIGENCE?

Input into his structure of intellect (SI) comes both from the environment and the soma or body, the latter being of both motivational and emotional types, and from the brain as well as the internal receptors. Filtering or screening occurs, shutting off some sorts of input, facilitating other types.

The foregoing pages deal mainly with the cognitive development of the child since birth. This is based on what the famous developmental psychologist Jean Piaget has traced in his book *Origins of Intelligence*. How a normal child develops intellectually up to two years of age, has been described above. Piaget has called this the period of sensorimotor development. Input (stimulus) is received from the external world, and also from the soma or the body or mind of the child. The child reacts to it according to the state of his sensorimotor development; and, his reactions also help him in the process of physical and intellectual development. While reacting to the stimulus, body and mind has to perform certain functions which again provide an occasion for having more experiences. Thus, the process of intellectual development continues. Guilford[5] writes "..... input into his structure of intellect (SI) comes both from the environment and the soma or body, the latter being of both motivational and emotional types, and from the brain as well as the internal receptors. Filtering or screening occurs, shutting off some sorts of input, facilitating other types".

5. Guilford, JP. *Intelligence*, 1965.

To meet the demands of the situation, to be able to solve the problem that one faces, successfully, are the indicators of intellect. Thus, it is through one's behaviour, that it can be assessed, how much developed one is intellectually. Behaviour has two aspects–external and internal; and—of course, the two are interdependent. It is only through the external behaviour, that a clue to the nature of internal behaviour, which is purely mental or emotional, can be found. While, conversely, it is the internal nature of behaviour which guides and controls the external behaviour. Henry Garrett writes:

"Efficiency in meeting everyday situations or solving everyday problems, is, perhaps, as useful a working definition of general intelligence as any. Intelligence, in the solution of problems, demands power as well as speed. To do a thing well, we must know how to do it; and we must not dawdle and blunder, in the doing".[6]

"Efficiency in meeting everyday situations or solving everyday problems, is, perhaps, as useful a working definition of general intelligence as any. Intelligence, in the solution of problems, demands power as well as speed. To do a thing well, we must know how to do it; and we must not dawdle and blunder, in the doing".

The two words used by Garrett in his definition of Intelligence—"power" and "speed", are very significant. In English, there is a famous saying—"knowledge is power". It means, it is the knowledge which breeds power or ability to behave in such a way, that one can do what is required to be done or one intends to do. This ability or power, is the same what J Piaget calls "SCHEMA". "Schema" is ability in reference to a certain type of behaviour. It means, for different types of behaviours, there is the need for the development of corresponding types of schemas or mental abilities. The other word "speed" indicates the time taken in doing a certain thing. "Power" increases "speed". With the increase of power, for doing a certain thing or for behaving in a needful way, speed also increases. The more the power, the less will be the time required for doing a thing or for behaving for the performance of something. This is why Garrett declares "power" and "speed" to be the sure indicators of intelligence.

Intelligence has been described by James B Stroud in terms as under:

"....Ability to learn, to make a good response, to think abstractly, to remember, to perceive relationships, and to display insight and good judgement in situations requiring thought".[7]

"Ability to learn, to make a good response, to think abstractly, to remember, to perceive relationships, and to display insight and good judgement in situations requiring thought".

How much a person is intellectually developed, we can know through his behaviour in situations demanding power or ability to learn, that is, how swiftly and properly one learns something new—a new action or a new information. How promptly and befittingly one responds to some stimulus that the environment presents; how far and how correctly one can think abstractly. Besides this, a good memory is also one of the indicators of the level of intelligence. Piaget has traced minutely how the power to

6. Garrett Henry E. *General Psychology.*

7. Stroud B James. *Psychology in Education.*

perceive relationships, develops along with age. Nevertheless, this power differs from man to man according to the level of intelligence. There may be problems, the solution of which depends upon the power of insight—this power is also a form of intelligence. Intelligence is also assessed according to the nature and ability of how one judges things. Proper judgment involves proper thinking; it means the ability to think over an incident or about an object, so that a just judgment about it may be made.

Guilford in his same book, on page 25, writes: "Awareness that a problem exists, and identification of structuring of the problems are cognitive operations ... during which ... there is evaluation of cognised information. In the effort to cognise the problem, there may be a seeking for new input information".

Now, it would be useful to explain what is implied in these words of Guilford:

- Awareness of the existence of the problem is the first condition for an intelligent behaviour.
- Then the organism needs to identify the problem with its relations to other phenomena; and to structure the problem in its entirety.
- For the identification and structuring of problem in its entirety, past references are must. This fact leads the author to conclude that "there is dependence on memory storage".
- For intelligent behaviour, the subject must be able to evaluate what part of the whole gamut of cognised information is relevant and of importance now. The subject must also know how much important that cognised information is.
- The subject may feel the need of some new/additional information in order to be able to better identify and for a better structuring of the problem.

The mention of new/additional information as additional needful input, verifies Nancy Bayley's definition:

"Intelligence appears to me, rather, to be a dynamic succession of developing functions, with the more advanced or complex functions in the hierarchy depending on the prior maturing of earlier simpler ones......"[8]

"Intelligence appears to me, rather, to be a dynamic succession of developing functions, with the more advanced or complex functions in the hierarchy depending on the prior maturing of earlier simpler ones....."

- First the simpler functions are mastered, then with the help of new information coming in as new input, the subject becomes able to perform new functions, more complicated and more advanced. Nancy Bayley at the end of the definition, as quoted above, adds a few words more within brackets—(given, of course, normal conditions of care).

These words refer to the importance of social environment in the process of the development of intelligence. If two children intellectually are too

8. Nancy Bayley. *On the Growth of Intelligence,* p. 807.

much different, one of the factors leading to this difference is the difference in their social environment. The one having got a more congenial environment will impress as more intelligent. He has been exposed to an environment of greater variety, more encouraging, more stimulating for activities. The environment, providing more varied desirable experiences, will more enrich the repertoire of the subject's information, with the result the subject will be able to behave more intelligently. By 'normal conditions of care', Nancy Bayley means that there should be no hindrance in the development of intelligence along with the maturity that age brings about.

The chain of S-R provides more and more input in the form of experiences leading to better, clearer perceptions and conceptions, and the intellect is the end product of all these developments.

The importance that is being accorded to environment in the development of intelligence is quite justified, as it is the environment, social or physical, which provides inputs in the form of experiences through the thresholds of senses, the end-result of which is intelligence. The environment for the child becomes varied where a lot of objects—toys, are available for the child to play with, to handle. These objects enable him to enrich his repertoire of information with the conceptions of hardness and softness; with the conceptions of size and shape; with the conceptions of different sounds that are produced while moving or throwing objects/toys about; with conceptions related to taste, smells and others, as the child matures with age, and, passes from the stage of sensorimotor to that of Formal Operations through that of Concrete Operational—as Piaget puts it. Piaget in his book *Origins of Intelligence*, has traced this development in great details graphically and mathematically.

Before coming to that, it would be proper to see what environment should be considered stimulatory and leading to intellectual development. An environment which stimulates the child to react, to respond fully to the stimulus, is called to be stimulant. The more stimulating the environment is, stronger and better will be the response. The chain of S-R provides more and more input in the form of experiences leading to better, clearer perceptions and conceptions, and the intellect is the end product of all these developments. Conversely, if the environment is dull, the child will not be moved to react, to respond and, if there is no reaction, no response, no development will be there.

This is why, especially, the parents and the teachers are advised to provide for their wards such an environment which is rich. Rich, in the sense that therein the child has a variety of experiences, where there are an umpteen number of objects to handle; and stimulating, in the sense, that it readily prompts the child to react or respond to it, and, do the same with its utmost ability—as this is the only way of further developing its abilities.

The affectionate treatment of parents, teachers and elders also make the environment stimulating for the children. Though we shall describe this in greater details when we shall deal with the emotional development of the child, yet to make a mention of this factor here, is also essential, as proper emotional development too has its salutary effect on intellectual development. All the three aspects of personality—physical, intellectual and emotional—are interdependent. If one's nervous system is innately impaired or weak, he or she cannot be intellectually strong. When in old age or in the presenile period, one suffers from alzheimer, a disease caused because of physical reasons, his or her intellectual ability would also seriously be damaged. Thus, an environment which the child does not feel secure; where the genuine affection is not felt for the child, and, he is not encouraged (and supported, if need be) for his reactionary attempts, not only the child's emotional development suffers but the child also fails to achieve intellectual development to the full level of his capacity. We have already seen how the child develops cognitively during the sensorimotor period. Now again, we shall be referring to Piaget when we describe the last two periods of cognitive development; that is Pre-operational and the period of Formal Operations.

PRE-OPERATIONAL PERIOD

The main development of the pre-operational period is the development of mental imagery.

The former part of pre-operational period extends from 2 to 7 years of age. The main development of the pre-operational period is the development of mental imagery. It is during the last stage of sensorimotor period that mental representation of events starts. Its full impact on the ability to cognise, can be felt only during this period. Piaget calls this ability as conceptual schema to differentiate it from sensorimotor schemas of the first period of cognitive development. The child can have proper conceptions of things perceived because of mental representation of the same. This is the ability to conceive or ponder things which are invisible. This is also the ability which makes possible "deferred imitation", that is, the child can imitate the model when it is no more present there.

Mental image is an internal phenomenon, and is the result of internal activity—during the development of which the child seems inactive or non-functional externally. Nevertheless, the fact remains that the first reaction was initiated in response to some stimulus from the external world. Mental image is different from perception because the latter occurs only in relation to a thing which is present, and, is perceivable by any of the five senses; the former is the reconstruction of the same previously perceived object/event in the mind not necessarily causing any external action.

The mental image does not necessarily contain all the details of what it represents. It is really the representation of a class of actions rather than the imitation of some specific event. Giving his explanation of what Piaget has written about Symbolic Schema; AL Baldwin clarifies "It (image) is not an after effect of perception or an attenuated perception of some kind; it is an independent schema....."

SYMBOLIC SCHEMAS

When one action represents another, not in its exactness but just to represent the characteristics of the genre, the ability involved is Symbolic Schemas. The child's fondling a doll is a pretense which represents the genuine action of the mother, but the child sometimes losses distinction between the two. The child shifts from the pretense to the genuine and vice versa. Doing this requires some degree of symbolic thought which is one of the important cognitive developments of the period.

Distinction between play and pretending should also be clearly understood. Play is a fun. "It emphasises assimilation rather than accommodation. The child can stop the game whenever it so likes. In imitation, the process of accommodation is important; imitation is an attempt to behave as the model does or did. A game may involve imitation too. Especially, the complex games are not possible without the role of mental imagery being therein.

"In the process of play, Piaget sees the first appearance of symbolic schemas, internal schemas that permit symbolic behaviour. Behaviour is symbolic when something in it is used to represent something else".

"In the process of play, Piaget sees the first appearance of symbolic schemas, internal schemas that permit symbolic behaviour. Behaviour is symbolic when something in it is used to represent something else". Symbolic schemas are of two kinds—Idiosyncratic and Communicable.

Symbolic schemas are of two kinds—Idiosyncratic and Communicable. Idiosyncratic schemas are something private with the person. They are quite different from the schemas which initiate, direct and control behaviours and which are the reactions to the stimuli that are there in the external environment. Idiosyncratic schemas colour the likings and disliking of a person; and affect the behaviour which the stimuli of the external world evokes, only indirectly. These schemas are incommunicable, non-verbal. Contrary to it, the other type of schemas are communicable and verbal. They are directly expressed through the reaction that the external stimuli evoke. These are only the latter kind of schemas that adapt themselves to other people of the situation. These schemas conform to social rules and customs (whereas the first kind of schemas, that is Idiosyncratic Schemas have nothing to do with the norms and customs of the society; nor do they need to adapt themselves to other people).

Idiosyncratic schemas are non-verbal; they cannot be communicated directly, even then they influence the thoughts of the person, which he expresses verbally. Idiosyncratic schemas directly control our dreams and fantasies, and the plays, especially, those of the younger children.

Idiosyncratic schemas are non-verbal; they cannot be communicated directly, even then they influence the thoughts of the person, which he expresses verbally. Idiosyncratic schemas directly control our dreams and fantasies, and the plays, especially, those of the younger children. Schemas' effect may either facilitate or hinder the solution of the problem. Our feelings

The level of intelligence much depends upon the level and nature of these non-verbal and verbal schemas.

Play, on the one hand, expresses the level of child's cognitive development, on the other, it helps in improving his cognitive development further.

Language is a verbal activity. What Piaget describes, has the implied inference that the development of language depends upon the development of symbolic schemas. It is the social environment which leads to the development of these schemas where each sound or word stands for a concrete object or for an abstract idea. Intelligence tests have two forms—verbal and non-verbal.

or emotional life is very much affected by these schemas. These non-verbal schemas have very strong elements of concrete imagery which can explicitly be expressed only symbolically as an artist would do; an artist attempts to communicate his private, feeling-laden, symbolic schemas to other people.

The level of intelligence much depends upon the level and nature of these non-verbal and verbal schemas. The more and the better exposure a child gets, the better developed will be the schemas of the child. The intelligence of a child can only be assessed on the basis of his non-verbal and verbal behaviour which themselves are initiated, conducted and controlled by the schemas—non-verbal and verbal. This is why so much stress is laid on providing good environment to the child at home, at school and outside in the society.

Play, on the one hand, expresses the level of child's cognitive development, on the other, it helps in improving his cognitive development further. So, a lot of games should be provided for the child, keeping in mind, his age and level of development—both physical and cognitive. If we consider play in reference to the development of non-verbal schemas, some very important facts may come to our notice. Symbolic schemas can very clearly "be seen and studied" through children's play. Play is often a non-verbal activity; and if words are used, they are not used so freely. Another reason that play is a good window on the child's symbolic schemas, is that it is less accommodated to reality than to routine or problem-solving behaviour.

Language is a verbal activity. What Piaget describes, has the implied inference that the development of language depends upon the development of symbolic schemas. It is the social environment which leads to the development of these schemas where each sound or word stands for a concrete object or for an abstract idea. Intelligence tests have two forms—verbal and non-verbal. Verbal form of intelligence tests, also assess the level of the development of the child's language; indirectly a good knowledge of language, and good verbal expression of the child-are indicators of higher level of intelligence.

Of course, intelligence is considered to be an innate faculty. It is innate to the extent that it depends upon the natural sharpness of the senses which are the thresholds of receiving experiences, the end-product of which is intelligence. So, in the long run, the sharper the senses, the higher will be the level of intelligence. Nevertheless, nurture has an important role to play. Through play-way method and other devices of providing activities to the child, the development of the senses of the young child at the nursery level, may substantially be influenced. The home of the child may also make important contribution towards it. So, it would be wrong to dismiss

Thomas Alva Edison's assertion that genius is ninety-nine per cent perspiration, as altogether unpsychological.

So, coming to the nurture; the better the environment, better in the sense of providing varied and richer experiences, still higher will be the level of intelligence. The parents, first of all, will have to see to it that the infant gets to play with the maximum possible number of objects, and reacts to the events, such as are helpful in the development of senses. At school, the environment should be rich with objects and activities which make it motivating and delightful, and where the child has full occasions for reactions and receiving experiences such as may help in further sharpening his senses. Individuals close to the child, other beings and objects of his environment, the pictures, excursions and a lot of other things that have their influence on the development of perceptions and conceptions of the child, are all parts of the factors which affect the intelligence of the growing child. Though the fact remains that a child can be benefited by nurture only to the extent that his brain or senses by nature are capable of.

Intelligence is considered to be an innate faculty. It is innate to the extent that it depends upon the natural sharpness of the senses which are the thresholds of receiving experiences the end-product of which is intelligence. Nevertheless, nurture has an important role to play.

INTELLECTUAL DEVELOPMENT AND PLAY

Piaget in his observation, found his subject, a child of 1;6 (30), saying "cry.cry" to her dog. Then she herself made the sound of crying. On the following day, she made her bear/duck, cry. Then she attempted to make her hat cry.

This illustrates Projection of Symbolic Schemas Onto New Objects.

- The child at 1;7 (12), pretended to be reading a newspaper; she also pointed with her finger at certain parts of it; she muttered to herself. On the following day, she pretended to be telephoning. Not only this, she made her doll also telephone. On the days that followed, she made all sorts of things telephone.

This is Projection of Imitative Schemas Onto New Objects.

- At 1;8 (30), Piaget's subject stroked her mother's hair, saying "pussy, pussy". The next day she saw a shell, picked it up saying it "a cup", and pretended to drink with it—the identification of cup and shell evoked the pretense.

This is Simple Identification of one Object with Another.

- At 1;10 (30), the child pretended to be playing with her cousin who had been away for a period over two months. She herself became her cousin, Clive. Clive is running; Clive is jumping;" and she imitated him strutting up and down.

This is the example of Identification of Child's body with that of other People of things.

- The child at 2;1 (9), put her doll's head out through the balcony railings with a turn towards the street, and, said, "you see the lake and trees. You see a carriage, a horse", etc. The same day, she seated the doll on a sofa, and, told it what she herself had seen in the garden.

In such a behaviour of a child, there is Simple Symbolic Combinations Involving Whole Schemas Instead of Simple Objects.

At 2; 4(8), not being allowed to play with the water being used for washing, she took up an empty cup, and went, and stood by the forbidden tub, and went through the actions saying, "I'm pouring out the water". At 2;6 (28), she wanted to carry Nonette (the new baby). Her mother did not allow her to do so, saying that she could do so later on. She folded her arms and told, "Nonette is there. There are two Nonettes". She repeated the game many times on the same day, but quite secretly. When Piaget went up to her, she stopped talking, and whispered to Nonette.

Another variety of this game is catharsis, at 2;9 (14) the child, the another subject of Piaget's observation, was afraid of a tractor in a field near a garden. The child then told her doll. "Dolly told me she would like to ride on a machine like that". At 3;0 (0) the same thing happened with aeroplanes.

Such a game of a child shows Compensatory Combinations.

- At 2;1(7), the child was afraid while sitting on a new chair at the table. Later in the day, she put her dolls in the uncomfortable positions, and said to them:" It doesn't matter. It will be alright". (—repeating what had been said to her).
- At 2;7(2) she had fallen down, and cut her lip. After the usual scheme, she consoled herself by projecting all on to her cousin Andre who took the form of a doll.
- At 4;6 the child's hand was hit with a rake which made her cry. The psychologist expressed himself to be sorry for the same. At first, she did not believe him to be sorry for the same. At first she did not believe him to be sincere. Some time later, she repeated the exact words spoken to her, of course, changing the order of words.

These are the examples how a child of this period, by dint of imagery would behave in the way which otherwise was not possible, and such plays, imitations and dreams or imagination are a great help in intellectual development also—though it's a fact, not directly perceivable.

Piaget has given these examples to illustrate Liquidating Combinations.

- Continuing with his observations, Piaget found that at the age of 4;6(23), Jacqueline was walking on a steep mountain road when Piaget warned her—"Mind that loose stone". And, she started saying—"Marecage once strode on a stone, you know, and didn't take care, and she slipped and hurt herself badly". On another occasion, when Jacqueline was 4;6(26), and was on a precipitous path, she was warned to be careful of the rushing stream at the foot of the mountain. She immediately started: "Do you know what my little negress friend did? She rolled right to the bottom of the mountain into the lake. She rolled for four nights. She scraped her knee and her leg terribly. She did not even cry. They picked her up afterwards. She was in the lake, she couldn't swim and was nearly drowned. At first, they could not find her and then they did."—"Now do you know all that?" she was asked. To this she replied: "She told me on the boat". It was the incidence of Jacqueline's seeing a negress that gave rise to this cycle.

These are the examples of Symbolic Representations. The first thing that stands out through such examples, or through our own observations, is that the symbolic representation has its relationships with things of the real world. In making such representations of objects and events, imagination, of course, plays its important role. Characters may even be imaginary; nor are events just opposed to those of the real world. Symbolic representation may be much similar to objects and events of reality, or it may be a representation of things in contrast—the implied motive there always being to prepractise in reference to what is the present need, or to lighten the strain which the impending situation is likely to cause. The child, of course, resorts to symbolic representation, during the time of difficulty as well as that of great pleasure and excitement—then the behaviour serves for catharsis.

To sum up this part, the following points may be noted:

- Symbolic representation is to compensate what the child cannot have or possess; it is to protect the tender child from the strain, which his inability to do something, may cause.
- Symbolic representation is a natural device for outletting excitement both bitter and caused by something pleasant, again to save the child from the strain of excessive excitement. Thus, it provides for catharsis.
- Thus, symbolic representation is in the interest of the child's mental health and development.
- Symbolic representation creates a situation for the child where he can have prepractice for the behaviour which the situation demands. It is during prepractice that the child gets new experiences, which lead to further intellectual development.

REVIEW QUESTIONS

Q.1. What is intelligence? How is it related to nature and nurture?

Q.2. How does a child develop cognitively, according to Jean Piaget, since birth to 2 years of age? Describe in brief.

Q.3. Supposing you have a small child in your family, what games would you propose for him for his cognitive development?

Q.4. Explain the following terms as used by Jean Piaget:

(*i*) Schema

(*ii*) Assimilation, accommodation and adaptation

(*iii*) Tertiary circular reactions

(*iv*) Symbolic schema

(*v*) Mental images

CHAPTER

8 DEVELOPMENT OF LANGUAGE

Chapter Outline

INTRODUCTION

"In the first place, words are our most nearly arbitrary signs. Although some words have an inherent resemblance to what they represent, they are, in the main, quite arbitrary, and there is no inherent reason to prefer "hand" "to" "dog", or "Chien" as the best word for signifying the barking mammal we have for a pet."

(*Theories of Child Development*–AL Baldwin)

A language, broadly speaking, is nothing more than a collection of words, the arbitrary nature of which, has properly been shown by Baldwin, as given above. Notwithstanding, lack of language development, in a person, would prove to be a big handicap. Nothing can provide for so fast an intellectual development as language can, and, the development of language is also a sure indicator of intellectual development. No society can work without language as it is the most important vehicle for communication. Its value, as such, cannot be over-estimated.

For the development of language, social milieu is a must. It is only in a social milieu, that the child can get to listen to the other people speak.

For the development of language, social milieu is a must. It is only in a social milieu, that the child can get to listen to the other people speak. It is through imitation of the people speaking, that he can learn which speech sound represents a particular object or event. The young child starts with the production of certain sounds almost as reflex actions.

".......... the child as practising his own crying responses, he is learning to respond to the voices of others. Adults who are feeding, fondling, and otherwise caring for infants, usually, talk to them, thus certain tones of the human voice, acquire a reward value, and may, later, be used to soothe the fretful child." (Miller and Dollard)

The language learning goes on along with the training that the child gets, for the development of his behaviour on desirable lines—a sharp "No" is followed by punishment; the child can escape it only by stopping or retreating. Such an escape is always rewarding for the infant. How a child responds to such instructions or directions, much depends upon the child's learning capacity of a language at a particular age. And, the learning capacity is affected by the fact as to how much particular the parents are in motivating the child to learn.

At the second stage of learning, the child starts responding to others verbally also. Such a response requires less efforts, and happens to be quite rewarding. During the previous stage, the child would be indulging in such effortful gestures which are dropped at the second stage of language development; and social value is also more of such a development. The child gets a meticulous training in the correct use of a particular word for a particular object. And, he gets a like training for connecting words to other words, that is "in combining words into sequences of stimulus producing responses." On the basis of his study of "The Psychology of talking birds", OH Mowrer has suggested a "Tentative hypothesis" that mother's loving care, combined with vocalisation–presumably creates a predisposition to react with emotional satisfaction, first to the vocalisations of others and later to his own vocalisations. "The child hears his own voice—babbling and jabbering—and feels a consoling, comfort—effect (a reward) when he is alone or uncomfortable."

The welcome and reassuring words of the mother or of the father, motivate the child to reproduce the same words again and again.

Gradually, recognisable words emerge from what had been, so far, only inarticulate sounds of his mother. The welcome and reassuring words of the mother or of the father, motivate the child to reproduce the same words again and again. He tries to perfect the articulation of words through trial and error; perfect articulation gives great satisfaction to the child. The main basis for trial and error is imitation. Where there is no welcome and reassuring words to encourage or motivate, it is emotional conditioning which makes the child continue with his trial and error efforts. Words are uttered like noises purely on autistic basis. It is, of course, the second stage of language development when a lovely child may be heard producing words having no other purpose or motive than to relieve itself from boredom, or fear of excessive annoyance. Cold or hunger may also make the child murmur or utter such words which have previously been associated with comfort and satisfaction. It is only later that the child utters words to react to the external world.

As the child grows up, his capacity to imitate increases. The words which were first uttered accidently, are now reproduced purposefully. The child imitates the sounds of the adults; he tries to approximate to their sounds, and his success in doing this, proves to be his greatest reinforcer. The closer the relationships in the family, the more secure and stimulating is the family environment, the more the child will try to perfect his verbalisation for the approval and satisfaction of the elders he is emotionally associated to, and for his own satisfaction. Studies conducted on infants, without families, have confirmed the hypothesis that if the children of the age under two, are separated from their families, they remain backward in the development of speech.

> As the child grows up, his capacity to imitate increases. The words which were first uttered accidently, are now reproduced purposefully.

RE Beckey[1], made a clinical study of 50 children who were delayed in speech development and of 50 other children whose development of speech had been normal,—it was a comparative study. The report concludes that there is close relationship between lack of emotional stimulation and speech retardation. Buxbaum, E also supports such a finding.

> There is close relationship between lack of emotional stimulation and speech retardation. Buxbaum, E also supports such a finding.

SEX DIFFERENCES

Some studies of fifties[2] and sixties[3], reported the superiority of female over male babies until they attained the age of 4. Children of both sexes, ranging between two and three, were studied for the development of their speech. The findings were, the female babies could utter more speech sounds and approximating more to the correct forms of articulation than the male babies could do. The comprehensibility of the female babies was also higher.

> Some studies of fifties and sixties, reported the superiority of female over male babies until they attained the age of 4.

1. Beckey, RE. *A Study of Certain Factors Related to Retardation of Speech,* 1942.
2. Irwin, OC, Chen, HP. *Infant Speech: Vowel and Consonant Frequency,* 1946.
3. Irwin, OC, Chen, HP. *Development of Speech during Infancy, Curve of Phonemic Types,* 1946.

   Harmes, Erene, and Spiker CC. *Factors Associated with the Performance of Young Children on Intelligence Scales and Tests of Speech Development,* 1959.

SOCIAL CLASS DIFFERENCES

Language is the basis of all social communications; and its importance in human behaviour can hardly be overestimated. For all higher mental processes, it is the means. "A host of dramatic new possibilities for psychological development" is present during the period the child learns to use language. It is during the second year that the ability to use language is rapidly enhanced. His vocabulary goes on increasing—the more stimulating the social milieu, the more rapid and richer will be the growth of vocabulary. But the child's passive vocabulary happens, always, to be richer by far; than his active vocabulary—he can follow the sense of many more words than the number of words he can actually use in his expression.

MM Shirley in a study of 25 children of about 2 years of age, found that the average vocabulary of them was 37 different words. Though the individual differences ranged from 6 to 126 words.

- With the development of vocalisation, the child's speech becomes more comprehensible.
- His own comprehension of questions and commands goes on increasing.
- MM Shirley in a study of 25 children of about 2 years of age, found that the average vocabulary of them was 37 different words. Though the individual differences ranged from 6 to 126 words.

The speech of a 2-year-old child consists of nouns, verbs and adjectives; and "typically, each is used to convey the entire thoughts"[4] that is, when the child says "hot", it means "The milk is hot." At this stage, the use of adjectives before a noun or to use prepositions, articles or conjunctions, is something unusual.

Parents of lower stratum of society, generally, get little time to fondle their child, to talk to them; and, because of their own illiteracy and poor social-cultural background, cannot prove themselves to be effective and good stimulators and trainers in case of the linguistic development of their wards.

The more stimulating social environment the child gets, the more will be the linguistic development of the child. The affectionate care of parents, and, of elder siblings; their fondlings along with utterances reassuring their love, go a long way in the process of language development of the baby. Parents of lower stratum of society, generally, get little time to fondle their child, to talk to them; and, because of their own illiteracy and poor social-cultural background, cannot prove themselves to be effective and good stimulators and trainers in case of the linguistic development of their wards.

Children from culturally disadvantaged backgrounds are, generally, found deficient in all aspects of language development, such children do not get enough stimulation. The most important research in this field has been that of B Bernstein, an educational sociologist of England. He found that mothers in the lower class families use short, grammatically poor, simple

4. Massen, Paul Henry, Conger John Janeway, Kagan Jeroame. *Child Development and Personality.*

sentences; some were found to be using restricted codes also. In comparison to this, mothers in the middle-class families pay more attention in instructing their children for better socialisation through linguistic interactions. Such instructions help children in learning operations and principles; and engender in them, a sense of autonomy in skill acquisition. The working class mothers use language more to teach basic skills; and their children learn more of operations rather than of principles.

The working class mothers use language more to teach basic skills; and their children learn more of operations rather than of principles.

Moreover, verbal achievements are more highly valued and rewarded in upper and middle-class families. So the children, generally, make a more rapid progress in the development of language, and, their levels of linguistic achievements also happen to be higher. Irwin[5] found that infants under the age of one, from professional and business families, vocalised more and more phonemes than from working class homes. Another study[6] indicated that the children with speech defects, on the average, come more from uneducated families of lower occupational status. Studies conducted on older children with age from 3 to 8 years, clearly demonstrated that those from lower class families, performed poorly on a variety of language tests. The performance of the children belonging to middle and upper class families, were better both in respect of vocabulary and the length of sentences with a proper syntax. Those of the lower class families were found to be poor in vocabulary, in sentence structures, in sound discrimination; poor in articulation with less vocalisation. Those of upper class homes were superior in all aspects of language behaviour. They had richer vocabulary, could frame longer sentences with the correct placement of words. They had a higher capacity to communicate, and, their usage of words, was far more flexible and efficient. The level of their comprehension, was also higher, and their sentences were more complex in terms of grammatical structure.

Early sentence stage A child of the age of about two years, generally, expresses himself through a mono-worded sentence; and that single word, happens to be a Noun. Later, at the second stage of sentence structure, he attempts to make a sentence of 3 to 4 words, and, sometimes the child even fails to articulate a word in full. Now he starts using a Verb, an Adjective, but the use of a Preposition is made at a still later stage. My granddaughter (whom we had nick-named Shalu), used to speak—"Shalu *ne kha liya*" (Shalu has eaten). The use of "I" and other Pronouns, is made even still later. Before the age of 4, a child can hardly make one or two complex or compound sentences out of fifty. Still, he lacks the mastery in the use of Inflections. A child of 4, can make complete sentences,

5. Irwin, OC. *Infant Speech: The Effect of Family Occupational Status and of Age on Use of Sound Types*, 1948.
6. Beckey, RE. *A Study of Certain Factors Related to Retardation of Speech*, 1942.

sometimes made of 6 to 8 words. Dorthea McCarthy[7] reports that the sentences of a child of 4, generally, happen to be "characterised by greater definiteness and complexity." Now, the child shows a fairly good mastery of Inflections and the number of relational words goes on increasing in his sentences.

The period of maximum and most rapid increase in articulation is that of between 3 and 3½ years of age. By 8, pronunciation attains the level of mature form. As for accurate grammatical usage, the four-year-old child can use Subjects, Predicates and Adjectives, in a correct sequence. A child of 10 may be considered to have attained the level of maturity, so far the construction of sentences and the use of words of different grammatical kinds are concerned. Vocabulary level continues to increase into adulthood.

Colin Fraser has supplied a complete list of sentences uttered by Mary at 2, and of Jane at 6. Tremendous was the development of language during this short period of four years.

(*i*) The sentences made by Jane were longer. (*ii*) There was a much greater variety in the use of words of different parts of speech, as made by Jane. (*iii*) The intelligibility of Jane was much higher in comparison to that of Mary. (*iv*) Jane could make use of some very sophisticated forms of grammatical constructions. But Mary could utter only shorter and simple forms of sentences. (*v*) The percentage of speech in the form of social interaction was greater, by far in case of Jane than in that of Mary. (*vi*) Mary's utterances, in many cases, were the immediate imitations of what she heard from some adults. Jane on the other hand, in most cases, made her own independent utterances, as the situation demanded.

Conceptualisation Language is the medium for the child to understand, to know his world. Almost at all times, the senses of the child remain active in getting sensual experiences of the objects and events of his world. With age, the level of his perception increases. The field of perception also increases as the child grows more mobile. By the time the child enters the pre-operational period, as Piaget has named it, objects of the world, and those related to his "soma", that is, body, start to be recognised as objects having some shape, size, colour and other attributes of their own. The increasing perception of objects and events as distinct items with separate language labels, enables the child to recognise similarities and dissimilarities. Such a knowledge of objects and events is called conception. Conception is the discrete knowledge of an object, developed in reference to the past experiences of the organism as well as in the wider perspective. All of which yields a comprehensive information regarding the nature and usage of an object along with its apparent attributes

7. McCarthy Dorthea. Language Development in Children. *Manual of Child Psychology*, 1954.

which may include shape, size (size as big, small; and, later comparatively), colour, and so on. When objects are thus conceptualised, only then the child can see different objects related to a certain number of classes. Grouping and classification is the result of cognitive development, but such a development is a hallmark in the development of language too.

Great is the importance of verbal mediators in tasks involving concept-formation and inferences. Tracy Kendler and her colleagues have provided impressive examples of it through their studies. The verbal mediators enabled the children to solve reversal-shift problems. That is, they could switch to the responses of just reverse nature, to what they had done previously under similar conditions. They could "integrate independently acquired responses in making inferences." Flawell David Beach and Jack Chinsky have reported through observations that the kindergarten children, who can name depicted objects, are less likely to use the same as verbal mediators.

Marion Blank and Frances Solomon worked intensively for 4 months with nursery children. Each day, the training session continued for 15 and 20 minutes for each child. Each one of them was actively involved in the training, and, it was found that they improved in language comprehension, thought abstraction, cognitive organisation and problem solution. The programme raised the IQs of the children, and, there were beneficial changes in the behaviour of the children.

The understanding and categorisation of the environment continues unnoticed. Yet, for the child's total development, conceptualisation of language is of utmost importance.

Conceptualisation and specificity of language With increase in conceptualisation, two kinds of changes take place—(*i*) Words increasingly represent some specific objects and events. A child of 3 is apt to use the word 'Dog' for all animals who are quadrupeds; and, 'Car' for all the four wheeled vehicles. Heinz Weener has called this kind of language usage as 'undifferentiated' or 'syncretic'. 'Syncretic', because during this pre-school period, one single word may stand for a combination or fusion of several concepts; the child may use the word 'eat' for 'food' and for 'the process of being fed.' But before the child is five years old, he will have started making differentiated usage of words. The words 'dog', 'eat', and so on, will be applied with some of the specificity that characterises the language of an adult.

(*ii*) Increase in the use of words representing Abstract Ideas or Conditions. A word like 'Man' is more abstract than 'Gopal,' 'Animal', in comparison to 'Cow', 'Goat' and so on. The child learns the use of such words only when he is of the age of about five. The words like 'Man' and 'Animal', stand for different classes of beings (of objects)—the use of such words increases along with the increase in maturity. The faculty of conceptualisation of the child also increases. So, the two types of important developments in the use of language are (*i*) to use specific words for specific objects, and (*ii*) to use words which stand for groups or classes. He gradually develops to the stage when he understands that the word 'animal' include all from 'dog', 'cats' to 'frog' and 'butterfly.' Of course, words stand for a child of five, only in the context in which he has learnt the same. "Money" stands for something abstract, but for a child in India its concrete form may be only the few currency notes that he has seen, while for an American child, it may stand for a few forms of currency notes of that country, and so on. "Conceptual development is roughly measured by the number of abstract concepts for which the child has acquired labels for the sub-categories." Some concepts are defined in terms of their actions or functions, for example, a 'dog' is one who barks, a 'monkey' is one that jumps high to cover long distances and so on—a child, between the age of three to four, develops his concepts in this fashion. He defines or conceptualises objects sometimes in abstract terms, such as money; sometimes through labelling, such as a 'dog' is an animal; but mostly through the functions that are the properties of the concerned objects—'a fire is that which burns.'

To sum up, the child, during the pre-school period, rapidly learns the following aspects of the language:

1. Using words which refer only to certain specific objects.
2. Using words which refer to abstract things.
3. Using words in a sentence at their proper places.
4. Using words which describe the properties of objects and events.

MEDIATED GENERALISATION

My granddaughter, of about two years of age, would call anyone in the picture as 'Da-da' (grandfather) who is old, his old age is an important property that is common with mine. She would, because of the same reason, call a man in picture as 'Pa-pa' because of some similarity in age, and, because of moustache, as her father wears. If the first experience of a child with a teacher has been unpleasant, the child would define any teacher as someone who is harsh—this is mediated generalisation. The child's reaction to the word 'teacher' would be that of anxiety and avoidance; his face would indicate feelings of happiness when he would call someone in the picture as 'Pa-pa.' This mediated generalisation plays an important part in the process of language development.

LANGUAGE LABELS AND SELF-CONCEPT

Self-concept is an important phenomenon in the process of personality development. What a person considers himself to be, is important in the nature of development that takes place. There are many factors responsible for self-concept. One very important among them being the label of 'Good' or 'Bad' that is used for a person. There are acts which cause pain or unpleasantness to others, and for such acts the adults react to the child with the label 'Bad' for him. And, for the acts which are approved by the society, the label 'Good' is applied. When a child is repreatelly labelled as 'Bad', he starts considering himself as such, and he ceases to make efforts to prove himself otherwise. Thus, a negative self-concept is developed. Such sort of self-concept is a big hurdle in developing the child on desirable lines.

It is not the case that the child cannot learn what is 'good' and what is 'bad.' By nature a child always tries to behave in such a way lest he should be labelled as 'Bad.' If his efforts are not properly appreciated, and seldom or never the label 'Good' is applied to him, and even for the unknowingly committed undesirable acts, he is called 'Bad', then such a negative self-concept is developed that he ceases to care for the pleasure or displeasure of others. Such a development is not good. A hardened negative self-concept may turn the child into a problematic child.

On the contrary, if the sincere efforts of a child, as every child, generally, always tries to see that none of his acts should be such which may displease his elders, are encouraged with language labels such as 'Good', or, with some such word which means approval, the child's character would develop on proper lines. Such is the importance of these language labels. If the elders, the parents and teachers whose language the child values so much, properly apply the same in reaction to the behaviour of the child, the child may learn that to destroy objects is bad; to disobey elders, hurts them; and that to be kind and helpful to others, is good. To cause pain to others, is bad; to work for saving others from discomfort, is good—in imparting such an important training to the child in social manners, the language labels such as 'Good', 'well–done', 'Nice', 'Quite good', 'Excellent', etc., go a long way. Such a training is very helpful in developing desirable moral character. If we call a boy 'Smart', he would spare nothing to prove and maintain himself as such. Contrary to this, if a child is repeatedly labelled as 'pest', or 'rotten' or with such other negative adjective, 'he will act in ways that are congruent with this label.'

If we call a boy 'Smart', he would spare nothing to prove and maintain himself as such. Contrary to this, if a child is repeatedly labelled as 'pest', or 'rotten' or with such other negative adjective, 'he will act in ways that are congruent with this label.'

Recently, two psychologists of the Columbia University in New York, Claudia Mueller and Cardine Dweck, published their report in the *British*

Journal of Personality and Social Psychology. Therein, they have warned, "Parents and teachers should congratulate the children on working hard instead of praising them for cleverness or smartness." Dr Dweck further writes—" "..... of the kinds who were praised for their efforts, and not intelligence, 90 per cent wanted to perform a challenging task where they could learn something."

STAGES IN LANGUAGE COMMUNICATIONS

In the development of language of the child, there are two important stages—Egocentric and More Sociocentric. A 5 or 6-year-old child, generally, speaks in reference to himself. He lacks the maturity to communicate with a consideration for others' point of view; he even lacks the concern for being understood by others. A child of two to three years of age, may speak to the other of his own age, like "it is the birthday of my sister." To this, the hearer, the other child, may respond without any sense of proper reciprocation, "My dog barks—hau, hau."

As the child grows older, he feels that socially-oriented speech is rewarded more frequently, more strongly and commands more attention. On the contrary, the egocentric speech is being discouraged; so, it grows less dominant as the child advances in age.

The child does not bother to whom he is speaking, he may either address to himself or to a character of his own imagination, or to someone who may be associated to his pleasant egocentric statements or conversation. Piaget made a study[8] of 20 children at the Roussean Institute in Switzerland to show how with the advancement of age, the language of the child progressively changes from egocentric to sociocentric. Through his study, he concluded that egocentrism at its highest, cannot be more than 90 per cent of the total language that the child uses during the peak period of his egocentrism. Personal characteristics and situations are the factors which immensely affect the proportion of egocentrism to sociocentrism during all periods of a man's life.

The more socialised a child grows, the higher will be the proportion of sociocentrism in his verbal expression. As the child grows older, he feels that socially-oriented speech is rewarded more frequently, more strongly and commands more attention. On the contrary, the egocentric speech is being discouraged; so, it grows less dominant as the child advances in age.

LANGUAGE DIFFICULTIES IN THE PRE-SCHOOL PERIOD

Proper development of language in a child is an important indicator of the proper development of his personality as a whole. Language has to

8. *The Language and the Thought of the Child.*

do not only with the intelligence of the child but with such characteristic traits also, as self-confidence (freedom from a feeling of inferiority), socialisation (freedom from shyness), a blithe spirit (freedom from unnecessary worries), etc. The language difficulties that occur during the pre-school period of the child, are mainly due to the lack of these and such other characteristic traits.

1. **Repetitions** A child, between the age of 2 to 5, finds great difficulty in speaking out what he means to tell, because of inadequate active vocabulary—only a small proportion of vocabulary that he hears others speak, can be used by the child himself. The child's repetitions of a word or a part of it, after uttering every four or so words, indicate his difficulty in expression because he actually needs more time to find proper words to express himself, but he tries to be as fast as he hears his elders speaking. DM Davis considers that there is a relationship between repetitions and language maturity and other situational factors. During moments of strain or anxiety, repetitions may occur. Repetition is caused because of hesitation also. Hesitation may also be caused because of a feeling of insecurity.

> The child's repetitions of a word or a part of it, after uttering every four or so words, indicate his difficulty in expression because he actually needs more time to find proper words to express himself, but he tries to be as fast as he hears his elders speaking.

2. **Stuttering** The second difficulty related to language is stuttering. Stuttering means lengthening the efforts for the uttering of a certain letter of a word, as a result of failing to utter the same in a flow and with ease. For example, in the pronunciation of the word 'Example' if one utters "Illgza:mpal" then there is stuttering on the letter 'I', which the utterer repeats many times before he can complete the pronunication of the word. We may take another example: a child who pronounces the word "Surround" as "sss..... raund", stutters at the initial sound. (The stammerer is one who makes involuntary stops and repetitions in speaking). The psychoanalysts consider emotional tension as the main reason for stuttering. Such a tension is mainly caused because of improper parent–child relationships. Because of emotional stress, the child hesitates and out of hesitation repeats a letter (or a part of a word) before he succeeds in pronouncing the complete word. Situational pressure, may be at home or outside the home, such as excitement over activities, attempts to direct a peer's activity or to gain attention, may cause stuttering. If the young child, especially as a new entrant, is coerced to do something against his will, he will be suffering from tension, which may result in stuttering.

> Stuttering means lengthening the efforts for the uttering of a certain letter of a word, as a result of failing to utter the same in a flow and with ease.

Johnson believes that children become chronic stutterers as a consequence of being so labelled by anxious parents.

So, the main factors, which cause stuttering or stammering, are difficulties in social and emotional adjustments.

We get to read some examples of difficulties in emotional adjustment. A girl of two and a half started stuttering when a new maid joined the family on the old one's (—who had been with the family since long–) departure. In two weeks' time, when the girl became well familiar with the new maid, the stuttering stopped for the time being. When a home-sick child is moved to a new place, he may start stuttering. The stuttering grows more frequent and of longer duration, if conditions at the new place/ house are such which increase the mental strain of the child. If father's attitude is dictatorial, it may also cause stuttering.

What the parents should do The only thing that the parents should do and can do, is to find out the source of disturbance, the cause of anxiety, and, attempt to remove it. If the parents attempt to correct the child's speech, it would further aggravate the problem.

Let the child have plenty of time to play with others, unnecessary restrictions in this, may cause tension to the child, and, it may make the problem more difficult. Parents themselves should play with the child rather than merely telling the child to do this or to do that. The child should never feel isolated or ignored. Whenever he means to tell something, a patient hearing ought to be given to him; the child should never get the impression that we are not interested in listening to him. Such a feeling on the part of the child, may make him frantic, and stuttering may also be a result. The child should neither feel jealous. Jealousy upsets his emotional condition. To avoid development of such a condition, the parents should do all that they can.

PERVASIVE EFFECTS OF LANGUAGE DEVELOPMENT

The pre-school period of the child is very important for the development of language. The child makes very rapid development in the use of vocabulary and sentence-structures. His vocabulary not only grows in respect of number of words, but also the child is able to use words and structures, more precisely and subtly. Both the use and understanding of language increase very fast. Symbolic representation also appears to be increasing fast. The child acquires basic rules of grammar (syntax, etc.), at such a fast rate that no traditional learning principles can explain this process. Induction or discovery of latent structures may be a factor involved in the "process". "Progress in language is, generally, antecedent to improvements in the process of thinking, perceiving, abstractions, reasoning, imagining, categorising, learning, problem-solving, and concept formation."

For the cognitive or intellectual development of the individual, language development is a must. Without language, the different mental processes, as have been mentioned above, cannot be possible, and these mental processes indicate the level of one's cognitive or mental development. As the child advances in his knowledge of language, he will be perceiving more and more objects of his environment, more and more events will be affecting him, and be meaningful for him. This growth in the volume of perception adds to his power of thinking, gradually making it multi-dimensional and deeper. By and by, the words, standing for abstract phenomena, grow in number. Reasoning is the development of thinking. When an individual thinks about an object or event from more than one angle, in reference to other objects or events, considering similarities and dissimilarities, or, the possible reactions or consequences of an event and so on, such a sort of mental process may be called the reasoning out of a phenomenon. Just passing through the process of cognitive development beyond the period of sensorimotor development, the faculty of imagining develops rapidly. It helps the child in practising various behaviours, and in relieving the child from mental tension, and, is helpful in other higher mental processes of reasoning, problem-solving and concept-formation. Again, it is a fact that, for all these different mental processes, language is a vehicle. These mental processes also help in the improvement of verbalisation.

Reasoning is the development of thinking. When an individual thinks about an object or event from more than one angle, in reference to other objects or events, considering similarities and dissimilarities, or, the possible reactions or consequences of an event and so on, such a sort of mental process may be called the reasoning out of a phenomenon.

The use of grammatically correct language is also an effect of the development of language. It is, in most cases, the result of "deferred imitation." The grammatically or syntactically correct structures that the child hears the adults speak, remain latent in the mind of the child, and come up or be directive in the child's later utterances. Sometimes, the child utters sentences in immediate imitation to his elders. It is said that language is picked up, rather than learnt. When there is unconscious learning of language, it may be called "picking up" language. Language, being the most important and very powerful vehicle of social communication, is, later, taught to children assiduously, and in a planned way.

It should not be concluded that the utterances of the child when grammatically correct, are so because of unconscious imitation only. Active mental processes are increasingly involved as the child grows in age.

THREE PROCESSES IN THE ACQUISITION OF SYNTAX

There was published some very important matter on the processes which lead the child gradually to the acquisition of syntax, in the "Harvard Educational Review", 1964, 34, No. 2. It is authored by Roger Brown and Ursula Belluge. According to these authors, the children utter the first intelligible word during the second half of the first year of their lives. A few months later, they start uttering words which are the names of household articles—chair, table, glass, water, milk, bread, doll, and also, names such as doggie, cow, and the word used for the sparrow, and so on. Then they start speaking words which stand for actions such as play, see, drop, etc. The use of words which stand for quantities is made still later, and, occasionally. By the time the child is about 18 months old, he can express himself using sentences made up of two words. The child utters in such a way that primary stress is given on each word. The unity of the sentence would appear because of the absence of a terminal contour.

The children utter the first intelligible word during the second half of the first year of their lives. A few months later, they start uttering words which are the names of household articles—chair, table, glass, water, milk, bread, doll, and also, names such as doggie, cow, and the word used for the sparrow, and so on.

The longitudinal study conducted by the investigators, yielded the results that Adam, aged 27 months, was only a little more advanced than Eve, aged 18 months, in speech—judging it from the single index, that is, the average length of the sentence uttered by each. The average length of utterance of each was 1.84 and 1.40 morphemes, respectively. During the succeeding year, the two children remained fairly together. A record was made of the utterances of the two for the succeeding period of thirty-eight weeks of the year. Now, Adam's average was found to be 3.55 and that of Eve to be 3.27 morphemes. The remark of the investigators is being quoted here: "Every second week we visited each child, for at least two hours, and made a tape-recording of everything said by the child as well as of everything said to the child. The mother was always present; and most of the speech to the child, was her's."

One of the investigators, would always make a written transcription of the scene, making a detailed mention about the speech of the mother and of the child with notes about actions made and the important objects that stimulated the children for speech and actions. From this transcription and the tape, a final transcription was made. These transcriptions constituted the primary data of the study.

Then, distributional analysis was made; the utterances were categorised, making the kinds of parts of speech a basis for the same. In sentences, there were an Adjective and a Noun, in some, a Noun and a Verb; in some the Verbs were in Past Tense; in some, Pronouns were used. The distributional analysis showed how the children were improving in syntactic regularities. Sometimes, extra experiments were made to see how many of them had learnt the use of a Noun, both as a subject and as an object; and how many of them could pluralise a sentence from its singular form.

Children use telegraphic language, using high-information words and leaving out the low-information ones. The sentences of the children are the results of adaptation to the sentences of the adults, in an optional way. The adults utter sentences with stresses on contentives, and the functors remain unstressed. The children are more likely to leave out functors rather than the contentives.

REVIEW QUESTIONS

***Q*.1.** Make a table to show how language develops since the beginning up to two years of age.

***Q*.2.** Trace how a child linguistically develops from a stage of "vocalisation to others" (Mowrer) to a stage where the child can independently "react to the external world".

***Q*.3.** Describe, with examples of your own experience, how social milieu affects the development of language.

***Q*.4.** Suppose there is a child underrating himself, narrate the steps that you would like to take to improve his self-concept.

CHAPTER 9

DEVELOPMENT OF REASONING

Chapter Outline

- What is Reasoning and How it Develops?
- INRC: Identity, Negation, Reciprocity and Correlative-Transformation
- Groups
- Grouping I: Additive Composition of Classes
- Grouping II: The Secondary Addition of Classes
- Grouping III: The Bi-univocal Multiplication of Classes
- Grouping IV: Co-univocal Multiplication of Classes
- Grouping V: Addition of Asymmetrical Relations
- Grouping VI: Addition of Symmetrical Relations
- Grouping VII: Bi-univocal Multiplication of Relations
- Grouping VIII: Co-univocal Multiplication of Relations
- The Development of the Concepts of Classes
- The Development of the Concepts of Classes
- Review Questions

WHAT IS REASONING AND HOW IT DEVELOPS?

There are innumerable objects, both living and non-living, that surround us—the multiplicity of characteristics or attributes of them, is quite baffling. But nature protects the neonate from being overwhelmed by so large a variety of objects, as the senses of the body, only gradually establish relationships with the objects, which are very important in the immediate environment of it. Up to two years of age, the child can hardly realise the existence of objects, as independent of himself. The sense-impressions received at the threshold of senses, activate the child, and both himself and the object stimulating him to activity, become part of the activity. By the time the child attains the age of two years, separate registration of sensory information begins; that is the child starts having sense-impressions, without necessarily indulging simultaneously in a sensorimotor activity. This sort of registration of sense impressions is what we call perception. A perception is the result of momentary sense impressions. It is the impression which may be visual, auditory, olfactory, tactual or related to taste.

Up to two years of age, the child can hardly realise the existence of objects, as independent of himself. The sense-impressions received at the threshold of senses, activate the child, and both himself and the object stimulating him to activity, become part of the activity.

Still, the child is too far away from the stage of reasoning. His understanding of the world, in many cases, is likely to be far removed from being accurate. As the child, during his pre-operational stage, is likely to make a distorted judgment of the length of a stick lying exactly parallel to another stick, equal to it in length; and may declare the removed stick either longer when brought nearer to the subject, or shorter, when removed farther away from the subject. This is perception; we have read much about such distorted perceptions in the familiar Miller-Lyer illusion. The distortion is caused because the judgment still happens to be based on immediate sense-impression. The child cannot integrate his present impression with his past impression when the two sticks were judged as exactly of the same length.

As the child, during his pre-operational stage, is likely to make a distorted judgment of the length of a stick lying exactly parallel to another stick, equal to it in length; and may declare the removed stick either longer when brought nearer to the subject, or shorter, when removed farther away from the subject.

Passing through the successive stages of cognitive development, the child reaches to the stage when he can integrate his present sense-impressions with that of the past. He can develop mental images; decentres his thinking; can think over an object or event from more than the perspective of his self only. This sort of thought process, results in the development of conceptions. The conceptions are less likely to be distorted, than is the case in regard to perceptions; since the latter being based on the present sense-impressions, with no reference to the past.

Nevertheless, conceptions may also be distorted. It is only through the thought process, based on logical rules of irreversibility, invariance or constancy, cause and effect sequences that hypothetical assumptions may be supported or rejected, thereby enabling the subject to make accurate judgments. This is the process of reasoning—a stage to which a child reaches starting from the stage of sensorimotor, and passing through pre-operational, concrete and formal operations. These stages of cognitive development, are not discrete. Each previous stage or stages, provide raw material for the succeeding one. The cognitive development, as a whole, is one continuous process. The stage of reasoning is the final stage of this development when one can visualise consequences through a sequential cause-effect thought process.

INRC: IDENTITY, NEGATION, RECIPROCITY AND CORRELATIVE TRANSFORMATION

Piaget opines that the process of reasoning happens to be based on INRC, where each letter stands for *Identity, Negation, Reciprocity* and *Correlative Transformation,* respectively.

Reasoning enables one to make accurate conception, regarding characteristics of an object; regarding cause–effect relationship in an event; regarding similarities and dissimilarities of objects and events of the environment, that one is related to. Reasoning is the process of logical thinking that one resorts to, when confronted with some problem. It leads one to the solution of a problem. Piaget opines that the process of reasoning happens to be based on INRC, where each letter stands for *Identity*, *Negation*, *Reciprocity* and *Correlative-Transformation*, respectively.

Identity The enormous variety of objects and events is baffling. For a better understanding of the environment consisted of the same, the mind searches for relationship among them. Some have similarity of shape with others; some are similar in colour; related to each other through similarity, may be said as having identity between the two. There may be a great number of objects which are identical. Such objects may be grouped as one discrete class. Again, in a single class, there may be some grouping, depending upon the number of factors that are identical among them. To illustrate the system of classification, an example as given in the book *Theories of Child Development* by AL Baldwin, is being reproduced here.

Now, because of broad identity, first of all, the different animals have been put into one single phylum, named chordata; then they have been further divided into classes, orders, genera and species. The classification depends upon the fact whether the identity, is in toto or part only. "The group of individual animals called setters can be combined with dogs of other breeds to form the class domestic dog. These dogs can be combined with various wild dogs to form the genus Canis, and so on."

Negation Under Identity, it is given how through the operation of combining classes, larger classes are formed, but the system may be reversed, through the operation of dividing the members of a large class, they may be sub-divided into sub-classes. This division is based on negation, that is, on the fact, that there is or are factors which are absent in the other group, thereby necessitating the other group to be put in a separate sub-class. Thus, negation of identity in some respect or respects, warrants the division of phylum into classes; of classes into orders; of orders into genera; and, of genera into species. Negation is the absence of some factor of identity, and such a negation necessitates the division of large classes into sub-classes. Setters are domestic dogs, but all domestic dogs are not setters;

in some of them we do not find all the characteristics of the setters, so they have been put into a separate sub-class.

So, both Identity and Negation are the operations, included in the process of reasoning, which are initiated for the better understanding of the physical and social environments. The lack of this understanding may render an individual unable to resolve some problems, especially, of the post-childhood period. Two objects may be identical but for the absence of one or some characteristic factors, each may have to be put in separate groups or groupings, which sometimes, may be classes, or orders, or genera or species. This absence of one or more characteristic features is the Negation.

Identity and Negation are the operations, included in the process of reasoning, which are initiated for the better understanding of the physical and social environments. The lack of this understanding may render an individual unable to resolve some problems, especially, of the post-childhood period.

Reciprocity The literal meaning of the word reciprocity is "giving and taking" so as to maintain balance. In nature, there is a system of reciprocity, a system which operates for maintaining balance. If there is addition on one side, it would be saved from being weighed down with weight, through some change being made to the other side, too. Piaget has illustrated this relationship through the example of a pair of scales. If there is increase in the amount of the article being weighed, there will have to be made increase in the weights, too, to maintain balance. Nature has a like system of maintaining homostatus through reciprocity. If temperature is falling down below the usual point, there will be shivering with hairs of the body standing erect, to work as insulators to maintain the body temperature. In all the natural phenomena, we find such a sort of automatic balancing process—vacuum caused by the hot air rising up, is filled by the air rushing in from the surrounding environment where the pressure of air is higher. This sort of balancing system works in human relationships also. Action leads to reaction in such a way that a particular action leads to a particular reaction. And, lack of a certain desired action leads to a reaction of a reverse kind. All these changes are controlled by the logical principle of reciprocity. Being guided by this principle, an individual may better understand relationships between cause and effect in events, that take place in physical as well as in social environments. Consequences may be predicted on the basis of the principle of Reciprocity.

Correlative transformation In nature, as well as in social relationships, there happen to be chained, continuous changes, when a certain cause has effected a certain change. One effect leads to another change, and that serves for yet another change—the initial effect starts working as a cause for the next effect, and, the chain of cause and effect keeps continuing endlessly. To understand this logical principle, it is essential to understand one's environment, without which one is very much likely to fail in the solution of the problems that one confronts.

In a previous chapter, we have read that it is only during the last stage of sensorimotor period of development, that is, between 18 and 24 months of age, that the child can internally represent the events of the external world. And, it is only then that the child can correlate the present effect or occurrence to some past cause. However, to correlate a whole series of cause-effect relationships, indicates the highest stage of the development of reasoning. This is correlative transformation.

A person whose reasoning has developed up to this stage, can effect transformation or change as desired, through a whole series of changes. Such a person can also analyse why an object or an event is, in its present form; he can mentally recreate all the stages of change, can think of the successive causes which must have brought about to form successive effects or transformations or changes, till the object or the event comes to its present form. By dint of such a reasoning, one can predict the occurrence of the likely events, and, if the same is not for the good of the individual, timely action may be taken so that such an event would not recur. A person with such an ability behaves cautiously; and generally, is able to avoid pitfalls, and always stands better chances for success. Usually, it is not before the age of eleven that the adult stage of reasoning can be achieved.

GROUPS

There appear apparent similarities and dissimilarities among objects of the environment. Looking to similarities in shape and behavioural characteristics, some objects or living beings are put into certain groups, which may further be divided into smaller groups or groupings. In doing this, first a child is guided by the factor of identity. Later on, he gets better knowledge of objects and events being guided by the logical principles of Identity, Negation, Reciprocity and Correlative transformation. This knowledge helps the child in sub-dividing classes into groupings. This knowledge is the result of reasoning and it gives more leverage to the person for handling situations or resolving problems.

"A class .... is a set of objects or events that has certain characteristics in common. The common characteristics define the class, and often some label of the language designates the class."

To see how Piaget has reported the gradual development of reasoning that works behind groupings that the child makes; here, we are reproducing the same on the basis of what is given by AL Baldwin in his book. *Theories of Child Development*.

"A class .... is a set of objects or events that has certain characteristics in common. The common characteristics define the class, and often some label of the language designates the class." Classes can have a variety of relationships. One class can be included in another, which means that the two classes have the same defining properties but that the sub-class has the additional defining characteristics which the class does not have. (see Fig. 9.1) The class of poodles, for example, is included in the class of dogs,

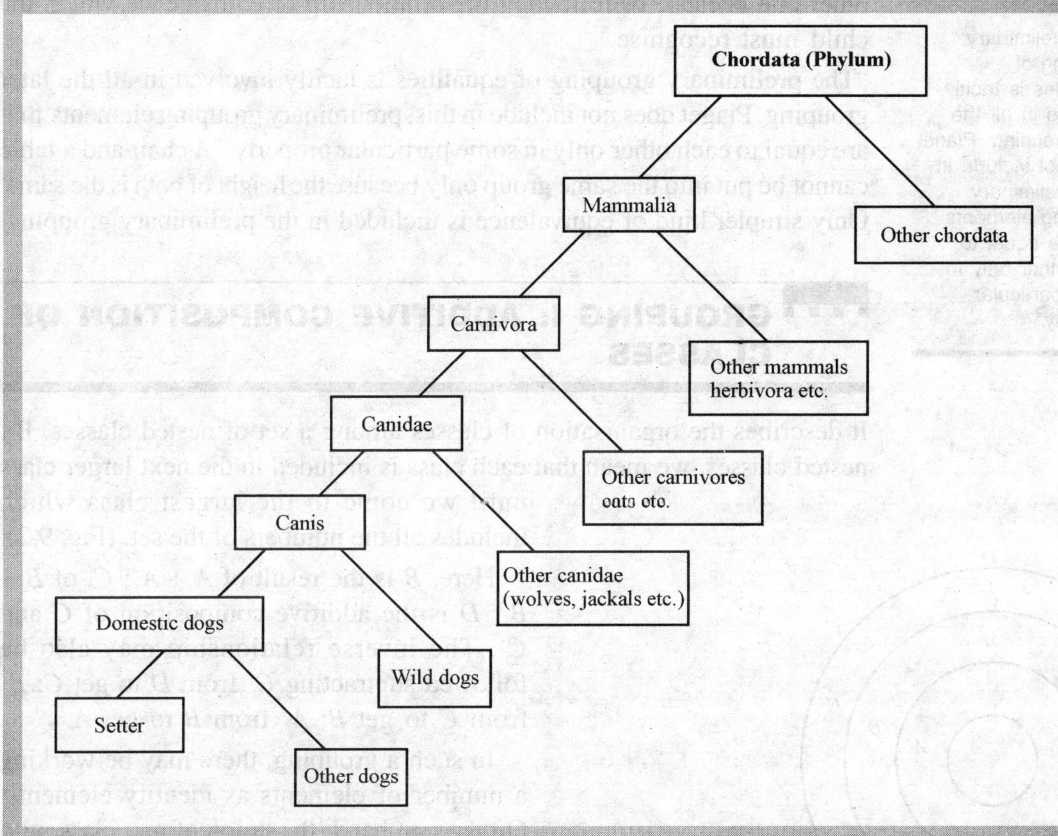

Figure 9 Classification-sub-classification of chordata.

but in addition to being a dog, a poodle must have some additional specific, characteristics that distinguish it from other dogs.

During the period of concrete operations, that is, between the age of 7 and 11, the child makes nine kinds of groupings in his pursuance to have a better understanding of his environment. These groupings have been called by Piaget, as the nine basic groupings—here, mention will be made of eight of them only.

Among the first category of groupings, we may include those which are formed because of equalities found in their characteristics. "If there are a number of classes or sets that are all completely equivalent to one another, the child must understand this fact." The example is, if *A* is equal to *B*, and *B* to *C*, then *A* is also equal to *C*. This is equivalence relationship. Understanding this kind of relationship, the child can reason out relationship or equivalence among things, not apparently or directly related to one another. The child can go forward as well as backward; for example if *A* is equal to *B* then *B* is also equal to *A*. The identity element is the basis for such a sort of grouping. The child may reason from any one to any

> "The preliminary grouping of equalities is tacitly involved in all the later grouping. Piaget does not include in this, preliminary grouping elements that are equal to each other only in some particular property."

other one because of following the relationship of equivalence which the child must recognise.

"The preliminary grouping of equalities is tacitly involved in all the later grouping. Piaget does not include in this, preliminary grouping elements that are equal to each other only in some particular property." A chair and a table cannot be put into the same group only because the height of both is the same. Only simpler kind of equivalence is included in the preliminary grouping.

GROUPING I: ADDITIVE COMPOSITION OF CLASSES

It describes the organisation of classes among a set of nested classes. By nested classes, we mean that each class is included in the next larger class until we come to the largest class which includes all the numbers of the set. (Fig. 9.2).

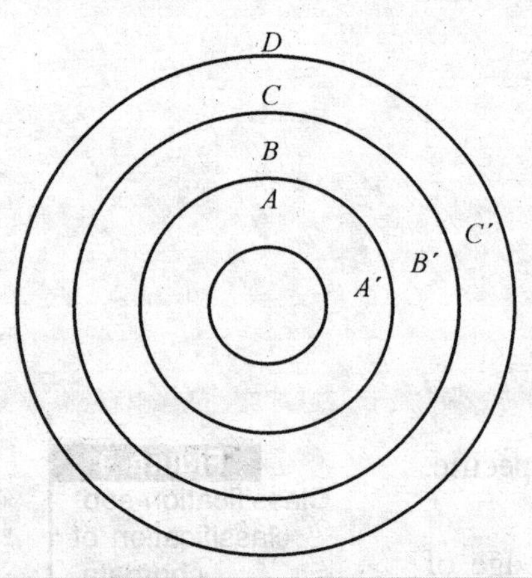

Figure 9.2
Additive composition of classes.

Here, *B* is the result of *A* + *A*′; *C*, of *B* + *B*′; *D* is the additive composition of *C* and *C*′. The inverse relationship may also be followed subtracting *C*′ from *D* to get *C*; *B*′ from *C* to get *B*; *A*′ from *B* to get *A*.

In such a grouping, there may be working a number of elements as identity elements. On the one hand, the union of any class with itself, is equivalent to the class itself, that is, *A* + *A* is equal to *A*. If zero is added to any class even then the group will remain unchanged. Such sort of organisation—does not fulfil the conditions required for the formation of a group. The elements which lie in vicinity to each other can only be combined together—only *A* and *A*′ can be combined together. Likewise, *A* and *B* can be combined. Piaget in his research has thoroughly studied this additive grouping of classes. The child's understanding of all the implications of this organisation of classes, develops only gradually.

GROUPING II: THE SECONDARY ADDITION OF CLASSES

"Whereas grouping I covers the relationships of inclusion of one class into the superordinate class that contains it. Grouping II is concerned with the relationship between alternative divisions of the same class." For example, mammals as a whole make a class which can be divided into dogs and non dogs. Piaget describes this algebraically as A_1 (dogs) plus A'_1(non-dogs) = B (mammals). The class of mammals can also be divided as cats and non-cats. There is an equivalence between the sum of two classes: $A_1 + A_1' = B$ and $A_2 + A'_2 = B$. Each sum represents the class of complete mammals. (see Fig. 9.3). These equivalences have been called vicariences by Piaget.

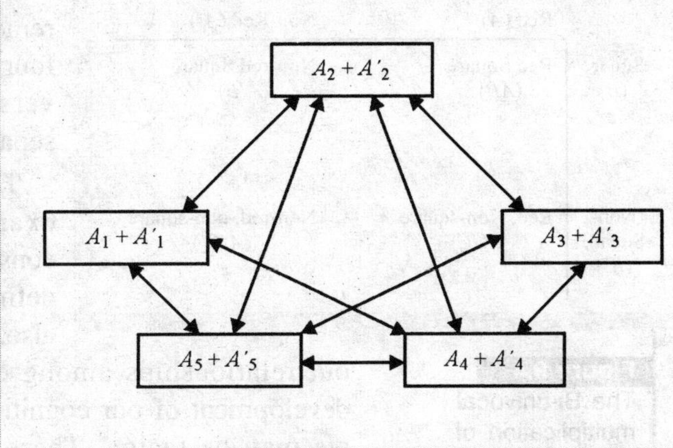

Figure 9.3
The secondary addition of classes.

It is through reasoning, which develops along with maturity, that the mind searches out such vicariences, and develops logical organisations of mutual relationship.

GROUPING III: THE BI-UNIVOCAL MULTIPLICATION OF CLASSES

Piaget describes four groupings that involve classes. The first two involve addition of classes; the second two multiplication of the classes. The first two groupings may be red [*A*] and non-red [*A*´]. At the same time they may be separated into square [*B*] and non-square [*B*´]. In each case, the set is total—$A + A'$ or $B + B'$ is total. The relationship between A versus A' and B versus B' is different from the relationship between A_1 (dogs) versus A_1' (non-dog); and A_2 (cats) versus A_2' (non-cats) described in the previous section; because A (dog) and A_2 (cats) are mutually exclusive, while A and B are not. We can thus multiply $(A + A')$.

Here, *A B* represent objects which are both red and square; *AB*´ correspond to objects which are red but not square. *A*´ *B*´ describe the objects which are neither red nor square. "Thus, by multiplying a dichotomy, we can divide the total set into four sub-classes, $A + A'$ is equal to the total set; $B + B'$ is also equal to the same total.

Considering red (*A*) and non-red (*A*´), and square (*B*) and non-square (*B*´) as elements of two separate classes, we can see that the separation (*A* versus *A*´) is connected to the separation (*AB* versus *A*´ *B* versus *A*´ *B*´) by a relationship of multiplication by (*B* versus *B*´). The separation can be multiplied further by (*C* versus *C*´) and we can obtain (*ABC* versus *A*´ *BC* versus *AB*´*C* versus *A*´*B*´*C* versus *ABC*´ versus *A*´*BC*´ versus *AB*´*C*´ versus *A*´*B*´*C*´). In this way, a whole series of separation can be arranged in a sequence. (see Fig. 9.4).

	Red (A)	Non-Red (A')
Square (B)	Red Square (AB)	Non-red Square ($A'B$)
Non-Square (B')	Red, Non-square (AB')	Non-red, non-square ($A'B'$)

Figure 9.4 The Bi-univocal multiplication of classes.

These multiplications are reversible; we can remove the classification (B versus B') from the fourfold classification (AB versus AB' versus $A'B$ versus $A'B'$), and we shall have the original separation (A versus A').

Thus, this whole set of multiplications is the example of an organisation, where there are consistent relationships among the elements. Piaget defines such an organisation as a grouping. It is, also, a concrete example to show how we reason out relationships among elements of the same grouping, for further development of our cognitive ability, and for resolving a problem which we may be facing. These relationships are logical relationships, the relationships between one division and a finer division.

GROUPING IV: CO-UNIVOCAL MULTIPLICATION OF CLASSES

The grouping III differs from grouping IV, in the sense, that while in grouping III, the multiplication of red versus non-red by square versus non-square leads to a division containing all four classes; red square versus red non-square versus square non-red versus non-square, non-red. It is not always the case in grouping IV, where the multiplication of two attributes does not result in all the four classes. For example, if we multiply the division (dogs versus non-dogs) by (cat versus not-cats), we find there are no animals which are both cat and dog.

For Piaget, grouping IV represents a logical completion of the grouping of multiplication. This grouping includes cases where each class in a classification corresponds to differing numbers of classes in another. We are reproducing a matrix here as given by Piaget to make the pattern of grouping clear.

This is grouping IV, based on co-univocal multiplication of classes. Here, classification K_1 has the classes A, B, C, included in it. The classification on K_2 includes the class A_2 A'_2 and B'_2. When these are multiplied together, we get the only classes as shown in the triangle on the lower left-hand side of the matrix. There is correspondence between the numbers of categories in the two classes, that is, K_1 and K_2.

To realise the classification concretely, we should take A_1 as the class of sons of a particular person P. B_1 is the class of grandsons of that person. And C_1 is the class of great-grandsons of P. This is the K_1 division of the male members of the family tree. Another classification is A_2, A'_2 and B'_2.

A_2 is a class of brothers; and A'_2 is a class of first cousins of people in A_2. It is implied that $A_2 + A'_2 = B_2$, the class of males who are children of the same grandfather. Class A'_2 consists of these males who are grandchildren of the same person; but who are not members of the same class A_2. They are remainder of the class C_2 who are not in B_2. The class C_2 is made up of great-grand children of the same person. And, when these two classifications K_1 and K_2 are multiplied together, we find that all those in A_1 who are sons of the same person, are all brothers. People, making B_1, may be either brothers (A_2) or first cousins (A'_2) or second cousins. (see Fig. 9.5).

		K'_2		
		A_2 A'_2	B'_2	
	A_1	A_1 A_2		
K_1	B_1	B_1 A_2	B_1 B_2	
	C_1	C_1 A_2	C_1 C_2	B_2 C_1 C_2

Figure 9.5 Co-univocal multiplication of classes.

Such sort of classification may, no doubt, appear quite arbitrary. Nonetheless, Piaget considers it to be a logically necessary grouping for the cognitive development of the child.

GROUPING V: ADDITION OF ASYMMETRICAL RELATIONS

Grouping V to VIII are all concerned with relationships, rather than with classes as we have seen to be the case in groupings I through IV. There is one-to-one correspondence between the four groupings of classes with the four groupings of relationships—grouping V corresponds with grouping I.

For understanding the logical significance of these groupings, we shall have to consider the different kinds of relationships and the names that have been given to them in logic and mathematics. *A* has relationship with *B*, and the same is shown through the notation *AqB*. The terms symmetric and asymmetric are used to show relations. The relation of sibling is symmetric; for example, if *A* is a sister or brother of *B*, then *B* is also a sister or brother of *A*. This relationship may also be shown as a relationship of equality. If *A* is equal to *B*, *B* is also equal to *A*. *A* relationship between an object and its element, is called the reflexive relationship. When we say *A* and *B* are the sons of the same father, we are showing the reflexive relationship. Unequal relationship can never be reflexive, though symmetrical it may be. When we say *A* is the son of the same father as *B*, then the relationship is reflexive.

"Grouping V describes relationship that are asymmetrical between two or more individuals, objects or classes. The analogy between grouping V and grouping I, stems from the fact that the sizes of the classes is a nested set, described in grouping I form, an asymmetrical series in which each member is asymmetrically related to other members of the series" [*Theories*

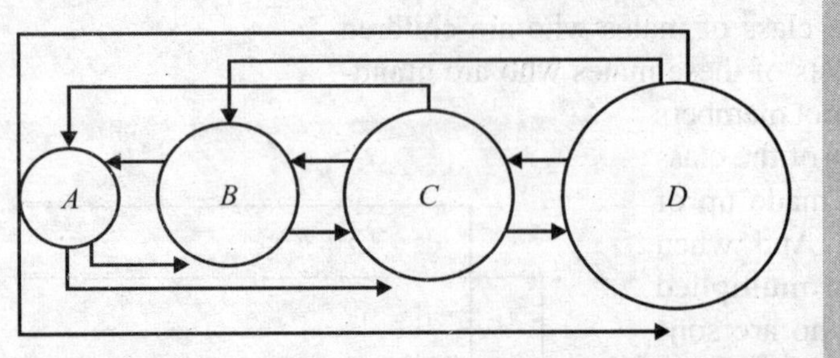

Figure 9.6 Addition of asymmetrical relations.

of Child Development: AL Baldwin]. The number of members in class *A* is the fewest. The class *B* has greater number of members. Then the class *C* has still greater number of members. The next is class *D* which has the greatest number of members in the existing four classes (see Fig. 9.6)

The classes may be arranged from any dimension—weight, size, and may be asymmetrically arranged. This asymmetrical arrangement may also be read as '*C*', is smaller than '*D*'; '*B*' is smaller than '*C*'; '*A*' is smaller than '*B*'.

A series of objects may, thus, be arranged in order of size. New elements may also be fitted into such a series. Arranging objects in such a series, is a cognitive operation which needs the knowledge of asymmetrical relationship existing between the objects. Such an operation forms a grouping of the same type, as it happens in case of the nested sequence of classes in Grouping I. Movement is possible both from *A* and *B,* from *B* to *C,* and so on, in an onward way, as well as in an inverse way from *D* to *C,* from *C* to *B,* and so on, as each one is related to its next in a nested sequence. In such a sequence, *A* is less than *B*, and, *B* is greater than *A*; relationship between each adjacent duo, is also of the same nature.

Piaget has pointed out the difference between the inverse relationship that exists in grouping I and that in grouping V. Grouping in I happens to be based on the operations of subtraction or addition-class *B* is reduced to class *A* when some of the members of the former are taken out, reducing the class into *A*. This relationship is based on negation. But relationship in grouping V, is reciprocal, when we say *A* is less than *B*, reciprocally, *B* is greater than *A*. "These two different kinds of inverses 'negation' and 'reciprocation', are important for some of Piaget's conceptualisations about the thinking of older children in the stage of formal operations. At that time, the child is capable of understanding an organised set of relationships in which both kinds of inverses exist within the same organisation. The combination of the two, makes it possible to define a special group called the "4-groups."

For the development of a true number system, conceptualisation of the relationship between grouping I and grouping V, must have been the basis. For example, the cardinal number 7, is a label for any set containing seven members. 7 describes a class that is included in 10 in grouping I. "That 7 is less than 10, is established when the two sets are juxtaposed, and cardinals in the first are exhausted at 7 while in the second set there are still more cardinals up to 10. Both groupings I and V are involved when numbers are used ordinally as points on a line to form an asymmetric series.

For the establishment of a unit, we move from an ordered series to a number system of integers. A set of five is transformed into a set of six, when one unit is added to the former set. This operation may be repeated over and over again. The numbers form a true group rather than a mere grouping, on the patterns of groupings I and V, the classes are given cardinal numbers.

GROUPING VI: ADDITION OF SYMMETRICAL RELATIONS

Preliminary grouping of equalities, illustrates cases of symmetrical relationships. Grouping VI, also, illustrates relationship within a genealogical tree. If "*B*" has the same grandfather as "*B*´", we can build up a hierarchical set as was illustrated in grouping IV. "These relationships can be combined; thus, if *X* is also a brother to *Y*; and *Y* is a first cousin of *Z*, then *X* is a first cousin of *Z*. Thus, there are logically necessary relations among these different kinship terms and altogether they constitute an organised system of relationship—which Piaget describes as Grouping VI."

GROUPING VII: BI-UNIVOCAL MULTIPLICATION OF RELATIONS

"This grouping is quite important as it describes the kinds of relationships that can exist when objects are ordered asymmetrically with respect to two attributes at the same time....." (see Fig. 9.7).

In the Fig. 9.7, there are a series of rectangles; the two attributes are the width and the height—in respect to which the rectangles have been ordered asymmetrically. One dimension of looking at the relationships of these rectangles, is horizontal–B_1 is wider than B_2, B_2 is wider than B_3, and so on. It is also possible to rearrange the rectangles in such a way that the widest one is in the first column, the next widest in the second column, the third widest in the third column, and so on. It is not always the case that the width decreases evenly from column to column. Likewise, the rectangles can be arranged in an asymmetrical sequence from the dimension of height. The elements in the first row are taller than those in the second; the second are taller than those in the third, and so on down to the shortest.

When the two sets of relations are multiplied together, "We get a matrix in which there is decreasing width as one moves from left to right across

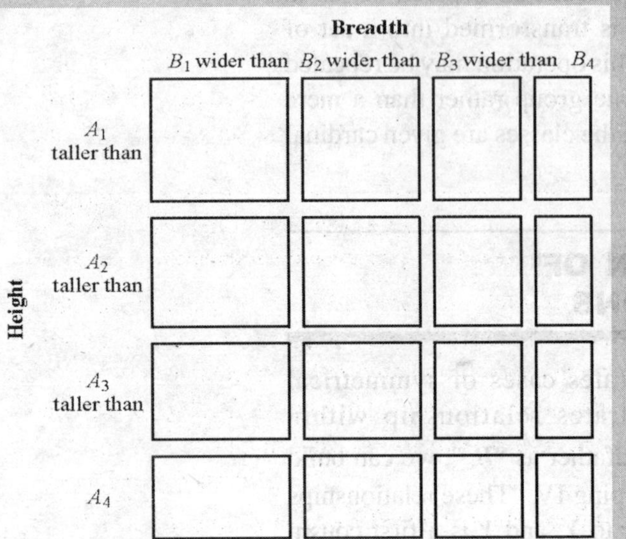

Figure 9.7 Bi-univocal multiplication of relations.

the table and decreasing heights as one moves from the top down through the table. If such sort of relationships are appreciated by a child then, he or she can understand the problems of invariance. Understanding such a relationship, the child can realise that the amount of liquid will remain invariant, when it is changed from a wider pot to a narrower one, as the latter is much taller in height than the former.

Piaget, in a very important experiment, asked a child to arrange a number of dolls in a series, in order of size and then, to arrange cones in a series, in the same sequence so that each doll will have its due place in order of size, vis-a-vis each cone, again, arranged in order of size. "This represents the multiplication of two asymmetrical series" where "the diagonal cells in the matrix are occupied. The tallest doll (A_1) has the tallest cone (B_1); the next tallest doll has the next tallest cone, and so on." .... no complete matrix but rather a series of diagonal cells running from the upper left to the lower right." Piaget contends, that putting two kinds of elements in correspondence with each other, when each is arranged in series of its own individual numbers, requires the understanding of the possibility of multiplying one asymmetrical series with another.

In an another research, the child is shown a matrix arranged in this fashion with certain cells missing. The child is asked to fill in the blanks looking from both the dimensions, horizontal as well as vertical, as to what would fit in that particular cell. The correct response by the child, verifies that he understands the essentials of this kind of multiplication of asymmetrical relationship.

GROUPING VIII: CO-UNIVOCAL MULTIPLICATION OF RELATIONS

Co-univocal multiplication of relations is to grouping VII what grouping IV is to grouping III. A_1 is the grandfather of A_3—this is one dimensional relationship. A_1, A_2 and A_3 make an asymmetrical series. Grouping VIII is concerned with the multiplication of such relationships, when we say B_2 is the brother of B_1, B_3 is the first cousin of B_1 etc.—we are referring to some other dimension. This kind of relationship can also be predictably multiplied together. If *A* is the father of *B*, and *B* is a brother of *C*, this implies that *A* is the father of *C* also. The other dimension is, if *A* is the father of *B*, and *B* is a first cousin of *C*, then *A* is an uncle of *C*; combination of these two kinds of symmetrical and asymmetrical relationship, forms a logical organisation which Piaget describes as Grouping VIII.

THE DEVELOPMENT OF THE CONCEPTS OF CLASSES

Piaget attempted to form consistent systems of logical grouping; but almost all the systems discussed above, were the results of abstract thinking. Only the first system of Grouping, based on the operation of addition, could be thoroughly investigated empirically. Piaget and Inhelder brought out a book *The Early Growth of Logic in the Child* in 1964, containing their findings regarding additive classification system. Inhelder and Piaget have listed the criteria for such a classification:

1. At the end of classification, not even a single object should remain isolated; that is, criterion or criteria of classification must be such that each object falls within one or the other sub-division. If there is only one object of a particular type, it must by itself form a class of its own.
2. There should be no isolated classes. Each class, making a sub-division, must have another class of objects as its complement to make one bigger classification. Objects may be divided into two classes as "red" and "non-red". To divide this complement into more classes, is also possible. Instead of classifying objects into squares and non-squares, the child may divide them into squares, triangles, rings, and half-rings. For any set of objects to form a class, it is essential that no further classification of the same, should be a possibility.
3. The basis for classification must remain consistent. The objects which have the attributes of being classified as squares, will always be so classified, and the criteria for that classification will always remain the same.
4. There can be no object which is included in both the classes—*A* and non-*A*, as the two are mutually exclusive.
5. For squares, the non-squares are the complement; but it is not always the case, that the complementary class has only single common attribute. The complementary class of non-square may be consisted of triangles, rings or half-rings.

6. "A particular class is included in every higher-ranking class that contains all its elements." For example, mammalian includes both carnivora and herbivora. Carnivora includes both canidae and cats etc., and so on. Another kind of example may be that of non-living objects; wooden objects making a higher ranking class which may include both squares and triangles. The criterion on which a classification happens to be based, helps the child in recognising that all members of a sub-class are included in the higher ranking class, but that they are not the only members in the higher-ranking class.
7. There ought to be simplicity, and the number of classes be the minimal.
8. When objects (both living and non-living) of the same rank, are to be divided into different classes, the criterion or criteria for doing this, ought to be the same.

REVIEW QUESTIONS

***Q*.1.** What is reasoning? Which, according to Jean Piaget, are the four factors which serve as bases in the process of reasoning? Describe.

***Q*.2.** Narrate in brief, what Jean Piaget means by the following groupings:
(*i*) Additive composition of classes
(*ii*) Co-univocal multiplication of classes
(*iii*) Bi-univocal multiplication of relations.

***Q*.3.** Draw figures to illustrate the above three groupings.

CHAPTER 10

EMOTIONAL DEVELOPMENT: FIRST TWO YEARS

Chapter Outline

Personality includes a great many aspects of a person's characteristics. Broadly speaking, it includes his physical, mental and emotional characteristics. Here, in this chapter, we are concerned with the emotional aspect of a person's characteristics. We find some to be easily upset, irritated, angry or otherwise awkward in his behaviour, while another may not get provoked or embarrassed even in the very unfavourable situations—this shows the difference in the emotional development of the two individuals. One is anxious without any reasonable cause to be so. While, on the positive extreme, there is another person who does not let himself be overwhelmed with anxiety, even in the worst of conditions. We may come across such persons whose fears may not be genuine, but, mainly, happens to be imaginary. Some remain balanced under impact of both the negative and the positive emotions; while there are some who express the same in an extreme way. We know the presence of emotions in one's mind, through one's behaviour.

We find some to be easily upset, irritated, angry or otherwise awkward in his behaviour, while another may not get provoked or embarrassed even in the very unfavourable situations—this shows the difference in the emotional development of the two individuals.

Emotions are feelings in their strongly aroused state; we know of their presence through the behaviour of the people. Fear, grief, joy, irritation, anxiety, love, anger, jealousy etc. are emotions when one's feelings are in a state of high intensity. Feelings are natural and very needful but their arousal, in too forceful a way, makes one's behaviour awkward and undesirable. And, repeated resorting to such a behaviour, would be a symptom of distorted personality. Such a personality can neither be

Emotions are feelings in their strongly aroused state; we know of their presence through the behaviour of the people.

considered wholesome for the person himself nor for the society that the person moves into, and reacts within. It being such, there is need to trace the causes leading to such a development.

In a previous chapter, it is mentioned that even during the prenatal period, there may be some factors affecting the emotional development of the baby. Both genetic and non-genetic biological variables affect the emotional growth. Though floating in the amniotic fluid, the unborn child happens to be fully protected from the outward factors of change, as well as, from the factors inside the body of the mother. The nutrition of the mother, her anxiety, fear and other emotions, however, indirectly affect the unborn child, by way of changing the biochemical nature of the blood of the mother. Before we take up the biochemical factors affecting the emotional build-up of the prenatal baby, it would be proper to refer, again, to the genetic factor related to the emotional development of the child.

GENETIC FACTORS

Genes are the carriers of heredity.

The tiny sperm penetrates the wall of the ovum, and immediately it releases 23 minute particles of chromosomes. At about the same time, the inner core of the ovum, the nucleus, breaks up, releasing another set of 23 chromosomes. These are further sub-divided and each particle is called "a gene." These genes are the carriers of heredity. Now, as to the question of what is actually inherited, the opinions of the geneticists differ. During the eighteenth century, the speculation was that even the singing faculty of the mother, and the father's penchant for learning, are inherited. Later geneticists discarded such speculation. Actually, the mother in no way can affect the embryo/foetus lying in her womb. The only connection she has with the embryo/foetus is through the umbilical cord, also called the life line. It joins a section of the uterine wall where the uterus and the chorion [the membrane covering the fertilised ovum] join. It extends from it. Two arteries carry blood and nutrients from the placenta, to the foetus; and one vein carries waste from the foetus back to the placenta [a tissue which grows inside the uterus during pregnancy, and links the baby to the mother]. It is only through placenta that exchange of oxygen and nutrients, all forming part of the mother's blood, takes place.

NON-GENETIC BIOLOGICAL FACTORS

When the mother is tense, is suffering from a sense of insecurity, remains strained with anxiety, is overpowered with fear, is jealous of someone or something and so on, the biochemicals inside her body are changed, because of the excessive secretion of some glands of hormones. Adrenal gland, for example, grows more active; chemicals, such as acetylcholine and epinephrene, are released into blood in more quantity. As the foetus is fed through the blood of the mother, all these changes in the blood of the mother, have their effect on the emotional build-up of the unborn baby. Due to tension, and increase of some hormones and chemicals into the blood of the pregnant mother, her breathing becomes irregular, blood-pressure rises up, pulse rate increases, and so on. All these changes have their indirect impact upon the growing foetus. Sontag[1] writes:

"Such an infant is from the beginning, a hyperactive, irritable, squirming, crying child, who cries for his feeding after every two or three hours, instead of sleeping through his four-hour feeding period. Because his irritability affects control of his gastrointestinal tract, he empties his bowels at unusually frequent intervals; spits up half his feedings and generally makes a nuisance of himself. He is, to all intents and purposes, a neurotic infant when he is born."

When the mother is tense, is suffering from a sense of insecurity, remains strained with anxiety, is overpowered with fear, is jealous of someone or something and so on, the biochemicals inside her body are changed, because of the excessive secretion of some glands of hormones. Adrenal gland, for example, grows more active; chemicals, such as acetylcholine and epinephrene, are released into blood in more quantity. As the foetus is fed through the blood of the mother, all these changes in the blood of the mother, have their effect on the emotional build-up of the unborn baby.

A neurotic personality develops because of improper emotional growth. It is characterised by the syndrome of suffering from anxiety and fear, when actually there is no genuine reason for the same. A neurotic person is likely to get irritated very soon on any real or imaginary hindrance in the fulfilment of his desires. Due to his nervous worrisome disposition, he cannot think cool-mindedly, objectively or judiciously. Nor can such a person make sustained efforts for achieving his objective. He will prove problematic for himself and for others as well. Lack of proper emotional development results in many psychotic[2] and psychosomatic[3] abnormalities.

A neurotic personality develops because of improper emotional growth.

There are some drugs which, if consumed by the prospective mother, may have their effect on the biochemical nature of her blood, and may eventually prove harmful to the emotional build up of the baby to be delivered. The unborn child or the neonate is also affected by the nutrition of the mother till the time, the child is having its feeding through the umbilical cord, and through breast after delivery. The malnutrition of the mother affects both the physical and the mental health of the child.

It has also been mentioned in the third chapter of the book that a house where a sense of belongingness is lacking, quarrelling and squabbling is a routine, the mother has to live in a state of constant strain; love and peace are conspicuous by their absence, the mother cannot feel secured and satisfied. Anxiety, fear, frustration would be the relevant terms to describe

---

1. Sontag, LW. *The Significance of Foetal Environmental Differences.*
2. *Psychotic*: Related to psychosis, which is a kind of serious mental disorder where the patient shows lack of insight, and touch with realities.
3. *Psychosomatic:* Related to a sort of mental disease caused mainly by bodily disorder as well as by a prolonged state of fear and anxiety.

Some drugs prove harmful to the emotional build-up of the baby to be delivered.

A long and painful delivery or because of obstetrical mishandling a traumatised baby may be born.

her psychic condition. A mother suffering from such emotions, is less likely to deliver a perfectly healthy child, so far as its emotional character is concerned.

Squalid and dingy physical environment in and around the house, ill-ventilated rooms with only the polluted air available for breathing—may also adversely affect the physical and the mental health of the prospective mother as well as, of the child, to be born. And, even after delivery, if there is not enough fresh air available for the neonate, it may cause anoxia or asphyxiation. A long and painful delivery or because of obstetrical mishandling a traumatised baby may be born.

A mention has already been made in the concerned chapter, that if conception takes place for the first time when the prospective mother is 35 or more, or if it is an unwanted conception or if the prospective mother herself has contracted some such disease which may pass on to the foetus, the neonate cannot be emotionally healthy.

Studies have also revealed the fact that immaturely born children, in many cases, happen to be not only less sensitive in auditory and visual perceptions, have speech difficulties, poor motor co-ordination and are awkward in movements but also shy, flighty, and "distracting or extremely persistent in work."

Now, we shall consider the factors which are related to the emotional conditions of a child up to two years of age. Broadly speaking, there may be four factors which work upon the emotional development of the child:

1. General Breeding
2. Family Environment
3. Nutrition
4. Living Cond itions in General

1. **General breeding** The needs of the child should be attended to properly and in time. If the child is crying out of hunger, and the mother does not respond to it in time, and with a feeling of affection, the child may emotionally get upset. Mothers, sometimes, complain of their baby not taking into its mouth the nipple for getting breast feeding as a reaction to the fact that there was no timely response to its demand for feeding or for water. If such a sort of negligence, on the part of the mother, is repeated often, the neonate may develop into an irritable, squirming and crying child. The child may show its displeasure through frequent defecation and urinating, more often than natural, spitting up a good part of its feeding. And, such a behaviour of the child may result in the emaciation of it, and, may cause dehydration. And, an emaciated child is, generally, found to be more peevish or irritated.

Sleep It is a common experience of each mother that whenever a child does not have his full stint of sleep, or take rest to the full, he gets uneasy and generally, keeps crying till he has not slept enough as per his need.

In a previous chapter, a mention has already been made to the "agewise needful durations of sleep for a child." Both for physical and emotional health, it is essential that the child sleeps well and for the needful period. For it, it is also essential that a peaceful environment is provided, lest the child's sleep should be disturbed. The place where the child sleeps, should be well-ventilated and congenial for it to have a sound and undisturbed sleep—congenial, in the sense that there the child should not suffer because of inclement weather conditions.

> It is a common experience of each mother that whenever a child does not have his full stint of sleep, or take rest to the full, he gets uneasy and generally, keeps crying till he has not slept enough as per his need.

If disturbance to the child's sleep is a general routine, it may not prove wholesome so far his emotional growth is concerned.

Emptying the wastes Emptying the wastes in the form of defecation or urination, is an experience of being eased. So, if the child, generally, always has to face disturbances during the time of his defecation and urination, there may be undesirable development in the emotional life of the child. Showing displeasure by the mother or by other elders on the child's emptying its bowels or bladder, if done repeatedly or often, may distort the emotional build-up of the child. To expect toilet-discipline from a child who is hardly two years old, is too much, if such a discipline is forced upon the tender child whose concerned sphincters are still not developed enough to effect full control, it will harm the emotional development of the child. The habitually crying and squirming child cannot be termed emotionally healthy; and disturbances during defecation or water making, or attempting untimely toilet discipline, may be a cause for the same.

> So, if the child, generally, always has to face disturbances during the time of his defecation and urination, there may be undesirable development in the emotional life of the child.

2. **Family environment** Family is expected to be the most well-knit unit. So far the feelings of each for the other members of it are concerned, a natural bond of love ought to be binding each to the other. Everyone of its members should feel a natural concern for each other member of it. A strong feeling of belongingness ought to be there (Fig. 10.1). Where such a feeling is not found, or if it is not so strong, emotional growth, especially of the children of the family, is bound to be adversely affected.

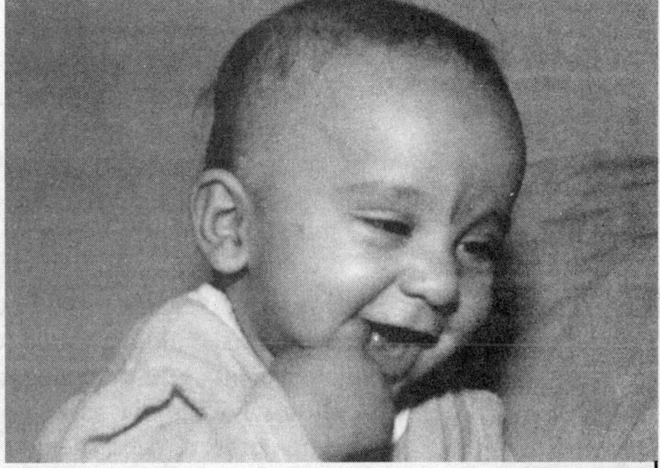

Figure 10.1 A strong feeling of belongingness helps in the emotional growth of the child.

If father and mother are not emotionally tied to each other; each is not feeling a natural concern for the well-being of the other, it would have its impact on the emotional growth of their small child. In some cases, it is found that father, generally, metes out harsh treatment to his wife, abuses her, rebukes or beats her. In the absence of a cordial relationship between the two, the wife lives in a state of continuous mental strain. A feeling of insecurity, humiliation and trauma haunts her always. This may result in hypertension, loss of sleep, loss of appetite, increased secretion of some hormones, or generation of biochemicals such as acetylcholine and epinephrene. The young baby depending on breast feeding, is affected by such a condition of the mother. A neglected wife, cannot give a smile of affection to her baby. All this creates an environment which disturbs the process of healthy emotional development of the child. The child would grow either irritable or sluggish causing trouble in all matters whether it is feeding or sleeping or emptying bowels or bladder. Later, the family may have to bear with a child who is aggressive or quite inactive, or very slow in the activities so natural to a child of that age. Under such circumstances, the child may grow neurotic.

If behaviour of any member in the family is not proper, it would have its effect upon other members of the family also, and the chain of action and reaction would vitiate the emotional environment of the family.

The relationships among other members of the family, among the siblings, are also important. A warm affectionate bond among them only can create a congenial environment for the wholesome emotional growth of the child. Nothing can be more desired for the proper emotional development than an affectionate care. If behaviour of any member in the family is not proper, it would have its effect upon other members of the family also, and the chain of action and reaction would vitiate the emotional environment of the family. Where the father is an addict or a drunkard, we can hardly hope for a harmonious environment (Fig. 10.2).

Figure 10.2
Children always like to be assured of affection by their nurturants.

In a family environment, where the mother is a working woman and the father is too busy to spare time to fondle the baby, to laugh and play with him, the child's development will be thwarted. Such a child who is neglected because of his circumstances, cannot grow emotionally healthy. It would grow less active than a normal child, he would learn walking and speaking later than other children of his age. Such a sluggish child would be more prone to frustration. A child who has not been brought up experiencing the full warmth of affection of its mother, should be considered one among the most unlucky lots. The child's hunger for motherly love, especially happens to be very intense, and, if it is not satisfied timely and in a proper way, would upset the emotional growth of the child (Fig. 10.3).

If the gap between the birth of two children of the mother is less than four years, chances are that the former child would become jealous of the latter one, presuming the younger one to be having the lion's share in the maternal affection.

Figure 10.3
Different gestures and moods are representing their different family backgrounds.

If mother is unwell, she would be losing patience often. Likewise, if the elderly member who has to look after the baby, is not physically healthy, and mentally of good humour, the baby would be receiving harsh treatment; would have to hear unpleasant sounds—and this all is, certain to distort the emotional growth of the child. The elders who are not tolerant enough to bear with the childish activities of the baby, and, cautious and prompt enough to meet the baby's needs timely and pleasantly, can only harm the emotional make-up of the child. And, emotions form a very important aspect of one's personality.

If because of any reason, it is an unwanted conception—the mother or the father does not want a child to be born; it may be because of penury of the family, or of some disease of the mother or of the father, or because of lack of emotional harmony between the two—this would definitely affect the emotional health of the child who is still unborn.

Proper nutrition is an important condition for physical health. If for want of proper nutrition, bodily health is spoilt, the emotional health, also, cannot be maintained.

3. **Nutrition** Body and mind can never be separated, the one affects the other, and the two work interdependently. One who is bodily fit, is, generally, found to be mentally healthy also. Proper nutrition is an important condition for physical health. If for want of proper nutrition, bodily health is spoilt, the emotional health, also, cannot be maintained. In the *Gita*, food has been classified into three categories—*Satwik*, *Rajas* and *Tamasik*—each one of them has been described as to what types of food items are included in a particular category. The emotional nature of a person very much depends upon the type of food that one takes. The ancient wisdom forbids the use of aphrodites or condiments in excess, if one desires to maintain the purity of celibacy or virginity. If during pregnancy, the mother does not get balanced food in an adequate quantity, it would harm not only the physical growth of the foetus but it may result in developing a child whom the mother would find to be a frequently crying, squirming and irritable one when born. In a previous chapter, it has been described how deficiency of a particular ingredient of food, causes disease of a certain kind, or harms the health of the person concerned. And, physical ailment also upsets the emotional balance, and the affected person cannot behave in a normal or desired manner. Deficiency of any sort—of some vitamin, of proteins, or of any mineral, may cause emotional/behavioural abnormality. So, care needs to be taken both during the prenatal and postnatal periods that the child gets proper nutritive and balanced food in an adequate quantity, and gets it timely with due intervals.

Nutrition is related to the secretion of certain glands and the generation of certain bio-chemicals in the body. For example, excessive secretion of adrenalin hormone would cause both physical and emotional abnormalities. We have already read about the ill-effect of the excessive generation of bio-chemicals such as acetylcholine and epinephrene—they would make the child overactive, irritable, and, so problematic.

The congested living in an ill-ventilated, squalid house, if it can be so termed, make the occupants prone to diseases.

4. **Living conditions in general** Families with very low socioeconomic standard, may have to live in a single thatched shed, where ventilation and other hygienic conditions are unimaginable. The occupants are left with no alternative but to spend the whole life living in a dark and dingy shed. The number of members in such a poverty-stricken family, often, happens to be quite large. The congested living in an ill-ventilated, squalid house, if it can be so termed, make the occupants prone to diseases. Such a shed can hardly protect them against inclement weather conditions. A sense of insecurity always haunts them. A sort of mental tension always tortures them. Personal privacy is difficult to be maintained under such conditions. Such living conditions disturb the emotional development not only of the children of the family but also of the babies who are still unborn. The mother would, generally, be more perturbed when her neonate or young baby is a crying, squirming and irritable brat. Mother of a neurotic child can hardly remain emotionally normal.

The mother would, generally, be more perturbed when her neonate or young baby is a crying, squirming and irritable brat. Mother of a neurotic child can hardly remain emotionally normal.

A wholesome family environment cannot be expected under such circumstances. The father would return home badly tired after a day-long labour; the mother may also have to do hard physical labour for paltry wages besides doing a lot of domestic chores. The illiterate father may even drink excessively in the night, and bawl at and beat his wife, mother of the baby or prospective mother of the baby. Proper emotional growth of a child of such parents, or of one living in, and brought up under such conditions, would be too much to expect. The family environment hot with frequent squabbles, would give rise to emotions, such as anger, hatred, jealousy, revenge, fear, anxiety, and so on. Under the impact of intense emotions, the heart-beating increases; the pulse-rate rises, appetite goes down, digestive system is disturbed because of changed biochemical conditions of the body, and because of the excessive secretion of certain hormones. The overall result would be subnormal emotional development; the new born infant would be handicapped in adapting itself to the external world.

MATURITY AND EMOTIONAL DEVELOPMENT

The emotions of a neonate, or, of a very young baby, are evoked, mainly, because of internal causes. Generally, up to the age of 6 months, the child has very little experience of the external world, to enable him to perceive stimuli for emotions. It is with age, that the child's sensations and perceptions grow in acuity. A child who is younger than four months, can hardly sense whether the person holding him in his arms, is in a pleasant mood, or, otherwise. Nor, can he discriminate between a face that is smiling, and the one which is angry and is frowning. Due to lack of perceptibility, such a situation cannot serve as stimulus for the arousal of emotions in a very young child. The repertoire of experiences of a young child happens to be very limited, so also is the scope for the arousal of his emotions. External situations can stimulate emotions only when the child is able to comprehend the meanings of the same, that is, he can perceive the nature of the situation, whether it is pleasant or otherwise. For such a perception, the relevant past experiences serve as a base. It is by the end of the second half of the first year, that the child begins to discriminate between a voice that is pleasant and the one that is unpleasant.

Child's receptivity of emotional stimuli and reactions to the same, also depends upon the constitution of the child. A child who is irritable as a neonate, generally, remains so throughout the period of his early infancy.[4] Other factors, as already mentioned above, affecting the emotional development of the child, are heredity, prenatal and early postnatal influences. With the advancement of age, response-patterns become more varied, differentiated and recognisable. Of course, individual differences will be there because of physiological state of each individual, and the activity of the moment of each of them. How much a certain stimulus would affect, also depends upon the period of its duration, and upon the degree of its intensity. A child begins his life with almost all its emotional responses being automatic or reflex; and it is through his living in the external world, that the number of learned responses goes on increasing.

A child who is irritable as a neonate, generally, remains so throughout the period of his early infancy.

A child who has had no adequate loving care of his mother, would remain emotionally dwarf for the rest of his life. For the development of positive emotions, the child needs to have much warmth of affection, many occasions of pleasant stimulations, and a wholesome environment where he was feeling himself safe and much cared after. Physical and mental developments alone are not enough unless one is developed emotionally too. An emotionally ill-developed, will be a nuisance for self as well as for others.

Emotions are natural phenomena. They are essential too, for a purposeful and good living. But their arousal too frequent, and, when a situation does not warrant for the same, or with the intensity that they are aroused or evoked, would be considered a symptom of ill-emotional development.

4. Shirley, MM. *The First Two Years, A Study of twenty five Babies.*

The emotions that are important during infancy are: 1. Fear, 2. Anger, 3. Anxiety, 4. Joy, 5. Jealousy, and 6. Love.

The emotions that are important during infancy are: 1. Fear, 2. Anger, 3. Anxiety, 4. Joy, 5. Jealousy, and 6. Love.

1. **Fear** An object that is too ugly, too big, fierceful or uncommon, in other ways that the child would like to avoid, becomes a source of fear for him. A child even gets afraid of darkness. A thing, or a person that has ever caused harm, or has in any way hurt him, would become a source of fear for him. A child may become fearful on looking at a big bull or camel for the first time; or at an animal or anything rushing at with great speed; on seeing one who once caused him fall down or get hurt, and so on. It is not only through the sense of seeing that the child perceives the object of his fear, he may even get fearful on hearing very loud and fierce sound.

Sometimes, parents and elder siblings evoke fear in the child to make him stop crying or to dissuade him from doing something that the elders deem unfit. Recourse to such a strategy, too often, would harm the emotional build-up of the child. It would not prove good for his physical health, and would distort the overall development of his personality.

The emotion of fear would make the child shriek, cry, run away crying, or he would tightly cling to his elder whom he trusts and feels closest to. The abdominal muscles contract, the heart-beat rises up suddenly, blood-pressure becomes abnormal. The face may also become whitened or discoloured, as a result of sudden arousal of fear. Fear may leave the child stunned and in a state of total immobility.

Fear is a state of a feeling of insecurity. A sense of security is its antidote. The child should be provided an environment where he can feel totally safe. A loving care would generate a sense of security in the child. To safeguard the child from the harmful effect of fear, it is essential that he must not be exposed to a situation which may prove dreadful for him. To adopt frequently, the strategy of frightening a crying or naughty child in order to silence him, would harm the emotional development of the child. For the proper development of the child, it is essential that the child should feel free and secured for activities of his interest. [Or, rather, for a young child, we should provide activities to be indulged in—the way to development lies through cheerful activities].

2. **Anger** The presence of the emotion of anger, becomes evident when the child is screaming, flinging arms in the air, or, is kicking with his leg/legs anything that may come his way; holding breath, is yet the other symptom of anger. A child is provoked to anger when he cannot get a thing that he wants or, do what he is inclined to do. And, when the child finds that anger helps him in being allowed to have his own way, he begins to show anger at the slightest opposition to his will.

Goodenough collected data regarding the behaviour of, as many as 1,878 children, when they were angry. His subjects were ranging from the age of 7 months to 8 years. This was a one month long study. The findings of Goodenough provide a clue as to what sort of elderly responses suggest to the child that angry behaviour is an effective means to achieve what is desired. Over-indulgent parents are more likely to yield to the motor or verbal resistance of their children made out of anger. Fourteen per cent of such resistances are rewarded. Sex-discrimination was found in this regard also—56 per cent of the outbursts of the male babies ranging in age between one to two months, are likely to be encouraged, but not those of the female babies to the same extent.

In case of children under two, the general causes which evoke anger are:

(*i*) Regarding clothing
(*ii*) Toilet training
(*iii*) Making the child sleep
(*iv*) Regarding feeding
(*v*) Restricting the child from doing what it is badly inclined to
(*vi*) Failing in making others behave as it desires
(*vii*) Other reasons

(*i*) *Regarding clothing* A child under two, sometimes does not let itself be wrapped with some quilt, blanket or cover, and gets more angry when it is done forcibly. It is only later, when the child is between two and five that it insists on putting on some particular clothes only. A child under two, rarely does so. It is also very rare, for a child under two, to try to take off some head-covering or footwear, and, when restricted from doing so, to burst out with anger.

Parents and other elders should acquiesce to the demand of the children, if it does not involve any harm. If children's demands are generally neglected or refused, they would grow irritable and become more problematic. However, this impression should also not be created that through their insistence or obstinancy, they would get everything done as they desire.

(*ii*) *Toilet training* Toilet training is the main occasion when the child gets angry. Parents, generally, try that their two year or so old child should always give some hint when it is to defecate or urinate; should do the same only at a time when it is not very inconvenient to the mother. But such a toilet training could be too harsh for the tender baby whose sphincters' control is still not so developed. So, the training will have to be given patiently and judiciously.

Even when the child defecates, or empties its bladder, no annoyance should be expressed on the part of the parent on account that the same is being done at an improper time, or with more frequency than usual.

Such a behaviour of the elders, upsets the child, it gets irritated because of this. Rebuking the child for a thing over which it cannot exercise any control, will only make it tizzy. If the child has to experience such a behaviour often, it would harm its emotional build-up. The elders would find the child to have grown aggressive. The parent will have to see that the evacuation of the wastes is done without unnecessary disturbances; nor any attempt is made on her/his part to induce the child for evacuation when the system is not prepared for the same.

(*iii*) *Making the child sleep* Sometimes, parents or elders of the child, try to make him sleep when he is not sleepy at all. This creates tension for the child. The child becomes emotionally upset. If the feelings of the miffed child, are often suppressed through such an attempt, it may lead to serious distortion of the child's behaviour. Later on, this may be one of the reasons for thumb sucking, stammering or stuttering. The parents should know the amount of biological need of sleep agewise; and, should make the child sleep only when it is felt that now the child is getting sleepy. The child should have an adequate stint of sleep each time, and, with no disturbance whatsoever. Undisturbed, adequate sleep is quite essential for both physical growth and proper emotional development. The mother's common experience also testifies the fact that the child happens to be very peevish when it has not had its full stint of sleep.

(*iv*) *Regarding feeding* Especially a working mother may not be able to respond timely to the child's demand for feeding, which it makes through crying. It so much angers the child that it would not take nipple or the bottle into its mouth, as a protest against the delayed response of the mother. And, if adequate feeding is not made, or if it is not to the liking and need of the child, this would also make the child annoyed. Causing annoyance, thus, repeatedly, would interfere with the emotional development of the child. The child would grow not only emaciated but peevish, too.

However, due gaps ought to be maintained between two feedings. And, while breast-feeding the child, the mood of the mother should be quite cheerful. If a natural maternal affection is meted out to the child, the effect would be very wholesome in the emotional build-up of the child.

(*v*) *Restricting the child* (from doing something that the child is badly inclined to). I have often seen my granddaughter, Manvi, getting infuriated when my wife would snatch a thing from her hand, the thing being such that could either hurt or harm her or be broken or destroyed. A child does not happen to be cognitively matured enough as to understand what to do and what not; what thing is fit for him to play with and what is not suitable for him to play with (Fig. 10.4). So it would always like to have its own way and behave quite obstinately. Such an obstreperous child should be tackled psychologically.

1. Let the child take a thing or do something, if there is no harm involved in doing so.
2. If harm is involved, let his attention be diverted by presenting some more attractive alternative for him.

Let the child take a thing or do something, if there is no harm involved in doing so.
If harm is involved, let his attention be diverted by presenting some more attractive alternative for him.

The reasoning has still not developed in your child, so do not get yourself annoyed at its unreasonable demand and recalcitrance, only diversion to some more attractive thing may be a solution. If the elders grow rough to a recalcitrant child, it would make the child more obstinate—"20 per cent of their outbursts" are due to verbal or physical restraints put in the way of their carrying out their desired activity.

(*vi*) *Failing in making others behave as it desires* Many a time, a child gets angry because he desires someone behave in a particular way, and failing to make the other do the same, becomes the cause of his annoyance. The baby may want another child not to touch it, likewise, he may want the other child sit on a particular place, in a particular manner. The child, many a time, attempts to direct the behaviour of other children or adults. The latter may not follow, or, for any reason, would not do accordingly. The child even may not tolerate his mother sharing out her affection with child even if he is sibling. The child even may not tolerate the other child touching his mother or anyone or anything which is very dear to it. Sometimes, a child is annoyed because of visitors coming to his house. Even, many adults living in the same house, may be a cause for the child to get upset. The reason for the behavioural change in the child, under such social circumstances, is that the child would get less care.

Figure 10.4 Children should be allowed to enjoy to the full.

(*vii*) *Other reasons* Other reasons making the child angry, may include ill-health or some physical ailment—innate or developed later on. As has already been described, some children may be easily excitable because of prenatal genetic or bio-chemical reasons. Such children need a careful and affectionate nurturing. And, to do this, the parents or elders, looking after the children, will have to be very patient or tolerant. Nevertheless, it is not the case that over-indulgent and permissive guardians only can keep such children in a proper mood. Sometimes, children have to be restricted, or refused a thing, not in a harsh manner but quite judiciously.

3. **Anxiety** A small child cannot feel anxious for achieving some future

goals. It is only his bitter experience of the past, that he has perceived, which the child happens anxious to avoid. A child remains anxious to avoid the situation causing unpleasant experience. Hence, he may try to avoid the person responsible for such an experience; the place where the unpleasant incident occurred; things which were involved therein. The child, as he grows older, becomes more and more anxious to avoid something which may result in the withdrawal of love or care of those who are very much affectionate towards him. The point for constant anxiety for a child happens to be to resist from a behaviour which may invoke displeasure of one who is so fond of him. Such is the sense of insecurity in the child, that he is constantly anxious not to lose the love and affection of his caretaker. Therefore, he tries to behave in a manner that pleases them.

A feeling of security and affection is among his important needs.

If the past experience of a child reminds him that his call for feeding was not inmediately responded to, he would cry more loudly, feeling anxious for the avoidance of the re-occurrences of a similar situation. The same thing is true with regard to the occasion when the child is in need of any physical thing, or, is to empty its bowels, or, has emptied its bladder.

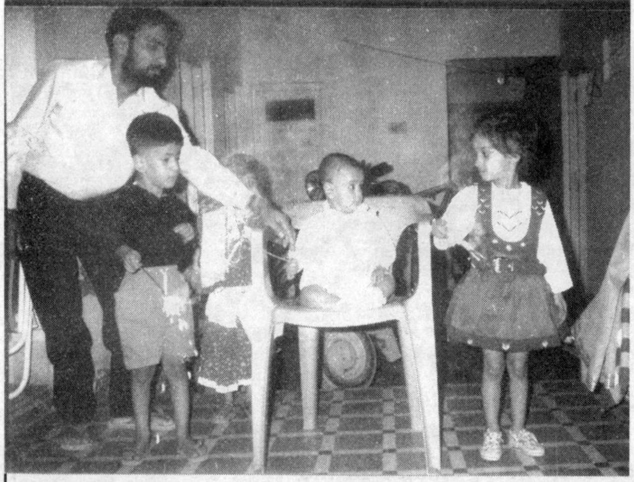

Figure 10.5
The youngest one is apprehensive of the new experience of the Diwali fireworks.

The needs of the child, both physical and mental, are only very few. Yet the child, along with the development of his power to perceive, grows more and more anxious to avoid the re-occurrence of an unpleasant experience related to any of his needs. A feeling of security and affection is among his important needs (Fig. 10.5). A child would anxiously resist himself from indulging in such a behaviour, which may engender a feeling of insecurity or may cause the withdrawal of affection towards him.

4. **Joy** A child would exclaim out of glee when his nurturer fondles him, or makes him feel excessively happy (Fig. 10.6). Playing with favourite toys also makes a child cheerful. In a child, the emotion of joy is manifested through jumping, shouting, singing, and so on. A smiling face is a sure sign of the feeling of joy; and it is only the human being who has been bestowed upon by nature with this mode of expression of joy. Other beings, too, have the emotion of joy which they express only through jumping or running to and fro, or through other kinds of frolicsome gestures.

The emotion of joy is good for our health. It boosts the process of physical growth, and brings about wholesome biochemical changes, as it stimulates such hormonal products which are helpful in the process of growth and development. One feels relieved of mental tension after going through the experience of joy. The antithesis of anxiety is joy. The feeling of joy is possible only during the time when one is altogether free of a feeling of anxiety. The feeling of joy lightens the mind, relieves it of all tensions or worries thus improving the working capacity of the mind itself. A feeling becomes an emotion, when it is aroused to the level of high intensity.

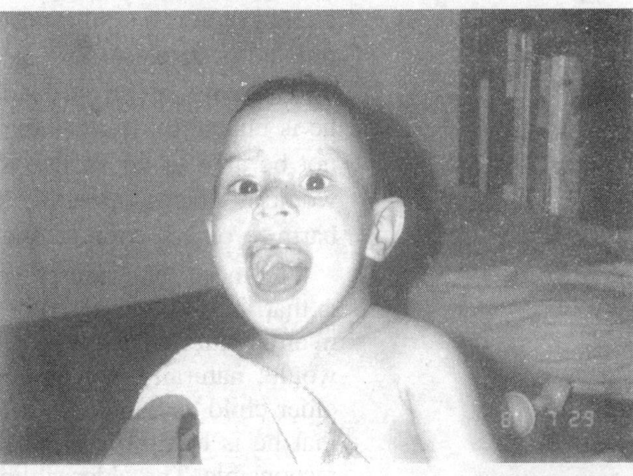

Figure 10.6
A child would exclaim out of glee when his nurturer fondles him.

Generally, a young child is not much obsessed with worries or tensions. So, to make him cry out of joy, is not so difficult to achieve, as it may prove to be in case of a grown up. As the child is passing through a period of rapid growth, arousal of joy, proves quite stimulating in the process of growth and development.

Let the child indulge in such plays and activities which it very much likes. It is only during such times that a child may be jumping out of a strong feeling of joy. An environment, where a child is not often led to playful activities or gestures of joy, cannot be considered to be wholesome for the growth and development of the child. So, the guardians need to see that their ward is not deprived of the occasions which can make him joyful, in a natural way.

5. **Jealousy** Jealousy is a strong feeling, which makes one intolerant, sharing one's dear possessions, with anybody else. This type of jealousy is possessive in nature, and, can be found in most children. A child, under two, can hardly tolerate someone else, even to touch its mother. It cannot tolerate anyone taking or even touching a thing of its liking or a thing of its possession.

Envy may also be an important characteristics of jealousy. When the child feels that his younger sibling is getting more of the motherly affection, he would grow severely envious of his younger sibling, and may even desire to harm the younger sibling. Also, when the child sees someone else in possession of something, or something being given to him, which is quite attractive for the child himself, then the child would grow envious of the one who is possessing such an article. Under the strong impact of envy, one would not like anything of the other person, especially, anything indicative of goodluck, would make him more envious.

A feeling of jealousy cannot be said to be something unnatural. It is, rather, a natural phenomenon. When aroused to a level of great intensity,it may lead one to some unnatural behaviour. Hence, the guardian or guardians need to be on guard, that child does not grow strongly jealous of anyone else. If effective measures are not timely taken to cure the child of jealousy, the child may grow into a jealous person by nature. The behaviour of such a child would be quite unsocial. He cannot even tolerate the presence of one, he is strongly envious of. He would withdraw from the company of others, and may be so distorted or frustrated in nature, when finding that he is unable to do anything against the object of his envy, that he would not be able to appreciate anything good of anyone else. Such a person would not be co-operative. On the contrary, an envious person may cause harm to others, even to one not directly related to the object of his envy.

The most important prevention against the development of this emotion is that, in no case, the child should feel that he is less preferred to others in any matter whatsoever. Generally, when a new baby is born, the mother would, naturally, not be able to give as much exclusive attention to the older child as before. As a result, the older child may get the impression that he is being discriminated against. For this, he holds the new baby responsible. The older sibling thinks that the affection which was reserved only for him, has been snatched by his younger sibling. The older child grows bitterly envious of the younger baby. To avoid the development of such a situation, the measures that may be effective are as follows:

(*i*) A new child should not be born till the youngest sibling is less than 4 years old.

(*ii*) The mother's treatment should make the older child feel that her affection has, in no way, been reduced because of the new born baby.

  (*a*) The mother should still devote adequate time fondling and playing with him.

  (*b*) When the younger one has grown old enough to play with toys and others, it is essential that, whatever item is purchased for him to play, or to wear, or to eat or drink, should also be purchased for the older sibling as well.

(*iii*) The mother should make the older child play with the younger one; of course, she should be vigilant lest any harm should be caused, wittingly or unwittingly, to the youngest baby.

(*iv*) The mother should make the older child feel that the baby is his or her own brother or sister. For this, the mother should make the older sibling sit beside the younger one; play with him; talk to him; kiss him; fondle him. In this way, intimacy would increase, would grow stronger.

6. **Love** Love may, very well, be called a master feeling. The reason being, love is a very strong feeling or emotion and also many other feelings get their strength from it, as it is a primary source of energy. It is the feeling of love which unites the mother to her child; and the father and the mother of the child are bound together because of the feeling of love. In the first case, it is the parental affection, while in the second, it is erotic—though Sigmund Freud and the other psychoanalysts do not find any difference between the two, so far the origin of them is concerned. According to them, both are erotic though the form of their expression, may differ.

Love is such a strong emotion which makes one tolerant to all sorts of difficulties. One may be prepared to undergo the most difficult troubles, make the greatest sacrifice for the sake of one's subject of love. A strong feeling of love that each mother has for her child, is a very important factor for the proper emotional development of the child. A child who has not had the affectionate care of his mother, as prompted by the emotion of love, cannot have a proper socialisation. His personality would remain dwarfed in respect of many traits of character. Love is the antithesis of jealousy which breeds hatred, and leads to repulsion. Love leads to the union of the two, having mutual concern for the well-being of each other. Love binds not only two or more persons, but it can unite the entire people of a land into a bond of one single nationality. The wider the field of the effect of love, the better it would be for the welfare of humanity.

Here, we are concerned with a baby up to two years of age, so the effect of the feeling of love ought to be considered in that reference only. First, it is the mother in whom the love of a baby remains concentrated. As the child grows older, his attachment with other members of the family also develops. It is love that is the base for such an attachment. And, when the child is still older, he develops contacts with other children of his age. The field of his love also goes on widening. Thus, love is a very strong binding force. The home environment, and later the environment of the nursery school, should be such which help in the generation or development of a strong feeling of love.

REVIEW QUESTIONS

Q.1. How would you define the term 'Emotion'? How is it important in the development of personality?

Q.2. How the phenomenon of 'genes' is related to emotions?

Q.3. "Such an infant is from the beginning, a hyperactive, irritable, squirming, crying child, ...". How does, according to Sontag, such a behaviour develop in a child?

Q.4. If there is an irritable child at your disposal, what steps would you take to cure it?

Q.5. Make a table, showing both negative and positive factors which would cause emotional build-up accordingly.

CHAPTER

EMOTIONAL DEVELOPMENT: THREE TO FIVE YEARS

Chapter Outline

- **Reflex Stage**
- **Manipulation Stage**
- **Interactive Play**
- **Aggressive Play**
- **Social Deprivation and Emotional Growth**
- **Review Questions**

> "An emotion is characterised by the occurrence of a fairly intense physiological response (sudden increase in heart rate, contraction of stomach muscles, increase in blood pressure, increase in muscle tension, release of adrenal hormones) in association with a specific internal need, image, thought, or external stimulus. The name we apply to the emotion—fear, joy, sorrow—is determined by the content of the image, nature of the need, or meanings of the external arousing stimulus."

"An emotion is characterised by the occurrence of a fairly intense physiological response (sudden increase in heart rate, contraction of stomach muscles, increase in blood pressure, increase in muscle tension, release of adrenal hormones) in association with a specific internal need, image, thought, or external stimulus. The name we apply to the emotion—fear, joy, sorrow—is determined by the content of the image, nature of the need, or meanings of the external arousing stimulus".[1]

Arousal of emotions is very much related to maturity. A very small child cannot realise what it is to lose, forever, the one that he loves so dearly, hence, is not likely to suffer from the emotion of grief at such a loss. No failure still causes any intense emotional upset. "..........an adult emotion is the product of a learned association between a specific thought or situation and a physiological or postural reaction." A bashful gesture can be a reaction of a three-year-old child when a stranger enters his room, but a small baby, only a month old, cannot be expected to indicate the presence of any emotion in such a situation. In the process of emotional development, the role of perceptions happens to be very important—the higher will be the emotional development as the perceptual capacities grow in acuity.

---

1. Paul Henry Mussen, John Janeway Conger, Jerome Kagan. *Child Development and Personality.*

REFLEX STAGE

It is the first stage in the series, when the children's movement towards one another happens to be unlearned or totally natural. Many a time, children may be seen, clinging to each other out of peer affection. They may be seen close to each other in ventral clasp. The mother, often, has to adjust their positions, looking to their physical needs. During the play-session of children, clinging and clasping episodes occur as reflexes, and, are indicative of the presence of a strong emotion of peer-affection.

MANIPULATION STAGE

During the per-school period, co-ordination goes on increasing, in case of movement of eyes, hands and other larger muscles of the body. This coordination gains in acuity as the child indulges more and more into exploratory launches. The movements of the child may be to the effect of bodily exploration of the mother, for the first instance. As the child grows in age, the area of its exploration and number of objects of exploration, also increase [Fig. 11.1 (*a*), (*b*), (*c*)]. The child becomes better able to explore its surroundings because of the growing co-ordination among the functions of different organs of the body. The manipulative activities happen

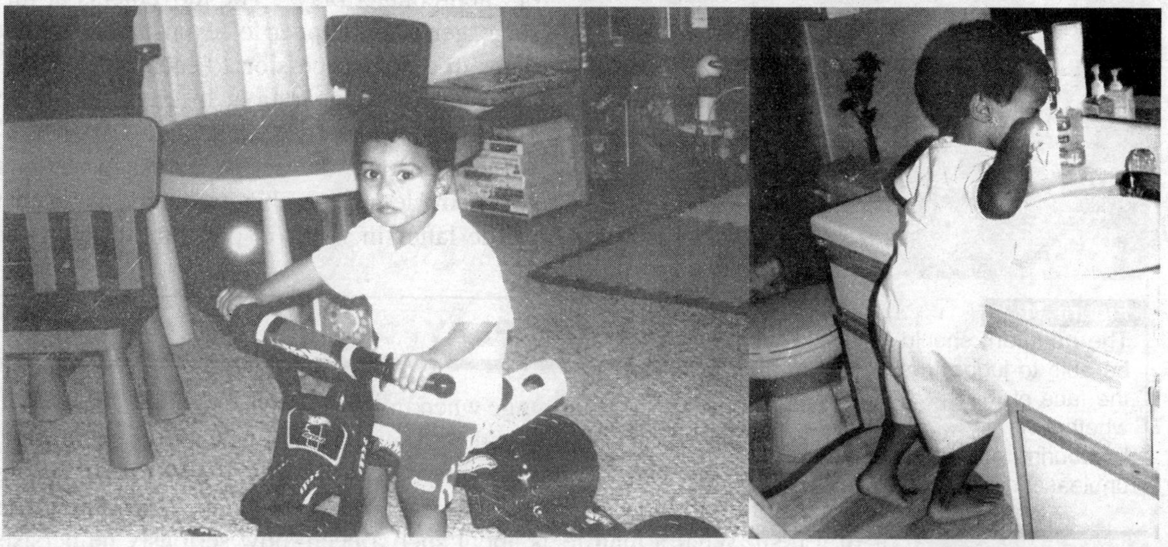

(*a*) (*b*)

Figure 11.1 (*a*), (*b*) (c) One who is not active cannot appear to be smart.

(*c*)

to be surcharged with a strong feeling of curiosity and attachment. Such a strong feeling may also be taken to be an emotion. The manipulative stage persists into the stage of interactive plays; and "social play emerges from the matrix of manipulatory play".

INTERACTIVE PLAY

The stage of interactive play is a step further in the process of child's socialisation. This is a step further, also in the development of peer-affection. "It marks the true social interactions among peers". It overlaps with manipulatory plays as they start being interspersed with many sequences of physical exploration. Plays are directed towards the age-mates, and may be towards the younger or the older. Social-interactions continue, subject to the availability of responsive partners. More complex type of interactive play develops. The rough and tumble play, is replaced by a play where close body contact is not so much required. This pattern has been described as "approach-withdrawal" or "non-contact play". The movements at this stage, generally, happen to be pursuit and retreat types in quick succession to each other. There is no clear-cut separation, in times, of rough and tumble play from that of the approach-withdrawal one; the occasions for the former type grow less in number gradually, as for that of the latter increase in the same proportion.

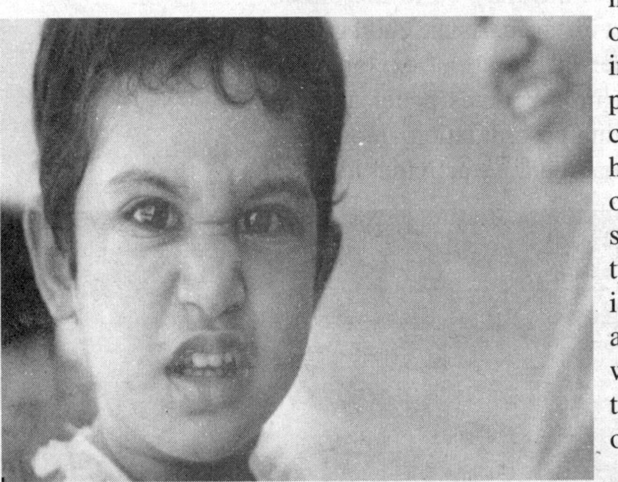

Figure 11.2 The nurturant should be able to judge from the face of the child whether he is harbouring some unpleasant emotions.

> Interactive play marks the true social interactions among peers.

AGGRESSIVE PLAY

It is the final stage. It is the stage when improved motor skills are displayed. The spirit of competition pervades throughout the period of such a play; the motive, working behind the motor activities, happens to be to secure a place of importance in society. Social status is among the important needs of a man. What a man feels about such a need, how seriously he persists in fulfilling that need—would depend upon his emotional character; and all this also affects as an important factor in the emotional development of a man. "Aggression is simply additional social mechanism operating in peer-interactions".

A strong intra-group affectional relationship develops. Every member of the group, is bound to all the other members of the group in an emotional tie. "The in-groups cohere against out-groups. Though, gradually, friendship develops among members of different groups; living together, playing or indulging in activities together, engenders relationships. Nonetheless, when a member of one's own group is threatened, all the other members of the group will unite to protect him, to rescue him, an evidence of *esprit de corps*.

The spirit of competition pervades throughout the period of such a play; the motive, working behind the motor activities, happens to be to secure a place of importance in society.

Suitable playful environment is helpful in a proper emotional growth. Suitability of a play is a relative term; it is relative to age and sex. By the time, the child is five years old, he or she starts preferring the company of the like-sexed playmates. Play is an important social behaviour; it is predominately an infantile behaviour which persists into adolescence, but continuously grows weaker with age. Play also shows the continuance of affectional ties which bind those, who are together in playful activities.

SOCIAL DEPRIVATION AND EMOTIONAL GROWTH

Many experiments have been conducted to study how social deprivation has its adverse effect on emotional growth. Monkeys were subjected to two kinds of social deprivation, partial and total. In the first kind, they were deprived of the close company of other monkeys but were kept where the other monkeys were in view. In the second kind, they were kept in such an isolated place, where none of their species could be seen; not even any animal was in view. A period of such a total deprivation, when prolonged as long as three months, left the monkeys with a sort of emotional shock. This proves that a social life knit with affectional fibres, is must for a proper emotional growth.

Many experiments have been conducted to study how social deprivation has its adverse effect on emotional growth.

In the experiment with monkeys, mentioned above, the monkeys were found to be self-clutching and crawling. When after a three-month-long total social-deprivation, they were allowed contacts with other monkeys, nearly of their own age, for a period of 30 minutes on each day, they very rapidly established effective social relationships with their peers.

Gregariousness is an instinct among the fourteen ones enumerated by McDougal. Though, the theory of instincts may not be enjoying acceptance among the modern psychologists, nevertheless, it tells that in almost all living beings, with individual differences, (though a few species are the exception) there is a strong feeling for living in a group of their own species. The feeling being so strong, as illustrated above in case of monkeys, it should be taken to be an emotion for social living in case of human beings, among whom the feeling happens to be the strongest.

Gregariousness is an instinct among the fourteen ones enumerated by McDougal.

Figure 11.3
A stimulating family environment can provide very rich experiences for the development of the children.

A child develops because of his reactions to the stimuli that his surroundings, both social and physical, provide to him. So, when a child is isolated, or is not living in a wholesome social environment, which is stimulating enough to make the child react fully and in a proper way (Fig. 11.3), he would not be developing emotionally, too, as his cognitive and motor development would suffer. Using the terms as used by the psychoanalysts, we may say that till the time, the child is living at the stage of ID, it would not be requiring the company of others of its society, but if it is to cross over to the stage of ego, then for the satisfaction of his ego, he would need the company of others of his society, beginning with his mother and moving towards the widening society consisted of his peers or classmates of the nursery level.

What has been described so far, proves Love to be the master emotion. Its forms may be different, in different situations, and in relation to different persons. A child's love for his mother or father, is filial love; that of parents towards the child, is parental love; love among brothers and sisters is fraternal love; and love for one's own self, is self-love. Though a female child's liking for her father, and, of a male child, for his mother, has been described by Freud, because of Electra Complex and Oedipus Complex respectively; and an overwhelming fondness for one's own beauty, is narcissism.

The source of energy for competition, is self-love, or, motive for social status, a demand of one's ego; or it may be *Esprit de corps*, which shows one's strong love for one's group.

LOVE

As mentioned earlier, Love is a Master Emotion; it is a key to the desired emotional development of a child. Many important social and moral qualities have their origin in it. Many animals, besides human beings, also have Love as a strong emotion; it affects their reactions and behaviour immensely. Here, we shall, particularly, see how the emotion of Love develops during the third to the fifth year of childhood; in what different forms it expresses itself in reference to different persons and situations; and how it is important in the development of different social and moral qualities.

If we consider the patterning of maternal affection, we find it to be changing through three stages. The first is the Protection Stage, when the

Figure 11.4
The elder sibling cannot feel elderly unless the younger one is four years younger to her.

mother's affection is total and fully caring. She looks after three functions in regard to the baby (*i*) feeding, (*ii*) maintaining proper body temperature of the baby, and (*iii*) handling the body's eliminative needs.

The second is the Transitional or Ambivalence Stage, when the mother wants her child to have less physical contact with her. She allows exploratory movements of the child to increase. Of course, her protective attention would be required more now. In the beginning, the number of negative responses of the child may be quite high, but the number of the same goes on decreasing as the child grows older; his skill in avoiding punishment increases along with decrease in physical contacts with his mother.

A necessary step in the process of socialisation of all mammals is the child's/young one's lessening dependence on its mother. How the mother weans away the child from the latter's habit of clinging to his mother, is a matter of skill—good mothering goes a long way in the process of the child's development. The child's decreasing dependence on his mother, would increase occasions for the child to make exploratory attempts into his physical and social environments. This change in the pattern of maternal love, is the time which would make the child more competent in meeting the problems of his larger world.

The progression of transition depends upon many factors. The main are mother's previous experiences with the child; mother's status in the group; personality variables of the mother, and, the behavioural characteristics of the child. The mother remains vigilant and greatly protective, lest the child should cross the point of danger.

The third is the Stage of Maternal Separation. This stage comes through a series of developments. The stage is the result of a long series of interactions between mother and the infant—it happens to be the cumulative effect of these series. This stage may be considered to be the final stage so far as the emotional development of the child, in its relations with its mother, is concerned. The child has, now, developed his emotional attachment with other members of his family, as well as with his peers and schoolmates. The love, which was previously only filial, has become divergent. Such sort of emotional divergence, is must for the child to grow into a social being. If a nursery level child, continues to be emotionally attached with the same fierce intensity, to his mother, the child cannot be considered to be emotionally normal. However, a sudden separation from his mother, which generally happens on the successive birth of a child before the older child is four years old, harms the emotional growth of the child, thus separated suddenly. The same thing will happen in case of sudden demise of the child's mother. In such a condition, the male parent needs to fill the vacuum to the greatest possible extent. The father (or some elderly sibling) will have to mother the child with an intense maternal affection, otherwise the adverse impact may become a life-long syndrome.

Maternal love loses its previous intensity, as the child advances in its exploratory expeditions, towards other attractive objects and places. "The age-mates become more and more rewarding companions". The mother ceases to be "The sole affectional object of the maturing infant". The peer's affectional tie, nevertheless, cannot supplant motherly affection, but they serve as additional ties (Fig. 11.4). The peer's affectional ties are essential to satisfy the new needs which are now dominant for the growing child. The juvenile also seeks satisfaction for his needs in the company of his peers. The peer affectional system also progresses under a certain pattern, and, through a number of developmental series.

JEALOUSY

A persistent strong feeling against someone, is jealousy. Jealousy is such a self-centred feeling which does not let others possess what the jealous person so dearly wants to keep to himself only. What is thus desired to be possessed, may be a person or a thing. A jealous person feels very envious of the other, who, he is afraid, is possessing that person or thing, or is likely to deprive him of the possession of what he desires to keep to himself only. One who is envious, cannot tolerate even the successes and achievements of the other that he is envious of. Successes and achievements of such a person, would rather, enrage the envious person. The one who is envious of the other, cannot tolerate the well-being of the latter. Jealousy is a burning feeling, and a jealous person cannot live with peace with himself; he may always be thinking of causing some harm to the other or others that he is feeling envious of. Now, we shall deal with jealousy in reference to a child ranging from three to five years of age. It is the age when a modern child, generally, happens to be in a nursery. We shall see here what are the reasons which may cause jealousy in a kid of that age.

> Jealousy is such a self-centred feeling which does not let others possess what the jealous person so dearly wants to keep to himself only.

> One who is envious, cannot tolerate even the successes and achievements of the other that he is envious of.

A nursery school child has to experience a sudden separation from his mother for a quite long period every day. To adjust to this changed situation is not so easy for a child. If the environment of the school is not appealing or affectionate, the separation of the child from his mother, may prove all the more shocking.

In addition to this, if a teacher in a nursery school praises one student too much, loves one too much, or seems to be loving one particular student too much, it may become a cause for envy for some other student or students. And, such an envious child may try to tease or harass one so greatly praised by their teacher. A teacher may encourage a student who does good things, or does good at his school work, or rather, a teacher should praise such a student because such a behaviour of a teacher proves to be a big reward for the student thus appreciated, and would make such a student do more efforts to do still better. Cheering up by a teacher happens to be highly reinforcing.

However, the teacher's praise for one, should not appear to be a humiliation for the other or others. While uttering the words "Good", "Well done", "Quite good", "Excellently done" or so on, he or she should not abuse any other student or students with the words such as "Stupid", "Foolish", "Donkey" etc. The teacher, instead of humiliating others, or putting them to shame, should try to teach them with patience and with a sincere feeling for their well-being that they should also emulate the example of a good student. Sometimes, parents' unwise praise for one of their children, spoils relationship among the siblings. One sibling grows envious of the other because of such a behaviour of the parents. The behaviour of a teacher or of a parent with a child should not be such as to provoke anger of others against such a child. The students who are lagging behind or are weak mentally, should be treated with more sympathy and patience. Treating them harshly, may make them envious of the one who is fast, and, is the subject of praise by one or more teachers.

A child who is grown up enough to understand that in some respects, he is less benignly bestowed upon by Nature than others, he does not appear to be so handsome or cute, is not so bodily healthy or stout; is not so quick in learning a thing etc, he may grow envious of such a lucky one who is benevolently bestowed upon in all these respects; and more so if on account of these, he is more endearingly treated. The only solution in such a situation is that, his natural short comings, in no way, should lead others to treat him with less affection or care. One who is discriminated against, is very much likely to grow vengeance against the one, against whom he is discriminated. In many cases, the behaviour of others, happens to be responsible for the engendering of a feeling of envy, and for its rousing to the level of emotion. The child should always feel that no one is being loved more than he is. Impartiality must appear in the behaviour of the teacher, and in that of the other elders, too. If recognition is to be given to the better performance of someone, and he is to be praised for the same, it should be done in such a way that none else feels humiliated or teased because of that. The teacher should rather involve other students in applauding someone for good performance.

JOY

> Joy is the antithesis of anxiety and fear.

Joy is the antithesis of anxiety and fear. No one likes to be in a situation of fear or anxiety. On the other hand, one likes to be immersed in a situation of joy. In other words, everyone likes to feel happy and seek ways of getting pleasure; joy is the result of an entertaining situation. Joy is such a heightening feeling, a recreating feeling that we see adults expending a good amount of money for a situation of joy.

The first main event that curtails the joy of a child, is that of weaning. It is with great difficulty, that the child has to be adjusted to the changed situation. The second situation, to which the child can adjust, only with much difficulty, is the one when he is separated from his mother, for his nursery school. Only the very affectionate behaviour of the teachers there, can help the child in adjusting to the changed situation. For the first time the child is separated from his home, for such a long period. For the first time, he has to face so many new persons to adjust to. It is a very difficult situation that the child has been put into. If the old belief "Spare the rod and spoil the child", is the rule in the school; and if the school has no broader target to achieve than the 3 Rs, then there would be no scope for joy there. What is badly needed is the parental affection on the part of the teachers to compensate the loss of affection of the mother, and of other elderly members of the family. The situation would be grim if sincere motherly affection is lacking in the teachers of the nursery.

> A school has to provide a joyful ambience for its students.

A school has to provide a joyful ambience for its students. No development of any sort is possible unless the children are free from fear or anxiety. A feeling of joy is very essential for development, may it be physical, cognitive or emotional development. A child, shocked or traumatised because of a sudden deprivation of the affectionate homely environment, or, is otherwise frightful because of the harsh treatment of a teacher, can hardly adjust himself to the school, and no learning can take place. The first motto of every school should, therefore, be to keep the child in a happy mood.

The first need for the joy of the child is that he should be able to indulge in such games or activities, liking for which is so natural to him because of his age and circumstances. In the book of Jean Piaget titled as *Play, Dreams and Imitation in Childhood*, it has been shown that initially, a play is only for the sensory-motor development of the child, but later, it gets significance because of its representational value or imitation. Where a child is restricted from such a play, he would grow unhappy. Both at home and at his nursery, the child should get adequate occasions for play. Nothing can fill a child with more joy than a playful activity. The school, which compels little kids to remain passive while the teacher is busy teaching some lesson to the class, deprives the kids of a feeling of joy. And, so long as the children are sitting passively with a long face, no learning can take place. No development is possible.

A child enjoys activities. It is through activities that he should be taught his lesson. Way to development lies through joyful activities (Fig. 11.5).

Figure 11.5 Colourful festivals, like the Holi, can provide stimulating environment for the children.

Children should never get the impression that the elders are too busy to listen to them. It is with great, sincere interest and patience that the elders should listen to the children. The behaviour of the elders towards young children should not make the latter feel that they are considered of no importance by the elders. The elders should not only listen to them but they should, also, talk with them, play and enjoy games with them—if not often, at least some times.

The parents should see to the physical and emotional needs of the infant. The satisfaction of these needs should be timely and adequate. Only then, the children can remain in such a mood that they can cry and bubble with joy, play frolicsome games and may otherwise be prompted by an emotional explosion of joy.

CURIOSITY

We have dealt with three important emotions above. Now, we are dealing with curiosity, as an emotion. Before coming to the psychological phenomenon of curiosity, it would be proper to rethink what is an emotion and how does it differ from a need or a drive. Now, a need is a want, a physical or psychological state which makes us feel that something is lacking, and, such a feeling makes one behave in a way that the need may be fulfilled. If the behaviour thus, initiated by a need, is surcharged by an intensely aroused feeling, such a state of feeling is called an emotion. Thus, we can say that need initiates an action, drive is the impetus for that action; motive is that which maintains the continuity of that action; and it is the action itself, which indicates the presence of the related emotion. If there is no action or reaction to some external stimulus or to some inner need or urge, presence of an emotion cannot be perceived.

> Need initiates an action, drive is the impetus for that action; motive is that which maintains the continuity of that action; and it is the action itself, which indicates the presence of the related emotion.

Curiosity is a desire to know about something or someone. This desire in its extreme form, with high intensity, grows into an emotion. Then, it makes its subject behave in a strong manner, sometimes in a rash manner,

The elders and the teachers should, rather, treat the phenomenon of the curiosity of the children at their disposal, in such a way that this endowment of Nature, may prove highly beneficial to the children in the process of development, especially, in that of cognitive and emotional fields.

to have an access to the object of curiosity. In such a state of intense curiosity, it is very difficult for its subject to resist himself from behaving in such a manner that his curiosity may be satisfied. Nor, it is easy for others to dissuade or desist him from such a behaviour.

And if, by force, such an intensely curious child is restrained from such a behaviour, which alone can lead to the satisfaction of his curiosity, he would get angry, and behave in an aggressive way to remove the hurdle. If he fails in removing the hurdle, or the hurdle appears to be too big for him to remove, he may become frustrated. Both the conditions are not good for a desirable emotional growth of the child. And, the period of his growth, from 3 to 5 years, is such when the intensity of curiosity happens to be very high.

The elders and the teachers should, rather, treat the phenomenon of the curiosity of the children at their disposal, in such a way that this endowment of Nature, may prove highly beneficial to the children in the process of development, especially, in that of cognitive and emotional fields. The satisfaction of curiosity means learning, the successful exploration of surroundings—both physical and social (Fig. 11.6). The elders and teachers should, rather, encourage such explorations, and, provide the needful facilities for the same. They are to work as facilitators in the explorations of their children.

Figure 11.6
The younger sister is curiously looking at her fingers.

Curiosity when ignored, or way to its satisfaction is thwarted, leads to the development of other emotions, such as anger or grief. Anger and grief, as frequent emotions, have their adverse effect on the emotional growth of the child. Hence, it is in the interest of the desirable emotional development of the child, to provide not only for the proper satisfaction of the emotion of curiosity but to provide such an environment also for the child, where he may grow more curious to know about a lot many new things. And, these things should be such, that the knowledge of which, may prove an important addition to the existing repertoire of the child.

ANGER

Anger shows the strong opposition of a person to an event or situation. It indicates the situation to be hardly tolerable. A strong opposition to a situation which is unjust, or otherwise harmful, is must for survival. However, when we speak of anger, in reference to a child who is not older than five years, then it means irritability, which makes the behaviour of a child aggressive. If a child becomes habitual to resorting to such a behaviour, it would be an indicator of an undesirable emotional growth. To avoid the development of such a situation, the first thing that the elders need to do, is to acquiesce to such of the child's demands where no harm is involved.

It is still too early to expect reasonable thinking from a child. Sometimes, he may insist on taking a particular thing, or on doing something, to agree to which, may cause some avoidable pains or trouble to the elders. Even then, it is in the interest of the proper emotional growth of the child to let him have his own way, provided no harm is involved therein.

There may be many internal causes for the child's irritability. The child may be hungry, or may be feeling thirsty. He may be feeling uneasy because of inadequate protection against inclement weather; or, the room of the child may not be properly ventilated. The child may not have had a full stint of his sleep, or some ailment may be a reason for the child's uneasiness. A state of frequent irritability would be provoking the child to anger, and, thus upsetting the process of his emotional growth.

The behaviour of the mother, and in case of a child ranging between three and five, that of the other elders and teachers, should be such that the child should not feel ignored, or as not getting full affectionate nurturance. ("nurturance"—Murray has used it in his book *Exploration in Personality*). If the elders of the family are too busy to listen to the childlike chats of their ward; are unable to play with the child; the teacher,

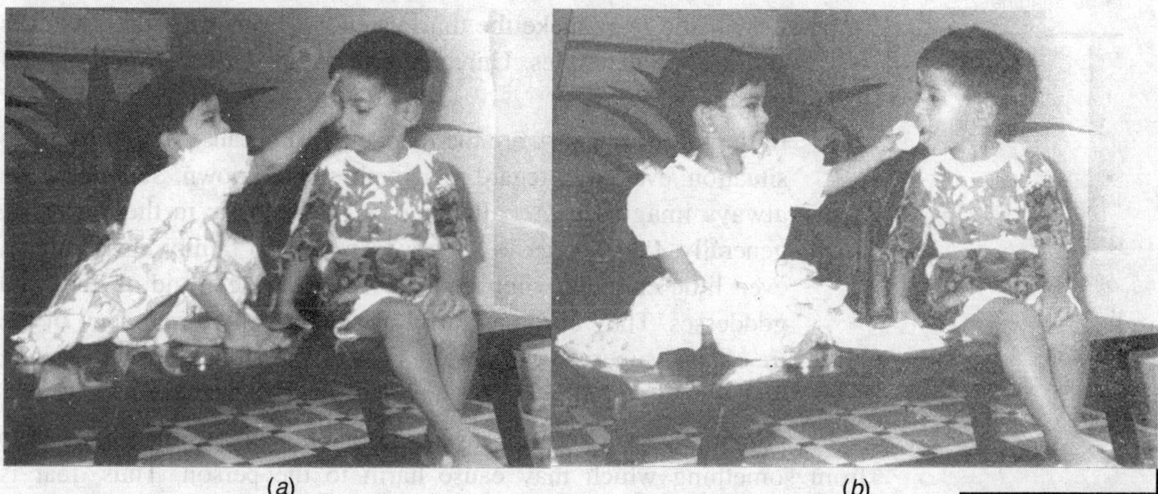

(*a*) (*b*)

Figure 11.7a, b Assigning work of the elders to young children makes them feel honoured.

himself, is annoyed because of the childish manners of the kids, and scolds or roughs them often, then the children too would grow miffed, and, anger would be an overwhelming emotion [Figs. 11.7 (a), (b)].

Getting angry at triffles, is such a characteristic weakness of personality, that it would prove a great hurdle in the progress of a person.

FEAR

One-third of the events, thus recorded, were related to the experience of fear.

In a study, a group of 10-year-old students were asked to record the most important event of their life. One-third of the events, thus recorded, were related to the experience of fear. In some cases, fear was the result of such events as being bitten by a dog (or by some insect etc.); being hit by something, or of such parental warnings as "Stay away from fires"; "watch out for some poisonous or harmful animal or insect". Some cases recorded were just of the symbolic nature. Jersild and Markey found 20 per cent of the children's fears to be imaginary—related to imaginary creatures, to darkness or being alone.

Dunlop GM[2] has classified fears into four categories:

Jersild and Markey found 20 per cent of the children's fears to be imaginary.

1. Realistic fears are the fears related to actual events, or are related to such events which could have happened.
2. Fears related to events which have very remote chances of occurring, are included in this category. The examples are: a child is looking at a lion in some zoo, and harbours the fear of being devoured by the same; is sitting safe on a step of a ladder but entertains the fear of falling down from the same, and so on.
3. Unrealistic fears make the third category. Fears of ghosts, witches etc. are the examples. Unrealistic fears are based on non-existed causes.
4. In the fourth category are the fears evoked because of a mysterious situation; evoked in regard to something not known. Such fears are always imaginary. A child who is alone, or is in the darkness, generally, falls a prey to such a fear. Due to family environment, even little children, younger than five, become afraid of gods and goddesses. They become fearful as they are often reminded of the ire of such supernatural powers. Fear of sin, and fear of the ensuing punishment should also be included in this category.

Fear is not always harmful. Fear makes one run away or protect oneself from something which may cause harm to the person. Thus, fear is an emotion which is essential for the survival of the living beings. A

2. Dunlop, GM. *Certain Aspects of Children's Fears.*

child becomes fearful of something or someone which, in the past, has caused pain or trouble or harm of some sort, to him. The painful experiences of the past would make the child avoid similar situations which were responsible for the bitter experiences. My granddaughter, Twishi, had once fallen down from a wooden horse, she would not ride it, in spite of all our assurances for her safety. If a dog, even once has run after a child, he would grow afraid not only of that particular dog but of all dogs.

Generalisation of a cause of fear, in many cases, would prove a big hurdle in the normal working of a child. So, through teaching the needful related facts, the child needs to be freed from unreasonable fears. He will have to be taught that it is not always the case that one falls down from a staircase or from a wooden horse, and so on. Nor, is every dog fierce and would cause harm. The child needs to be taught, that in most of the events leading to bitter, fearful experiences, the fault was that of the child himself. Teaching a child how to behave for full safety, is an important part of informal education. While lighting a match stick, a child may have realised that it could burn someone; but for that we cannot let our child grow fearful of a match stick even when he is grown up enough to use it.

A young child roughed by a nursery teacher, may generalise the experience, and, grow afraid of all teachers. Examples are there that because of such a sort of generalisation the child fails to pursue his education, and, the entire direction of his life is changed. Fear is a persisting emotion, obsession with it, leaves one non-attentive to other important issues. A child fearful in the class, would fail to pay attention to the lesson of the class. Hence, it is not advisable for a teacher or parents or elders, to adopt fear as a strategy to make the child calm and obedient. It is because of the detrimental effects of fear, that corporal punishment is considered unpsychological. Do not coerce a child to work evoking fear, rather, make the work so interesting that the child is automatically attracted to it, and, continues to attend his lesson with longer span of attention.

Parents who are very strict, harsh and howling would cause the greatest harm to the emotional growth of the child. Only a reasonable strictness of affectionately caring parents, can help in desirable emotional growth. Parents of the first category may leave the child terrified, timid or shy for the entire life. Even when such a child has grown up, he would be feeling shy of the company of others, and, would be of a withdrawing nature.

A young child may feel fearful of someone or something very big and ugly, very fast moving and producing very loud sound. It is only with age that many childish fears become extinct. However, if during childhood, fear had been regularly used by the parents and elderly siblings to silence the child, the child would grow into a timid adult. So, it is in the interest of the proper development of the child that his unrealistic fears, ought to be removed by way of convincing him that there exists no cause for such fears.

Long illness or hospitalisation affects adversely, not only the physical growth but also the emotional development of the child. Not knowing exactly what he is suffering from, he grows fearful "........... he may take it to be some punishment, especially, if parents have related it to some shortcoming of the child. He may revert to earlier social and emotional behaviour; he may react rebelliously; he may enjoy being sick because of the care he receives."[3]

Sometimes, such a situation may prove helpful in the development or emotional maturity. It can be possible only if the child's relationship with his parents, is full of warmth, and, rational, too; the elders, looking after him, have understanding and resourcefulness of the desired level; and the child himself is not emotionally unstable. If all these favourable factors are present, the experience of illness, and for that matter, of any trouble or mishap, may have its constructive effect in the development of emotions ... the child may develop more patience and fortitude in the face of adversities. Of course, this is applicable in case of children who are nearing adolescence.

But, if a child is not progressing normally in motor activities as he grows in age, it would also have its adverse effect on the emotional growth of the child. During early childhood, one should have learnt walking, started taking solid food, talking, controlling elimination, relating oneself to others, and so on. A school-going child should be able to adjust to his school; should learn reading and writing; should learn to get along with his age-mates; should be independent in many of the routine activities. If a child lacks in all these matters even after getting adequate time to adjust himself, or learn, he will start suffering from a feeling of frustration.

---

3. Gofman, E. et al: *The Child's Emotional Response to Hospitalisation*, 1957.

REVIEW QUESTIONS

***Q*.1.** What are the non-genetic biological factors that affect the emotional build-up of a child?

***Q*.2.** What are the three stages that the maternal affection passes through? Describe each of such a stage.

***Q*.3.** (*i*) How a child's growth-bodily, emotional, and socialisation, is related to his plays?

(*ii*) Suppose you are a teacher in a school, what precautions would you take lest jealousy should spoil the emotional build-up of your students?

(*iii*) What is the importance of love in the personality development of your ward?

CHAPTER 12

DEVELOPMENT OF SOCIAL TRAITS

Chapter Outline

- Family
- Friendship
- School
- Motives Behind the Development of Social Traits
- Gender-based Social Learning
- Environment and Social Behaviour
- Sublimation of Undesirable Responses
- Review Questions

"The important milestone in the average child's social development in the first year, is the occurrence of the smile to people, beginning between 3 and 4 months of age...... Smiling response is also subject to the effects of reward and extinction. If the adults reciprocate by lifting up a smiling child, he is more likely to do the same on future occasions, too ... if not rewarded, occurrence will decrease."

Man is a social animal. He cannot live without society. A man without society would be no better than a brute. He develops a lot of qualities only through living in a society. These are the qualities which make his life good for himself, and important for the society that he lives in. While living in a society, he imbibes many traits because of his natural tendency for imitation of his elders and peers; many social traits are inculcated as a result of his reactions to the actions of other members of the society.

"The important milestone in the average child's social development in the first year, is the occurrence of the smile to people, beginning between 3 and 4 months of age...... Smiling response is also subject to the effects of reward and extinction. If the adults reciprocate by lifting up a smiling child, he is more likely to do the same on future occasions, too ... if not rewarded, occurrence will decrease"[1] [Fig. 12.2].

People living in the same society, differ so greatly in their social traits, because of the difference of the other very important units of society, which are family, neighbourhood and school. It is because of the impact of family,

1. Paul Henry Mussen, John Janeway, Jerome Kagan. *Child Development and Personality.*

Figure 12.1
Children too, are social beings.

neighbourhood and/or school, that some grow into luminary personalities of society, whose contribution to society can never be forgotten. On the other hand, because of the other type of family, neighbourhood or school environment, such personalities are also developed, who prove to be a permanent source of trouble to the society.

The important social traits are adaptability, friendship, co-operation, sympathy/empathy, love, social service, sacrifice (for others), courtesy, initiation, leadership, sincerity and obedience. These are the qualities, which are important for the proper functioning of a society. This is why society considers these as very valuable virtues, and strives for the inculcation of the same in its members. Here, we shall see which are the social agencies that work for the inculcation of these social qualities or traits in the child.

FAMILY

Family is the basic unit of a society. A society happens to consist of an umpteen number of families. It is the most important unit of a society. The child is born in a family. He is born to his mother, and, is the result of the combined genes of both of his mother and father. And, as genes are the carrier of heredity, he is born with some of the characteristics inherited to him prenatally. If any or both of his parents possess positive social qualities, it would be easier for the social agencies concerned to develop the same as the child grows up. If the child has congenital negative traits, the agencies will have to struggle hard for liquidating the same, with no prospects for a cent per cent success. Thus, heredity also plays an important role in the development of social traits.

> The process of socialisation of the child because of the following four reasons:
> 1. **Identification**
> 2. **Imitation**
> 3. **Reward**
> 4. **Motive of anxiety**

The process of socialisation of the child begins with the imparting of toilet-training. A child would, gradually, adopt the adult behaviour because of the following four reasons:

1. **Identification** The child desires to be like his parents.
2. **Imitation** Here, the difficulty is that the parent does his/her eliminations in a closed toilet.
3. **Reward** The child is rewarded when he makes a correct response.
4. **Motive of anxiety** This fourth mechanism is, also, very effective—the child learns to prohibit immediate reaction because of anxiety over potential punishment.

The most important functionary in the family, so far the development of social qualities in the child is concerned, is the mother. Her intense parental affection goes a long way in moulding the social character of the child. *Affection or love* has marvellous power to affect its object. This emotion releases so much energy, develops so much patience that the person loving the other, may *sacrifice* anything for the object of her or his love; can undergo all sorts of sufferings for the person that she or he loves. First, we are to discuss the impact of the mother in the development of social traits in the growing child. ... No single person influences so much the development of social qualities in the child, as his mother does. An intense relationship of affection between the mother and her child, may be the foundation stone for the inculcation of a lot many social qualities in the child. Goldfarb, W, on the basis of case studies of orphan children, reared in an institution during the first three years of their infancy, found them to be inferior in all respects—motor, intellectual, language and social development, to those who were brought up by their mothers.

The mother can sacrifice all her comforts and everything for the welfare of her child. Her sleep, rest, food, everything may be neglected if it is so needed to look after and to bring up her child. She does not care for her own health, and always tries to safeguard the well-being of her child. The qualities of love and sacrifice, thus, affecting the emotions of the child, make the child reciprocate his mother with like behaviour. Soon, the feelings of love and sacrifice may be witnessed motivating the mutual behaviour of the members of the entire family. There would be more and more people whom the child, when grown up, will be loving and making sacrifice for, if proper social education is imparted to him.

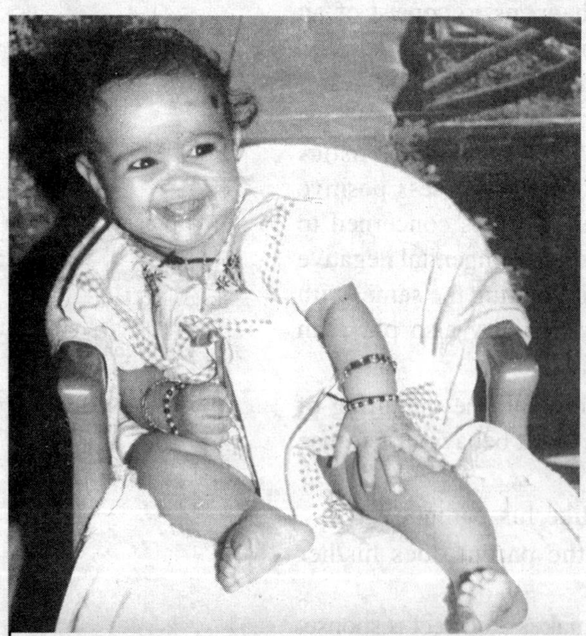

Figure 12.2
Smile is the first step towards socialization.

Love and sacrifice are such moral characteristics which sweeten the overall social milieu as these are the virtues which only can make the stronger support the weaker. In a society, there are always people of different physical, mental and financial capacities; some are very strong, some very weak, and others in between the two. It is love and sacrifice, which can motivate the stronger people to assist their weaker brethren. In every society of the world, there have been examples of love and sacrifice. Prompted by the strong emotions of love and sacrifice, people have shown little attachment to their own physical self, their money, comforts etc. This is the reason that society has been attaching so much importance to these social virtues.

On the contrary, if the child could not get the maternal affection in the beginning, it would affect his behaviour towards others in years to come. The situation may sow seeds of mistrust and hostility, which would spoil his future social relations, too. Rheingold's experiment on 16 babies, not older than 1 year, led him to the findings: "The experimental babies showed more social responsiveness to the experimenters, that is, to the mother, the examiner and the stranger than did the controls; *i.e.,* smile in response to smile, or showed more social reaction to the adults than the normally treated children-the effect being more marked in response to the experimenter. Social acts learned in response to a nurturant and socially stimulating caretaker, will be generalised to other people."[2]

Social acts learned in response to a nurturant and socially stimulating caretaker, will be generalised to other people.

It is through practical examples, that other members of the family can, also, help in inculcating the virtues of love and sacrifice. Father's role in this context, may be second only to the mother. Siblings also have or can have their wholesome effect, in this respect. Elder sisters and brothers also assist their mother in upbringing the younger child (Fig. 12.3). They can do this only, when they, too, feel affection for their younger brother, and, are prepared to make sacrifice for his good.

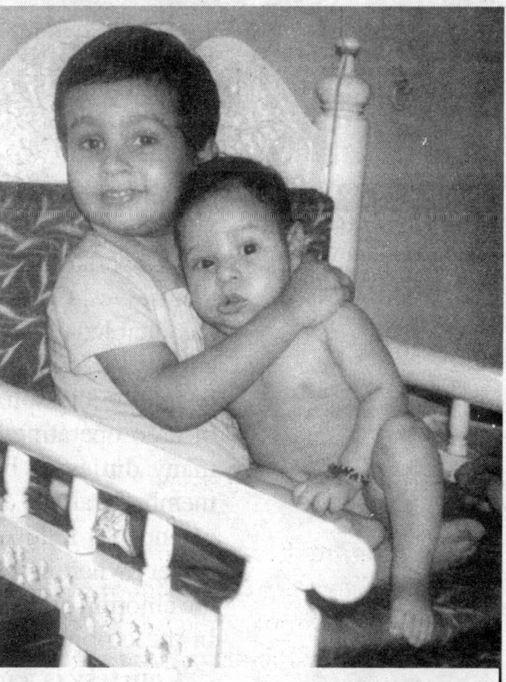

Figure 12.3 Elder siblings also assist their mother in upbringing the younger child.

In an environment, where this kind of, action–reaction, charged with a feeling of affection, does not exist, the child can never grow into a social being in the real sense of the word. The trio authors[3] of the book *Child Development and Personality*, write that if during the first year a child experiences external neglect, "there may be irreparable damage to the child's capacity for development" and "interpersonal relations in the future. His reactions to his mother form the nucleus of his later behaviour toward others."

Judith Rich Harris, a recipient of "George A Miller Award", in her recent book, published in 1998, has made a heretic blast, that Mom and Dad are not paramount, and that, the other kids on the playground, matter more.

Over-protection and over-nurturing are equally harmful to the process of making a child social and developing in him desirable social qualities.

By nature, a child happens to be jealous of others. He cannot tolerate others to possess, what is denied to him, and, what he himself would like to possess. A child who is not yet two years old, may be seen snatching his toy whenever someone else takes it. He may be seen protesting through crying or throwing out his legs and hands, when some other baby is picked up by his mother in her arms, he even cannot tolerate his mother to share her affection with someone else. In most cases, jealousy is "a normal response to actual, supposed or threatened loss of affection." Such sort of jealousy, is a strong

2. Rheingold, Harriet. *The Modification of Social Responsiveness in Institutional Bodies,* 1956.
3. Mussen, Paul Henry; Conger Jane Janeway; Kagan Jerome. *The Child Development and Personality.*

Figure 12.4
The elder siblings are good nurturants too.

antisocial feeling, which would develop into rivalry if no proper channelisation is given to it. Jealousy is a divisive emotion, which is strong enough to split a family, if it continues in the growing child. Sewall, M in the book *Two Studies of Sibling Rivalry: Some Causes of Jealousy in Young Children* has also suggested how to avoid jealousy—good interpersonal relations in the home, consistency in discipline, reassuring affection and continued gratification of the older child's basic needs—are the means.

Its antidote is the feeling of co-operation. From the very beginning, a child should be persuaded to co-operate in his sibling's activities. A child should never [even when he is a school-going child] be taught only to excel others, to go ahead of others at any cost; but should be taught to co-operate in the efforts of others, and thus, assist them in improving themselves. Co-operating with others is an important social quality, which has enabled society to achieve so much, in the form of civilisation and culture. A good family provides a very congenial environment for the child to imbibe the spirit of co-operation. In the family, he sees each member of it co-operating with the other in a work. A family has to perform a lot many duties; it becomes possible, only with the co-operation of each member. Parents and elders should see to it that this important social virtue extends its field of operation beyond the family. That is, into the wider society wherein the child has to move and work later on. The energy, which the emotion of jealousy would be otherwise generating, will, then be utilised in the co-operative efforts being done in the interest of many.

> Courtesy is the axis, around which our manners must revolve.

Courtesy is a must for the smooth functioning of society. It is essential for strengthening the social bonds, which keep the society united. Why is so much emphasis being given on the teaching of manners? It is because, good manners relate one to the other; one may be moved to co-operate with the other, as an impact of good manners only. Moreover, good manners are the yardstick to assess how much civilised a society is. Again, the first school for the teaching of good manners, is the family. And, courtesy is the axis, around which our manners must revolve.

Courtesy is an acquired quality like some other social qualities. The child acquires it, in imitation to others, to his seniors especially. And, when he finds courtesy to be helpful in getting a thing done, he adopts courteous manners. A growing child's experiences teach him that, what cannot be achieved through coercion, can be achieved through requests made politely. Such experiences of the child reinforces his courteous manners. The mother, as the first teacher of the baby, and other elderly members of the family, should teach the child consciously, and painstakingly, good and courteous manners, mostly through their own practice, and, sometimes may be through preaching. Good manners have become a part of the school curriculum.

Obedience to elders, to seniors, is an important social virtue, which the family has a duty to inculcate in a child. If willing and sincere obedience is not there, family will fail to perform its functions. Obedience is the response for co-operation. If the seniors cannot command obedience of their juniors, of their youngers, there will be arbitrariness, pursuit of individual interests only, and breaking down of the social fabric. A chaotic situation would be the result. The psychological analysis would be to the effect that, initially one will obey others only, when, one finds doing the same to be in his personal interest. Obedience elicits immediate commendation. This is a reward for the child which motivates his future behaviour also. So long as one is a child, most of the instructions and orders that the elders of the family happen to give, are usually, in the interest of the child himself. When the child would have realised this fact, the obedience would become more willing and automatic.

If the seniors cannot command obedience of their juniors, of their youngers, there will be arbitrariness, pursuit of individual interests only, and breaking down of the social fabric. A chaotic situation would be the result.

This quality of obedience, needs to be observed in reference to a wider circle of relationships. It is this quality, which can be a guarantee of discipline, in different professional and social establishments. Obedience is quite essential for a smooth working of any organisation. For the development and sustenance of a proper work culture, the habit to obey the orders of the authority will have to be inculcated. No organisation can develop and work if there are no sincere and firm followers to its leaders. We all are well-aware of the importance of discipline in defence, which can only be possible if obedience to the commanding authorities, is unquestioning.

Sympathy/Empathy is the feeling which enables us to feel for those who are in trouble or are the sufferers. To feel concern for those who are the sufferers, to feel grief for those who are aggrieved; or to be sensitive to the sufferings of others, is sympathy. This sympathy binds persons together so that they can work for the relief of one another from sufferings. Lack of sympathy means lack of sensitivity for the troubles and the sufferings of others. If in a society, majority is insensitive to its fellow members, it would not be a closely bound society. It would be, rather, a loosely-knit society where people do not feel sorrow or happiness if the predicament of others, so demands. Sympathy is a fellow-feeling, that is to have similar feelings as the others do. It is such a feeling which strengthens society, through the commonness of feelings of the people of the society. And, when it is so, they can work together for a common cause.

Sympathy/Empathy is the feeling which enables us to feel for those who are in trouble or are the sufferers.

Empathy means to put oneself mentally into the predicament of the others so as to be able to comprehend the feelings and conditions of others. Through teaching and persuasion, the mother and other elders of the child can develop this habit in the child that he thinks about the condition of others; always tries to know what the other or others would be feeling in relation to or in reaction to a certain action, what others would be feeling in a particular situation. A person who behaves always with such a thinking, is least likely

Empathy means to put oneself mentally into the predicament of the others so as to be able to comprehend the feelings and conditions of others.

to do anything unjust or wrong to others. The higher the number of people with a sense of sympathy for others, or who can comprehend the predicament of others through empathy, the better the society would be, where one would be co-operating with others, would be working for the good of others so as to relieve them of the sufferings that they are undergoing. It would be a well-knit and strong society, too.

Members of the family, and especially the mother, can realise the needs of the child because of their empathy with the child. Through empathy, a mother can know when her baby would be feeling hungry, would be thirsty, would be feeling sleepy. Empathy, or mental identification with others, enables one to realise the needs and troubles of others, and, out of sympathy one would do what one can, to relieve the other of his trouble.

The child imbibes the quality of sympathy and empathy as an impact of his mother's behaviour, and of those of the other members of the family. When the child is a little grown up, the mother can teach him through words of mouth that he should realise the difficulties and troubles of others, and behave in such a way that may help the others in being relieved of their difficulty or trouble. It may also be asked of the child what he would feel if his thing is snatched off, or if he is hit as he has done to the other, and so on, to make him realise the sufferings of others. Thus, lessons in sympathy and empathy may be taught. Short tales, illustrating kindness to others out of sympathy, should be told to the child to make him sympathetic to the sufferings of others.

Spontaneity gets a more congenial situation for the development when a child is reared in a permissive family.

Spontaneity or self-learning is also an important social quality. This quality gets a more congenial situation for the development when a child is reared in a permissive family. During the period from 1 to 3 years, the child rapidly improves his motor activities, and realises, gradually, that he himself can manipulate things of his environment—can change the place of an object, can throw it down or elsewhere, can spill water, can scuffle with the papers of his daddy, can make marks on the floor/wall with a pencil etc. These exploratory motor activities engender self-confidence in the child. An understanding parent would handle the situation in such a way, that the child continues with his explorations—a way to enhance knowledge and spontaneity. Contrary to this, if the child's activities are harshly and insensitively inhibited, it would be very difficult to develop the quality of initiation, in his future life.

FRIENDSHIP

Man is social because he can make friends, and can be befriended. Plays are the main means to provide suitable ground where friendship thrives. RC Challman[4] studied 33 boys and girls in their free play situations, and,

4. Challman, RC. *Factors Influencing Friendships Among Pre-school Children.*

identified certain factors which influence the formation of friendship: (*i*) Frequency of contacts—number of times that the children were members of the same group. (*ii*) Sociality—some children easily mix up with others, while some shy off the company of the unknown people. (*iii*) Physical activity–if the physical activity suits one, he or she would join the group. (*iv*) Similarity in chronological age—those of the same age, are more likely to join easily, to one another in a play. (*v*) Sex—like-sexed peers are more likely to develop friendship among themselves. (*vi*) Common interests — those having common interests, feel it more satisfying to play together.

RC Challman studied 33 boys and girls in their free play situations, and, identified certain factors which influence the formation of friendship

Friendship pattern changes with age. Between 2 to 3 years, the number of playmates, increases, though the children then happen to be more interested in play-materials. After that, the strength of friendship increases with increasing age. The child is exposed to new social situations, his skill of making friendship also improves, and he succeeds in befriending a few who were unfamiliar. The spirit of competition, of course, sometimes causes friction but with age the quarrelsomeness–friendship ratio decreases.

SCHOOL

When the child has grown still older, he goes to his school. There, he is taught not only 3 Rs but, gets an environment which greatly helps in making him social. Previously, his interaction was limited to a few members of his family. Now, he comes in contact with a big number of other children, his classmates who are more or less of his own age. He may, also, come in contact with older or younger children. He interacts with them, while earlier, he had been shying off the new faces. His own behaviour is affected by the behaviour of others. He imbibes a lot many new social qualities, and the most important among them, is the *quality to adapt* to others. The child plays with so many other children, he learns to make friends. His living with them in different situations—in the classroom, while taking his tiffin, attending classes of music, drawing, of physical and cultural education and activities and others, too, much increases his adaptability to different situations that as a grown-up member of the society he would have to live in. His intimacy with his peers, his classmates and schoolmates goes on increasing, and members of his family and others, who have experienced his pre-school period behaviour, feel that much change has come about in his behaviour. He has become more understanding, more adjustable and social. As wider grows the circle of movement, the more pliable one grows, and pliancy is essential for one to succeed in society, or rather, to live in society. It is unknowingly impressed upon the child that he has to depend on others for a lot many of his activities and for the satisfaction of many of his needs. This interdependence makes man a social being.

Then, there are teachers who have been entrusted the duty, not only to impart the narrow education of 3 Rs to the child but are the custodians of all the children coming to school for their all round development. The heart is equally to be developed along with the head. The education now, is not limited to 3 Rs only but it has been widened, and is now desired to be the education of 3 Hs, that is Head, Hand and Heart. As, before coming to school whatever, social traits are developed in the child, happen to be, mainly due to the impact of the behaviour of the members of the family; and upon the school-going children, the influence of their teachers happens to be very important. The children observe everything very curiously; are very impressionable, hence the school environment plays an important role in the development of the child. The school happens to be the first, wider social organisation outside the family that influences the development of social traits in the character of the child.

The school happens to be the first, wider social organisation outside the family that influences the development of social traits in the character of the child.

Playing together, the children learn the lesson in *team-spirit*. They study together and happen to be together for a number of school activities. This enhances adaptability and team-spirit in the children. They learn to co-operate with one another. The teacher can, consciously, try to inculcate the spirit of co-operation rather than of rivalry, which is so natural to the children. Competitions should be held between groups, rather than between individuals. Thus, members of the same group would be co-operating with one another, to make the group, a winner. Of course, healthy competitions, even among individuals, may also be encouraged where each should make full efforts to excel others but with no intention to thwart the efforts of others to do the same.

Some cultures are competition-oriented. There, exalting over others, and striving for higher-status, are frequently and consistently rewarded. PJ Greenberg[5] studied the development of the spirit of competition with age. The facts revealed were:

- a two-year-old child does not compete.
- competition begins by the third year.
- competition grows more intense between 4 to 6 years.

Some are highly and violently competitive, others mildly and calmly so. Some are not competitive at all.

- familial background also affects.
- socioeconomic status, also a factor to influence the competitive spirit.

5. Greenberg, PJ. *Competition in Children: An Experimental Study.*

The spirit of co-operation may be raised to the level of sacrifice, when one becomes prepared to suffer for the sake of others' well-being. If children come across practical instances of sacrifice and *social service*, they would be more likely to imbibe such social qualities. Poems, stories, plays and other literary forms may, also, serve as tools, for encouraging children for co-operation, sacrifice and social service. Those whose personalities are devoid of these traits, happen to be egocentric and self-centred. They can contribute little to the society that they live in.

The first object of a child's love, is his mother. Then, he starts loving other members of the family. The school can do much to widen the circle of his love. Attachment to others with a feeling of love, goes a long way in strengthening social solidarity. Again, if the behaviour of teachers towards the school children is warm and affectionate, it would cause a wholesome contagious effect. With the help of poems, narration of historical anecdotes, stories, plays and others, personal love may be widened to include the entire nation into the ambit of love.

All these developments in the child that a family and a school ought to strive for, are less related to cognitive domain, and are more related to the conative aspect of personality. Lop-sided development of the child, cannot be termed as a wholesome development. It may even prove harmful for the individual, and a source of trouble for the society. A well-educated person, who is bodily too very strong, but emotionally or so far his feelings are concerned, is not desirably developed, would be egocentric, selfish, and might be indulging in any sort of deeds, may be unethical and even criminal, to achieve his ends. So, the family and school will have to fulfil as their obligation, the duty of assisting each child in the development of proper feelings. Feelings are what make that aspect of one's personality which we call heart (a colloquialism), so that his personality may have an all round development, and such a development may prove good for the self of the child, and for the society, too.

In a school, *social service* programme ought to be organised from time-to-time so that the children would get practical training in activities of service to the society. It may be in the form of cleaning or even repairing some public place or pathway, may be assisting the administration in controlling traffic, especially in a fair or on occasions when the common people gather in crowds, may be cleaning some reservoir or pond, attending on some patients in a hospital, who have none else to look after them. School and colleges, through their students, may provide very substantial service during periods of natural calamities, such as earthquake, land-slide, flood, famine etc. Such activities would develop feelings of social service among the students, and they would become competent to render such services.

Sympathy and empathy are very effective in establishing close bonds, in moving one to come to the help or rescue of the other. 'Sympathy' is 'fellow-feeling', to feel what the other is feeling, and 'empathy' is identification with the other in such a way that his predicament can fully be comprehended. These are the qualities which should be developed by further evoking feelings, by asking such questions—"What must he be feeling then, under those circumstances?" "What would you have done for the redressal of his grief?" "Whom do you consider responsible for his miseries and why?" and so on. Whenever the behaviour of a student indicates the presence of sympathy in his heart, he should be praised. Children are greatly encouraged when good things in their behaviour get prompt recognition.

Courtesy or proper manners are taught to the students in every good educational institution. They form part of the school curriculum. The importance of good manners in society, cannot be over emphasised. Only through good manners, a harmonious social milieu can be maintained, as lack of the same would generate bitterness and clashes, and this may result in the disintegration of society. Again, both devices, "practice" and "preaching" should be operative, side by side, to achieve the objective.

Good manners also demand obedience to the seniors or elders. The society cannot work if directions of the elders and seniors are not complied with, so the quality of obedience also needs to be inculcated. Only that society can work effectively and properly, where there are good leaders and good followers who sincerely obey their leaders. In the classroom, the students are taught to do as their class monitor asks them to do. They have to obey their teachers, and have to behave in compliance with the instructions of the school authorities.

Society needs good leaders, too. Leaders who can initiate actions, and lead others along with themselves till the objective is achieved. *Leadership* is a social quality. Preparation for leadership needs a psychological approach. Some children by nature, and also because of good physique or stature, can command following or compliance. Such children deserve proper guidance by the elders of the family and teachers of the school. They should be encouraged, too. For class control, the teacher requires a monitor, monitor is the leader of the class. For making the students play in a proper system and with discipline, a captain is the leader. When a student is entrusted the duty of a monitor or of a captain, the qualities of leadership get a boost. A sense of responsibility also develops. For a society to prosper, both capable leaders and sincere followers are needed. School can play a major role in developing the qualities of leadership through a variety of curricular and co-curricular activities. Society can have responsible citizens and competent leaders, only if responsibilities are assigned during the developing periods of childhood and adolescence. Leaders should always be selected whether the students are going out on an excursion, or some scouting or social service camp is being organised. They will learn how to seek co-operation of one another. The leaders will be, further, skilled in the art of organising their fellow-students in groups, in such a way that they can work like a team, co-operatively and in a harmonious manner.

The quality of *initiation* is also essential in a leader. There may be occasions when the leader needs to take his own decisions. He should be so trained that he can do it objectively, in a judicious manner. The more opportunities a student gets for leadership and for initiation, the more developed these qualities would be. The speed of socialisation is influenced by the rate and speed of physical, motor and language development. With age increases the mobility of the child, he can come in contact with more and more persons outside his family. The motor development of the child, enables him to have interaction with more and more of his peers, and with older and younger ones. In such interactions, the role of language is very important. Language is the means of communication. As the linguistic development goes on, the ability and skill for communication also increases, and this all helps in the widening of circle of contact, and the result is that the child grows more and more social.

Language is the means of communication. As the linguistic development goes on, the ability and skill for communication also increases, and this all helps in the widening of circle of contact, and the result is that the child grows more and more social.

Parten[6] has classified the nature of social participation into six categories: (*i*) Unoccupied behaviour; (*ii*) Solitary play; (*iii*) onlooker; (*iv*) Parallel play; (*v*) Associated play; (*vi*) Co-operative or organised play—especially, the plays of the last category immensely contribute in socialising the child, in emulating the spirit of co-operation, team spirit and co-ordination among the children.

In the words of the author, "composite social participation scores were highly correlated with chronological age" [r = + 0.61].

As social interactions become more frequent, they also become more complex. Many aspects of social behaviour, change simultaneously—children may become more aggressive, bossy and competitive, but they may also become more co-operative, friendly and sympathetic.

Sincerity is a moral virtue which is very much praised in every society. The reason being, sincerity is the quality of the thinking and working habit of a person, who would never do anything half-heartedly, or without involving the best of himself, may it demand the severest of labour that he is capable of. One who is sincere in one's work, will also be sincere in regard to time, that is, he will be doing his work on time, would reach his duty point or to any programme on time. His dealings with all, and

6. Parten, MB. *Social Participation Among Pre-school Children.*

in regard to all matters, will always be fair and transparent. And, fairness and transparency are the qualities very much needed, in the unscrupulous consumerist society of today. Shirking from one's duty, irregularity and non-punctuality, and doing a work not to the best of one's ability, to deal with others in matters of money and others, with an intention to serve one's own interest only, even at the cost of others, are the forms of insincerity for which a society has to suffer.

MOTIVES BEHIND THE DEVELOPMENT OF SOCIAL TRAITS

The period of childhood, ranging from 3 to 5 years, is very important for the developing of social traits. The motives, which work in the development of proper social attitudes, are three—1. Praise and Acceptance; 2. Anxiety over loss of Nurturance, and 3. Identification.

1. Praise and acceptance is a sort of nurturance substitute, that can act as an incentive and reward for learning. The behaviour of the child, which is accepted or praised, is reinforced, and is repeated in future. Thus, a child would behave with the motive of winning acceptance or praise from his elders or peers.
2. Anxiety over loss of nurturance also acts as a strong motive, to make **a child behave** in a socially approved manner. A child would be **anxious not to** behave in a way regarding which, his anticipation is that, he would lose nuturance because of that—it is prohibitive learning, and, has great social significance.
3. Identification is the conceptualisation of the various aspects of personality development. "It refers to the process that leads the child to think, feel and behave as though the characteristics of another person or group of people, belonged to him. The term 'model' is used to refer to the person or group with whom the child is identified."

Identification may even be unconsciously done. The process of identification is subtle and often proceeds without conscious awareness. "The phenomena of reflected glory or shame are frequently the products of an identification." If father wins in some competition, the child feels proud of it, as if he himself were a winner. And, when the son commits something wrong, the father feels ashamed of the same. Both ways, it is identification.

In middle childhood and adolescence, identification may not be confined only with individuals but may be with groups and institutions also. If in a match, a school wins, its students are jubilant; and in the same way, they would be depressed if the school loses in a match. "To be identified with a strong parent, can be an important source of security for a young child." Thus, identification is an important natural tendency which leads man to his socialisation. Identification to the model is possible only when (*i*) the child feels that for him, it is possible to emulate the model, and (*ii*) he feels that there are some similarities between him and his model.

GENDER-BASED SOCIAL LEARNING

There are some social characteristics which the society approves in the behaviour of girls only, while there are some others which the society likes to be developed in boys only. It is natural, too, that girls tend to be motivated by models of their own sex, and boys would have inspiration, mainly, from male models. "Sex-typing refers to the adoption of the beliefs, attitudes and activities which the culture defines as appropriate for one's sex."[7] Most boys have their father as their model; and the girls, their mother. Our society does not allow the model to be of the opposite sex, sometimes, it rather punishes for it being so. The father is gratified to see the recreation of his own qualities, attitudes and masculinity in his son; and, the mother that of her qualities, attitudes and feminity, in her daughter.

> Sex-typing refers to the adoption of the beliefs, attitudes and activities which the culture defines as appropriate for one's sex.

But when there is strained relationship between the couple, the child would be in a dilemma, as his attempt to identify himself or herself to either of the parents, would incur anger of the other.

ENVIRONMENT AND SOCIAL BEHAVIOUR

If a child's relationship with his mother is gratifying, he is likely to generalise his positive responses towards his mother, while behaving with others, too. In case, the reverse is the fact, the mother is harsh towards the child, the child would withdraw from social relationships with others. Before the child is three years old, peer's role may not be very important as little reciprocation occurs among children younger than that. From age 3 onwards, the reactions of the children vary so widely, because of their having had different experiences in their respective home environments. In due course, the process of affecting one another goes on in the group situation, and the impact of peer group soon begins to be felt, in the changing patterns of behaviour of each child of the group.

> In due course, the process of affecting one another goes on in the group situation, and the impact of peer group soon begins to be felt, in the changing patterns of behaviour of each child of the group.

7. Mussen, Paul Henry; Conger, John Janeway, and, Kagan Jerome: *Child Development and Personality*.

Figure 12.5 Celebrating anniversaries is also a way for socializing children.

The social behaviours which continue to be rewarded in the new situations of the peer groups, and nursery, become consolidated, while others which are rather, likely to invite punishment, are dropped.

The social behaviours which continue to be rewarded in the new situations of the peer groups, and nursery, become consolidated, while others which are rather, likely to invite punishment, are dropped. In a democratic, freedom-giving, calm and happy home, group contacts are considered desirable, and they are felt to be gratifying. Those who are relatively independent of their adults, are more likely to establish friendship with their peers.

Freud A and Dann S[8] studied the development of behaviour patterns of six orphaned children, who had been growing together with no one else providing warmth of affection to them. A very close relationship developed among them, leaving no room for jealousy against one another. Each was sensitive to the difficulties of the other, and would feel happy in co-operating to remove the same. "These orphans reacted to the first adult, with the same intense feeling of attachment as they had done with one another." Their feelings differed in quality from that of a child towards his mother. Their approach was based on group feelings. The authors further write. "... Their companions of the same age were their real love objects.... This explains why the feelings of the six children toward each other, showed a warmth and spontaneity, which is unheard of in ordinary relations between young contemporaries."

SUBLIMATION OF UNDESIRABLE RESPONSES

106 children were subjects of a case study. The experimental group of the children had been in the nursery school for nine months, and the control group had been there only for a few weeks. The 106 children were divided in these two groups. A comparison of the behaviour patterns of the two groups revealed the changes that had come about during the period of their schooling. The new patterns were indicative of their growing emancipation from their dependence on adults. Undesirable infantile habits were eliminated through a continuous process of change. In most of the cases of the experimental group, now, there were fewer maladaptive reactions, such as avoiding strangers, shirking from notice, giving in easily, gnawing at the nail, tenseness, wriggling, refusing food, enuresis, leaving the work

8. Freud, A, Dann S. *An Experiment in Groups Upbringing*.

incomplete, dawdling with food etc. As many as 60 kinds of behaviours were studied. Schooling immensely facilitates the process of sublimation, making the kids adaptable, improving their routine habits and along with these improvements, there was witnessed a remarkable reduction in social inhibitions and nervous tendencies. Of course, all the children were not improving equally—pre-school family experiences and some other factors may have been responsible for the individual differences that were there. Hattwick BW writes: ".... the influence of nursery school may be greater for social behaviour and routine adjustments, than for emotional traits *per se*."[9]

The impact of the nursery school was evident in the form of advances in sociability, self-expression, independence, initiatives and growing interest in the school environment. Yet, all the schools do not effect these changes with the same speed and intensity, as they differ in their curricular and co-curricular activities, in their teaching methods/techniques and approaches, and in their general atmosphere. The teacher is the most important factor in this regard—"Frequent, warm, friendly interaction with teachers also fostered more leadership, greater constructiveness when faced with possible failure, and a lower incidence of nervous habits."

REVIEW QUESTIONS

***Q*.1.** How can you say that man is a social being? What is the importance of social traits for us?

***Q*.2.** "The important milestone in the average child's social development in the first year, is the occurrence of the smile to people, beginning between 3 and 4 months of age...."

Why "the occurrence of the smile to the people" has been called "the important milestone" by the author, in the process of socialisation?

***Q*.3.** What are the four reasons which make a child 'Social'? Describe each of them.

***Q*.4.** What is the importance of the peer-group in the desirable and non-desirable social development of a child?

***Q*.5.** What are the important social-traits that a family should be expected to inculcate? Describe each in brief.

***Q*.6.** How far do you agree with the views of PJ Greenberg regarding the spirit of competition as a social emotion? Discuss.

9. Hattwick, BM. *The Influence of Nursery School Attendance Upon the Behaviour and Personality of the Pre-school Child.*

CHAPTER

13 MORAL DEVELOPMENT

Chapter Outline

- **Motives leading to Moral Development**
- **Dos and Don'ts for a Child**
- **Self-control is Crucial in Morality**
- **Current Theories of Morality**
- **Sex Differences in Conscience Development**
- **Other Aspects of Moral Development**
- **Review Questions**

The sense of morality is the sense of right and wrong; it is conscience; an internal censor, and is the result of experience that the child goes on having.

Mother's approval or disapproval of the child's action or behaviour proves to be the foundation stone whereon develops the child's conscience, the internal guide for distinguishing right from wrong.

A child is neither MORAL nor IMMORAL, he is AMORAL (Fig. 13.1). The sense of morality has still not been developed in it. Every behaviour of it, is the result of some instinctive urge. A psychoanalyst would term it, the stage of ID. The sense of morality is the sense of right and wrong; it is conscience; an internal censor, and is the result of experience that the child goes on having. These are the experiences that the child has in its social environment. Its social environment is made up of the behaviours of the members of its family only and, thereto, the role of its mother is most important. Social environment is the result of actions and reactions (to the actions) of the people living together. Barring the reflex actions or unlearned actions of the young child, every other action of it, bears the impact of the behaviours of its family members; and, particularly, that of the mother. Mother's approval or disapproval of the child's action or behaviour proves to be the foundation stone whereon develops the child's conscience, the internal guide for distinguishing right from wrong.

MOTIVES LEADING TO MORAL DEVELOPMENT

By the time, the child is two years old, we can feel three motives working behind the behaviour of the child—(*i*) fear of rejection; (*ii*) desire for acceptance or praise; and (*iii*) identification. The fear of rejection makes the child stop himself from doing something; and the desire for acceptance, to behave in a particular way. The effect of the first, is prohibitive in nature, and, that of the second, is inducive—it induces the child to behave in such a way that is likely to be praised. But motive behind such a prohibitive or positive behaviour happens to be effective, in proportion to the degree of nurturance of the mother, whose rejection or acceptance/praise is important for the child. The more nurturant or affectionately caring the mother is, the more valuable becomes her acceptance praise for the child; and more will be the child's fear for the rejection by his mother. Child rearing attitudes of the mother, have a major role to play in the formation of conscience. The mother can take a number of steps to encourage or discourage a certain behaviour. She can (*i*) distract the child; (*ii*) directly tell of her acceptance or rejection; (*iii*) punish him by way of spanking; (*iv*) threaten withdrawal of love, or (*v*) she can make the child suffer maternal deprivation. However, as mentioned above, the degree of efficacy of her step, or, for that matter, of any of the members of the family, would depend upon the fact how warm one is towards the child.

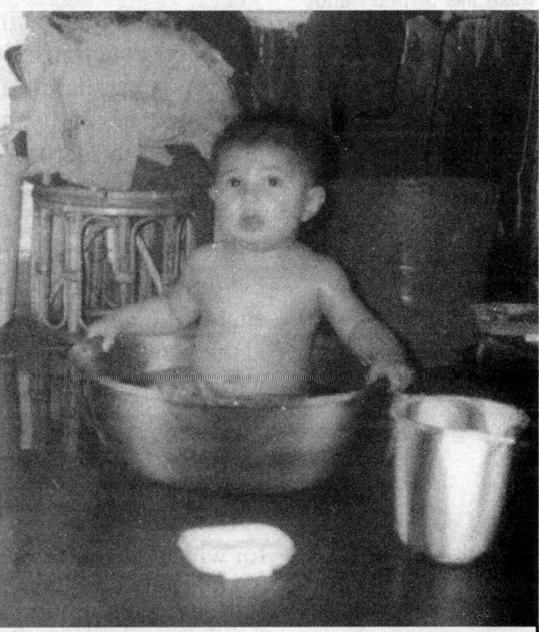

Figure 13.1
A child is amoral.

It is the child's fear of rejection or/and desire for acceptance/praise of the mother or of the other elders, which first develop him from the stage of Id to the stage of Ego. Id is the stage, when the child has no consideration of right and wrong. It is prompted by animal instincts to behave like some animal to satisfy its hunger and other such needs. The child would attempt for an immediate satisfaction of his need. The stage is, still, to develop when it would start thinking about the reactions of its nurturant/nurturants to its behaviour. That would be the beginning of the stage of the development of Ego—as Sigmund Freud has explained it. Prohibitions by the elders—"Don't do this", or, "Don't do like this or that", and the standards of behaviour of the elders are important factors in the development of Ego. Ego is the stage when the child realises the existence of "I"; and desires the acceptance of "I" by those whose nurturance he values. Now, he starts behaving what is in the interest of "I" or his own "self". And, his greatest

By the time, the child is two years old, we can feel three motives working behind the behaviour of the child—(*i*) fear of rejection; (*ii*) desire for acceptance or praise; and (*iii*) identification.

Prohibitions by the elders—"Don't do this", or, "Don't do like this or that", and the standards of behaviour of the elders are important factors in the development of Ego. Ego is the stage when the child realises the existence of "I"; and desires the acceptance of "I" by those whose nurturance he values.

interest lies in the acceptance of "I", in the praise of "I" by the elders, whose affection he values most.

The third motive, Identification, for the pre-school child, appears in the imitative behaviour. Imitative behaviour of the child leads to his development, as well as, prepares him for his acceptance by the elders. The elders would accept only such an imitative behaviour of the child, which is in conformation to the set standards of behaviour of the society. Identification, through emulation, begins by the time child is seven years old. Identification becomes the same as the hero worship. For the female child, mother becomes the ideal for identification, and, for the male child, his father. The child emulates the qualities of his ideal or hero. Thus, the three motives—fear of rejection, desire for acceptance/praise and identification, are the important factors in the development of conscience or Superego, which is the internal guide to enable the child to distinguish right from wrong. Conscience or Superego is the censor which checks one not only from wrong-doing, but also from wrong thinking. One feels guilty when an idea or thought, inconsistent with the conscience or superego, comes to one's mind.

The above-mentioned three motives, working into the development of conscience, without which no moral life is possible, can be effective only in reference to someone having nurturant care for the child. In other words, for what the elders consider to be the moral development, a sincere affection on the part of the elder/elders of the family, looking after the child, is a must. If mother is not affectionate enough, the child would neither have fear of rejection by her, nor would he desire for acceptance or praise by her. Now, the child's reaction would much depend upon the nature of nurturance that he gets. Behaviour of the mother towards her child may be very affectionate, of highly nurturant kind; or it may be harsh and cruel; or, she may be indifferent or insensitive towards the child. A fourth situation is also possible, where the mother may be fondly attentive sometime, but very strict at other times. Now, the important thing to see is what type of behaviour of a mother, or of an elder, would be more suitable for developing the child into such a member of his society, who may be considered morally sound.

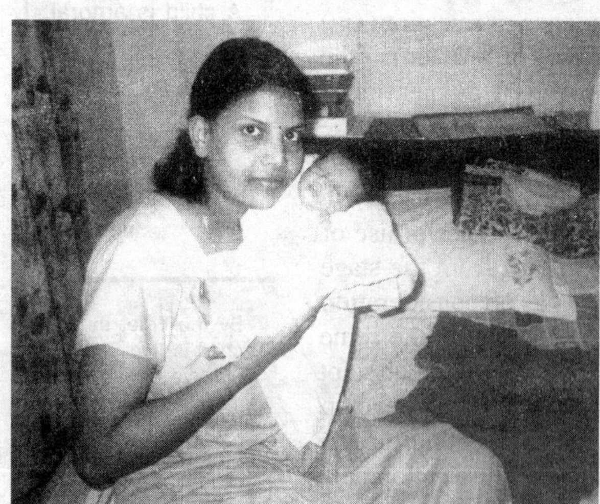

Figure 13.2
There is nothing like mother.

The authors[1] of the book, *Patterns of child rearing*, write, "If the mother is relatively cold to begin with, than using withdrawal of love, should have little effect on conscience development..... The children most prone to behave in the ways we have considered indicative of having a well-developed conscience, were those whose mothers were relatively warm, and

1. Sears, RR, Maccoby, EE, Levin, H. *Patterns of Child Rearing*.

who made their love contingent on the child's good behaviour (Fig. 13.2). These were the children who truly were risking the loss of love when they misbehaved."

For the development of Conscience or Superego, it is essential that:

(*i*) the child must get affectionate care;

(*ii*) the mother, or anyone else looking after it, must be neither too much permissive nor too prohibitive—a just discipline ought to be maintained;

(*iii*) if the mother is very strict sometime while at other time she is too much indulgent-such an inconsistent behaviour would obfuscate the situation, and would not be so helpful in the development of conscience. The child should be able to know, in advance, which of his behaviour/action, would arouse what kind of reaction from his mother, or from the one nurturing him;

(*iv*) a social environment where there is/are some nurturant/nurturants to react to the actions of the child, is a must for the development of morality in a child. Again, it is a particular society which sets standards of behaviour, called moral behaviour. "Moral standards refer to rights and wrongs of the child's society, the do's and don'ts."[2]

DOS AND DON'TS FOR A CHILD

Now, what are the dos and don'ts for a child which are considered important for the development of moral character:

		[*i*] should not be aggressive or destructive;
		[*ii*] should obey the elders;
for the	:–	[*iii*] should be amiable to playmates;
children	:	[*iv*] should be quiet at dinner;
who are +4	:	[*v*] should speak the truth;
	:–	(And the children who have grown still older—)
		[*vi*] should be sexually modest.

[*i*] First, let us consider what are the possible reasons which may make a child aggressive or destructive. A child needs feeding when it is hungry. If this basic need of the child is not satisfied timely, it would upset the child. And, if indifference to the basic needs of the child is something common in the family, the child would grow aggressive in nature. He would become recalcitrant—would not follow the directions of the elders, or, may be doing just contrary to what his elders want. Care should be taken about the clothes and cleanliness of the child. There should be proper ventilation in his room. The physical environment should be wholesome for the child. Parent or nurturants should always be affectionately careful towards the child. If a mother is very strict or harsh to an erring child, it would not help in making a child modest or obedient—a harsh behaviour may prove

2. Mussen, PH, Conger, JJ, Kagan, J. *Child Development and Personality.*

counter-productive. If an elderly family member is harsh, often rough to an erring child, it would be instilling aggressive characteristics in the development of the child's personality. If a child wants to play with something, and if it is not harmful for him to do so, his demand should pleasantly, and immediately be met. A child cannot tolerate the deferment of the gratification of his desire; [though a training should be imparted later, to make the child tolerant to the deferment of gratification of his wants]. If the child has wetted the bed, the child should not be made to keep lying on the wet bed. The mother should immediately change the wet cloth/clothes and/or bed sheet. The mother's indifference or insensitivity to the child's need or trouble, would naturally make the child peevish or aggressive. Nor, should the mother be too strict in matters of toilet-discipline, especially, when the child is still not even two years old.

The likings of the child should be accorded due importance. Indifference to his likings, or, doing just contrary to what the child likes, would make him irritated. If this thing happens often, the child would grow habituated to behaving aggressively to get his demands met. Fear or anxiety of punishment may make the child frustrated, and result in complex effects. Sears, after observing the aggressive responses of the children (*i*) who had non-punitive mothers; (*ii*) who had mildly punitive mothers, and, (*iii*) who had highly punitive mothers, concluded:

".... the best way to prevent aggression in a child is to discourage him, punishment seems to have complex effects. While, undoubtedly, it often stops a particular form of aggression, at least momentarily, it appears to generate more hostility in the child and to lead to further aggressive outbursts at some other time or place, ... they (parents) are providing a living example of the use of aggression at the very moment they are trying to teach the child not to be aggressive."

[*Patterns of Child Rearing*]

".... the best way to prevent aggression in a child is to discourage him, punishment seems to have complex effects. While, undoubtedly, it often stops a particular form of aggression, at least momentarily, it appears to generate more hostility in the child and to lead to further aggressive outbursts at some other time or place, ... they (parents) are providing a living example of the use of aggression at the very moment they are trying to teach the child not to be aggressive."

Too much fear and anxiety, may make the child very frustrated and neurotic, and such a one would prove a highly problematic case, from morality point of view also.

Anna Freud refers to the adoption of the behaviour of the aggressive model with the label "IDENTIFICATION WITH THE AGGRESSOR"—the motive behind such an identification happens to be anxiety of the threatened aggression, differentiating it from the developmental identifications, Mowrer has called the process as "defensive identification." [Sanford, RN *The Dynamics of Identification*, Psychol. Rev; 1955, 62].

A child suffering from some physical disability, may also grow aggressive, Myerson writes, "Emotionally, he may be unable to satisfy his needs for security, affection and success, and thus, be driven to compensate for the lack either by withdrawing or by showing aggressive behaviour." [Some youngsters may be suffering from body dysmorphic disorder (B.D.D.), a severe preoccupation with an imagined or slight defect in appearance may lead to drop out of school, shun social contacts, and even commit suicide].

Chronic diseases, also, have emotional implications. They may interfere with the steady process of personality development and emotional stability. (Freed, EX and Cruickshank, WM *The relation of cardiac disease to feelings of fear*); and, may make the children rebellious. About a neurologically damaged child, Bradley, C writes that such a child would be impulsive, hyperactive, irritable, distractable, unpredictable in his behaviour, and has difficulty in abstract thinking.

Chronic diseases, also, have emotional implications.

[*ii*] Elders would, naturally, want a child to learn to behave as their society considers it proper to do. And, the child's behaving in an inconsistent manner, may be construed as disobedience. Little consideration is given to the maturity level of the child. We, the elders, often forget that still the child is dominated by Id. Self-esteem is, still, to be developed in him; and the stage of superego is still farther beyond. The elders need to be conscious of the fact that the child is still passing through the stage of amorality—a stage when the child should not be considered immoral for any action of his; nor should morality, as elders take it to be, be expected of him. In no case, the elders' treatment towards the tender child, should grow harsh or rough. A child would care for the pleasure, of that only, who is greatly nurturant to it. Nor, would inconsistent reactions of the elders help in improving the child's behaviour.

If repeatedly such things are expected of the child, for which he is not matured enough to accomplish, he would develop a habit of disregarding the demands of his elders. The main difficulty is caused because of the fact that the child generalises his reaction to other elders also—so the child should be so treated that only desirable reaction may be elicited from him.

What is very much essential is, the adults' sensitivity to the child's mental state of tension, caused because of his separation from his mother. And, also of the difficulty of the child in adjusting to the situations of his first nursery school, and, to his playmates and others. Adjustment to school is often an emotional strain, "first grade children frequently suffer from lack of appetite, sleep disturbances and loss of weight as a consequence to tension. The adults' attitude should be very sympathetic and helpful to these children, otherwise, they may grow more disobedient and indifferent to the demands of the adults.

What is very much essential is, the adults' sensitivity to the child's mental state of tension, caused because of his separation from his mother.

Punishment to the children may make them adopt defense mechanism, which would invite more punishment, cause fear to the child—and a vicious circle would be created.

The important thing to remember is "..... that uncurbed drives were no better than completely suppressed ones." A judicious balance is needed.

If adult patterns are forced upon children, ignoring their basic needs and capacities, antagonism or neuroticism will be the result.

If adult patterns are forced upon children, ignoring their basic needs and capacities, antagonism or neuroticism will be the result.

[*iii*] We expect the child to be amiable to his playmates; it is taken as a desirable indicator towards a proper socialisation, and, moral development of the child. Up to the age of three, the child has very little reciprocal plays. He mostly plays alone with his toys. After 3, the importance of playmates, grows continuously in the socialisation of the child, so it is desirable that the child must have an amiable relationship with his playmates. His experiences with his playmates, are significant in his moral development also. Here again, the child's learnings at home, are important. His reactions to other social situations, reflect his learnings at home. The pattern of behaviour that is rewarded in the home situation, is likely to be rewarded in other situations also.[3]

It is in the self-interest of the child, that he becomes amiable to his playmates in reciprocal plays, otherwise he would not be able to continue the play which he is finding so interesting, so entertaining. Thus, he learns sharing his interest with the interests of others. This may prove as an initial step towards the development of the spirit of accommodation, which is so essential for the development of moral traits.

Some behaviour-patterns which were rewarded in home situations, are also liklely to be rewarded in the nursery school situations by his playmates also, while others may not be rewarded by the group of playmates, or may provoke punishment. The behaviour-patterns which do not get favour with his playmates, are likely to be reduced in strength, and, eliminated eventually.

Children, depending too much on adults, care for the rewards by adults only, and such children are likely to be rejected by their peers. Contrary to this, "Youngsters who have not experienced gratification in their social contacts with adults, are also likely to fall into the dragnet of bad company, if there, the environment is not so dull, or, otherwise rewarding."[4]

The study of Freud and Dann of six orphaned children, also brings out the fact that early experiences of the children, play an important role in the development of amiability in them. There was great attachment to one another among them. They could not tolerate separation from one another—there was complete absence of competitive rivalry and jealousy among them. Their common experiences of extreme privations in concentration

3. "Into (the) wider community the child carries whatever behaviour equipment he has succeeded in developing as a part of his growing personality, in the more intimate and protected home environment. He will have learned at home some of the essential social techniques used in associating with other persons in group situations; and in behaving himself as the member of a group." [Cameron, N. *The psychology of behaviour disorders*].

4. Freud, A; Dann S. *An Experiment in Group Upbringing.*

camps, had made them so intimate or emotionally attached to one another. MORALITY DEPENDS UPON THE NATURE OF EMOTIONAL BUILD-UP. "These children reacted with the same intense feeling of attachment with the first adult that they came in contact with. Their approach was based on group feelings, and was different from that of a child who has contacts with the mother only. The feelings of these children, were positive; they had grown sensitive to the needs and feelings of others; which is so essential for the development of amiability.

Amiability is possible where there is no jealousy. There are some factors which are likely to make children jealous:

> Amiability is possible where there is no jealousy. There are some factors which are likely to make children jealous.

- If another sibling is born to the mother of a child, who himself is four years or so. It is natural that the new born child would seem to the elder one, as to have snatched his mother's affection to which he had so far been the sole claimant. But a four-year-old or older child may feel affection for its younger sibling.
- If a partial treatment is meted out to a child, giving preference to one against the other, may be because the mother is a step-mother; the younger child is more handsome, or less aggressive or irritant; or because of preference—the elder sibling being a female child; or because the mother gives more affection to the younger because of its age; the child which feels to be getting less affection, would grow jealous of the child which gets or seems to be getting more motherly affection.

  Jealousy, thus engendered at home, may be generalised at the pre-nursery and nursery stages when the child lives and plays with other children outside the house.
- The elders at home, and, the teachers in the school, should not pass very plain and blunt remarks against a child, while applauding the other. It would make the former child jealous of the latter. I have seen such a jealous child spoiling the exercise-book of the latter, or trying to otherwise harm him.

Sewall[5] has given some symptoms of jealousy in pre-school children:

1. **Aggression** A jealous child would react aggressively against the one that is the object of his jealousy. He would not obey the demands of such an elder, who favours the object of his jealousy, in preference to him. He may try to harm the object of his jealousy.
2. **Regression** A jealous child, a child threatened by actual or supposed loss of affection, may regress to infantile behaviour of a child much younger than him. Such a child may refuse to eat food, may lose bladder and bowel control.

5. Sewall, M. *Two Studies in Sibling Rivalry. Some Causes of Jealousy in Young Children.*

3. **Withdrawal** A jealous child would withdraw from the elder, whose behaviour is actually responsible for causing jealousy against someone else. Not only this, such a child may withdraw to himself, in isolation, from others also, who in no way are related to his present state of frustration.
4. **Indifference** Far from being amiable to his playmates, a jealous child, when feeling himself helpless in improving the situation in any way, in his favour, grows so frustrated that he loses all interest in the development of events about him—no reaction is elicited, howsoever stimulating an occasion may be.

A child suffering from these four symptoms, should be taken as a case, demanding special measures for his desired socialisation and moral development.

Sewall[6] found that a large number of the children who were suffering from jealousy, were the first born. They were emotionally insecure and upset. Such children, if not treated in time, can never grow into amiable playmates for their peers. The author has suggested the following four measures:

(*i*) Spend more time, exclusively, with the older child.
(*ii*) There should be good interpersonal relations at home.
(*iii*) There should be consistency in discipline—if the elders are sometimes very strict while at other times undesirably permissive, it would not help in nurturing proper discipline.
(*iv*) The basic needs of the older child too, should be gratified always, without avoidable delay.

As social interactions become more frequent, their nature gets more importance in the development of social/moral qualities. Such is the importance of friendship, that many aspects of social behaviour undergo changes, as a result of its impact. Along with friendship, many other social qualities, such as co-operation, sympathy, sacrifice, patience, tolerance, also develop on the playground.

(*i*) Too strong competitive drives; (*ii*) prejudice; and (*iii*) some other undesirable responses are the very formidable blocks in the development of amiability.

(*i*) Too strong competitive drives; (*ii*) prejudice; and (*iii*) some other undesirable responses are the very formidable blocks in the development of amiability. Competition is unhealthy, if the child's own "estimation of himself and of his worth is tied to the extent to which he can undo others."[7] Though to a certain extent, competition may be necessary for the accomplishment of something important, yet, too much emphasis on it may turn one bitter, vengeful and callous.

6. Sewall, M. *Two Studies in Sibling Rivalry. Some Causes of Jealousy in Young Children.*
7. Jersild, AT. *Child Psychology.*

Prejudice means lack of objective assessment of cause–effect relationship. A study was made in America with 5 white and 5 Afro-American children as subjects. The findings proved that physical difference is also a cause for making one prejudiced. Socioeconomic status, differences in family backgrounds, intelligence, parental attitude, and even age, are the other factors which may cause prejudice.

Prejudice means lack of objective assessment of cause–effect relationship.

There are some other kinds of responses, too, which would make the child maladjusted in the group of his playmates, and, in other social situations. Hattwick, BW[8] divided 106 children into two groups—the experimental and the control ones. The experimental group had attended the nursery school for nine months, while the control group only for a few weeks. He wanted to study the impact of the nursery school in developing sociability/adaptability in children. He rated the children, on 60 kinds of behaviour-patterns. Fewer maladaptive reactions were found in the children of the group which had attended the school longer—avoiding strangers, shirking from notice, giving in easily, twisting their hair, tenseness, playing with finger, wriggling, refusing food, enuresis, leaving task incomplete, dawdling with food are some of these maladaptive reactions. Such a reaction may be found in a child who lacks in amiability with his playmates; and if corrective measures are not taken timely, may cause difficulty in developing adaptability. A maladjusted child is less likely to develop moral traits in his behaviour. Development of tolerance is essential for the moral and social qualities of adaptability and amiability.

(*iv*) Should be quiet at dinner. When a child feels hungry, he would make an urgent demand for his gratification. And, if no immediate gratification is made, or some convincing explanation presented, for the little unavoidable delay, in case of children who are not younger than plus 4, undesirable reactions would be there. In order to avoid the development of such reactions, the following alternatives are desirable:

(*a*) Do not delay in gratifying the hunger or any of the other basic needs of the child; it would be better if timings are fixed for his feeding.

(*b*) While feeding the child, or meeting any of his demand, a touch of affection should always be present.

(*c*) The child who is not younger than two years of age, should be taught table-etiquettes, which include, that while taking one's food, one should not be noisy or quarrelling with others. Food should be taken quietly and in a pleasant mood. Table-etiquettes also, demand that one should take one's food neatly—without either greasing or spoiling the mouth, finger or the spot where food is taken.

8. Hattwick, BW. *The Influence of Nursery School Attendance upon the Behaviour and Personality of the Pre-school Child.*

Proper food habits are taken as an indicator of the development of good personality traits.

Great is the importance of diet so far health—both physical and mental, is concerned. It has been a firm belief with the Indians, that one's mind would be as the food one takes. In the *Gita*, one of the most important books of the ancient India, food has been classified into three kinds, each liked by the people of different (moral) categories—*Satwik* (modest, disciplined and enthusiastic), *Rajsi* (short-tempered, rash, greedy and violent), and *Tamsi* (mannerless, rude, wicked....), respectively.

(*v*) Should speak the truth. Speaking the truth is an important moral quality, highly desirable in society. One who tells a lie, is not liked by anyone. No one believes him. So, from the very beginning, we should be careful that the child does not tell a lie.

Notwithstanding, we should take a child's telling a lie, with a due consideration to his tender age. As mentioned in the beginning of this chapter, a child happens to be amoral; because of his immaturity, he can commit nothing immoral intentionally. But we find the child to be telling lies very often. My three-year-old granddaughter, who very often tells innocent lies and quite interestingly—"I have got fever", (because it would make everybody behave with her more affectionately, more caressingly); "I have brought these shoes from bazaar", or, "I will bring shoes for you (to her grandfather) from bazaar", (in order to enjoy a feeling of being important; of being able to do things which only the adults can do). If the child sees a grown up to be sad, he may ask him who has beaten him, and may give out his assurance—"I will beat him."

Also, in order to seek attention, a child lies "I have got fever."

These are the child's ways of trying to relieve himself from the tension, which is caused by his constant awareness of the fact that he is weak, and cannot do things which the adults can do. It is a device, that the child adopts to have a momentary satisfaction of becoming as able in all respects, as adults are.

A child often develops such illusory things about himself in order to compensate for his weaknesses. The adult should not see anything immoral in such a behaviour of the child. Such a behaviour is, rather, good for his mental health or development.

There are other reasons, also, which may make the child tell a lie:

- When the truth may displease the adults.
- When speaking the truth may lead to corporal or other severe punishment.
- When speaking the truth is not to the liking of the child.

- When the child feels that mentioning of mere facts would not be so interesting, so impressive.
- The child also tells lies for compensation, for practice of his adult life.

Sometimes a child just, per chance, stumbles upon the possibility of lying.

It is natural, that none would unnecessarily like to displease others by his behaviour. A child happens to be very sensitive, and understanding in this respect. He cares most for the pleasure and displeasure of those who are so affectionate towards him. The child values their pleasure very much, and, would try to keep them in a good mood, even by telling a lie. But a child who is still about three years of age, would tell innocent lies, as the child's intention in telling lies, rarely or never happens to harm others.

The best way to wean a child from such practices, is to tell him in a happy mood, "ah, you are making a fool of me." The child would realise that he or she can see through the lies that it tells.

Our behaviour with a child should never be very harsh and threatening. It should be, rather, of such a nature that the child can dare tell the fact to us.

When we feel that the child is telling lies only to make his report more interesting or impressive, or, just to clip out things which are not as per his likings, we should, rather, listen to him interestingly. During such moments, a child may be flying on the wings of imagination. Let the child continue. Such things may be helpful in his growing into a creative adult.

We often find a child playing the roles of adults, especially, of the mother or of the father (generally a female child would play the role of her mother, and, a male child that of the father) or of a teacher. Such a role playing, though, cannot be taken as telling lies, yet while playing such roles, a child would tell a lot of lies. These innocent lies are in the interest of children's emotional, as well as sensorimotor development. The child through such imitative plays, practises for the duties and chores of adult life. Such a play, also provides the child an occasion to compensate for his weaknesses, because of which he cannot do what he sees the adults around him doing—at least for a while he has the satisfaction that, he also can do as the adults do, though only in his make-believe world.

What we need is to let the child enjoy his make-believe world. Playing imaginary roles, playing with imaginary objects and imaginary characters—is the psychological need of the child. It is helpful in his development. Hence, let us provide suitable environment to the child for such games.

Sarvis, MK and Garcia, B[9] have, however, warned against the extreme form of autism (absorption in fantasy as an escape from reality). Such a case will be termed as schizophrenic.

9. *Etiological Variable in Autism*. Psychiatry, 24, 1961.

When a child tells a lie to avoid punishment, we need to impress upon him, through our behaviour, that if he tells the fact, we will not be angry and rebuke or punish him, because speaking the truth is liked by all.

We should, rather, teach a child that telling a lie is something bad which none would like. And, the most important thing, in this respect, is that we ourselves should not tell a lie. Generally, what happens, we give assurance to a child to make him stop crying or weeping, or to make him give up his insistence for something, which we never honour. Such a behaviour on our part, will instil the habit of lying in the child; so, it ought to be avoided, and, the child be made to face the reality which is unavoidable. The affectionate care of the elders should, however, never be slackened. The accusation—"you are a liar, we cannot trust you" if made seriously and repeatedly, would turn the child into a hardened liar. However, it ought to be impressed upon the child that only truth is expected of him.

(*vi*) Should be sexually modest. Sex is a very strong instinct which has its impact, even on the behaviour of a small child. It is, perhaps, the most powerful of all the instincts, and, provides a very strong motive for a number of activities of the child. Sigmund Freud has divided the period of childhood into three parts, as the behaviour of the child goes on changing, in reference to the impact of the instinct of sex upon it.

1. **The oral stage** It is the stage, when the child finds pleasure in sucking food from the breast of his mother up to the age of one year. The mouth is the main organ that the child seeks pleasure through. He puts everything that he takes hold of, into his mouth, to have the pleasure of doing it. Psychoanalysts, like Freud and Alfred Alder, find this to be the motive behind such a behaviour of the child, though a behaviourist, would like to link this behaviour to the theory of action–reaction, and would take the behaviour as being indulged into, in order to be acquainted with the objects of the environment.

   The mouth of the child is the most sensible part of the body, and, he finds it to be pleasant when someone touches his lips or any part of his mouth—a child likes to be kissed.
2. **The anal stage** A child finds great relief when the waste matter passes out from his bowels. As a child finds release from tension in this anal-activity; the guardian can quite effectively impart toilet-training to a child who is about two years old. Contrary to this, if the child is unnecessarily disturbed in the activity of defecation, or if toilet-training is imposed upon a child who is still not even two years old, the efforts of the guardians would be counter-productive. The child may even grow into an obstreperous child and an obstinate adult.

3. **The phallic stage** From third to fifteen years of age, a child may be seen growing curious about his genitals. He looks at his genitals and also that of the others. A female child feels that she lacks in some respects in bodily structure, in comparison to a male child. Some compensation for this deficiency seems to have been made when the female child is grown up into an adult, and, is a mother of a male baby.

The phallic stage is the stage when a male child feels more attraction towards his mother, and, a female child towards her father. Not only this, a male child starts harbouring jealousy against his father, and a female child against her mother. In Freudian psychology, the male child's jealousy against his father, of course, in his unconscious mind, has been termed as Oedipus complex[10]; and that of a female child's against her mother, as Electra complex.[11]

At present, we are concerned with the sexual modesty of a child, as a moral quality. We shall not discuss here, how a child, when proceeding towards adolescence, first grows amorous towards one's own body, then towards those who are of his own sex, and, then, towards those who are of the opposite sex. Such sorts of erotic inclinations have been termed as Narcissism, homosexual and heterosexual respectively—here we shall only mention what precautions should be taken to avoid unnecessary repression of infantile sexuality.

The child's curiosity regarding genitals; his feeling a sort of pleasure when the genitals and the area about the same are touched, is not unnatural. Hence, no harsh step on the part of the elders is warranted to suppress the child's curiosity or inclination.

What is required, is to tell the facts regarding sex differences, in such a way that the curiosity is wisely satisfied, and the child will not have to repress an emotion unnecessarily. Contrary to it, if every curiosity of the child related to sex, is repressed in an insensitive manner, it would aggravate the curiosity of the child further, and its repression would only help in making the child neurotic.

For developing and maintaining sexual modesty in the child, such an environment ought to be maintained, that the child's attention hardly, if ever, inclines towards anything related to sex. Proper clothing of the child, and of others, too; highly interesting games for the child to be busy with; company of other children and elders that the child may neither feel unhappy nor bored; timely satisfaction of the child's needs, and that, too, with an

Proper clothing of the child, and of others, too; highly interesting games for the child to be busy with; company of other children and elders that the child may neither feel unhappy nor bored; timely satisfaction of the child's needs, and that, too, with an affectionate touch of the elders, are all helpful, directly or indirectly in maintaining sexual modesty of the child.

10. In a Greek mythological story, Oedipus unwittingly killed his father and married his mother.
11. Electra is a girl in a Greek mythological story, who, because of her love for her father, helped her brother kill her mother.

affectionate touch of the elders, are all helpful, directly or indirectly in maintaining sexual modesty of the child.

After a prolonged longitudinal study, Peck and Havighurst[12] concluded—"There does seem to be such a thing as individual character; a persisting nature of attitudes and motives which produce a rather predictable kind and quality of moral behaviour." Character is a by-product of many other developments. The twin authors further write—"character can be regarded as a special aspect of personality; or, otherwise stated, as a function of certain personality characteristics." They have listed six aspects of personality as relevant—(*i*) moral stability; (*ii*) ego strength; (*iii*) superego strength; (*iv*) spontaneity; (*v*) friendliness; and (*vi*) a hostility guilt complex.

Though apparently, it seems that here, we are concerned only with one of the six aspects, that is moral stability; but, by what has been discussed above, it should be clear that moral stability is such a wide aspect of character, which is related to all the other five enumerated here. Moral character is made up of self-control, awareness of self (that is, ego), skill and insight into others, (pre-thinking as to how others would react to a particular behaviour), reaction to the authority of parents (a child would always try to avoid a behaviour which is likely to evoke the displeasure of parents, or, to result in the withdrawal of affection by them).

> In the classic book, *Child Development*, six things have been given as requisites for good moral growth: (*i*) Good physical health (*ii*) Emotional security (*iii*) Proper avenues for the expression of excitement (*iv*) Continued discipline in self-control (*v*) Consideration for the rights and privileges of others (*vi*) Religious programmes as a source of Inspiration.

When a child grows older, and has to move and behave in wider circles of society, he also develops conscientiousness in his relations with the church and in regards to cultural mores. He accepts group codes. His ability to restrict his own selfish, impulsive behaviour, in order to adjust to the interests of the wider groups, grows stronger.

In the classic book, *Child Development*[13], six things have been given as requisites for good moral growth:

(*i*) *Good physical health* Good physical health is very much helpful in enabling one to resist immoral pressure. The saying 'sound mind in a sound body,' is relevant here also.

(*ii*) *Emotional security* A child who is properly cared after, and loved, does not feel isolated or lonely; and has not to feel grudge against anyone, or harbour bitterness for anyone. Revenge would never be his motive, when he behaves with others. He can be expected to love his neighbours as he loves himself.

(*iii*) *Proper avenues for the expression of excitement* A child may more often be excited when it is an occasion for glee. If proper avenue is not provided for the expression of such an excitement, it would not be good for the health of the child. The repressed emotion may

12. Peck, RF, Havighurst, KJ. *The Psychology of Character Development* (1964).
13. Marian E. Brekenridge, MS; E. Lee Vincent. *Child Development.*

lead the child to express the same in an unhealthy way. Care needs to be taken that, a child does not feel bored because of lack of recreation and excitement.

(*iv*) *Continued discipline in self-control* The child should be trained in exercising proper control over childish impulses. Nevertheless, the child must not be made to observe adult standards in his behaviour. The activities which are natural to a child, should be allowed to be pursued, in a wholesome manner. Self-discipline is, no doubt, important but our expectation of the same should not lose sight of the fact that the child is still not fully matured physically, cognitively and emotionally.

(*v*) *Consideration for the rights and privileges of others* With age, the child's social horizon also gets widened. This enables him to know others in a better way, to tolerate differences with others, or the situation which is not as he had expected, or desires it to be. The widening social horizons only can make a child sympathetic to others—otherwise he would remain self-centred and grow selfish. A child who moves in a wider social circle, develops a better understanding of others, and, may have genuine consideration for the rights and privileges of others. There can be no morality without such a consideration for others.

(*vi*) *Religious programmes as a source of inspiration* Religion has got a very great psychological significance, especially for the development of moral character. All religious books teach us good things; inspire us for a life of sacrifice, devotion, truthfulness etc. Saintly teachings are to the same effect; biographies of saints provide examples of moral lives which, if told to children in a proper way, may prove as a source of effective inspiration for them to imitate and emulate. If, throughout the year, some such religious programmes are held, which practically involve us in deeds of devotion and co-operation, which touch our emotions through holy psalms sung on the occasions, impact of the same is definitely to be there in the development of moral character.

> "Only in the more mature stage can the child see that the rightness of an act lies in carrying out the spirit rather than the letter of the ruling."

Piaget, in his book *The Moral Judgment of the Child*, 1948, views that a child learns the rules that are not objectively real, but they are made by people, and, can be modified as demanded by the circumstance.... "only in the more mature stage can the child see that the rightness of an act lies in carrying out the spirit rather than the letter of the ruling." Piaget's studies in Switzerland and Durkin's[14] studies in the United States, led to the similar findings that the concepts of justice increase with age. Each child "re-works"

14. Durkin, D. *Children's Acceptance of Reciprocity as a Justice Principle*, 1959.

> Moral rules are not assimilated by the child as readymade principles, handed down from one generation to the other—"he can integrate into his own life, in terms of his own individual needs, and his own identification with and respect for the other people in his environment." Jean Piaget.

the moral principles that are handed down to him. Moral rules are not assimilated by the child as readymade principles, handed down from one generation to the other—"he can integrate into his own life, in terms of his own individual needs, and his own identification with and respect for the other people in his environment." Conflict within the mind continues till the child has not made the rules thoroughly his own. As the child grows in age, and, has to move in a constantly widening circle of society, his capacity to identify himself with others, his interest in others, also grows, and his capacity to judge situations on a wider basis, develops. He would be depending less on adult authority, less on the majority rating by his peers—he develops the capacity to judge situations for himself.

SELF-CONTROL IS CRUCIAL IN MORALITY

Enough control over primitive impulses, has to be exercised to live in a social group. Emotional energy has to be directed into desirable channels, in order to be accepted as a good member of society, and for leading a personal life which is not conscience-smitten. Resistance to temptation is a necessary part of self-control. There may be situations when one is tempted to distort the truth, and tell a lie for the benefit of the self. Training needs to be given that one must refrain from telling a lie, with a consideration for others. Likewise, titillating situation may be there when one is likely to violate sexual modesty, again self-control will be needed. Experience teaches one that self-control is essential for living a happier life with others. ID loses its energy in favour of EGO and SUPEREGO in the process of socialisation, where efforts are made in the form of self-control. The more we become considerate for the rights and privileges of others; for the difficulties and inconveniences of others, the more co-operative and sacrificing we shall grow.

However, a balance has to be maintained between consideration for the self and consideration for others. One needs to preserve one's health and a balanced frame of mind, while sacrificing the interests of the self, in favour of the benefits of others.

CURRENT THEORIES OF MORALITY

Martin, WE[15] refers to 'conscience' as "one's social inheritance." Kohlberg says that according to current investigators, morality or conscience is

15. *Rediscovering the Mind of the Child, a Significant Trend in Research in Child Development*, 1960.

"a set of cultural rules of social action that have been internalised by the individual."

Peck and Havighurst[16] write that there are four qualitatively different kinds of conscience. The first is the most primitive, and is made up of a big number of crude and harsh "Don'ts." They act only in a repressive way. As internal inconsistency persists very strongly during this period, so the child is, often, likely to be frustrated as regards to the feasibility of always behaving in accordance with these "Don'ts."

The second kind of conscience is the result of conformity to the rules. The main impact happens to be of the people around the child, whose approval he values the most.

The third type of conscience, or, we may say the third stage of conscience development is that which Freud has called superego. And, it is an authority which does not permit anyone question it or test it on rational basis. It maintains its own autonomy. This third kind of conscience is "made up of a firmly organised body of internalised moral rules."

The fourth stage of conscience development is, when it becomes "a firm set of internalised moral principles that are accessible to rational questioning and testing." A man developed up to this final stage of conscience development would, no doubt, be firm in his behaviour, yet he would never be rigid. He would be prepared to listen to others' points-of-view, and without trying to impose his outlook on others, would only try to win over others to his point-of-view, persuading them through rational arguments.

Regarding the "internalisation of rules", Kohlberg writes that, when rules are conformed to, in absence of the situational incentive or sanctions, if conformity is intrinsically motivated, then rules are said to be internalised.

The second criterion when moral standards can be said to have been internalised, is that every guilt or transgression of moral standard must be self-punitive; self-critical reactions must follow each and every violation of cultural standards.

Bennel's (1960) theory of the development of conscience, again, gives stress upon identification. The child begins with identifying himself with the person who loves him most. He cannot tolerate a stage of withdrawal of love by such a person. Naturally, such a person would be his parent. As a child grows older, he tries to be independent even of the person that he has been emulating, but again, by way of identifying with him. It is through identification that he seeks his independent personality to develop. The strength and reliability of the child's conscience, directly depends upon the strength of love of the person that the child identifies himself with.

16. Peck, RF, Havighurst, RJ. *The Psychology of Character Development*, 1960.

Douvan (1962) points out that the boy has an internal representation of the parents that he must placate. This internal identification serves, as a source of reinforcement for the child's acts. In case where the identification is partial, and only primitive, the parent influences the behaviour of the child, as a source of reward and punishment only.

Strength of conscience, depends upon the condition of reinforcement (*Reinforcement Theories of Learning*). The psychoanalysts define this phenomenon in terms of mechanism of identification of the child with parental patterns and approval. Kohlberg (1963) says that both these theories suggest a focus upon "anxiety" and "guilt"; and upon the inhibition of impulses, such as sex, aggression, and so on, as the expression of morality. Some writers conceive family antecedent to be as an important factor in the development of "superego strength" or morality.

Those believing in the "learning-theory" approach, conceive morality to be a matter of "habit acquisitions." Bad habits have to be weaned out, and the good ones have to be appreciated, encouraged. Good habits may be helped to be developed by way of good examples, through teaching and reward. Bad habits are prevented from being practised through rejection, disapproval, or punishment in the form of withdrawal of love. Some researches on the development of morality, show the impact of Hull's ideas of learning through conditioning. Conditioning occurs because of reward and punishment. Moral behaviour learned at home, are generalised outside.

Heredity has its impact on the conditionality of moral anxiety. Bandura et al, 1963, are of the view that "film mediated" models are more effective in modifying the reactions of the subject, to a frustrating situation than do the real life-models.

"If a child were cared for but never disciplined, he would presumably show only developmental identification and would develop skills but no character."

Many studies have been conducted to find how and to what extent home environment affects the development of moral conscience. Glueck and Glueck, 1950, and Bandura and Watters, 1963, found that more primitive, inconsistent, and unreasoning methods of discipline were used in homes of delinquent than of non-delinquent adolescents. Researchers have also tried to know to what extent the nature of discipline at home, is related to delinquency; and the capacity to resist temptation. The findings of the researchers, are not the same on these counts. In all cases "altruistic morality" seemed to have developed, where the parents were loving and wise. The findings of Peck, RF and Havighurst, RJ[17] are to this effect:

"If a child were cared for but never disciplined, he would presumably show only developmental identification and would develop skills but no character."

17. Peck, RF, Havighurst, KJ. *The Psychology of Character Development* (1960).

[Mowrer, OH. *Cognitive dissonance or counter-conditioning?—A reappraisal of certain behaviour "paradoxes"*].

For the development of character, it is also important that clearly understood standards of evaluation are provided to the child. It is also essential to do so for the child's self-critical responses. The punishment of transgression must have sufficient verbal and understood context.

SEX DIFFERENCES IN CONSCIENCE DEVELOPMENT

The following are the findings of Grinder, RE and Rou, L:

1. Girls are more conforming to rules and authority than boys.
2. No substantial general differences between boys and girls in conforming to internalised moral standards. Few sex differences in resistance to temptation. No differences in cheating.
3. Boys and girls feel themselves guilty, equally strongly after committing some omission.
4. Boys are more rules or justice-oriented in their expressions of indignation or sympathy.
5. Boys are more willing to accept rules for their own behaviour when they insist for others to observe the same.
6. Girls are expected to be more obedient, more fearful, more affectionate and more dependent than boys; the girls expect themselves to be so.

OTHER ASPECTS OF MORAL DEVELOPMENT

In the beginning, a child eschews an act, not with the idea of its being morally unsound, but only because it is not being liked by the elders, whose caring affection, he can hardly tolerate being withdrawn. The reasoning that such an act is wrong because it causes harm to others, causes pain to them, impinges upon the rights of others, develops only later on when the child is about 9 years of age. It is the period when reasoning, sympathy, aesthetic sense and tolerant love "make excellent progress" (Cole). The morality can be said to have developed to its desired level, when it is the result of reasoning, sympathy, aesthetic sense and tolerant love. What is reasoning, a mention has already been made about it; and, sympathy is the fellow-feeling—feeling sorrow for one who is in trouble; aesthetic sense, though a term more commonly used in reference to a work of art, is a sense of perceiving beauty in a natural way, and is free from morbidity. A person with aesthetic sense developed in him, is less likely to be having unhealthy interest in things immoral. The tolerent love is the love which is enduring, and does not wane even in the face of adversity or difficulties. With adolescence, truth and justice also come to have deeper meanings. He can, now understand the abstractions that are there behind most of the moral rules and principles.

For a child, entering an elementary school, the role of the school is very important, in developing the quality of resistance to temptation. A child of 5 to 6 may be tempted to steal a thing which is of interest to him, which attracts his attention. Even if a child of this age steals an article, it should be taken as an incidence of mistake, and the child be made to return the same. The memory of being, thus, made to return the stolen article, would be an unpleasant one helping in the development of conscience, that can resist temptation to indulge in pilfering. Contrary to this, if the child is declared to be a "thief" for such a pilferage, it would turn him into a habitual thief.

A proper attitude towards school, its property and programmes, will help the child grow into a responsible adolescent, considering public property as valuable as his own personal property, and would be honouring the time and work of others, by way of co-operating with them. Living and playing with peers in a group or team, develops team-spirit. One's interest grows wider beyond one's own personal concerns, and, one may learn a practical lesson in sacrificing one's own interests and comforts for the sake of others. Games and sports at school develop the sportsman spirit, in accepting failures as challenges for greater efforts. His achievements in motor and scholastic activities, make him realise the worthwhileness of efforts. A sense of attachment to school, widens. In due course, if the teachers at the school, have this objective in view, this attachment widens to include his society, his nation and may develop into an attachment to the international community also. The school can teach the lesson, or, can consolidate it that cheating is bad, is immoral in all matters, whether it is a work or a play.

Though the process of development goes on throughout the school years, yet, the first three years of the school life are more important. Lessons in morality, learnt during this period, have their permanent impact on the later developments. Honesty towards work, whether one likes it or not, is also a contribution of the school. False systems of merits and demerits on the other hand, may teach the children to work for artificial ends—such a situation should be rectified, otherwise they may even be inclined to use dishonest means to achieve end results.

"It is apparent then, that the friends a child goes with, his classroom codes, the nature of school adjustment, and the example of his parents, are definitely related to his sense of responsibility and his tendencies to be of service."

Family environment A child imbibes many moral qualities in his family environment. He has been experiencing the sacrifices of his mother, being made for him and for the welfare of the entire family. The child sees his father's sense of responsibility in rearing his family and the hard labour that he puts in for the cause. He sees the elder siblings of the family making sacrifices and working for the well-being of their youngsters. All this is done out of a feeling of affection and belongingness. This situation brings to bear a permanent impact on the mind of the child.

Repeated story-telling by the adults, with some moral to teach, makes the child over-conscientious as to what is wrong and what is right. Moralising overdone would have a negative effect. The child may have to suffer from an over-acute sense of guilt, he may even lose his interest in didactic stories.

The desirable condition to develop is that the child must have a sense of honour for himself. Self-esteem is essential for a good moral life; no external fear should be goading his behaviour. Superstitious fear in the child and the 'super-conscientious over analysis' of his behaviour, are not in the interest of proper emotional growth of the child. He may grow nervous or emotionally unstable because of them.

Religious training is good, if it can help make Love the governing principle of life; make life serene and bring about "peace within."

> Moralising overdone would have a negative effect. The child may have to suffer from an over-acute sense of guilt, he may even lose his interest in didactic stories.

Landies remarks how the current circumstances have slackened the previous chaperonage of adults in matters of practical training in morality. According to him, there are three factors responsible for this state of affairs:

1. Most young people have to leave the family and neighbourhood very early.
2. Due to rapid changes in all phases of experience, the age-old moral standards no longer hold good now. As a result of the changed situation, even parents, in many cases, cannot be sure of rightness of an issue; and such an uncertainty makes the moral precepts lose their positiveness.
3. A good many adolescent/youth groups have come into being, codes of which hold sway over the new generation, and, the familial impact has been weakened.

A specific mention has to be made of the deep impact of the television, on the psyche of the growing child. I do remember to have read a news in a daily, that in a case of juvenile crime (murder), the judicial magistrate declared that it was more specifically due to the impact of the television, that juvenile crimes are on the increase. In case of the deadliest school massacre with a toll of 23 school children, two heavily armed young men entered a suburban high school in Littleton, near Denver (Colorado), and sprayed the crowded classrooms with bullets indiscriminately; it happened in April, 1999. Again, it was felt that the video electronic media had its effect in such a case, too.

As mentioned above, story-telling can play an important role in the development of moral character, but the present-day condition of it, as I read in a daily, I would like to quote verbatim:

"Today, story-telling is one of those art forms that have vanished. Thanks to Enid Blyton or Carolin Keene, not to mention Alfred Hitchcock, some fiction is read by children. There is a lot to learn from stories...... Can we update Vishnu Sharma's technique to improve the quality of our education system?"

REVIEW QUESTIONS

***Q*.1.** Fill in the blanks:

(*i*) The sense of morality is the sense of .... and ....

(*ii*) Our .... works as an internal censor in matters related to morality.

(*iii*) .... is the external censor to check immoral practices.

(*iv*) For the development of Superego, the child must get ......

(*v*) Inc ...... behaviour of the mother cannot help in the development of conscience.

***Q*.2.** What are the Dos and Don'ts for a child?

***Q*.3.** Elaborate with examples, what are the four motives which lead the child to adopt the adult patterns of morality?

***Q*.4.** There is a student who behaves aggressively against a good student who earns affection of all.

What negative emotion do you think, is working behind the former (aggressive) student's behaviour and what other characteristics would you find in his behaviour? Suggest how can such a one be improved upon?

ANSWERS TO OBJECTIVE TYPE QUESTIONS

***Q*.1.** (*i*) right, wrong, (*ii*) conscience, (*iii*) social environment, (*iv*) affectionate care, (*v*) inconsistent

CHAPTER 14

MASS MEDIA AND ITS ROLE IN SOCIAL AND MORAL DEVELOPMENT

Chapter Outline

- **Television and Cinema**
- **Print Media**
- **Review Questions**

Personality is the cumulative and dynamic result of so many factors which affect the different aspects of it—Physical, Cognitive and Affectional (or conative). Of these so many factors, the broad categories are the three—Hereditary, Environmental (Social and Physical) and Educational. These factors have interactionary effects for one another. So far as Heredity is concerned, little or nothing can be done to change it after the birth of the child; but its effect on what the environmental and educational factors do for a person, persists throughout the life. The social environment is the creation of society. The family, the school and so on are its different units or agencies. That way, Education is also a function of society, which it performs through the agency of school but looking to its importance, it has been put in a separate category. The school is an organisation which carries on efforts for the development of an individual in a formal manner. In this chapter, we are concerned with the non-formal factors such as Print Media (Newspapers, Journals and others), Radio, Electronic Media (Television) and the Cinema which immensely affect the children of our era. Especially, the moral and social aspects of their personality bear the impact of these mass media.

First, we shall see how the television and cinema affect the moral and social behaviour of our children and adolescents. It was sometime back, that a judicial magistrate in England while considering a case of juvenile crime—two boys together had killed another younger boy—emphatically declared that in criminal cases of such nature, the electronic media had its impact. Though we have begun with an instance of negative impact of mass media, we shall now, first, see its possible role in bringing about positive changes in the development of the personality of the child. The event referred to here, is just to show how strong is the impact that such media make on the personality of an individual.

I do remember there was a time when children of a family would gather around their grandmother, who would tell them very interesting tales, befitting their age and need. The style of narration was such that the children would be spell-bound while listening to their grandmother. The stories were based on the popular epics of the land or stories wherein animals and birds were the characters; sometimes they were like the fairy tales, or supernatural characters performing some supernatural feats. They were always didactic in motive. The impressions that such stories create are always good, and they help very much in developing desirable social and moral qualities in the personality of the child.

Then, there were frequently held religious programmes with psalms or hymns being sung. As was the case, particularly in England, that Miracle and Morality plays were staged by the people associated with the Church; entertainment programmes were, generally, held within the ambit of religion itself. Religious discourses and reading out or recitation of holy books were very common. All these social institutions were there, to inculcate desirable social and moral traits in the people of the society. Now, such programmes are few and far between and they have lost their old times' impressiveness.

TELEVISION AND CINEMA

During the present times, it is the television and the cinema which have the strongest impact. In every house there is a television set, and, to find even a baby younger than two, being attracted towards it, is not surprising. As its appeal is very attractive, and it involves the greatest possible number of senses, therefore its impact is strong. Parents may be heard complaining against the obsession of their school-going children with this electronic media. What is true of the television, is also true of the cinema. The two are the most stimulating means of entertainment.

> As the television and the cinema make so strong an impact upon the growing child, their educative value is also very high.

As the television and the cinema make so strong an impact upon the growing child, their educative value is also very high. If educative serials, which are both highly interesting and educative, are produced, keeping in consideration the physical and mental maturity levels of the children, no teaching aid can surpass these. For the teaching of both physical and social sciences, the electronic media would prove very interesting and very effective.

Good manners may effectively be taught through demonstration in serials on the television screen. Short stories, teaching lessons in co-operation, truthfulness, service and so on, may be the themes of serials to help in inculcating these moral or social qualities. Almost in all developed, and in many developing countries, video cassettes have become an indispensable material in the system of distance education. Other educational organisations of higher national and even regional levels, prepare their educational programmes for the interested television viewers. We, in India, are well-acquainted with the UGC programmes which serve the educational interests of students/scholars related to different faculties or branches of learning. Now, important scientific experiments can be telecast for a number of people. Knowledge of many researches can effectively be spread among the masses. Especially, since the beginning of the latter half of the twentieth century, we have been experiencing explosion in knowledge. The electronic media, and also other means of mass communications, the latest being Internet, have immensely boosted this explosion.

For the teaching of both physical and social sciences, the electronic media would prove very interesting and very effective.

Since here, we are to limit ourselves to the effects of mass media on children, and, that too, in respect of social and moral qualities, our main thrust will be on this aspect only.

Here, I am quoting a few words from a book published in the seventies: "Children tend to react emotionally, physically and morally to movies". "... too frequent attendance at movies may prove far too stimulating to a nervous or high strung child ... there must be definite restriction on the type of movie, he is allowed to see."

"... too frequent attendance at movies may prove far too stimulating to a nervous or high strung child ... there must be definite restriction on the type of movie, he is allowed to see."

Since then, the use of the television has very much increased, hence its evil effects should be properly highlighted. Long hours spent in front of the television sitting, with full concentration on the screen, is strenuous and causes fatigue to the child. The sleeping hours of the child are disturbed. A child can play less because of his attending to the television for long hours. Thus, too much of a television is not in the interest of the physical/motor development of the child.

To a young child, everything that happens on screen, seems like real events, with the result that he views with rapt attention for a long period. That may harm his vision, too, more so if the child is not sitting at an adequate distance from the television set. Sometimes, the scenes or events happen to be so full of violence, and terrifying that the child is horrified. His mental condition becomes so disturbed that he can hardly be at ease or sleep—we know, the child takes all the scenes and events to be real happenings. And, if the adults in the family continue watching the television programmes till late in the night, again, the child will not be able to have full sound sleep. All these conditions have their deleterious effect upon both the physical and mental health of the child.

To a young child, everything that happens on screen, seems like real events, with the result that he views with rapt attention for a long period.

If too much attachment to the television continues through adolescence, it proves highly detrimental to the moral development of the child as the television serials (or the cinema pictures), generally, happen to be full of sex and violence. Crime pictures may suggest an undesirable type of behaviour pattern by which the innocent children are more likely to be affected. And, the delinquents, may like to escape to that screen-world for the time-being. The more unpleasant, non-stimulating and unhappy situation a child has to live in, the more likely he would be inclined to escape into the screen-world for temporary relief. Such a child may grow too weak to boldly face the hard realities of the world. Increase of violence in the child's games, is also a result of serials and pictures suggesting aggressive behaviour patterns. In April' 1999, in the suburban school of Littleton, near Denver (the USA), in one of the deadliest school massacre, children fell prey to the firing by two students of another high school, who too were found dead in the school library—the death toll was as high as 25 (23+2). The impact of the television or the cinema was suspected to be there in that incident.

Nevertheless, it cannot be denied that movies have tremendous educational utilities—what the children would not like to listen when taught by their teachers or elders of the family, would pay utmost heed when taught through a television programme or a movie. Mahatma Gandhi has written in his autobiography that the play of Raja Harish Chandra made him adhere to the policy of honesty and truthfulness strictly throughout his life. The television programmes and cinema pictures can stir the feelings of the viewers, more so of the youngsters, and broaden their outlook in such a way that they may start thinking more of their society rather than of their own self. These programmes may awaken the adolescents to the burning problems of the society. Serials or pictures based on life-stories of the great personalities of the past or present, may prove very stimulating, and set in the process of identification or emulating. Thus, the spirit of social service, patriotism or love for the widest society of the entire world, may be inculcated.

> If they see how one behaves with the other, how the youngsters show their respect to the elders, and how the elders sacrifice their own comforts for the sake of their youngsters, these would prove very effective lessons in social manners.

The children and adolescents are more impressionable; and the impressions created upon their mind happen to be more enduring. If they see how one behaves with the other, how the youngsters show their respect to the elders, and how the elders sacrifice their own comforts for the sake of their youngsters, these would prove very effective lessons in social manners. The songs, dances and other forms of artistic expressions, may sweeten our life, and may greatly help in the inculcation of aesthetic sense, and in sublimating us to a higher level of living. Acting is a strongly effective means of sublimation, and hence, of making our society more cultured. But, the cumulative effect of serials and films with the dominance of sex in them, may result in the laxity of character in our youth.

The cumulative effect of serials and films with the dominance of sex in them, may result in the laxity of character in our youth.

PRINT MEDIA

Children's interest in magazines, journals and newspapers, is first stirred because of pictures and cartoons, if the same are there. Only when they have developed practice in reading the newspaper and magazine, they can be interested in reading them. The other way round is also correct—good and attractively illustrated newspapers may make the children feel interested in attempting to read the same. However, the newspaper is an effective mass media only for adolescents and youngsters, not so much for the young children. Up to the age of 12, a child, in general, prefers to read comics. By the time he attains the age of 14, he inclines more towards sports news. It is, generally, not before 16 or so that an adolescent starts showing keen interest in general knowledge. Now, he would like to know news of different sorts related to politics, diplomacy, peace and war, science and explorations or inventions, and of course, those related to sports, television programmes and films, and other matters of interest. It is the time by which some develop a keen penchant for arts. It is a little later that news related to economics attract the youth.

Thus, for the adolescents and youth, the print media serves as an effective means to widen the horizons of thinking. As a result of the media's impact on them, they would start thinking of issues in a wider, social perspective. The print media can keep their knowledge abreast with the latest social developments, and, hence they should be expected to be in a better position to address to the social and moral problems that our society may be facing. Thus, the regular reading of the newspaper is very much likely to develop such social qualities as objectivity, sympathy/empathy, co-operation in the solution of social problems, leadership and so on. Due to these, and such other qualities, one's moral standard would also rise.

Regarding the total impact of mass media, Mead wrote as early as 1963, that the present low standards of ethical behaviour in many parts of our society reflect the breakdown of parents' ability to give children clear ethical direction, within a scene that has been changing too rapidly.

Regarding the total impact of mass media, Mead wrote as early as 1963, that the present low standards of ethical behaviour in many parts of our society reflect the breakdown of parents' ability to give children clear ethical direction, within a scene that has been changing too rapidly[1]. It was her estimation of changes during the early years of the seventies. Now, in the 21st century, we can better recognise the tremendous change which the mass media has brought about.

A few words of Mead should be quoted here for a better appreciation of how correct she was in her estimation, "when television and radio were

1. Mead, M. *The Changing American Family, Children.*

brought into the home, ... the capacity of the parents to give moral direction further reduced." If parents want their authority to be revived in this respect, they will have to develop new and more powerful ways to issue directions for desirable moral and social development of their wards.

> Delhi school authorities who already have their hands full with infinite adolescent blues, are now grappling with a new malaise—cyber mania.

Before summing up the chapter, I would like to refer to what was published in a largely circulating daily, as it warns the guardians against the novel problem that advancement in computer technology has posed before them. The Internet has made contact with friends of the opposite sex both easy and swift. A girl asked the counsellor, "Should I meet him?" She confessed that she had met him on the web several months ago. The paper reports: "Delhi school authorities who already have their hands full with infinite adolescent blues, are now grappling with a new malaise—cyber mania. An alarming number of senior students spend more time on the Net than with their books, ... at least six hours a day, adversely affecting grades and home life."

Thus, surfing porno sites on the web, puts a new and serious onus on the guardians, and on the society as a whole, to develop a strongly effective agency, which may successfully counter the misuse of such a beneficial scientific technology.

REVIEW QUESTION

***Q*.1.** Write an essay, giving your views regarding the utility of the mass media for the youths of our society. If you feel they are making their negative impacts too, elaborate the same.

CHAPTER

15 PERSONALITY

Chapter Outline

- **What is Personality?**
- **Factors Affecting Personality and Types of Personality**
- **Review Questions**

WHAT IS PERSONALITY?

"__________ *a dynamic totality of systems.* " Kurt Lewin[1].

"*Personality can be broadly defined as the total quality of all human behaviour.*" Woodworth [The behaviourist].

"*By personality we refer to a pattern of traits rather than to a mere list or collection of characteristics.*"—Gates.

"*Personality is the integration of those systems of habits that represent one individual's characteristics adjustment to his environment*"—Kemph [The behaviourist].

Personality is a very common word. Every one of us uses this word off and on. We use this to speak of an impression that a person creates upon us, and we say, "His personality is very impressive" and so on. Some times, we speak such things about a stranger too, and in such a case, it is the physique of the person that creates the impression. In all cases, the bodily structure, the height and the overall appearance of a person are the first to impress others. These are the external features of the personality which make others to pass their immediate judgment about a person.

But personality is an end product. It includes many internal factors too, besides what can externally be perceived. It includes all the attributes of

1. Lewin, K. *A Dynamic Theory of Personality.*

a person when we speak of one's personality, actually we speak of the whole of his person—his physical, cognitive or intellectual and emotional or affective build-up. The factors which affect the build-up of these different aspects are so many; we have been referring to the same in the preceding chapters.

Thus personality is the result of the growth of a person's bones, whether one is broad-boned or narrow-boned; of the growth of one's muscles, whether they are big and strong or small and weak; of one's whole nervous system, whether the same is properly developed or its development has been thwarted because of some ailment, or malnutrition or some hereditary reason. Whether the bodily growth—height, weight and others, is in due proportion or not, so far the size and shape of different parts of the body are concerned. The overall outward appearance of a person makes one impress others as handsome or otherwise. If the finer motor skills of a person are well—developed, he may impress as sharp; one who is hesitant in motor activities, demanding better co-ordination of eye, hand and other parts of the body whose involvement is there, would impress as—sluggish. Thomas and Chess[2] studied temperamental differences in very young children on the basis of the following nine dimensions:

1. Activity level—the amount of physical activity.
2. Regularity of bodily functioning.
3. Adaptability to near situations.
4. Response to near situations.
5. Level of sensory threshold—the amount of external stimulation required to produce a response.
6. Intensity of response—the energy content of responses regardless of their quality.
7. Positive or negative mood—amount of pleasant and unpleasant behaviour throughout the day.
8. Distractibility—the effectiveness of external stimuli (sounds, people, toys and so on) in interfering with ongoing behaviour.
9. Persistence and attention span—duration of maintaining specific activities with or without external obstacles.

A person who is bodily well-built, and fully developed but is aggressive, short-tempered, greedy, lax in character and so on, cannot be deemed as one having a good personality; such a person is not adequately matured or developed emotionally. Likewise, if he fails to establish a just relationship between cause and effect; and has not had enough exposure to have earned needful experiences of his physical and social environments, and cannot reason out things justly, cannot be considered to be fully developed cognitively.

---

2. Thomas, A; Chess, S: *Temperament and Development, 1977.*

Thus, personality is the end-product of a person's physical, cognitive and emotional development. But when we say that "personality is the end product", we do not mean that the development has ceased to continue, but we only mean that at the time of speaking about or mentioning of the personality of someone, it is the stage up to which development has occurred. The term "end-product" is thus in reference to a particular point of time. Otherwise, "personality is a dynamic and complex organisation of a person's physical, intellectual and emotional characteristics".

These are the characteristics by which a person is recognised. His behaviour in a particular situation can be predicted because of these characteristics. Nevertheless, there is no end to the process of development, it starts since the time sperm enters the egg (female ovum), and continues with no end—if we mean to put the phenomenon in a precise way: this is why the organisation of personality has been described as "dynamic".

None the less, it is a fact that, almost in each case, there is a point of maturity when development reaches to its adult level, and it is considered to have reached to the highest point in the process. But examples are there to show that the process of evolution does not, exactly, come to a final halt at any age of a person; the process almost, in a number of cases, may bring about changes throughout life. Of course, after adulthood, the changes are neither frequent nor rapid, nor they happen to be in a general or a strong way.

When a person, because of hereditary reasons, or because of the nature of his physical, intellectual or emotional development, reacts in the same manner many times, to a particular inner or external stimulus, in a particular situation, it becomes a habit of that person to behave in that particular way when a similar situation arises. Habits are also important components of personality. Habits go on gaining in rigidity as time passes on, and the well-known saying is "habits die hard".

Bobroff,[3] describes personality as "a blend of ... predispositional temperament, an accumulation of emotional and cognitive experiences and genetic maturity".

But this accumulation that Bobroff has referred to, is dynamic in two senses, first, because the amount and nature of accumulation does not remain the same for all times, a change in the same goes on; secondly, the three components—physical, emotional and cognitive—interact among themselves, and each influences the other two in the process; they are inter-related.

A person takes some time for the development of his personality; Ausubel has put this fact showing a hierarchical order of development. The order of development is Self, then Self-concept, Ego and then Personality. Each

3. Bobroff, A. *Child Development*, 1961.

stage is a higher stage of development also because of growing complexity and inclusiveness. He writes, "The self is a constellation of individual perceptions and memories consisting of the visual image of the appearance of one's body; the auditory image of the sound of one's name, images of kinesthetic sensations and visceral tension, memories of personal events and so on. The Self-concept, on the other hand, is an abstraction of the essential and distinguishing characteristics of the Self that differentiate an individual's "self-hood" from the environment and from other selves. In the course of development, various evaluative attitudes, values, aspirations, motives and obligations become associated with the self-concept. The organised system of inter-related self-attitudes, self-motives and self-values that result, may be called the Ego. ..... Personality is a still more inclusive term than Ego. It includes all of the individual at a given moment in his life history."

The definition given by Ausubel, highlights the following characteristics of personality:

(*i*) It is more inclusive than any stage of development that a man reaches to—it includes all of a man's special features related to his physical, emotional and cognitive development.

(*ii*) Personality is an organisation of man's physical, emotional and cognitive characteristics.

(*iii*) The organisation is complex in nature. It is complex because of its inclusiveness of so many aspects in a highly complex way of inter-relatedness.

(*iv*) The organisation is in no case "final", but as it is "at a given moment in his life"; this means that the organisation is dynamic.

Sigmund Freud classifies the stages of the development of personality as:

1. ID
2. Ego
3. Super Ego

ID is a stage when one is not aware even of one's self, and behaves mostly through reflexes, being motivated by the animal force of instincts—no stage for "Do's and Don'ts".

EGO is the stage of self-consciousness. Now, an individual thinks of his good, of his prestige, of his interest and would try to refrain himself from doing what may harm his self.

SUPER EGO, is the stage when, one is guided by one's conscience—now he considers what is morally good and what is wrong. The bases of his evaluating the justness or otherwise of a behaviour, are the social norms.

Landis[4] defines personality in the following words: "Personality is dynamic, a growing entity. Physically, it is vested with the capacity for maturation. Except as mutilated by environment, physical traits follow their predestined course from childhood to maturity. Psychologically, it is plastic, capable of an infinite number of modifications by external stimuli. Sociologically, it is dependent on the group product."

In brief, Landis has also referred to the factors which are responsible for the development of personality of an individual.

(*i*) For physical development, nature has set a fixed schedule, according to which, each organ of the body and its functions mature: the "physical traits follow their predestined course from childhood to maturity". Of course, this predestined course is liable to be influenced by environment; the environment in some cases, may help for better, that is, more rapid and qualitatively of superior type of development; and, it may also slacken the process of development and make the individual lag behind the others of his age in growth and development. So, suitability of environment is an important condition for the normal course of development of desirable personality.

(*ii*) Psychologically, personality has been described as "plastic" because it is "capable of an infinite number of modifications", again it shows that personality is a dynamic organisation of many characteristics. But these modifications are caused by external (from the socio-physical environment) or internal stimuli; that is, socio-physical environment is the main factor which can cause modifications in personality. If modifications are desired, suitable environment for the same will have to be provided.

(*iii*) Landis, in the definition of personality, as given above, says that "human nature is a group product", this shows the importance of the company of other human beings for the development of sociological aspect of personality.

FACTORS AFFECTING PERSONALITY AND TYPES OF PERSONALITY

Murphy[5] concludes that no definite laws of development can be known in spite of a life-long intensive research. Factors which influence the development of personality are many, and, the process is very complicated. Nevertheless, all these factors may be classified under two heads—Nature and Nurture.

4. Landis, PH. *Adolescence and Youth—The Process of Maturing*, 1952.
5. Murphy, LB *et al. Personality in Young Children*. Vol. 1 *Methods for the Study of Personality in Young Children*. Vol. III.

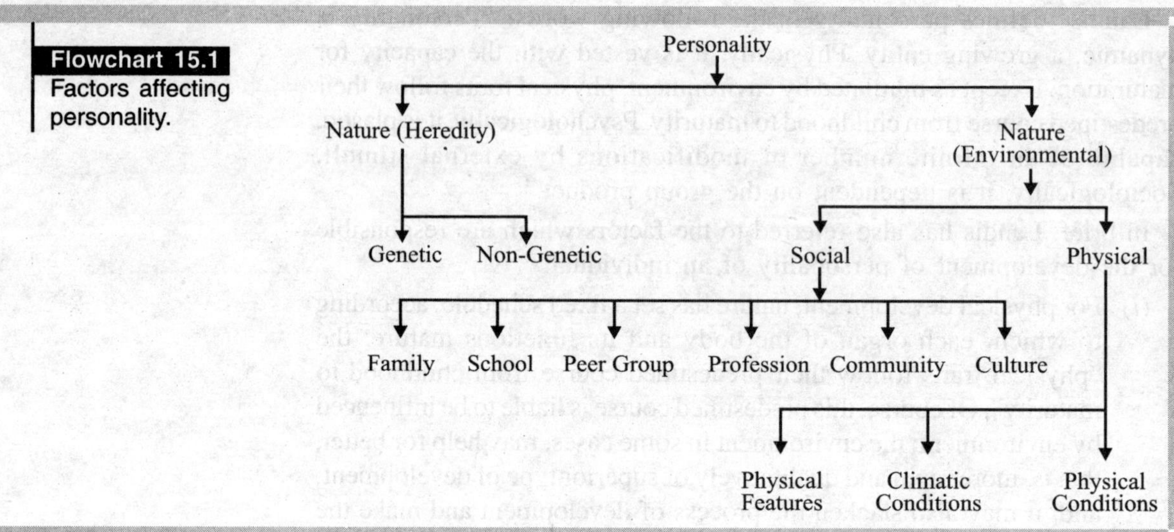

Flowchart 15.1 Factors affecting personality.

GENETIC

As in the growth of a vegetation, immense is the importance of the seed and of the soil. The type of seed that is used, and the nature of the soil where the seed is sown, determine very much as to what will be the nature of the growth of the vegetation that is desired to be grown; the same is the importance of the sperm of the father and the ovum of the mother. The resultant fertilised nucleus—cell is divided into two rod-like or thread-like structures, each such a pair is called a chromosome; the process of breaking down continues till the number of chromosomes grows to 23 pairs. These chromosomes contain genes; and genes are the carriers of heredity.

Aristotle classified personality into three types:

1. Endomorph. Short, fat-built persons fall into this category.
2. Ectomorph. Those having long and thin physique, have been put in this category.
3. Mesomorph. To this third category belong the persons who are muscular and have a well-proportioned body structure.

This classification is based on the apparent condition of the physique of a person. The condition of physique is mainly the result of heredity; it, generally, depends on genes. People would link one's height and body-build to one's parentage. This aspect of one's personality much depends upon the genetic factors of a person.

Aristotle in the past, and Stanford and his associates in our times, have linked temperamental and other characteristic traits to the type of body-build as mentioned above. (Considering the body-build or physical characteristics, Kretchner and Sheldon have also made a like classification into three types). The psychologists of our age conducted experiments too but they could not come out with conclusive results; at the most, their results may be said to be suggestive. To what they have reached, may be put in brief as under:

1. Genetic factors determine both the physical attributes and the other personality characteristics.
2. The individual's physical characteristics may affect his temperament and behaviour.
3. A thin, non-muscular, and poorly co-ordinated person in motor development, is less likely to achieve success in physical tasks; or, in athletic games—the activities that the school boys value highly; with the result that he cannot enjoy popularity with his peers. This would make him withdrawn and timid and introvert. The strong, well-muscled, is more likely to become popular with his peers; he would be more involved in group games—all this would make him an extrovert; he may grow aggressive, too. On the contrary, an ectomorphic would withdraw from "gangs"; and it is there that most delinquent acts occur.

In the above paragraph we have mentioned personality of two types 1. Introvert and 2. Extrovert—showing their relationship with the physique of a person. Later on, we shall see how many types of personalities the different authors have shown, assessing the same from different angles.

NON-GENETIC

The physique of a person is dependent not only on the genetic factor, but there is one more prenatal factor which affects it. It may be called non-genetic or biological factor.

When the embryo/foetus is in the womb of its mother, it is hardly affected by the external environment. It is fed through the umbilical chord, and its feeding depends upon the food of the mother. The malnutrition of the mother, would affect the physique of the unborn baby; and not only its physique but the temperamental or emotional build-up of the child is also affected by it.

The mental condition of the mother, though cannot directly affect the emotional conditions of the child yet indirectly it does. If the prospective mother is suffering from a sense of insecurity; is tense because of anxiety, is hot because of anger, it would affect her physiology—the heart-beat would increase, the body temperature may also be affected, there would be more secretion of glands; chemicals, such as acetylcholine and epinephrene, may increase in amount and the same would adversely affect the digestive system. All these constitute the non-genetic or biological

Aristotle to classify personality into three categories:
(*i*) Endomorph;
(*ii*) Ectomorph;
(*iii*) Mesomorph;

factor, the effect of which becomes apparent only when the child is born. The mother feels that the neonate is too much crying, squirming or peevish. Later on, the personality that develops, may be of a person who is irritating, short-tempered, aggressive and problematic, if not proper handling in childhood is made.

The ailment of parent and the home environment of the prospective mother also have their effect on the physique and emotional build-up of the child to be born.

This nature, through genetic and non-genetic factors, affects the physique which led Aristotle to classify personality into three categories:

1. Endomorph;
2. Ectomorph; and
3. Mesomorph;

and also classify temperamentally or emotionally into:

(*i*) Active—Lively, talkative, playful, creative, good physical co-ordination with greater strength and energy.

(*ii*) Inactive—Sluggish, passive and poorly co-ordinated.

(*iii*) Timid—Physically small in status, poorly coordinated, relatively weak and apathetic, shy, fearful, depending more on others; such a child would remain more absent from his school than others.

NURTURE

All the factors that make the environment, and, affect the development of an individual into a personality, may be put under the heading Nurture; Nurture includes all that are there in the environment, both physical and social. The nature of land, mountains, plateau or plains, rivers, lakes and so on, geographical location; and flora and fauna of the place in addition to the climatic conditions, all affect the nature or kind of personality that is in the process of evolving. Besides these, the architecture and size of the house, its sanitary systems or hygienic conditions, ventilation, cleanliness of the house and so on, all have relationship with the development of the personality of the individuals living therein. The kind of food used (balanced and fresh or stale and unwholesome); the water drunk, clothes put on, and so on, all have their share of effect in making the kind of personality that an individual grows into. They all make the physical environment.

From what has been written above, it becomes clear that socioeconomic conditions of a family, make the living style of it different from that of the others. Thus, socioeconomic conditions make an important constituent of social environment. The social environment happens to be the result of what the people of the society do. Hence, it also includes the behaviour of parents and siblings, of peers and teachers, and of people of wider and wider society into which the child or adolescent progressively moves on. Now, before going into details, it would be quite proper to speak something about Bronfenbrenner's[6] conceptualisation of development. He has conceived ecological development as a set of four nested systems: (Fig. 15.1) he has explained how an individual develops or what are the factors affecting this development; the same set of four nested systems can explain the conception of the development of personality.

At the first level is the "microsystem"—it is related to the individual experiences of the young child that he has:

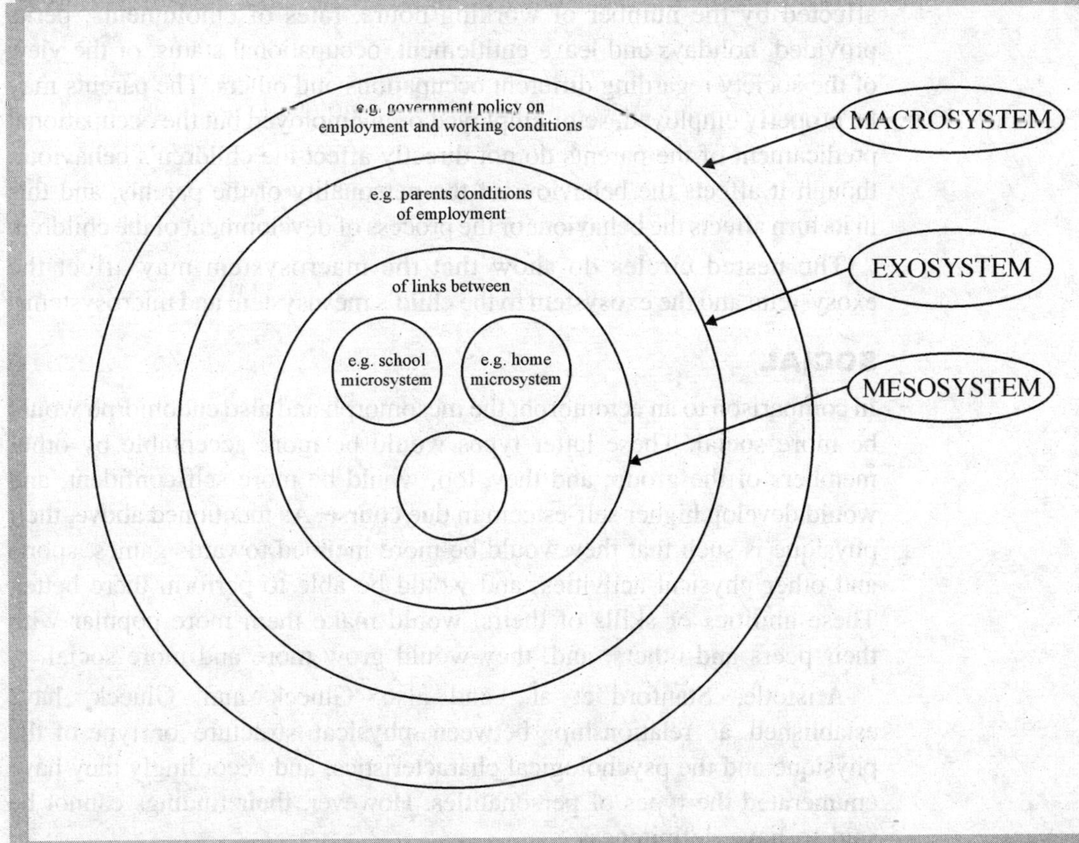

Figure 15.1
A set of four nested systems showing ecological development.

(*i*) in the home environment, living with his parents and siblings; and
(*ii*) in the school environment, living with his teachers and peers.

At the second level is the "mesosystem"—it refers to the links amongst settings where the individual child directly participates in. For example,

6. Bronfenbrenner, U. *The Ecology of Human Development*, 1979.

the home and the school are such settings; and the quality of the home environment may affect the child's performance in the school, and his adjustment with the peers.

The third level is the "Exosystem"—this refers to the settings where the child does not directly participate in; the father's or the mother's work environment is the example in which there is no direct participation of the child but their work environment does affect the child-care that the parents take.

The fourth and the final level is the "macrosystem"—it refers to the general pattern of ideology and organisation of the different social and the sub-cultural institutions. For example, the parents' stress at work is affected by the number of working hours, rates of emoluments, perks provided, holidays and leave entitlement, occupational status, or the view of the society regarding different occupations and others, The parents may be properly employed, semi-employed or unemployed but the occupational predicament of the parents do not directly affect the children's behaviour, though it affects the behaviour of the personality of the parents, and this in its turn affects the behaviour or the process of development of the children.

The nested circles do show that the macrosystem may affect the exosystem: and the exosystem to the child's mesosystem and microsystems.

SOCIAL

In comparison to an ectomorph, the mesomorph and also endomorph would be more social. These latter types would be more acceptable by other members of the group; and they, too, would be more self-confident, and would develop higher self-esteem in due course. As mentioned above, their physique is such that they would be more inclined towards games, sports and other physical activities; and would be able to perform there better. These abilities or skills of theirs, would make them more popular with their peers and others, and, they would grow more and more social.

Aristotle, Stanford et al., and also Glueck and Glueck have established a relationship between physical structure or type of the physique and the psychological characteristics, and accordingly they have enumerated the types of personalities. However, their findings cannot be said to have definiteness.

FAMILY

In a family, the greatest impact exerted is that of the mother, the loving care or the affectionate nurturance of the mother goes a long way in building up, especially. the emotional aspect of personality. Whether the child grows into a healthy adolescent or into aggressive or neurotic or otherwise a problematic one, to a great extent, depends upon the treatment that he, as a child, has got at the hands of his mother. The smiling face of the mother lays the foundation stone for the socialisation of the child. Stone and Church write that in the beginning, individuals and things have only emotional significance for him, their qualities he can realise only later on.

Though the child has been born with some prenatal effects but they also happen to be mostly because of his mother, and, now again, after birth, for a period of few months, what counts most, is the affectionate nurturance of the mother. A mother who attends and fulfils the needs of feeding, elimination and clothing of the child without delay, and with patience and love, would be helping in developing a child who would grow into a youth with balanced temperament. He would, generally, remain in a good mood, and would not get peevish on any small hurdle coming his way. On the contrary, if the mother is not healthy, gets irritated often, roughs the child, cries at him, neglects his needs and lets him cry long before his needs are fulfilled, would be responsible for the child's developing the habit of crying even when no genuine cause for the same is there, such a child would refuse taking his feeding, or would take out the milk and so on, that is put into his mouth. He would go on crying, or throwing out his arms and legs or squirming with discoloured face. If this continues for a good part of infancy, it would be difficult to sublimate the child from gestures of aggressiveness.

Already present temperamental characteristics make a central core of personality, a centre of gravity which lends stability to personality, and reactions to all environmental experiences that are affected by this central core.

Thomas, A et al[7] studied 130 children from birth through the first two years, and concluded that changes in temperament cannot exclusively be attributed to environmental factors. Temperamental characteristics already present during the first few months, make a fundamental difference. Personality is a result of interaction between these and an environmental complex. These already present temperamental characteristics make a central core of personality, a centre of gravity which lends stability to personality, and reactions to all environmental experiences that are affected by this central core.

A few months after birth, other members of the family, who are emotionally attached to the child, start having their impact in the evolution of the child's personality. It counts much whether the face that the child encounters is smiling or crossed; the tone of the elders, rearing the child, also affects it.

A few months after birth, other members of the family, who are emotionally attached to the child, start having their impact in the evolution of the child's personality. It counts much whether the face that the child encounters is smiling or crossed; the tone of the elders, rearing the child, also affects it.

Baldwin, AL[8] worked on a sample of 67 children, all ranging about 4 years of age, and were attending their nursery school. The objective was to study the impact of the home on the development of the child. The author visited homes with both types of environments—democratic as well as controlled.

7. Thomas, A et al. *Behavioural Individuality in Early Childhood.*
8. Baldwin, AL. *Socialization and the Parent–Child Relationship, Child Development*, 1948.

In the homes with controlled environment, there was found clear-cut restriction on behaviour. All were working with a discipline externally imposed upon them.

The homes with democratic environment were characterised by more permissiveness, avoidance of arbitrary decisions, and a high level of verbal contact between the parents and the child, consultations about decisions, explanation of reasons for family rules, supplying satisfactory answers to the questions of the child which may have been prompted by his curiosity.

Contrary to this, in the homes with controlled environment, there was found clear-cut restriction on behaviour. All were working with a discipline externally imposed upon them.

Now, the important thing to see is how the two different types of home environments, effect the development of two different categories of personalities:

Table 15.1 Home Environment and Personality

Children from Democratic Homes	*Children from Controlled Homes*
1. Active (with initiation)	1. Active only as per directions issued
2. Competitive	2. Content
3. Outgoing	3. Shy
4. Having qualities of leadership	4. Less of originality
5. More curious, assertive	5. Curiosity less expressed
6. Assertive (but also appearing)	6. Submissive
(*i*) non-conforming	(*i*) conforming
(*ii*) a bit disobedient	(*ii*) obedient
(*iii*) aggressive	(*iii*) quiet

Note: A child reared in a home with more of democratic atmosphere, is more likely to develop as an author, scientist or leader because of his having more of fancifulness, curiosity, originality and better expression.

But the highly indulged, babied and overprotected children grow to be timid, awkward and apprehensive.

SCHOOL

School provides a very important landmark in the process of the development of personality.

School provides a very important landmark in the process of the development of personality. Suddenly, the child is shifted to an environment where he gets to see almost all faces to be new. The homely affectionate environment is not there. According to Bowley et al, the separation produces a permanently disturbing effect on the child. Casler (1961) found that loss of maternal love, probably, has ill-effects on the child only if the separation occurs after specific affective responsiveness has been achieved. The result may be less rapid social and motor development. The child has to deal with a big number of children who initially happen to be strangers to him.

But a few things are common with them. They are almost of the same age, and, must be having their likings and dislikings common to a great extent. They all have suddenly been weaned out of the environment that they have so closely been attached to, though the separation happens to be only during the school hours. These common factors help in getting children, gradually, closer to one another.

Next to home, the school is the social agency which the society has entrusted with the work of co-operating the home in inculcating in the child the needful social habits of living, in developing attitudes befitting the values of the society and so on. Since early years, both the family and the school instil in the behaviour and thoughts of the child the important cultural characteristics of the society that give it its separate identity.

The school caters not only for the physical and intellectual development of the child but being the custodian and transmitter of culture from generation to generation, it includes such topics in its curriculum that may inculcate the desirable values of culture. The attitudes, habits and if the same are of the desirable sorts, can make the person social and cultured. Nevertheless, because of difference of "central core", each person has his own attitudes and habits by which he is recognised as a personality separate from others. Along with family, the school is also expected to inculcate wholesome habits indicative of discipline, co-operation, truthfulness, diligence, punctuality, creativity and so on.

The school is to play a very significant role through a host of its activities, and by way of creating a very congenial environment, in the development of the child into a personality that is sound in body, and mind, and emotionally strong and noble.

Personality is what a person is—it includes everything of a person. And, what a person is, can be known through the behaviour of a person. And, one behaves as he is directed by his attitudes, and is accustomed to or habituated to. The school is to play a very significant role through a host of its activities, and by way of creating a very congenial environment, in the development of the child into a personality that is sound in body, and mind, and emotionally strong and noble. The school broadens the experiences of the child both intellectually and socially. In school the child has to live in the company of teachers and so many other students; it enhances his ability to adapt to new social situations—this is why school is considered to be the most effective agency which works for the socialisation of the child. The school through its routine activities develops a lot many social qualities in the growing child. Here, the child takes many conduct prohibitions on faith. "School increases the child's concern with what happens to other children, and, also increases the scope of their interpersonal relationships" (Fig. 15.2).

"School increases the child's concern with what happens to other children, and, also increases the scope of their interpersonal relationships."

Dodge and his colleagues[9] suggest how a child can earn social behaviour through peer interactions:

9. Dodge, KA, Pettit, GS, McClaskey, CL, and Brown, MM. *Social Competence in Children*, 1986.

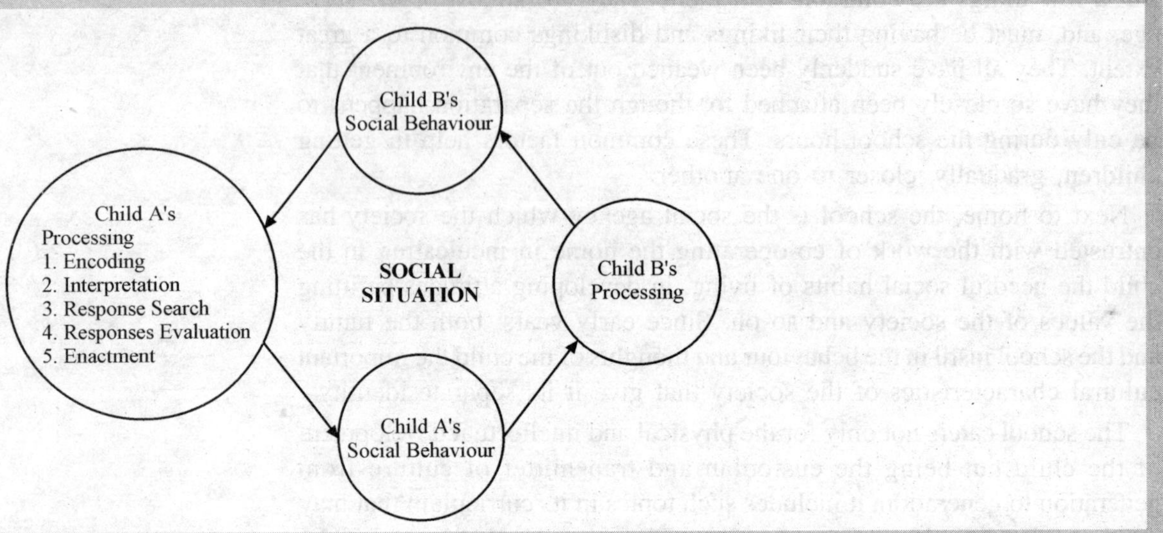

Figure 15.2 Dodge and his colleagues suggest how the process of socialisation goes on.

The supposed situation is that child A is interacting with child B. B is running forward with arms raised, shouting and smiling. A will pass through certain steps of the process before coming to the final response.

(*i*) He will encode the incoming information-perceive what child B is doing;

(*ii*) Interpret the information whether the behaviour of B is friendly or aggressive;

(*iii*) Search for appropriate responses whether he should run away, or ignore or play fight;

(*iv*) Evaluate these responses, and select the best; and then

(*v*) Enact the response—will do it effectively.

In response to the behaviour of A, the child B will also pass through the similar steps of the process.

A school through its teachers, curriculum, approaches to teaching and overall physical and social environment, so impresses its pupil that it leaves an indelible impact on the personality of its products by which they are recognised. Among these factors, the teacher is the crucial one; he alone is the living factor and the impressiveness of other factors; is dependent upon his skill and personality; upon the fact how good a teacher he is.

A classic study was conducted by Lewin et al[10] to see how the teaching style affected the development of skills in the taughts, their output and social behaviour.

10. Lewin, K; Lippit, R; White, RK. *Patterns of Aggressive Behaviour in Experimentally Created Social Climates*, 1939.

The students were divided into three groups, each under the leadership of a teacher with a different style as regards the providing of guidance. The first was authoritarian; the second, democratic, and the third a laissez faire. The activity was making masks of paper-mache. They all were 11-year-old boys.

1. The authoritarian leader was providing directions, was highly critical of work; kept distance from the boys; made all the decisions himself with no explanations for the same.

   The impact. The output was quite high. There was discipline in the class but as soon as the leader (teacher) was away, the work stopped. No initiative, no enthusiasm or creativity was seen in the group.

2. The democratic leader talked about the aims of the course; boys were a party in decision-making, dialogue and discussions during classes. The boys, to some extent, were also free to choose the partners for their group.

   The impact. The output was less; but quality was better; the work continued even when the leader was away; there was much of enthusiasm, initiation and creativity.

3. The laissez-faire leader allowed the boys to do as they liked; gave no guidance or direction about the mask-making activity; not any feedback was provided regarding the quality and the quantity of the output.

   The impact. The group fared the worst of all. The quantity was low, the quality was poor; the mentality was that of apathy. The boys were confused as no directions or guidance was available. The boys were not happy working in such conditions.

The nursery teacher's behaviour should be such that she may make up, to some extent, the absence of the child's mother from whom he is taken off suddenly for attending his nursery school.

Especially, the nursery teacher's behaviour should be such that she may make up, to some extent, the absence of the child's mother from whom he is taken off suddenly for attending his nursery school. The teacher's personality should be characterised by a natural affection for the kids of the school. Her patience and painstakingness should be indicative of her affection for the kids. On the contrary, if a teacher is rough with, and, is howling at the students all the time, the students may develop a repulsive attitude for the school, and for all related to it. This would change the whole direction of the development of their personality.

I am quoting a few words from a book which describes the great impact of the school in the making of a child into a good personality.

With entrance in the school, a sense of responsibility begins to be developed; without this there can be no development. His attitude towards, or his sense of the worthwhileness of efforts, a sense of attachment towards the school property, his sharing of teacher's time and attention, and his learning to team up with his peers, are all in the making from the day he enters the school. The school age is a period of learning how to accept defeat in sportsman spirit, how to accept failure as a challenge for greater efforts; for learning not to cheat in work or play; and, of expanding groups' participation and responsibilities. although most of these lessons are continuing through the school years. The first three years in school, usually, determine the child's attitude towards school and the job of school for the rest of the school life, and, perhaps, even for the rest of his career.

Moral attributes make a very important aspect of a person's personality; from the above paragraph we may very well follow what an important role a school plays in developing good moral qualities in an individual.

PEER-GROUP

Generally, initiation has to be taken by the newcomer as he knows that now he will have to live with the group. He has to learn the cues and the responses which are likely to be rewarded by his peers. The process of integration progresses only slowly because the peer-group is not exactly consisted of members of the same type; and the socioeconomic status of their families also happen to be different, and then each happens to be having its own "centre of gravity" or "central core" because of their having had different prenatal impacts besides having heterogeneous family backgrounds.

Factors which affect peer acceptance.

The following are the factors which affect peer acceptance:

1. Those who are bodily well-built and strong, are liked by their peers.
2. Those who are good looking, they become popular among the peer group.
3. Children better in physical activities or sports, win more friends.
4. Habits of tidy-living are also liked by the members of the group.
5. A happy child, friendly in nature, would naturally win more friends. The frequent laughter is a sign of friendly invitation.
6. Those who are good at studies, may attract some for friendship with them while at the same time some may become envious of their class-achievements.
7. Rough and tumble, and having some aggressiveness also get favourable attention from many.
8. During the middle childhood, such children are befriended who are skilled and competent in the work befitting their age and sex.

Patterson et al,[11] through a diagram have shown how the rejection by peers and failure in academic work has its cause in the nature of family care (see Fig. 15.3).

11. Patterson, GR, Debaryshe, BD, Ramsey, E. *A Developmental Perspective on Antisocial Behaviour,* 1989.

"Rejection" by normal peers may be caused by the conduct of the child himself; he may be a problematic child. "Poor parental discipline and monitoring" may have been a factor responsible for the child's growing problem. And, because of this factor (that is, poor parental care), he may not be doing well in school. A child so poorly looked after at home, and rejected by the normal peers, (and being punished frequently by his teachers because of his academic failure), is very much liable to be attracted towards the deviant peer group. And, moving in that group means that he is definitely to grow into a delinquent.

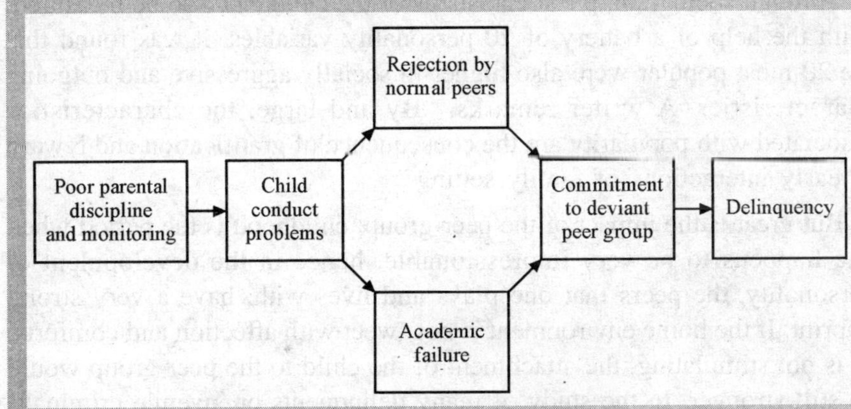

Figure 15.3 Patterson et al. show how family environment may be responsible for rejection by the peers and failure in scholastics.

So, "acceptance" by the peer-group is very important if the child is to be protected against delinquency. And, for the peer acceptance, the conduct of the child should be such that the normal peers may like him. Again, the conduct of the child would be good only if the desired parental care (discipline) and monitoring had been there.

As the children get older, they become more independent of their parents; more of their time would be spent with their peers. The norms and values of the peers become more important to them. For acceptance by the peer group, each child tries to conform to the norms and values of his peers; he chooses the type of clothes as worn by the popular member/members of the group; he copies; and he would imitate them in the way of speaking; and, would have the same cine-stars as his favourites as his peers (especially the favourite peers) do. He feels a pressure to conform to the attitudes and behaviours of his peers for fear of being left out.

Acceptance and rejection by the peer-group has a long enduring impact on the behaviour of an individual. It affects the development of personality. Those accepted, happen to be extrovert and sociable, they, generally, also happen to be out-spoken. Since their school times, they are active and participating in different activities, their social qualities may be expected to be further strengthened, and it is out of such a lot, that some with leadership qualities, come out as leading personalities.

But those who are rejected by the peer-group, generally, already happen to be shy of the company of others; and because of this they grow more withdrawing, introvert and escapist. Some of them may grow neurotic for life; some, of course, may develop into writers or thinkers.

Bonny, ME through "sociometry", and Tuddenham, RD through his reputation test, studied correlates of popularity among elementary school children.

Through sociogram, the social status of the child can also be measured. With the help of a battery of 20 personality variables, it was found that the 20 most popular were also higher in socially aggressive and outgoing characteristics. A writer remarks, "By and large, the characteristics associated with popularity are the consequence of gratification and reward of early interactions of family setting."

But great is the impact of the peer-group; childhood is the period when one happens to be very impressionable, hence in the development of personality, the peers that one plays and lives with, have a very strong imprint. If the home environment is not sweet with affection and comforts, or is not stimulating, the attachment of the child to the peer-group would be still stronger. In the study of many delinquents or juvenile criminals, the non-democratic or dull families were found to be responsible for the children's falling into bad companies. A family where the father is very strict, or the elders are wavering in their response to a particular behaviour of the child; or are too busy to sit in an easy mood chatting to the child, sometimes to play with the child, the child's attraction towards his peers would grow stronger.

Once, a child therapist, in a conference organised on the topic "Relationships and Families" told "children when ignored and misunderstood by their elders, develop a deep sense of rejection which also erases their trust in others." (*The Times of India*, Nov. 28, 1998). She also remarked, "Parents must learn to hear the voices of their children before they become manifest in actions like self-abuse including drugs or aggressive behaviours towards their peers and adults."

Judith Rich Harris, declares that mom and dad are "not paramount that the other kids on the playground matter more ....

Judith Rich Harris,[12] a writer of New Jersey, and recipient of George A Miller Award, in her book declares that mom and dad are "not paramount that the other kids on the playground matter more ... They tailor their behaviour to the group". Peer-group dynamics, she claims, influence everything from smoking to gender roles.

12. Harris, Judith Rich. *The Nurture Assumption: Why Children Turn Out the Way They Do.*

PROFESSION

Though the book is related to child psychology but personality is related to the whole life of a person even though its development is very rapid during childhood. Personality, almost in its full bloom, is a subject related to adulthood. None the less, we have included the topic in reference to child development because the personality is mainly the resultant of factors which are most effective in childhood. But profession is such a factor which is related only to adulthood. It also exerts its impact in bringing about changes in one's personality. Every profession leads to the development of certain habits, attitudes and values in life of the professional. This is why people can guess the profession of a person correctly in a majority of cases. A doctor reacts to a social event differently than does a man of accounts, or a lawyer; it is because of the impact of one's profession that develops an attitude by which the professionals are recognised. The profession so fixes ways of behaving and thinking which are unique of that profession, that to predict one's response to a stimulus, can be possible. All this shows that a profession is also a factor to count with when we speak of the development of personality.

COMMUNITY

Community is a very wide term which may be made up of many social groups. Many entities, like a family, and agencies like a school may be operative therein to bring about a collective and cumulative impact on the individuals belonging to the community. With the result that an Israelite may be easily distinguished from a Japanese, and an Indian from an African because of some unique characteristics of each of them. We can differentiate the one from the other because of distinctive habits and attitudes of each of them. Each community has its own traditions, history and culture influencing its people since centuries. The geographic and climatic conditions of each of them, may be very dissimilar; each factor affecting the other, the interactions between so many different factors result in the development of a unique and complex character of a community. And, community in its turn serves as a factor in developing each of its individual member into a personality distinguishable from each other member of another community. Nevertheless, it is not the case that each individual of a community has the same kind of personality in all respects as do others of the community—it is because each individual person has his own "central core" of personality which can hardly be changed, and makes each individual, even of the same community, a unique personality.

Community is a very wide term which may be made up of many social groups. Many entities, like a family, and agencies like a school may be operative therein to bring about a collective and cumulative impact on the individuals belonging to the community.

The effect of community happens to be very strong on the individuals as well as collectively on all the different organisations and agencies working therein. We see that in some communities; democracy, if it is

> Each community has its own traditions, history and culture influencing its people since centuries. The geographic and climatic conditions of each of them, may be very dissimilar; each factor affecting the other, the interactions between so many different factors result in the development of a unique and complex character of a community. And, community in its turn serves as a factor in developing each of its individual member into a personality distinguishable from each other member of another community.

ever established, cannot survive long, the people there being more belligerent, and the individual quality of aggressiveness may be getting higher value than the quality of co-operation, the quality of offering sacrifice in the interest of the benefit of the majority. People of some community are found to be very intractable while that of the other may be pliant or adjustable; some happen to be easily provoked while others are more peace-loving and tolerant; some are more assertive than others.

These differences in the behaviour of peoples representing different communities are because of many factors, the chief among them being the socioeconomic status of a community which includes the level of education of the majority; geographical conditions and the political history of a community also affect the habits, attitudes and the overall lifestyle of the people of a community, and each individual in his personality represents more or less the characteristics of his community. Coming to the divisions in a community, we find that an urban community effects a different type of personality development than does a rural community. In adult personalities. the differences are easy to mark, on a child, the impact of differences may not easily be perceived. The congenial countryside environment is more suitable for making people rich in imagination; for inculcating love for nature, attachment to animals, for physical health with a variety of chores being there to be done.

But the city life has its advantages, too; there may be more occasions for cognitive development—big libraries, educational institutions of all levels and types being there. Art museums, concerts, theatres, grand markets, and all provide a stimulating environment for having variegated experiences helpful in cognitive development. Both the rural and city communities inculcate different sorts of values and lifestyles.

We, in India, are having a heterogeneous community, with people of different religions, speaking different languages and wearing dissimilar clothes, using dissimilar foods, and so on, have been living together—this situation has made us more tolerant and pliant. A segregated community, generally, would affect in making its people more rigid and fundamentalist.

CULTURE

> Culture represents the best product of human mind in the fields of arts and intellects. It is the result of the cultivated human mind which has been making constant efforts for achieving perfection.

Culture represents the best product of human mind in the fields of arts and intellects. It is the result of the cultivated human mind which has been making constant efforts for achieving perfection. The stage up to which a particular community has reached by dint of its efforts, can be known through the works of that community in the fields of architecture, fine arts, dance, music, different literary forms, styles of living and values of life, consumer items that make life more comfortable, more secure; sanitary care (including ways of disposing wastes), means of recreation and so on.

While on one hand, the achievements in all these varied fields depend upon the types of personalities that the society consists of; on the other hand, the culture of a society through its concrete forms and through its values that direct behaviours of its people, has immense impact upon the development of personality of its people.

Tastes, hobbies, and likings and dislikings of the people happen, mainly, to be the result of the impact of their culture. Literary and artistic pursuits reflect the nature of culture of the people. The food one eats and the clothes one wears, also reflect the culture of the people. Culture affects each behaviour of the people of a community; how a younger greets an elder, is different in different communities according to the culture of each. An Indian boy would touch the feet of his father to see him off while departing for a journey but an English boy would shake hands with his father. Manners and etiquettes differ from community to community, according to its culture. How an old member is treated in his family; what type of behaviour a woman gets at the hands of her husband, and in her family, to a great extent depend upon the values that the culture teaches. Some people are hospitable while others shy off strangers, so on and so forth.

The models that the parents present before their children; the patterns of rewards and punishments; the attitudes that the people share with other members of their community—all indicate the culture of a community—when both parents belong to the same cultural group, the types of behaviour that they would be teaching to their children, would be alike, and, there would be little or no scope for confusion for the children. Technique of child rearing, and of discipline, will also be the same in the same cultural group. In the families with low socioeconomic status, physical punishment to children with all its harmful effects, are more frequent. Honesty, though is rewarded in all social groups, yet is more cultivated where the cultural demand makes the parents the living models of honesty.

Danis, A[13] writes that the child's behaviour which is rewarded and encouraged in one family, may be disapproved and punished in another family because of sub-cultural differences. Parents teach responses, values and beliefs to their children befitting to their sub-culture. The manner of eating food, and the choice of playmates—all form the part of parental teaching. The educational and occupational goals cannot be decided without an impact of culture in so doing. The times and places of recreation, the chores required of the child by his family; the rooms and articles of the house, that the child can use: the wearing of certain clothes at certain times, the amount of study required of him, the economic control to which he is subjected, indeed, the very conception of right and wrong of parents—all have bearing with the culture that the parents belong to.

Danis, A writes that the child's behaviour which is rewarded and encouraged in one family, may be disapproved and punished in another family because of sub-cultural differences.

13. Danis, A. *Child Training and Social Class.*

Those belonging to the same culture, would behave differently in regard to their children because of socioeconomic class differences. Middle-class mothers would be more affectionate and less punitive in comparison to that of the lower class. Interviews of 178 mothers of each, upper middle and upper lower class, whose children were in the kindergarten, indicate that mothers belonging to the former class, were warmer and more demonstrative.

REVIEW QUESTIONS

***Q*.1.** Give three definitions of "personality" as given by the renowned authors.

***Q*.2.** Which are the nine dimensions as narrated by Thomas and Chess to study temperamental differences among small children?

***Q*.3.** What are the four characteristics of personality that are highlighted by the definition of personality as given by Ausubel?

***Q*.4.** Describe in brief the three stages of personality development as mentioned by Sigmund Freud.

***Q*.5.** Describe the types of personality that you are aware of?

***Q*.6.** "Thus, personality is the end product of a persons' physical, cognitive and emotional development."
Discuss if personality is an "end product" or, is it a "dynamic totality of systems" as narrated by Kurt Levin.

***Q*.7.** Which are the factors that affect the development of personality? Describe in detail how the "Genetic" factor, and the 'family' as a factor are important in this respect?

***Q*.8.** What characteristic differences would you find, in general, in the behaviour of the people belonging to a democratic society, in contrast to, that of the people from an autocratic one?

CHAPTER

16 THE ABNORMALITIES AND THEIR TREATMENT

Chapter Outline

- Neurosis
- Causes
- Remedial Measures
- Two Approaches of Play Therapy
- Cause of Schizophrenia
- Remedy
- Modification of Racial Attitude
- Feeble-mindedness
- Learning Disabilities
- Characteristics of a Child with Learning Disabilities
- What Should be Done for the Learning Disablement?
- Review Questions

There are children who apparently strike as abnormal. Physical abnormalities can be perceived at first sight. If a child is dwarfed or short for his age, or is abnormally tall; is too much overweight or underweight, will immediately be recognised as such. If the bones or muscles have not developed normally in due course, the fact will easily be perceived without any diagnostic exercise. But there are a number of other types of physical or bodily abnormalities for the perception of which expert diagnosis will be required. The deficiency of some particular vitamin or of any other ingredient, of hemoglobin, or of excess of some particular fluid secreted from some hormonal gland and so on, requires some expert investigation for its diagnosis. Deficiency of a serious nature, as that of iodine, for example, may result in serious physical, intellectual and emotional abnormalities, too. Particularly in chapter six, it has been given what are the main ingredients of food which are necessary for health, and what ailments may be caused because of their deficiency.

There may be some prenatal factors responsible for physical deformity or abnormality. A mention of the same has been made in chapter three of the book. Some diseases are caused because of the genes carrying hereditary effects; or, because of malnutrition of the prospective mother; or, because of her tension, anxiety or a sense of insecurity disturbing physiological functions of the mother; or, because of biochemical changes (excessive secretion of adrenaline glands and increase of chemicals such as acetylcholine and epinephrene and so on), with the result that the embryo/foetus, getting its feeding from the blood of the mother through umbilical chord, is affected, and physical growth may be adversely affected. A mongoloid may be born if the number of chromosomes increases by one more than the normal.

Unhygienic living conditions and malnutrition are both prenatal and postnatal factors which affect the physical and so also the mental and emotional health of the child. A home characterised by routine brawling, father being too busy to chat and play with, or fondle the child, and the mother is also an insensitive working woman or is herself ill, or remains tense and fearful because of unwholesome home environment, cannot take care of the physical needs—feeding, clothing, elimination and so on, of the child, nor, of its emotional need which is affectionate nurturance. The child's health may be affected because of obstetrical troubles; or, because of inadequate oxygen in the labour room; the latter situation may cause asphyxia. Even after birth if the physical conditions of the house is not hygienic, that is, if no proper ventilation, light and sanitary system is there, the child cannot remain healthy.

We have already read previously, in a concerned chapter that if feeding to the child is not made timely and with affection, in a pleasant mood; proper care regarding the elimination and cleanliness of the child is not taken; proper clothing is not provided according to the weather conditions, and the bodily need of the child; and if the child is not provided a congenial environment for having its full stint of sleep with no disturbance whatsoever—the child cannot develop normally in its physique. And, such a child would develop the habit of crying, squirming; and of spitting out its food when the same is belatedly given and in not a happy mood. If such a one grows up as aggressive in nature, these situations of his infancy may be a cause.

Some cases of imagined or of a slight defect in appearance, have been reported leading to devastating disorder. Body dysmorphic disorder, in some cases, led to dropping of school, shunning social contacts, and even to suicide.

Awakening to just reasoning, is the only remedy to such a disorder. In this chapter we shall take only some serious types of psychological abnormalities; have a look into their causes in brief, and, suggest remedies. Some of the abnormalities that have been mentioned above, may be remedied if the causes leading to abnormalities, are removed at the initial stage.

NEUROSIS

Etymologically, "neurosis" means "disorder of nervous system". The word has been developed from the Greek term "neuron" which means "nerve". Its apparent symptoms are "irrational behaviour" and "depression". A neurotic person is found to be abnormally anxious or obsessed with something. I remember of an acquaintance of mine, who whenever happened to come across me, would appear highly troubled or puzzled, he would continuously complain of one or the other problem haunting him. It was not the case that his anxiety was always genuine, many times he would be jittery only in connection with imagined reasons. To grow anxious had been his mental habit which he could hardly improve upon. Just an idea would come to his mind, and he would be so obsessed with it that he could not find respite.

Etymologically, "neurosis" means "disorder of nervous system". The word has been developed from the Greek term "neuron" which means "nerve". Its apparent symptoms are "irrational behaviour" and "depression".

I would like to refer to a colleague of mine to illustrate how a neurotic behaves. We were travelling together in a train. Each was accompanied by wife. That colleague of mine was sitting just in front of me. He had put a bag of his on the wooden slab meant for the purpose; the bag was in front of him, and was above my seat. He would rise from his seat off and on, touch his bag to be assured that it was safe. Now, his obsession for the bag was unreasonable, his jitters for its safety were without a genuine cause. The same colleague of mine once sought my help in getting a shirt of his sewn. I sent for a tailor. He noted the measurement. But, as soon as the tailor, after putting into his pocket the slip of measurement noted upon it, and the piece of cloth in his hand, climbed down the stairs, my colleague desired me to call back the tailor. On my asking "why", he replied, the tailor might sew a shirt not fitting to the size of his body.

Both instances given above illustrate how a neurotic person behaves, and what type of psychology he has.

1. He remains anxious even when the reason may not be a genuine one.
2. He fears of things which actually evokes no fear for a normal person.
3. He remains troubled mostly for no reason to be so. He cannot have peace of mind.

4. Such a person is not likely to enjoy a sound sleep, and have a full stint of it.
5. Because of such an obsession of jitters and fear, he would lose both his mental and physical health, and would become a patient of some psychiatrist.
6. Such a person would not be having that much of vigour or mental zest that he may persevere long and properly for the performance of some serious and important mental work.
7. Depression would be a general symptom of a neurotic.
8. If a survey may possibly be conducted into the cases of suicide, majority of those who commit it, would be found to have been neurotics.

CAUSES

(*i*) If during the period of pregnancy, the prospective mother had been suffering from a feeling of insecurity; would have been anxious or tense due to the unwholesome home environment, and, especially because of the rough or harsh treatment meted out to her by her husband who may often have been inebriated, or because of her ill-health and low socioeconomic status of the family, or so on, would give birth to a child prone to neurosis.

(*ii*) If the child is a result of unwanted delivery; the mother is a step-mother, or for any reason she fails to give a sense of security and warmth of affection, the child would grow neurotic.

(*iii*) A child may grow traumatic because of obstetrical complexities.

(*iv*) If both father and mother are too busy to attend to the needs of the child in time and in a happy mood, the psychology of the neglected child would be distorted, and the result may be neurosis.

(*v*) Too harsh toilet-training to a babe who is still not two years old, would make it tense and fearful.

(*vi*) A sense of insecurity is the main cause for neurosis. When the child first attends his nursery, he experiences too much tension. To adjust to an altogether new situation, where there are so many unfamiliar faces behaving in a strange way with the new entrant; and over it all, if the teacher is of a serious or frowning kind, would be very difficult. If such a situation continues for long, the child would be greatly disturbed mentally, and, the traumatised child may grow into a neurotic for his whole life.

(*vii*) A long period of hospitalisation may also harm the psychology of the child, and if, his aftermath experiences are also not good, he is very likely to be neurotic.

(*viii*) Body dysmorphic disorder may also make the child shy and withdrawn, and the eventual result may, sometime be neurosis.

(*ix*) Experience of some riot or any such event presenting scenes of gruesome killings, or undergoing some terror-evoking incidence, or the death of one's dear and near one, may so upset and horrify the mind of the child that he may never be free from its traumatising effect.

(*x*) An innocent child if happens to have been physically or sexually-abused, may also grow neurotic. Physical abuse has been defined by Gil[1] in the words "... the intentional non-accidental use of force on the part of the parent or other caretaker interacting with child in his or her care aimed at hurting, injuring or destroying that child".

Kempe[2] defines the sexual abuse as under:

"... The involvement of dependent, sexually immature children and adolescents in sexual activities that they do not fully comprehend, to which they are unable to give informed consent or that violate the social taboos of family roles."

REMEDIAL MEASURES

Psychotherapy Psychotherapy provides the child a free atmosphere where he can express himself with no fear of being punished, rebuked or laughed at. For the success of psychotherapy, the first thing that is needed, is a very cordial and close relationship between the child and the therapist. Even the teacher may work as a therapist. The child must be treated with regard and dignity. Dollard and Miller[3] write that psychotherapy is basically a learning process for adopting attitudes and behaviour which may replace less adequate responses learned in the family setting. It is for unlearning the undesirable behaviour or habits, and for learning non-neurotic habits.

Techniques of therapy Play therapy is an important technique which helps the child in releasing his feelings, and expressing his problem. Axline[4] underlines the importance of this therapy with the words as follows.

1. Gil, D. *Violence Against Children*, 1970.
2. Kempe, CH. *Incest and other Forms of Sexual Abuse.*
3. Dollard, J, Miller, ME. *Personality and Psychotherapy.*
4. Axline, VM. *Play Therapy.*

"Play therapy is based upon the fact that play is the child's natural medium of self-expression. It is an opportunity which is given to the child to play out his feelings and problems just as in certain types of adult therapy, an individual talks out his difficulties."

When the feelings are played out, they become open on the surface. Now, he develops the habit of facing them openly. He learns to control them without being mentally perturbed. He may even abandon them. The feelings which, previously, he was so afraid of their being there in his mind, he has developed courage to face them in the open. Play therapy has provided emotional relaxation to him. He starts realising power within himself, and finds himself to be an individual in his own right. He feels that now he can think for himself, he is free and able enough to have his own decisions. Such a therapy helps one in achieving timely maturity, and self-hood.

TWO APPROACHES OF PLAY THERAPY

The play-therapist may either keep the reins of the situation subtly in his own hands, or/may allow full freedom to the child to handle the play situation in his own way. The former would be the example of *directive approach*, the latter, that of the *non-directive one*.

Directive Approach The approach is directive when the therapist decides what material (dolls, or other play material) to use, what plot to adopt, what questions to ask—when to ask and how to ask. Besides this, the therapist performs the following activities:

- Systematically observes the play;
- Reports what day dreams or dreams the child is having;
- He so organises the situation that the child may have a free association with the therapist;
- Has direct discussions with the patient (child) whenever situation permits, and he deems proper.

While observing the child at play, he always remains cautious to be assured that the play is developing on desired lines, and no hindrance is likely to be there. He observes the changes coming over the face of the child, indicative of the dreams passing through his mind. While the play is going on, he finds out occasions when he should ask questions to the child to know more about the feelings and emotions that are evoked by the different situations in the play—it is through the answers of the child thus elicited that he can have a better understanding of the problem of the child.

Directive play technique, more than other techniques, makes use, at least partially, of the theory and procedures of the psychoanalysis school of psychology. This technique demands controlled and standardised situations. If the main problem in a family is that of sibling rivalry, and, the patient (the child) is a prey of the same, the therapist encourages the child to play with the plot, and may supply more actors and scenes if for the fulfilment of the objective, it is so needed. The objective in such a controlled play is always the release of pent up feelings or emotions, as he has always been too afraid to give vent to the same. This is why its leading exponent has called it "release therapy". While playing with the actors of the play, he would express his grievances which he may have harboured against any of his siblings or any of his parents, or against any of his peers or teachers. The therapist, thus, provides an occasion for releasing severe anxiety, fear, reactions or night terrors which may have been precipitated by traumatic experiences such as death or divorce of a parent, some surgical operation or so on. David Guy suggests that this technique should not be used in case of a child older than ten years.

I have often seen the newly admitted nursery or kindergarten students playing 'sir' or 'madam'. While thus playing, a child who is greatly fearful of his 'sir' or 'madam', would give vent to his suppressed feelings regarding him or her. The "sir" or "madam" may be very rough or harsh, and may have rebuked and even beaten the child; the child because of fear may not be able to express his resentment otherwise. Such feelings of his, the child may express in the free atmosphere of the play. On the release of his repressed feelings, the child feels much relieved, feels to have got courage to face the situation. Thus, the play therapy helps in the restoration of emotional health. Though in such an instance if there are no directions from the side of the therapist, and the children are fully free to behave in their own way, the technique would be called as Non-directive.

We are taking another instance of Directive Approach to illustrate how a therapist may provide a situation for the "release" of the suppressed feelings. Suppose there is a child who, generally, remains sad, he hardly ever smiles; he has lost his hunger also. He seems to be growing weak in body. Such a child would grow neurotic, and if timely therapy is not provided, the case may become chronic when the child grows older as adolescent or adult. The father of the child is responsible for a development of this sort. He is very strict and non-feeling, he is not sensitive to the feelings of his young child. Whenever the child seeks permission to go out and play with his peers, he gets only a threatening rebuke along with refusal. The poor child may only be looking at his peers playing their evening games, while himself sitting in his balcony, wearing a long face.

The therapist provides dolls as material. The actors would be a father and his son. Then, there would also be dolls of small size which would be like the peers of the son, with whom he would like to play. But on the stage there are brought a number of small dolls; there is a ball which each one of them is kicking now and then. Now, the therapist asks the patient:

T. (Therapist): Who are on the stage?
P. (Patient): There are a number of boys (dolls).
T. What are the boys doing?
P. They are playing.
T. Do you also like to play?
P. Yes, I do.
(Then there is presented a bigger doll on the stage with its face very serious or expressing anger.)
T. Who has come now?
P. A father (expected answer.)
(The bigger doll takes hold of the arm of one of the playing dolls, and pulls the same away).
T. Who is this that has come now?
P. He is also a father.
T. What is he doing?
P. He is looking at the boys play.
T. What kind of father is he?
P. He is good.
T. Why is he good?
P. He allows his son to play.

In this way the therapist may ask more questions to elicit the repressed feelings or emotions of the child whose main cause for problem is the refusal to him for play by his very strict father.

If the therapist deems it easy to arrange a set of pictures, and use the same, he may use the same in place of dolls. Some such sets of pictures may be kept ready in the clinic for the diagnosis and treatment of such a common abnormality as neurosis is. Alternatively, the therapist may orally make the child open his mind in response to the appropriate questions asked by him. But for it, first, a very close rapport has to be established with the child; the child needs to be made free of fear in exposing his pent up feelings; otherwise, he may choose to keep mum, or, may just evade by making any response which is not a sincere one. This is why *projective method* is better where unfinished pictures are displayed by turn, and the child would express his mind when asked to tell what he is seeing in the picture, and what type of person has been represented in the picture, and so on. Such a therapy may be needed to be applied for either of the parents when one of them is the cause for the trouble of the child. David Guy writes, "... to a child suffering from the results of maternal rejection or overprotection ... mother is the exclusive object of therapy."

Active play therapy Active play therapy as a controlled method, has also been suggested by Solomon.[5] The therapist asks parents to give freedom to the child to express his feelings without fear. Solomon gives the example:

T. (Pointing to a doll) How does the boy (doll) look like?

C. It is sad (angry, and so on).

(The therapist may ask questions to elicit the child's reactions to a particular situation).

T. What would you do in such a situation?

In response to such questions, the child would be unfolding himself. This will help him in a better understanding of himself. It will give him self-confidence. His behaviour would improve after going through a series of such a play. The therapist would thus be able to pinpoint the nature of the problem, and would be helping the patient in being cured of the same through his own behaviour. The patient (child) himself may be now having an understanding of the problem or conflict with more confidence in himself. He begins to be less fearful of his hostility and guilt because he has been allowed to express them in a permissive and unthreatening situation. Direct suggestions as, "you don't have to feel badly about that" (Solomon) may also be used to help the child.

Non-directive approach Under this approach, the therapist provides altogether a free situation to the patient (child) where he can express his feelings and emotions with no fear of being rebuked, criticised or otherwise punished, nor of being considered guilty by others and by even himself. The approach is non-directive when the therapist gives no direct suggestion, he allows the child to do or say anything he wants. The behaviour of the therapist remains friendly and interested throughout. Alert, of course, the therapist remains all the time the therapy is being carried out so that his observation may be thorough, and he may indicate his acceptance or understanding of the behaviour of the child. The therapist is alert to note what the child is expressing in the play or in his conversation. Axline[6] writes, "the child is given the opportunity to play out his accumulated feelings or tension, frustration, insecurity, aggression, fear, bewilderment and confusion".

When the pent-up feelings have been brought out, the child feels relaxed emotionally. Now, he can see what the trouble is. He can now control them or, can abandon whatever is not desirable. He "begins to realise power within himself to become an individual in his own right". He can think

5. Solomon, JC. *Play Technique as a Differential Therapeutic Medium.*

6. Axline, VM. *Play Therapy.*

for himself, he can make his own decisions. Psychologically he is more matured, and is in a position to realise self-hood.

In the play therapy-room the child is the most important person. He feels himself fully secured, is in command of himself, and of his situation. There is no one here to suggest him anything, none to criticise him. He is fully accepted by others. He feels "here he can unfold his wings; can play in any way he likes, and is accepted completely. He can hate, love or be indifferent as a stone, still he is accepted completely. It is a unique experience for the child to find all adult suggestions, mandates, rebukes, restraints, criticisms, disapprovals, supports, intrusions—gone. They all are replaced by complete acceptance and permissiveness to be himself."

For the therapist, and for the parents, too; it may be a unique experience to find the same child so active, so progressive, so open and so happy, who otherwise—in the highly restrained situation—behaves so recalcitrantly. The child, who appears so problematic when parents bend upon disciplining him through strictness, and through showering upon him a lot of didacticism, starts behaving pliantly. Change in the behaviour of the child would not be sudden, only gradual; as the unfolding of the child would continue, he would be improving. Excess of his shyness, fear, anxiety, frustration, jealousy, anger all will be cured as the child would be releasing out all these emotions in the hot, unrestricted pursuits of his game.

The spontaneous play technique is, especially, useful in case of children with longstanding neurotic traits. It is a very effective treatment. Let the child play freely in his own way—he may run, kick at a ball, jump, cry, push his peer, pull some one or some thing—no restraint is advisable unless any harm is likely to be caused. This is non-directive play therapy. The therapist observes and notes which of his repressed feelings or emotions are getting a chance to be expressed: how they are expressed, and what changes come about in the bahaviour of the child because of such an emotional relaxation. The children who are "inhibited, repressed, extremely hostile, excessively timid or overly ridiculous" are most likely to be benefited. The child, under his changed mental state, can adequately deal with previously upsetting situations. He himself starts attempting at new solutions to his problems.

The exponents of the non-directive approach of play therapy forbid the therapist, and all those interested in the treatment of the child, from referring to the events of the past to the child, the child needs to be fully absorbed into his present activities. Allen, F[7] writes " ... Emphasis on present activities, statements, feelings and emotions rather than on past circumstances and events which have influenced his behaviour. Difficulties and problems are

7. Allen, F. *Psychotherapy with Children.*

discussed in terms of what is happening at the moment. Sessions are treated as growth experiences."

Thumb sucking, staggering (or stammering) and enuresis are also abnormal behaviours. The causes of these abnormalities and their remedies have already been given in the previous concerned chapters, hence we are skipping over them just mentioning their names. Likewise, the very serious abnormality **aggressiveness** which also becomes apparent even in early childhood, and if the cause, giving rise to it, continues, the abnormality would be hardened and more difficult to be cured. Aggressiveness has also been dealt in detail proviosuly. Play therapy that we have described in great details in above paragraphs, is an effective remedy for it also.

Shyness, fearfulness, anxiety, prejudice all are abnormalities when they are in excess, out of proportion than the cause warrants. One is shy (or withdrawn) because one feels something to be there in his personality which he does not want others to look at as he is afraid of the laughter that others may make him subject to. One shies the company of others because of his experiences with others have not been good; he may have been neglected, scoffed at or rebuked, or may have been otherwise maltreated. A shy person, whether a child or a grown-up, also harbours some sort of fear in coming in contact with others. Other people, especially, when their number is big, would make him uneasy, and, he would prefer to avoid them. He shuns the company of others, and likes to remain alone. Such a person is liable to develop a more serious type of abnormality, that is, *schizophrenia*.

Shyness, fearfulness, anxiety, prejudice all are abnormalities when they are in excess, out of proportion than the cause warrants.

The word **schizophrenia** is derived from the Greek words schizo + phren; the meaning of the first is "split" and that of the second is "mind". The schizophrenic is one whose mind becomes split. Split in the sense that his mind is not absorbed in the action that he is doing. There is no unity of "action" and "thought" or "feeling". He develops a dual personality. He is not what he seems to be externally; he may be doing something related to his routines yet, internally, he may be lost in his own world of fantasy. Outwardly he likes to remain idle so that he may be able to think about his own problems which generally happen to be the creation of his own fantasy.

The word schizophrenia is derived from the Greek words schizo + phren; the meaning of the first is "split" and that of the second is "mind". The schizophrenic is one whose mind becomes split. Split in the sense that his mind is not absorbed in the action that he is doing. There is no unity of "action" and "thought" or "feeling". He develops a dual personality.

- A schizophrenic tries to avoid the company of others, lest there should be disturbance in his phantasmagoric flights.
- Schizophrenia is a mental disorder, its patient has less relationship with realities, and remains absorbed in imaginary problems.
- He is always doubtful, anxious, and fearful though no genuine reason for the same is there.
- He appears troubled; and sometimes becomes violent, even against one who tries to teach him realities to end his imaginary troubles.

A schizophrenic is rarely seen indulging in a loud conversation with imaginary characters, but if no proper handling is done, the condition may further be precipitated, and the patient may start behaving totally like a lunatic.

Though schizophrenia and some of the other abnormalities develop to the perceptible level only during adulthood yet, we are dealing with them in a book related to child development because the process of development of abnormalities, generally, starts when one is still a child.

CAUSE OF SCHIZOPHRENIA

A sense of insecurity is the main cause of schizophrenia. The baby feels insecure when either or both of the parents are punitive, are sometimes indulgent and sometimes unnecessarily harsh. The behaviour of the elder sibling may also cause a sense of insecurity.

When the need of feeding of the baby is not timely fulfilled, and the child has to cry for long, it starts feeling insecure. If care is not often taken in regard to elimination and other needs for the health and protection of the child, even because of that also a sense of insecurity is engendered.

Schizophrenia may also be caused when the family environment is not peaceful and wholesome because of frequent brawls between father and mother, because of the father being a drunkard, and of his beating the mother or other members of the family.

If the home environment is not stimulating enough, and a sense of belongingness is not there among the members of the family; the child does not enjoy a parent's warmth towards it; would feel neglected, and the child would have to keep itself lying idle with no smile on his face nor on those of the others.

If the nursery teacher is not sensitive enough towards the child who is already too much disturbed because of being suddenly weaned out of the warm and protective environment of home. Or, rather, the teacher is rough and harsh in her treatment towards the new entrant, such a fear would be caused that the child will be constrained to remain silent and lonely—as he has still not been able to adjust itself to other children of his class either. Such a situation may lead to the development of schizophrenia.

Some highly unpleasant event of life may cause someone to be shocked into schizophrenia, one is traumatised because of such an event. If a child is often rebuked to silence by someone elder to him; the child would lose courage to express himself in future, with the result, the child may grow either neurotic or schizophrenic in the long-run because of continuous repression of feelings and emotions. Even cruel treatment meted out to a girl at her in-laws, if continued for long, may leave the girl schizophrenic.

REMEDY

The best remedy is the warm and loving treatment meted out to the patient so that the patient may again be assured of his safety.

A schizophrenic patient should never be left alone for long though he would like to be so. The patient should get an environment where he may be kept engaged in conversation on some pleasant topic. The patient should never be reminded of the past, particularly, which has not been pleasant for him.

An attempt should be made to attract the patient towards some hobby so that his diversion towards the world of his fantasy would be less likely.

The patient needs always, to be persuaded to contact members of the family and other acquaintances so that he would not remain lonely, as loneliness always precipitates the problem.

The patient may be taken out on excursions, or to some other place with congenial environment, to stay there for some time so that he may be dissociated from the environment which is responsible for the problem.

The psychotherapy, as suggested above for the treatment of a neurotic, is also effective in curing a schizophrenic, either or both of the approaches—Directive and Non-directive—may be tried.

Fearfulness in its extreme form makes one's behaviour abnormal, and one suffering from it cannot lead a normal life. It also has its root in infancy, or susceptibility to it may have prenatal origin. During the period when the child is still in the form of a foetus, if the prospective mother remains tense or jittery, the future child is definitely to be affected by it, as the chemical biology of the blood of the mother is changed because of tension or anxiety; and the child is fed through that blood. If the child is the result of unwanted delivery, it may also be a factor in causing it. A child traumatised because of obstetrical complexities, may also grow fearful.

After birth, if the home environment continues to be tense because of noisy squabbles going on as a common routine; because of rebuking, scolding, beating, crying and so on, being a general experience of the child, the child would develop fearfulness. Experience of long hospitalisations, and that of operation, injection, or of some hard restrictions that the doctor may deem essential to prescribe, may also make the child timid.

A child, because of his age, happens to be very curious, and would go on asking many questions to acquaint himself with his environment; but when in reply, the child is often silenced through words of rebuke, the child may grow timid or fearful in expressing himself, in talking to others, in meeting others—and the timid child may even grow neurotic or schizophrenic if no timely cure is there.

The causes of fearfulness as mentioned above, are the genuine ones, but fearfulness may also be caused because of imaginary reasons. In a study, Jersild and Markey found 20 per cent of the children's fears to be unrealistic—imaginary creatures, the dark, and being alone. Some children cannot go into dark, and if asked why, they may tell of ghost or of some such imaginary things which they may have been told of living in the dark just to make them silent while crying, or to dissuade them from doing what they may have been insisting upon doing.

Dunlop[8] classifies the fears of children into four categories:

(*i*) Realistic, that is, could have happened to the child.
(*ii*) Remote—not much chances of happening.
(*iii*) Unrealistic—no chances of happening.
(*iv*) Mystical—where everything is shrouded with mystery, no basis for being definite about the cause.

An unpleasant experience of childhood, may leave one fearful for life in a particular situation. If a child was severely slapped for eating some sweet without permission, it may lead to phobia for sweet, and when that child has grown into an adult, even then the very sight of sweet, may make him shiver with fear.

Most kinds of fears, in most cases, disappear as the child grows older. The development of the faculty of reasoning, also helps one in being free from the feeling of fear.

Parents or elders should appeal, too, the reasoning of the child if fearfulness continues even during the period of formal operations, as Piaget has termed the period when the child attains the adult level of reasoning. Through arguments the child may be convinced that his fear is quite imaginary or unfounded.

The insecure child would, naturally, grow timid; in such a case the child needs convincing assurance of safety by his nurturants. In many cases, a feeling of insecurity engenders because of lack of care or affection from the side of parents or elder siblings. In such a situation, the warmth of affection of the person nurturing the child, is the only effective cure. The child recently admitted into a nursery, would grow fearful or timid if the teacher there is rough and harsh. Such a teacher cannot be expected to be sensitive to the fact that the child just weaned from the over-protective

---

8. Dunlop, GM. *Certain Aspects of Children's Fears.*

and warm environment of the home, is already much disturbed, and, needs parental affection to be assured of safety.

Anxiety An all-time or frequent obsession of anxiety, is something abnormal; it often, leads to other serious types of abnormalities such as neurosis and schizophrenia. Tendency to anxiety, may either be the result of circumstances which do not augur well for the future of the child, and, he may be feeling a mental strain brooding the harm to be caused, or, the danger to occur. Or sometimes the parents or elders of the family, or the teacher at the Kindergarten may be instrumental in the child being anxious. The targets fixed by them may be too ambitious, and so, too difficult for the child to achieve. And, such unrealistic targets, rather, harm the child; he ceases to behave in a normal way because of tension caused by anxiety. If over-ambitious parents expect too high scholastic achievements from their child, it is just possible that because of constant mental strain, he may not even achieve that much which he otherwise would have done.

Likewise, in the field of motor activities, or in the field of intellectual activities, or in regard to the planning for the career of the child, if the attitude of guardians or teachers is not realistic, anxiety would be the result. It may cause loss of appetite, and so emaciation.

Because of excessive parental love and their severe prohibition on aggressive and sexual behaviour, an adolescent, would feel constant strain and anxiety. Temptation to lie, to hit and to masturbate may arouse a sense of guilt in the adolescent, or in a child of school-going age—it causes mental tension, and anxiety haunts him. If such a condition continues for long, the behaviour of the child may grow abnormal.

In some cases health or body-condition may be source of anxiety. If one is not normal in weight and height, or is not well-built, or good-looking, comparing to others who have been endowed with a good looking and a well-proportioned and stout body, would always be thinking about the means to improve upon his physical drawbacks. Ailment or poor-health would be considered a genuine ground for anxiety. In such a case, effective treatment ought to be arranged by the parents. And, in case of anxiety regarding body-structure, or bodily condition, if all measures to improve the same have failed, the child's anxiety may be mitigated by telling him that if in some aspects he is poorly endowed, he is better than others in other respects, his strengths need to be highlighted, and he be cheered up for his achievements. When grown-up enough, an appeal to his reasoning, should also be made to lighten or remove his anxiety. Again, play therapy is useful here also.

Prejudice Prejudice to some extent is, perhaps, unavoidable; but when the same grows in excess, the behaviour of the person appears abnormal. We criticise a grown-up for his prejudice, and do not do so in case of a child because the behaviour of a child does not so much influence others. During childhood, the impact of the attitudes of the adults of the family happens to be very strong and lasting. The adults say about and behave with others as per their attitudes towards them. The child imbibes like attitude towards the same persons, or persons of the same group or class. If the mother of a girl often speaks ill of her mother-in-law, blaming the very institution of mother-in-law, the impact of this would be in the form of prejudice, and, when the girl herself is married, she would go to her in-laws with a prejudiced attitude towards her own mother-in-law. Thus, a child can easily grow prejudiced against certain categories of persons through generalisation.

If the mother of a girl often speaks ill of her mother-in-law, blaming the very institution of mother-in-law, the impact of this would be in the form of prejudice, and, when the girl herself is married, she would go to her in-laws with a prejudiced attitude towards her own mother-in-law.

Communal hatred or racial hatred is thus permanently ingrained into a child because of the hatred and hostility of the parents and other elders against people belonging to other religions or race. Thus, traditional hostility is the main source of prejudice. Prejudice means pre-judgment about other persons, institutions, castes, religions and so on, without first observing or assessing the same for their good or bad points. Thus, the judgment of a prejudiced person can never be just or objective. Such a person has his opinions ready-made about persons, organisations, events and so on, before he comes in contact with them. His opinions do not happen to be based on his observations or on the facts that are there, but they happen to be based on pre-conceived thoughts which others have caused to be instilled into his mind.

Communal hatred or racial hatred is thus permanently ingrained into a child because of the hatred and hostility of the parents and other elders against people belonging to other religions or race.

A lot many problems of our society, and I can say, of the international community, are because of prejudice. If a child belonging to one religion, hates the other belonging to a different religion, it is not because of his personal experience of the other, it is the product of the prevailing milieu. A lot many clashes, or battles may be having their roots in some or the other sort of prejudice. A lot of blood-shedding may have been because of prejudice. Coming to our personal relations, in many cases, they grow bitter because of pre-conceived opinions, that is prejudice. In a good many family clashes, prejudice may be the main culprit.

Prejudice is thus a distorted mind-set, we the grown-ups have a moral duty to save our future generation from being a prejudiced lot—the children being very impressionable, are easy to fall a prey to this mental ailment. If A has been telling his children against B with no serious fault of B the children would grow prejudiced against B; and no amount of good deeds done by B even for the children of A, can change the children's opinion for B.

The children of minority groups inherit a fear of hostile prejudice and rejection from their peers and adults. Children acquire prejudice from those with whom they identify themselves. They identify themselves with their parents and with their sub-cultural groups, that is, religious, ethnic or racial groups. Bigoted people are the product of prejudiced and fundamentalist parents or society. We are witness to it, and history provides umpteen number of examples how the bigots have been butchering and shedding blood of the innocent. In a society with the majority being consisted of bigots, democracy cannot thrive. If we look at the political scenario of the world, we see that there are nations where democracy either fails to have its birth, and, even if it has had its birth, its life always happens to be of a short duration.

School-going age, is the period of life when the children identify themselves most with their parents and sub-cultural groups. Years back (1974), Clark and Clark[9] in a study of 253 Negro children found that with increase in age, the percentage of children who identified themselves with Negro idols, increased. When the children were asked, "Give me the doll that looks like you"; 36 per cent of the 3-year-old, 48 per cent of the 5-year-old, and 87 per cent of the 7-year-old children chose the coloured dolls. This study proves that mid-childhood years, is the period when identification with one's sub-cultural group is firmly established. The motives, or the entire psychological make-up is influenced by this identification. The result is the prejudice which becomes apparent through the behaviour of the person. Radke and Traques[10] have shown how relations between the minority and the majority groups in a country get strained because of communal, religious or social prejudices. As the children grow older they wear their racial or religious labels with stronger convictions. As already stated above, prejudices are the feelings, emotions, opinions and convictions developed not through one's own experiences but are always the result of the behaviour and the oral teachings of the older members of the group.

> As the children grow older they wear their racial or religious labels with stronger convictions. As already stated above, prejudices are the feelings, emotions, opinions and convictions developed not through one's own experiences but are always the result of the behaviour and the oral teachings of the older members of the group.

The prejudiced adults tend to be rigid, authoritarian, highly conforming and overly moralistic. Frenkel's[11] study demonstrates that children's ethnic prejudices are also related to general personality structure. Five hundred Californian boys and girls were the sample. With the help of a tool, developed for the purpose, the views of the children, aged between 11 and 16, were sought in regard to Jews, Japanese, Mexicans, and out-groups in general. The views of the ethnocentric (prejudiced) children would always be-"Only people who are like myself, have the right to be happy." One hundred and twenty children were found to be most prejudiced, and they were of the view that they should think only of the Americans first.

---

9. Clark, KB, Clark, MP. *Racial Identification and Preference in Negro children—Readings in Social Psychology.*
10. Radke, M, Traques, HG. *Children's Perception of the Social Roles of Negroes and Whites*, 1950.
11. Frenkel-Brunswick, EA. *A Study of Prejudice in Children/Human Relations.*

Attitude of a person is greatly affected by the prejudice that he has been subject to.

Attitude of a person is greatly affected by the prejudice that he has been subject to. The narrow or rigid personality is indicative of the nature of prejudice that one is subject to. A strong opposition to a change in the apparel of girls, shows rigidity of attitude of the concerned society. Such a rigid attitude is because of the adults' prejudice against all that is modern. I do remember the sense of a Sanskrit shloka which is to the effect that all that is old, is not good, nor all that is new is bad, what is required, is to have an objective assessment of good and bad on the basis of their merits. Such an attitude as implied in the message of this shloka, can be considered to be free from prejudice. With the passage of time, a lot many old practices lose their utility, and a good many new ones may prove to be of more use and benefit to us, but the social prejudice developed for all that is old, stands in the way of social reforms, and in the way of ushering in new things or practices. Again, the teacher will have to shoulder the onus of freeing our new generation from a prejudice against all that is new. So far the developed countries are concerned, prejudice against the new is not such a problem there, but in the underdeveloped, and in some of the developing countries, prejudice against anything that is new, is a big problem—fundamentalism being ambient there. If greater is the socio-educational backwardness, the greater will be the prejudice against all that is new.

Harris et al,[12] write that prejudiced mothers score high in the authoritarian and rigid behaviour. They further write,—"What children learn is not specific attitude but a whole complex of attitudes and personality characteristics which reveal themselves in interpersonal relationships of various sorts." Tolerant children often speak of affection, co-operation, companionship while the prejudiced ones would, generally, complain of lack of affection, and of submission to stern, harsh and primitive treatment. Interviews with parents confirmed the general hypothesis that the tolerant child learns at home the equalitarian and individualised approach to people as the ethnocentric child learns the authoritarian hierarchical way of thinking.

A prejudiced child would be rigid in his approach to a problem; he would not easily change his original conception of a problem.

A prejudiced child would be rigid in his approach to a problem; he would not easily change his original conception of a problem. His approach to an intellectual task will be less effective than that of a less prejudiced child. The prejudiced child would "persist with a poor hunch or hypothesis". And, would thus have more difficulty in solving the problems. Such a child may not avail of the hints provided to him. Rigidity of approach, is an indicator of prejudiced attitude.

12. Harris, DB, Gough, HG, Martin, WE. *Children's Ethnic Attitudes. Its Relationship to Parental Beliefs Concerning Child Training.*

MODIFICATION OF RACIAL ATTITUDE

To modify racial attitude, is a difficult task; it requires intensive clinical treatment. For such a modification, "intolerance" will have to be replaced by "tolerance", for which basic personality structure will have to be changed. Children who have become intolerant because of their living among the bigoted people, will have to be shifted to an environment characterised by tolerance and co-operation. A democrat living where an equalitarian philosophy prevails, would be the congenial environment for the slackening of hardened prejudice, and, it would be only gradually that a change may come about in the attitude of looking at things and persons. Those who are well-accepted by their peer-group, will have "ability to relate to others". They would complain less about interpersonal relations, would be more satisfied with whom they live.

The children who live in segregated cabins, feel constant tension leading to the development of many abnormalities in them—enuresis, nightmare, crying, repeated accidents and uncommon physical symptoms may be the consequents.

Prejudice may be reduced by educational measures—to teach the child or adolescent whenever there is expressed a prejudiced attitude or behaviour, that how his thinking is not based on facts. Guardians and teachers may promote positive feelings towards those against whom the child is prejudiced.

FEEBLE-MINDEDNESS

There are children who become a source of anxiety to their parents, and of tension for their teachers. They cannot follow easily what is taught to them. And, when they have learnt a thing, their forgetting the same much earlier than others, is more likely. This learning and retaining difficulty, is the main symptom of feeble-mindedness. In 1973, the American Association on Mental Deficiency (AAMD), now the American Association on Mental Retardation (AAMR), provided the definition of mental Retardation as under:

"Mental retardation refers to significantly subaverage general intellectual functioning existing concurrently with deficits in adaptive behaviour and manifested during the developmental period."

Feeble-mindedness is a mild mental retardation. It is also characterised by a lower level of intellectual capability, less behavioural adaptability, and backwardness in the process of development.

Feeble-mindedness is a mild mental retardation. It is also characterised by a lower level of intellectual capability, less behavioural adaptability, and backwardness in the process of development.

Reasons There may be many reasons for this mental weakness. Generally, this weakness happens to be innate. A mention has already been made of mongolism, a congenital mental deficiency caused when the number of chromosomes is increased by one beyond 46—I read a report to the effect that IQ would be reduced by 7 points if the prospective mother had been a thyroid patient. If we measure this weakness in terms of intelligence quotient (IQ), then it may be said that all whose IQ is below 90, would be categorised as feeble-minded.

Family environment may also be responsible for the development of this. If, because of poor economic condition, the prospective mother, and after the birth of the child, the mother is not given balanced and rich food, containing all the needful ingredients, malnutrition may cause nervous weakness, and cerebral debility may be the result. Spies et al, in a study concluded that deficiency of niacin resulted in poor school grades, poor marks. Even very young children with "Kwashiorkor", behaviour in a queer way—dull, apathetic, miserable, indifferent to the surroundings, would impress as feeble-minded.

If the home environment is not wholesome, it is lacking in sanitation: proper ventilation—air and light is not there; or the house is congested; is situated in a slum or in a dirty narrow lane with no proper drainage system, and foul smell is coming out all the time because of dirt and stinking water; the occupants would always be ill, or prone to illness—both physical and mental.

If there is strained relations between father and mother of the child; or, for other reason, there, generally, goes on squabbling all the time—maybe, with beating and crying, the atmosphere would cause great tension to the child. The constant mental tension would not only weaken his mental ability but would harm his physical health also. In such a disturbed atmosphere, it is just possible that the affected child may not have a full stint of his sleep and rest.

Even in a dull atmosphere where there is no stimulation; the family relations lack belongingness; the father may be an addict and an insensitive person, or too busy a person who has no time to sit and fondle his child, to talk to it, play with it, the mental health of the child would suffer. In some cases, mother may also be failing to give a warm nurture; may be because of her ill-health or because of her own being too much tense due to disturbed home environment. In such a dull environment, a child gets so much stunned that he loses whatever mental sharpness he may innately have been endowed with; or, just possible, the child may start behaving like a dullard because of losing all interest in activity of any sort.

So far feeble-mindedness is concerned, the impact of nature is always greater, nevertheless, nurture may precipitate or reduce the gravity of the problem. Under the wider factor nurture, taking it in its broader sense, we may include the impact of school on the intellectual condition of the child. The pivotal role in developing the atmosphere of the school is that of the teacher. If the teacher of the school is authoritarian, rebukes the child who comes to him with his queries to satisfy his curiosity, creates fear in the growing child's mind through punishments or rough handling—would prove to be the greatest stumbling block in the intellectual development of the child, and the child would behave to impress as more feeble-minded than actually he is. Methods adopted in the school, and the entire physical milieu and human relationship prevailing between the teacher and the taught, and in the peer-group, all have their effect on the problem.

Measures If feeble-mindedness is of a very serious nature, no measure whatsoever can bring about perceptible results, otherwise the removal of the causes as mentioned above, should help in reducing the gravity of the problem, and if the feeble-mindedness is not innately very acute, the problem may be fully resolved.

- Balanced and rich diet ought to be given to the prospective mother, and to the mother of the young baby.
- The home atmosphere should be peaceful and pleasant, lest the prospective mother or the mother of the young child should remain mentally tense, and also physically uneasy.
- The physical environment of the house should be congenial to mental and physical health of the mother, of the child, and of all its occupants.
- The interpersonal relationship between mother and the child, and between child and other members of the family should be characterised by a warm feeling of belongingness; and a caring nurture by parents and siblings should generate in the child not only a sense of security, but a feeling of delightfulness while it is in the lap of any of them.
- Psychologists tell that the child learns to smile, it is the most important first step in the direction of socialisation in the home environment; the atmosphere of the school must not make this smile disappear. The teacher should make "learning new things an exciting adventure"; and it depends, mainly, upon the teacher that the second most important socialising agency as the school is, may perform its function as such through comforting and solacing the child when he is troubled. The physical environment of the school should be hygienic, comfortable, pleasant and helpful in learning. The situation should be stimulating and leading the child to be pleasantly engaged in different activities.

There was a time, up to early years of 1970s, when the mentally retarded children were put in segregated classes, and there were institutions specific for such children. That isolation for the mentally retarded was given up in favour of integrated classes where the environment may be more stimulating, and more inspiring because of the presence of brilliant students in the class; and here, the mentally backward would not be suffering the social stigma with the label of backwardness that segregation had put upon them.

- To make things graspable for the feeble-minded, things will have to be taught with the help of concrete objects, such children have difficulty, especially, in understanding abstract ideas. A lot of teaching aids, as per need of the lesson to be taught, ought to be used. The teaching aids should be big enough to be clearly perceptible, and interesting enough to attract the attention even of such students.
- The feeble-minded students will learn more if Dewey's maxim—"Learning by doing" is applied as a method.
- And, the most important thing is that such children need more of personal attention to be given to them with a lot of affection and patience.

LEARNING DISABILITIES

Learning disabilities may have different forms; they may be related to listening, comprehending, expressing—oral (or through any other form of motor activity) or writing, calculating numerical problems and so on. It is through the behaviour of the child that a learning disability is manifested.

Learning disability is not because of physical, mental or affectional disability of any sort but it is in spite of the child's being physically, mentally and affectionally quite able for a learning function.

Now, we shall see how "Learning Disabilities" have been defined; but one thing is always common in all the definitions, and, it is "difficulty in learning".

The definition of learning disabilities was first notified at the federal level in the USA; with variations, it was adopted by all the 50 states (it was done in the sixties):

"Specific learning disability means a disorder in one or more of the basic psychological processes involved in understanding or in using language, spoken or written, which may manifest itself in an imperfect ability to listen, think, speak, read, write, spell, or to do mathematical calculation."

Now, all sort of learning disabilities are included in the terms; the term may indicate perceptual handicap, brain injury, minimal brain dysfunction, dyslexia and developmental aphasia. But it does not include such children who have learning problems because of visual, hearing or motor handicaps, of mental retardation, or of emotional disturbance; nor, does it include handicap caused by environmental disadvantage—environment may be physical or social or both.

When a child fails to achieve learning to the level commensurate with his age and ability in one or more of the following fields even when appropriate learning experience are provided to him, it would be a case of learning disability:

Listening comprehension;
Oral expression;
Written expression;
Basic reading skill;
Reading comprehension;
Mathematics calculation;
Mathematics reasoning.

As mentioned above, the discrepancy between ability level and achievement level, must not be the result of any sort of visual, learning or motor handicap; nor, of mental retardation, emotional disturbance or environmental disadvantage.

CHARACTERISTICS OF A CHILD WITH LEARNING DISABILITIES

Characteristics of a Child With Learning Disabilities.

Actual learning level of such a child would be much below the level of his learning potential.

Hyperactivity.

Hyperactivity This hyperactivity is identified because of attention deficit. Because of hyperactivity a child fails to concentrate on any work for a minimum needful period of time. Such a child cannot work or play quietly. He cannot even wait for his turn. He cannot follow through the instructions or have patience to abide by the rules. His span of attention would be much shorter than what should be expected of a child of his age. Over-talking, without much substance, is also a characteristic of hyperactivity. He may be impatiently intruding into the conversations of others. He appears not to be serious regarding anything. Losing papers, a book or anything may not be uncommon with him. Though childhood is the period of life when none happens to be careful about an important work, but his degree of carelessness may cause concern.

And, such a child when attains adolescence, lacks in self-esteem. Shaywitz[13] (1987) writes that the child would be characterised by "oppositional behaviour", and may at times feel "depressed". The author is of the view that from 33% to 80% of the students having learning disabilities, suffer from hyperactivity disorder.

Lack of co-ordination.

Lack of co-ordination Such a child is found to be below-average looking to his age so far co-ordination of different organs are required for a particular function. When a child is playing a ball, he needs co-ordination of hand, vision and mobility. When a teacher is teaching something with the help of a blackboard, the student needs to attend to it, co-ordinating the senses of seeing and hearing; if the proper co-ordination is not there, such a student would not be able to learn, and would be lagging behind. For clean, correct and beautiful writing, again, co-ordination is must—mind, hand and eyes have to work simultaneously in co-ordination with one another. Generally, awkward or clumsy movements in a play [the hesitant mood of the child may also be indicated therein], may also be the consequence of lack of co-ordination. If one is lacking in co-ordination, he would find difficulty in assessing the relative positions (distances) of things in space, and in estimating weights of things.

Attention fixation.

Attention fixation The difference between attention span and attention fixation should be clear, as the first is related to the time for which one can concentrate attention upon a subject; attention fixation is the term to show the ability to shift attention from one subject to another as per need. Some children become so absorbed in one particular subject that it becomes difficult to divert their attention to another subject which now deserves to be the centre of consciousness or the focal point of attention. This is a problem of "involuntary over-attention". This problem leads one to be hyperactive in one particular respect at the cost of other subject.

Perceptual disorder.

Perceptual disorder Below-average perceptual ability may lead to educational retardation. A child who, in spite of having normal sensory acuity, is unable to perceive experiences in a normal way, there is a case of perceptual disorder.

A child who confused between "b" and "d" in his calligraphy exercise, or later who feels difficulty in learning spellings; and who cannot distinguish between the sounds of "dz" and "z"—in words like "jet" and "measure"; between that of "sh" and "s" as in words like "ship" and "slip"; may be said to be a case of perceptual disorder. We must be knowing persons who can easily distinguish the sounds of scooters belonging to different people; the persons who can distinguish one colour from the other very much similar to the first; contrary to this there are others who confuse the one with the other; the latter category illustrates "perceptual disorders".

13. Shaywitz, B. Hyperactivity/Attention Deficit Disorders in Learning Disabilities 1987.

Perceptual abilities develop through normal developmental devices as used in the process of learning. But if the same do not yield the desired results, there may be an occasion for concern; and some expert ought to be consulted to know if it is a case of perceptual disability.

Memory disorders.

Memory disorders Because of poor—imperfect, indistinct or ambiguous perception, the items perceived would not be retained in memory for long. Such a person may not recall even what has been perceived only recently through the sense of hearing, or the sense of seeing. He may not locate a place he has been many times to. Even things put somewhere, a little ago by him, may miss his memory as to where the same was put. A child with such memory disorders, is, naturally, to face difficulty in learning.

The factors that have been mentioned here—hyperactivity, lack of co-ordination and attention fixation; and perceptual disorders have their share of responsibility in the development of memory disorder as such.

The expert diagnosing a child with learning disabilities, is likely to confuse the same with mental retardation or handicaps of other types caused by impairment, or because of environmental deprivation, or diverse cultural impact—the behaviour of the child being alike in both (learning disabilities and mental retardation or physical handicap) the cases.

WHAT SHOULD BE DONE FOR LEARNING DISABLEMENT?

What Should Be Done For Learning Disablement?

In the regular classroom, while teaching the same topic to the whole class, it is needed to pay individual attention to children with learning disabilities. The teacher should ask them individually, to be assured that they have followed. And, if they have not, time will have to be given to them for **individual instruction.**

Individual instruction.

The methods and devices, and the teaching aids, will all have to be chosen or oriented as per individual need of each of such children. As different students may be having learning disabilities of different types, no single approach can do; a number of methods may have to be tried for different such students.

Such a student may have developed a "failure syndrome", so quite a new method should be adopted to attract attention, and motivate afresh for refurbished efforts to learn the topics of studies.

Positive reconditioning.

Positive reconditioning needs to be made. Fernald and Gillingham did pioneering work in this field, and, they recognised the value of this principle. Unfortunately, the majority of our teachers go on harping repeatedly—"you are a failure"; "you are a dullard; an idiot", with the result that a negative conditioning is caused. Hence, what is very much needed, is the positive reconditioning. For it, the students' self-esteem will have to be developed through rewarding them with positive remarks for their achievement, howsoever small it may be, or it may have come after long persistent efforts.

High motivation.

High motivation is related to the affective domain; the more vigorously the child is motivated to achieve something in the field of school learning, or in other fields of learning, the higher would be the attention of the child directing his efforts with an eye only on the target. On the contrary, if the child is not motivated for learning a thing, all the efforts of the teacher, would not be better than that of a blacksmith striking a cold iron repeatedly with his hammer. There are so many techniques for motivating a student, the teacher may adopt the one which may best suit the learning background, instructions and learning abilities of the child. Some living model, some picture example, poem, some problem, something attracting the attention of the child and retaining the same, may serve for the motivation of the same.

Great is the importance of the use of teaching materials; especially, in a case where a senior student has been suffering from the problem of retarded reading skill, the exposure of which he has been circumventing since long, and, to pin-point the nature or cause of the problem has not been possible. Such teaching materials should be used which commensurate with the age and interests of the student. The materials should be such which may make the student keenly interested in learning the point that the teacher means to teach; and make the study more easy, meaningful and pleasant.

Meaningful practice.

Meaningful practice alone can provide a permanent remedy to the problem. If a student has problem in outlining the material read by him, he should be taught to outline the very material which is of the concerned content areas. If for the sake of practice only, any material, irrelevant to the syllabus of the child, is made use of, it can neither retain the student's interest for long, nor can motivate him for learning.

A student with learning disabilities may be helped for better learning if the teacher besides knowing what the student is to learn, also knows how he learns; the teacher should adopt the student's strategies of learning, for enabling him for better learning, for more learning. Every student, howsoever skilled, or backward he may be, adopts some strategy of his own to learn each item of studies, the teacher can improve or accelerate the student's learning by guiding him how to use that particular strategy of his to make it more effective rather than by imposing a strategy from his side. This is the skill of organising the learning material; the teacher should be able to assist the students suffering from learning disabilities, to organise their material in such a way that better learning may be there.

Multisensory approach.

Multisensory approach may be more effective. If more senses are involved, even in case of normal students also, the learning becomes more effective; and it is more so in case of a student with learning disabilities. If the disability is more because of visual sense only, or because of the auditory sense only, an approach which involves the senses of vision, hearing, touch (tactile) besides the channel of kinetic activity, learning would definitely prove more effective. A nursery student would learn alphabet earlier and with better retention if he is not only asked to read the letter from the book but is also asked to select the particular letter from the scrambled lot of cardboard letters, and is made to colour each letter. Other mnemonic devices, and drawing letters or words, completing the incomplete letters or words through writing, or rewriting the scrambled letters in a way that some meaningful word may be made, and so on, are also good devices.

Many techniques have been suggested for cognitive training. Without going into all of them I would like to sum up this chapter after mentioning the six steps suggested by Wong and Jones[14] as under:

1. Ask. Why am I reading this?
2. Locate main ideas and highlight them with a marker.
3. Write down a question about each main idea.
4. Think about an answer for each question.
5. Read the passage or chapter.
6. Re-examine the questions and compare your mental answers with the answers in the passage just read.

Divide lengthy passages into sections so that this strategy may be used effectively.

REVIEW QUESTIONS

***Q*.1.** Explain the following terms, each in a sentence:

(*i*) acetylcholine
(*ii*) epinephrine
(*iii*) mongoloid
(*iv*) neurosis
(*v*) body dysmorphic disorder
(*vi*) psychotherapy
(*vii*) withdrawn
(*viii*) enuresis
(*ix*) schizophrenia
(*x*) prejudice

14. Wong, B Jones, W. *Increasing Meta Comprehension in Learning Disabled and Normalcy Achieving Students Through Self-Questioning Training.*

(xi) feeble-mindedness

(xii) learning disabilities.

Q.2. How would you recognize that a child is suffering from learning disabilities? What measures would you adopt in such a case?

Q.3. What would you do as a parent and as a teacher if your ward is feeble-minded?

Q.4. What are the behavioural traits of a person suffering from schizophrenia? What may have caused it? Suggest measures for its cure.

Q.5. Have you ever come across a person suffering from neurosis? How should you have recognized one as such? Imagine, what circumstances may have developed him into a neurotic? What should be done for the benefit of such a case?

ANSWERS TO OBJECTIVE TYPE QUESTIONS

Q.1. (i) A body chemical released from the adrenal gland which causes excitement.

(ii) An adrenaline secretion causing stimulation.

(iii) A mental abnormality caused because of increase in number of a chromosomes by one to 47.

(iv) Neurosis means "disorder of the Nervous system"-symptoms are "irrational behaviour" and "depression."

(v) Body dysmorphic disorder-some defect (real or imaginary in the bodily appearance) which becomes an obsession with a person leading to neurosis?

(vi) 'Psychotherapy' provides a free environment to express one self, with no fear whatsoever.

(vii) One who shys away from the company of others, is called "withdrawn."

(viii) Involuntary passing of urine.

(ix) "Schizo" means 'split' and "phren" means a mind—when one's mind is not, in what one is doing.

(x) When an opinion for a person or event is pre-made before assessing the same.

(xi) Mild mental-retardation, characterized by low intellectural capability.

(xii) Learning disabilities refer to difficulties in learning in spite of there being normal mental capability in the learner.

CHAPTER

17 ADOLESCENCE

Chapter Outline

- Physical Growth and Onset of Puberty
- Characteristics of Adolescence
- Adolescence—A Period of Storm and Turmoil
- Identity Crisis
- Adjustment to Sexual Relationship
- Generation Gap
- Emotional Instability
- Career Consciousness
- Treating the Adolescents
- Sublimating Emotions
- Moral Education
- Good Literature
- Socialisation
- Proper Teaching Methods
- Sex Education
- Review Questions

Adolescence is a transitional period between childhood and youth. A transitional period always happens to be a difficult one as new developments occur rapidly during this time, and the difficulty is in adapting adequately to the changes. During 2 to 5 years of age, there is the period of very fast developments—mainly physical, but mental developments also synchronise. Then, there is a period of slow developments, slow changes—generally, it ranges from 5 to 11 years, and is called a period of moratorium. Then again, generally, ranging from 12 to 18 years, there is a period with a spurt in physical, mental and emotional developments. It is the period of adolescence. A great many biological changes occur, but mainly it is

> Then again, generally, ranging from 12 to 18 years, there is a period with a spurt in physical, mental and emotional developments. It is the period of adolescence.

called a period of the onset of puberty. Rapidly the individual moves towards maturity in biological growth. The genital or reproductive organs become fully developed and functional during this period—this explains why it is called the period of pubescence.

PHYSICAL GROWTH AND ONSET OF PUBERTY

Individual variations, of course, are there, but each boy and girl gains in height very rapidly during this period. Sex difference is also there, in the beginning, the rate of growth, in case of girls, happens to be higher but later on, the boys surpass the girls in this growth of heights. This variation applies to the general body-build also. Children who are short and stocky, mature earlier than those having slim and linear body build. Variations may be genetic. But environmental factors have very significant impact. The growth of the malnourished children is slowed down or retarded whereas proper nutrition helps the growth. The wholesome and stimulating physical and social environment accelerates growth, but an unwholesome and dull one, would decelerate it. As a child grows in age; and puberty advances, he requires more of calories, and if the food given to him, does not contain the same in adequate quantity, the growth may be hindered. Thus, the socioeconomic class differences, and cultural differences have their impact on the growth and development patterns very significantly during adolescence, too. In case of less wealthy countries, there may be difference of one year when the age of menarche starts; but in wealthy countries, generally, this difference is not found. Tanner[1] found the average difference in the age of two randomly selected girls to be 19 months; for two sisters, it was 13 months, but in case of the identical twins, it was only 3 months.

The wholesome and stimulating physical and social environment accelerates growth, but an unwholesome and dull one, would decelerate it. As a child grows in age; and puberty advances, he requires more of calories, and if the food given to him, does not contain the same in adequate quantity, the growth may be hindered.

Fig. 17.1 and Table 17.1 show velocity of growth in height for boys and girls.

On the basis of records, Tanner found out that during the century beginning from 1860s the average age of menarche has decreased from 16 or 17 in the 1860s to around 13 in the 1960s. The change averaged about 0.3 year per decade. The trends in height has also been alike. Over the same period; the average height of 12-year-olds, increased by about 1.5 cm per decade. But since 1960s, changes in growth rate in height and in age of menarche, seem to have ceased. Throughout the school years the average increase in height remains steady at about 5 or 6 cm per year; but with the onset of pubertal period there comes about a spurt increasing

1. Tanner, JM. *Growth at Adolescence*, 1962.

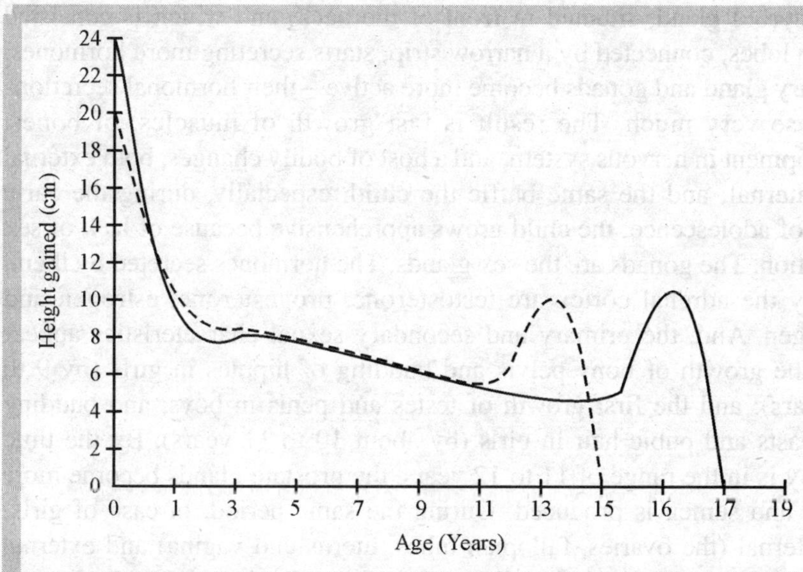

Figure 17.1 Typical individual curves showing velocity of growth in height.

the average growth to about 9 cm per year in girls, and 10 cm per year in boys.

Table 17.1 Approximate Age and Sequence of Appearance of Sexual Characteristics. (Adapted from Katchadourian[2], 1977)

Age (Yrs)	*Boys*	*Girls*
9-10	—	Growth of bony pelvis, budding of nipples
10-11	First growth of testes and penis	Budding of breasts, pubic hair
11-12	Activity of prostate gland producing semen	Changes in lining of vagina. Growth of external and internal genitalia
12-13	Pubic hair	Pigmentation of nipples, breasts fill out
13-14	Rapid growth of testes and penis	Axillary hair (under armpits) Menarche (may be anovulatory for first few years).
14-15	Auxillary hair (under armpits), down on upper lip, voice change	Earliest normal pregnancies
15-16	Mature spermatozoa (average: 15 years; range: 11.25-17 years)	Acne, Deepening of voice
16-17	Facial and body hair, acne	Skeletal growth stops
21	Skeletal growth stops	

Spurt in physical growth and changes, is caused because of internal biological changes—hormonal changes accelerate the physical changes.

2. Katchadourian, H. *The Biology of Adolescence*, 1977.

The thyroid gland, situated in front of the neck, and which is consisted of two lobes, connected by a narrow strip, starts secreting more hormones; pituitary gland and gonads become more active—their hormonal secretions increase very much. The result is fast growth of muscles, of bones, development in nervous system, and a host of bodily changes, both external and internal; and the same baffle the child, especially, during the early years of adolescence; the child grows apprehensive because of lack of sex education. The gonads are the sex glands. The hormones secreted by them, and by the adrenal cortex are testosterone, progesterone, estrogen and androgen. And, the primary and secondary sexual characteristics appear with the growth of bony pelvis and budding of nipples in girls (by 9 to 10 years): and the first growth of testes and penis in boys, and budding of breasts and pubic hair in girls (by about 10 to 11 years). By the time the boy is in the range of 11 to 12 years, the prostate glands become more active and semen is produced. During the same period, in case of girls, the internal (the ovaries, fallopian tubes, uterus and vagina) and external genitalia (the vulva, including the clitoris) grow in size, and with changes in lining of vagina, they become more sensitive and the process of the growth of reproductive organs gets started. Pubic hair (the adrenal glands located on top of the kidneys, are paired organs: cortex and medulla; pubic and axillary hair grow because of secretion of hormones from cortex), in case of boys grow later than in case of girls, and the average time of their appearance is 12 to 13 years; the time when the breasts of girls fill out. During 13th to 14th year, the growth of testes and penis becomes rapid, followed by first ejaculation; and it is the average period when a girl menstruates for the first time—though the range for menarche may be as wide as 9 to 17 years. By 14th to 15th years axillary hair appears under the armpits, and on upper lip in case of boys; and their voice deepens. In both sexes, there is growth of body hair. In case of boys, the body becomes more coarse and the facial hair grows. There are skin changes in both the sexes, and the sweat glands become more active often leading to acne (the hormones secreted from cortex cause acne). The average period when spermatozoa attains maturity is 15 to 16 years. This is the period for girls when their voice changes, and pimples appear on their face (acne). In case of girls, skeletal growth stops during the period 16 to 17, though in case of boys, skeletal growth is possible up to the age of 21.

The sex hormones are produced by the adrenal cortex, and by the gonads. The growth of the gonads is stimulated by the hormones secreted by the pituitary gland. Puberty is the period when the 'setting' of the hypothalamus is changed. The hypothalamus controls the work of the pituitary gland. It "shuts down" when the sex hormones in blood grow to an excessive degree.

CHARACTERISTICS OF ADOLESCENCE

Characteristics of Adolescence (1) A period of rapid physical/biological changes, has psychological repercussions too.

1. *A period of rapid physical/biological changes, has psychological repercussions too* We have read in the previous paragraphs how a spurt in physical growth and changes synchronises with or characterises the period of adolescence. The growth of the pelvis bone, the filling out of breast, growing in size and sensitivity of genitalia, growing of pubic and axillary hair, deepening of voice, acne, and the menarche are the main physical and biological developments in girls which make them confused and apprehensive. Both in boys and girls, the secretion of hormones from adrenal and gonads, and supported by what is secreted from the glandular anterior and the posterior neural portions of the pituitary gland, bring about rapid changes in size and strength of bones, muscles, nervous systems and especially in the reproductive organs which become fully matured for the sexual function. The growing of pubic and axillary hair, deepening of voice, change in the nature of body skin with the sweat glands becoming more active, and because of the sudden growth of testes and penis, and functionally their growing stronger and the ejaculation that the boy experiences, all make him muddled.

   All these physical and biological changes in the adolescent make his or her adaptation to the changed situation very difficult. The adolescent sometimes feels shy of the company of others, may blush when looked at by others, or may grow escapist. The girl because of her menstruation and the boy because of his ejaculation, especially, grow apprehensive. The adolescents may at times suffer guilty consciousness. They grow appearance conscious, and become obsessed with the concern "what others (the imaginary audience) may be thinking of my appearance and behaviour", David Elkind[3] has called it a new sort of "egocentrism". Again, according to Elkind, the adolescents construct a personal fable of their own taking themselves as very important in the eyes of others. They confuse their own feelings about themselves with what they think the others are feeling about them. It is also the period when the closeness of the young person with his parents, decreases, and, he either remains more absorbed in his own feelings and thoughts or feels a strong attraction towards his peers. Steinberg[4] writes that it is also a period when his conflict with parents, increases.

   A number of studies have been conducted to know the psychological impact of menarche on girls. Retrospective studies reveal the event

3. Elkind, D. *Egocentrism in Adolescence*, 1967.
4. Steinberg, L. *Reciprocal Relation between Parent–Child Distance and Pubertal Maturation*, 1988.

to be something unpleasant—more so because of the lack of social support. After menarche, the girls report of more negative emotions or experiences. According to Ruble and Brooks-Gunn[5], though the experiences do not happen to be traumatic, they happen to be of inconvenience and ambivalence. In case of early maturers, the negative feelings were greater. There may be positive impact of the menarche too; the girl would move closer towards her mother, and the changes associated with it, may make the girl behave with more maturity.

In traditional families or cultures, both girls and boys, are initiated to adolescence with ceremonies. The period of menarche, in case of girls, is better handled. Greif and Ulman[6] have reviewed such studies. The rituals signal a transition from childhood to adulthood.

Now, coming back to physical growth, a mention should be made of the pituitary gland; the anterior lobe of which produces many growth promoting hormones during adolescence. And, the excessive secretion of the same, may produce a giant, whereas deficit of it may leave one a dwarf. Over-growth or under-growth—both are the conditions which make one seriously concerned about one's physique and appearance. Physiological and psychological processes are mutually dependent variables. Endocrines play an important role in the process of physical growth, and adolescence is the apex period for growth; these very endocrines through physiological processes, affect the behaviour of the person concerned, and the whole of his personality is also affected. The adjustability of a person much depends upon the kind of physical growth that one has, especially during the period of adolescence when the endocrines happen to be the most active.

(2) Appearance-consciousness.

2. *Appearance-consciousness* During adolescence, both the girl and the boy, grow very much conscious about their appearance. As physical changes are very rapidly taking place, affecting the appearance of the adolescent, "how do I appear?" becomes his or her haunting concern. An adolescent would do all that he or she can to develop and maintain an attractive look. One grows very particular regarding one's dress, hair-style and so on. One may have to come before a mirror many times a day, just to know how she or he may be looking now. It is the period when the narcissism of the psychoanalysts becomes relevant; narcissism stands for self-love, when one becomes enamoured of one's own appearance. But this state of feeling is not to last long; the adolescent feels a strong pull towards the opposite sex. Now, his or

5. Ruble, DN, Brooks-Gunn, J. *The Experience of Menarche*.

6. Grief, EB, Ulman, KJ. *The Psychological Impact of Menarche on Early Adolescent Females*, 1982.

her main concern becomes how he or she must be looking in the eyes of the opposite sex.

The obsession of appearance would, naturally, make the adolescent very uneasy at times. Its side-effect may be jealousy against someone that he or she cannot compete with. This persistent concern for one's appearance may distort one's behaviour. One may grow shy or withdrawn in case of physical defect or lack of attraction, imagined or real, is there. If the defect is innate or developed postnatally but to the level of incurability, in general, the development of personality would be adversely affected. Such a one cannot behave in a normal way. The body dysmorphic disorder may prove very devastating when it becomes an obsession with someone. The author would like to refer again to a report recently published in a famous daily, which is to the effect that a severe preoccupation with an imagined or slight defect in appearance may lead one to drop out of school, shun social contacts, and may even try suicide—especially an adolescent happens to be very sentimental and rash, and is likely to take any reckless step.

(3) Attraction towards the opposite sex.

3. *Attraction towards the opposite sex* The pubic changes in the girl, and in the boy, make one feel a strong attraction towards the other. The physical growth during the period of adolescence, makes one attractive for the opposite sex. Nevertheless, it entails the problem of adaptability to peers of the same sex, and to those of the opposite sex. The adolescents who fail to adjust themselves to those of the opposite sex in a proper way, would prove awkward in their behaviour. Such a maladjusted person would ever be having a feeling of strain.

The curiosity regarding sex matters, and regarding that of the opposite sex, increases with age, and if the elders only go on suppressing such feelings of an adolescent, it will not help in having a wholesome understanding of the sexual matters and the repressed feelings may either explode more devastatingly or may lead to other abnormalities. The adolescent undergoes a great strain as to how to handle these newly awakened sex impulses, and what do these strong impulses mean. A great part of the adolescent's energy and attention is occupied by these impulses. Not only the adolescent but sometimes the elders of the family also get worried as sex behaviour happens to be the greatest concern regarding the development of the moral character. The inextricably interwoven two aspects of sex behaviour—physical and psychological, may be illustrated in the sex behaviour of the adolescent. Until adolescence, the child is considered to be innocent of sex or sexual urges—though psychoanalysts have effected a change in such a consideration, and the roots of sexual urges may be traced even into infancy, yet anatomy and physiology make it understand why adolescence is a period when sexuality happens to be the strongest. And, if no proper sensitivity on the part of the adults is there in handling the situation, and the only mechanism of repression is resorted to, the consequence may be neurosis, or some other abnormality. With the onset of puberty, the child starts feeling interested in manipulation of his genital organs. On the part of the adult members of the family, a frank and an honest dealing with the situation of masturbation and ejaculation/menstruation needs to be done. Horracks[7] advises the guardians to treat their adolescent wards reasonably so far their sexual behaviour is concerned, lest the latter develop a feeling of guilt for life, and they become seriously maladjusted psychologically.

(4) Cognitive development.

4. *Cognitive development* Adolescence is the stage when a person attains maturity in physical development, in respect of sexual behaviour, and also cognitively. From year eleven onward, Jean Piaget considers it to be the stage of formal operations when the growing adolescent starts thinking logically and persistently. It is the adult stage of cognitive development, and is characterised by the following features:

(*i*) Now, one can follow logical relationships that exist among those which/who belong to the same class, and among the ones belonging to different classes. Uptil now the child could follow the existing relationships that were there among different events, but now the adolescent has developed the abilities to visualise the future possible relationships, and, by dint of that the adolescent can design situations. He can think of all the possible kinds of relationships that can exist among events that are likely to occur in future. Though the future may confirm some of his hypotheses and reject the others, his thinking always happens to be based on logic, and, is carried on persistently.

(*ii*) Now, he has the ability of combinatorial thinking—he can review all the choices systematically, he can go through them sequentially if it is so needed, and can exhaust all of them. The adolescent can use the entire system of formal logic in an intuitive way also, to obtain the kind of information he wants.

Adolescence is also the period when one attains an advanced stage of the development of imagination—it helps a lot in intuitive thinking.

(*iii*) It is during this period of life when one acquires some additional concrete constructs. For example, he can understand the problem of equilibrium in which there are two different inverses, and which lead to the development of 4-groups. It is during the period of formal

7. Horracks, JR. *The Psychology of Adolescence: Behavior and Development*, 1991.

operations that the child acquires the concept of the volume construction. Now, he can follow the rule of equilibrium that operates in the kind of balance that exists between density and quantity.

Now, because of so much development in the cognitive field, the adolescent becomes career-conscious. Musing upon his future, he is in a better position to make a proper choice of subjects of studies for a brighter career—of course, variety and complexity in the field of vocations, may require an expert guidance, nevertheless, his career-consciousness is a big step, and is indicative of his cognitive development.

However, an adolescent is more likely to make a hasty decision as one, generally happens to be rash during this period.

5. *Career-consciousness* A mention, by the way, has already been made that an adolescent starts thinking about his career at this stage. Now, one happens to be mature enough to think of the importance of a good job in life. Looking to his own parents and to others, he can very well realise the importance of a good job for a respectable and comfortable life. He also knows that a good job is must for attracting a good life-partner for marriage—adolescence is also a period when mating starts. In many countries, the problem of unemployment is very acute, this fact makes our adolescents feel more concerned about their career even when their studies are still not over. Banks and Ullah[8] have reviewed the situation, and the fact emerges that youth unemployment is a factor for distress or anxiety to a majority of early school leavers in the developed countries. Gurney[9], employing Erikson's developmental model. studied the psychology of both—those who were to leave their schools shortly, and who had left theirs four months back. The findings are to the effect that obtaining a job was an important factor for the perception of identity, especially for the females. a short period of unemployment does not cause a much distressing experience. Other studies reveal that a long period of unemployment causes not only a distressing feeling, but it brings a sort of stigma. and lowers one's self-esteem.

(5) Career-consciousness.

6. *Emotional conditions* Wilkins[10] writes that hyperthyroidism is more common in adolescence. Hyperthyroidism is caused because of excessive secretion of thyroid gland. Hyperthyroidism is characterised by emotional instability and excessive movements. Because of

(6) Emotional conditions.

8. Banks, MH, Ullah, P. *Youth Unemployment in 1980s: A Psychological Analysis*, 1986.
9. Gurney, RM. *The Effects of Unemployment on the Psychosocial Development of School Leavers*, 1980.
10. Wilkins, L. *The Diagnosis and Treatment of Endocrine Disorders in Childhood and Adolescence*, 1957.

emotional instability, an adolescent has no patience to think over the pros and cons of a step that he is going to take—though cognitively he or she is developed enough to do it. An adolescent boy or girl may take any rash or reckless step out of anger or frustration. An adolescent lacks in emotional maturity. Failure in education, in love affairs, in pursuing an act of his or her interest—may it be playing or loitering with his or her peers, or seeing a picture or watching a television serial and so on, soon upsets an adolescent; cool or objective thinking, generally, should be taken to be too much to expect of an adolescent. Sometimes, an adolescent may even take an extreme step of committing suicide when persistently insensitive surroundings leave him or her with no other alternative.

For the needful physical changes, the hormones released by the pituitary gland further stimulates the function of adrenal cortex and of gonads. The overall impact of these physical and biological changes is the development of an emotional state which generally makes the adolescent short-tempered and rash; sometimes his repressed emotions may result in an explosive outburst or a temper-tantrum.

The adolescent is rich in emotional energy but for want of proper channelisation, it may prove disastrous.

(7) Flight on imagination.

7. *Flight on imagination* The adolescent often rises high and above the limitations of realities into the unbridled sky of imagination, seeking the fulfilment of a lot many of his desires which stand no chances of being fulfilled otherwise. Adolescence is also a period when imagination can help him in visualising likely consequences, and enable him think persistently. Thus, imagination may either make the adolescent a day-dreamer, or an escapist losing himself in the phantasmagoria, or in a world which is the creation of his own fancy, or may turn him into a creative artist. To imagine of good things, of high ideals or targets, is essential for the upliftment of a person, provided a touch with the hard realities of the world, is not lost.

Imagination is an asset with the personality of an adolescent, provided, a judicious scope is provided for its development and creativity. An environment of fine arts, rich with the performances of good artistes, can further stir and enrich the imagination of the adolescent, and his overflowing energies can find a field for sublimation and creative rise of his feelings and emotions.

An appeal to the imagination of an adolescent is easy to make through poetry or through any form of art. He may, with the help of such a work, be turned into a great patriot or a true cosmopolitan, a great social worker or so on. Hence, great is the importance of environment for an adolescent. The more possessed of imagination he is, the more will be his interest in poetry and other fine arts, of course, a congenial environment will have to be provided.

(8) Hero worship.

8. *Hero worship* Some living character, maybe, some hero of the screen, a member of his peer-group, or someone among the acquaintances, or of the family, may have caught the imagination of the adolescent, and he starts emulating him keenly. What attracts him, may be the physique—good height and well body-build plus good appearance; may be the skill in games or sports; adventurous nature; outspokenness and so on are also the qualities for which the adolescent may choose his hero. The adolescent may choose his hero from history or from some piece of literature; or an imaginary character may also occupy the place of a hero in his mind.

   Sometimes, because of the influence of a bad company, some gang leader or someone who is boisterous and belligerent, may become an ideal for him to emulate. Psychologists also say that the hidden motivation in such an emulation, happens to be self security—for the sake of security, a member of the gang tries to emulate one who is very aggressive and assertive.

   Elderly members of the family, and teachers in school may be instrumental in the development of the desired type of personalities by way of presenting great characters before the students. The character may be someone living, or may be from the recent or past history or myth. In some instances, even the teachers are emulated by their students. Presenting ideal characters for emulation, is a holy duty of the teachers.

   In most of the cases, heroes are changed with age. The hero of the middle childhood, may be replaced be someone else with characteristics more appealing to an adolescent's imagination. One with some inclination towards arts, is likely to emulate some artists of excellence. The family background also affects the choice of a hero.

(9) Hobbies.

9. *Hobbies* Adolescence is also a period when one is inclined to a number of hobbies, or at least to one or the other of the hobbies. He may join some gym, or a club of table-tennis or lawn-tennis. Some may like to compose poems or write stories. Music or dance may attract a few. Others may opt to be cricketers or hockey-players. Girls, especially, may choose knitting, sewing, embroidery work and so on, as their hobbies. Sex-identity, hero-worship and others, are also the factors influencing the choice of a hobby.

   Adolescence is a period where the growth and development are very rapid in all the fields—physical, intellectual and emotional. Energies are brimming out, so hobbies can provide very desirable channels to the adolescents to make use of their excessive energies—though, some of their energies are made use of in the process of growth which is so rapid during this period. The elders in the family, and teachers, and others who work voluntarily for the welfare of the youth, should see to it that the adolescents choose some or the other hobby—channelise their energies there, pursuing some creative work.

If during this period, the growing youth are having no work to indulge into, nothing that they can entertain themselves with, the situation may prove very harmful. They are likely to go astray, fall into a bad company, and spoil their career, turning themselves into delinquents, and later into hardcore criminals. Contrary to this, hobbies of this time may turn many into men of letters, artists of name, good athletes, or may enable them to shine in one or the other creativity.

Schools, colleges and voluntary organisations should run hobby classes. They may be related to photography, may be for computer-training, or be related to the latest devices of information technology.

(10) Sex-role identity.

10. *Sex-role identity* We have read in the relevant chapters that girls have their identity in the choice of play, in the choice of their companions; and also in the way they behave. A distinct identity of the sex may be marked in the selection of dresses and other items to wear. Some hobbies are there for which girls have preference; for example, fine needle or embroidery work is, generally, liked by girls only; and, hard gymnastic exercises or some rigorous games are liked by male youth only.

Sex awareness comes about much earlier than this; even the nursery school children may be seen playing with peers of their own sex. During adolescence, both boys and girls try to acquire a set of behaviour patterns, acceptable, and liked by the society for a particular gender only. For example, an aggressive and boisterous boy may be liked at times but a girl is expected to be quiet, and even bashful. Sex-role identity has always reference to the culture or to the sub-culture to which the adolescent boy or girl belongs.

Especially, during the last three or four decades of the twentieth century, we have been witnessing significant changes in the "sex-role identity" of adolescent females. Douvan[11] has called this development, in the modern urban societies, to be the most difficult. Adolescent girls prefer to put on the garb of the boys more amusingly. Because of sex-egalitarianism, girls prepare themselves to compete with boys for any job whatsoever—many of the jobs which were previously considered fit for males only, are no more so considered, females have significantly registered their entries therein. It is so, because modern education

11. Douvan, E. *Sex Role Learning*, 1979.

encourages the girls for independence, competition and higher achievements. But the general trend even in our urban traditional societies, does not favour this development, and still, the guardians would not allow their girls to go in for a number of jobs which have traditionally been considered as male-specific. When the girls are thus debarred from what they may have set their heart on, they feel frustrated. This situation adds to the strain of female adolescents in many cases. After marriage, when girls have to assume a motherly or domestic role, independence, competitiveness and assertiveness are not the qualities that would be approved at the in-laws'. But since the time Douvan and Adelson[12] conducted their survey, a significant change in the thinking, especially, of the urban society has occurred, and independence, assertiveness and job-orientation in young females, is more acceptable now.

Nevertheless, strain related to sex-role identity, in case of boys is not common anywhere in any society, but the adolescent females are more subject to it. Conger[13] remarks that for young men there are no options of so different characters open, as career-orientation and motherly-role are for the young women. It is also a conclusion of research that cross-sex interests or behaviour, are more tolerable in case of girls than in that of boys.

Coming to the conventional sex-role, girls are expected to assist their mothers in performing domestic chores and child care. Cleanliness and decoration of the house is mainly considered to be a concern of girls. Sewing, stitching clothes and so on, are expected to be done by girls of the family. If car is to be repaired, it would be a concern of the men-folk. The question of self-esteem, is very much related to sex-role identity, but, some researches are to the effect that among the ultramodern society, especially of the USA, "androgyny" is now considered to be boosting self-esteem. A man who performs baby-minding and car-repairing with equal dexterity, will be called "androgynous".

Margaret Mead[14] has reported that amongst the Tchambuli tribe, the women were more dominant, and men were more emotional and concerned about their appearance; amongst the mundugamor, females were equally ruthless as the males were found—the females are masculine in their tastes and behaviour. But some later writers[15]

12. Douvan, E, Adelson, J. *The Adolescent Experience*, 1966.
13. Conger, JJ. *Adolescence and Youth*, 1977.
14. Mead, M. *Sex and Temperament in Three Primitive Society*, 1935.
15. Blurton Jones, NG; Konner, MJ. *Sex Differences in Behaviour of London and Bushmen Children*, 1973.

criticised her for being selective in presenting results. Mead was found to have exaggerated the cultural factor, while, as in sex-role development, it is the biological factor which is dominant. Archer and Lloyd[16] have also shown the importance of biological factors in the development of sex-roles.

Impact of the peer-group is the strongest.

11. *Impact of the peer-group is the strongest* During early childhood, parents, and more especially, the mother, enjoys the greatest influence upon the child. The child values its acceptance by the parents to be the highest. The child's greatest reward is the praise for his behaviour by the parents, and the severest punishment is the withdrawal of parental affection. With the child's entry into the nursery, his social circle expands. Now, he also cares for his acceptance by the peer-group. He cannot tolerate isolation from a peer of his who happens to be very close to him.

For an adolescent, the peer-group grows more in importance, sometimes, more than even the parents do. He is influenced by his peers in matters of dress, hair-style, likings-dislikings, hobbies, recreations and so on. If the home environment is drab, his attachment to the group of his friends, will be greater. And, if that group, or his friend or friends do not happen to be good, he too would be spoilt.

The adolescent, as a child, has learnt that to get a respectable entry into the peer-group, he will have to imitate those among them who are more active. Through imitating their remarks, gestures and actions, he gets more and more integrated into the group. The newcomer adopts the behaviour pattern of the one who is successful.

Up to the period of middle childhood, the groups happen to be informal, but during adolescence, boys and girls join such organisations and clubs which are governed by certain rules. Now, observance of certain rules, gets importance. In higher structured organisations, certain rituals are also observed. Some join Boys Scout, the girls go to the Girls Guide; then there is NCC, and a number of other groups related to different games in the school. Some have their friendship developed in a club—a hobby or a literary one, that they join. Sex-role identity becomes more conspicuous now. A boy of eleven would feel embarrassed if he is surrounded by a group of girls. The tastes and items of the game become different for different genders. Whether a boy or a girl, each one feels secure in one's own sex identifications. Relationships with peers, teach each of them to work co-operatively; and to earn competence-knowledge and skills for integration into the group. Interests, attitudes and skills ought to be

16. Archer, J; Lloyd, B. *Sex and Gender*, 1986.

identifying with that of the group, especially, organised with a due consideration for a particular gender.

Bonny[17] measured popularity in the social group through sociogram. He found that the most popular were those who had the qualities of leadership, enthusiasm and active and aggressive participation in the activities of the group. Now, these positive qualities have more chances of being thriving if the same have been encouraged in the family environment.

When peers, parents and teachers are in agreement regarding the appropriateness of certain values and actions, few problems arise for the adolescent. Otherwise, he or she will have to bear a situation of great tension or strain, and ambivalence would be the result. And, adolescence is the period when he or she gives more importance to the values rewarded by the peer-group rather than the values that his or her parents have been rewarding. For acceptance by the peer group, the behaviour-patterns of the peers are adopted. Now, one can interact better with one's agemates who are of the same sex. The adolescent learns how to behave for dominance, and, when hostility needs to be shown, and how it should be shown. Because of the development of formal operational skill, he or she can have discussions regarding his or her problems—conflicts or complex feelings. And, when an adolescent finds that some of his or her peer is having the same sort of conflict or problem with his or her parent, it provides some relief in the tension. The discovery that other too is angry with his father or is concerned about sexuality, relieves one from a sense of guilt.

The peer-group also helps in developing self-concept. One can realise one's strengths and limitations on the basis of when the peer-group acceptance is accorded to one, or, when one is rejected by the group.

Whitlery and Hallock[18] write:

"......... It is fair to say that the crucial arena for self-esteem is the arena of one's age-mates."

As the adolescent seeks independence from his parents, he spends more time with peers, and turn to them for identity and social support; he is shifting from a period of "parent-orientation" to "peer-orientation". Hargreaves[19] has documented the importance of the values of the peer groups; to abide by the same, the adolescents may even transgress the patterns of behaviour which their parents were at great pains to inculcate

17. Bonny, M.E. *The Constancy of Sociometric Scores and Their Relationship to Teacher Judgments of Social Success and to Personality Self Ratings* (Sociometry, 1943).
18. Whitlery, GM, Hallock, GT. *Health Observations of School Children.*
19. Hargreaves, D. *Social Relations in a Secondary School*, 1967.

in them. Studying the mentality of the adolescents in the USA, Coleman[20] has concluded alike. Studying anxieties about friendships with peers JC Coleman[21] reported that anxiety of being rejected by the friends, increased between 11 to 13 years, and then to 15 years; by 17 it starts declining. Such an anxiety was found to be stronger in girls.

Notwithstanding, in matters of education and career, the adolescents would like to consult their parents rather than to their peers. But a good number of students start taking to drugs as a result of peer-orientation. The nature of social relationships with peers is not the same as with parents. Parental relationship happens to be one of "unilateral authority"; what parents strive to teach is a "constructed set of knowledge and attitudes". Relationship with friends, on the other hand, happens to be that of "mutually reciprocal" nature; here, it is possible to have divergent views regarding an issue, and more freedom is there to air one's views, and have discussions on the same.

Hunter[22] prepared a questionnaire to study the reactions of adolescents in case of disagreement with father, mother or a friend. He administered the questionnaire on 180 adolescents in the age group 12 to 20 years. Through the responses that were got, again it was confirmed that parents are more unilateral, and friends are more mutual. Democratic parents can develop better relationships with their adolescent children along with giving them greater independence and confidence.

Adolescence—A Period of Storm and Turmoil.

ADOLESCENCE—A PERIOD OF STORM AND TURMOIL

Adolescence[23] has been described a period of "storm and stress"; a period of life when one experiences the greatest "turmoil" and "crisis". In this part of the chapter, we mean to go through the reviews of these traditional conceptions regarding this most important period of life. In the development of these conceptions, there had been contributions of some important psychoanalysts and of socio-psychologists, nevertheless, a review was very much justified. I shall be depending upon these reviews besides giving my own views regarding the subject.

Adolescence is a transitional period when one is not so young that he or she can live wholly depending on parents, nor he or she is so mature

20. Coleman, JS. *The Adolescent Society*, 1961.
21. Coleman, JC. *The Nature of Adolesence*, 1980.
22. Hunter, FT. *Socialising Procedures in Parent-child and Friendship Relations During Adolescence*, 1984.
23. Hall, GS. *Adolescence*, 1980.

as to be able to live independently, and have one's independent decisions on important matters of life. It is a period of pubescence, and sexually one grows mature enough as to have got the potentiality of being a father or a mother. A host of physical changes occur, and the teenager fails to decide how to adapt to the same. Along with physical changes, a lot many biological changes also take place; excess in secretion of some hormones, including the sex hormones, generally, makes the individual rash, short-tempered and reckless. Inclination to masturbation, and the events of ejaculation and menarche further upset the adolescent. It is a period, when he or she has to establish his or her identity, for it also, a lot of struggle has to be done. Too much concern for physique and appearance also makes one uneasy. Above all, is the anxiety for career. An adolescent starts thinking about his future job also. These are the main factors which make this period so difficult. Though we have dealt all of them in the previous section of the chapter, here we shall take the most important of them, and touch the crucial points regarding them to see how far the description of the period as a period of "storm" and turmoil" is a fiction and to what extent it is a fact.

IDENTITY CRISIS

The child who was totally dependent on his parents, with age, goes on striving for independence. Coming to adolescence, his desire to be more independent is natural, and, is in the interest of his development. He wants to establish his identity, and tries to make others feel it, and give due recognition to it. But difficulties are there:

(*i*) The first difficulty is that he himself fails to have a sense of identity for his own physical self—because of rapid physical and biological changes; for the adaptation to which he needs much time. The adolescent girl, because of widening pelvis bone, filling up of breast; the boy because of pubic hair, and hair on the upper lip and beard, becomes uneasy regarding his appearance. The most difficult experience happens to be that of menarche for the girl, and of ejaculation for the boy. To reconcile to this situation, is not easy, especially, for want of social support.

(*ii*) Parents are still not prepared to believe that their children are grown up enough, in some respects at least, so as to take them into confidence; to discuss with them before taking a final decision—when the matter is purely related to the adolescent son or daughter of theirs. Such an insensible and insensitive behaviour of the autocratic parents, makes the situation tense for the growing teenager.

Naturally, the adolescents too, would like their personality to be given due honour. In a democratic home atmosphere, the adolescent would not find much difficulty in adapting himself or herself to widening social atmosphere, and to new responsibilities of more serious nature. Adolescents' altercation with parents, was not found to be a general problem; the findings of Rutter et al, are given in the table (Table 17.2) as under:

Table 17.2 Adolescent's Adjustment Many a Time Poses a Problem (in percentage)

	Boys	*Girls*
Parental interview		
Any altercation with parents	18	19
Physical withdrawal	12	07
Communication difficulties	24	09
Adolescent interview		
Any altercation with parents	42	30
Any criticism of mother	27	37
Any criticism of father	32	31
Any rejection of mother	03	02
Any rejection of father	05	09
Often feel miserable or depressed (questionnaire)	21	23
Reported misery (psychiatric interview)	42	48
Observed sadness (psychiatric interview)	12	15.

Source: Rutter et al, 1976.

(*iii*) During adolescence, the social circle of interactions rapidly widens. The peer-circle grows bigger and more varied than was the case in childhood. So, the difficulty of adaptation becomes further acute. As the peers happen to come from different family milieus, they so differ among themselves in patterns of behaviour, in their attitudes and thinkings. The adolescent finds it difficult to adapt himself or herself to the widening, varied social groups of peers besides to those of the family relationships. Especially so, because still the adolescent has not been able to develop a sense of his own physical self, an identity of himself or herself. The adolescent is still passing through a state of flux—a lot many physical changes are appearing rapidly, entailing a state of psychological indecisiveness. Erikson[24] has divided the entire life of an individual into eight developmental stages (see Table 17.3); has shown adolescence, the fifth stage, to be

24. Erikson, E. *Identity: Youth and Crisis*, 1968.

Table 17.3 The Eight Developmental Stages Proposed by Erikson

Normative crisis	*Age (yr)*	*Major characteristics*
Trust v/s Mistrust	0–1	Primary social interaction with mothering caretaker; oral concerns; trust in life—sustaining care, including feeding.
Autonomy v/s Shame and doubt	1–2	Primary social interactions with parents; toilet training; holding on and 'letting go' and the beginnings of autonomous will.
Initiative v/s Guilt	3–5	Primary social interaction with nuclear family; beginnings of "oedipal" feelings; development of language and locomotion; development of conscience as governor of initiative.
Industry v/s inferiority	6–puberty	Primary social interaction outside home among peers and teachers; school age assessment of task ability.
Identity v/s Role confusion	Adolescence	Primary social interaction with peers, culminating in heterosexual friendship, psychological moratorium from adult commitments; identity crisis; consolidation of resolutions of previous four stages into coherent sense of self.
Intimacy v/s Isolation	Early adulthood	Primary social interaction in intimate relationship with member of opposite sex; adult role commitments accepted, including commitment to another person.
Generativity v/s Stagnation	Middle age	Primary social concern in establishing and guiding future generation; productivity and creativity.
Integrity v/s Despair	Old age	Primary social concern is a reflective one; coming to terms with one's place in the (now nearly complete) life cycle, and with one's relationship with others; 'I am what survives of me'.

the stage of "identity crisis" because of psychological moratorium—the adolescent still cannot make final decisions regarding his relationships with his or her peers; nor regarding other adult issues. The following figure adapted from Marcia[25] shows that still the "identity status" of the adolescent is in a state of "moratorium" as concluded from the responses of the adolescents (a sample) to the questions asked through the technique of interview, regarding, mainly, to occupation, religion, political belief and attitudes.

25. Marcia, JE. *Development and Validation of Ego-identity Status*, 1966.

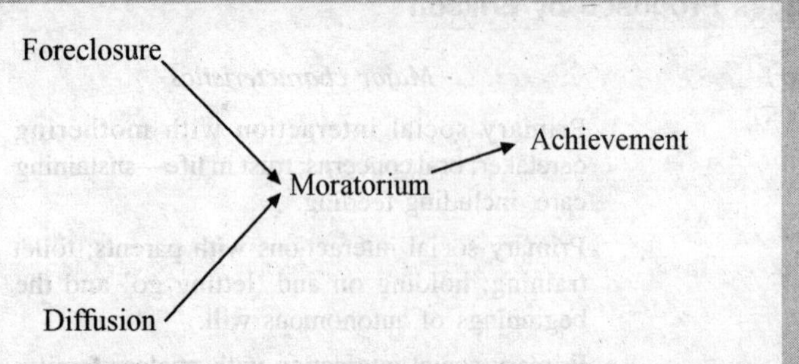

Figure 17.2
Changes in identity status.

Before one achieves the final decision, he or she passes through the three previous stages. The first one is the stage of "foreclosure"—when one adopts the beliefs or views of adults as they are told by them to the child, there is no struggle of any sort in the mind. As the child grows in age, he starts developing his or her own view or belief regarding a subject. Yet, the child does not take things seriously, and, is not keen having his own independent view on a subject. It is the period of "diffusion". But the most difficult period starts with adolescence when he or she is serious about his or her views regarding an issue. It is the period of "moratorium". It is so called because during adolescence no final decision can be achieved regarding important issues of life; such as, religion, politics, vocation, marriage and so on. But a state of ambivalence continues throughout the period, and the adolescent feels disturbed. Adulthood is the only period of 'achievement' when one achieves a final decision regarding an issue. The beliefs and views are finally formed when one is matured during adulthood.

More studies were conducted regarding the development of adult commitments to different issues of life; the studies were both cross-sectional and longitudinal; and the sum and substance of the same may be summarised as under:

- *Identity achievement* was much higher in the working youth than in the college students of the same age. (Munro and Adams[26]).
- Family background affects the identity status; close relationships to parents prolongs the period of foreclosure. Those who were in the status of *moratorium* or achievement, reported distant and critical relationships with parents.
- Children from divorced families scored higher in regard to identity status in comparison to those from intact families.
- Those who had achieved identity status, were found to be having more interest in cultural and literary activities (Waterman[27]).
- In a study, 51 of the college students were found to be at the post-conventional level in reasoning; 31 per cent out at the *moratorium*, 12 per cent at the *foreclosure*, and 9 per cent at *diffusion* level.

26. Munro, G, Adams, GR. *Ego Identity Formation in College Students and Working Youth*, 1977.
27. Waterman AS. *Identity Development from Adolescence to Adulthood: An Extension of Theory and a Review of Research*, 1982.

- Authors, like Matteson[28], Cote and Levine[29] have questioned the validity of classifying individuals on the basis of identity status correlating the same to different age periods. A person of a certain age was found to have reached to the achievement status in some fields while still at the moratorium or foreclosure status in some other content areas. In some cases even reversion was found to have occurred from the achievement status or moratorium status to the foreclosure or diffusion status.

Nor, it is the case that an adolescent is at the moratorium status in regard to all the topic areas. At one particular time, the adolescent may be found stable in the particular content area, but may be experiencing crisis in some others. Crisis may occur during any period of adult life also.

ADJUSTMENT TO SEXUAL RELATIONSHIP

Adolescence is the period of the onset of pubescence. Biologically, it is a period when a boy and a girl become ready for sexual function. The genitalia (penis and testicles in male, and vulva in female) increase in size and get stronger in sensitivity because of hormones secreted from gonads; the production of these hormones is stimulated because of the secretion of TSH and ACTH hormones which the front lobe of the pituitary gland (called adenohypophysis) secretes. Some muscles and bones also increase in size; such as pelvis bone in a girl, and, the filling out of her breast; growing of pubic and axillary hair in case of both sexes; and some other changes because of certain hormonal secretions. Ejaculation, in case of the adolescent boy, and menarche, in that of a girl, make them uneasy, apprehensive; and sometimes even guilty-conscious for lack of sexual education. And, masturbation is, generally, considered to be devastating for the physical and mental health of the growing adolescent. All these things make the period very difficult for the adolescents. It is also the period of experiencing oedipus complex. The situation is further aggravated because of the fast growing of a very strong attraction towards the opposite sex. The adolescent becomes totally diffused; he or she feels—they would not be able to decide, would not be able to adjust in face of so strong a sexual urge. Of course, the situation would not be so acute for those whose energies have been channelised to some creative motor or literary activities; for those who have been engaged in suitable hobbies.

---

28. Matteson, DR. *Exploration and Commitment: Sex Differences and Methodological Problems in the Case of Identity Status Categories*, 1977.
29. Cote, JE, Levine, C. *A Critical Examination of the Ego Identity Status Paradigm*, 1988.

Studies[30,31], showed that the average age of having first sexual experience in the western societies had decreased. It may have been the impact of television serials and the increasing trend of permissiveness that has been prevailing all around. Other factors are—early physical development and the "lively gregariousness".[32] The parents' control is less, and the peer-group is having more influence; with the result that adherence to teenage norms is stressed instead of conformity to adult norms. Consciousness to physical attractiveness has also had its impact on sexual behaviour.

However, finding a life partner, and being bound into a happy wedlock, cannot be a general experience for the adults; as adolescents, they must have passed through a lot of ambivalence before a happy married life is achieved.

Wide publicity is being given regarding the risks of contracting AIDS and other venereal diseases. It has had its desirable effect in restraining further sexual behaviour and changing attitude regarding this behaviour.

GENERATION GAP

It is the adolescent who happens to be the most affected because of generation gap. The adolescent lives in the peerage company, representing a changing society, a society in a state of flux. Those are the changes which the established society of the adults cannot accord recognition; it would, rather, be protesting against the emergence of such a society. The adolescent is still not matured enough to have developed his own personality to assert his views or attitudes. The society of the adults has ever been ignoring the ideas and the views of the adolescents, entailing a constant struggle between an established society and the society labouring to be emerged. And, the adolescent is the worst prey of this struggle. He or she will ever have to remain in a state of tension to have his or her own way in regard to the fashion of dress, the hair-style, the ways of talking and in behaving according to his or her own beliefs and convictions. The generation gap is apparently perceivable in the clash between the adolescents and the established society of the adults.

Stone et al,[33] and Hopkins[34] have shown how the adolescents gradually cease to be "parent-oriented" and shift into "peer-orientation"; and a clash

30. Schofield, M. *The Sexual Behaviour of Young People*, 1965.
31. Farrell, C. *My Mother Said*, 1978.
32. Smith, PK, Cowie Helen. *Understanding Children's Development*, Second Edition, 1996.
33. Stone, LH, Mirrane, AC, Ellis, GJ. *Parent–Peer Influence as a Predicator of Marijuana Use, Adolescence*, 1979.
34. Hopkins, JR. *Adolescence: The Transitional Years*, 1983.

ensues between the society of the adults and the society of the adolescents. The drifting away of the adolescents, in some cases, may make them drug-addicts and lax in character—so strong happens to be the impact of the peer-group.

Times are fast changing; explosion of knowledge, because of super-computer era as at present, is so bewildering for the ageing generation that they cannot understand why the adolescents believe as they do, and, behave as they do. Since authority is vested in the adult society, the adolescents have to struggle hard to establish their identity. In some cases, the knowledge and skills of the adult generation become obsolete for the adolescents, and the adults cannot earn what is so important a knowledge for the present age; nor, can they acquire skills in the use of new technologies. Generation gap, because of this fact, also aggravates difficulty for the adolescents.

EMOTIONAL INSTABILITY

The period of adolescence is a period of difficulty also because of emotional instability. As, during the period one moves fast towards the climax of development—physical, mental and emotional, one has to traverse through a period of fast changes also. Fast physical changes, and fast growing mental abilities and self-consciousness, make one more jittery because of the difficulties in adjustment to so many changes, and because of consciousness to new problems, to new responsibilities which the adult generation wants him to shoulder, while at the same time, he or she is not considered matured enough to be entrusted with the same. Because of excess of sex and some other hormones, the restraint over the flow and bursting of emotions, becomes very difficult. The adolescent gets angry very easily; grows jittery because of physical changes, especially because of menstruation or ejaculation.

Now, the boy or girl is cognitively very much developed; he or she can better understand his or her situations, is more conscious of problems ahead, and, is matured enough to think of his or her career also. All this makes the adolescent prone to anxiety. In spite of the fact that the adolescence is a period of development in all fields, emotionally, he or she suffers the short-comings of being unstable, rash, and sometimes reckless.

An adolescent happens to be very emotional; very sensitive. Sometimes, he gets nervous through the ebbs and flows of emotions. He is having more of self-consciousness, and when he feels his self to have been hurt, he loses control over himself; he may either get very upset, or, may grow nervous when he finds the entire situation to be against him. The adolescent should be treated with sympathy, with sensitivity. Of course, it is a period

An adolescent happens to be very emotional; very sensitive. Sometimes, he gets nervous through the ebbs and flows of emotions. He is having more of self-consciousness, and when he feels his self to have been hurt, he loses control over himself; he may either get very upset, or, may grow nervous when he finds the entire situation to be against him. The adolescent should be treated with sympathy, with sensitivity.

of extremity; in case of favourable situations, in case of successes and recognition of his work and worth, he feels highly exulted; but in case of reverses, he may feel very dejected. Lack of patience and tolerance is witnessed in his behaviour. An adolescent needs to be taught lesson into temperance, into moderation, the qualities which he or she, generally lacks.

A strict handling to crush the bursting of adolescent's emotions, may distort the temperamental health of the adolescent. In many cases, too strict fathers, were found to be responsible for spoiling their children; the latter grow rebels on attaining adolescence or adulthood—due freedom of work and thinking ought to be allowed to the adolescent, lest his/her development should be thwarted. Valentine[35] studied 2,000 students, and found the girls to be, rather, more sensitive than boys. Though, sometimes, both of them grow extremely nervous—it is the age when one may even attempt to commit suicide. Adolescents, generally, happen to be very ambitious, too—they dream of becoming great (often emulating their models); and when hurdles, one after the other, break their dreams, they get frustrated.

In his book,[36] Valentine writes that the main reasons behind the mental trouble of his subjects were—too much self-consciousness, an uncommon state of inferiority complex, bitter relations with parents, sometimes a repulsive attitude towards religion, and growing repulsive to its tenets, getting apprehensive and harbouring a sense of hatred at the initial experience of sex ... or the social evils which he or she still considers himself or herself quite unable to do anything about, until freedom of action is allowed.

An adolescent also gets uneasy when there are no occassions for self-expression, for which he or she happens to be so keen.

Rutter et al.[38] conclude—"adolescent turmoil is a fact, not a fiction, but its psychiatric importance has probably been over-estimated in the past."

Through the tools of a questionnaire and interview, Rutter et al.,[37] have tried to find out how far psychiatric disorder is a fact and a fiction as regards the adolescents. Their findings are to the effect that only one-fifth of the adolescents reported on the questionnaire that they often felt miserable or depressed; but that nearly half of the subjects were suffering from miserable feelings—though in interviews, a much smaller number actually appeared sad. (Table 17.4). Severe clinical depression was rare to be found though inner turmoil to some degree was there.

Rutter et al.,[38] conclude—"adolescent turmoil is a fact, not a fiction, but its psychiatric importance has probably been over-estimated in the past."

35. Valentine. *Psychology and its Bearing on Education Year.*

36. Ibid, p. 565.

37. Rutter, M Graham, P Chadwick, O, Yule, W. *Adolescent Turmoil: Fact or Fiction*? 1976.

38. Rutter, M Graham, P Chadwick, O, Yule, W. *Adolescènt Turmoil: Fact or Fiction*? 1976.

Table 17.4 Psychiatric Disorder at Different Ages (%) (a longitudinal study)

	10 yrs	*14–15 yrs*	*Adult (parents of teenage sample)*
Males	12.7	13.2	7.6
Females	10.9	12.5	11.9

Source: Rutter et al

CAREER CONSCIOUSNESS

During the latter years of adolescence, as one proceeds towards adulthood, one starts feeling concern about one's career. The selection of courses and subjects, is made with the targeted career in mind. The adolescent attains the adult level of cognitive development before he or she is actually adult. Because of this development, an adolescent understands where lie the best chances for his bright career; and how he needs to prepare himself for such a career.

The adolescent attains the adult level of cognitive development before he or she is actually adult.

In some cases, the adolescent may not have attained that level of career-consciousness, and, the fact makes the parents jittery; they go on goading their children for working hard and regularly for the desired career. The situation may cause tension for the adolescent.

But a state of short-timed unemployment does not leave a traumatic impression, it may make one apprehensive. Those who have to leave the school early because of economic pressure, or other reason in the family, would naturally be distressed if they fail to get a job.

Banks and Ullah[39] have presented a psychological analysis of the personal consequences of youth unemployment. The studies aimed at gauging distress, anxiety, and so on of the unemployed youth; how far such a state was responsible for a feeling of dissatisfaction or unhappiness among the school leaving adolescents. If youth have attained the age of employability, and do not get a job in spite of making all efforts, it lowers self-esteem and brings a kind of stigma to them.

The problem starts not only on attaining the age of employability but the adolescents start feeling concern for the problem even when they are still students—such acute is the problem of unemployment. Some unscrupulous people in our society, may even think of swindling such youth through assuring them of good jobs.

39. Banks, MH, Ullah, P. *Youth Unemployment in 1980s: A Psychoanalysis*, 1986.

TREATING THE ADOLESCENTS

Adolescence is a period of great importance as it is the period of fast and vast development in all fields—physical, mental and emotional. It is through adolescence that a child grows to full adulthood. Nevertheless, it is a period of storm and stress (G Stanley Hall)—as has already been described above. Hence, a very sensible and sensitive handling of the adolescent is required. A rough handling, blind to the developmental nature of adolescence, and to the needs of the adolescent, may spoil this most creative period of the life of a person. Here, are given some suggestions as to what ought to be done in regard to an adolescent so that this period may actually prove to be a channel to lead a child through, to the stage of a wholesome adulthood.

Physical activities There is spurt in physical growth. The adolescent would naturally be inclined to join a lot many physical activities. Depending upon the family environment and the peerage, he or she may join some gym, sports-club, or may like to play a game that is offered to him or her. In a good school, physical drills are conducted regularly for a proper physical build of the adolescents. Games and physical activities should be in adequate variety looking to the age, physique and gender of the children. They should be such that the children may indulge into them with great interest and gusto. If a congenial environment in this respect is not provided to the adolescent, it will cause a life-long loss–physical, and indirectly mental and emotional also.

An adolescent happens to be full of energy, and a desire to do something of remark so that others may be attracted towards him, is natural. If no scope for proper activities is available to him, he may go astray, and turn a delinquent, and a criminal also, if guardians do not care about the company that their ward is having.

Surging sexual urges may get a sublimating channelisation in the form of physical activities, otherwise the innocent adolescent, under the onset of pubescence, may ruin himself or herself. The importance of physical activities is two-folds; first, it is the most suitable period of life when, through appropriate physical exercise, a well-built muscular body may be developed; secondly, the brimming youthful energies may be creatively utilised for physical development.

If this period is suitably utilised, some may turn out into outstanding players, sportsmen, gymnasts, swimmers, shooters and others. Contrary to this, if this period is wasted with no physical efforts, later on, achievement cannot be of the desired level. Outing, tracking, mountaineering, *Yogasana* (boy scouts and girl guides)—a lot of activities are there, the adolescent should be given a chance to try one or some out of these many, and, develop himself or herself enjoying the activity to the full. Such activities make the environment stimulating, sublimating and developing.

Adolescence is the period when emotions of happiness, of grief, of anxiety and frustration, of anger and love, have great force.

SUBLIMATING EMOTIONS

Adolescence is the period when emotions of happiness, of grief, of anxiety and frustration, of anger and love, have great force. They are strong enough to do or undo. If the energy released by these emotions, is properly utilised constructively, the life will develop as desired, and if the emotions are let loose with no reins over them in an environment with no constructive programmes at all, they will prove to be forces which can undo life.

Music, drawing and painting; collecting rarities, reciting and composing poems or stories or expressing oneself in one or the other literary or artistic form, are the activities that an adolescent would like to be indulged into. These activities would provide a sublimating channel for the forceful emotions of the adolescents. These are the activities which moderate the emotions, and channelise their force for the development of a better personality. None can morally be good whose emotions have not been sublimated through literary and artistic pursuits, or through some programme of social service. Games and sports help in emotional development, too.

None can morally be good whose emotions have not been sublimated through literary and artistic pursuits, or through some programme of social service.

Emotional training may be provided to students through their playing dramas where emotions are expressed with wholesome impact both upon the performers and the audience. Emotions prove good for development when the same are utilised for literary and artistic activities. Parents should encourage their wards to pursue such activities. Suitable environment ought to be provided for the pursuance of the same. Schools should also provide motivation and guidance to their students in developing themselves in the fields of art and literature. Let there be umpteen activities to be selected from, as hobbies for the adolescents. Let there be hobby clubs for photography or activities based on the use of a computer, and so on. The students will not only be earning skills in different fields but their emotions will also be getting sublimated along with.

Emotions prove good for development when the same are utilised for literary and artistic activities.

MORAL EDUCATION

A child, up to the age of five, should be considered amoral; as up to that time, he or she has no conception of morality. Superego or conscience is the result of a long series of actions and reactions to one's own experiences. During adolescence, superego or conscience starts working as an effective censor. The adolescent starts thinking whether a certain behaviour is morally proper or not. But because of lack of maturity in this respect, many times, he or she gets confused, and fails to decide whether a certain thing should be done or not. For guidance, during such difficult occasions, the adolescent needs a good amount of repertoire to fall upon for reference.

Superego or conscience is the result of a long series of actions and reactions to one's own experiences. During adolescence, superego or conscience starts working as an effective censor.

And so is the importance of moral teaching which may even be orally delivered by the adults who themselves are good enough in moral character to serve as models, and, source of inspiration. Good, interesting stories or poems may be the media for such an education. Sometimes, a picture, a television serial or cinema may very effectively serve as media. Much depends upon the resourcefulness of the adults imparting such an education, and upon their character. Subjects like history, civics and even language books, generally, contain a lot of material which may be invoked for moral education. Even the sums in mathematics may be given an additional dimension to teach a moral lesson to the students. The adolescents very much need such an education to assist them in resolving dilemmas which they face not infrequently.

There are some qualities which can effectively be inculcated in the class-room situation—the students may be turned into diligent youth; they may be taught to work sincerely and to help others in times of need. An adolescent is full of energy and is keen on doing something remarkable—he is passing through the most creative and developmental period of his life. He may, on many occasions, be confused what is morally good, and what is not; hence, he would be seeking moral enlightenment.

The adolescence is the period when one grows mature also for moral reasoning. This being the period for Formal Operations, as Piaget has described it, the best approach for moral reasoning may be "cognitive-developmental approach". According to Piaget, it is the third stage of Moral Judgement characterised by the following:

1. Moral subjectivism.
2. Growing importance of mutual consent.
3. Evaluating actions by intentions.
4. Punishment in proportion to crime.

Piaget distinguishes "moral realism" from "moral subjectivism"—when punishment is in proportion to the damage caused, it is "moral realism"; but when the intentions of the subject are taken into consideration while deciding punishment, it is "moral subjectivism"; only an adolescent or an adult can have "moral subjectivism"; and not the children younger than that.

The children have to observe rules as they have been made, or as they are there conventionally developed; but during adolescence, the faculty of reasoning starts developing, and it reaches to its maturity point during this very period; hence, directly to issue instruction in matters related to morality, in the long-run, may turn the youth into a rebel. As the adolescent is fastly gaining ability to reason out things, his opinion ought to be sought when confronted with some moral dilemma.

The work of Kohlberg[40] called neo-Piagetian in the sense that working on the same lines, he suggested revisions through his studies. According to Kohlberg, making sub-divisions, there may be six stages of the development of moral judgment. The first level is that of **Pre-conventional**, when the child reasons in relation to himself. A child younger than nine, cannot think in terms of society expectations or conventions—he is interested only in his own self, in the good of his individual self.

The second level of development is that of **Conventional Morality**. It is the level when an adolescent starts giving importance to societal rules, conventions and expectations over his own individual interests. Hence, it is the right time that the adult society of parents, teachers and others, should more and more acquaint adolescents with the relevant rules of the spheres of activities that they are related to. They should be taught what are the healthy conventions of our society, and what may be the other expectations of the society which each adolescent must endeavour to fulfil.

The third and the final level of moral development is the level of **Post-conventional or Principled Morality** when the adult is cognitively developed enough to evaluate even laws, and would raise voice against such laws which violate the "universal principle of justice", the principle of the "equality of human beings" and respect for the "dignity of human beings as individual persons".

Though this final **Moral Development** is the result of maturity, yet, environment plays an important role in the process. The school can directly help in leading the child through these three levels (each level has been further divided into two stages by Kohlberg) with better development.

GOOD LITERATURE

Interest in reading rapidly grows during adolescence. This interest should be further inculcated by the adults of the family, and teachers of the school. If during this period, one does not develop interest in reading, it would hinder one's scholastic progress. Only such students can grow into eminent scholars who are voracious readers.

40. Kohlberg, L. *Moral Stages and Moralisation: The Cognitive Developmental Approach,* 1976.

But equally important is the fact that the children should read only the good books, with contents which can instil wholesome and useful ideas and feelings into their fast growing and highly impressionable minds. Especially, the period of pubescence is such when the children are likely to be inclined towards the reading of pornographic literature. It is the duty of parents at home, and of teachers at school to see that the boys and girls of this age easily get to read interesting and useful literature befitting to their mental level. These books may be of varied types—picture books, illustrated stories, biographies, books on travels and adventurous deeds—historical or fictional, poems, novels, dramas and so on. The curiosity of the children should be fully satisfied. Books on geography, history, science and other subjects, should also be made available as per interest of the children.

A good library, and a well-set and rich reading room—is an important need of every school.

SOCIALISATION

The process of development is concerned with the individual child, and is the result, mainly, of biological maturity—social perspective does not get its due importance in Piaget's postulation.

When we read Piaget for his theory of cognitive development, we feel that the process of development is concerned with the individual child, and is the result, mainly, of biological maturity—social perspective does not get its due importance in Piaget's postulation. Margaret Donaldson[41] and her colleagues demonstrated how the child's competence to take others' perspectives into view, in regard to tasks which have social significance, increases with age. This shows the individual child's social development which is important for cognitive development also. The importance of socialisation from this angle was never realised by Piaget. According to Piaget, the years when one reaches to the apex level of cognitive development, are the years of adolescence; in achieving this stage, socialisation has its very important contribution to make. Hence, it is for the parents and teachers to see that the growing child gets a very suitable social milieu where he can indulge himself into a variety of activities offering occasions for rich interactions. The cognitive and moral development has very positive correlation with the social milieu of an individual.

Adolescence is the period when one moves into a continuously widening circle of companions. First, his peerage was confined to a few of his class-fellows; by and by he crosses the boundary of his class, makes friendship with many of his school-mates. Students come in contact with one another while indulging in curricular and co-curricular activities such as games,

41. Donaldson, M. *Children's Minds*, 1978.

sports, scouting, outing, excursions or tours or picnic and so on. An adolescent becomes keenly interested in moving with his companions. Their number rapidly increases. An adolescent may like to join clubs of different types. All this makes the adolescent very much social; and, the environments provided by these different social circles, help in his multi-faceted development. The parents and teachers should provide guidance to the adolescents in making suitable choice of social circles. If the urge for companionship makes one blind as to its nature, he or she may ruin his or her career. It is here that the parents' and teachers' role is called for.

The impact of teachers, and, of some other adults that the adolescent comes in contact with, also happens to be very important. But the greatest impact happens to be that of the peer-group. In some matters, the adolescent even may not listen to his parents neglecting his peers; the parents need not lose temper but should persuade their child to see the reason if peers' effect is for a wrong choice.

When Vygotsky writes that human beings are subject to dialectical interplay between biological and cultural factors—he underlines the importance of cultural factors, that is of the social environment; he thus challenges the Piagetian lopsided developmental psychology.

PROPER TEACHING METHODS

The adolescent happens to be very creative, very active so the creative approach would suit him in the process of teaching–learning—a lot of activities should be introduced as means to learning and development. This is the period of life where the child grows argumentative; he achieves adult level of development in reasoning, hence the approach and methods should be such which boost the natural process of cognitive development. Instead of spoon-feeding the students with ready-made answers, they should be actively involved in the development of the lesson through Heuristic method, that is, question-answer method. Problems should be presented before the students to make them think; think seriously, think deeply to find out answers to the problems. Such methods would greatly help in further sharpening their faculty of reasoning. Probing questions will very much enhance the faculty of thinking. Some practical problem, related to real life, may be presented, and through questions, such a matter may be elicited which alone can lead to the solution of the problem.

Question-answer method provides maximum occasions for interaction in the class. A state of suitable group-dynamism develops. Wright HF[42]

42. Wright, HF, (et al.): Towards a psychological ecology of the classroom, 1951.

and his colleagues write that seventy per cent of the events that happen to a child in a school, happen to be the result of interactions that take place in the school every day because of varied activities. The teaching method should be such which gives maximum occasions for interactions; and which organises these interactions into very useful repertoires of experiences to fall back upon for learning new items.

Project-method is also a very suitable method for adolescent students. It would provide adequate occasions for creativity where the best learning, through doing, will take place and the students will be amply interacting to one another.

Discovery or inquiry method would suit to the inclination and needs of the adolescent. The problem should be distinct to him. The situation should be suitable for the student to conduct discovery freely and properly. All the needful physical facilities ought to be available to the discoverer. The role of the teacher should be that of a facilitator; supporting the onward journey of the learner towards the target. The teacher should remain an alert observer to step in only when he feels that the taught is likely to go astray.

First hand information, through observation, happens to be more distinct, more enduring. And, an adolescent can like nothing more than learning through tours and excursions. The adolescents should be taken for outings to observe zoos, museums, exhibitions and others; and, to factories, bank and post-office to teach them their functions and so on.

The adolescent day dreams; generally, someone or the other would catch his imagination as a hero—hero-worship is an important characteristic of an adolescent.

Learning by doing is a very important maxim as given by John Dewey who favoured the empirical approach. For imparting education to the adolescents, this would prove to be a very effective guiding principle.

And, the most important thing that the school should do, is to provide effective sources of inspiration to push on and to endeavour hard to emulate. The adolescent day dreams; generally, someone or the other would catch his imagination as a hero—hero-worship is an important characteristic of an adolescent. It is for teachers to present such models before the students who can inspire them to develop themselves into the desirable form of personalities.

And, the last but not the least, that is required for the adolescent student, is an understanding teacher, a sensitive teacher who knows and can realise under what strain an adolescent is working—he and she are confused because of sudden spurt of physical changes, because of strong onset of sexual urges, and, of emotional disturbances, and so on. The teacher should serve as a very trustworthy counsellor for them. His behaviour should be sympathetic and encouraging. He should possess the qualities of an erudite teacher whose moral character is very high so that he may very well serve as a model for the students to emulate.

If the parents are authoritarian, and the teacher is insensible, the adolescent would either grow frustrated and neurotic, or may turn into a delinquent.

SEX EDUCATION

It has already been described how for lack of sex-education, and social support, an adolescent girl and a boy are confused, and sometimes, fall a prey to continuous tension caused because of a spurt of physical changes along with an onset of strong sexual urges during this period of pubescence. Not only the adolescent grows tense, he or she may develop guilt-consciousness because of ignorance to the fact that whatever physical and emotional changes are taking place, are the results of natural evolutionary developments.

Curiosity of the child, even when he is about the age of five, regarding the difference in genitals of the children of two sexes, is natural. With age, this curiosity further increases, and other bodily differences between the two sexes and the bodily changes that come about during pubescence, naturally attract the attention of the children. But, in a society where everything related to sex is a taboo, the sex-related curiosity during adolescence, may lead one to unhealthy or harmful behaviour. While as imparting knowledge, regarding the naturality of the occurrence of menarche, may relieve the girl from great tension which otherwise is caused to her because of its first experience.

> In a society where everything related to sex is a taboo, the sex-related curiosity during adolescence, may lead one to unhealthy or harmful behaviour.

Ignorance regarding sexual matters is a fact in a traditional society, like that of the Indians. Goldman and Goldman[43] found that only 3 per cent school children of the age group 15, could make fully appropriate responses to the questions regarding puberty in North America and England, and 5 per cent in Australia; of course, the percentage of such children was 48 in Sweden. Likewise, the percentage of fully appropriate responses was found to be different in regard to questions related to terms such as pregnancy, virginity, venereal disease and rape.

It is the arrangement of nature that the two partners get ready biologically for procreation. The state of maturity for procreation is marked by some physical changes, by some bio-chemical and emotional changes. To teach about gender differences in terms of genitals, and about all these changes and developments that occur during adolescence, should be the contents of sex-education. For want of such education, and, if the natural curiosity of the children and adolescents regarding all these facts is suppressed, the curiosity may just grow stronger, leading the boy and girl to adopt such

43. Goldman, R, Goldman, J. *Children's Sexual Thinking*, 1982.

means to satisfy the same which would spoil the youthful pleasures of their individual lives, and can help only in vitiating the social milieu.

Presupposing consensus regarding the need of sex education, let us pose three questions to ourselves about sex education:

1. What to teach under sex education?
2. When to impart sex education?
3. Who should impart it, and, how—collectively or individually?

1. Sex education should consist of knowledge about gender differences. The attention of the children may be diverted to the fact of gender differences in animals and in birds also. It is natural for children of the opposite sex to feel that one is not the same as is the other of the opposite sex in body structure; this feeling is mainly because of their difference in genitals. If the curiosity of the children is not satisfied and they are just hushed down, it may further strengthen their curiosity and they may resort to unhealthy ways to satisfy the same.

   Children, generally, feel eager to know as to how they have been born, whence he or she has come. They were given by the god from above, or bought from market, or given by such and such person, and so on. Such answers do more harm than satisfy the curiosity of a child.

   Instead, the child may be taught that before birth the baby grows into the womb of the mother where his feeding is done through the mother—the two happen to be connected with a cord.

2. Sex education should be imparted and spread over the early years of childhood, and, especially, during the years of adolescence when the onslaught of sexual urges happens to be the strongest. What has been mentioned above should form part of sex education during early childhood; not only the children should be taught gender differences in reference to genitals and so on, but adequately, the nature and purpose of gender-differences should also be made clear to them.

   During the period of pubescence, when a lot of anatomical changes take place, the students ought to be taught what changes, apparent and non-apparent, take place; what biochemical reactions occur and to what effect and purpose. If this much has been taught to them, they would not be afraid of having first experience of menarche or ejaculation. Otherwise, such an experience may make the adolescent feel herself or himself as guilty of some immoral commission. Some boys feel the need of consulting some physician in this respect.

3. To children, of the age between 5 and 7, an idea should be given that of the gender differences; that are there created by nature not in case of human beings alone but in case of animals, birds and others also. The children can learn of apparent difference between a boy and a girl when the fact is made clear to them by their parents at home.

   As regards gender differences being made apparent because of physical and biochemical changes that take place during puberty, it is the biology teacher of the school who should be considered to be the most proper person to impart sex education. Only an elderly person of some serene temperament can do this in a desired way. The health and pleasure of life, much depends upon how sex is taken. To make one's life wholesome and pleasant, sublimation of the sexual urges is must, and, sex education, if properly imparted, may prove very helpful in doing this. The imparting of this education must never cause excitement to sexual urges. Hughes and Hughes have underlined the importance of sex education both for a good individual life, as well as for a better society.

If we compare the findings of Kinsey et al[44, 45] with the warnings contained in the parents' manuals published in 1909, and with that of the Mother Craft Manual published in 1928; and also with the findings of Schofield[46] and Farrell[47], we can appreciate the changes that have continuously been coming over in the sexual attitudes and behaviours of the adolescents and the adults over the years.

The spread of AIDS and other venereal diseases in recent years, has also had its impact upon the attitudes of the youth regarding sexual matters. Studies of Hopkins[48] and that of Griffitt and Hatfield[49] have suggested that teenagers of the higher social groups are likely to have greater sexual experience. Hence, along with the imparting of sexual education, restraint and high moral discipline must also be taught. During the period of pubescence, the energies of the teenagers, ought to be channelised to physical activities and to other social and literary hobbies, so that the period of high spurt of growth may prove to be the period of highest development.

During the period of pubescence, the energies of the teenagers, ought to be channelised to physical activities and to other social and literary hobbies, so that the period of high spurt of growth may prove to be the period of highest development.

---

44. Kinsey, AC, Pomeroy, WB, Martin, CE. *Sexual Behaviour in the Human Male*, 1948.
45. Kinsey, AC, Pomeroy, WB, Martin, CE, Gebherd, PH. *Sexual Behaviour in the Human Female*, 1953.
46. Schofield, M. *The Sexual Behaviour of Young People*.
47. Farrell, C. *My Mother Said*, 1978.
48. Hopkings, JR. *Adolescence: The Transitional Years*, 1983.
49. Griffitt, W, Hatfield, E. *Human Sexual Behaviour*, 1985.

REVIEW QUESTIONS

***Q*.1.** Adolescence has been called a period of "storm" and "stress" by GS Hall. How far do you agree to it? Discuss and elaborate.

***Q*.2.** What is meant by "Identity Crisis?" Narrate in detail your own experiences as an adolescent when you may have had to struggle for your own identity in the world so heavily dominated by the adults.

***Q*.3.** How the following terms are significant for the study of adolescent?

(*i*) pubescence
(*ii*) hero-worship
(*iii*) sex-role identity
(*iv*) hyperthyroidism (as used by Wilkins)
(*v*) appearance-consciousness (refer David Elkind)

***Q*.4.** Complete the following chart which shows the biological changes that come about in case of adolescent boys and girls.

Age (in years)	*Boys*	*Girls*
9-10	—	Growth of bony p....., budding of n.....
10-11	First growth of t ....., and p	Budding of b....., p..... hair
14-15	A ..... hair (under armpits), d ..... on upper lip, v ..... change	Earliest normal p .....
15-16	Mature S	A ....., D ..... of voice

ANSWERS TO OBJECTIVE TYPE QUESTIONS

***Q*.4.** *Age (in years)*	*Boys*	*Girls*
9-10	—	*pelvic, nipples*
10-11	*testes and penis*	*breast, pubic*
14-15	*auxillary, down, voice*	*pregnancies*
15-16	*spermatozoa*	*Acne, Deepening*

CHAPTER

18

THEORIES OF CHILD DEVELOPMENT—FREUD'S PSYCHOANALYSIS THEORY

Chapter Outline

Development is a characteristic of every living being. The human child develops the most. The study of the process of the development of a child has been very important for psychologists of different schools. Hence, different theories of child development are available. Freud's psychoanalysis theory is an important one among them. Freud has traced the development of a child not on the basis of his overt behaviour but his study of the development of the child is based on his psychological functioning. The psychological functioning which is consisted of the child's feelings, perceptions, thoughts, memories, ideas and so on, provides the raw material for the study to a psychoanalyst. Freud's psychoanalysis theory of child development is the result of such a study. Thoughts and feelings could be studied only as they came to consciousness of the patient of Freud's pathological clinic; because a clinical patient can report of his feelings and thoughts when he is conscious of the same, or as they flow through his consciousness.

> Freud has traced the development of a child not on the basis of his overt behaviour but his study of the development of the child is based on his psychological functioning. The psychological functioning which is consisted of the child's feelings, perceptions, thoughts, memories, ideas and so on, provides the raw material for the study to a psychoanalyst.

Freud assumed that all pathological functioning could be taken as a maladjusted form of normal functioning. Freud's subjects were the maladjusted pathological patients who would come to him for treatment or relief. Thus, the raw material for the development of Freudian theory

Freud's subjects were the maladjusted pathological patients who would come to him for treatment or relief. Thus, the raw material for the development of Freudian theory of child development was made available through the report of the clinical patients as feelings and thoughts flowed into their consciousness.

of child development was made available through the report of the clinical patients as feelings and thoughts flowed into their consciousness. Freud found that the motivation which makes one behave, is the same both in case of a clinical patient and a normal person.

AC Baldwin[1] writes that the Freudian "theory is more obviously concerned with an individual's thoughts and feelings than his behaviour." Freud has traced development, mainly, in respect of thoughts and feelings, how they undergo changes as the child grows biologically as well as in experiences through the three personality structures—ID, Ego and Superego. To personality structures, we shall come later on; first, let us see what are the basic concepts of his theory.

BASIC CONCEPTS

In 1951, Freud's article "Instincts and their Vicissitudes" was published. In it he describes instinctual drives to be the source of all covert and overt activities of the individual. The instinctual drive has three aspects:

(*i*) Its source; (*ii*) Its external aim; and (*iii*) Its object.

In 1951, Freud's article "Instincts and their Vicissitudes" was published. In it he describes instinctual drives to be the source of all covert and overt activities of the individual. The instinctual drive has three aspects.

Source Source of a drive, is its basic property. Excitation arises in some region or part of the body; that region or part of the body, is the source of the instinctual drive. Such a source has some internal aim. As in case of hunger as an instinctual drive, satisfying or gratification of the same, is the Internal Aim—in respect of each drive, an internal aim remains constant to it. Likewise, the sexual drive has a strong internal aim as seeking gratification.

External aim External aim in case of the drive of hunger, is eating some such thing, and, in such an amount that the drive of hunger may attain satisfaction, it may be gratified. In case of sex, some sexual activity will be sought to be done.

Now, when the personality of an individual develops, changes occur in case of external aim which is manifested through the overt behaviour of the individual—the internal aim in case of each instinctual drive remains constant.

Object The third aspect of the instinctual drive is the object. In case of hunger as an instinctual drive, the object is food or what is consumed to satisfy hunger; in case of sex, there must be someone, as an object in respect of which the individual's sexual activities—exhibiting organs, touching, kissing, sexual intercourse are directed. Freud has described how in the beginning, all the sexual activities of a child are carried on in respect

1. Baldwin, AC. *Theories of Child Development.*

of oneself as an object; and, how the external aim and object change as the child grows in age, and he goes on earning experiences.

Study of the external aims and objects is possible, but no definite number of sources can be given, nor can we be sure regarding the internal aim of each drive—the sources being purely internal phenomena, and, because of the possibility of the regions of excitation being both conscious and unconscious mind.

The internal phenomena remain constant; what change, are the external aims and objects. The vicissitudes that Freud describes in his article "Instincts and their Vicissitudes" are in reference to external aims and objects. As the child's personality develops, vicissitudes occur both in case of external aims and objects. The overt behaviour of the person makes these vicissitudes evident. They are the indicators of development in the personality which is the result of biological maturity and the experiences earned.

LIBIDO

Libido is the sex instinct. It provides the most important instinctual drive. No other drive is so significant in the process of personality development as is the libidinal one. The satisfaction of the instinctual drive of hunger will not bring about any significant change so far the development of personality is concerned, but, what external aim is there in the pursuit of the gratification of the instinctual drive of sex, and, what object one adopts for its gratification, is very significant. The overt behaviour of the individual in reference to the external aim and object of sex, is a very important indicator of the nature and level of personality development. While the gratification of all other drives are for the preservation of the self, the gratification of the libidinal urge is for the preservation of the species. It has been labelled as a basic drive in the Freudian theory. It is a source of a good many significant personality adjustments. Libido is the special name that Freud gave to the sexual excitation. What particular action discharges how much energy can be described in term of libido, this is a quantitative indicator of sexual energy.

Libido is the sex instinct. It provides the most important instinctual drive. No other drive is so significant in the process of personality development as is the libidinal one.

Freud has used the term sexual in a wider sense than is customary. Even the sympathisers of the theory could not digest the far—fetched usages of the term. As, for example, in the action of ploughing the land, Freud sees a symbolic rape of the mother. Freud had to face strong opposition because of such sexual flavour of many psychoanalytic explanations of behaviour. But, when the psychoanalyst explains the child's anxiety over physical danger, as a fear of castration—psychoanalytic evidence is there, that the child harbours the unconscious fear that his penis will be cut off. The fundamental importance of sexuality cannot be "explained away".

Though the sexual drive is important for procreation, and, the preservation of the species, yet, none of the partners of sexual intercourse, is motived to it as a biological function but by pleasures of the act. But much more than sexual intercourse, is required for the preservation of the species, and Freud uses the term sexual for all such functions which are directly or indirectly related to the maintenance of the species. Indeed, a number of other feelings and pleasures have been integrated into the pattern of mating and child rearing, so it is difficult to decide which one has the element of sexuality and which does not. Of course, kissing, embracing, caressing and snuggling close together, have the element of sexuality. But in early childhood, no genital sensations are involved in them. Freud calls them "organ pleasures". But as the child grows up, these sensual feelings are integrated into a coherent set of sexual feelings which promotes the biological procreation of the species. Freud has labelled all these pleasures as sexual; and they have been distinguished from genital activities by speaking of them as pregenital.

Psychosexual maturity involves the integration of these sexual pleasures into a pattern of genital pleasure in sexual activity. One more important characteristic of psychosexual maturity is the material faithfulness between the partners of sexual relationship in all circumstances. Parental love can result only as a result of psychosexual maturity; it makes the parents provide a warm and secure environment to the child for his wholesome development. Thus, sexuality has been dealt as a genuine cornerstone of psychoanalysis theory.

CATHEXIS

In some region or organ of the body instinctual drive is excited (as for example, Libido is the term that has been used for the excitation of sexual drive); an "idea" cannot lead to behaviour unless, first, it is carried to consciousness. The force which carries a drive or an idea representing a drive, to consciousness, has been termed as cathexis by Freud.

The force which carries a drive or an idea representing a drive, to consciousness, has been termed as cathexis by Freud.

Excitation is caused because of some feeling, perception or thought or action. Excitation discharges energy, the source of which is some instinctual drive. Personality mechanisms make use of this energy; no overt behaviour is possible without this energy, and, it is disposed of when something is operated. "..... the drive energy operates by cathecting various psychological structures in the personality." Freud views cathexis as an electric charge which energises the region or the object which is involved in the process of the behaviour. Cathexis describes how energy is distributed or deployed.

Drive excitation is essential for a behaviour. But drive excitation cannot directly express itself in the form of some behaviour. "The intervening mechanism is cathexis." The cathexis is the force that drives the idea into consciousness. The idea represents the drive which is then felt as an impulse. All the ideas are not acted out into behaviour though they may have been brought to consciousness; but it is always through cathexis that ideas are brought to consciousness; "objects of a drive are cathected". The mother is the best example of an object cathected for the child; she is valued by the child. The ideas of a child that are related to its mother, have a strong cathexis. In other words, we may describe the fact of this relationship that mother "commands a lot of cathexis in the child's psychological functioning"—the fact is evident through the behaviour of the child who carries out whatever is asked to be done by his mother. The mother is the object that occupies the child's mind for most of the time. The basic psychoanalytic assumption is that all kinds of feelings, thoughts or other psychological processes, or behaviour of an organism, have their genesis in the instinctual drives; but cathexes are the forces which can make their presence felt only by others. The influence caused by these drives are carried to consciousness, and, eventually to overt behaviours by the force which has been termed as "cathexis" in psychoanalysis explanations. Overt behaviour is essential for the gratification of the drive motivated need.

Drive excitation is essential for a behaviour. But drive excitation cannot directly express itself in the form of some behaviour. "The intervening mechanism is cathexis."

"..... objects of a drive are cathected". The mother is the best example of an object cathected for the child; she is valued by the child. The ideas of a child that are related to its mother, have a strong cathexis.

The nature of cathexes, changes as the child's personality structure develops from "Id" to "Ego" and from "Ego" to "Superego". This change is perceived through the behaviour of the subject. What does not change, or remains constant, is the instinctual drive. Then, what makes a change in the behaviour as the personality develops, psychoanalysts say that it is the cathexis that changes with maturity, with environment; so, here is the importance of environment for psychoanalysts. Defense mechanisms is a result of the sublimation of cathexes.

The nature of cathexes, changes as the child's personality structure develops from "id" to "Ego" and from "Ego" to "Superego".

An idea reaches to consciousness when it is at a critical level of cathexis. Some other factors also contribute in the process when an idea is cathected to some object—the idea must be related to some basic instinct, or to the drive, deriving from it. The common assumption among the people is that we are inclined to think of things which we want, and which have emotional significance for us. The higher the intensity of motivation, the stronger will be the thoughts intruding upon consciousness.

But if thoughts are painful, the individual would try to exclude its intrusion into consciousness. The defense mechanism used is Repression. A defense mechanism is used only when an individual is developing to a higher structure of personality—from "Id" to "Ego"; or from "Ego to "Superego". Repression is the result of Counter Cathexis. Counter Cathexis subtracts energy from the region energised by some drive cathexis, and, generally, in relation to some object. Counter Cathexis is used to repress an idea which threatens the development of some unpleasant situation, or

Repression is the result of Counter Cathexis.

Counter Cathexis is used to repress an idea which threatens the development of some unpleasant situation, or when the idea itself is painful, and so causing fear. An individual at the level of "Ego" or "Superego", has his "Self-image" developed, and if an idea threatens his "Self-image", or is against his "Self-esteem", he would attempt to repress such an idea.

when the idea itself is painful, and so causing fear. An individual at the level of "Ego" or "Superego", has his "Self -image" developed, and if an idea threatens his "Self-image", or is against his "Self- esteem", he would attempt to repress such an idea. If I consider my worth to be as a man of tolerance, I would get afraid if an idea or drive representative seeks intrusion into my consciousness through cathexis, and to lead me to some such overt behaviour which may harm my self-image; and to exclude that idea from intruding upon my mind, I would resort to the defense mechanism called repression. Sometimes, the thought may be too strong to be excluded fully from consciousness. A repressed idea is most likely to continue its existence in the unconscious mind, and may be playing very important role in a dream, or in a state of hallucination. Ideas thus suppressed in our unconscious mind, do affect our overt behaviour also. For a person who is keen in maintaining his sexual loyalty to his wife, the very idea of sexuality towards another woman, is immoral; and he would try his utmost to repress this idea through counter-cathexis-leaving little energy for the drive cathexis to be acted out. It is thus that a person avoids an otherwise threatening anxiety-provoking situation. Likewise, as the child grows older, he would learn to resist the instinctual drive of hunger when food is not available, as otherwise the situation would be very painful and derogatory. The use of counter-cathexis is an indication of the development of the child's personality from the "Id" structure to the "Ego" structure. An adult or even an adolescent may have developed to the level of "Superego" structure when one tries to avoid the acting out of such a drive cathexis which is not acceptable to the society, or is considered outlandish.

Hypercathexis is for focusing attention to realities or to ideas other than those aroused by the immediate basic drive; these may be the ideas that had come to consciousness in the remote past, or may have been lying repressed in the unconscious mind.

Finally, there is a third type of cathexis which Freud has termed as hyper-cathexis. Hypercathexis is for focusing attention to realities or to ideas other than those aroused by the immediate basic drive; these may be the ideas that had come to consciousness in the remote past, or may have been lying repressed in the unconscious mind. The two important functions of hypercathexis are—focusing on an idea, and to integrate it with relevant ideas in a sequence or system with an objective to solve the problem. While cathexis focuses attention on the object to be achieved, hypercathexis leads the subject to think realistically and logistically also about means and modalities which are essential for the achievement of object. Freud has used this term to describe the fact that we can voluntarily concentrate on any object or can think of an idea before it comes to consciousness of its own. Hypercathexis cathects many ideas and thoughts in a system based on logical rules. For chalking out plans, or for searching out a needful information, a proper sequencing of ideas or thoughts is needed. It is hypercathexis which enables the subject to do it.

Hypercathexis is a stage of development in one's personality when one's thoughts are not bound by drive cathexis only. With the development of hypercathexis, one can bring to consciousness ideas and thoughts which are not tied to drive cathexis; sequence and organisation of one's ideas and thoughts may not be determined by drives alone. Now, "attention can control access to consciousness and change the organisation. Ideas are partly under voluntary control; the sequence of the ideas is governed by realities related to the plan, and by logical rules. The sequencing of ideas and thoughts in accordance with a certain plan, or as per certain rule, is the essence of what Freud has termed as Secondary Process. In the primary-process thinking, thought of the drive is the only connecting thread. The primary-process thinking may lead to only some single drive satisfaction whereas the secondary-process thinking is to have the satisfaction of achieving something which has social significance also. As for example, if a hungry person thinks of food, his thoughts may roam to foods of different kinds; to some dinner party enjoyed by him in the remote past; and to his mother who may have been cooking delicious food for him. But when the same person rises above thoughts related to his own person only, and thinks of a plan to arrange food for the hungry people to the extent that he can, he starts the Secondary Process, and it is the result of Hypercathexis.

> Hypercathexis is a stage of development in one's personality.

> The primary-process thinking may lead to only some single drive satisfaction whereas the secondary-process thinking is to have the satisfaction of achieving something which has social significance also.

Repression is to avoid a pain-producing thought; nevertheless, facing realities squarely, may sometime be needed to tackle a problem effectively. Under such a situation hypercathexis brings ideas of relevance to consciousness; had there been no relevance or significance of such ideas to the resolution of the problem, they may have been ignored, and a major part of them may have been relegated to unconsciousness—at least for the time-being. The idea of being poorly prepared for an examination is definitely anxiety-producing, and hence painful, but one would not attempt for its repression; one would rather have hypercathexis to chalkout a plan sequencing and organising ideas or thoughts in such a way that the motive of success in the examination may be achieved.

Thus, hypercathexis indicates an important stage of development in the personality of a person.

DEFENSE MECHANISMS

A reference has been made above to only one kind of defense mechanism, that is repression, when an idea or drive representation is excluded from having accessibility to consciousness. The defenses are the indicators of the development of the personality structure from the level of Id to Ego or Superego level. Id is the stage when each drive or drive representation seeks immediate and direct gratification of its need, it cannot tolerate any

A reference has been made above to only one kind of defense mechanism, that is repression, when an idea or drive representation is excluded from having accessibility to consciousness.

deferment. Each idea or drive representative is cathected to consciousness, and leads to overt behaviour. Still, the person is too immature to harbour any other consideration in reference to his self-image or self-esteem; or social or moral propriety to defer or detour or suppress the gratification of the drive representative through some mechanism depending upon counter cathexis or hypercathexis so that the two aspects of the instinctual drives, that is, the external aim and the object, are affected. The defenses that have clearly been identified, have been classified as under:

1. Repression 2. Displacement 3. Reaction formation
4. Isolation 5. Projection 6. Denial.

All these defenses distort the consciousness of the individual in a way that the expression of the drive may be prevented. Describing the common feature of these defenses, AL Baldwin[2] writes: ".....they distort the individual's consciousness in a way that prevents or alleviates the pain and anxiety that would be caused by a more realistic awareness of his environment or of his own ideas and feelings". This shows why a defense mechanism is adopted, and when it is adopted; it is adopted when the situation is painful or anxiety-provoking; for such a situation either the external environment may be responsible for some idea or feelings of the individual himself. The objective behind the adoption of a defense mechanism is always to prevent or alleviate the pain or anxiety.

The defenses that have clearly been identified, have been classified as under:
1. Repression
2. Displacement
3. Reaction formation
4. Isolation
5. Projection
6. Denial.

Such is the importance of these defense mechanisms that an individual's life-style is indicated because of these. These mechanisms are the corner—stones of one's personality, and, the behaviour of an individual can be predicted because of the mechanisms that one would adopt under certain circumstances.

Now, let us see how each of the above-mentioned defense mechanisms, has been described by Freud and the psychologists of the school of psychoanalysis. But before we describe these defenses, their difference from Controls should be made clear:

Defenses by one means or the other distort consciousness to prevent the expression of the drive while Controls only inhibit the expression or modify it—"they do not really block the drive itself".

1. Repression Repression is the cornerstone of all the defenses, to a certain degree, repression is exercised in all sorts of defense mechanisms; the motive there being to raise the threshold level of access to consciousness. Repression can occur only when cathexis is subtracted from a drive cathected idea. The threshold of access to consciousness is raised to prevent the drive cathected idea from reaching to the critical level of intensity when the individual would be consciously aware of its presence.

2. Baldwin, AL. *Theories of Child Development.*

2. Displacement A drive-cathected idea is repressed for protection from pain or anxiety. But other ideas that have only associative link with the drive-cathected idea, escape repression, and become expressed in the form that is not painful or anxiety-laden. This psychic function of the escape of the ideas having only associative link with the drive-cathected idea, and of their being expressed through such an overt behaviour which is for the present not likely to be threatened by the censor, has been called **Displacement**, it is a common accompaniment of repression.

Repression can occur only when cathexis is subtracted from a drive cathected idea.

The example given is that of hand-washing so often, and with great care. In some cases, the root for this symptom, has been found to be in the idea of masturbation, a result of the libidinal drive. Washing the hand is not considered to be a dirty habit, and hence is not anxiety-laden as masturbation. So, hand-washing has been quoted as an example of displacement, also a sort of defense mechanism. At the same time, "The tender care of the hands, expresses some of the cathexis of the genitals".

The ideas which are associatively linked with the idea that is repressed, but which themselves are not repressed, are the examples of displacements. The displacement is the mechanism through which the forbidden idea is expressed in disguise, gets its "message through to consciousness".

The ideas which are associatively linked with the idea that is repressed, but which themselves are not repressed, are the examples of displacements. The displacement is the mechanism through which the forbidden idea is expressed in disguise, gets its "message through to consciousness".

Freud describes how the mechanism of repression tends to spread. Once the link between the repressed idea and the associatively linked ideas that have got an expression through displacement, is consciously recognised, such associatively linked ideas also start causing anxiety, with the result that the same are also repressed.

3. Reaction formation Let us begin with an example. Suppose a person has an idea of hatred against his father, but the same makes him feel, or may cause an immediate unconscious reaction that harbouring such an idea is immoral. The energy released because of the drive of hostility is inhibited, tamed or civilised through counter-cathexis, and a counter-drive leads to the impulses of excessive love or respect for the father. The counter drive differs from the primary instinctual drive as:

(*i*) the former is established against a primary drive, as a reaction to it;

(*ii*) it is a more tamed, inhibited and a civilised drive than the latter.

But, whenever the subject has a little feeling that his overt behaviour has leaked the original drive of hatred, he would further inhibit his counter drive too through more controls and defenses.

One more characteristic of the counter-drive is that it has a life of its own; whenever its maladaptiveness is realised, it too requires defenses and controls; and it is possible that in respect of each counter-drive, again and again, defenses and controls may be required each time layering the new ones upon those of the previously used ones; and each time the cathexis of these derivative motives becomes more and more inhibited, and less and less demanding and peremptory.

The example is, one, as a reaction formation, indulgences into acts of kindness only to realise that his behaviour has been maladaptive. He may grow pessimistic or disillusioned to find that the object on one account or the other, did not deserve that much kindness, or that in a bid to show kindness to the object, he has exceeded the reasonable limit. In such a situation some sort of defense and control may be established over kindness. In a neurotic form of kindness, one may be giving out, and giving more only to feel hurt and angry that the object is not grateful enough for it. Here, the subject may give acceptable conscious expression to less repressed hostility along with the counter-drive.

4. Isolation Isolation is the mechanism to isolate the feeling associated to an idea, but not the content of the idea itself. This isolation is executed through repression; the more exact word for which here, would be "Intellectualisation". The example is, some people do not respond with anger or hostility when they are insulted or imposed upon; it appears as if they were unconscious of such a behaviour of others towards them or were unaware of their intent. By and by, they grow so habitual or structualised of responding to such a situation isolating the feeling of anger or hostility that they always appear to be playing cool to such a situation though actually they may be pondering upon the situation to take action more appropriately against those inflicting insult or imposing something upon them.

The close relative of isolation, is intellectualisation. Intellectualisation is a cognitive function; it consists of understanding situation cognitively so that appropriate means may be thought out to accomplish the objectives without being swept off by the affective side of the drive expression. But one negative impact of such a structualisation is that the person thus structualised may not have that force in his behaviour which the affective side of the drive may cause to grow because of the energy released by it.

Intellectualisation is a cognitive function; it consists of understanding situation cognitively so that appropriate means may be thought out to accomplish the objectives without being swept off by the affective side of the drive expression.

Affect serves as a signal which guides the subject in adapting the behaviour to the purpose to be achieved. Affect seeks emotional discharge in an explosive manner only until mature ego is developed, and the affect is at the primary process level; but, when personality has developed to the structure of mature Ego level, that is, the affect is at the secondary process level, it serves as a signal indicating the significance of the problem, and, helping in setting a goal for the adaptive behaviour. So, repressing affect would mean preventing it from functioning as a signal.

Isolation is a psychodynamic process which saves a person the anxiety which may be caused by the impinging of two mental events upon each other while occurring simultaneously, and which are of such nature that they cannot co-exist harmoniously. In such a situation, separation of the one from the other is essential to save the individual the difficulty of reconciling the two, or of dealing with the two simultaneously. Such a separation is the defense mechanism of isolation. Suppose I go to a temple, and there, along with a feeling of devotion, an idea occurs impinging upon the feeling of devotion that the idol that I am bowing to, is nothing but a work in stone or in some metal. The psychological situation causes anxiety, mental trouble; and the only way out is **Isolation**. For the time-being, at least, I would make a psychological separation of the two mental events which are irreconcilable.

Other example of isolation is that a man having the tender feelings of love, may not have sexual relationship with a woman; and may not be loving tenderly another woman with whom he has sexual relationship. In such a case, tender love and sexual feelings have to be separated through a device of defense mechanism; though feelings of both types are expressed but on different occasions, and in relation to different persons.

5. Projection A drive motivation which is undesirable, but which being too strong to be prevented from consciousness, makes one to adopt a defense mechanism of attributing that undesirable characteristic or drive motivation to another person; this mechanism is called **Projection**—one projects something undesirable into one's character, into that of another. A prudish spinster may be complaining against over-sexuality into another persons. And, she herself may grow into militantly non-sexual as a reaction formation. Such a complaint expresses both sexuality and hostility that have come to the consciousness of the complainant. A person who always strives to give the impression of himself being a religious man, would project such feelings of his into the character of other persons, which are incompatible with religion.

It, generally, happens that a person who, because of his own selfish behaviour, is cut off from other members of his family or society, would complain aggressively against unsociability of others, and would himself grow more unsocial.

One more form of projection is also witnessed in the behaviour of people in general. Suppose, my son has scored very high marks in an examination; since my praising my own son on this account would be immodest, so I may start speaking of other cases of high scores only to bring to the notice of others the fact of my son having scored so high.

AL Baldwin writes—"Projection is not so much a modification of the actual content of consciousness as a modification of the organisation of consciousness." It means, whatever content comes to consciousness, remains there in its entirety; the defense mechanism of projection is to effect a change in its organisation only—whatever content is there in the consciousness of a person, is projected as a characteristic in the personality of someone else, or in others; what originally was in reference to one's own self, is reorganised in reference to others. Only such a one adopts this defense who has developed self-image or self-esteem; to protect the same, for example, one would express one's sex-related drive- cathexis through describing someone else engaged in sexual actions; attributing the motive to another person.

"Projection is not so much a modification of the actual content of consciousness as a modification of the organisation of consciousness."

In a given situation, what we imagine the other would behave, actually, in most cases, projects what our instinctual drive might have driven us to behave but for our Ego or Superego.

6. Denial It is the most primitive of all defenses. It distorts cognition in a more severe way. To deny the existence of a reality is denial. A very young child hallucinates things as still the faculty of perceiving reality is not developed, nor has he developed his Ego. A seriously psychotic person also distorts cognition through denying the facts because he cannot face realities. A grown-up denies a reality to protect himself from an anxiety-arousing situation or when it is otherwise unpleasant to him. A grown up may deny facts when they are minor or unclear. We may have seen people denying an impending unpleasant event; for example, when a driver says, "I do not feel sleepy when I so determine," the probability is that he may be feeling the impact of sleep while he so declares. "Denial is perceiving the world in the way that one wants it to be rather than the way it is." (AL Baldwin).

"Denial is perceiving the world in the way that one wants it to be rather than the way it is."

Now, we should distinguish hallucination from denial. Denial is the distortion of cognition, but hallucinations do not imply distortion of cognition as the child who hallucinates, has still not fully developed the faculty of perceiving facts; still, he cannot distinguish what he is hallucinating, and what he is perceiving. He hallucinates things for drive-satisfaction, a grown-up denies things to protect himself from pain or anxiety.

As the child grows older, he cannot deny realities, his Ego is also stronger now. Of course, he can deny realities in a play or in a day-dreaming; there, things may be taken to exist as he would like them to be, rather than, as they are. A grown-up also day-dreams. Both playing and day-dreaming may provide respite from burdensome or hard realities only for a while.

A person with a fully developed Ego, would adopt other types of defenses than Denial to protect himself in an anxiety-arousing situation.

As already told in the beginning that this list of mechanisms, does not exhaust all the defenses, there may be a lot of others, too, but Freud has described these six as the most important among them. Later neo-Freudians viewed these defenses in a broader context as to how they affect the styles of perceiving and thinking besides serving as defensive devices. They have described these mechanisms as cognitive controls and cognitive styles. In the development of the personality of a child, these controls and styles play an important part. The personality of a person has three aspects—physical, cognitive and conative. It is the cognitive aspect of personality which is mainly represented and affected by the defense mechanisms.

Cognitive controls and cognitive styles Though defense mechanisms are mainly concerned with the cognitive aspect of personality, yet, their effect may be perceived upon the over all functioning of the individual. How a person controls his cognitive functions, that is, his perceptions and thinking; what is the way of his knowing of things, or of being conscious of things or of facts, and his judgment about the same—all this forms an important part of an individual's personality. In wider perspective, defenses are cognitive controls and cognitive styles. These controls and styles are adopted in general forms to protect oneself in an upleasant or anxiety-arousing situation, none the less, individual differences are there which, besides other characteristics, make personalities distinct. The general cognitive functioning of an individual influences the kinds of defenses one develops.

Though defense mechanisms are mainly concerned with the cognitive aspect of personality, yet, their effect may be perceived upon the overall functioning of the individual. How a person controls his cognitive functions, that is, his perceptions and thinking; what is the way of his knowing of things, or of being conscious of things or of facts, and his judgment about the same — all this forms an important part of an individual's personality.

Using stroop colour—naming test, George Klein and his colleagues investigated one particular cognitive style as Constricted Control as distinct from Flexible Control. Those who have developed constricted controls in their functioning, happen to be very precise and meticulous; and, do not allow intuitive or affective factors to influence their cognitive as those with flexible controls do. The high interference group shows more vulnerability to interfering stimuli from the periphery. Just to concentrate on the main content, the central content, such a group would adopt the defense of isolating the peripheral objects, and the style of constricted control develops. Of course, the need that is present at the moment, would affect the nature and intensity of control. Baldwin writes, "The same procedure is even stronger when there is a compelling need present which threatens to impinge upon the perception." "If the season is hot, and in a picture the central item is "ice-cream", the pictures of other items, given on the periphery, would be ignored through the mechanism of isolation, and concentration would be high on "ice-cream" and other related words if the same are given there. The subject would be vulnerable to the intrusion of words related to hot-relieving things; such a situation would make not only the visual movement of the subject constricted, but also his association to other objects. The mechanism is both a defense and a result, "the entire pattern of interaction with the environment is coloured".

THE ESTABLISHMENT OF PERSONALITY STRUCTURES

Freud describes the development of personality through three structures—Id, Ego and Superego. Each of the three structures has distinct patterns of reactional behaviour that is caused by the arousal of some motive. Each structure determines how drive representations would appear in consciousness and lead to drive discharge. We can know what is the development structure of personality, looking at the dispositional properties of the subject. It means, each structure is characterised by its own dispositional properties. Id, Ego and Superego—each has its own distinct dispositional properties which indicate the type of structure that one is having; it gives the idea how a person functions, what are the various properties that are evidenced during the period of drive discharge; and how the various properties are related to one another.

Id is the structure of personality when a primitive instinctual force reigns supreme, it is highly impulsive and rash, and, can tolerate no delay in the gratification of a drive. It is the primitive source of energy which is blindly utilised to serve the urges of the wild "Self" only. It is uncultured and thoughtless. A child, in the beginning, happens to be at the Id stage when it has no thought of right or wrong but immediately rushes into an action being prompted by some instinctual impulse. It is only gradually that the personality develops towards the structure of Ego. Even when the Ego structure has been developed, it is not the case that one gets totally above, and beyond the properties which characterise the structure of Id—a constant struggle goes on between the urges of the Id, and the directions given by the Ego.

Id is related to primary process only when no defense mechanisms have developed. Rappaport[3] has described the models of the functioning of primary process, separately in reference to action, cognition and affect. In each case, the primary process is consisted of three stages. Here, we are giving each of the three models as given by Rappaport:

The primary model of action:

Restlessness	®	Sucking breast	®	Quiescence
(drive accumulation)		(drive satisfaction)		(drive absence)

The infant grows restless as drive accumulates and it demands immediate gratification. The child starts yelling and would not be affected by any means that may have to be tried at, to make it tolerate even, a little delay in the fulfilment of the motive. The drive is satisfied when the child gets to breast sucking. With it the motive is achieved and the final stage of quiescence is reached to when no drive happens to exist there.

Drive reaching ® Absence of drive object threshold intensity

® Hallucinatory idea of previous gratification

Drive determines the experience; it determines what the organism is to be conscious of; but for the drive to become conscious, memory of the previous gratification serves as a vehicle. In case of previous cognition,

3. Rappaport, D. *The Structure of Psychoanalytic Theory*, 1960.

drive discharge is not as effective as it happens when the object is present, hence cognitions cannot be taken as effective substitutes for the behaviour.

The child is very young but he has learned what it is he wants, and he thinks about it. Still, he is not mature enough to have sensing and thinking as separate functioning—sensing and thinking, generally, go simultaneously; and, his thoughts are hallucinatory, they being not based on the realities of the situation but are related to the object he wants to achieve, and, the object is not present. "Cognition, or conscious experiencing of the drives representation, occurs where the aim of the drive is not achieved".

But as the child matures, he perceives the present situation also besides remembering the past gratifying experience; with the result that gratification occurs in reality, and not in hallucination only.

The third of the primary models, as described by Rappaport is the model of affect:

Drive—Absence of drive object—Affect discharge.

Again, drive is there but no object is there for its gratification, and the result is that the drive discharge does not happen to be so effective as it would have been in case of the presence of the drive object; whatever discharge is there, is only an emergency discharge of the drive cathexis—here again, the gratification is hallucinatory.

So long as Id is the only system present, the process happens to be consisted of three stages—restlessness of the organism, his experiencing the affect, and his experiencing a hallucinatory gratification followed by a state of quiescence when there is no action, no cognition, and no affect.

Ego is the second structure which personality attains in due course of development. Ego is realistic and makes the person appreciate the realities of the situation and makes him behave in the wider interests of his self. "It represents the role of enlightened self-interest in the personality." Though Ego is not unaware of the drive, and of the impulses which the drive may give rise to, yet, its role is to restrain the person from behaving on the spur of an instinctive drive in a reckless manner. It may prepare the person for a detoured or delayed gratification of the drive, if an attempt for an immediate gratification of the same may harm the self-esteem of the person. Ego would not permit such a step of behaviour which the people would not approve of. It is in the interest of the person, living in a society, that it (Ego) controls the drives by way of delaying, inhibiting or restraining them so that their aims may be achieved realistically, and with no harm to the self of the person. The Ego may arrange for the maximum gratification of the drives for which it may have to inhibit drives for a certain period of time; may have to detour the gratification, and reconcile incompatible impulses arising out of instinctual drives.

"Cognition, or conscious experiencing of the drives representation, occurs where the aim of the drive is not achieved".

Ego is realistic and makes the person appreciate the realities of the situation and makes him behave in the wider interests of his self.

The Ego performs the following five functions:

1. It raises the threshold for drive discharge. The drive object may be present even then it controls the subject from behaving impulsively to achieve that object. Though such a control may result in the frustration of the subject, yet it develops tolerance in the subject for such a frustration, and it prepares the subject for better adaptation; of course, in extreme cases, such a control may make one neurotic.
2. It controls the access of ideas to consciousness. For a behaviour, the access of an impulse to consciousness is essential, but the same is prevented by the Ego, and thus it distorts consciousness. The various defense mechanisms that we have described earlier in this chapter, are the part of the Ego.
3. The Ego directs the behaviour towards the acceptable goals. Acceptability can be judged only through a cognitive function. The Ego selects an effective means to the goal. If necessary, the Ego may make the individual take detours; and balance "one value against another". Thus, the Ego may make an individual plan an action well in advance before he actually indulges into it.
4. Logical thinking is the fourth function of the Ego. The individual thinks in a logical sequence because of the Ego. He thinks according to some set of rules in contrast to what he does at the structural level of Id—there, the sequence of thoughts going "from one drive representative to another regardless of logical rules or realistic factors".
5. The Ego directs the individual what goal to select. The Ego makes use of the affect as a signal to be guided in the selection of a goal which should be such that it may relieve of a feeling of frustration—may it be despondency, anger or some other unpleasant feeling, as well as it should be important, too. Again, the functioning is at the secondary process level, and affect accompanies the drive frustration as a signal to help the person select the right goal.

Ego performs five functions:
1. It raises the threshold for drive discharge.
2. It controls the access of ideas to consciousness.
3. The Ego directs the behaviour towards the acceptable goals.
4. Logical thinking is the fourth function of the Ego.
5. The Ego directs the individual what goal to select.

The Ego-cathexes are basically derived from the instinctual drives, but here the effect that accompanies the frustration of instinctual drives is controlled, indicating thereby that the situation demands some sort of adaptive behaviour. To the Id, Freud attributes "dynamically unconscious content, primary process functioning, the pleasure principle and drive cathexes. In contrast, the Ego is partly conscious and partly not so. It operates following the secondary process. Nevertheless, no distinguishing line can be drawn between the Id and the Ego. There is a continuum from one structure to the other; the higher level controlling the lower one, and evolving out of the lower.

Superego marks the difference in the aims that comes about when an individual has further developed to the third structured system of the personality. To describe the development of personality theoretically, Freud has used these three terms—Id, Ego and Superego. He has distinguished the first two on the basis of means adopted. When an individual is very young, it happens to be very impulsive and labile, and cannot tolerate any delay in the gratification of a drive; Freud calls his first structural system of the personality by the name Id. And, to the second structural system as Ego, when one grows more realistic, and, would work for the maximal drive satisfaction. Sometimes, Ego may inhibit the expression of an instinctual drive when such an expression is considered not to be helpful in the attainment of maximal drive satisfaction. But in case of both the structural systems, that is, Id and Ego, there is no difference in aims. These are the means adopted that distinguish one from the other. In case of Superego, the aims are also different from the ones that activate the young child who is still at the structural level of Id.

The Ego-cathexes are basically derived from the instinctual drives, but here the effect that accompanies the frustration of instinctual drives is controlled, indicating thereby that the situation demands some sort of adaptive behaviour.

To describe the development of personality theoretically, Freud has used these three terms—Id, Ego and Superego. He has distinguished the first two on the basis of means adopted.

Superego is the guide that enables a mature individual not to adopt such an aim which is irreconcilable with the social order. An individual at the structural level of Id or Ego, is not mature enough to allow only such a drive discharge which may serve for the satisfaction of the person without disrupting the social order. It is possible to do so when the structural system of Superego has developed. The social system can remain constant over the generations only when social rules become incorporated into the individual personality; for it, conflict between the egocentric satisfaction of the individual and the maintenance of social order, must be resolved. The Superego is the result of the resolution of this conflict as well as it is system of the personality which enables an individual to resolve such a conflict.

Superego is the guide that enables a mature individual not to adopt such an aim which is irreconcilable with the social order.

There is a dynamic relationship among these three systems of personality—Id, Ego and Superego. For all these systems, Id is the basic source of motivation. It represents the forces which lead to direct, immediate expression of the instinctual drives. The Superego represents the cultural restrictions on the expression of instinctual drives. The E go seeks maximal satisfaction within the restrictions imposed by superego and the realities of the world. Superego begins to be acquired even during the period of childhood. As for example, the child would try to acquire the parental interpretation of sexual prohibitions. Later on, as an individual grows in age, his capacity to feel the restricting nature of the societal rules, increases; and the realities of the world also exert a restricting impact—all this represents the development of the system of Superego in the personality of the individual.

In some cases, the restrictions and fears that stem from the Superego, may be unrealistic and rigid. In such cases, the Ego plays the arbitrary role by way of bringing some compromise between the Superego and the Id. Now, reconciliation has to be found between the impulsive nature of the Id, seeking direct expression of the instinctual drives, and, the restrictive nature of the Superego demanding strict observance of the societal rules.

The psychoanalysts have described the mechanisms of Ego—Id relations in greater details than they have done in case of ego-superego

REVIEW QUESTIONS

***Q.*1.** In what particular way is the Psychoanalysis Theory of Child Development is different from other theories of child development?

***Q.*2.** What are the basic concepts of Freud's Psychoanalysis Theory of Child Development?

***Q.*3.** What is meant by "Defense Mechanism" when Freud uses the term? How does a defense mechanism indicate the concerned person's development from a lower to a higher personality structure?

***Q.*4.** In what sense has Freud used the term "cathexis?" How is it related to our overt and covert behaviour?

***Q.*5.** Fill in the Blanks:

(*i*) ..... is the special name that Freud gave to the sexual excitation.

(*ii*) The personality of a man is judged not on the basis what one's instinctual urge is but, on the basis of what ....., and ..... are adopted to satisfy the same.

(*iii*) The force which carries an idea, representing a drive, to consciousness, has been termed as ..... by Freud.

(*iv*) E ..... is caused because of some feeling, perception or thought or action; ..... discharges energy.

(*v*) The nature of cathexis changes as the child's personality structure develops from ..... to ....., and from ..... to .....

(*vi*) Repression is the result of C ..... the C .....

(*vii*) Freud has used the term ..... to describe the fact that we can voluntarily concentrate on any object, or, can think of an idea before it comes to consciousness of its own.

***Q.*6.** On the left is given a situation in each case, you are to write on the right which defense mechanism one would use or is being used in such a situation.

Situation	*Defense Mechanism*
◆ When strange idea relating to sex tries to intrude into my	

consciousness, I would resort to counter-cathexis leaving little energy for the drive cathexis to be acted out.

- Your Superego would not permit you to snuggle someone other than your own wife, but you may cuddle a cute baby with parental affection.
- A timid student had an idea of hatred flashed against his teacher, but the very moment that the idea is flashed out of his mind, he bowed down to his teacher, apparently to show great respect to him.
- A weak old man declares—"I am not tired at all." But the very next moment he sats down thumping.
- A selfish man is cornered or isolated, but would complain against others calling this world as 'self-centred.'
- The servant of that spinster tolerated coolly the harsh treatment of his mistress. (And his hatred against her, was only exposed when the police could prove him to be the murderer of that lady).

ANSWERS TO OBJECTIVE TYPE QUESTIONS

***Q*.5**. (*i*) Libido, (*ii*) external aims objectives, (*iii*) cathexis, (*iv*) emotion, emotion (*v*) Id, Ego, Ego, Superego, (*vi*) controlling, cathected idea, (*vii*) Hypercathexis

***Q*.6.** Displacement; Displacement; Reaction Formation; Denial; Projection; Isolation

CHAPTER 19

THEORIES OF CHILD DEVELOPMENT—PIAGET'S COGNITIVE THEORY

Chapter Outline

- The Schema
- Adaptation: Assimilation and Accommodation
- Period I–Infancy: Birth to Two Years
- Period II–Preoperational: Two to Seven Years
- Perceptual Activity
- Perceptual Constancy
- Conceptual Invariance
- Mental Images
- Symbolic Verbal Schemas
- Classification
- Egocentrism v/s Decentring
- Intuitive Solution of Problems
- The Periods, 3rd and 4th, of Concrete and Formal Operations
- Operational Thinking
- Consistent Thinking
- The Groups and the Groupings
- Conservation of Quantity
- The Period of Formal Operation
- Understanding Logical Relations among Classes
- Combinatorial Thinking
- Achieving Some Additional Constructs
- Review Questions

Piaget traces the development of the child since its birth. He observes day-to-day changes that come about in the behaviour of the child. His theory of child development is the result of his long and minute observations of the child's behaviour that goes on changing from the day the child is born till such time when he attains adulthood or reaches to the maximum possible point of development—though, to some extent, the process of development ever remains dynamic. Thus, the approach of Piaget was empirical; his findings are, mainly, based on case studies or cross-sectional studies. He observed closely how a neonate starts, apparently, with reflex reactions, and, in due course of time attains the stage of Formal Operations by the time he is 11+.

Piaget's theory of child development is the result of his long and minute observations of the child's behaviour that goes on changing from the day the child is born till such time when he attains adulthood or reaches to the maximum possible point of development—though, to some extent, the process of development ever remains dynamic.

Jean Piaget was basically related to Biology. He received his doctoral degree in biological science in 1918 at the age of twenty-two. He was professor in the university of Geneva. But his first research was related to the development of reasoning in children, and it was published in 1921. He was then offered the post of Director at the JJ Research Institute at Geneva. Ever since he held that post along with the post of Principal at the Center of Genetic Epistemology, Geneva; and came out with so much work on child development that he impressed as the most prolific writer and the theorist on the development of the child.

Three factors influenced the research and the theorising work of Piaget—(*i*) biological studies related to the adaptations of fauna and flora to their natural environment; (*ii*) philosophical study of the genesis of knowledge, that is, Epistemology; and (*iii*) studies on developmental psychology. Though the entire work of Piaget falls into the category of developmental psychology, his approach throughout bears evidence to the impact of biological background that he had. Adaptiveness and the development of the biological structures, have been made the basis of his showing the genesis of epistemology or the development of knowledge.

Three factors influenced the research and the theorising work of Piaget—(*i*) biological studies related to the adaptations of fauna and flora to their natural environment; (*ii*) philosophical study of the genesis of knowledge, that is, Epistemology; and (*iii*) studies on developmental psychology.

As mentioned at the outset, Piaget's conclusions are the results of empirical researches conducted through the clinical device of observations and questionings. Besides those of the children of his own family, his were the cross-sectional studies widely conducted—had he conducted more longitudinal studies, the findings, related to cognitive development, would have been more coherent.

There are some terms which are very important for understanding the theory of Piaget, such as SCHEMA. It is not possible to follow the elaborated explanation of his theory without being clear what he means by the term 'schema'.

THE SCHEMA

The schema is "behavioural parallel of structure in biology." A biological structure may be unitary and as simple as a finger, but it may also be a wide system of different structures, as complicated as the digestive system. A finger reacts in response to a stimulus, overt or covert, and so does the

The schema is "behavioural parallel of structure in biology."

digestive system, but the action of a unitary structure illustrates a single reaction to a single stimulus; that of the digestive system, illustrates how different structures work in correlation to one another in an integrated way.

Piaget starts with the 'sucking reflex' as one of the earliest schemas. Apparently, it appears to be a one-to-one response, that is, a single response to a single stimulus. But actually it is not so, many acts are involved in the process. The mother touches the cheek, the infant turns its face towards the mother, the touch on the lips, makes the baby open its mouth; sucking when the inside of the mouth is stimulated; and swallowing when the liquid reaches the throat. The sucking structure is developed as a result of the child's sucking behaviour. This behavioural structure is a 'schema' as Piaget calls it. Thus, each schema is a result of a unitary behaviour or a set of behaviours, that is, consisted of a series of actions enabling the organism to achieve some specific end.

Another simple schema is that of looking at an object. Even a neonate can see an object when its eyes are pointed to it, but it is not looking at an object. Looking involves the actions of moving the eyeballs, adaptive movements of the lens of the eyes, and paying attention to the object—it is not merely fixating the eyes upon the object. Thus, looking at an object needs the development of a schema, the role of which is very important in the overall development of the child.

For picking up a big doll, and for picking up a small thread, different sorts of muscular movements are required; the child's skill of lifting both of them, indicates his adaptability to the situation, and the equilibrium that comes about in his behaviour because of the development of the different variants of the schema of grasping. And, the development of the different variants of a schema, illustrates his mobility. Until the time these different variants of the schema have developed, there would be a state of unequilibrium, and efforts would continue till equilibrium is attained.

To be able to grasp an object, indicates that the schema to do the same has developed. But a child's being able to grasp objects both big and small, or thick or thin, illustrates how the schema of grasping has adapted itself to the demands of the situation. For picking up a big doll, and for picking up a small thread, different sorts of muscular movements are required; the child's skill of lifting both of them, indicates his adaptability to the situation, and the equilibrium that comes about in his behaviour because of the development of the different variants of the schema of grasping. And, the development of the different variants of a schema, illustrates his mobility. Until the time these different variants of the schema have developed, there would be a state of unequilibrium, and efforts would continue till equilibrium is attained. But equilibrium is not finally attained with the development of a schema, a change in situation demands a new schema for the organism to perform the now needful function. Again, there would develop a state of unequilibrium; the present state of equilibrium is disturbed to be restored again only when a new schema or a new variant of a schema, which enables the organism to perform the new function, is fully developed. An adaptation does not take place in isolation. There is interrelatedness in the process, and a complex, coherent pattern is formed when changes take place for adaptation to the environment. The new adaptations are rooted in the old ones to suit the new demands of the environment; and thus, there is continuity in the process-"the development of new structures to fill old functions under changed circumstances" (AL Baldwin). The biological principle of teleological adaptation is based upon the mechanism governed by causal laws. Each adaptation is to serve some specific purpose, and each is related to other adaptations, and to the demands of the environment. Thus, there is interrelatedness, continuity and complexity in the process leading to the development of new structures, new schemas or schemata. A child learns to walk—the development of a new sensorimotor schema enables the child to perform the function of walking, which in turn enables the child to perform still other such functions which cannot be possible unless the child can walk. This is an example of teleological adaptation. The development of the structure or schema of walking is quite essential to enable the child to explore its widening environment; which again, is so essential for enabling the child to perform so many other functions which the continuously changing circumstances, as the child develops, will be demanding from it. Walking and holding some object in the hand simultaneously, requires still a new variant of the schema of walking; a change in the nature of the function of walking also depends upon the shape, weight and so on, of the object being held while walking. And, the development of so many variants of a schema, indicates its mobility.

The new adaptations are rooted in the old ones to suit the new demands of the environment; and thus, there is continuity in the process-"the development of new structures to fill old functions under changed circumstances" (AL Baldwin).

So far, we have been referring to the development of sensorimotor schemas only. By the time the child moves from the stage of infancy to the peroperational stage, generally beginning by the end of second year, the development of the cognitive schemas becomes apparent though this development is rooted in the sensorimotor schemas themselves. The development of cognitive schemas, marks the beginning of the internalisation of the sensorimotor functions. For example, looking is a sensorimotor function, and the visual image that is created in the mind of the child, is the internalisation of the same function, and, is a result of the development of a cognitive schema. Interpreting Piaget's theory, AL Baldwin[1] writes: "cognitive processes are best conceptualised as actions."

For example, looking is a sensorimotor function, and the visual image that is created in the mind of the child, is the internalisation of the same function, and, is a result of the development of a cognitive schema.

Sensorimotor schemas involve overt actions as cognitive schemas involve the internal function of the mind. The child's knowing of the number system, and his concept of space, and the laws of logic, all mark that, there must have developed the cognitive schemas for the same. The development of cognitive schemas enables the child to think in abstract. Thinking is the internalised use of language. Different cognitive schemas rapidly develop, enabling the growing child to perform mental functions beginning from very simple, such as, integrating two different pieces of experience to

Sensorimotor schemas involve overt actions as cognitive schemas involve the internal function of the mind.

1. Baldwin, AL. *Theories of Child Development*.

perform a sensorimotor function, to integrating a whole series of logical thinking to make conceptual conclusions. During the stage of formal operations, the adolescent child can perform very complex mental functions after going through a long exercise based on the logico-mathematical principles of groups and groupings, and cause and effect relationship.

ADAPTATION: ASSIMILATION AND ACCOMMODATION

'Assimilation' is 'taking in' something from the situation. But an organism would not 'take in' or 'assimilate' anything unless the situation can activate the schema to do the same; the situation must be motivational for the organism, for the initiation of assimilation. And, the situation becomes motivational only when there is some challenge in it.

Adaptation is an important term which Piaget has borrowed from Biology. Adaptation is a process consisted of assimilation and accommodation of something into the structure; a schema is an element of a structure as Piaget explains it. 'Assimilation' is 'taking in' something from the situation. But an organism would not 'take in' or 'assimilate' anything unless the situation can activate the schema to do the same; the situation must be motivational for the organism for the initiation of assimilation. And, the situation becomes motivational only when there is some challenge in it. When challenge ceases to be there in the situation because of the fact that the organism has adapted to that particular aspect of the situation, it would now endeavour to adapt to some other aspect of the situation which demands for the same; it is such a demand of the situation which activates a schema for assimilation.

The next development, after assimilation, in the process, is 'accommodation'. Accommodation implies changes that take place in the structure, or in the schema so that the organism may adapt to the demands of the situation or to the new situation.

The next development, after assimilation, in the process, is 'accommodation'. Accommodation implies changes that take place in the structure, or in the schema so that the organism may adapt to the demands of the situation or to the new situation. It was the biological background of Piaget which led him to describe the development of the child in terms of **Adaptation**, **Assimilation** and **Accommodation**. According to Piaget, it is the schema which assimilates, provided, the situation can activate it for the same; that is, the situation must be motivational for the process to start. A change in the covert or overt behaviour is the result of accommodation and it testifies that the process of adaptation has been completed. Now, we shall take one or two examples by way of illustrations.

First, we are taking an example of general nature, related to the adaptation of system of schemata. A young one of an animal, and so also that of a human being, changes the items of food as it grows older; for the digestion of those new items of food, the system concerned has to accommodate itself. And, when such an accommodation for the needful changes in the functioning of the system has occurred, the organism may be considered to have covertly adapted to the situation, and a state of equilibrium ensues.

Let us take another example. A child, say of eight months or so, sees a lot of things in the situation. Some are big items, like a table, a pitcher, a stone; and, some are tiny things—a doll, a small piece of paper and a small piece of thread. Now, which of these items attracts the attention of the child for an attempt to pick up, depends on two factors; first, the thing must be graspable to the child; second, it must contain the element of challenge; that is, the child must not be already perfectly equipped with the skill of picking up the same. These two factors are essential for the activation of a schema. And, when a schema or a whole system of schema is activated, the existing schema assimilates the ailment or food, which is the experience that the organism has while being active in reference to the new function that the situation demands to be performed. The performance of that new function entails some changes in the schema or the system of the schemas; the changes thus occurred constitute the Accommodation. And, the result is Adaptation to the new situation. Adaptation alone can lead to a state of equilibrium. The organism continues to be in a state of unequilibration until it has developed the skill to perform the new function as demanded by the situation present before it.

Adaptation alone can lead to a state of equilibrium.

This process of adaptation, which includes both assimilation and accommodation, serves motivational as well as learning purposes. One is motivated to be active when the situation poses some challenge, and it contains the element of feasibility with which one can meet the challenge. And, the skill to perform a new function is developed as a result of the action done. In the Piagetian terms, a schema develops when some action is done through the process of adaptation. Development of each schema is a measure of new learning. Each schema serves as a tool in the process of future development of a new schema.

This process of adaptation, which includes both assimilation and accommodation, serves motivational as well as learning purposes.

In the Piagetian terms, a schema develops when some action is done through the process of adaptation. Development of each schema is a measure of new learning. Each schema serves as a tool in the process of future development of a new schema.

As regards other terms that are important for understanding the Piagetian theory of child development, we shall be explaining the same while describing the main characteristics of the different periods that the child develops through.

Piaget has divided the child's development into four periods: 1. Infancy, 2. Pre-operational, 3. Concrete Operational, and 4. Formal Operational. Piaget measures development cognitively. Each of the four periods of development is characterised by distinct schemas. Development of the different schemas synchronises with biological maturity. Piaget has quantified development on the basis of various schemas that distinguish one period from the other. Though time-scheduled development of each stage has been quantified, nevertheless, it is not the case that there is a water-tight compartment separating one period from the other.

Piaget has divided the child's development into four periods:
1. Infancy,
2. Pre-operational,
3. Concrete Operational, and
4. Formal Operational.

PERIOD I—INFANCY: BIRTH TO TWO YEARS

Infancy is the first period of life beginning since birth and extending up to the end of second year. Piaget calls it **Sensorimotor** period because it is the period when motor schemas develop as a reaction to the different sense experiences. The visual, the auditory, the olfactory, the tactual are the different senses which serve as sources of information; they are the various sensory modalities which the child grows and is able to coordinate. The sensorimotor schemas are the historical roots out of which the cognitive schemas develop.

The sensorimotor schemas gain the following three characteristics as they develop; these characteristics show the trend of development of the sensorimotor schemas:

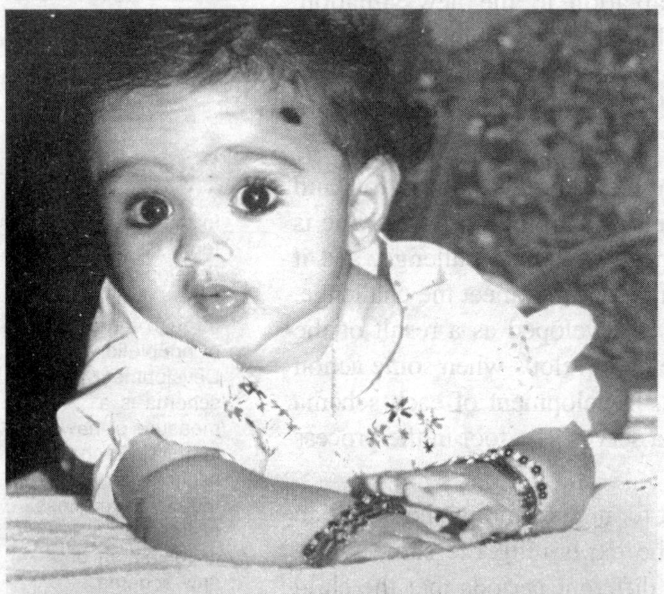

Figure 19.1 The development of the prehension schema is the result of the co-ordinated action involving eyes and hand.

1. SENSES WORKING IN CO-ORDINATION

The eye, the ear, the touch (skin) are the senses which work in co-ordination in reference to a single object. Looking at his hand, held still, is a motor action of the child. Both, the eye and the hand are, involved therein. When the motor schema of holding the hand still, has been developed, the child can now hold an object in his hand. Thus, the development of the schema of prehension is the result of the co-ordinated action involving eyes and hand (Fig. 19.1). The process of the development of the schema of prehension, may involve the function of both the hands working co-operatively. The object happens to be the same which makes the various sense-organs work in an integrated way. Sometimes, the infant looks at an object being diverted to it because of hearing a certain sound being produced by the same object. And, if the child has acquired the schema of walking by that time, it would walk to it also.

2. ACQUISITION OF THE KNOWLEDGE THAT THERE IS PERMANENT SPACE SURROUNDING THE INFANT

Initially, when an object disappears, the child has no idea that the object removed from his sight, still exists. But before this period of sensorimotor ends, the child would have acquired the idea that the object that has been removed from his sight, still exists in the space. The child would search for the same, walking through the space and towards the direction it was carried to. He even can take a different route to reach to that object. The idea of a surrounding space is a very significant acquisition of this period.

Figure 19.2 Three schemas are evident in this figure: Sucking, Looking at something and Prehension.

3. GOAL-ORIENTED BEHAVIOUR

The third significant acquisition of infancy is that the child develops or constructs schemas which are activated, involving more than one actions, all directed towards the same goal. Such an integrated activity of the child is intentionally motivated. The child is motivated to reach to the end point of the sequence. The child, who could so far prehend a doll, can now pick up a ball as well as a thin long cylindrical object also; and even a very thin fibre too—as a result of continuous attempts or trials at objects one after the other using the schemas already acquired, and thereby developing new schemas as per demands of the situations. The child achieves its objectives varying its actions spontaneously and deliberately.

But still, the child lacks conceptual schemas which develop very late. His behaviour is very concrete. Because of this limitation, the child, still, cannot plan his action ahead; that is, he cannot visualise through the sequence of future actions. This, of course, limits the child's capability to adapt.

Piaget has divided the period of infancy into six stages to describe in greater details how the child, through his attempts (initially non-voluntary), adapts to the surrounding situations, thereby continually developing sensorimotor schemas. Three of Piaget's books are related to the developments occurring during these stages. The books are: *The Origin of Intelligence in Children,* **1952**; *The Construction of Reality in the Child,* **1954**; *Play, Dreams and Imitation in Childhood,* **1954**.

The first book describes how the development of intelligence is rooted in the development of the sensorimotor schemas of the childhood, that is, of the first two years of infancy. It is during these twenty-four months that a good many adaptive behaviours develop. The second book analyses a child's assumptions about different objects, space, time and causality. The book gives an idea as to how long the child takes before he is able to perceive the reality of things. The third book also contains examples of his observations to illustrate how the child grows from the stage of purely reflex action to the stage when he can behave in a voluntary manner, in many cases, accidental behaviour leads to the voluntary trials to achieve

Table 19.1 Stages of the Sensorimotor Period

Stage	*Age (months)*	*Characteristics*
Reflex activity	0-1	The child practises reflex activities, for example sucking, looking and so on. Behaviour, mainly assimilative, but not entirely so.
Primary circular reaction	1-4	The behaviour mainly made up of reflexes or motor responses—and so primary. The tendency is to repeat such a behaviour, and so, circular reactions centre on the child's own body; for it, there is no difference between the self and the external world.
Secondary circular reactions	4-10	Now, the infant focuses on objects rather than on its own body. Now, it has started changing its surroundings by way of making movements like hitting a hanging toy, and so on. Now, it can behave intentionally.
Co-ordination of secondary schemas	10-12	The child is now able to combine schemas to achieve its goals. It does so to solve problems in new situations. The hitting schema may be used to remove a barrier in achieving a goal.
Tertiary circular reactions	12-18	His active use of trial and error methods, helps in learning about objects. His growing mobility helps in the widening of environmental explorations. New ways of solving problems are learned.
Internal representation	18-24	Now, the child can have symbolic representation of people and objects of the external world in his mind. This helps in finding insightful solutions to problems. Now, deferred imitation is possible.

some goal. But still, the child is guided by his fancy rather than by logical rules. In the beginning, the child imitates its model only when it is present before it; deferred imitation develops later on.

Piaget has described the period of infancy, dividing it into six stages. The characteristics of each are given here in a tabular form (see Table 19.1).

PERIOD II—PRE-OPERATIONAL: TWO TO SEVEN YEARS

The pre-operational period of cognitive development is characterised by the following features:

1. Perceptual Activity
2. Perceptual Constancy

3. Conceptual Invariance
4. Mental Images
5. Symbolic Verbal Schemas
6. Classification
7. Egocentrism v/s Decentring
8. Intuitive Solution of Problems.

PERCEPTUAL ACTIVITY

Registering in the brain of an object, or of an event through a sense organ, is perception. It is the result of the momentary fixating of a sense organ upon an object. The perception is liable to many distortions because of the momentary fixating and because of the child's failure to integrate different perceptions temporally distributed and spread over space.

This is compensated, to some extent; as the child grows, he is more and more able to move his attention from one aspect of the object to the other. He may do it repeatedly. If the child looks at two different objects spatially separated, he would move his sight from the one to the other. All this is perceptual activity, as it has been called by Piaget. Perceptual activity is a step forward from mere perception, and towards conceptual thoughts—which develop during a later period. Perceptual activity enables the subject to have a view of the object from different angles with wider perspectives; and all this leaves less chances for the perception being distorted. But still, the subject cannot develop logical conceptions, as still, he cannot integrate his past experiences with those of the current times to come to conceptions which are almost free from distortions; this can be properly done during the last period which Piaget calls the period of Formal Operations, and is the period of 11+.

> If the child looks at two different objects spatially separated, he would move his sight from the one to the other. All this is perceptual activity.

PERCEPTUAL CONSTANCY

It is during this period that the child assumes that the size and shape of an object remains constant; change of place of the object makes no difference. But before this perceptual constancy develops, one passes through a stage when the perception is distorted because of change of place. A circle surrounded by smaller circles, appears bigger than when the same circle is surrounded by the bigger ones. Likewise, a gray square in the middle of a white background appears darker than when it is in the middle of a black background. The proximity of other objects thus distorts the perception regarding a particular object. But with age, it decreases; and

> The child assumes that the size and shape of an object remains constant; change of place of the object makes no difference. But before this perceptual constancy develops, one passes through a stage when the perception is distorted because of change of place.

the child can perceive the constancy of objects—change of place or time makes no difference in size, shape or colour, though the retinal image of an object may be reduced to half of its present size with the removing away of the object to the double of its present distance.

CONCEPTUAL INVARIANCE

A child of pre-school age would declare the amount of liquids to be equal when they are there in containers of the same shape and size, and the height of the liquid in each case is equal. But if the liquid from one of them is poured out into a third container which is narrower but taller in shape, the child would declare, now the liquid is more in quantity than as it is in the other container because now the level of the liquid is higher.

It is because of the pre-school child's failure to integrate data of the past experience with that of the present, although the liquid was poured in the very presence of the child itself.

A simpler example of two sticks—when the two sticks were lying just parallel to each other; the one just above the other, the child told the two to be equal in size. But when the above one was moved a little to the left or right, the child told that they were not equal in length. This is the famous Piaget–Taponier experiment (1955–56) which illustrates Muller Lyer illusion.

It is during this period that, to a great extent, the child becomes free from this illusion, as his ability to integrate the past experiences with the present ones develops. This is conceptual invariance that the child achieves before he can develop himself for other cognitive functions of the period of formal operations.

MENTAL IMAGES

> The mental images are the models of the external actions or events; they represent some specific actions or events, and are the results of the internalisation of the external activities or events.

Mental images are mental schemas, they are constructed in the mind as the sensorimotor schemas are constructed. But the latter are the result of some external overt behaviour as the former are not. The mental images are the models of the external actions or events; they represent some specific actions or events, and are the results of the internalisation of the external activities or events.

The mental images are different from conceptual constructs also. Though a conceptual construct may contain some imagery associated to it, but such an imagery is different from a mental image. It is the mental image which enables the child to imitate an activity or an event that is no more present;

such an imitation is called deferred imitation. A child can have no deferred imitation till the end of the final, that is, the sixth stage of the period of infancy or the period of sensorimotor.

A mental image is not an after-effect of perception, nor it is "an attenuated perception of some kind", it is an independent schema, an internal act of the mind. A mental image differs from the external activity or event, also in the sense that it may not have all the details of the external activity or event.

It is only during the pre-operational period, extending up to the age of seven, that such mental images develop which serve as models to guide a subject through the conduct of a behaviour when no other model in the external environment is present. But such a mental model is always the result of the internalised imitation of an external action or event whereas a conceptual construct is the result of conceptual thoughts. Such a mental model is a very significant mental schema that cannot develop before the pre-operational period.

SYMBOLIC VERBAL SCHEMAS

During infancy, the subject perceives things as a result of sensorimotor activity. His perception is a mental activity but still the thing and his perception are not distinguished as separate. It is during the Pre-operational period that the child realises the existence of an object as separate from his perception as mental representation of the same. It is during this period that a word is taken to be a symbol for what it signifies; the word is distinguished from its significate. The word is a verbal symbol for an object that it signifies. In the play of a Pre-operational child, both mental images and verbal symbols are very important; they are profusely involved in his plays.

The word is a verbal symbol for an object that it signifies.

For the development of conceptual schemas, verbal symbolic schemas are must. The verbal symbolic schemas prepare the child for the final stage of cognitive development, that is, the Formal Operational Period which is mainly characterised by conceptual schemas of various sorts.

During the period of late Infancy, and early stage of the Pre-operational Period, we can see how in the play of a child, a pretense is confused with a reality. A child, while pretending to hit something or someone, genuinely performs the action of hitting the same. Thus, the child confuses the mental representation for the reality that he pretends. When a child can genuinely pretend, it is an evidence that the child has developed some sort of symbolic thought. On such an occasion, he has some sort of mental representation of the action he is pretending to perform, and it is distinguished from the action he is really performing.

Verbal schemas are developed because of the child's living in a social environment.

Verbal schemas are developed because of the child's living in a social environment; a child bereft of social environment can develop no verbal symbols or verbal schemas—for such a child, the word "dog" would signify nothing. It stands for a quadruped mammal with certain characteristics only because the child has heard the word used for that animal for so many times in his social environment. In most of the cases, there can be no answer to the question why only a certain word is used for some particular object, and why not any other sound can be used to signify the same object—it is something arbitrary. Of course, some words are onomatopoeic; as for example, 'cuckoo' is the name of a bird which makes such a sound.

The development of verbal schemas during Pre-operational Period, is a very significant cognitive development of a child. During infancy, that is, the period extended up to the end of second year, an external object remains involved into the sensorimotor schemas related to it. The object cannot be distinguished from the actions performed in connection with it; the actions, the result of which are the sensorimotor schemas which represent or describe the object. For an infant, at the first stage of cognitive development, the very word 'ball' involves the sensorimotor schemas of grasping, throwing, bouncing, rolling, and so on. But it is only during the Pre-operational Period that the word 'ball' stands in the mind of the child as distinguished from the object that it signifies. The word becomes a verbal symbol, a verbal schema for the object, such a development goes a long way towards the development of conceptual schemas.

The verbal schemas only can enable one to define an object. When one defines an object, one distinguishes it as belonging to a class of objects having certain distinguishing characteristics assimilated in the experiences of the subject. When a pre-operational child uses the word "ball", he includes in it all kinds of balls, making together a class of their own having certain characteristics.

In the beginning, a word uttered by an infant, happens to be a part of its sensorimotor activity. When it utters the word "mama" in the appearance of its mother, psychologically it is not much different from hugging its mother. Likewise, on the appearance of something strange, big or otherwise fear-arousing, a child may produce the sound "ahh", and it would cling simultaneously to its mother or other protector. On the appearance of a like object on any other occasion too, the child would repeat a similar behaviour uttering the word "ahh". Here, the word "ahh" does not stand for any particular object, but a symbolic schema, of course, it is. It represents rather a situation.

Both Freud and Piaget consider that symbolic thinking is possible even without its being verbal or logical. Like the former, the latter also takes the symbolic thinking to be a primary process which develops with age, as the child gets more and more verbal stimulation to react verbally in his continuously widening social environment. Notwithstanding, the major difference between the two is that Freud considers symbolic thinking to be primitive while Piaget takes it to be a psychological phenomenon having its origin during the post-infancy period. Even then, they have many points of similarities in their conceptualisations.

Especially during the beginning years of pre-operational period, there seems to be a spurt in the growth of language which we would like to call the development of verbal schemas. But we need to appreciate the difference that is there in the use of verbal schemas or language of an adult and that of a child at the threshold of Pre-operational Period. I do remember my little granddaughter, Manvi, calling an elderly man, almost daily passing by our house, as 'Nana', the Hindi word for maternal grandfather. When she uttered this word, she did not mean what an adult means by that word, though the word as all other words are, a symbolic representative of some living human object. When an adult uses this word, he means "father of the mother" but for Manvi it stood for all the male people with grey hair and having a little resemblance to her relative who had been introduced to her as "Nana", especially by her dear mother.

Especially during the beginning years of pre-operational period, there seems to be a spurt in the growth of language which we would like to call the development of verbal schemas.

Piaget's Jacqueline, at the age of 2½, used the term "slug" for the creature seen almost daily while walking along a road. On going a little further, another slug was seen, and she told, "Here it is again". She was asked if it was not some other slug. She went back to see the first one. "Is it the same one"? She was asked, "Yes", was her reply. "Another slug?" Again, she replied "Yes". Her answer illustrates that the word "slug" did not represent for her a class consisted of many creatures belonging to it, but only to one particular creature assimilated in her experience.

Another very interesting example I would like to give here. It is again related to my granddaughter, Manvi. Now she is about 2½, whenever she is angry with anyone, on any account, she would always react with the words—"Gande chore", meaning thereby "bad boy". She has been reacting thus since the time she had hardly attained the age of two. She remarks thus in regard to anyone, without distinction, the object may even be her old grandmother. It shows, her remark is neither concerned with sex nor with age, it represents only a situation of displeasure that she happens to be passing through. Symbolic schema, of course, it is, but not a verbal schema in the same sense as it is for an adult.

As Manvi would grow older, this phrase would lose its present connotation for her as then, she would be knowing the correct meanings of the words "Gande" (bad) and "chore" (boy); the use of the phrase would be discontinued in its present sense.

Should we use the terms of Piaget, we should call these terms used by Manvi as "preconcepts". When a child really understands what a noun signifies, he should be considered to have genuinely achieved conceptual thinking. Since at that stage, he would be realising the fact that a class cannot be pointed to, it is only an individual member of a class that can be thus demonstrated. A child of two, failing to understand what classes or classification is, may form aggregates of two objects belonging to different classes, only because of similarity of the two in some single respect or so. For example, a child of about two, may call a herd of cows and buffaloes combined by a single noun "cows". AL Baldwin writes—"The formation of such aggregates takes place by a different psychological process than conceptual thinking". The former is the result of "merely a momentary" clustering while the latter, that is, conceptual thinking, would be based on some "defining criterion".

CLASSIFICATION

A class "is a set of objects or events that have certain characteristics in common". AL Baldwin.

What is the nature of classification, and, what are the relationships that may exist among individual members of a class? AL Baldwin writes about a class that "it is a set of objects or events that have certain characteristics in common". A class is often designated by a certain label. The members of a class may not always be physically forming a cluster; spatially they may be dispersed apart. When we say 'squares', we are referring to a certain class of geometrical figures having certain defining characteristics though we may get to see them at different places and different times.

This environment of ours is made up of so many objects of different kinds, both living and non-living, and having a variety of defining characteristics that it is quite baffling to think of them unless a proper classification is made of them on the basis of certain characteristics which distinguish one class from the other. Again, a class may further be divided into sub-classes. When we say "canidae", we are referring to dogs as well as to wolves, jackals, the dogs and others, all being the members of the same class, that is, "canidae". But the class "canis" does not include the wolves, the jackals, it is a sub-class of "canidae".

For mastering the logic of classification, the child must understand three things:

1. What a class is?
2. What are the elementary relationships among classes?
3. What complex relationships are there among classes?

These relationships are described in formal logic, to which Piaget calls Formal Operations. For a child, before the Pre-operational Period, it is not possible to understand even the elementary relationships; and it is during the period of 11+ that a child develops formal operations; that is, can develop conceptual schemas through thinking logically in the abstract regarding more complex relationships among different classes.

It is during the period of 11+ that a child develops formal operations; that is, can develop conceptual schemas through thinking logically in the abstract regarding more complex relationships among different classes.

But in this section of the chapter we are dealing with the Pre-operational Period when only the cognitive schemas develop which enable the child to understand what a class is, and, what elementary relationships are there among different classes. Piaget and Inhelder made serious investigations (1974) as to when at the earliest the child can understand the relation between two classes. Very significant experiments were conducted. A number of counters were spread before some children. Some were circular in shape, and the others were square. And the set of counters was only in two colours, red and blue. In answer to the question whether all the blue ones were circular, the youngest among the children, not older than three, answered in negative, "No, it is not true that all the blue ones are round because here is a round one that is red."

In another experiment (1952), Piaget showed a box of wooden beads to a child; some beads were white and some, brown. The question that was put to him, was whether there were more wooden beads or brown beads. The young child usually answered that there were more brown beads than wooden beads. When further asked "why", the answer was, "Because there are so few white ones". Piaget concluded that a child cannot solve this problem before the age of seven. The answer of the child was based on the comparison of brown beads with the white beads; in his cognitive system, he could not include a separate property of the beads at the same time; he failed to recognise the fact that both the brown and the white beads were included in the class—of "wooden beads". The problem is because still the child has not developed conceptual schemas which require some sort of a representation of a class of objects, events, or instances. "A child during the period of pre-operations, has no cognition that each member of a class is an individual in its own right besides being a member of the class".

Baldwin, by way of an example, writes that a poodle is a dog. It has all the properties of a dog; it means it is a member of the class of animals designated as "dogs". But at the same time, it has some such additional characteristics which dogs other than poodles, do not have. It qualifies poodles to be considered as a sub-class of the class of animals called "dogs". Thus, a class has the characteristic of inclusiveness, as it includes the specific characteristic of a sub-class which distinguishes it in its own class.

The classification also implies something. When we say—"this object is metallic", it implies that "this object is a conductor to electricity." In this way, statements about different objects, have many other things implied therein which happen to be related to their characteristics.

Classification helps in making conclusions. The individual goes on gathering information. He designs ways for the formulation of the same into relevant groups. Conclusions are the end points of the process.

Classification helps in making conclusions. The individual goes on gathering information. He designs ways for the formulation of the same into relevant groups. Conclusions are the end points of the process. One can reach to these points only when one can understand what a class is, what elementary relationships are there among classes, and what are the complex relationships among them.

EGOCENTRISM V/S DECENTRING

For a pre-school child, it is difficult to grasp—1. The separation of appearance from reality, 2. Perceptual constancy, 3. The size constancy, and 4. The diversity of views.

To a pre-school child, the moon appears to be following him as he himself moves on. It is only later on that he understands that the following of the moon to him, is only an appearance, and not a reality, as another child moving opposite to him also makes the same claim. He muses, the same object cannot be moving simultaneously in two different directions. As the child grows in age during the Pre-operational Period, he becomes able to integrate experiences temporarily scattered, and the same further enables him to distinguish an appearance from a reality.

He cannot grasp the perceptual constancy until he becomes able to view the same object decentralising his perspective, and this he can do first during the pre-operational period only when his cognitive schemas develop as a result of viewing the same object from different perspectives. Only then he can realise that each object has its shape constant.

Now, the child's difficulty in grasping perceptual constancy during the beginning stage of the Pre-operational Period may be illustrated experimentally. A child of three or four cannot understand what is the actual shape of a landscape; a view that he grasps, is egocentric, it is from his own perspective. He cannot grasp the perceptual constancy until he becomes able to view the same object decentralising his perspective, and this he can do first during the Pre-operational Period only when his cognitive schemas develop as a result of viewing the same object from different perspectives. Only then he can realise that each object has its shape constant, and what appears to be different from different angles, is only an appearance and not a reality, constancy of objects is a reality.

When a young child of Pre-operational Period, views a ball lying just near him, it appears bigger than what it appears when it is removed to a distant place. Double the distance; an object would, roughly, appear half in size in comparison to what it appeared previously. Still, the child cannot grasp the size constancy. He can do this only when he is able to integrate his previous experience of the object to that of his present experience of the same. The integration of the present experiences with that of the past, is a result of the development of the very important cognitive schema which is also essential for concepual schemas.

The main limitation of a child during the major part of the pre-operational period is his egocentric thinking which renders him unable to know what others may be thinking about an object or event from their own individual perspectives. So long as the child can see and take things from his own perspective alone, he would remain insensitive to the feelings and thoughts of others. For the socialisation of an individual, for the intuitive solution of problems, decentring is must. This decentring, of course, develops before the period of Pre-operation ends. Using the Freudian terminology, we should say that decentring indicates an onward journey in the development of personality from Id to Superego through Ego.

INTUITIVE SOLUTION OF PROBLEMS

Experimentally, Piaget demonstrated the role of intuition in resolving a problem. Three beads were strung on a wire like a miniature clothesline. In the middle of the wire there was a tube which could hide the beads when they were moved through it. First, the beads were moved from the left to the right through the tube. The order of the beads was fixed as first red, then yellow, and the third one was blue. The experimenter repeatedly moved the beads through the tube, and would be asking the child "Now, which one will come out first?" Making mental picture of the event, the child, but only such a one who was not younger than four, could make a number of correct responses. Piaget has divided the Pre-operational Period into two parts—the first from 2 to 4 years, and, the second from 4 to 7 years, Piaget has named the latter as intuitive stage. The child before attaining this stage, cannot have the feel of the solution of a problem—such a feel marks the attainment of the intuitive stage.

Coming back to the Piagetion experiment, referred to in the above paragraph, it was found that when the experimenter, holding in the middle of the tube, reversed the process, the child failed to answer in a correct way which bead would come out first, and bead of what colour would be the last one.

Reversing the process would reverse the order of beads, and, a second reversal of the process would restore the original order, and, the child may fail to make a correct response to the question regarding the order of beads until the time the child has developed the conceptual schema.

A child of five can mentally manipulate the development of an event, but his limitation is that he cannot formulate laws conceptually and see the problem through; for the formulation of conceptual laws, proceeding logically in his mind, he is still too young to do. A child at the intuitive stage, sometimes has a feel of the solution of a problem but is likely to

A child at the intuitive stage, sometimes has a feel of the solution of a problem but is likely to blunder at the other time.

blunder at the other time. AL Baldwin writes of such children, "They just cannot revolve a mental image seven times and keep track of all of its parts".

The child can grasp the principle that one turn reverses the order, the second one restores it, and the middle one always stays in the middle. It is only by the age of seven, that the child starts concrete operations. A child during the period of Formal Operations, would behave in a different fashion, nevertheless, intuitive approach continues to be a part of his repertoire, and proves of great help in the solution of simple problems involving interpersonal relations. We must frequently imagine ourselves in the position of others so that we may formulate our behaviour in the light of the likely reactions of the others.

THE PERIODS, 3RD AND 4TH, OF CONCRETE AND FORMAL OPERATIONS

The third and the fourth cognitive development periods have been designated by Piaget as the **Concrete Operations Period and the Formal Operations Period,** respectively. The third ranging from seven to eleven years, and the fourth, from eleven onward.

The third has been called the Concrete Operational because during this period the mental and the sensorimotor operations of the child are in relation to objects or events that are concretely there in the environment. He can hardly integrate past experience to the present one for a consistent chain of thinking in the abstract—this he can do only during the fourth period of cognitive development, that is, during the period of Formal Operations. Though during the period of Concrete Operations, sometimes, solutions are made, almost intuitively, where pure mental operations have an important role to play, however, before the age of seven, such mental operations do not have equilibrated and stabilised forms in the abstract to fall back upon for a logical conclusion of something. Piaget has shown empirically the cognitive limitations of a child during the third stage, and the achievement of conceptual schemas during the fourth period marking distinct cognitive development achieved through the third period and during the fourth period.

THE PERIOD OF CONCRETE OPERATIONS (AGE SEVEN TO ELEVEN)

It is during this period that the child's thought processes become much more stable. The child gives indications of having started thinking reasonably. His placing things in order of size, is an indication of the kind. He can compare two sets of objects, thinking similarities between each object of the one to the corresponding object of the other. Now, he has developed the perceptual constancy, thereby is able to grasp that spatial rearrangement of objects, does not change the number of objects in the set. He can follow simpler relationships between different classes. His cognitive schema tells him that the number of members in a class is equal to the total number of members in its sub-classes; or, at least, the number of members in the class cannot be fewer than what it is in its sub-classes altogether. He also knows the results of reversal of the order of objects, and can tell in advance about the result of the second reversal. He has achieved the schema which can guide him regarding distance between two objects; he can also realise that the length of the path between two objects may be more than the distance that is there between two objects.

For a proper understanding of events and objects, sedimentary conceptions regarding time, space and number must have been achieved, and the period of Concrete Operations, is the time when the same are achieved. The child now starts thinking with some logic. All this, helps in a better understanding of events and objects.

None the less, there are some fields of conceptual limitations for the child during this period. His conception of volume does not happen to be adequately developed, with the result that he fails to realise the relationship between quantity and density in a correct way. Still, the child has no schemas to enable him to arrange situation in his mind before he has actually to confront the same in his environment.

The period of Concrete Operations (between age seven and eleven) is characterised by the following factors:

1. Operational thinking
2. Consistent thinking
3. The groups and the groupings (classes and classifications)
4. Conservation of quantity.

OPERATIONAL THINKING

It is during the period of Concrete Operations that the child's thinking assumes operational character in the sense that an event or object in the environment, not merely evokes some thought but it sets in motion a series of thinking; and it is what is meant here by the term "operational thinking". The operational thinking is the basic factor, for want of which the remaining three factors, mentioned above, cannot be possible.

It is during the period of concrete operations that the child's thinking assumes operational character in the sense that an event or an object in the environment, not merely evokes some thought but it sets in motion a series of thinking; and it is what is meant here by the term "operational thinking".

Now, thinking relates itself not only to different perspectives but it also integrates the past experiences to the present ones. And thus, the cognitive development moves towards a better perception of objects and events. But still, the thought process gets started as a result of some concrete object—some object or event in the environment working as a stimulus. The child cannot still start thinking with some idea coming to mind without there being any concrete stimulus in the external world to evoke the same.

CONSISTENT THINKING

During the Pre-operational Period, sometimes, a child may give the evidence of the presence of logic in his thought process but it is not generally the case. It is only during the Period of Concrete Operations that the child achieves some logic to give direction to his thinking process, though intuitive solution of problems would continue even during the period of adult cognitive development. Nevertheless, there is consistency in the child's thinking now. He thinks with some logical sequence, and the thought process becomes organised. The system of thinking becomes stabilised. It happens to be the result of equilibration. All the logical implications of a belief are available to a child whose thought process has thus got organised.

The child gets prepared for the formal operations of the next period as a result of the development of interrelated systems in the organisation of operational thoughts. The behaviour of the child indicates that now, he has started searching for some logic for what he does or says but whatever he says or does, is in reference to something concretely present in the environment. Notwithstanding, his behaviour is not a mere response of some stimulus in the environment, it is a result, on the one hand, of the unfolding of a maturational process, and, on the other hand, it is a result of the concatenation of experiences—all aspects of the child's behaviour are thus active. His experiences are acquired through his active involvement in responding to the stimuli received from the environment, and, a simultaneously going on thought process leads to the organisation of operational groupings which Piaget would like to call well-organised cognitive schemas. Consistency in thinking, is the evidence that the thinking process is well-organised now. Every piece of thought is the result either of some new experience or is the natural consequent of the piece of thought preceding the present one—consistent thinking process is the achievement of the third period of cognitive development, that is, the period of concrete operations.

Every piece of thought is the result either of some new experience or is the natural consequent of the piece of thought preceding the present one—consistent thinking process is the achievement of the third period of cognitive development, that is, the period of concrete operations.

THE GROUPS AND THE GROUPINGS (CLASSES AND CLASSIFICATIONS)

According to Piaget, the organisation of mental actions in operational thinking "can be described in terms of mathematical groups and groupings."

The interrelated intellectual actions are organised into certain sets which have properties of mathematical groups or groupings.

GROUPS

In Mathematics, a group is a set of certain elements having relationships with one another based on certain properties. These elements may be numbers, points, people, classes of objects operations or anything. These elements combine together through certain operations. These operations are numerical or logical operations. The result of an operation may be the combination of two classes into a single one, or, may be the formation of a third number when two separate numbers are added together. Only such a set of elements can become a group where the elements have been combined under some law. This operation may be multiplication, though in character it may not exactly be an arithmetical multiplication. If the two elements of a group are two events or actions, the two actions or events must follow one to the other in succession, so as to make a combination.

Let us consider an example to illustrate how non-quantitative elements may be treated to form different permutations of the same set. Let us suppose the set to be that of three beads—red, yellow and green in colour respectively. Now, six different permutations are possible on this set: 1. (RGY) 2. (RYG) 3. (RG) (Y) 4. (RY) (G) 5. (R) (GY) 6. (R) (G) (Y). In each case R goes to G, G goes to Y, and Y goes to R. The elements in the set, are the six rearrangements as shown above. These rearrangements have been possible through a succession of operations conducted on elements. Here, the elements are not the beads of three different colours but the rearrangements of the same. The set becomes a group where its elements are combined under some law. The operation conducted here should be labelled as "multiplication".

Many other operations besides thus permutating the order of beads, are possible. If the path is combining the two regions A and B; and if B is combined to C, then to combine A to C is also possible. But the path from M to N cannot be joined to that from A to B. Another example of operations may be the rotations of a wheel to 120 degrees, 240 degrees and 360 degrees—the three positions making three elements of the set. There is a relationship among the three elements of the set governed by some law of combination, and thus these three elements of the set make a group. To assess whether a set is a group or not we should see three things:

1. Is the law of combination applicable to every pair of elements in the set?
2. Is it possible to combine an element with every other element in the set?
3. Is every such combination making an element of itself of the set?

If answers to all these three questions are found to be positive, then the set should be taken to be a group. The set of elements would be closed when the possibility of all the rearrangements has been answered: In the example of three beads, given above, when the six rearrangements have been made, the set is said to have "closed" under that operation.

The second requirement for a group is that it be associative. That is, each element in the set must be so related to each other element of it that the result of any two elements of the set may be associated with the remaining elements making no change in the total value of the set. To make the point clear, let us take the example of an arithmetical group consisted of three elements as 1 + 7 + 8, the total value of which is '16'; now, it makes no difference whether '1' and '7' are added first, or the result of '7' and '8' is added to '1', the total value of the group will remain unchanged; that is, there is no difference between (1 + 7) + 8 and 1 + (7 + 8).

The third requirement of a group is that one of its elements be called the identity element; adding of it to any other element in the group, makes no difference. Zero is such an element, the addition of which to any other element of the group will cause no change. In the set of permutations (R) (G) (Y) is the identity element. It leaves the arrangement just as it was with no effect of a change in the order of beads.

The fourth and the last criterion of a group is that every element of it, has an **inverse**. The entire set forms a group when a negative integer and an identity element are added to it, the positive integers alone cannot form a group, "they are closed and associative but contain neither an identity element nor inverses". As mentioned above, 'zero' is an identity element, and if +5 is a positive integer, the negative integer which works as its inverse is –5, all together they make a set, a group of elements. In the set of permutations, there is an inverse for every element. (RGY) and (RYG) are inverses of each other. The combination of the element and its inverse, is the identity element.

GROUPINGS

Piaget has coined the word 'grouping' for a set of operations that has many of the properties of a group but which does not form a 'group'.

Piaget has coined the word 'grouping' for a set of operations that has many of the properties of a group but which does not form a 'group'. When a larger class is divided into such classes, there occurs a sequence of legitimate operations which can be undone through another sequence of operations. Thus, there is closure as well as reversibility, and the system of operations resembles a group in some respects. But actually, the system of operations does not form a group because only certain classes may be legitimately combined. As for example, the child during the period of Concrete Operations, can understand that setters can be combined with dogs of other breeds to form the class—domestic dogs; these dogs can be combined with various wild dogs, and they together make the genus called canis, but there can be no class representing the combination of domestic dogs and non-carnivorous mammals. Thus, because of lack of certain things, and because of certain resemblances with the characteristics of groups, Piaget has used the term 'grouping' for the system of operations leading to it. One can realise the characteristics of closure, completeness and reversibility in the system leading to such groupings, by the time one is in the range of the second half of the period of Concrete Operations. Piaget distinguishes eight types of groupings and he considers their role to be very significant in the cognitive development of the child during the period of Concrete Operations commencing from the age of 7 years.

CONSERVATION OF QUANTITY

The child's perception regarding size, volume or mass happens to be illusionary till he attains the stage of Concrete Operations.

The child's perception regarding size, volume or mass happens to be illusionary till he attains the stage of Concrete Operations. The example of famous Piaget–Taponier experiment or Muller–Lyer illusion, has already been given previously which illustrates how the two sticks appeared to be of unequal size when the place or the physical position of one of them was changed. Likewise, the child declared the liquids to be unequal when the liquid from one of the two containers was poured into a container narrower in size but one having more height. Though the changes were made in the presence of the child even then he could not perceive or have the conception of the constancy or conservation of size, mass or volume because a child up to that period of age cannot integrate his past experience with that of the present one. For, the development of the conception of conservation of quantity, size, mass or volume or of weight without the same being affected by the change of place, or due to the passage of time, is possible when the child is able to integrate his past experiences with that of the present ones.

Mass or volume of an object remains unchanged even when its shape is changed. The example given is that of two chapati-like structures of clay, which are equal in mass. But when one of the two structures, is reshaped as a roller, the child declares that now its mass has grown more in quantity. This conception is illusionary, illusion being caused because of this structure's length being much more than that of the other. Even when this reshaping is done in the presence of the child, he will not be able to perceive the conservation of mass.

When an object is broken into parts or pieces, the weight is conserved, that is, the weight of the parts, generally, remains the same as was that of its previous intact position. It is after many years of maturity that the child obtains the conception that an object loses its weight in proportion as it is carried to a point higher and higher, away from the centre of the gravitational force. An object becomes almost weightless when it is on the moon, or high in the space.

Conservation of quantity as a perception, is an important cognitive achievement of the period of concrete operations.

Nevertheless, conservation of quantity as a perception, is an important cognitive achievement of the period of Concrete Operations.

THE PERIOD OF FORMAL OPERATION

The period of formal operations is the period of early adolescence. It is the period when cognitive developments reach to their adult or highest levels. Now, the adolescent has the fundamental grasp that "underlies the logical thought." His mode of thinking appears to have undergone a major change from accidental thinking to a sequential causal thinking which enables him for scientific experimentation, and for deducing proper implications.

The main characteristics of the period of Formal Operations are:
1. Understanding logical relations among classes;
2. Combinatorial thinking;
3. Achieving some additional concrete constructions.

During the period of Concrete Operations, the child sorts objects of the concrete world into groupings but he fails to understand the relationships which are there among different groupings. It is during the period of Formal Operation that the adolescent starts understanding such relationships. The main characteristics of this period are:

1. understanding logical relations among classes;
2. combinatorial thinking;
3. achieving some additional concrete constructions.

UNDERSTANDING LOGICAL RELATIONS AMONG CLASSES

During the period of Concrete Operations, the child is able to divide the numerous objects of the concrete world into classes. This is his way of perceiving objects in reality and with greater details. But the relationships that exist among classes, can be grasped only during the fourth period of cognitive development, which Piaget has named as the period of Formal Operations. Formal means "of constructs"; the child has now entered into the stage of adolescence, and it is during this period that constructs or conceptions develop and become the bases for abstract thinking or logical thinking. An adolescent, by the period of 11+, starts thinking of relationships that exist among the various classes that he distributes the objects into. Thus, his thinking assumes more and more abstract forms, based on concepts related to concrete objects: dealing with mental constructs rather than only with the concrete forms of the objects. Now, one starts surveying the logical relationships among classes that he has distributed the objects of the concrete world into. During the period of Formal Operations, the adolescent becomes cognitively so developed that he can visualise the possible relationships that may develop in future among different objects; and so, can design future plans accordingly. Such operations of the mind, are the formal operations, are of indispensable importance in scientific surveys or experimentations. Importance of a factor in the causation of an event may be established in advance when one can conduct Formal Operations.

So far, the child was able to realise simple relationships that existed among the events that presented themselves to him but now, he can design or create situations required to establish the needful relationships among the events and thus, now he is able to confirm or disconfirm a hypothesis.

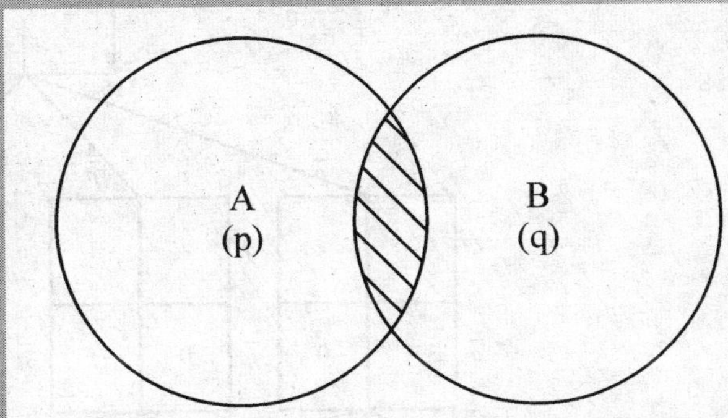

Figure 19.3
Multiplication of two characteristics.

Through a number of examples, AL Baldwin has tried to make clear how logical operations enable one to obtain the matrix of possibilities through multiplication of two characteristics together. The Fig. 19.3, given here, illustrates this matrix of possibilities. In this figure, two classes of objects A and B are intersecting each other in such a way that four divisions have been made:

One area is both A and B; the area where A cross-hatches in one direction, and B in the other

(The area where one circle overlaps the other).

Then there is area which represents only the object A.

There is another area which represents only B.

And, there is one more area, the fourth one, which is neither A nor B.

"These are the four cells in the two-by-two matrix that emerge when two classifications (A versus non-A) and (B versus non-B) are multiplied together."

Now, if we think these four as elements of statements, the four positions are:

p represents where the statement is true.

$\bar{p}$ represents examples where the statement is not applicable.

q represents another statement about the same class that the statement *p* is related to; and is true.

$\bar{q}$ represents examples where the *q* is true and $\bar{q}$ is false.

The same situation has been expressed through another (Fig. 19.4).

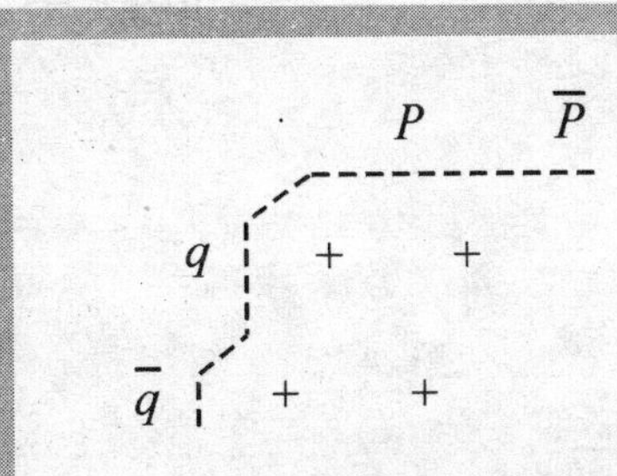

Figure 19.4
The four possibilities of changing the elements of an expression.

Here, four possibilities have been expressed:

(*i*) *p* is true

(*ii*) *q* is true

(*iii*) *p* is true *q* is false

(*iv*) *p* is false, *q* is true.

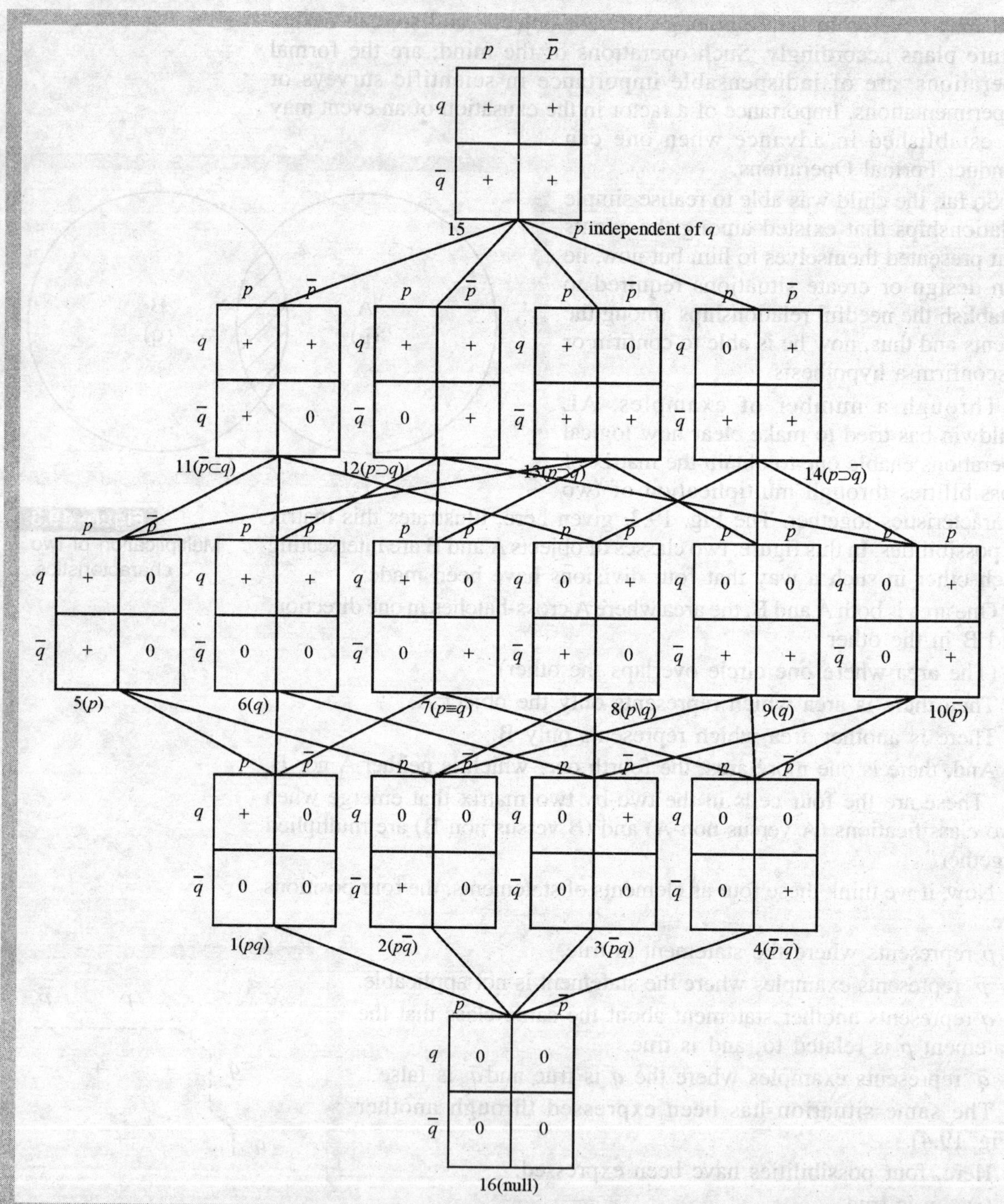

Figure 19.5
Truth table for sixteen binary operations.

Piaget has given such logico-mathematical examples to illustrate how an adolescent during the 11+ period has his faculty developing with age and enrichment of environment, so far formal cognitive operations are concerned. One grows continually more able to understand his environment, and can perform better in relation to his environment, his mental faculty for formal operations being more developed. It is, thus, that an adolescent grows proficient in solving very complicated problems through a consistent sequential thinking in an abstract way. AL Baldwin in his book *Theories of Child Development* has given the truth table for 16 binary operations (Fig. 19.5)—This shows how in due course an individual cognitively develops so much so that he can perform formal operations of such a complicated nature.

COMBINATORIAL THINKING

Combinatorial thinking is the second important characteristic of this period. It is this ability of combinatorial thinking that enables the adolescent to go through all the choice sequentially or systematically. One, during this period is cognitively so developed that he can cover all the different aspects of an issue, and, can exhaust all possibilities relating to the development of an event. One can obtain the needful information using the entire system of formal logic; sometimes even intuitively. Formal Operations always happen to be based on formal logic which enables one to survey exhaustively the possible relationships that may be there among classes of different objects.

The truth table for sixteen binary operations (Fig. 19.5) is the result of logical thinking which illustrates how combinatorial thinking can enable one to understand the relationships between two statements of a fact exhaustively. It is not enough for the child to understand the relationship among the sixteen binary operations. First, each of the four classes has to be taken systematically, one at a time. Then, every possible pair of classes has to be described. Then, every possible triplet of classes is considered, and finally comes the combination of the quadruplet of classes. Such a combination is possible only because of a certain kind of thought process. Each binary operation represents a kind of possible combination. The thought process enabling one for one, such an operation is possible only during the period of formal operations. An adolescent during this period only can be cognitively developed enough to appreciate the difference between all the combinations that occur; and he can also acquire ability to process the entire range of possibility.

I shall describe here the experiment devised by Piaget and Inhelder to illustrate how formal operations of combinatorial thinking lead one to certain conclusions.

There were four bottles containing some colourless liquid in each; and they were labelled as 1,2,3 and 4. The first bottle contained sulphuric acid; the second water; the third oxygenated water; and fourth, thiosulfate. There was a smaller vial which contained potassium iodide, it was labelled as *g*.

The subject was presented two glasses; in one of them there were liquids from bottles first and third; and in the other it was from the second. While the subject was watching, the experimenter dropped liquid from the vial '*g*' into each of these two glasses. The liquid in the first glass (which contained liquids) both from bottles 1 and 3 turned yellow, while in that of the other glass, no change in colour occurred.

Later, the child was asked to describe how each liquid had functioned in effecting change in colour. The child could tell the function of each liquid only on the basis of trial—watching the effect of each liquid separately, and in combination with some other liquid, upon some other liquid. The child by no way, can tell of such a change ahead of a concrete operation. The trial and error is an important method in developing conceptual schemas in such a situation. The combinatorial thinking is an important characteristic of the period of Formal Operations. As here, the subject enhances his conceptual knowledge through the function of combining liquids. Likewise, adolescent during the period of Formal Operations, thrusts ahead cognitively by way of combining different pieces of information to come to new conclusions. This is combinatorial thinking—pieces of a wide range of knowledge related to far off places and times are combined together with the result of the development of new/advanced cognitive forms/schemas during this period. To achieve the result, all possible combinations may have to be tried. Ability to form systematic combinations is a characteristic of this period. If a subject belongs to this period of cognitive development, then only he can have the ability to cover systematically all the possibilities; in the example given above, he will try *g* with each.

ACHIEVING OF SOME ADDITIONAL CONSTRUCTS

It is during this period that the child is able to understand the problem of equilibrium. In such a problem there happens to be two different inverses leading to the development of the 4 groups. In Fig. 19.6 there is a beam, on both sides of its fulcrum, the weights are equal; the weights are at equal distance, too. But with the addition of weight on any one of the two sides, the beam is thrown out of balance. There are several ways for the restoration of

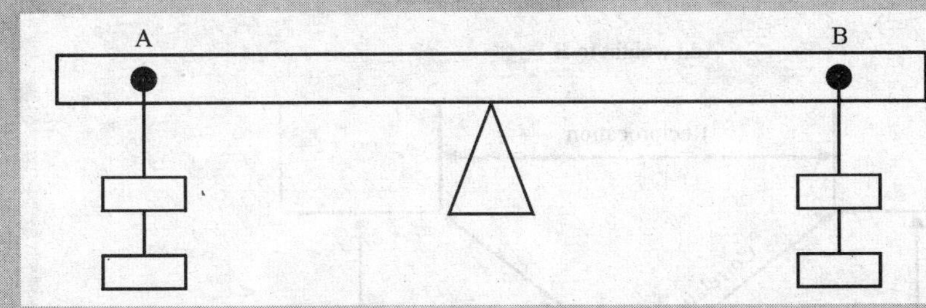

Figure 19.6
Restoring balance.

balance. The balance may be restored by inverting the previous function; that is, by subtracting the weight previously added. The other way for the restoration of balance or equilibration is to add weight to the side where it is less.

To resolve the problems of equilibration, the same double inverse is resorted to in a number of fields. By way of another example, the velocity of an object depends upon the distance it covers over a period of time. The velocity is said to have increased in the proportion as the time taken remains the same in spite of there being increase in the distance covered. To bring the object to its original velocity either the time factor is increased or the distance covered is decreased.

The problem of equilibration may likewise be resolved in cases of relationships in the fields of gravity, volume and weight of a liquid. The simple law of proportion works everywhere—one variable equals the quotient of two other variables. We can restore the value of fraction to its original one either by changing the numerator or the denominator. Two kinds of operations are involved in the solution of an equilibration problem. These two operations are inverses of two kinds—a negation of the original change or a reciprocation which changes some compensating factor. An actual mathematical group is the result of such a system of negation or reciprocation. The Fig. 19.7, illustrates this relationship.

The total operations involved here are—negation, reciprocation, correlation and identity, these four have already been explained in some other relevant part of the book. Negation attains a balance through subtraction; reciprocation through addition; the relationship between the opposite corners is that of correlation—the corners are the equivalent results of negation and reciprocation.

A clear cognitive improvement during the period of Formal Operations is witnessed over that of the Concrete Operations in the sense that during the period of Formal Operations, the child acquired the ability to understand relations of different groupings to one another. He can also have a preview of possibilities that may develop in future. It is because of combinatorial thinking, during the period of Formal Operations that one can have a full

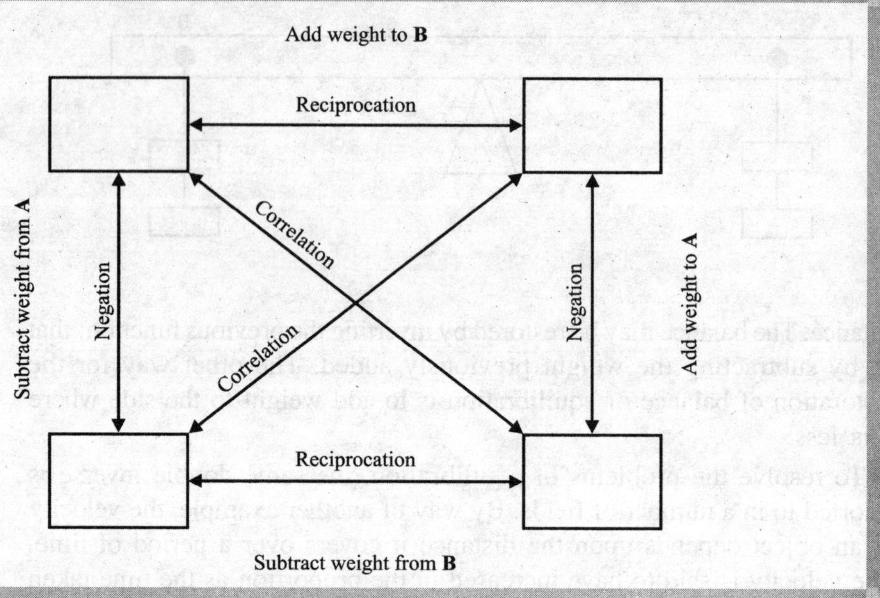

Figure 19.7
A system of negation and reciprocation.

understanding of the full implication of propositional thinking as well as that of the equilibrium problems. His understanding of the variety of relations that exist among different classes of elements, also becomes complete during this period.

REVIEW QUESTIONS

***Q.*1.** Describe in brief the main characteristics of the preoperational period, as described by Jean Piaget.

***Q.*2.** What new cognitive schemas are earned during the periods of Concrete and Formal Operation; describe each such a schema in brief.

***Q.*3.** On the left is given description of some sensorimotor/cognitive schemas; write the name of each schema in front of each of them:

	Description	*Name of the Schema*
(*i*)	An adolescent can go through all the choices sequentially or systematically, can cover all the different aspects of an issue.	....
(*ii*)	Grasping of relationships that exist among classes.	....

(*iii*) The child can now conceive that change of place, and, the passage of time, make no change in the mass or volume or size of an object. ....

(*iv*) When a larger class is divided into such classes, there occurs a sequence of legitimate operations which can be undone through another sequence of operations. ....

(*v*) Active use of trial and error method is made in pursuance of learning more and more about objects. ....

(*vi*) Internalisation of external activities or events; it enables the child to imitate an activity or an event. ....

(*vii*) The child realises the existence of an object as separate from its perception as mental representation of the same. ....

***Q*.4.** For the development of a Schema, three things are required; name them.

(*i*) a ..... (*ii*) a .....

(*iii*) a .....

***Q*.5.** Fill in the blanks:

(*i*) Registering in the brain, of an object, or of an event, through sense organ, is ..... The ..... is liable to many ..... because of the ..... fixating of a sense organ over an object.

(*ii*) The child's ability to integrate experiences of the past with that of the present, leads to the development of the schema of .....

ANSWERS TO OBJECTIVE TYPE QUESTIONS

***Q*.3.** (*i*) combinatorial thinking, (*ii*) classification, (*iii*) conceptual invariance (*iv*) grouping, (*v*) tertiary circular reactions, (*vi*) mental image (*vii*) symbolic verbal schemas

***Q*.4.** (*i*) assimilation, (*ii*) accommodation, (*iii*) adaptation

Q.5. (*i*) perception, perception, distortions, momentary

(*ii*) perceptual constancy

CHAPTER

20 THEORIES AND PRACTICES OF CHILD EDUCATION: MADAME MARIA MONTESSORI

Chapter Outline

- **Theories and Practices Advocated by Dr Montessori**
- **What is Needed for the Child's Development:**
  1. **Creation of learning situations allowing due autonomy to the child.**
  2. **Putting the senses into use in a planned way to achieve the potential capacity.**
  3. **Putting the child into effective co-ordination with the external reality.**
  4. **Self-instigated personal change.**
  5. **Active use of the learning materials.**
  6. **Creative diversion of emotions.**
  7. **Socialisation.**
  8. **Religious fervour.**
- **Review Questions**

Still, very little is being done in the field of pre-school education, especially, in a developing country as India. There is a fast growing trend for sending children to nurseries by the time they are three-year-olds or even earlier. It is a new trend; in bygone times, children were hardly sent to school before they were five-year-olds. Actually, nursery is not a stage for imparting formal education; luckily some good nurseries have come up with a true conception of pre-school education. Talking with the Indian perspective in view, I may remark that a good many of our nurseries start schooling at that stage rather than preparing our kids in a better way for future schooling.

Let us first consider what is pre-schooling, and its need or importance. Schooling is a period when direct efforts are made to educate the children what is considered necessary for their persons as well as for the society that they belong to; and pre-schooling is to prepare the children for school education so that they may learn more, learn in a better way, in less time, and requiring less efforts on the part of the teachers. If we consider the second part of the question, that is, whether the pre-schooling is needed or not, or what is its importance, the nature of pre-school education would be further defined. The representative assembly in the USA passed the resolution in 1966 for expanding the general system of universal public education so as to provide opportunity for compensatory education, beginning "at the age of four for those children who, through economic or social deprivation, may be seriously impeded in their progress through public schools and consequently in participation in a democratic society ...".

Differing from the views of Mabel M Mitchell who had suggested amendment to delimit the Resolution for the disadvantaged children only, other educationists expressed their opinion that pre-school education should not be considered something required as "compensatory" for those only who are from families which are economically and socially deprived. Though such an education is essential for the disadvantaged yet it is nice for all.

The period of three-four and five-years is a root period; only such fruit can sprout later, seeds for which are sowed during this period. This is the most impressionable period when maximum learning occurs. But, as learning occurs in proportion to the experiences offered by the environment, such an environment needs to be provided which may enable the child to enrich his experiences more. Actually the child, because of his innate curiosity, is keen in exploring his environment intently, so what is needed is the programming of the environment so that it may be highly exciting, stimulating, and, may prove greatly helpful in learning to learn.

The period of three, four and five years is a root period; only such fruit can sprout later, seeds for which are sowed during this period.

Only such environment may be exciting which provides umpteen opportunities for activities to the highly curious child, and, to the child who is full of energy, and enjoys remaining engaged in one or the other activity untiringly. Consequently, deprivations during this period are "most disastrous". To modify the harms caused because of deprivations during this period, is more difficult to do than to adopt preventive measures for all the children of this period—in some cases modification may not even be possible.

But this realisation should always be there that such a pre-school educational institution is not to replace the child's home, it is only to complement it. No institution, howsoever well-organised to the end of the maximum welfare of the child, can replace his home or family. A pre-school educational institution should work for the objectives related to the four major areas—intellectual, emotional, social and physical.

A pre-school educational institution should work for the objectives related to the four major areas—intellectual, emotional, social and physical.

"The intellectual goals include the promotion of curiosity, growth of language and generation of readiness for the intellectual activities that will

"The intellectual goals include the promotion of curiosity, growth of language and generation of readiness for the intellectual activities that will come in later years."

come in later years." The intellectual activities also include ability to observe and listen, to perceive things, to handle concepts and meet problems. The range of the child's experience is enhanced as a contribution of the intellectual development. The child's early education can open new possibilities of learning by programming and enriching the environment to the end of his development. The educator's skilled guidance proves a very facilitating factor in furthering the intellectual growth of the child. The child comes in contact with many new items, and new situations in his environment and he indulges into a number of activities which provide him a lot many new experiences fostering his intellectual growth. His home environment cannot open up so many vistas of learning as the programmed environment of the child's educational institution can. It is literally the period when the child learns to learn.

For achieving the emotional goals of early education such an environment needs to be provided for the child where he may interact in the new extended social milieu consisted of so many other students and teachers with a feeling of security and self-respect.

For achieving the emotional goals of early education such an environment needs to be provided for the child where he may interact in the new extended social milieu consisted of so many other students and teachers with a feeling of security and self-respect. For a wholesome emotional growth, it is essential that the child feels himself safe and important, but at the same time his egocentrism needs to be balanced by the development of a perspective where others become a part of this 'me's'. Even for a proper intellectual growth, nothing can be more important than a sense of security and self-respect. The child's happiness or mental health would be depending upon such a sense. For making the environment of the nursery or kindergarten congenial for the emotional growth of the child, it is essential that the child feels that he can learn by himself, and he can also help others in learning. This generates a sense of self-respect and self-importance which is of crucial importance for the emotional growth of the child.

Early education can achieve its goals only if it is exciting for the child. The child has got a lot of curiosity, creativity and 'spontaneous energy'—his education can be exciting only when it allows for a free positive play for these innate characteristics. These are the sources "from which a life-time of learning can develop".[1] The school programme should be such which may enhance these qualities.

Of great importance is the teacher-parent co-ordination, for the emotional development, too, besides its being greatly helpful in the intellectual growth of the child. Off and on meeting of the mother to the nursery teacher, may help the child in adjusting to the new environment that its school presents to him. If the mother involved in the school experiences, the association of the teacher and the mother may be mutually beneficial; the teacher can better understand the child, and the parent can better assist the teacher in the achievement of goals of early education.

1. Frost, Joe L. *Early Childhood Education Rediscovered.*

The third objective of early education is to develop the child as more social. With his entry into the nursery, wider social arena opens itself for the child where he needs to adjust himself. He happens to be surrounded by so many new faces, it is a major objective of early education to enable the child to learn how to befriend his classmates, and how to behave towards his elders. "A young child tends to see himself as the centre of the world," what needs to be done for such a child, is to "balance his egocentricity with a concern for and responsibility toward others." Such a development is a very important objective of the early education, and is basic towards the socialisation of the child.

The third objective of early education is to develop the child as more social.

One important thing in this respect is that the child is not to be taught only always to obey others, he must be assertive too when his self-respect is hit, or when it is the other or others who need to adjust and not he. Respecting the rights of the child would always help in a better socialisation.

Child's physical well-being or development is not an objective of lesser importance for early education. Sound mind in a sound body is a saying which, in general, is to remain a fact forever. One who is physically weak, cannot have a zeal for learning, nor does his body permit him for exploratory pursuits to satisfy his curiosity, and thereby enhance his experiences which only can serve as a source for intellectual development. Body and mind are interdependent, inter-related; the one affecting the function of the other. It is the common experience of each one of us, that a physical disturbance of any sort, disturbs our mind. The physical disturbance may be overt from the external physical or social environment, or it may be caused in our body itself; the result is ever to be emotional upsetting.

Child's physical well-being or development is not an objective of lesser importance for early education.

If the school campus is not clean, open, adequately spacious; the air there is not cool and pollution-free, there being no lawns, plants and so on; and there are not suitable grounds and apparatus for the children to play, they cannot have an emotional attachment to their nursery school or kindergarten. Nor, such an institution, and an institution with no airy, spacious, well-ventilated, furnished, suitably equipped and attractive classrooms, can be good for physical and emotional health of the child. Intellectual growth of the child is also definitely to be adversely affected under such physical conditions.

An institution with no airy, spacious, well-ventilated, furnished, suitably equipped and attractive classrooms, can be good for physical and emotional health of the child. Intellectual growth of the child is also definitely to be adversely affected under such physical conditions.

Play is the indispensable activity for the desirable physical growth of the child. Selection of games should be in keeping with the age and physical capacity of the children; they should be such that the liking of the children for the same is natural. In the school, being run by the society that the author is associated to, we are having *yoga* as one of the physical activities, of course, a great care has been taken in the selection of the yoga-exercises that are perfectly suitable to the tender kids as they are.

Let our tots run, jump, throw a ball, kick at the same, and enjoy swings of different sorts—all is good for their physical health, and for their mental health, too. The children should have occasions when they can sing and dance freely, and also as a part of their education.

THEORIES AND PRACTICES ADVOCATED BY DR MONTESSORI

Robert Travers finds certain of Dr Montessori's propositions having their roots in psychology dating as back as Aristotle, some are of obscure origins or they represent speculation, while others constitute her novel contributions made to early child education. J Mcvicker Hunt advises fans of Montessori, who consider the Madame as "sacrosanct", to rediscover her methods. But in spite of these and other reservations, her contributions have occupied an important place in the annals of educational innovations.

"The recent upsurge of interest among psychologists in cognitive processes, in individual differences, in structural arrangements of cognitive processes, and in the intimately related area of the development of specific cognitive skills, all contribute to a current Zeitgeist in psychology in which a closer look at the Montessori method is especially pertinent."

Riley W Gardner considers the contributions of Dr Maria Montessori "of signal importance in their own rights". In an address to the annual meeting of the American Montessori Society, in 1965, Gardner remarked, "The recent upsurge of interest among psychologists in cognitive processes, in individual differences, in structural arrangements of cognitive processes, and in the intimately related area of the development of specific cognitive skills, all contribute to a current Zeitgeist in psychology in which a closer look at the Montessori method is especially pertinent."

The operation Head Start was a programme in America which involved various agencies of social service to provide such social experience to the children which are commonly available to the children of that age group but to the children from the low-income group families. These social experiences were such which led to confidence, self-respect, better peer-relations, families' ties more strengthened, broadening horizons for cognitive development and language competencies. I feel the impact of Maria Montessori to have unconsciously worked upon the operations of Head Start which put so great a stress on social experiences that, generally, the children from the low socioeconomic strata of society happen to be deprived of; Dr Montessori looked at this deprivation as the inadequate sensorimotor preparation rather than inadequate cognitive potential. She declared that lack of adequate sensorimotor experiences, was the cause of failure in later school years. The great psychological theorist of the twentieth century, Jean Piaget, also considers sensorimotor schemas to be basic in the cognitive development of the child; the same have been likened to the ground floor of the intellectual structures. Both Piaget and Montessori believed that the sensorimotor nature of the young child's intelligence could be understood only through an astute observation of his behaviour. Montessori developed methods which could make it possible to achieve the maximal acceleration of cognitive development. The common thing in both the educationists was to evolve their theories, mainly, through observations of the children's behaviour.

One very important similarity between Montessori and Piaget is that, they both believe that during the pre-operational stage, a child can manipulate transformations and other mental operations "only when he manipulates the object concretely". This led Montessori to suggest the use of a number of sports-items and other gadgets or teaching-aids to concretise the teaching of the child. The pre-operational period that succeeds the sensorimotor period ending by the end of the second year of the child, is the period when symbolic functions just start their appearance in their primitive forms, so concretisation of teaching items is of immense importance during this period of pre-schooling.

Dr Montessori underlines the importance of environment as did Piaget, Rappaport and others during the latter half of the twentieth century. Only "richly varied early experience" can provide "an ample array of preliminary schemata". The previously developed schemata go on assimilating new experiences and the process of the development of cognitive abilities remains a continuum one. But the limitation that Montessori suffers from, is her belief that environmental deficiencies can be fully compensated through the specially manufactured, and ingeniously handled teaching devices or materials. Such devices cannot broaden the range of sensorimotor interactions to the desired level and in the desired way—a broad range of affective and motivational factors can be available only in a naturally enriched environment. Nevertheless, Montessori had given great importance to the interactions of the child with his environment for his intellectual development.

The Montessori method seems to encourage accommodation to external realities in place of assimilation to the fantasies of the playful child.

WHAT IS NEEDED FOR THE CHILD'S DEVELOPMENT (MONTESSORI METHOD—STRIVINGS AND LIMITATIONS)

1. Creation of learning situations allowing due autonomy to the child.
2. Putting the senses into use in a planned way to achieve the potential capacity.
3. Putting the child into effective co-ordination with the external reality.
4. Self-instigated personal change.

5. Active use of the learning materials.
6. Creative diversion of emotions.
7. Socialisation.
8. Religious fervour.

1. Dr Maria Montessori's first and foremost emphasis for an effective child education is on the creation of situations congenial for learning. Her conviction is that only such situations can be considered congenial for learning which instigate the child to be active to explore the same, and keep him active, moving from one object to the other, handling them one after the other till his curiosity is satisfied. The child's sensorimotor activities that are conducted uninhibited would result in learning fast. Dr Montessori is a strong advocate of autonomy for the child to play and work; authoritative directions or restrictions, dampen the child's zeal for being active in exploring his situations, and, in handling different objects of his situations. Montessori considers autonomy as an essential condition for the creation of a situation congenial to learning. She writes, "with my methods, the teacher teaches little and observes much". "The child educates himself." Feedback loop is not possible unless the child has the liberty of movement and activity. The Montessori method is for the effacement of the teacher from between the child and his learning situation, nevertheless, she favours some design, some sequence in the process of learning, which cannot be possible unless the teacher's indirect role of a facilitator is there. And, there may arise an occasion when some timely corrective communication, from the side of the teacher, may be urgently needed. Though not much corrective communications, would be required as the materials being used by the child, happen to be self-corrective.

> Only such situations can be considered congenial for learning which instigate the child to be active to explore the same, and keep him active, moving from one object to the other, handling them one after the other till his curiosity is satisfied.

2. In a Montessori school, the three-year-old child is introduced to a world wider than that of his house, where he physically interacts with his environment yielding more experiences, and, sharpening his senses. This is done in a phased way. During the first phase, a child of 3 years is motivated to such daily activities of the house as washing, dressing, sweeping and so on. These are the chores which a child sees daily being performed by his mother or by some other elder member of the family; and so he enjoys doing the same in imitation, and, more so in doing in reality. The experiences that such of his activities provide, help a lot in developing manual dexterity (or sensorimotor schemas, as Piaget would put it).

In the second phase, Montessori has prescribed the use of teaching materials with the objective of developing sensory sensitivity. The Montessori approach is for real "sense education". It is based on the conviction that sensory sensitivity can be increased through practice. "One should proceed from a few stimuli contrasting to many stimuli in gradual differentiation always more fine and imperceptible." In a Montessori school, there would be a good many materials to develop the activity of senses. The child playing with pieces of wood or with plastic blocks of different sizes and shapes, develops the sense of touch as well as vision, and learns of various geometrical shapes and sizes. He learns of colour with the help of 64 spools of different colours and shades. A set of musical bells is used to distinguish one sound from another. Tablets of wood of the same size but of different weights are used to educate the children in appreciating volumes or mass. These and a number of other materials become instrumental in developing the senses of the child so much so that he can distinguish the minute differences that may be there between two things in shape, size, colour, weight, pitch of sound, softness or hardness.

It is during the third phase that the child is to get practice in the controlled and skilful movement of fingers along with the use of eyes in a co-ordinated way. A proper co-ordination is also established between the eye and the ear. Visual and auditory senses are so much developed that they can work in a fully co-ordinated manner in an exercise of dictation. A child of six can properly read, write, and do his exercises in Mathematics with due rapidity.

The crux of Montessori's approach to education is "the development of the senses to the level of potentiality". Children, especially, of the low socioeconomic strata, are feared to be deprived in this respect. The Montessori approach is essential for the deprived but it is nice for all. Children from middle and upper classes of society are also benefited by the Montessori methods in developing the senses and making perceptions quicker and more accurate. The impact of this development may be studied when such children are compared in the field of scholastic achievement with those who had directly started with 3 Rs.

> The crux of Montessori's approach to education is "the development of the senses to the level of potentiality".

Evidences are available as results of studies conducted by Skeels and Dye (1939), and by others to prove the importance of early experiences in cognitive development or the development of the IQ levels. Skeels and Dye got transferred a group of 13 infants, ranging in age between 7 and 30 months, and with the mean IQ of 64.3; and a range between 36 and 89 from an orphanage to a special school for the mentally retarded. There, they remained very much attached to, and played with, for the most of their waking periods, with girls older than them and also brighter. Such a stimulating environment was available to infants for a period ranging from six months to 52 months; for an infant of seven months, it was of six months; and for the one 30 month-old, it was for the duration of 52 months. They were retested after the periods of rich experiences and stimulation. Each of the 13 infants showed a minimum gain of 7 points. This verifies Madame Montessori's conviction that the deprivation caused because of poor socio-cultural milieu, may, to some extent, be compensated by way of programming an environment which can provide rich experiences and stimulation to the infants, and by way of making a planned use of the sense with the help of teaching materials especially prepared for the purpose. Neuropsychological theorising of Donald Hebb (1949) led some psychologists in education to conclude that early experiences influence very much the mental and motor behaviour of an adult organism. Hebb found the cell assemblies to be "based upon early learning involving perceptual experiences". The other important term used by Hebb is phase sequences based upon the sequential organisations of later learning.

3. The Montessori approach aims at introducing the child to the world of reality as he happens to be too much absorbed into a world of phantasies. The Montessori method makes the child learn through making him do such house-chores as sweeping, cleaning, washing, dressing, decorating and such others. A child automatically is inclined towards performing such activities; the Montessori method avails itself of such a natural inclination of the child. These are the activities of the real world, and can help in weaning the child out of a world of phantasmagoria. A child is inclined to do such activities in imitation to his mother and other elder members of the family, and enjoys doing the same. The method prescribes a number of materials, plus the use of dolls to enable the child do it all in a proper way.

The Montessori approach aims at introducing the child to the world of reality as he happens to be too much absorbed into a world of phantasies.

With the child's admission into a Montessori school, a wider world confronts him. He sees a good many objects making this world. These objects are of different shapes and colours. He hears sounds of different tones being produced by different living and non-living objects. There are things which are soft to touch and some are hard to touch; some make us feel that they are hot while others, as cold. There are edibles of different tastes. This world, consisted of so many varieties of objects, is the main theme of our study. The senses are the thresholds for experiencing all these multifarious objects. The Montessori method is based on a plan to study these realities through a variety of toys, appliances and teaching materials, each helping to teach realities through the thresholds of different senses.

Figure 20.1
Outings can have educative value too.

It is for a thorough experience of realities that children are taken out on excursions, to exhibitions and others (Fig. 20.1).

Learning takes place through "contiguity of stimuli", through Aristotle's "association by contiguity", that is through introducing of names of objects while presenting the objects themselves. What is "rough", what is "smooth"—the child learns through tactile sensation by way of touching the objects with these properties. The teacher may repeat the qualitative word while the child is feeling the property through touch, and uttering the word, too.

4. All round development as an objective has become a hackneyed term in pedagogy. Development is always a change, a change for better, a desirable change. As already mentioned under point one, for a proper learning situation, due autonomy to the child is essential. To highlight this factor further, we intend to emphasise here that the role of the teacher in bringing about a change in the person of the child, should be the minimum, for the most part the process of change ought to be self-instigated. A mention has already been made of a "feed-back loop", it always involves "situation-response-new situation". And, when liberty of movement and activity is there, whatever change occurs as a result of "situation-response-new situation", will be self-instigated. The change is not externally imposed or thrust upon. The Madame believes in self-discipline; in a change that automatically occurs while the child goes on indulging into activities that he is inclined to by nature. Such a change would be something like a natural growth; so more in keeping with his innate attributes and potentialities. Such a change would be not only more enduring but more wholesome as well.

For a proper learning situation, due autonomy to the child is essential.

Madame Montessori's ideas regarding self-instigated change reflect the need and maturity theories of development also. The motor behaviour of the child is related to his particular physical proportions. "The baby loves to walk on all fours because like the quadruped animals, his limbs are short in comparison with his body." The supine child's stretching out its legs in the air, is an expression of physical needs related to the proportions of his body. Such, and a lot of other activities or movements of the child happen to be self-instigated and they result in some desirable change—physical and cognitive.

For the child to learn "to regulate conduct from inside himself", Montessori considers the creation of appropriate conditions as an essential factor. Thus, environment assumes special importance in the change that is desired to be made in the person of the child. A congenial environment so affects the functioning of the body that a change becomes self-instigated from within the body. The process of physical as well as cognitive and emotional development becomes smooth and natural.

In a Montessori school, there are found at hand creative materials such as easels, paints, clay, scissors and coloured papers. A child likes to work with such materials, it is a play for him to make use of the same under the needful directions of the teacher, he enjoys it.

5. In a Montessori school, there are found at hand creative materials such as easels, paints, clay, scissors and coloured papers. A child likes to work with such materials, it is a play for him to make use of the same under the needful directions of the teacher, he enjoys it. But working with, or playing with such materials leads to the child's learning significantly. His skill at handling such materials, rapidly improves along with the improvement in movement of fingers, wrist, and so on.

A child is let play with dolls, toys, and with blocks of different sizes, shapes and colours. Playing with all these, and with a lot of other materials, a child earns experiences which facilitate his learning about colours, shapes, sizes, weights, mass, volume and so on. A child would also enjoy making simple scientific experiments in the fields of physics and chemistry; it all would depend upon the resourcefulness of the Montessori teacher who would decide what type of experiment would suit the child looking to his age, abilities and inclinations; of course, sometimes a teacher may have to motivate a child for a particular kind of activity. The teacher should give due importance to the joy of achievement of the child.

A child learns first by taking in impressions, then involving himself actively in doing something in response to the same. The child has a natural eagerness to master the project; for it he would be making corrections when and where he would feel a need for the same—his hope for success remains persistent. Nevertheless, a Montessori school would proceed more systematically making the child realise "the inherent order and structure in nature."

Montessori stressed the importance of sensory experience in learning. A long list of learning materials was developed, and it may further be lengthened with the motive of involving the children in their active use in such a way that sense impressions may prove to be the threshold points for learning. Montessori desired two objectives to be achieved through the active use of the learning materials by the child: first, the education should be based on sensory experiences; second, the child should be motivated to develop skill in the use of learning materials, or in performing activities in real life. The Montessori materials are so designed that when they are used in the proper sequence they gradually lead children, over a period of several years, into an understanding of abstract ideas with a minimum of adult explanation and interference. After the adult has introduced them to the child one by one, she "can retire into the background while he teaches himself."[2]

2. Spock, Benjamin. Hathaway, L Mildred. *East Cleveland Schools.*

The child handles rods for the visual perception of lengths: geometric solids for touching; spools of different colours for colour discrimination; a set of musical bells for distinguishing sounds; tablets of wood to be able to tell of difference in weights; "guinea pigs to be cared for seeds to be planted, mud to mould, cookies to make, a stethoscope to play doctor with," so on and so forth. The child realises relationships between different materials; and the discriminatory knowledge leads to the development of a variety of mathematical and physical concepts. The child's manual dexterity is also developed. All this proves to be a better preparation of the child for reading, writing and doing mathematical exercises.

Emotions are the natural sources of energy which activate one physically and mentally. Madame Montessori recognised the power of emotions, and devised means for their creative diversion through a number of activities of plays.

6. Emotions are the natural sources of energy which activate one physically and mentally. Madame Montessori recognis-ed the power of emotions, and devised means for their creative diversion through a number of activities of plays (Fig. 20.2). The Montessori methods suggest the use of a number of learning materials, they all help in the creative diversion of emotions.

Figure 20.2

John Holt advises the school to be a smorgasbord of activities.

Emotions make an important aspect of one's personality hence their proper channelisation is must for a wholesome development of personality. Montessori had always desired self-discipline, and proper habits of conduct to be inculcated—nothing by way of imposition from outside but as a natural growth from within.

A Montessori teacher recognises the important role of emotions in learning. She would be giving as much focus on guidance of the child's feelings as on that of his intellectual growth. The feelings of anger, fear, jealousy, for instance, are very important; the energy released by them if is not diverted to creative channels of learning, they may not only disrupt the process of learning but may even render the child uneducable if the child often falls a prey to such a tantrum. A child who is emotionally maladjusted, may have his ability to learn seriously hampered, and the teacher may fail to inculcate sociability in such a case.

For a happy future of the child, a Montessori teacher would be expected to keep the child 'on the right emotional track'. And, this can be possible only through the diversion of emotions towards a creative learning situation.

For a happy future of the child, a Montessori teacher would be expected to keep the child 'on the right emotional track'. And, this can be possible only through the diversion of emotions towards a creative learning situation.The Montessori teacher knows that the kids at her disposal need her help in understanding their own feelings and in managing them. "Feelings are not to be denied, but their appropriate expression must be learned." The child should be taught the names of each of his emotions, and also, how to manage the same. Let the child be made aware that the adults too are susceptible to the onslaught of emotions, what is important, is the 'appropriate expression' of the same, and the proper diversion of the same for the benefit of the self, and for the good of all related to the situation.

A child in a Montessori school may be found playing with his dolls, blocks, cars and so on, as well as dressing-up costumes, and playing out all kinds of human dramas—these are the desirable outlets for the raised-up feelings of the child, and also the means of managing the same. Such games develop the child's imagination and creativity, and, may be the effective ways of mastering his strong feelings. Story-telling or story-reading also indirectly serves to let out some brimming emotions. Role-playing or dramatisation is a direct means of managing strong feelings (Fig. 20.3). At one time, the teacher may encourage the expression of feelings, at another time, he may have to provide a situation for the diversion of the same in the interest of learning and creativity.

Figure 20.3 Role-playing or Dramatisation is a direct means of managing strong feelings.

Generally, educationists of all schools of thoughts believe that when a child is taken out to school, trying to wean him out from so strong of his attachment to his mother, he happens to be sad, anxiety-ridden and sometimes frustrated or angry. For want of a proper management of his negative feelings, the same would get expression through some disruptive behaviour. The Montessori teacher should be expected to provide situation which may make good the loss to some extent caused because of the child's weaning out of so affectionate an environment as his home happens to be, this is possible only when his nursery teacher is sweet and loving like his own mother. Secondly, the teacher should provide situations for him, where he can express his strong feelings through creative activities leading to effective learning.

Child's interactions with his peers is essential for overcoming his egocentrism which otherwise may stand in the way of desirable management of emotions.

The Montessori method is important in managing emotions because it encourages accommodation to external reality rather than, "assimilation to personalised motives and fantasies". The history of human evolution on the track of development, is made up of control mechanisms which involves both inhibition and facilitation. In the conative field of learning, the Montessori method suggests which emotions to control through diversion, and when, and where they may benefitially be allowed to be expressed.

The principal feeling that is keenly aroused in a Montessori school is the "joy of achievement". A child and a teacher would always be seeking the satisfaction of achieving something in a proper way. For it, and under its spell, many negative feelings may be benefitially managed or diverted to creative learning.

7. We may often find a Montessori child engaged in some individual game or activity, and it leads to some learning. However, this should not give the impression that the Montessori methods may only make the child individualistic in his thoughts and behaviour. In a Montessori school, children get opportunities for co-operation and companionship in games and also in formal learning exercises. There are some such activities which provide more opportunities to play in co-operation with one another, and sometimes jointly in a team. The need to work together, fosters sociability; a trait which society desires to be developed in its children. Nevertheless, the fact is that the child in a Montessori school is encouraged for self-learning, and an environment is prepared for the same. Edison Responsive Environment Equipment, and the electric 'typewriter' device developed by OK Moore, are the examples of learning appliances or devices which engage a child in an individual pursuit of learning.

> There are some such activities which provide more opportunities to play in co-operation with one another, and sometimes jointly in a team. The need to work togothor, fosters sociability; a trait which society desires to be developed in its children.

The Montessori approach is for the maximal autonomy to the child, yet, this autonomy cannot exceed the limit of collective interest; the child would always be taught to do nothing which may offend or annoy others. The Montessori school aims at helping the child develop into an adult who is comfortable with himself, with his work and with the people with whom he would be working. Thus, the Montessori methods cannot overlook sociability as an objective to be achieved.

Excursion is also a device under the Montessori method to make the children learn. But when children are taken to a new city, there they get a chance to see a lot of new people, may be living with different styles, and having clothes and language of a different sort. This helps the children to adjust to differences, and widen the vistas of their knowledge, and, indirectly it also helps children in growing more sociable.

Children are made to march in co-ordination with one another, to sing together in unison, perform dramatic and domestic plays; they share in block-building and in the use of tricycles and seesaws. Thus, a peerage bond is strengthened. The widening circle of human contacts makes the child more sociable. A shy or lonely child may not learn so much as one who can learn anything from anyone and who does not feel shy in asking anything of anyone that his curiosity may prompt him to do. Of course, even sociable children also sometimes may busy themselves in isolation with some such plays or activities which are good for learning or development. But a lot of individual help is desired to be given by the teacher concerned in a Montessori house where a child is shy, aggressive or gloomy. If timely measures are not taken, a child may not be weaned out of egocentrism, and, may grow excessively a day-dreamer, or even schizophrenic.

The children should be made to realise what a fun it is to perform shared work and friendship. Children, by nature, observe one another working or playing; and also, one teaches the other—this also helps in bringing one closer to another, and sociability is fostered. The teacher is expected to play a helping role in such a development. A "genuinely loving, tolerant, gracious, intellectually curious, and in harmony with life" teacher would prove to be a very effective factor in children growing sociable.

Parents are always the "compelling models" for the child in earning language, imbibing beliefs, idiosyncrasies and values, and a lot of social traits which are so important in the development of sociability in the child. But where the children are not lucky enough to get congenial social milieu at home, the school is expected to make good the loss caused because of deprivation.

Again, parents are the "compelling models" in instilling "religious fervour" in the children. It is the home environment which may cause pious feelings to be aroused since the early, highly impressionable years of childhood.

8. Again, parents are the "compelling models" in instilling "religious fervour" in the children. It is the home environment which may cause pious feelings to be aroused since the early, highly impressionable years of childhood. Biographies of many old time great personalities, verify this fact—in most cases we get to read that the spiritual excellence of them was because of their devout mothers.

The significance of religion should be explicit in the ability to distinguish evil from good. The Montessori house prepares the child for self-discipline so that he can "regulate his own conduct". The various activities in the house, help in the development of such a conduct. We may agree or not, Madame Maria is of the firm conviction that mere exposure to some environments may lead to complex learnings. Even the extra-ordinarily beautiful picture of 'Madonna della Seggiola' made by Raphael, may leave "a religious impression" as a result of

For the regulation of one's conduct, Montessori gives more importance to "internal source" rather than to "external forces."

constant companionship with it. The Madame desired some such pictures to be hung in the house, which may awake religious fervour through an impression of the beauty and piety of the universe being created by them. This is so in spite of the fact that children can hardly interpret the symbolic significance of such pictures.

Again, for the regulation of one's conduct, Montessori gives more importance to "internal source" rather than to "external forces"; so, the real punishment of a normal man is "the loss of consciousness of that individual power and greatness which are the sources of his inner life". The educational philosophy of Madame Montessori stems from her "deeply religious orientation to life". Education, as Madame takes it to be, prepares an individual not merely for temporal achievements but for the revelation "of his own triumphant inner force".

To sum up, we can say that Madame Montessori has given the highest importance to the sensorimotor experience as the corner-stone of all learnings:

- for her the early experiences are of utmost importance;
- she is of the conviction that "learning proceeds first by perceiving objects and then by undertaking motor activities in relation to the objects";
- her education is the education of senses; and the graded "didactic materials" being used in her houses, are for the "refinement of differential perception of stimuli";
- there is no lock-step system in a Montessori house; the child is free to choose the materials and items of learning; no break-up of education into classes for children in the age group of three to six years;
- her conviction is that the enrichment of early experience during the pre-school period, may serve as an antidote to cultural deprivation; it underlines the importance of the organism's informational interactions with the environment.

In the end of this last part of the chapter to quote a few lines from a publication of the Association for Childhood Education International, may further help in understanding the epochal contribution of Madame Maria Montessori to pedagogy:

"We want to have children get to know everyday phenomena in many first hand sensory ways to question thoughtfully and think for themselves. They need to enjoy the satisfactions of problem solving and learning-skills, lest they stop seeking. They also need to express their feelings and sense of self through dramatic play, dance, graphic art, literature. We want to help children to begin to symbolise ideas with pictures and signs as well as with spoken words we want to cultivate in them, a delight in language used playfully and imaginatively, in ways other than just labelling or demanding. We want them to have fun as they play, since play is a young child's natural way of working."

REVIEW QUESTIONS

***Q*.1.** What is the need and importance of the preschool education? Give your own views regarding the opinion of Mabel M Mitchell about it.

***Q*.2.** Piaget opines that only richly varied early experience can provide "an ample array of preliminary schemata." In this reference both Montessori and Piaget give importance to environment, describe how they differ in one particular aspect.

***Q*.3.** Madame Maria Montessori has narrated eight things as essential for the development of a child; and the same are also the objectives of education for the children. Name the same, and, elaborate each point.

***Q*.4.** Madame Montessori writes "with my methods the teacher teaches little and observes much."

Why, according to Madame Montessori, the teacher needs to teach less? And what is there to be observed, and what for?

***Q*.5.** The Montessori approach aims at introducing the child to the world of reality as he happens to be too much absorbed into a world of phantasies.

How has she proposed to achieve such an aim?

***Q*.6.** The term "feed-back loop" has been used in the chapter, expand the idea contained there in.

***Q*.7.** A child likes to play with different materials, what importance has such a play got in the scheme of Montessori education?

CHAPTER 21

THEORIES AND PRACTICES IN EDUCATION — JEAN PIAGET

Chapter Outline

- **Intelligence**
- **Memory has Two Components: Figurative and Operative**
- **Psychological Growth and the Teacher**
- **Development and Learning**
- **Review Questions**

The significance of the contributions of Piaget has been likened to a bomb in intensity as well as in the area of effect. During the last fifty years, there has hardly been any attempt to develop curriculum for pre-school and early school children which has not been affected by or, rather, has not drawn heavily upon the notions of Piaget. Great are the implications of Piaget's ideas so far the enrichment of early childhood education is concerned. Carol Honstead has highlighted his contribution in this regard: "The emphasis on enriched experiences in early years of life has resulted in governmental programmes such as Operation Head Start, and, other educational efforts for young disadvantaged children, and a general increase of interest in intellectual activities in pre-schools and elementary schools. Piagetian theory, the primary impetus to all this action, will be of special interest to educators of young children."

Piaget's long clinical observations of children, mostly longitudinal, and his theorising of the cognitive or intellectual development of the child, have great educational implications which may be put as under:

- Education is for guiding children towards higher levels of learnings.
- Experiences mature in learnings.
- Social and physical environments provide experiences, so programming environments is very significant for the enrichment of experiences of the desired nature.

- Learnings only take place when the new experiences are related to the old ones, and appear as further development of the former.
- "Crucial learnings take place during the first six to eight years of life"—hence this period of life is very important for the intellectual development of the child.
- Cognitive or intellectual development occurs in a constant sequence; an attempt to teach a child something for which the proper stage of development has not yet been attained, stands little chance of success—a significant implication for the curriculum framers.
- The sequence of the stages of cognitive development, is related to the needs which an organism has as he advances in age.
- Learnings result in development which occurs in the form of the formation of structures or "schemata" (as Piaget calls them).
- 'Structures,' are the result of both sensorimotor and mental or cognitive activities.

To elaborate, in some detail, the ideas of Piaget as mentioned above, and which have very significant implications for education, will be very helpful in understanding Piaget's contribution to education.

Since birth, a child starts getting sensations. Sensations which have meanings for someone, are his perceptions. And, such sensations should be called experiences which have their effect on the mental or conative development of an organism.

Since birth, a child starts getting sensations. Sensations which have meanings for someone, are his perceptions. And, such sensations should be called experiences which have their effect on the mental or conative development of an organism. If development is the result of experiences which mainly are earned through overt or covert activities, and experiences are provided by the physical and social environment that a child is living in, then what is the function of education?

Education is a process which is meant to guide a child towards higher levels of learning. Piaget observes each child to be learning as his environment motivates him to indulge into some overt or covert activity. Education is for stimulating or programming the environment for more learning or for higher levels of learning. But Piaget has discovered a sequence of stages of cognitive development which those who are related to the education of the child, would do well to keep into consideration while selecting the items of learning or the points of teaching. Thus, very important has been the contribution of Piaget in the field of curriculum-making for the pre-school and early school children.

Education is a process which is meant to guide a child towards higher levels of learning.

So far the stages of sensorimotor period are concerned, the child develops cognitively or intellectually through a sequence of innately motivated activities. Piaget has divided this period, starting from birth till the end of second year, into six stages. This is the period when no formal education is possible, nor required. The next is the Pre-operational Period, ranging upto seven years. It is during this period when conceptual thoughts develop through a long process of perceptions beginning from the stage of fundamental ambiguity of sensory information, so well demonstrated by

Ames.[1] The ambiguity happens to be the result of momentary sensory information, and because of the subject's (child's) failure in taking other information into account. The teacher at a proper stage can provide different perspectives to the child for an accurate perception of an object.

Piaget affected the curriculum-framers immensely in deciding the items of information to be included for the education of the children of different age groups or at different levels of cognitive development, and also in deciding approaches and devices for children of different ages. The sequence of items and approaches are strictly in order of the intellectual or cognitive development of the child.

- After the age of five, a child is able to co-relate his previous knowledge with that of the present one, and so ideas may be built upon ideas by the teacher; writes A.L. Baldwin[2] "one of the important developments in the child's acquisition of conceptual thought is the gradual appearance of the effects of previous knowledge upon his thinking."
- Piaget and Lamberier concluded, "....some illusions that depend upon the distortion of momentary perceptions decline as the child becomes older and compensates for them through perceptual activity." During this period, the teacher would do well if he makes the child indulge in perceptual activities more and more.
- The automatically moving child towards conceptual invariance, that is, a change in place, in order or positions, does not affect the size of an object, may be helped by the school to have this conception developed earlier, and, in a clearer way through a number of experiments.
- Education as a process may be made greatly helpful in developing the child from the stage of sensorimotor adaptations towards more conceptual and cognitive types of adaptations, and the child develops new conceptual—intellectual ways to tackle problems. The long and continual observations of Piaget suggest ways and means to help the child do this.
- Again, it is during the early stages of Pre-operational Period that there develop mental images. These images represent specific external events in specific ways, and are different from visual imageries; as images do not have the generality of the imageries but are, rather, the internalised imitation of a sensorimotor action. It is reproducible over and over, though all the details are not represented in an image.

> After the age of five, a child is able to co-relate his previous knowledge with that of the present one, and so ideas may be built upon ideas by the teacher.

> Some illusions that depend upon the distortion of momentary perceptions decline as the child becomes older and compensates for them through perceptual activity.

> Child towards conceptual invariance, that is, a change in place, in order or positions, does not affect the size of an object, may be helped by the school to have this conception developed earlier.

> Images do not have the generality of the imageries but are, rather, the internalised imitation of a sensorimotor action. It is reproducible over and over, though all the details are not represented in an image.

1. JR A, Ames. *Visual Perception and the Rotating Trapezoidal Window*. Psychol. Monogr., 1951, 65, No. 7.
2. Baldwin, AL. *Theories of Child Development*.

If desirable sensorimotor activities are conducted under a well thought-out plan, such ideas would develop, strongly supported by images, that the intellectual development would be not only rapid but better also in all respects—"ideas build on ideas"; sensorimotor schemas are the foundations upon which perceptual and then conceptual schemas are built.

The most important development of the Pre-operational period, is the development of symbolic schemas—language is the climax of such a development.

The most important development of the Pre-operational Period, is the development of symbolic schemas—language is the climax of such a development. With the entrance of the child into the period of Pre-operations, there commences a stage when the child develops symbolic schemas very fastly.

But symbolic schemas are of two kinds—non-verbal and verbal.

But symbolic schemas are of two kinds—non-verbal and verbal. Non-verbal schemas are non-communicable, and are related to one's idiosyncrasies; they are mainly responsible for the emotional personality of an individual. Plays, dreams, reveries and others, represent one's symbolic schemas. Symbolic schemas of this first kind, affect a man's behaviour, and the interpersonal relations are affected because of the same.

Much guidance has been sought from the works of Piaget, not only in planning syllabi for academic classes but also, he may provide guidance in chalking out syllabi for plays at different age-levels. Piaget's book "Play, Dreams and Imitation" is a guide in this respect. The book illustrates through his observations that the plays of the child through successive chronological stages are the evidences of a child's psychoneurological development in the field of symbolic schemas. The stages of development, since the time the child is shortly to cross over to the period of Pre-operations, are as Projection of Symbolic Schemas onto new objects; projection of Imitative Schemas onto new Objects; simple identification of one object with another; Identification of child's body with that of other people or things; Simple Symbolic Combinations involving whole schemas instead of simple objects; Compensatory Combinations; the stages of plays for Catharsis, of liquidating combinations; and, with anticipatory symbolic contributions and so on.

The guardians or teachers who are interested in the development of the child in all fields, and especially in that of cognition or intelligence will do well if they select or provide plays for him in the order, and of nature considering the stages of natural development of the child.

The guardians or teachers who are interested in the development of the child in all fields, and especially in that of cognition or intelligence will do well if they select or provide plays for him in the order, and of nature considering the stages of natural development of the child.

Of immense importance is the stage when the child so rapidly goes on developing verbal schemas. The importance of verbal schemas in the development of concepts is second to none. Between the second and the fifth year, the child earns language with a marvellous speed—it shows how much developed he grows in verbal schemas. But, it is only later on that the words become definable, transmissible and constant; initially, they are the sounds which involve the whole range of sensorimotor actions done in connection with the object. For a child, about two years of age, "ball" involves throwing, grasping, bouncing, looking and so on. The school can play very effective role in conceptual development through helping in the formulation of verbal schemas. The faster the child formulates verbal sehemas, the faster he would be developing conceptually. For the formulation of verbal schemas, social environment is required, and the school can prove itself to be the best agency to provide a desirable social environment for the same. Piaget suggests that for the development of verbal schemas, many contextual situations can be provided by the school where the children get to listen words being used in connection with certain activities in which they themselves are involved.

The importance of verbal schemas in the development of concepts is second to none.

In his book "Play, Dreams and Imitation", Piaget gives the example of the use of the term 'slug' by Jacqueline to illustrate that a child upto the age of 4, cannot use a term as representative of a specific object of a class, for him it would be the same 'slug' everywhere, wherever it may be seen. Piaget speaks of the use of such terms as '**preconcepts**'. It is later on that the child genuinely achieves conceptual thinking, and he comes to know that a class cannot be pointed out.

It is during the latter stage of the period of Pre-operations that the child should be assisted in classifying objects when he has already started putting similar things into groups. As the child further develops into conceptual thinking, the teacher and other elders may ask such questions to him that he is engaged in more abstract discussion of classes and classifications. Now, the child can follow that a class "is a set of objects or events that has certain characteristics in common". The child can understand, and, have a better knowledge of his physical and social environment when he is asked to classify and label objects and events of his environments.

The child may be led to discuss relationships among classes. The child can now think with some logic, and, in abstract how a sub-class has characteristics in addition to the defining characteristics of a class. At a further stage, the child starts grasping the "**relationship of implication**"; and when the child is told "this object is metallic", he understands that the statement implies "this object conducts electricity". It is during the final period of cognitive development that the child starts mastering the more complex relationships among classes; it is the period of formal logic, and Piaget has described it as the period of Formal Operations.

These stages are constant so far their sequence is concerned, and, it is very important for curricula-framers and teachers to select and set the items of teaching accordingly.

The pre-school child cannot think how an event would seem to be from different points of view; it is not possible until the child has developed from the stage of sensorimotor or perceptual schemas, to that of the conceptual one. The role of the school, can be very important in freeing the child from the egocentrism of early childhood. For this, the teacher should ask him such questions as—"there is a plant with a lone flower growing on it; what would you feel if it falls down?" The child—"I shall be happy. "And, what would the gardener feel?" The child, "He would not be happy, he would be, rather, sad." Such questions may help the child develop cognitively and conatively that he can think over an event from different perspectives. This is also a way to help the child grow more social. Thus, the child will be able to distinguish between "the view of the object, and the properties of an object itself".

The pre-school child cannot think how an event would seem to be from different points of view; it is not possible until the child has developed from the stage of sensorimotor or perceptual schemas, to that of the conceptual one. The role of the school, can be very important in freeing the child from the egocentrism of early childhood.

Piaget labels the latter Pre-operational period, that is, the stage from 4 to 7 years as intuitive stage. Baldwin writes, "During this stage, the child acquires a mode of dealing with many of the problems of integrating different view-points and information from different sources." Again, it is implied here for those who are practising education, that the approach of the teacher should be such that he may lead the student to integrate information from different sources. The stage has been called 'intuitive' because sometimes, a solution to the problem is found with no clear conceptual representation. The example of three beads strung to a wire was an experiment to verify the fact that sometimes solution to a problem is found intuitively.

Generally, after 11, the child enters the period of Concrete and Formal Operations. The period has been so called by Piaget because it is the period when the child (shortly to grow as an adolescent) starts thinking operationally in a consistent way "—the stable, equilibrated type of thinking results from the organisation of operational thoughts into inter-related systems". Thus, according to Piaget, the period of "Concrete and Formal Operations" is characterised by stable thinking; and thinking can only be stable when it is equilibrated, that is, when proper accommodation has taken place, and the child can behave in a perfect logical fashion.

Piaget suggests that this is the stage when education related to mathematical groups and grouping, can be imparted with much probability of success. The nine basic groupings as given by Piaget, show the logico-mathematical development during the adolescent period. This is the period when cognitive development attains its climax.

For an effective teaching, the teacher dealing with such adolescents should put such problems to the students for which they should now be expected to be able to tackle successfully.

For an effective teaching, the teacher dealing with such adolescents should put such problems to the students for which they should now be expected to be able to tackle successfully. The teacher should begin with the preliminary grouping of equalities, and, proceed further gradually through secondary additive and bi-univocal multiplication of classes to co-univocal multiplication of relations. Thus, the reasoning of students can be enhanced to the maximum possible level of development. Piaget suggests that to help achieve the maximum in a still shorter period, and, in a better way, the teacher should make the students solve a number of such exercises which may activate their reasoning faculties in search of finding relationships in different situations. Such exercises should require "the ability to think of all the possible kinds of relationships that can exist among events ....". All this would help in further developing combinatorial thinking. The objective of the teacher should be to enable his taughts, but only those who are, generally, in the plus 11 age group—to review all the choices in a system so that they may be able to go through them sequentially, and exhaust all possibilities.

Again, Piaget would like to make categorical suggestion by dint of his minute observations that no attempt should be made to make the child acquire the concept of conservation of volume until the period of Formal Operation The conception of the conservation of mass, of weight and of quantity, of course, he would have acquired earlier—volume involves both density and quantity; a kind of balance between the two.

Piaget would like to make categorical suggestion by dint of his minute observations that no attempt should be made to make the child acquire the concept of conservation of volume until the period of Formal Operation.

It is during the last period of cognitive development, that is, the period of formal operations, that the adolescent acquires the ability for formal logic. It is the period for logical operations. He can assess the validity of the logical relationship between two statements. An adolescent developed to this stage, can search for instances which may suit the statement.

The teacher teaching such adolescents, should put such questions, the solutions of which demand logical thinking, leading to such logical conclusions which may make clear the relationship between each two statements or among more statements related to one another.

Inhelder and Piaget put a number of problems to the students to test the capability of their logical thinking as well as to improve the same. The students were asked to formulate and test hypotheses regarding a number of possible factors pertaining to different events or developments. Such an experiment has been reported in one of their volumes. In the experiment, the student Dei, aged 16; 10 could appreciate the relationship among three variables—weight, material and length of the rod. Her hypothesis also included form of the rod as a possible factor. She was asked to test her hypothesis. The way she conducted her experiment, made her understanding of various logical relationships explicit—such an understanding marks the period of Formal Operations; and a teacher should do all that is possible to further develop such understanding through presenting situational problems before the students which demand logical thinking for their solutions.

During the period, the teacher should engage his students to experiment with gravity, volume and weight as variables so that there may grow a proper logical understanding of the relationship among different variables.

INTELLIGENCE

For Piaget, intelligence is both an open as well as a closed system. It is open in the sense that it goes on developing as it reacts to the environment—"intelligence derives knowledge from the environment". So, for the development of knowledge, the school should provide such an environment that to derive knowledge from which the child possesses readiness, both physical and cognitive. It is a closed system as "intelligence incorporates environmental attributes into its existing structures". There are two basic functions of intelligence (1) adaptation, and (2) organisation. These are functional invariant.

For Piaget, intelligence is both an open as well as a closed system. It is open in the sense that it goes on developing as it reacts to the environment—"intelligence derives knowledge from the environment". So, for the development of knowledge, the school should provide such an environment that to derive knowledge from which the child possesses readiness, both physical and cognitive. It is a closed system as "intelligence incorporates environmental attributes into its existing structures".

Piaget writes[3] "... intelligence is an adaptation ... life is a continuous creation of increasingly complex forms and a progressive balancing of these forms with the environment. To say that intelligence is a particular instance of biological adaptation is thus to suppose that it is essentially an organisation and that its function is to structure the universe just as the organism structures its immediate environment."

The role of the teacher may be very important in the creation of increasingly complex forms, by way of putting problematic questions for the better understanding of the environment and for the perfect formulation of structures. Sometimes, balancing of structures or forms may need external assistance which a teacher may provide. This assistance may be provided by the teacher through probing questions or through providing clues, or supporting with examples or illustrations.

One very important conviction of Piaget, regarding assimilation, adaptation and accommodation or the restoration of equilibrium is that "Accommodation, then, is the accommodation of old experiences to new, while assimilation is the assimilating of new experiences into the old ones" (as William so explains the ideas of Piaget in his book *Introduction to the Psychology of Learning*). Years back, Herbert Spencer had introduced a very important term—"apperception mass" in pedagogy. "Apperception mass" is a term which expresses "old experiences". New experiences can only be assimilated in a way that again a state of equilibration is restored. This can be possible only if they are properly related to the old ones. Piaget speaks of correlating ideas upon ideas, of correlating new ideas with the old ones.

"It is in this sense that intelligence, whose logical operations constitute a mobile and at the same time permanent equilibrium between the universe and thought, is an extension and a perfection of all adaptive processes."[4]

"It is in this sense that intelligence, whose logical operations constitute a mobile and at the same time permanent equilibrium between the universe and thought, is an extension and a perfection of all adaptive processes."

3. Piaget, Jean. *The Origins of Intelligence in Children*, 1952.
4. Piaget, Jean. *Psychology of Intelligence*, 1950, p-9.

MEMORY HAS TWO COMPONENTS: FIGURATIVE AND OPERATIVE

Piaget theorises—"Then the most likely hypothesis is that the memory code itself depends on the subject's operations and therefore this code is modified during development, and depends at any given moment on the subject's operational level." (Jean Piaget[5]).

Memory does not represent merely mental images being reproduced through a system of coding and decoding. Memory is not consisted of mere copies of internal and external realities. Memory is affected by the operational level of the subject, or it is modified along with the development of the subject.

This fact is very significant for the teacher; his expectation from the student will be more realistic; and he can contribute towards the modification of his taught's memory by way of doing something for the cognitive development of his taught. Thus, memory ceased to be considered as a mere retention of matter. "The material retained improves with time as far as recall is concerned because operations have progressively developed."[6] On page 4 of his book *On the Development of Memory and Identity* Jean Piaget writes—"What the subject retains is not the perceptual model as such, but the way in which he assimilated it to his operational schemata, in terms of the operational level of each individual subject". The teacher needs to see that the way of assimilation is such that better retention may occur in respect of clarity, exactness and period of retention.

On page 14, in his book *On the Development of Memory and Identity* Jean Piaget writes: "..... The figurative component, which is perceptual in the case of recognition, imperative in the case of reconstruction, and mental imagery in the case of the memory images necessary for evocation. The other is the operative component, which consists of action.... 'schemas' or representative schemas." (either Pre-operational or Operational, 1968).

The memory has two components—the figurative and the operative. The three functions are possible because of the figurative component of memory—1. Perceptual, 2. Imitative and 3. Evocative. The recognition is possible because of the perceptual component of the figurative memory. One can recognise a thing only when the same has been perceived previously by him. One can imitate something because of the figurative component of the memory. When a teacher makes a child describe something orally or in writing that he has perceived previously, he reconstructs it; it becomes possible because of the imitative function of the figurative component of memory. Feelings arise related to some event of the past, again because

> Piaget theorises—"Then the most likely hypothesis is that the memory code itself depends on the subject's operations and therefore this code is modified during development, and depends at any given moment on the subject's operational level." (Jean Piaget).

> "The material retained improves with time as far as recall is concerned because operations have progressively developed."

> "..... The figurative component, which is perceptual in the case of recognition, imperative in the case of reconstruction, and mental imagery in the case of the memory images necessary for evocation Jean Piaget."

5. *On the Development of Memory and Identity.*
6. Sahakian, S William. *Introduction to the Psychology of Learning*.

of the figurative component of the memory; it is evocative function of the component. The other component of memory is operative; it consists of 'schemas' or 'schemata' which are the result of actions. The 'schemas' may be representative of past actions. The period concerned may be Operational or the Pre-operational one.

PSYCHOLOGICAL GROWTH AND THE TEACHER

Psychological development is a process which continues with 'equilibrium' as its goal; development is 'progressive equilibrium'.

'Mental equilibrium is possible only when the 'mental structure' or 'schema' has fully been developed in relation to some activity, and through the performance of that activity.

Of course, psychological growth parallels with physical growth, it commences with birth and continues till full maturity in adulthood. Psychological development is a process which continues with 'equilibrium' as its goal; development is 'progressive equilibrium'. Learning is an activity to which a school is formally related. 'Learning is an activity directed towards equilibrium'. Mental equilibrium is a 'mobile equilibrium', and not a static one. The process towards mental equilibrium is enhanced because of learning that a school provides through different activities. The end, both of learning, and that of the processes of psychological development is '**adaptation**' which happens to be consisted of '**assimilation**' and '**accommodation**'. '**Assimilation**' is 'taking in' and '**accommodation**' is the change that has been required to be done in the environment so that the organism may find himself fully adapted to the changed milieu. Learning is a process initiated through some activity, through such an activity which brings about some change in behaviour. JP Guilford defines learning as 'a change in behaviour resulting from behaviour'. It is the behaviour of the teacher, and as a result of its impact upon the behaviour that of the taught, a change comes about, and it is learning. Piaget would like to put the same in the words that the activity of learning helps in bringing about 'mental equilibrium', 'Mental equilibrium is possible only when the 'mental structure' or 'schema' has fully been developed in relation to some activity, and through the performance of that activity.

So, for learning, activity is a must; this is why John Holt writes, "In short, the school should be a sort of smor-gas-bord of intellectual, artistic, creative and athletic activities, from which each child could get whatever he wanted; or as much as he wanted, or as little."

DEVELOPMENT AND LEARNING

There are mainly two views regarding the process of development. The one is that development is the result of the 'unfolding of the growth process'. Prediction is possible if development is the result of maturational process. But the behaviour of an organism cannot be fully explained if we view development as a process of continuous growth linking different stages as the previous ones leading to the next one. Learning has its impact too, and it is quite important.

The realisation of learning as an important variable in the process of development led some to formulate an alternative view of development according to which 'child's development is essentially the accumulation of the learning'. According to this view, development in behaviour is the result of experiences that the environment provides. Learning is always acquired from experiences. The purely maturational view cannot recognise the impact of learning in the process of development. The behaviourists, of course, recognise the importance of learning in the modification of behaviour.

But Piaget formulated a third view as he found both the above mentioned views to be incomplete in defining the process of development. To this third kind of developmental process, he has termed 'equilibration'. Piaget's theory is not merely an amalgamation of the two; he has rather exposed the limitation of each of them in describing in full the development of a child. When he describes the cognitive development of the child, he seems more to be criticising learning as a sole factor affecting the process of development. He has described the development of the concept of class, of the object conception, or conservation of quantity etc. relating the same to different chronological stages.

Piaget objects to the theory of learning, it being passive when learning is taken to be imposing some habit without allowing the organism to be active in the process. His belief is that the child is always active; he is active in relation to his environment—to adapt to it through accommodation; and in relation to the drives related to his inner needs. His being thus active, or his own activity results in a concatenation of experiences. And, the end result, as Piaget has termed it, is equilibration. New experiences are merged into the existing operational groupings, and each time a developed operational organisation emerges, characterised by full equilibration. The schemata go on being organised into more and more developed operational groupings as a result of an organism's being always active in relation to his social environment, and, to his own empirical experiences.

Piaget objects to the theory of learning, it being passive when learning is taken to be imposing some habit without allowing the organism to be active in the process.

The school provides such a social environment where direct teaching of experiences acquired by others, is conducted. AL Baldwin writes, "The combination of the social learning and its empirical effectiveness could account for the acquisition of the belief system." Very little is taught directly in the wider society outside the school, and a huge amount of learning is the result of empirical experiences. Organisation of operational groupings characterised by equilibration, indicates development; such a development cannot be defined merely by the first view of development, that is, the 'maturational', nor merely by the second, that is, 'accumulation of experiences'. Of course, Piaget recognises the importance of maturity for

"The combination of the social learning and its empirical effectiveness could account for the acquisition of the belief system." Very little is taught directly in the wider society outside the school, and a huge amount of learning is the result of empirical experiences.

cognitive development too, and, accepts the role of learning in the process of development, but his belief is that for development equilibration is must. The maturity enables the child for social and empirical learning; but they both serve as variables in the process of development only when equilibration is there.

Equilibration is a state of development when a child has risen from a state of incoherence, irrelevance, as the behaviour of the child up to the state of Pre-operational, is more often characterised by. The behaviour of the child, his beliefs, all is marked by contradictions till equilibration is there. Harmonious behaviour, and a coherent system of beliefs, are the evidence of the presence of equilibration, of a state of well-organised operational system or a system of beliefs. To Piaget, as to a number of other psychologists, a child is active, even apparently, when he seems to be only receptive—a feeling child or a thinking child is also an active child, and such an activity too, furthers the process of development.

Equilibration is a state of development when a child has risen from a state of incoherence, irrelevance.

Equilibration also needs to be developed in face of differences evidenced in the behaviour of other or in their points of view. The result is always, conflict in the behaviour and belief of the child confronting such a situation. But human nature is such, each state of conflict makes the child active in such a way that the final outcome is a reorganised operational system of beliefs, which is 'coherent, harmonious, and equilibrated'.

Thus, Piaget's hypothesis for explaining the process of development contains the following four kinds of forces:

1. Maturational.
2. Experiences acquired through reactions to the environment and to one's own inner urges.
3. Teaching to the child by the school teacher or by other people of the social environment; it includes both the explicit and the implicit teachings.
4. The process of equilibration.

Piaget's hypothesis for explaining the process of development contains the following four kinds of forces:
1. Maturational
2. Experiences acquired through reactions to the environment and to one's own inner urges.
3. Teaching to the child by the school teacher or by other people of the social environment; it includes both the explicit and the implicit teachings.
4. The process of equilibration.

We, the teachers, are part of the third force as mentioned here. The teachers must not forget that for teaching the concept of invariance of physical objects, they will have to wait till the child has matured to the level of Concrete Operations. But we cannot expect the child to have acquired the concept of invariance of an object merely by attaining the age of 7 or more—it is by dint of experiences acquired by the child as a reaction to his environment that a matured child may develop the concept of object-invariance. And, the teaching may serve to help acquire such an experience directly or through the organisation of some experiment. But no coherent system of beliefs (or operational system) can develop till contradictions are reconciled through a self-initiated, natural system of equilibration.

Thus, we can say that no other theory of development has so much emphasised the importance of the organisation of knowledge; and, has tackled the question of organising information with such clarity as Piaget has done. His theory of equilibration may not be adequate, but it, at least, points to the problem of the acquisition of the organised knowledge.

REVIEW QUESTIONS

***Q*.1.** Fill in the Blanks

(*i*) The most important guidance from Piaget related to education, is in regard to .....

(*ii*) Piaget puts emphasis on e ..... e ..... in early years of life.

(*iii*) According to Jean Piaget, the objective of education is leading children towards ..... of learnings.

(*iv*) Experiences mature in .....

(*v*) ..... are the results of both sensorimotor and mental or cognitive activities.

(*vi*) Cognitive or intellectual development occurs in a ..... sequence.

(*vii*) Learnings result in the development which occurs in the form of the formation of .....

(*viii*) Crucial learnings take place during the first ..... to ..... years of life.

(*ix*) Learning can only occur when the ..... experiences are integrated into the ..... ones.

(*x*) It is during the last period of cognitive development that the adolescent acquires the ability for f ..... l ....

***Q*.2.** Piaget suggests that this is the stage when education related to mathematical groups and groupings, can be imparted with much probability of success. Describe the stage, referred to here, and also what is meant by mathematical groups and groupings.

***Q*.3.** "Memory has two components."
What are they, describe each in detail.

***Q*.4.** For Piaget, intelligence is both an open as well as a closed system. Discuss.

***Q*.5.** On the left side are given items of teaching, you are to write, on the right, the names of the period of Piagetian cognitive development, when each of these items, ought to be taught:

Item of Teaching	*Piagetian Developmental Period*
(*i*) Making structures with plastic blocks of different shapes and sizes.	

(*ii*) Asking to tell names of items shown for a short view then covered from sight.

(*iii*) To compare the mass of two liquids both of which were first poured in plates of equal size and shape, but later, liquid from one of them, was poured into a beaker.

(*iv*) Now the child can realize how his work would affect others.

(*v*) It is only now that the child suddenly feels through the solution of a problem.

(*vi*) An event, or object sets in motion a series of thinking.

(*vii*) He (the child) thinks with some logical sequence, and the thought process becomes organised.

(*viii*) The child goes ahead by way of combining different pieces of information to come to new conclusions.

ANSWERS TO OBJECTIVE TYPE QUESTIONS

***Q*.1.** (*i*) curriculum, (*ii*) enriching environment, (*iii*) higher levels, (*iv*) learning, (*v*) Experiences, (*vi*) constant, (*vii*) schemas/schemata,
(*viii*) six to eight, (*ix*) past, present, (*x*) formal logic

***Q*.5.** (*i*) Sensorimotor-final stage/or early Pre-operational Period [2 to 4 years]
(*ii*) Sensorimotor-final stage/or, early Pre-operational Period [2 to 4 years]
(*iii*) Concrete-operational Period [7 to 11 years]
(*iv*) Pre-operational Period [2 to 7 years]
(*v*) Pre-operational Period [2 to 7 years]
(*vi*) Concrete-operational Period [7 to 11 years]
(*vii*) Concrete-operational Period [7 to 11 years]
(*viii*) Concrete-operational, or Period of Concrete Operations [7 to 11 years]

CHAPTER

22 IDEAS THAT I AM SEIZED WITH

Chapter Outline

- **Philosophical Background of Education**
- **How the Goal of Education Can be Achieved?**
- **Components of Education:**
  (*i*) The Teacher;
  (*ii*) The Learning Material;
  (*iii*) The Learning Situation.

The author started his teaching career when he was not even eighteen years old. It was a long professional journey of more than 42 years which ended with my superannuary retirement as a reader in a Government Institute of Higher Studies in Education where I served for the last mature years of my service career. Before that I had worked as a Head in some Secondary and Senior Secondary level schools. Thus, passing through a long period of teaching, monitoring or supervising educational—curricular and co-curricular activities, plus my penchant for reading books on education equipped me with certain ideas or rather convictions that had been prompting me to write on education.

After retirement, I was more free to think about society from a still wider perspective. The idea that something must be done for the good of the society, kept me goading, and this led me to work on two fronts—first, writing this book; and, second, starting a school wherein the solution of some of the problems that our society is suffering from, was expected to be lying. A few like-minded persons joined the team; persons who were of the view that seeking on, only benefits from the society, right from cradle till it is time when one is carried to the graveyard, is not the purpose of

> The idea that something must be done for the good of the society, kept me goading, and this led me to work on two fronts—first, writing this book; and, second, starting a school wherein the solution of some of the problems that our society is suffering from, was expected to be lying.

life; we can feel consolation that something has been done in life only when some selfless service has been rendered for the good of the society. It was felt that our Indian society was suffering from the three main problems—character-crisis, unemployment and illiteracy. Towards the solution of the first problem, the school was selected to be the most effective means. To help in the solution of the problem of unemployment, it is enshrined in the constitution of our Association that every year a camp for self-employment will be organised to impart training in some skill or branch of some vocation so that the unemployed may start his or her own job. And, it was also decided that our Association or Samiti would organise literacy camps to fight the problem of illiteracy.

A mention of all this has been made just by the way, as my working under the umbrella of our Association has provided me a field for working practically on my convictions, and, has been further enriching my educational thoughts.

Now, I am coming directly to my educational thoughts.

PHILOSOPHICAL BACKGROUND OF EDUCATION

What has ever been grieving me is the narrowing down of education to such an extent. The students, in general, set before them the passing of the examination as the only target for their educational pursuits; likewise, the objective before the teachers is only to enable them (the students) to get through. Given such a situation, the education has been narrowed down for the teacher to mere selecting of a few questions that seem to be likely to be set for the coming examination, and making students cram their answers. And, for the students, the only work is to cram the prepared answers of the same questions. The teacher, too, would like the students to do the same, and, would assist, or rather, make them do the same. The entire system of education is examination-ridden; the students always suffering from the acute examination fever.

Knowledge is no concern for a big majority of students, their only concern is to get a degree somehow or other with flying colours so that by dint of that they may get a decent—white collared job. But with the fast moving process of privatisation in India, and, an all-round trend of globalisation, competitiveness is growing so strong that only such candidates would be able to find a niche in the race who are really proficient for the job they are seeking to get—proficiency both theoretical and practical is required.

Information technology has gained, an over-riding importance in all fields of occupations, hence, proficiency in it has become an essential qualification for anyone who aspires for a good placement after the completion of education.

Now, I would like to consider the question of the objective of education in historical perspective. I would begin with what the ancient *rishis* or sagacious saints of India thought about education. For them, the education was a way for spiritual emancipation—"सा विद्या या विमुक्तये"—"only that is education which can enable one to free oneself from the temporal bondage (and achieve self-realisation)". The objective that a society or a country sets for its education, reflects the level and nature of its culture and civilisation. The Indian rishi were awakened to the fact that the only aim worth-aspiring for a human being was the attainment of self-realisation. This resulted in the main thrust of theirs being on spiritual upliftment.

What the ancient *rishis* or sagacious saints of India thought about education. For them, the education was a way for spiritual emancipation—"सा विद्या या निमुक्तये"

No spiritual upliftment is possible unless both the body and the soul attain the perfection that they are capable of. Plato, the great Greek philosopher has put this in words: "a good education consists in giving to the body and to the soul all the beauty and the perfection of which they are capable".[1]

Plato, "a good education consists in giving to the body and to the soul all the beauty and the perfection of which they are capable".

In ancient civilisations, education was taken as a process leading to the enlightenment of mankind. The process was bi-pronged, it was concerned to the upliftment of the individual while at the same time, the upliftment of the individual was to be judged in social perspective. Education should lead to self-realisation, and the self-realisation of the individual should always be in the interest of the society. In Athens, stress was given to that aspect of education which might prepare individuals for good citizenship. The Spartan society was under a constant strain of warfare, so militarism was declared there to be the goal of education. The Hebrew civilisation being of a different sort, there the fundamentals of ethics along with the rituals got stress in the system of education.

Situations for the Romans were such that they took a more practical view of education. Warfare leading to a cycle of victories and reverses, made them abhor speculative philosophy, and they aimed at making education a system which could produce such people who would not be disheartened by reverses; and so, they wanted temperate and moderate habits to be inculcated among their people, and equanimity was the quality that was highly appreciated in one's character. The need of the Roman society was the production of such people who would sacrifice everything for their fatherland; and so, it was through education that they attempted to inculcate the feelings of sacrifice for one's fatherland. Quintelian best represents the Roman ideals of character and education. He was of the conviction that only such education could do good to the society which had practical

The Romans aimed at making education a system which could produce such people who would not be disheartened by reverses; and so, they wanted temperate and moderate habits to be inculcated among their people, and equanimity was the quality that was highly appreciated in one's character.

1. Mayer Frederick. *A History of Educational Thought.*

Quintelian considered early education to be very important. He was against corporal punishment, and pleaded for positive rewards for leading children to good practices.

utility for its people. For the development of the child, he considered early education to be very important. He was against corporal punishment, and pleaded for positive rewards for leading children to good practices.

Education and religion remained inseparable. All the great teachers of different religions have given serious thought to the systems and contents of education. For the vedic rishi theological knowledge was most important. For them such an education was useful which helped the individual in enhancing his control over the self as well as over the nature around him. According to the old-time Indian thinkers, real education was not possible without 'obliteration and absorption of the self in a larger unity.' Buddhism taught, and, as also did the *sankhya* philosophers that real education must lead the individual to the 'detached intellectual love of God'. The life of spirit was to be superior to the life of senses. The *Upanishads* taught the same thing. Though in the system of education the needs of the contemporary society were considered. Earlier than this, the vedic rishi taught how this universe came into being, what forces were at work behind the vast varieties that were there in the fields of flora and fauna, as well as in regard to metals and other non-living things. Besides all this, education related itself to health and medicine, to weaponry—their making and use; architecture and so on. Thus, education aimed at uplifting man from the level of mere senses, to that of spiritual level so that the way to "emancipation" may open itself for him; but, at the same time, it prepared individuals in such a way that they might contribute as useful members of their society.

The Jainism teaches three *Ratnas*—right knowledge (the knowledge of reality without doubt or error), the right faith (as an essential preliminary for right knowledge; the *Gita* teaches—"श्रद्धावान् लभते ज्ञानम्") and right conduct it consists in controlling the passions, the senses, the thoughts, the speech and action so as to cultivate an attitude of "neutrality without desire or aversion towards objects of the external world."

The Jainism teaches three *Ratnas*—right knowledge (the knowledge of reality without doubt or error), the right faith (as an essential preliminary for right knowledge; the *Gita* teaches—"श्रद्धावान् लभते ज्ञानम्") and right conduct-it consists in controlling the passions, the senses, the thoughts, the speech and action so as to cultivate an attitude of "neutrality without desire or aversion towards objects of the external world."[2] If education works for the achievement of these three Ratnas, it would be a perfect education.

Lord Buddha bids—"Go forth on a journey that shall be for the good of many and for their happiness. Go forth in compassion towards the world".

The Buddhistic monastery would impart education 'for the good of many', that is 'Shivam' or 'Bliss'; 'for their happiness' that is, 'sundaram' or 'Beauty'. And, as Keats declared centuries later 'Beauty is Truth; Truth, Beauty', so this idea flashed to my mind that a complete or ideal education is that which works for truth, Bliss and Beauty (*—Satyam, Shivam and Sundaram*); I shall elaborate on this idea later on.

2. *Religion*. An unpublished work of the author.

Some six hundred years before Christ, Confucius preaches a religion based on the following five maxims:

(*i*) Love for all, goodness of behaviour towards all.

(*ii*) Restraint over verbal and non-verbal behaviour, bewaring of self-praise.

(*iii*) Stress on good family, and social relationship.

(*iv*) State must have the confidence of the people in it.

(*v*) Man must cultivate fine arts in his life, such as, music, drawing and painting, poetry and the other cultural pursuits.

Confucius preaches religion based on the following five maxims: (*i*) Love for all, goodness of behaviour towards all. (*ii*) Restraint over verbal and nonverbal behaviour, bewaring of self-praise. (*iii*) Stress on good family, and social relationship. (*iv*) State must have the confidence of the people in it. (*v*) Man must cultivate fine arts in his life, such as, music, drawing and painting, poetry and the other cultural pursuits.

Now, education is the only means to achieve it; this is why all religious gurus or teachers, social reformers or political leaders have always shown so much concern for education, and, have even worked for its reform. But I feel, broadly speaking, these five maxims of Confucius may also be seen including the three constant ideals of life—*Satyam, Shivam, Sundaram*, that is, the **Truth**, the **Bliss** (or the good) and the **Beauty**, in them.

The Zend Avesta, the scripture of the Zorastrians, stresses on the right choice. Again, that choice should be considered to be **Right** which fulfils the three ideals of life, that is the *satyam*, the *shivam*, the *Sundaram*.

For Lord Christ, real religion and real education were identical.

For Lord Christ, real religion and real education were identical. He stressed upon the blossoming of the child to reality. His methods for teaching the Truth to the people was through innumerable parables. The universe was His Text book; His classroom was the open field and the marketplace. Pascal, during the Renaissance made the people realise—"The heart has Reason that Reason does not know". Again, I feel the teachings of Lord Christ includes all the three supreme ideals of life "*Satyam, Shivam, Sundaram*".

Sri Rama Krishna Paramahansa, during the nineteenth century taught that education must be for enlightenment. For him the rule of Love was more important than the rule of knowledge. His disciple Vivekananda taught that the essence of education was "service to mankind". He considered knowledge to be essential for achieving the real meaning of life. For him Activity and Love were equally important for the achievement of the purpose of life.

Sri Rama Krishna Paramahansa, during the nineteenth century taught that education must be for enlightenment. For him the rule of Love was more important than the rule of knowledge. His disciple Vivekananda taught that the essence of education was "service to mankind". He considered knowledge to be essential for achieving the real meaning of life. For him Activity and Love were equally important for the achievement of the purpose of life.

With this, rather a philosophical preface, I would come to deal with *Satyam, Shivam, Sundaram* as the ideals of life, as well as the ideals of education. Again, though this dealing of mine would be something philosophic, yet soon after that I would elaborate upon the methods, devices and approaches as how to achieve these ideals—and for doing this I shall have to depend upon educational psychology as it has been appealing me, and, as I have been practising it through my life-long educational career.

Satyam, Shivam, Sundaram—the **Truth**, the **Bliss**, the **Beauty** are the three bases in reference to which all our activities should be conducted. The life is a long journey, a stage where the entire behaviour of homosapiens should be assessed in reference to these three aspects. These three aspects cover the entire life, or all the multifarious functions of humankind. If we look at the syllabi of different branches of learning, we shall find each to be linked to the one or to the other of these aspects of life. The varied branches of science deal with the truth of the physical environment. The social sciences are concerned with the truth related to social environment. These branches of studies are to impart knowledge about the Truth (*Satyam*) related to the universe where forces of nature are active in respect of the first, that is, physical environment; and the human beings, in respect of the latter, that is the social environment. Physics, Chemistry, Biology, Mathematics, and dozens of others developed from the same, such as Astronomy, Space Science, and even Information-Technology, Biochemistry, Medical and Engineering courses, with their varied branches. Veterinary science, Agriculture and Agronomy, and a number of specialities, all are related to the truths of physical environment, the *Satyam*. We read History, Political Science, Public Administration, Sociology, Economics and a lot of other such subjects related to social activities, to acquire knowledge or Truths pertaining to activities of human beings, in their social environment. Even Law is a subject developed for a better living, and is a branch of knowledge related to social environment. As a conception, it would be proper to say that all the subjects that we have been studying, and may have to study in future, enable us acquire the Truth—and the same should be an objective of an educational institution. Knowledge of the Truth, gives a unique power to a person; this is why there is a saying— 'Knowledge is power'. A knowledgeable person can do that, can achieve that which others cannot even think of doing because of their ignorance. Knowledge changes the personality of someone. Such a person being equipped with a particular sort of power, influences others in his own way; and can be of great use for himself, and more so for his society.

As a conception, it would be proper to say that all the subjects that we have been studying, and may have to study in future, enable us acquire the Truth—and the same should be an objective of an educational institution.

The old time rishi of India used to pray to God for leading them from untruth to Truth (असतो मा सद् गमय). Truth is very important, even, to achieve self-realisation.

Next comes the *Shivam*—The Bliss. To do such things which are good for the self as well as for all. This is more the behavioural aspect of life. The truth is cognitive aspect of life, and so is education, it must be directed by *Shivam*, that is, the *Truth* must lead one to behave in such a way which is good for the self, and good for all others also. *Shivam* is related to motive also, one should be motivated towards some behaviour with a feeling of doing good. Thus, it is also the conative aspect of behaviour.

Shivam—The Bliss. To do such things which are good for the self as well as for all. This is more the behavioural aspect of life. The truth is cognitive aspect of life, and so is education, it must be directed by *Shivam*, that is, the *Truth* must lead one to behave in such a way which is good for the self, and good for all others also. *Shivam* is related to motive also, one should be motivated towards some behaviour with a feeling of doing good.

But the rishi says that no behaviour can result in Bliss which is not based on **Truth**. What is untruth, can never be blissful. And, what is blissful can contain not even an iota of untruth. Philosophically considered, **Bliss** is the highest **Truth;** and the knowledge of **Truth** must result in **Bliss**; only such a knowledge should be considered as consisting of **Truth** which can lead to **Bliss**. **Truth** must be leading to **Bliss** both for the individual and for the society as well. Ravana in the *Ramayana* exemplifies the achievement of knowledge without bliss. The knowledge of Dr Faustus of Christopher Marlowe caused his ruin because it was divorced of bliss. Ours is an age of running after knowledge with a neck-break speed, but knowledge without **Bliss** as its result, can only be ruinous.

Equally important is **Beauty** as an ideal of a perfect life, as it is an aspect of a perfect education. Beauty, as an ideal of life is related to the pleasures that different objects of physical and social environments may yield. Keats declares 'Beauty is Truth; Truth, Beauty' and, 'A thing of Beauty is a Joy for ever'. In education we have an independent faculty of Fine Arts; it may consist of drawing-painting, music, dance and a lot others such as fabric-painting, and fashion-designing related to different fields. Beauty provides food to our emotions, and is so essential for our emotional health and development. Life will be dull and boring unless things of beauty, make it worth-living and enjoyable. A life devoid of joy, is a life devoid of **Bliss**, hence, the scheme of education must make man see beauty, hear beautiful tones, experience beauty in its varied forms. As the great romantic English poet declared, we can aver that Beauty and Truth are the two aspects of the same coin.

Equally important is **Beauty** as an ideal of a perfect life, as it is an aspect of a perfect education. Beauty as an ideal of life is related to the pleasures that different objects of physical and social environments may yield.

In education we have an independent faculty of Fine Arts; it may consist of drawing-painting, music, dance and a lot others such as fabric-painting, and fashion-designing related to different fields.

HOW THE GOAL OF EDUCATION CAN BE ACHIEVED?

So far, I have been concerned with the philosophical approach regarding my views as to what education should achieve; now I am to deal the practical side as to how the goal of education can be achieved. Hence, I shall have to seek support from psychology, which alone can tell what is practically possible to achieve, and how it can be done. Before coming to the methods, devices and techniques, I would like to mention the six things as required for the all round development of the child. In the Principal's chamber of the school, run by our Samiti, there is a big board displaying these six things with illustrations:

1. His happiness
2. His activities
3. A challenging situation
4. Encouragement
5. Guidance
6. Discipline.

Six things as required for the all round development of the child. 1. His happiness, 2. His activities, 3. A challenging situation, 4. Encouragement, 5. Guidance, and 6. Discipline.

Again, these six things are to show a psychologically sound approach to the education of a child. They are also related to the congeniality of the environment where an education as desired to achieve *Satyam, Shivam, Sundaram*, can possibly be imparted.

1. His happiness There can be no coerced or forced development. Development is possible only through activities that are indulged into willingly with a sense of happiness. This is why so much importance has been given to motivation, to teach a child who is not mentally prepared for his lesson is like hammering a cold iron, and such efforts are definitely to yield to failures. Years back, there was a period when education was considered something to be thrust upon a child forcibly even with the help of a rod.

Edwin R Guthrie writes: "We learn only what we do." And, doing something is a response which is elicited by some stimulus which the environment provides. And, if the response is not leading to some positive feeling, one would try to be away from such a response. No attention to such an activity would be there; again to quote Guthrie "A failure of attention, for instance, may prevent response."[3] The child would attend to such an activity only which yields satisfaction, which generates a feeling of happiness.

Edwin R Guthrie writes: "We learn only what we do." "A failure of attention, for instance, may prevent response."

The founder of the learning theory in the United States, Edward L Thorndike writes that an organism does nothing to avoid a 'satisfying state of affairs' and does nothing to preserve an 'annoying state of affairs.'[4] Thorndike's third principle of learning is the Law of Effect, about which he writes.

Edward L Thorndike writes that an organism does nothing to avoid a 'satisfying state of affairs' and does 'nothing to preserve an 'annoying state of affairs.'

"Of several responses made to the same situation, those which are accompanied by satisfaction to the animal, will, other things being equal, be more firmly connected with the situation, so that, when it recurs, they will be more likely to recur; those which are accompanied or closely followed by discomfort to the animal, will, other things being equal, have their connection with that situation weakened, so that when it recurs, they will be less likely to occur. The greater the satisfaction or discomfort, the greater the strengthening or weakening of the bond."[5]

The greater the satisfaction or discomfort, the greater the strengthening or weakening of the bond."

Thus, the psychologists of the bond learning theory averred that without a sense of satisfaction, no learning can occur. In our school, we are always careful that there should be nothing-neither the behaviour of the teacher, nor any physical factor which may make the child feel threatened or discomforted. This is why 'happiness' of the child has been displayed on our board, as our first motto. A state of 'set' can be possible when the activity of the child makes it happy. It would like to indulge in such an activity repeatedly, and, in as best a way as it can. Contrary to this, if the

3. Guthrie, Edwin R. *Association of Contiguity*, 1959, p. 179.
4. Thorndike, Edward L. *Man and His Work*, 1943.
5. Thorndike, Edward L. *Animal Intelligence Experimental Studies*, 1911, p. 244.

situation fails to generate a sense of security in the child, it would try to avoid such a situation. So, for learning or development—every learning is development in the wider sense of the term—the school should follow 'happiness' of the child as its guiding principle.

The *Gita* tells that we cannot live without activity; and a child is all the more active because of his age. Nature prods him to be superbly active as therein lies the way for his development. No activity, no development. Guthrie declares "We learn only what we do."

2. His activities The *Gita* tells that we cannot live without activity; and a child is all the more active because of his age. Nature prods him to be superbly active as therein lies the way for his development. No activity, no development (Fig. 22.1). Guthrie declares "We learn only what we do", that is, there can be no learning if there is no activity. Dewey theorised for learning the activity approach. And, Mahatma Gandhi propounded the Basic Education as a system of education wherein activity occupies the axial position through which all sorts of learning occurs. If a school attempts to keep its children inactive in the class wherein only the teacher is verbally active, almost throughout the period, the situation cannot be considered congenial for learning, and would prove, rather harmful, for development of children thus compelled to remain mum for longer durations, especially the children who are at the sensorimotor state of development; it would tantamount to punishment, and, deprivation of them from chances of development which a school is expected to provide through a number of activities for the school-children to be engaged in. This fact made the modern educationist John Holt remark: "In short, the school should be a sort of smor-gas-bord of intellectual, artistic, creative and athletic activities, from which each child could get whatever he wanted, or as much as he wanted or as little."

Figure 22.1 Co-curricular activities also facilitate development.

The sound educational principle for learning is that, more the number of senses are involved in the process of teaching and learning, the more learning for the taught will be there; and, more will be the retention of the matter that is being learnt. Only 20 per cent of what we hear, is retained in memory for a certain limit of time; 50 per cent of what we hear and see both; whereas 80 per cent of the sensory-experiences earned through the performance of some activity, are retained in the memory.

Again, I would like to quote Guthrie,[6] "teaching consists in inducing by one means or another some desired pattern of movement, whether of

6. Guthrie, ER. *Conditioning: A Theory of Learning in Terms of Stimulus Response and Association*. (1942).

Figure 22.2
Exposure to natural surroundings, makes congenial environment for development.

the whole body, of hand and eye, or of speech. The movement must be induced in the presence of the stimuli that we wish to make its cues or signals."

Thorndike also treats the principle or Law of Effect, operationally or objectively in terms of activity. So, that way we are not performing anything novel when we attempt in our school to concretise the class-lessons to the maximum possible extent with the purpose of involving at least both the senses of hearing and seeing of our kids—we make the maximum possible use of the blackboard or of the roll-up board, of the illustrations of various sorts, of drawings and so on—teaching of alphabets is performed, mostly, through the drawing work to begin with. Our efforts also happen to be to the effect of enabling our children see the things or items to be learnt, in reality; for this we, on and off, take our children to some outing programme; to some zoo or to some other natural environment; to some fort or exhibition. The process of teaching and learning is conducted through different games, activities or competitions that our children enjoy as play-items; and they are so motivated that they always try to put their best foot forward.

When there is no activity, the senses cannot be activated; no experience of the physical or social environment can be earned when the senses, the thresholds of experiences, are given no chance to become active. The more the sensory experiences are there, the more learning will be there. JP Guilford says that learning is "a change in behaviour resulting from behaviour". And, for the small kids, the behaviour of the teacher as a lecturer pouring forth ready-made information, does not constitute such a behaviour which should be expected to usher in desirable behavioural changes in the former.

John Holt (1964, 1972), Paul Goodman (1966), Edger, Z Friedenberg (1965), Charles Silberman and a number of others protested against the system of education which curbs the child's natural urge to know, to behave in a creative and original way. The remedy lies in providing a number of activities—physical and mental or artistic, towards which the children may naturally be attracted, and be absorbed in.

John Holt (1964, 1972), Paul Goodman (1966), Edger, Z Friedenberg (1965), Charles Silberman and a number of others protested against the system of education which curbs the child's natural urge to know, to behave in a creative and original way. The remedy lies in providing a number of activities—physical and mental or artistic, towards which the children may naturally be attracted, and be absorbed in. Their absorption in such activities would yield such varied experiences that the most effective learning, the desired learning would be the outcome.

The Project Method will ever be an effective one in the pedagogy as it engages the students in useful activities. It makes the students, first fix their target, then under the guidance of the teachers, they decide their modalities of approach, the devices and techniques are adumbrated, and finally there is launching upon the projects. Through a series of activities, enriching the cognitive aspect of the children, the target is achieved. But the project method can suit to the students studying at the level upper than the elementary one. The project method provides for practical education to which John Dewey declares as "Learning by doing." For such a learning, empirical approach best suits.

Figure 22.3 Let the children fully express their emotion of joy; it is in the interest of their development.

The work of the school is to provide such an environment which may make the children active—physically, mentally and emotionally. Children feel glorified when they learn a piece of information through their own activity. When, made to swallow dried-up, ready-made or second-hand information they feel themselves subjected to some wrong being practised by the elders. So, for a proper and adequate learning, voluntary involvement of children in activities that they feel to be their own, is must.

For proper and adequate learning, mere narrating of facts from the side of the teacher, is not enough. The teacher should, rather, make the students activated through asking questions and through providing congenial environment, tools, apparatus and so on, so that being highly motivated out of curiosity, they may indulge in their own discoveries. It is through activities only that the students may get a chance to think, to discuss or react physically and mentally both, to the demands of the situation. So, we can say, the more a child involves himself in activities, the more chances he stands for development.

Now, let us take an example, which I have already given in an article of mine. Suppose we want to teach our students the relationship between the pressure of air and its mass, at some constant temperature. One way to do this may be to tell the students verbally how the mass of air affects its pressure; while the other way is to make the students learn the relationship empirically through some activity or experiment. Needless to say, the latter would be better for learning.

It generally happens that a teacher makes a child write or read something which he has already done many times previously, too, that piece of academic activity loses attraction for the child, and such an activity cannot give the satisfaction of accomplishing something important or good.

3. Challenging situation If a child is made to indulge in an activity which poses no challenge of any sort; that is, it is such an activity which he has already performed independently in a proper way previously also, it would not motivate the child to do it still, or for going on doing it repeatedly. In such a case, the situation will be very dull and uninspiring. It generally happens that a teacher makes a child write or read something which he has already done many times previously too, that piece of academic activity loses attraction for the child, and such an activity cannot give the satisfaction of accomplishing something important or good. Generally, a teacher does so because some other students of the class are lagging behind, and, have not properly done that piece of curricular activity. What is advisable is to put the fast students to work/activity which is a bit harder to do. Only such a work or activity can motivate the child, and, make the child involve the best of himself, and such an involvement would highly be in the interest of the further development of the child.

A work or activity that appears to the child to be too easy or too difficult, would not motivate him to take it up.

A work or activity that appears to the child to be too easy or too difficult, would not motivate him to take it up. Put the child in such a situation where he feels the need of indulging himself into some activity which alone can lead him to the satisfaction of doing something useful, of doing something important. Whatever the point of knowledge the teacher teaches, should not be something ready-made, something being imparted from the side of the teacher when the student remains merely a passive receiver. Such a situation can pose no challenge of any sort for the taught. The teacher may intermittently be calling upon his taught to remain very attentive, but their attention cannot be had on the mere asking for the same. Attention will always be positively proportionate to the interest that a child feels in some activity. And, for a child to be interested in an activity, it is important that an element of challenge must be there for the child in the activity.

Figure 22.4 After climbing up the tree, the younger one is apprehensive, the challenge being too big for her; the elder one is celebrating the achievement.

Instead of imparting something of knowledge directly, the teacher would do well if he puts some problem before the students in the form of some question or some project, requiring study, discovery or experiment. It is only in such a way that the student may be motivated towards such an activity which may lead to the solution of the problem, or to the accomplishment of something which can yield satisfaction. The situation should be such which has "initially a high probability of evoking response." (William K Estes[7]). Among the 17 postulates of Clark L Hull, one is "Stimulus—intensity dynamism" (*V*)—a situation which has an element of challenge in it, further helps in increasing intensity of the stimulus. Of course, the role of "primary motivation or drive" (D), may be very important in furthering stimulus intensity. For a behaviour leading to learning, Woodworth et al[8], consider "objective situation" as an essential variable. As a behaviour aimed at "objective-situation", would always contain an element of challenge in it. A challenge tantamounts to a "definite goal", and makes the behaviour

7. Estes, WK. *Towards a Statistical Theory of Learning* (1950).
8. Woodworth, RS, Marquis, DG. *Psychology*, (1948), p. 224.

"purposive"; in another book[9] Woodworth writes "purposive behaviour has a definite goal or end, with means adopted to reach the goal".

4. Encouragement Encouragement is a sort of reinforcement, it serves as a cue to the subject for continuing in the same direction, or for a like performance in the future when faced with a situation or problem alike to the present one. Encouragement is a positive sign of approval, made in a way which enhances the subject's zeal for going ahead. If a child is trying to do something as desired by his teacher, or his elders, but no sign of approval or disapproval is there, the child may get confused, or be led astray by the influence of some other factor in his environment, or he may get slackened and even give up the activity. So, a teacher's "yes"; "Good"; "well-done"; "Fine"; "Quite Good", "Excellent" and so on, may go a long way towards cheering up the child in persisting to the right-track, and, for performing better. Clark L Hull[10] has enumerated 17 postulates as primary laws of mammalion behaviour; the 4th in the list is "incentive motivation" (K). It is the encouragement which keeps the activity going on, maintains the excitatory force of the reaction.

Encouragement is a sort of reinforcement, it serves as a cue to the subject for continuing in the same direction, or for a like performance in the future when faced with a situation or problem alike to the present one.

The teacher's nodding, or making "humh", "humh" sound, is also a way of approving, and, of thus encouraging the child for going on with the activity properly and with full zeal for the same. There may be some gestures also to provide encouragement for the activity of the child. Encouragement may be given through the award of grades or marks also but that has to be done very judiciously, it should convince the child that the assessment has been done objectively, that is, with no discrimination, or allowing any other factor than the quality of the performance, to influence it. Once a teacher asked her nursery students whether they would like her to award them "three stars" or an "Owl" ; the prompt response of almost all the students was in favour of an "Owl". It indicates that the children must be knowing the value of grades or marks, that are awarded to them—the purpose of encouragement can be served only then.

Hull's theory of encouragement or reinforcement is based on his conviction that such an activity serves as a reinforcing variable in the process of learning which leads to the reduction of need or the primary drive. In Hull's theory of learning, "Little Argie" (rg) acquires the value of reinforcing factor as it occurs along with the primary reinforcement. While adopting different devices to encourage the students, the teacher would be more effective if he is aware of this aspect of Hull's theory of learning.

Hull's theory of encouragement or reinforcement is based on his conviction that such an activity serves as a reinforcing variable in the process of learning which leads to the reduction of need or the primary drive.

Teachers in our school would do well if they act upon the advice that the students should be avoided from committing mistakes, as the most effective factor leading to better performance is the success that is achieved in an activity. BF Skinner's theory of operant conditioning is based on

9. Woodworth, RS. *Dynamics of Behaviour* (1958), p. 125.
10. Hull, L Clark. *Mind, Mechanism and Adaptive Behaviour* (1937).

Teachers in our school would do well if they act upon the advice that the students should be avoided from committing mistakes, as the most effective factor leading to better performance is the success that is achieved in an activity. BF Skinner's theory of operant conditioning is based on it.

it. Skinner writes, "If the occurrence of an operant is followed by presentation of a reinforcing stimulus, the strength is increased." " Skinner uses the term "Operant" to signify "behaviour which operates on the environment and produces reinforcing effects".[11] Conversely, "if the occurrence of an operant already strengthened through conditioning, is not followed by the reinforcing stimulus, the strength is decreased."[12] Here, I have been using the term "encouragement" in the sense of this sort of "reinforcing stimulus", the absence of which, as Skinner writes, may cause the weakening of learning.

Underwood and Shultz[13] experienced the efficacy of serial teaching or serial learning, as we do in case of teaching of the alphabet or numbers to the beginners. In a serial learning, each preceding letter or number serves as a reinforcer in the recall of the next one. Nevertheless, so far the teaching of the writing of the alphabet is concerned, I advised the teacher in charge of the Nursery class to teach in the order as given below:

I T L H F E X O Q D P C J S A Y U N M B Z G K R V W

After teaching the recognition of the 26 letters of the alphabet in the fixed order, the teacher taught the writing of the same, changing their order from easy to difficult. As for example, the writing of "A" is much more difficult for a nursery kid, than that of a number of other letters, and, if the teacher sticks to the fixed order, the child may take a long period before he learns even the first letter of the alphabet; and this may dishearten the child, and the teaching and learning in case of such a child, may be very difficult. Success in the work being done, is a very effective reinforcement, failure causes a reverse effect. Clue is most required for a recall when one is about the middle of a series or of the matter. CI Hovland in a research found that his subjects after learning a series of 12 non-sense syllables, reached to the height of errors between the sixth and the seventh of a series of twelve when asked to recall. This has been termed as the serial position effect. Anticipatory error and backward error are also related terms here.

Thorndike's Law of Effect is recognised as "reinforcement by reward".

Thorndike's Law of Effect is recognised as "reinforcement by reward". By the Law of Effect, he means—"The greater the satisfaction or discomfort, the greater the strengthening or weakening of the bond"[14]. According to this law, the learners should be avoided from the discomforts that errors may cause. And, the reaction of the teacher in case an error is committed by a pupil, should not be such which may break his heart, and, he may even give up his efforts.

5. Guidance For more than half a century, I have been associated with the practice of teaching, and, what I have been feeling is that, in many cases, the scholastic weakness of students happens because of the fact that

11. Skinner, BF. *The Man and His Ideas* (1968).
12. Skinner, BF. *The Behaviour of Organisms* (1938).
13. Underwood, BJ, Shultz, RW. *Meaningfulness and Verbal Learning* (1960).
14. Thorndike, EL. *Animal Intelligence: Experimental Studies* (1911).

no proper guidance is being provided to them. And, the work becomes all the more difficult when the number of students in a class is more than thirty or so. Providing guidance means "enabling each student to know where he is committing a mistake or error as well as what is correct." To be able to do this, the teacher will have to be observant regarding each student. *Gyanaytan* is the name of the school being run by the society that I am associated to, we have decided to keep the strength of students in each class only to the level that our teachers can pay individual attention to each student. For this, the teacher must also know the fields of general weakness of each student, and the field of their strength, too. For their weakness the students are neither to be punished in any form, nor are they to be put to shame. To do so, will result in making the students shy, hesitant and even frustrated. They may grow so non-responsive that the teacher himself may become disheartened, and, put the label "Dunce" in case of each such a student; while the fact may be that the unpsychological handling of the teacher may have made the student behave as such.

Providing guidance means "enabling each student to know where he is committing a mistake or error as well as what is correct."

Errors are the occasions which only can enable a teacher to know where and how should his efforts be conducted for the scholastic development of the students. Each individual mistake of each student is an occasion for the teacher to avail of for the improvement of the student; but the same is possible when it is done in such a way that the student, rather, feels encouraged to go on, to push on, though sometimes it may not be so easy to do so.

The language teacher's is the most arduous task so far the checking of written work is concerned. The approach of the teacher should be such that the student is not frustrated, nor he gets the impression that he can hardly do anything better regarding studies, nor should the teacher feel that the work is too difficult to accomplish. The written work may be of two kinds—controlled and open; the written work that is uniform, such as—"Fill in the right form of the given verb in each blank"; "Fill in each blank with a proper preposition" or "with a suitable article", and so on, is easy to check. The teacher may get answer in each case elicited from students by turn, involving the maximum number of them; may write the elicited answer on the blackboard so that each student himself may correct if there is a mistake. A mistake must always be corrected by the student himself. A teacher corrects mistakes in his own hand, the students may not take the trouble of even going through the mistakes, and the entire labour of the teacher may get wasted. Only in case of very young children at the kindergarten, the teacher may have to correct and present the model himself. But if it is so done, the students should then be required to practise the same, copying the teacher; or, guide your student in such a way and to such an extent that each student may realise his mistake, and, may do things in a right way. For the teacher to correct himself, a mistake committed by a student, is not sound psychologically, instead, make your student know what is wrong there, and, make him correct the same with his own hand.

First, I (the author) would go to each student to see whether he had done his home work/ class work or not. Then, I (the author) would make as many students read aloud the written work to be checked as the time of the period would permit. It would give the students more practice in reading, and, would enhance their ability to comprehend as I would be asking questions here and there, especially so where it was doubted that the expression was of the student himself.

The real difficulty arises when it is a free written work, each student has written in his own language, in his own way. Naturally, the number of mistakes will be the highest if it is a free composition work—it is more likely to be in case where the medium is a foreign language. I have ever been concerned with the teaching of English—a foreign language (in an Indian school, and more so in a state of Hindi belt as is ours). I had been teaching quite big classes, sometimes, with the number being about seventy. As I did not have enough free periods to check the written work so I experimented with different ways to do the same effectively.

(*i*) First, I would go to each student to see whether he had done his home work/ class work or not. Then, I would make as many students read aloud the written work to be checked as the time of the period would permit. It would give the students more practice in reading, and, would enhance their ability to comprehend as I would be asking questions here and there, especially so where it was doubted that the expression was of the student himself. This device of checking the written work, gave chances to the class of listening to how other students had done their work—and thus umpteen occasions of learning were provided.

(*ii*) In some cases, especially for senior classes, Secondary and Higher Secondary, I also experimented with another method. The classes being preponderantly big in number of students, I found it very difficult to maintain the ideal thing of checking the written work of each student, each time, thoroughly well. What I did, was to divide the class of seventy or more students into seven or eight groups, each headed by a group leader, selected so on the basis of the record of performance of each of them in English. I would thoroughly check the written work of each of these leaders plus that of the students of one of the groups—each time changing the group so that each group might get a chance to have its written work thoroughly checked.

The teacher should correct in his own hand only such of the mistakes regarding which the teacher feels that the student himself may not be able to correct it.

Of course, in checking, the teacher should correct in his own hand only such of the mistakes regarding which the teacher feels that the student himself may not be able to correct it. Otherwise, the spelling mistakes may be underlined, and the linguistic mistakes of other kinds, may be encircled; and the same may, better be numbered. The student should then be asked to correct each mistake, if need be, seeking help from some elder at home, or from someone who is in a position to guide; some dictionary or other book may also be consulted; and the concerned teacher should also be available for guidance regarding the same. If the leader of the group or some other student can assist in the work of correction, each student may correct the mistakes with the assistance of the same one.

Thus, each time, when some written work was assigned, the teacher would thoroughly check the written work of each of the leaders, plus that of the students who belong to the group of the turn. And, each leader would then check the exercise books of the students of his group. Of course, we cannot expect the leader to be capable enough to detect each mistake committed in the free composition by the students of his group, nevertheless, he would be able, at best, to point out some mistakes, and would thus lighten the work-load of the teacher, and, at the same time, be benefited himself through such a routine of looking through so many exercise books each time when some work is assigned to the class. And, the mistakes which the leader would not be able to detect, would be so done when by turn the teacher would be checking the exercise books.

> The student should be asked to correct each mistake, if need be, seeking help from some elder at home, or from someone who is in a position to guide, some dictionary or other book may also be consulted; and the concerned teacher should also be available for guidance regarding the same.

One very important thing is to change the attitude of the teacher regarding mistakes committed by the students. The Piagetian view is—mistakes should not be punished but treated as responses that can give the teacher insights into the child's thinking processes at one time. According to Piaget, committing a mistake by a child provides an occasion to the teacher to see how the child, in his custody, thinks—the mental behaviour of the child is revealed because of the same. The study of that behaviour happens to be very important for the teacher to enable himself to provide effective guidance to his pupil.

According to Piaget, committing a mistake by a child provides an occasion to the teacher to see how the child, in his custody, thinks—the mental behaviour of the child is revealed because of the same. The study of that behaviour happens to be very important for the teacher to enable himself to provide effective guidance to his pupil.

If a teacher is not harsh, and, has not threatened the tender children to silence, they themselves would be seeking the needful guidance from their teacher. How, with a sense of intense feeling, Froebel warns the parents against meting out harsh treatment to the children:

"..... ye fathers ..... Do not harshly repel, show no impatience about his ever recurring questions. Every harshly repelling word crushes bud or shoot of his tree of life. It is a warning to teacher as well."

"..... ye fathers ..... Do not harshly repel, show no impatience about his ever recurring questions. Every harshly repelling word crushes bud or shoot of his tree of life. It is a warning to teacher as well."

Guidance wrapped in harsh language would be counter-productive. Herbert Hoover underlines the importance of children in the words: "Children are most valuable natural resource."

When we speak of guidance, the reference should not be taken to be limited to the academic field only; guidance is valuable in the field of physical and the other co-curricular activities also, a lot of which a school should be expected to be providing. In *Gyanaytan*, the school of our society, we make use of a specially developed mechanism to measure the condition of each child in regard to physical or motor activities, physical health, emotional development, creativity and moral character, too. For guidance, assessment is an essential step which must precede it as it is the result of assessment in the light of which it may be decided whether any guidance is needed or not; or if it is needed, what sort of it, and how much of it is needed. On the basis of observation by the staff of the school, assessment is recorded in the anecdotal form of each student, twice a year. Of course, anyone from inside or outside the institution may make an entry regarding the position of a student in any of the fields of personality as mentioned

Guidance wrapped in harsh language would be counter-productive.

above—a notebook is always available for such an entry. Guidance would be required in all these different fields for an all-round development of the child.

6. Discipline We would, generally, hear the word discipline when special features of a school are mentioned. Of course, for the creation of congenial environment for proper functioning of any institution, discipline is must; and it is more important in case of a school where desirable habits of working are to be developed. Discipline is required in all fields of life for proper working, for effective working and success in life. There can be no game if there is no discipline on the playground. The army on the battlefield would change into a multitude of unruly people if the soldiers are not disciplined. The school is the most proper and important place where habits of discipline must be developed, and a spirit of discipline be inculcated.

For the creation of congenial environment for proper functioning of any institution, discipline is must; and it is more important in case of a school where desirable habits of working are to be developed.

But the conception of discipline has undergone some change. A class where pin-drop silence is prevailing need not always be considered as a sign of discipline; even a class where there may be some noise because of the class being actively engaged in some activity of their interest, and an activity so good for their development, should be considered equally disciplined. Discipline must never curb the behaviour of the students prompted by their curiosity. Children happen to be keenly eager to observe their physical and social environment, and, know about it—this spirit needs to be encouraged and all should be done to satisfy the curiosity of the children which would always result in their cognitive development. One's behaviour should be considered disciplined when it is helpful in achieving the desirable goal.

Discipline must never curb the behaviour of the students prompted by their curiosity.

Whether a child is disciplined or not, can be known through the behaviour of a child, that is, when a child indulges in some activity. How a child conducts the activity, how a work is performed—much depends upon how much disciplined the child is. A disciplined child is one who obeys the rules of the place and activity, who follows the instructions that are issued or given by the teachers or monitors or by others of his elders. And, the following of the same should not merely be physical or overt but in spirit, too. The wilful observance of rules, and the following of instructions, is a sure sign of one's being disciplined. And, such sort of discipline is must for a proper conduct of an activity to its success.

Whether a child is disciplined or not, can be known through the behaviour of a child, that is, when a child indulges in some activity. How a child conducts the activity, how a work is performed—much depends upon how much disciplined the child is.

For success in life, it is essential that one's behaviour should be disciplined. A disciplined person is one who does his work without being influenced by exterior factors or by his own psychological weakness, both of which may divert his attention away from his target or may weaken or slacken his pursuit towards the goal. Discipline includes concentration, discipline includes firm decision or iron determination. Discipline also includes courage, patience and tolerance. A mercurial, whimsical, wavering or in anyway suffering from some psychological abnormality, can never impress us as a disciplined person.

Nor, a person whose activity causes hindrance or hurdles in the ways of others, can be termed as a disciplined one. A person who is not disciplined in his habits and likings, cannot lead a wholesome life in matters of studies, games and other curricular and co-curricular activities; he would not be adjusted with himself and may be a source of trouble or nuisance for others. A person who may eat anything, at any time, and in any amount, would also be called as an indisciplined one. One who has no time-table for his studies, nor for other daily activities, would also be called indisciplined.

So, discipline is the proper way of doing things without being swayed and led astray by undesirable physical or mental forces. It being so, the word 'discipline' is very important for the school. It is one of its prime duties to see that its taughts are well-disciplined in all fields, and, bear good manners. These days, the student-community is especially described as an indisciplined lot. I feel, it is so because we fail to engage this most energetic part of our society in activities that are good for the society, as well as are good for the wholesome development of the different faculties that they are born with. When the overflowing energies of them fail to be beneficially utilised, the same would lead them to indulge into activities that are negative, and, are harmful both to the individual of each of them as well as to the society they are related to.

Discipline can never mean mere checking or prohibiting someone from doing something; it always lies in doing things in a way which leads to a better and desirable performance of an activity. Discipline is not a thing to be imposed upon externally; it is a habit of thinking and doing things in a way which does not interfere with the work of others, and, enhances the chances of things being performed as desired.

Discipline can never mean mere checking or prohibiting someone from doing something; it always lies in doing things in a way which leads to a better and desirable performance of an activity. Discipline is not a thing to be imposed upon externally; it is a habit of thinking and doing things in a way which does not interfere with the work of others, and, enhances the chances of things being performed as desired. If one is disciplined only in letter, it means that it is the result of something being done externally upon a person, but, to be disciplined in spirit, means that someone has become so used to thinking and doing things that nothing otherwise can be expected of him.

COMPONENTS OF EDUCATION

THE TEACHER

I have nothing to say against those who are in favour of assigning our child the central place in the whole process of learnings, and, to their preferring to call the teacher nothing more than a facilitator. They prefer

Teacher should provide such an environment, and, provide all such material which may greatly facilitate the process of learning.

to call the teacher a facilitator because they are of the conviction that a child himself would go on learning being strongly prompted by nature itself, hence the most important role that a teacher is expected to perform is that of a facilitator only—which means that the teacher should provide such an environment, and, provide all such material which may greatly facilitate the process of learning (Fig. 22.5).

It is the personality of the teacher which may either attract the child to school or make him repulsive to every-thing related to school.

But I feel that the role of the teacher is so vital, a pivotal one that something more needs to be said regarding it. In the formal process of learning, where school has still not been dead in spite of its being declared so more than a quarter century back. Great may be the impact of the teacher on learning. It is the personality of the teacher which may either attract the child to school or make him repulsive to every-thing related to school. The teacher should be an example of patience and affection so that he or she may make up to a great extent for the absence of mother, and, the child may be weaned without much difficulty. A child happens to be very sensitive, he cannot be befooled by just a show of affection, only a genuine affection for the child can attract him to his teacher. And, only then, every direction or teaching of the teacher assumes overwhelming significance for the child, and, the chances of the process of teaching and learning, being successful become very strong. This is something about the personality of the teacher, about his personal traits or characteristic qualities.

Figure 22.5
The children are quite enthusiastic towards their school.

For a teacher to be a good hand at writing, and, to be a drawing hand, would be very important additional qualities by dint of which he can concentrate the attention of the child on the lesson being taught. Small children's learning is greatly facilitated when the teacher can concretise the lesson, and, make it greatly interesting through drawing work. The students' attention may also be caught if a teacher can introduce a lesson with the recitation of some rhyme or poem, or, can sing some relevant song in a melodious tone. This is why drawing and vocal music should be taught in a training institute.

Teacher is the chief executive in the whole scheme of the education of each child in her custody. It is she who should, actually, be entrusted the work of planning for the education of each child; curricula-framers may be different but it is for the teacher to decide how much of the curriculum or syllabus is to be covered in a scheduled time; and it is also the teacher who is to decide as to how the same is to be done. Years back, I read a book on educational psychology wherein it was given that the teacher should know not only Latin but John, too. That is, for the success of the teacher in her or his mission, it is essential that she or he must have studied, and must continue studying each child psychologically, too, mere knowledge of the subject is not enough. It is the teacher who can be the best judge as to what method or methods, technique or device would best suit a particular student. During our times, computer has greatly facilitated the work of self-education, nevertheless, the importance of the teacher in the process, should not be under-rated.

Teacher is the chief executive in the whole scheme of the education of each child in her custody. It is she who should, actually, be entrusted the work of planning for the education of each child; curricula-framers may be different but it is for the teacher to decide how much of the curriculum or syllabus is to be covered in a scheduled time; and it is also the teacher who is to decide as to how the same is to be done.

For up-dating the knowledge of our teachers, and for keeping them abreast with innovations in educational thoughts and practices, refresher or orientation programmes need to be organised after a fixed duration.

THE LEARNING MATERIAL

It is at the level of lower primary classes that the question of the selection of books, assumes so great importance, as in case of higher classes only such books have to be taught as have been prescribed by the Board or the Department that conducts the examinations for the same. In the market there are books galore. A hard competition is there among the publishers to grab the market. Some considerations, other than academic, affect the selection of books; that is not proper, as it would cause the interests of the children to be ignored. While making selection of a book, the following things should be considered:

1. Contents of the book; 2. Order of the units and lessons; 3. Presentation of the contents (it includes language, sentence structure, arrangement of items of learning, illustrations, printing, and so on). 4. Exercises.

1. Contents of the book Contents of the book should be befitting to the age group, maturity level, needs and interests of the children. Jean Piaget can be a good guide in this respect; he has divided the cognitive development into four stages, and, the author should be aware as to what the average student can grasp at a particular stage of development—we should not expect one to be interested in learning what one is not matured enough to grasp. The contents, always, have to be graded standardwise, and, thus books have to be got written to provide experiences classwise in a series. The child goes on developing physically, cognitively and conatively; the books and other supplementary materials should assist in the process of this natural development while at the same time the contents of the same must not be above the level of maturity of the average child.

Contents of the book should be befitting to the age group, maturity level, needs and interests of the children. Jean Piaget can be a good guide in this respect; he has divided the cognitive development into four stages, and, the author should be aware as to what the average student can grasp at a particular stage of development.

The child, as he grows, is exposed to a continually widening social and physical environment, that he has to interact with; for a successful interaction to his environment, he needs to be equipped with new experiences which the new books of different subjects should provide to him, of course, his widening environment also provides new experiences—and learning is the end result of experiences. Books, generally, provide the second-hand experiences accumulated through the ages, one cannot depend merely on the first-hand experiences earned by oneself. So much development has been possible only because man could devise a means to communicate the ever-increasing lot of accumulated experiences. The writers of books need to decide the teaching points for different classes looking to the maturity levels of students of different age groups plus the individual and the social needs of them; and, the teaching items have to be graded in series of books for different classes.

2. Order of the units and lessons The contents of a book are arranged in units, and each unit may contain one, but, generally, it would have more than one lessons. But the order of units and lessons should be such that each succeeding lesson or unit is a bit more difficult than the previous one. The preceding matter should have fully equipped the student to be able to grasp what comes after, that is, it must serve as previous knowledge for the new experiences to be graspable. In more simple way, we may say that the order of units and lessons should be from easy to difficult. But it is not always the case that the units and/or lessons of a book, are so arranged; in such a case, the teacher should be free to decide what should be taught first and what afterwards; of course, his guiding principle would be from easy to difficult, as well as, he will have to see as to for a particular point of learning what ought to have been the previous knowledge.

3. Presentation of the contents We come across a huge number of books dealing with the common topics of learning, nevertheless, one book may be considered better by far than the other because it presents the matter in such a clear and concise way that to grasp the same becomes easier. The language should be of the level of the class, and, should appear to be interesting to the students. No superfluous word should be there; no repetition of the same thing should be there—the expression should have a perfect compactness, and beauty of its own. Nor, the sentences should be very long and cumbersome. Roundabout expression poses difficulty for the students to grasp it. The word 'compactness' used here is to say that each sentence should be well-knit with its preceding and succeeding one—each sentence should appear to be flowing from its previous one in a natural way. 'Compactness' also indicates that each word in a sentence should have its own importance, and, cannot be removed without impairing the sense meant to be conveyed.

The matter of each lesson should also be so arranged that each part, and each paragraph has a logical relationship with the one preceding, and succeeding it. In a book on Geography, 'Vegetation' cannot be taught before teaching about the "climate" of a particular place; in History, the governance of a ruler cannot be taught without first telling something about the early life and characteristic traits of the same.

The most important thing, especially, for the children at the primary level, is illustration. There should be a good many illustrations—clearly given in bright, beautiful colours. These illustrations, for the small children, would mostly be in the form of pictures. They attract the attention of the children, and, help a lot in making the point of learning clear to them. In higher classes, the illustrations may be in the form of charts, graphs, or tables of different sorts.

The most important thing, especially, for the children at the primary level, is illustration. There should be a good many illustrations—clearly given in bright, beautiful colours.

The resourceful teachers can themselves arrange a lot of illustrations to make the lesson more interesting, easy to understand, and, enhance its chances for longer retention. At the level of school administration, a list of articles—charts, maps, globe, pictures, overhead projector, epidiascope, television-set with VCR ought to be prepared to get procured as teaching aids so that the lesson would not be only much more interesting and easily graspable but enriched as well; and such a teaching aids a lot in a longer retention, too.

Printing is an important part of presentation. Some books are found to be very good examples of the printing art. The printing is an art, a skill, it has professionalism of its own kind which greatly increases the value of a book. The book meant for children, should have bold and beautiful fonts. The printing should be very attractive for the children. The arrangement of words, sentences and paragraphs should be such that it may further add to the attractiveness of the book for the children. The key words may also be given in a different colour. In a chapter, meant to teach prefixes or suffixes to begin with, the same may be given in a different colour than that of the root word—to exemplify the point of learning. The paper of the book for the Nursery and L.K.G. kids, may be glazed one, or may otherwise be of such a superior kind which may have its own attraction for the children. These things have great psychological significance; the child may not be interested in reading the matter of the book but its attractiveness would make him take it out off and on, and look into it. Thus, a book of this sort gives many more occasions to the teacher to teach what he wants to teach to her students.

4. Exercises Of course, an author of a book for the nursery class, would give no exercises therein as the same are neither required nor desirable. A light beginning may be made at the kindergarten stage. In case of classes higher than of this stage, the exercises go on acquiring increasing importance. The exercises are important for recapitulation or revision; recapitulation or revision consolidates the matter that has been read. A consolidated matter would have much longer retention as exercises, also help in making the point of learning further clear, and, depending upon the type of questions, the same may give different perspectives to the knowledge acquired by the child through the book.

Through exercises, the teacher may achieve objectives of different sorts. There should be exercise which make the students recall the learnt matter; there should be exercises for the enhancement of students' faculty for comprehension. In case of the former, the questions will be such which make the students recall the facts read by them in the lesson, while in case of the latter, the students will have to read the matter thoroughly well so that they may understand the implied meaning or sense as well as the explicit meaning as to what the author means to convey. There should be some thought-provoking questions also.

Through exercises, the teacher may achieve objectives of different sorts. There should be exercise which make the students recall the learnt matter; there should be exercises for the enhancement of students' faculty for comprehension. In case of the former, the questions will be such which make the students recall the facts read by them in the lesson, while in case of the latter, the students will have to read the matter thoroughly well so that they may understand the implied meaning or sense as well as the explicit meaning as to what the author means to convey. There should be some thought-provoking questions also, the answers to which are not directly given in the lesson but the students will have to infer from what is given therein the lesson. Such questions test the students' ability to apply their knowledge in different situations; such questions help in developing the faculty to assess different situations with their similarities and dissimilarities with the situation that they are already so well-acquainted with.

Format of questions should also be of various sorts. For recall, there may be questions requiring students to fill in the blanks with the given words or grammatical terms or structures as each of them suits for an individual blank. There may be questions with multiple choice to select an answer from, or, the students may be required to complete contextual sentences, or answer contextual questions recalling their knowledge of the lesson. Then, there may be matching questions, too. "True" and "False" type questions are also sometimes asked. All these types of questions, and, some of other types also may be asked to test the knowledge of the students. In such a case, the questions will be based not on the matter of a lesson in a textbook or in a Supplementary Reader, but will be related to some item of Grammar, or, may be to test or enhance the ability of free expression.

Questions serve as a device to teach new items as well as the means to test what has been taught. Hence, a teacher needs to be well-skilled in the art of framing questions of different sorts. And, this ability is all the more required in the author of a book so that exercises of various sorts may be there to serve the purpose of recapitulation and testing the efficacy of teaching. In some books, testing exercises are found to have been prepared with great skill, and they can help in achieving the objective of exercise in a proper way, and with full interest of the students in attempting the same.

Students, especially, of the lower classes may beneficially be required to do some sort of activity which needs the use of the knowledge or skill already acquired by them. The application of knowledge or skill consolidates the same, and, may even help in the further development of the same. In case of nursery students, the befitting activity would be to colour the beautifully drawn letters of the alphabet or digits of the number. They may also be asked to write the first letter of the word labelling a picture. At a little later, they may be asked to fill in the blanks first with letters, and then with words. At the upper primary and secondary levels, we may ask our students to verify facts given in a book of Science through some experiment. In teaching Geography, requisite amount of practical work can or should also be got done in the form of drawing some map, colouring the outline map of a country or state to show the different kinds of land surfaces or climatic or vegetation conditions, and so on. In History, a chart may be made to show lineage of a dynasty; to show reforms in different fields—social, political, agricultural, industrial, economical, and so on.

To foster creativity, students may be made to speak a few sentences about some animal, some object—living or non-living, a personality of History, and so on. Oral or written competitions may be held to develop oral or written expression of the students. The way of my holding the extempore speech competition had been to make my students come to my table one-by-one, to pick up one of the slips lying thereon, with a topic written on each of the slips; and the student had to start speaking on the same, extemporaneously. It was to avoid preparing for a topic through cramming. Though, sometimes, a topic may be assigned to prepare on; the students would consult different sources, and collect matter to speak on the topic with a spirit of competition. Such a programme would inculcate the habit of preparing for a literary or artistic work, resulting in the enhancing of knowledge and skill.

To foster creativity, students may be made to speak a few sentences about some animal, some object—living or non-living, a personality of History, and so on. Oral or written competitions may be held to develop oral or written expression of tho students. The way of my holding the extempore speech competition had been to make my students come to my table one-by-one, to pick up one of the slips lying thereon, with a topic written on each of the slips; and the student had to start speaking on the same, extemporaneously. It was to avoid preparing for a topic through cramming.

The Project Method is also a method having an activity approach. This method is good for students of senior classes. John Dewey was a strong exponent of learning by doing. In India, Mahatma Gandhi introduced the Basic Education which is an education to be imparted co-relating the same to some activity. Psychologically and pedagogically, the soundness of the approach was beyond doubt, though basic education failed in India because of our having been too much accustomed to a system which has been extremely bookish. Basic Education demands that geographical facts regarding the climate and soil suitable for the production of cotton, should be taught while the students are being given practice in spinning on a *takli*, or on a *charkha* or in weaving on some loom, and so on. Likewise, some relevant units of measuring lengths, should also be taught along with the continuance of the activity. Therein lies the way to relieve our system of education from its extreme bookishness, and the importance of cramming that it has got. But we failed to conduct it in a proper way. I feel the computer based education would also be an education through activity.

THE LEARNING SITUATION

Physically, the classroom environment should be quite congenial; it should be rather pleasant for the learning kids. Of course, a proper ventilation—provision for light and air, must be there. The students must feel comfortable in their classroom in every season whatsoever. Their furniture should be

Physically, the classroom environment should be quite congenial; it should be rather pleasant for the learning kids.

of the size and shape according to their age. In some schools, I have seen students being required to remain sitting for eight periods, each not less than of 30 minutes' duration, on stools with no provision of back-support. It would cause earlier fatigue leading to distortion of posture, and the net result would be ill-health, and diversion from the lesson of the class, as the span of attention would be adversely affected.

The nursery class should be well-equipped with toys of different sorts which may serve as objects of attraction for the nimble kids to play with, as well as means for learning what the teacher deems as essential items of their curriculum. At the nursery and pre-nursery levels, the thrust is to be on the development of senses—eye, ear, nose, tongue and touch (skin).

Especially, the nursery class should be well-equipped with toys of different sorts which may serve as objects of attraction for the nimble kids to play with, as well as means for learning what the teacher deems as essential items of their curriculum. At the nursery and pre-nursery levels, the thrust is to be on the development of senses—eye, ear, nose, tongue and touch (skin). A lot of such objects may be developed or procured, through which the resourceful teacher may teach the kids to recognise different colours; different shapes (circle, triangle, rectangle, square, and so on); different living and non-living objects; different letters of alphabets and digits of number—all in a play-way method; and all these are related to the sense of eye; and pictures and models should also be used abundantly to teach all these things. A trained eye of the child can very well distinguish which is bigger, which is smaller and catch the slight difference that may be there between two objects in colour, shape or size. At a latter stage, the children may be made skilled in measuring different things through guess work only, with no instrument whatsoever.

Initially the toys may serve as such for the playful kids, and later some sorts of real musical instruments, such as piano, flute, drum and so on, may be used with great benefit to the lot of learning students. Video and audio cassettes may help a lot in the development of eye and ear.

Children like to produce sounds of different volumes and at different pitches—their ear may be trained in the grasping of niceties of sound through procuring musical instruments—initially the toys may serve as such for the playful kids, and later, some sorts of real musical instruments such as piano, flute, drum and so on, may be used with great benefit to the lot of learning students. Video and audio cassettes may help a lot in the development of eye and ear. Some channels telecast wildlife on the screen of the television set; arrangements should be made for the students to be benefited by such programmes. For the same reason, drawing, music and dance should occupy important place in curricula of the primary level classes, too. To the beginners at the nursery level, the teaching of letters should be commenced, and, in many schools, actually, it is so done with colouring differently the different letters. Then, out of a jumbled lot of letters of plastic, the children, one-by-one, may be asked to pick a particular letter, so on and so forth. Distinguishing the roaring of lion from the howling of a wolf, of the hooting of an owl from the cooing of a dove being produced on an audio record, may be a very beneficial play for the primary level children. In our school, we have masks, with which the tots may play different animals, and, they may be taught to produce voices of the same as well. For the same reason, visiting a zoo or a sanctuary is educationally highly beneficial.

Eyes and ears are the organs whose role is crucial in the process of teaching and learning—we will have to adopt the various means to develop the acuity of these senses. Sharp eyes will grasp things in less time and with more exactness. Likewise, the oral teaching of the teacher, can be better grasped by those who have got an acute sense of hearing—in case of dictation by the teacher, only such a student can do well.

Eyes and ears are the organs whose role is crucial in the process of teaching and learning—we will have to adopt the various means to develop the acuity of these senses.

Playing different games may also help in the development of senses. On many occasions, more than one senses (organs) have to work simultaneously in co-ordination with one another. To use the term of Piaget, for the development of schemata, the school will have to be like some "smor-gas-bord" (John Holt) out of which the students should be free to select activities of their own liking.

In a good Montessori school, we may find the aid available for teaching what is hard, and what is soft; what is hot, and what is cold, so on and so forth. Thus, the sense of touch may be helped to be more acute.

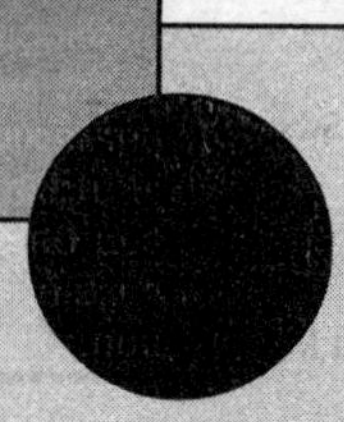

BIBLIOGRAPHY

Baldwin, AL (1968): *Theories of Child Development*, New York: Wiley.

E. Douvan (1960): "New Sources of Conflict in Females at Adolescence and Early Adulthood," in Bardwick et al. *Feminine Personality and Conflict*, Belmont: Brooks/Cole.

Elkind, D (1967): "Egocentrism in Adolescence", *Child Development,* 38, 1025-1034.

Frost, Joe L (1968): *Early Childhood Education Rediscovered*, New York: Holt, Rinehart & Winston. Fair, rebound.

Goldman, R. and Goldman, J (1982): *Children's Sexual Thinking: A Comparative Study of Children Aged 5 to 15 Years in Australia, North America, Britain and Sweden.* London: Routledge & Kegan Paul.

Guilford, JP (1967): *The Nature of Human Intelligence,* New York: McGraw-Hill.

Hall, G.S. (1905): *Adolescence*, Boston, MA: Harvard University Press.

Hull, CL "Mind, Mechanism and Adaptive Behavior", *Psychological Review,* 44: 1-32, 1937.

Leahy AM (1935): *Nature-Nurture and Intelligence*, London: Collins.

Lewin, K (1935): *A Dynamic Theory of Personality*, New York: McGraw-Hill.

Mayer, Frederick (1973): *A History of Educational Thought,* Columbus, Ohio: CE Merrill Publishing Company.

Piaget, J. (1936, 1963): *The Origins of Intelligence in Children,* New York: W.W. Norton & Company, Inc.

Piaget, J. (1963, 2001): *The Psychology of Intelligence,* New York: Routledge.

Stroud, James B (1956): *Psychology in Education*, New York: Longmans, Green and Co.

Tanner JM (1955): *Growth at Adolescence* (1st ed.), Oxford: Blackwell Scientific.

Thomas A. & Chess S (1977): *Temperament and Development,* New York: Brinner-Mazel.AM935) Nature-nurture and intelligence.

Thomas, A. et al (1963): *Behavioral Individuality in Early Childhood*, New York: New York University Press.

Woodworth, RS (1958): *Dynamics of Behaviour*, New York: Henry Holt.

GLOSSARY

Acetylcholine–a body chemical secreted from adrenal gland-causing excitement.

ACTH–Adrenocorticotrophic hormone.

Agglutinate–to form into groups (as bacteria cells group together, when blood cells of different types are mixed).

Androgyny–characteristics common both to male and female or related to both the sexes.

Antigen–substance (such as a virus or germ) which produces antibodies to attack the body.

Aphasia–caused because of damage to brain centres resulting in difficulty in learning to speak or write, or to understand speech or writing.

Atherosclerosis–a condition where deposits of fats and minerals forms on the wall of an artery, and prevents blood from flowing easily.

Asphyxia–physical disorder caused because of lack of oxygen.

Body Dysmorphic Disorder (BDD)–a severe (obsession) of anxiety with an imagined or slight defect in body.

Cathexis–the force which carries a drive, or an idea representing it, to consciousness, has been so termed by Freud.

Cephalocaudal–of the head.

Chromosome–a rod like or thread like structure occurring in pairs in cell nucleus of animals.

Ciliary muscles–muscles controlling vibration of eye lashes.

Colic–interalgia, pain in any part of the intestinal tract.

Conception–idea formed of something.

Correlative transformation–transforming in a series-each time the effect becoming a cause, and so on.

Cretinism–condition of being a cretin (= patient suffering from congenital hypothyroidism).

Croup–acute infection of the upper respiratory passages which block the larynx–a children's disease.

Cytoplasm–a fluid substance in which a zygote floats.

Development–increasing and expanding of capacities.

Dyslexia–"word-blindness" where a person is unable to read or write properly and is confused.

Ego–in the process of personality development, the second stage when one can think of one's good, of one's prestige.

Epinephrene–an adrenaline secretion causing stimulations.

Epistemology–knowledge (a Piagetian use).

Equilibrium–a stable state of adjustments competent to perform a function.

Erythroblastosis–presence of erythroblasts [mature non-nucleated red blood cells] in the blood, usually found in harmolytic anaemia.

Fontanelles–membraneous spaces in an infant's skull.

Gregariousness–an instinct driving one to live within one's own flock or community.

Growth–increasing of an organ or limb of the body in size and weight.

Hypothalamus–part of the brain above the pituitary gland which controls the production of hormones by the pituitary gland, and regulates important bodily functions such as hunger, thirst and sleep.

Id–the initial stage in the process of development of the personality of the child when he is hardly aware of his 'self', and behaves motivated by the animal instincts.

Kwashiorkor–anaemia, wasting body and swollen liver, mostly among small children of tropical countries, caused because of malnutrition.

Labile–unstable.

Libido–a sex instinct which provides drive for sexual activities.

Maturity–a stage of fitness for performing a particular function.

Myelination–filling in of the membraneous spaces in a baby's skull and other parts.

Neurosis–disorder of nervous system characterized by irrational behaviour and depression.

Nurturant–one taking care of in a child's proper upbringing (a term used by Murray in his book "Exploration in Personality").

Nystagmus–rapid movement of eyes up and down or from side to side.

Obstetrical–related to obstetrics, that is, the branch of medicine and surgery dealing with child-birth.

Ossification–hardening of cartilage.

Osteomalacia–protein in blood which helps blood in clotting (or coagulation).

Paresis–partial paralysis.

Perception–meaningful sensation.

Phenylketonuria–a disease caused by excessive secretion of phenylpyreusic acid in the urine—mental impairment and pigmentation of hair, are the results.

Plasma–yellow watery liquid which makes up the main part of blood.

Protoplasm–a minute dot like constituent of a cell.

Proximodistal–from the entire to the periphery.

Psychosomatic–related to a sort of mental disorder caused mainly by bodily disorder as well as by a prolonged state of fear and anxiety.

Psychotic–related to psychosis, a serious mental disorder where the patient shows lack of insight, and touch with realities.

Schema–a behavioural skill developed through activity (a Piagetian term).

Sensation–registration of impressions on the threshold of senses.

Sperm–semen.

Stutter–a speech defect causing involuntary stops and repetitions in speaking.

Super-ego–the final stage (according to Sigmund Freud), when one has developed enough to think and behave for the good of society.

Trophoblast–the outer layer of the small cavity formed within uterus.

TSH–thyroid stimulating hormone.

Ventral–of or on the abdomen.

Zygote–the first fertilized ovum.

SUBJECT INDEX

D

E

G

L

NAME INDEX

A

B

C

D

E

F

G

H

V

W

Y

LIST OF TABLES

LIST OF FIGURES